MW00830863

Trinitarian Personhood:

Investigating the Impications of a
Relational Definition

Dr. William Ury

Wipf and Stock Publishers
EUGENE, OREGON

Wipf and Stock Publishers
199 West 8th Avenue, Suite 3
Eugene, Oregon 97401

Trinitarian Personhood
Investigating the Implications of a Relational Definition
By Ury, William
Copyright©2001 Ury, William
ISBN: 1-57910-879-2
Publication date: February, 2002
Previously published by Npp, 2001.

ABBREVIATIONS

The Ante-Nicene Fathers: Translations of the Writings of the Fathers down to A. D. 325. eds. Alexander Roberts and James Donaldson. 10 vols. Reprint. Grand Rapids: Eerdmans Pub. Co. 1977-1979. Abbreviation: ANF.

Augustine, St. De Trinitate: Libri XV. ed. W.J. Mountain. Corpus Christianorum, Series Latina, vols. 50, 50A. Brepols: Turnholti Typographi Brepols Editores Pontificii, 1968. Abbreviation: CC.

Church Dogmatics. Karl Barth. eds. Geoffrey W. Bromiley and Thomas F. Torrance. Various trans. 4 vols. Edinburgh: T. & T. Clark, 1936-1969 (1975 edition). Abbreviation: CD.

Denzinger, Henrich and Adolph Schömetzer. Enchiridion Symbolorum: Definitionum et Declarationum de rebus fidei et morum. 33rd ed. Freiburg: Verlag Herder, 1965. Abbreviation: Denzinger.

The Fathers of the Church: A New Translation. Various editors. Washington: Catholic University of America Press, Abbreviation: FC.

Patrologiae Cursus Completus Series Graeca. ed. J.-P. Migne. 162 vols. Paris: Migne-Garnier, 1857-1912. Abbreviation: PG.

Patrologiae Cursus Completus Series Latina. ed. J.-P. Migne. 220 vols. Paris: Migne-Garnier, 1844-1890. Abbreviation: PL.

Select Library of Nicene and Post-Nicene Fathers of the Christian Church. ed. Philip Schaff. 14 vols. Reprint. Grand Rapids: Eerdmans, 1978. Abbreviation: NPNF.

Select Library of Nicene and Post-Nicene Fathers of the Christian Church. Second Series ed. Philip Schaff. 14 vols. Reprint. Grand Rapids: Eerdmans, 1978. Abbreviation: NPNF2.

Theological Dictionary of the New Testament. ed. G. Kittel and G. Freidrich. trans. and ed. Geoffrey Bromiley. 9 vols. (Grand Rapids: Eerdman's Pub. Co., 1964-1974. Abbreviation: TDNT

Note: All Scripture references are from the Revised Standard Version. Harper Study Bible Edition. Grand Rapids: Zondervan Bible Publishers, 1965. Abbreviation: OT and NT

Table of Contents

...both Unity in the Trinity
and Trinity in the Unity
must be worshipped.
He therefore that will be
saved must then think this
of the Trinity.

Pseudo-Athanasian Creed 6th c.

Introduction

Reflecting on one of the more disconcerting anathemas of the Quicumque, Dr. Robert
South, a learned Englishman of the seventeeth century is purported to have said, "As he
that denies the fundamental article of the Christian religion may lose his soul so he that
strives to understand it may lose his wits."[1]   Following the explosion of critiques upon the
well-worn battlements of orthodoxy brought on by the Enlightenment, there are many who
share this resignation. This resultant capitulation has meant the almost universal relegation
of the doctrine of the Trinity, and consequently the notion of 'Person' in Trinity, to a
tenuous and highly suspect position. The creeds and decrees once hidden behind the
monolithic granduer of the Vincentian Canon or conciliar dictums have been systematically
submitted to scathing critiques. What may have been "believed everywhere, always and by
everyone," as truly and properly Catholic remains fair game for theology's most critical
thinkers; many of whom view theological consensus as anachronistic and restrictive.[2]

The Fichtean dissection of traditional theism was adumbrated in the analysis of
Feuerbach which discerned contemporary concepts of God as mere idealisms which, when
unmasked, were nothing more than unconscious projections of human attributes and values.
This appraisal coincided with Nietzche's claim that God was dead and Heidegger's
existential pronouncement that the uncritical nature of ontotheological metaphysics, or talk
about God as highest being, had forced Christian theologians and philosophers to "remain
silent" when it came to the topic of God. As Pannenberg reflects on one hundred and
seventy years of onslaught from various forms of atheism, agnosticism and unitarianism he
concludes that the Christian Church has not yet recovered, especially at its most vulnerable

---

[1]According to the American Russian Orthodox thinker, Anthony Ugolnik, "The Trinity
is the cross upon which the mind is crucified." The Illuminating Icon (Grand Rapids:
Eerdmans, 1989), 103.

[2]Vincent of Lerins, Commonitories 2:1, FC vol. 7, 270. Augustine said similarly,
"Securus iudicat orbis terrarum." Contra epistolam Parmeniani libri III, 3:3, PL 43, see
section from cols. 95-97.

1

pressure point, the Trinity.[3]

The impact of this marginalization of traditional dogma is subtly revealed in Schleiermacher's trinitarian discussion placed as an appendix to his theology.[4] We have heard on the one hand Neibuhr's resignation that modern Christianity is only a form of radical monotheism, and on the other the prophetic voice of Rahner who warns that Christianity, if not willing to take up the modern philosophical or metaphysical gauntlets which confront the Church, will be reduced to mere monotheism.[5]

It would appear then that theologians who accept the traditional formulations must come entreatingly to the Church, and even more imploringly to the greater society in hopes of a reappraisal of the doctrine which is fundamental to all that is Christian.[6] Arthur Wainwright, fully cognizant of the unique place the Christian view of God has taken amongst other theologies, consistently refers to the "problem of the Trinity" throughout his exegetical discussion.[7] To the unreflective it may seem audacious, even blasphemous to put "problem" and Trinity side by side. But even a short excursion into its intricacies and implications will prove otherwise. Problems, however, can be viewed from different perspectives which yield varying results. The lure of rational assessment may produce

---

[3] Wolfhart Pannenberg, "The Question of God," trans. Carl E. Braaten, Interpretation, 21:3, 289-314, esp. here 289-290. Pannenberg sees prior attempts at projecting human values and calling them divine from Anaxagoras' idea of divine reason to Max Scheler's concept of a personal God. He sees a line of critique from Spinoza through Fichte and more recently in Hartmann against this alleged projection of ideals. The modern atheistic controversy in Western thought found its ideological impetus with Fichte's 1798 article,"Über den Grund unseres Glaubens an eine göttliche Weltregierung," which Pannenberg quotes. Ibid., 309-310.

[4] Cf. Kant's similar glance at the Trinity has been seen by some as a radical statement of commitment to this "article of faith" in the interpretation of "God is love." I. Kant, Religion Within the Limits of Reason Alone, trans. with intro. and notes T. M. Greene and H. H. Hudson (New York: Harper and Row, 1960), 136.

[5] My point regarding Schleiermacher's placement of the Trinity is challenged by the late Robert F. Streetman in "Friedrich Schleiermacher's Doctrine of the Trinity and Its Significance for Theology Today" Ph.D. diss., Drew University, 1975; whose contentions are generally reiterated in "Some Questions Schleiermacher Might Ask About Barth's Trinitarian Criticisms," in Barth and Schleiermacher: Beyond the Impasse? ed. James O. Duke and Robert F. Streetman (Philadelphia: Fortress Press, 1988), 114-137. I, as yet, remained unconvinced by Streetman's interpretation.

[6] Not all are so irenically inclined. In Protestant circles the voice of Thomas C. Oden has been heard in a clarion call to eschew "modern chauvinism" and return to the tradition of the historical Church in Agenda for Theology: After Modernity...What? (Grand Rapids: Zondervan, 1990), 35-38, passim. See this theme worked out in his Systematic Theology 3 vols. (San Francisco, Harper and Row, 1987, 1989,). He has an informative personal interlude in vol. 2, 217-220 on a post-critical consciousness.

[7] John Courtney Murray, Problem of God, 1-3, insightfully discusses God as "problem" in relationship to the recent appearance of the "godless man".

problems which are of a foreign nature to divine mystery. Definitional difficulties ought
not dissuade analogical discernment of Trinitarian 'vestigia'.

In spite of the modern aversion to metaphysics which includes the Christian Trinity
there is no doubt that the doctrine is slowly being re-integrated into the self-contemplation
of recent theological discourse.[8] In some corners of the Church, this repristinated
metaphysic may possibly be one of several watershed doctrines in the deliberations between
factions within larger denominations.[9] Yet, there is at least one glaring omission that
directly pertains to our understanding of this complex doctrine. Though most works
mention 'person' as it relates to the formulation of trinitarian orthodoxy, any survey will
reveal that in most; - neither an adequately comprehensive historical survey of 'person' is
given and thus its usage tends to be self-serving in light of the larger project, - nor is

---

[8]Ecumenical thrusts have produced amazingly orthodox statements with regard to the
Trinity. See the World Council of Churches' commitment to trinitarian discussion though
in varying degrees of orthodoxy. Awareness of the Christocentrism of the 1948 Amsterdam
statements has produced a more trinitarian basis for further theological discussion, though
for the most part theological constructs are secondary in importance to praxis. The 1952
Lund, Faith and Order Conference requested a Theological Commission which speaks of the
"threefold manifestation of God, the centrality of the Incarnation in trinitarian discernment,"
and sees that "the mystery of the inter-relationship of the persons of the Trinity remains
beyond the grasp of our human understanding," from One Lord, One Baptism, preface by
Keith Bridston (Minneapolis: Augsburg Pub. House, 1961), 13. In 1960 that emphasis was
deepened by a "general desire to include a reference ...to the Three Persons of the
Undivided Trinity." Evanston to New Delhi: Report of the Central Committee to the Third
Assembly of the World Council of Churches (Geneva: World Council of Churches, 1961),
37. At points it is difficult to ascertain if the trinitarian clauses are fundamental to the
theological basis of the proceedings or to the desire to include churches whose roots are in
the Patristic traditions, which was one of the major themes at Montreal. See Fourth World
Conference on Faith and Order: Montreal 1963, ed. P.C. Rodger and Lukas Vischer (New
York: Association Press, 1964), 24; Faith and Order Studies, 1964-1967 (Geneva: World
Council of Churches,1968), 42-43; hardly any mention of the Trinity at Uppsala 1968, cf. The
Uppsala Report, 1968 ed. Norman Goodall (Geneva: World Council of Churches, 1968). The
growing tendency to acknowledge the Eastern abhorrence of the filioque is seen in "Spirit
of God, Spirit of Christ," Faith and Order Paper, no. 103, ed. Lukas Vischer (Geneva: World
Council of Churches, 1981). Last, 1989 saw the culmination of five years of consultation
based upon the 1985 Crèt-Bérard draft concerning the Nicene creed. Background found in
"Faith and Renewal," Faith and Order Paper, no. 131, ed. Thomas F. Best (Geneva: World
Council of Churches, 1986), 107ff.

[9]Cf. the rise of trinitarian conflict within the United Methodist Church. The issuing
of the 1987 Houston Declaration challenged the waning commitment to orthodox positions,
including trinitarian commitments, within that denomination. The written statement of the
Houston convocation came out of meetings held December 14-15, 1987. It is possible that
complaints of this nature may have been instrumental in the reintroduction and
reaffirmation of distinctly trinitarian language in the Book of Discipline of the United
Methodist Church, 1988 (Nashville, The United Methodist Publishing House, 1988), see
para.68, section 3, and para.432. See Geoffrey Wainwright's discussion in "From Pluralism
towards Catholicity: the United Methodist Church after the General Conference of 1988,"
Asbury Theological Journal 44:1 (Spring, 1989): 17-27, reprinted from This World #25
(Spring, 1989).

sufficient theological consideration given to the term. The bankruptcy of modern thought with regard to personhood may be in part due to to the lack of proper theological anchoring.

It is quite common to find predicates of personhood along the lines of: 'rational individuality' or 'psychological experience' and 'consciousness'. Although these may be partially adequate, theology and philosophy, primarily in the West have come to equate, rather than approximate, intellectual, psychological and moral qualities centered on the axis of consciousness with 'person'. The unavoidable result is a notion of self-determination which stems from a fundamental tenet of the modern world - isolationism. Personality then is defined exclusively by the complex of human individuum. Monadic islands signifying little if anything.

This prevalence of egocentric categories is often found in theological discussions of person, which, beyond mere acculturation, is the direct result of a lack in solid theological consensus based on sound historical analysis of the idea of 'person'. It is the estimation of this author, to use the words of Boethius, that this "is a topic which deserves a moment's notice."

Of the many brave, and often obscure, attempts to do justice to the Christian doctrine of the Trinity there is this element of the discussion which is riveting because of its cruciality yet distressing because of its elusiveness. For the recovery of a rich trinitarian basis for the church it would be advantageous to confront the present difficulty with the necessity of proposing a cogent and reasoned discourse in ecclesiastical circles on the Trinitarian concept of person.[10] Tangentially this discussion is replete with implications for modernity's conception of personal worth and existence,

It is my contention that the Triune nature of the Godhead is integral to everything we call Christian, problems and all. Of the thicket of controversies, the notion of triune personhood is among the thorniest, a rather untidy issue. Yet the struggle may be worth it on several fronts, for preserving analogically heuristic categories of a relational trinity promises a substantiation for both the worship of a self-giving God and the wholeness of human persons offered by the Church.[11] In a period, when historiographers are blaring the

---

[10]Many have posited that the Christian doctrine of the person is the basis for all secularized comments on the same. The Christian tradition laid a foundation of discussion which might at first appear quite esoteric and tangential, if discounted, the concept of person is bereft on much of its content. See the argument of Thomas Torrance, "The Goodness and Dignity of Man in the Christian Tradition," Modern Theology 4:4 (July 1988): 309-322. Bavinck has said in his Doctrine of God (Grand Rapids, Eerdmans, 1951), that three questions must be raised in discussing the Trinity: the meaning of essence or being, the concept of person, and the relation between the persons and essence, Ibid., 297.

[11]Heuristic, as a term denoting the ever-increasing knowledge, or discovery, of a self-revealing God who is the originator of any language or understanding about divine things, is used in a specific way in the following text. It is meant to carry the idea of real

excesses and errors of the Church's chequered past, it might be advantageous to note its revolutionary ontology. Hammered out by the communio sanctorum, the implications of divine personhood devolved upon human persons. What the Church has failed to grasp in our day is that the deliberations regarding divine personhood continue to be, however unconsciously, the basis of all human dignity and the rights we have come to expect.

There would be little disagreement that in Western culture there are few terms, if any, which are of more importance than 'person'. There is certainly no word which excels it in a general description of the human essence. However, when the basis of that statement is explored, immediately we are caught in the web of a diachronic aversion, usually a philosophically-based reaction, to placing these themes together: Trinity and person, divine individuality or simplicity with divine multiplicity. Our modern attempts at understanding, 'person' are suffused with either resultant conundrums or illogical assertions which, we are often told, logically negate its use in terms of Trinity.[12] Thus, Pannenberg can conclude with the intriguing capitulation that:

> Obviously the word 'person' automatically brings to the fore an image which seems impossible to connect with the idea of a power determinative of all reality. If I see the matter correctly, the crisis of the idea of God since the eighteenth century is connected chiefly with the problem of how the power determinative of all reality can be conceived of as a person.[13]

One might agree with Pannenberg's theological historiography but at the same time might be hesitant to so easily capitulate to the call for a rejection of a significant term and its train of implications. The issue here is not with the term itself, but the denial of the term's significance in trinitarian discussion, often due, it seems to me, more to the clout of certain schools of thought or individual popularity of theologians who discount its meaningfulness, rather than to the results of reasoned discourse.

Instead of rejecting it as passé, or irretrievably replete with difficulty, I am endeavoring to look at the conception of person as one of the bases, the sources, of a rich trinitarian doctrine for the Church. It may be that the Church discerned a "proper and true sense of the word" 'person' which is not devoid of ontological connotation, in spite of the

---

discovery, not a nominalistic definition. Thus, 'person' bears strong evocative power when used of the Triune God.

[12]Laurence Porter's article lays out the major thinkers' reservations concerning the use of person in Trinity in "On Keeping 'Persons' in the Trinity: A Linguistic Approach to Trinitarian Thought," Theological Studies 41 (1980): 530-548. Part Two of W.J. Hill's The Three Personed God: The Trinity as a Mystery of Salvation (Washington: Catholic Univ. of America Press, 1982), 83-216 is focused on a variety of modern reservations with the problem of the Trinity and divine Persons.

[13]Pannenberg, "The Question of God," 309.

cultural implications it has appropriated in the modern era.[14] Implicitly, and thus not exhaustively, due to various constraints, we will point to the subsequent analogical and practical consequences of this discussion for those who claim personhood as essential. There may even be a 'personalizing' implication for ministry in a world whose philosophy has become progressively what de Chardin described as a world-view "where only one reality seems to survive ... that floating, universal entity from which all emerges and into which all falls back...the new spirit: the new god. So, at the world's Omega, as at its Alpha, lies the Impersonal."[15]

The clamoring for wholesale rejection of the "trappings" of tradition has often been the signal and reason for some not to do so. More often than not, underneath the accumulated scales of by-gone eras, reside productive beliefs, quite similar to the notion of a 'philosophia perennis', which are only finally discarded to the misfortune of their loudest critics and entourage of indiscriminate followers. The lack of clarity on this subject directly impinges upon the viability and value of the term 'person' in theological contexts.

Statement of Thesis This thesis will establish that an identifiable constant, i.e., relationality, is central to a proper comprehension of divine person and is discernible throughout specific periods of formulative trinitarian thought. Categories pertaining to cognition and volition in an individual sense, though constituent of, are not necessarily equivalent to a complete concept of personhood.

Description of the Methodology Our proposed historical constant: the theological concept of person as most adequately defined, primarily but not exhaustively, in relation to 'another' - or an 'other-orientation', will be explored both historically and systematically in the selection of three crucial periods of thought in which a relational interpretation of divine personhood has come to the forefront.

The immediate purpose of this trans-historical method is two-fold: 1) to focus on the 'watershed' figures, texts and decisions which have most influenced this one concept and, 2) to reveal a distinct uneasiness that the Church has expressed in propounding a relational

---

[14]This phrase comes from Niceta of Remesiana's Power of the Holy Spirit 5, FC vol. 7, 28.

[15]The Phenomena of Man, trans. Bernard Wall (New York: Harper and Row, 1959), 258. While I do not agree with much that de Chardin offers in his attempt to allow theology and science to dialogue, I am in complete agreement with his assessment of the disparagement of modern society due to the incursion of impersonal categories at every level of modern discourse. Cf. Mary T. Clark's quote, without reference, by the same author, we are "lost if it (the Universe) did not converge on a person," in her "The Human Person and God," The Downside Review 84:274 (1966):16.

definition of person.[16]

The history of person as a relational distinctive coincides with the major periods of Christian thought. Within the periods selected, four specific thinkers will form the fulcrum of our discussion. Gregory of Nazianzus, Augustine, Richard of St. Victor, and Heribert Mühlen will be assessed in that area of their thought which specifically pertains to the doctrine of divine 'Person'. Although the periods are indisputable in terms of theological importance, the figures chosen may raise some hesitation for the doctrine of person in each has not often been given careful consideration. They are found here due to their penetrating insightfulness pertaining to the theological notion of 'person' and the perduring impact of their relational views of the Trinity in spite of either their relative silence or obscurity on the topic. Each provides the rudiments of a theological paradigm shift.

Chapter One will explore several methodological approaches required to make cogent claims regarding trinitarian personhood in light of some key modern reservations regarding the cogency of using 'person' in reference to God. There is a ontological disagreement between the Eastern and Western traditions which revolves around the notion of 'person' and its relation to nature. Possible points of amelioration include: a rethinking of the category of mystery, the use of analogical language, proper hermeneutical endeavor within the Christian community of faith - both past and present, and a reassessment of the person of the Holy Spirit.

Chapter Two will examine the early concept of substance as it led into the etymological background for the sister terms, 'prosopon' and 'persona'.[17] Well aware of the plethora of opinions/disagreements regarding the concept of substantia as the Greek philosophers conceived it. Though not always precise, reference must be made to the acceptance in the early Church of a troublesome distinction, based on the lack of clarity in Aristotelian metaphysics, between primary and secondary substance. Primary ousia, found strong critics in the Eastern tradition. Its origin, they disparaged as a monistic world view, which fundamentally posited immutable being, or a Being who possessed a nature that

---

[16]Throughout the formative periods of theological thought, when "three persons in One" is discussed there is an evident, though at times unwitting, dialectic between the substantial and the relational, the static and the dynamic, the objective and the subjective regarding 'persona'. Instead of balancing the complementarity of both sides of the dialectic it will be shown that, historically, all too often the modal, or oneness, or simplicity position has gained universal acceptance and the personal, pluralistic, or relational case has been repeatedly regarded as insufficient and often rejected as a result.

[17]Though there will be no attempt to repeat the convoluted histories of both the trinitological or christological controversies there must be some background laid for highlighting the prominence of the discussion of divine personhood. Thus, several of the important philosophical terms and ideas will be explored. **Substantia, prosopon, persona,** and **hypostasis** are the pinions upon which the argument of this work will be built.

implicitly contained all that the being could ever become.[18] The Cappadocian response was to advocate two notions of substantia, a generic and a particular. The impersonal qualities of prote ousia, as it was perceived in the East, was reinterpreted for use in the ecumenical councils. Secondary substance, deutera ousia, that which was generally or commonly understood as the components of things that bore a nature, provided the elements for an epistemological shift from the being of nature to a personal entity, pertaining to the individual and the concrete.[19] It is at this point we will judge the merits of the use of these philosophical concepts in the larger discussion of how to view the divine substance of the Triune Persons. After laying an etymological and philosophical basis for the origins of the 'person' in the Patristic period, we will turn to the crucial theological junctures where 'persona' was crafted as a perennially evocative symbol of reality.[20]

Chapter Three will consider both the Cappadocian and the Augustinian contributions to our proposed topic. It is my opinion that of the Cappadocian fathers Gregory of Nazianzus is the least recognized in his view of trinitarian personhood and has some distinct additions to the thesis proffered which have been overlooked.[21] Due to the intricate historical milieu and mutual verification or the Cappadocians, it is difficult to attempt a discussion of Gregory excluding either his predecessor, Athanasius or his famous counterparts Gregory of Nyssa and Basil. In essence, it is a Cappadocian concept of person we will present, with Gregory as a strong connecting link.

It was the Eastern emphasis on 'perichoresis', or the mutual indwelling of divine persons, which provided new groundwork for theologizing about the inner life of the Trinity. The view of God's internal life which resembled a co-inherent "dance" of mutual love and honor was proposed as the best means by which to worshipfully access the

---

[18]It should be noted that the incorporation of the idea of 'entelechia,' by the Greek philosophers, produced the notion of substance as a being with a certain potency inherent in its nature, rather than the static notion of simple being, which they are often caricatured as advocating. See discussion in chap. Two, 68-72

[19]This of course, provided a Pandora's box of difficulties christologically. The Monophysitic controversy stemmed from this well-meaning but problematic distinction. We shall also comment on the Essence-Energy antinomy that was a product of this Eastern philosophical tradition.

[20]Brief mention must be made of Tertullian, who sought to protect the Church from viewing God as mere 'object' rather than as an active 'subject' in the world. His use of 'persona', presented as a basis though not central to our thesis, was the first systematic attempt to bring analogical terms for a human role, mask, or face into defensible theological presentation of trinitarian personhood.

[21]It is usually Nyssa who is looked to for reasoned discourse, but Nazianzus "The Theologian" offers as much, if not more, on this topic that is cogent and subtle. Interestingly, Calvin was nick-named 'ho theologos' by Melanchthon because of the former's indebtedness to Nazianzus, "the theologian."

intimate union between the three trinitarian 'hypostaseis' in the identity of the divine nature. Although the term is not directly applied to the trinitarian essence until John of Damascus, this emphasis is prefigured in the Eastern tradition by Gregory of Nazianzus and Cyril of Alexandria. For Maximus the Confessor, this mutual indwelling pointed to the unveiling of Faith for the return to the principle, or the trinitarian 'arche' in the contradictory conditions of time. Without a doubt this period and the crucial idea of coinherence will prove to be a key in the fuller definition of person with which this dissertation is concerned.[22]

The second major section of this chapter must be given to a new understanding of Augustine's observations on divine personhood. Though he is seen as one of the Fathers of the Western trinitarian tradition there are indications that he vacillated between absolute unity statements and more relational categories, possible reflecting connection with the East, in spirit if not in letter. His christology is posited as a place to consider reevaluating his conception of the divine inter-relationship.

In Chapter Four specific attention will be given to the post-Augustinian 'oneness' tradition which strongly influenced the Middle Ages as is seen in Boethius' definition of person. The resemblance to earlier static notions in his choice of rationality as definitive of the person is clear. The one distinctive voice which reminded the church of a relational Trinity was the Victorine mystic and scholar, Richard. His De Trinitate was unique in its emphasis on the trinity in communal terminology and its re-definition of Boethian categories. He is consistently posited as the opposing, or at best, complementary thinker as regards person in Trinity in connection with the medieval period's nearly unanimous equation of person and nature. It will be necessary to extract the unique contributions of Richard in the discussion of intra-trinitarian love as the basis of his definition of person.

The second part of chapter Four will consider the theological transition in Richard's own thought. Drawing upon, but then taking his own course away from the Aristotelian/Augustinian category of unity, the view of persons which Richard introduced was dissimilar from the major medieval thinkers who set the course for the church on this issue. In a christological setting, dissatisfied with the lack of clarity present in the church, Boethius proffered the famous dictum, natura rationalis individua substantia. Aquinas, after him, would slightly alter the definition as subsistens distinctum in natura rationalis.

---

[22] Surprisingly, Augustine did not offer much new material to the concept of person. It was the inclusiveness of his thought and the breadth of its implications which is remarkable. His keen desire to accentuate the 'unity' of God, what the predominant direction that the Western Church would take. Because of the fear of being called tri-theistic the Church resorted to the safer emphasis on the unity or oneness of divine personhood. Thus, the relational aspects which the Cappadocians had offered in the Greek East did not find the acceptance that the 'oneness' ideas of the North African doctor enjoyed, however misunderstood they might have been.

Both Richard and Duns Scotus after him, countered the Boethian strain with person as an rationalis naturae incommunicabilis exsistentia. Richard's "ontological exemplarism" based on the scriptural statement of the essence of God as love led him to some intriguing conclusions with which both Bonaventure and Duns Scotus worked. We will explore each facet of his definition of 'person' and the responses of Aquinas to them.

Granted, we live in a world epistemologically, methodologically and theologically removed from the heuristic realism of Gregory of Nazianzus, Augustine of Hippo or Richard of St. Victor, but it remains to be seen if the inheritances bestowed upon our generation are as easily retrieved as they have been squandered. Aquinas' stature and work over-shadowed that of Richard, and in line with the dialectic proposed in our thesis, his Summa served to re-direct medieval trinitarian thought back to the security of its more rationalistic/essentialistic Augustinian roots.

In the modern period, the influences of the Enlightenment which have fed into the last two centuries of trinitarian discussion, has exacerbated the loss of a fundamental relationality in defining person.[29] One of the most evident shifts in approaches to personhood is lucidly discussed in John MacMurray's Gifford Lectures of (1953-54). In radical contrast to the prevailing Cartesian categories, MacMurray makes two fundamental points: First, to define person as an self-reflective "I" alone, that is removed from relationship, is to posit a thinker who does not move or act, a non-agent. Thinking must be joined to acting, moving, or 'agency' to make one responsible. If the two are not joined the result is half a person. Action is inchoate without a context. Second, in order to act meaningfully as persons there must be 'another'. He claims that all meaningful knowledge is for the sake of action, and so, all meaningful knowledge is for the sake of friendship - an 'other-orientation'. MacMurray's theses have clashed with the majority view in both philosophical and theological sectors. However, his theses find resonance in an ever increasing number of theologians who are dissatisfied with the bias of cognitive/volitional definitions alone for person.

A survey of recent literature on 'person' reveals that the German Catholic theological

---

[29]The Enlightenment proposed a highly philosophical view of 'person' which fed directly into the nineteenth century theologians' approach to the Trinity and consequently into their views of humanity. We are not unaware of the Reformers' basic recapitulation of Augustinian and Thomistic categories but latent in the present thesis is the awareness of a similar 'incapacity' to deal with personhood relationally. In both periods, broadly speaking, the ascendancy of the will as descriptive of the person prevails. Generalizations at this point are more detrimental than constructive. There are important distinctions to be made between Calvin's view of person and the other Reformers. According to Torrance, Calvin had a strong Eastern proclivity, in ecclesiology, in eucharistic theology which placed him at variance with the Latin tradition. T.F. Torrance, Theological Dialogue Between Orthodox and Reformed Churches (Edinburgh: Scottish Academic Press, 1985), 12-14.

community has once again brought the discussion of relation categories to the foreground.[24] Chapter Five will provide a brief survey of the present theological definitions of person but will primarily focus on one specific personalistic thinker. Heribert Mühlen, the Catholic charismatic leader and systematician from Paderborn has written a work, Heilige Geist als Person which has been deeply influential in circles outside North America. His approach is in many ways a modern re-appraisal and application of several of the themes which the Cappadocians and Richard St. Victor sought to make clear.[25] Apart from assessing Mühlen's pneumatology, research has revealed no work specifically related to his doctrine of person and its connection to former thinkers, thus another important facet historically contingent upon precedents on personhood will be explicated. The work of the Australian Jesuit, David Coffey, who has been instrumental in introducing Mühlen to the English-speaking world, has done so in a criticism Mühlen's foundational categories, especially his pneumatological constructs. It appears that the relationship between the social analogy of the Trinity and its psychological counterpart has fared the same in recent days as it has in the fifth and the twelfth centuries.

For the theologians we will deal with, the Christian trinity: a) is the source for an understanding of the personhood, divine or human, b) involves an implicit intra-personal giving and receiving between divine persons, c) and therefore finds clearest expression in vestigial or analogical similarities with human relationships of mutuality and committed interrelatedness. Though clearly aware of the volitional and cognitional factors of their contemporaries they explicitly draw lines which open the discussion in the direction of the relational.

Chapter Six will serve as a conclusion in drawing upon the strengths of the social analogy of the Trinity within a theological context which is less than favorable to it. The relative merits of the major options for Trinitarian personhood will be explored. An

---

[24]Few of these, however, express an intense interest in inter-relational explanations of person. Karl Rahner's strong emphasis on the external acts of God being inseparable from the internal attributes of the Trinity has been persuasive in most trinitarian discussion, that which transpires within the Godhead. Catherine LaCugna appraises Rahner properly in "Re-Conceiving the Trinity as the Mystery of Salvation," in Scottish Journal of Theology 38:1 (1985): 1-23 when she states that he predicates "relationality as being of the very essence of God," Ibid., 13. However she does not deal with the problems Rahner has with the use of 'person' and the impact that has on his entire trinitarian discussion in relation to humanity. While we will not disagree with the main desire to keep 'immanent' and 'economic' attributes together, it will be correctively advantageous to explore personhood in light of the analogies revealed in the work of Heribert Mühlen.

[25]Der heilige Geist als Person: Beitrag zur Frage nach der dem heiligen Geiste eigentümlichen Funktion in der Trinität, bei der Inkarnation und im Gnadenbund, Münsterische Beiträge zur Theologie, vol. 26 (Münster: Aschendorff, 1963), is the key text which we will deal with alongside his articles on the subject. His thesis correlates with ours closely. As the bibliograpy entries indicate his ecclesiastical interests have caused him to write much on the implications of relational unity as it is worked out in the Church.

Appendix will also be included to provide further illuminative historical and sociological background for Victorine personalism. The trinitarian analogy which came from the Abbey of St. Victor found its source in a remarkably unique philosophical and spiritual milieu.

Contributions and Rationale

If in fact ideas have consequences, further significance of the proposed topic is offered in light of the present stalemate between two heresies: the threat to de-personalize God which reflexively results in arid deism, and the corresponding danger in advocating a tritheism which strikes a blow at the root of traditional monotheism.[26] To combat these trends, recent discussions on the Trinity have produced analogies in the areas of familial and ecclesial intersubjectivity and personal intrasubjectivity which need to be assessed and corrected for use in the Church at large.

The logical basis for our thesis is that the past holds both profound supports and heuristic correctives for the present.[27] Tradition has shown that with each rise in the interest of personhood there has been a corresponding denial of its presuppositions and a continual return to monistic or rationalistic concepts. If we are correct, it may be attributed to inadequate theological definitions of personhood which require immediate attention. The exclusion of the past due to claims that it is irrelevant, while, at the same time, giving ascendancy to the present, is a common theological phenomenon. Its premise bears faulty reasoning however. A present divorced from the past has no fundamentally higher claim to perspicacity or applicability than the past. In fact, it is self-defeating because of the brevity of the present. Process theology has adequately noted that what has transpired passes away. What that says of the claims to concrete reality in the present is of little consolation to the many who claim that there is permanent, some would even say transcendent, truth. Can the present hold any truth beyond itself? If so, then maybe the past is a neglected harbinger of necessary data. The theological notion of person is a good case-study for this diachronic discussion.

---

[26]Theological history and historico-political events evidence intriguing results from an anthropological standpoint when these aberrations are allowed in the Church. See, for instance, the East's criticism by C. Giannaras, "Consequences of an Erroneous Trinitology in the Human World," in Les Études Theologiques de Chambesy, vol. 2, 497-502, La signification et l'actualité du IIe Concile Oecumenique pour le monde Chrètien d'aujourd'hui. (Chambesy-Geneve: Editions du Centre Orthodoxe du Patriarcat Oecumenique, 1982). An impersonal idea of God spawns extreme de-humanization in cultures where it is found. Tritheistic tendencies nearly always feed a rampant individualism, or at least, divorces the reality of an ontological connectedness resident in persons from their actual experience. It is an ancillary contention of this thesis that that the Trinity is basic to the highest ideals of any true and fundamentally good society or community.

[27]Gerald O'Collins, "Criteria for Interpreting the Traditions," In Problems and Perspectives of Fundamental Theology, ed. René Latourelle and Gerald O'Collins, trans. M. J. O'Connell, 327-339 (New York: Paulist Press, 1982).

And the Catholic Faith is this:
That we worship
one God in Trinity,
and Trinity in Unity;
Neither confounding the Persons:
nor dividing the Substance

Pseudo-Athanasian Creed

CHAPTER ONE

Methodology:
The Possibility of Relational Trinitarian Language

In a post-Enlightenment, post-modern era, theology has been both helped and
hindered by the assessments of the harder sciences and philosophy. The sacred boundaries
of objectivity often exclude metaphysics. Censorius adjudications of irrelevance or
unverifiability devolve upon those disciplines which trade upon unseen realities. The
epistemological chasm hewn by Kantian agnosticism, fed by the fires of empiricism and
then positivism produced an incendiary assortment of relativisms. Protracted by disciplines
like linguistic analysis, or modal logic, the autonomous "sciences" have become virtually
tyrannous forces to be reckoned with as they pervade and critique topics pertaining to
"spiritual" reality.

As a result, the notion of revelation shares, at best, an uneasy alliance with analytic
philosophy; and topics which are distillations of revealed truth find themselves outside the
pale altogether. Confirmation of this assessment comes immediately upon the mention of
two terms especially if in proximity to one another; "Trinity" and "Person". Language
concerning the Trinity has been bombarded from every point on the epistemological
spectrum. To speak of Trinitarian persons is tantamount in many circles to
"remythologizing" that which has all but freed itself from such anthropomorphistic
trappings.

Nonetheless, both categories persist despite the tenacity of those who propose their
extraction from theological discourse. It is with a desire to recognize the merit of those
criticisms, as well as to reveal the epistemological and ontological pinions upon which this
work is built, that it is incumbent upon us to look at the possibility of speaking about
divine persons. It may be that precisely at this point theological tradition has something to
offer its former handmaidens, turned heady disparagers.

The Christian Church has consistently agreed that the highest essence statement

13

about divinity is that "God is love" (I John 4:8).[1] An intriguing theological recapitulation in our generation is the reconsideration of the claim that this love is related to a triune Godhead and as such is fundamental to a proper understanding of reality. Divine love, then, is not only God's initiative towards humanity but is the essential nature of the Godhead. Historically and theologically, the best, howbeit the most controversial, analogy of that love has been expressed by an interpersonal dynamic and relatedness within the Christian doctrine of the Trinity.

Theological consensus confirms that the modern notion of person finds its ultimate origin in the early Church discussions on christology and trinitology. The uniqueness of the individual person is a distinctly Christian phenomenon.[2] "The value of the person emerged first in the Christian context where God's action first touches man as a particular person and only from there reaches mankind as a whole....In Him (Christ) is established both the possibility and the necessity of developing the concept of person."[3] This statement is refreshing in its clarity and brevity but its premise, shared by many thinkers, has not gone unchallenged. A historical discussion of "person" will follow, but in anticipation, we must clarify what is meant by these claims. There is little doubt that philosophy and metaphysics preceded the early Church discussions on such things as person. What is claimed here, however, is that the trinitarian and christological controversies crystallized certain factors pertaining to personhood which the other disciplines left to themselves

---

[1]This love is revealed in both of the Testaments, though it is the holiness of God which provides the basis of a progressively revelatory picture of God. The love of God is discerned a holy love. Lv. 11:44, Dt. 7:6-9, Ps. 95:3-5, Is. 43:14, Ez. 36:23, Hb. 1:12. R. N. Flew confirms the same interconnection in the New Testament. The Idea of Perfection in Christian Theology (London: Oxford Univ. Press, 1934), 116. See Thomas C. Oden, Systematic Theology: Volume One, The Living God (New York: Harper and Row), 118-126. I recognize with Jüngel that this essential statement is not a univocal one, it does not follow that all love is God. Though E. Jüngel would not follow my thesis entirely, there would be general agreement here that the Trinity is fundamental to comprehending divine love, God As the Mystery of the World: On the Foundation of the Theology of the Crucified One in the Dispute between Theism and Atheism (Grand Rapids: Eerdmans Pub. Co., 1983), 314-330.

[2]Origen, Against Celsus Bk 4.23-25, 99, Ante-Nicene Fathers, (Grand Rapids: Eerdmans, 1979), 506-507, 541. Hereafter ANF. It might be possible to compare individual merits within and without the Judeo-Christian schema, but the distinction which Christianity made from other anthropologies was that each individual was of extreme importance to God.

[3]Christian Schutz and Rupert Sarach, "Der Mensch als Person," in Mysterium Salutis, ed. Johannes Feiner and Magnus Löhrer, vol. 2 (Einsiedeln, Benzinger Verlag, 1967), 637-639. Due to sensitivities regarding language, it must be stated that every attempt will be taken to be inclusive where it does not alter the original texts or intents. The use of masculine pronouns to refer to God is used in such a spirit. Speaking of the category of the person, Romano Guardini writes, "If I am not mistaken, antiquity did not have a true concept of person - indeed one does not seem to find it outside the realm of revelation," The World and the Person, trans. Stella Lange (Chicago: Henry Regnery Co., 1965), 115.

would never and have never fully comprehended. There is a distinctly hollow ring to metaphysical discussions of person apart from the Triune reality.[4]

Due to the prevalent "dissociation of sensibility," or the prevailing uncritically accepted dichotomy between faith and reason, there is a resultant reticence in making knowledge-claims about that which is not immediately sensate.[5] Yet, syllogistic, or worse, skeptical reasoning aside, it is difficult to dispute that the historical basis for our idea of person, properly understood, "resulted from the dogmatic struggles of early Christianity and has no roots in pre-Christian thought."[6]

Supported by a perspective that reveals yet another inherent difficulty, Thomas Torrance states:

> It cannot be stressed enough that it was this Trinitarian doctrine of God that actually gave rise to the concept of person, which was quite unknown in the world before, and to the realisation that God has created human beings in such a way that their inter-human relations are meant to be inter-personal, and as such are meant to reflect on the level of the creature the inter-personal relations of God himself.[7]

From the crucible of truth-claims based on revelation, Torrance's statement points to the often confounding category of analogous thinking, the only means whereby it is possible to

---

[4]One example of critique is C. J. De Vogel's argument in "The Concept of Personality in Greek and Christian Thought." Studies in Philosophy and the History of Philosophy 2 (1963). Even if one concurs with the early Greek philosophical elements of individuation, including microcosmic/macrocosmic conceptions, and self-determination, the question still remains as to the source of such propositions. Platonic and Plotinian "forms" are indeed metaphysical, but to what reality do they point? It will be seen that the accusation of projection cast upon traditional theological constructs can be applied to their philosophical forebears. On the other hand, there may be intimations of reality in the eighth to the second century B.C. which reveal a prevenient "philosophia perennis", which set the stage for interpreting revealed categories.

[5]This phrase is T.S. Eliot's which A. Louth draws upon for his critique of the division of thinking from feeling as a synergistic means of verification of reality. Discerning the Mystery: An Essay on the Nature of Theology (Oxford: Clarendon Press, 1983), 1-16.

[6]Robert Thomas Sears, "Spirit: Divine and Human. The Theology of the Holy Spirit of Heribert Mühlen and its Relevance for Evaluating the Data of Psychotherapy," (Ph.D. dissertation, Fordham University, 1974), 59. From a more critical vantage point, though quite fair on this element, Herbert Wolf acknowledges, "Historically speaking, the concept of person (and personality) had its origins not in the attempt to comprehend man as a person, but in the philosophical-theological task of defining both the relations of the three "persons" within the Trinity and the "person" of Jesus Christ." "An Introduction to the Idea of God as Person," Journal of Bible and Religion 32:1 (1964): 27.

[7]Thomas F. Torrance, "The Goodness and Dignity of Man in the Christian Tradition," Modern Theology 4:4 (July, 1988):320, (Author's emphasis). See also his The Mediation of Christ (Grand Rapids, Eerdmans Pub. Co., 1984), 58-59. One difficulty that I recognize and must continually confront is the tendency to speak in anthropological terms due to their accessibility rather than acknowledge the use of analogy in theological categories which are, by their nature, elusive. Cf. Oden, The Living God, 218. This seems to be the main message, and really only positive contribution of M. Durrant's agnostic approach in Theology and Intelligibility (Boston: Routledge and Kegan Paul, 1973), see p. 195.

approach the discussion of transcendent being. Of course, language is never fully specific. Dorothy Sayers enlightens this point where she speaks of the images behind the words we use due to the fact that:

> Every word is a unique event: there is nothing exactly like it in the universe: a meeting-place of images, each of which comes...bearing gifts, and attended by a long and glittering train of associates.... We can never permanently empty a word of all meanings save one: we can at most choose to restrict ourselves temporarily to a particular meaning in the context of a particular argument.[8]

The history of the 'person' as a term points to a Christian elucidation of a concept which had been expressed in faint glimmers of self-recognition attached to the idea of 'prosopon'.[9] The transfer of personal categories, or the reification of the person, demanded an enlargement of definition in both philosophy and theology. By nature, re-definition disallows total expurgation of a concept's former content from the resultant representation. In this light, perhaps theologians ought not be so quick to respond in defensiveness to accusations of lack of intelligibility and imprecision of terminology. It may be that through a concerted effort to eschew the factor of planned obsolescence, modernity might be rightly challenged by a reminder that past articulations bear images, and meanings, that would deepen our present thinking about reality.

The desire here is to analyze a theological term without destroying the context out of which it arose. This reflection must be done while maintaining cognizance of the illuminations found in modern insights, whether anthropological, psychological or linguistic. It would appear that a close analysis of the contributions of the theological origins to former contexts might confirm a productive encounter between original conceptions and present construction. Though the explicit theological intention of this thesis has been stated, it recognizes the value of "a meeting-place of images." If analogy is a requisite for talk about God, then this work will have to risk the use of language which might be criticized as anthropomorphistic, in the hope of clarification.

Our task is to lay a basis for a cogent discussion of person which has to do with a broader picture of the Trinity, especially as it is seen in the West. In order to do so several barriers must be faced and overcome. First is a problem in the orientation, or fundamental positions of the traditions. As has often been noted, theological treatises which have originated in the West have tended to bifurcate the reality of the Trinity.

---

[8]Dorothy Sayers, "The Poetry of The Image in Dante and Charles Williams" in Further Papers on Dante, 1957, Reprint (Westport, Conn.: Greenwood Press, 1979), 183. P.T. Geach paraphrases a quote by Sir William Hamilton regarding this same battle but specifically pertaining to 'person', "A good new term is like a fortress to dominate country won from the forces of darkness; but those forces never sleep and will strive by their Philological Arm to recover lost territory." The Virtues Stanton Lectures 1973-4 (Cambridge: Cambridge Univ. Press, 1977), 75-76.

[9]Further discussion of this point will come in chap. Two.

Quite rightly the scholastic separation of **De Deo Uno** and **De Deo Trino** has been ✗
criticized for its propensity to threaten the theological necessity of an inseparability between
unity and differentiation within the Godhead.[10] The result over two millenia of trinitology
in the West has been the casting about of vitriolic epithets such as; 'tritheism' or
'modalism', 'speculative' versus 'non-theological', ad infinitum. For the theologians that
form the groundwork of this dissertation this misunderstanding provokes concern. The
relationship between divine personhood and the divine nature is neither anachronistic or
stylish, but requires adequate and subtle articulation. Unless the two can be reconciled,
any discussion of Triune personhood is relegated to implausibility or incoherency.

But the problems go deeper. Second, and a corollary of the first, a more
fundamental barrier to talk about a Trinity, much less the persons that comprise it, falls
along a philosophical line. Modern thought has been infused with the premise that any
deliberations about God in himself must necessarily be suspect because it is an inscrutable
mystery and thus by the subject's immensity necessitates a contemplative apophaticism or a
disinterested agnosticism. Much has been done in the area of ontology to further alienate
divine being from created nature, while in other circles the conflation of the two has
produced a modern version of panentheistic monism. Even though Tillich's warning may
have intended the differentiating of the being of God from all other being, and in spite of
the Bultmannian insistence that to speak of God is to objectify the non-objectifiable, it
remains a cogent question to ask what the essential character of the Being is behind the
revelation that the Church has traditionally interpreted as one of a Triune nature.[11] No

---

[10]Found in many of the Church doctors, Aquinas is often pointed to as paradigmatic
here and appears even as late as Lonergan. See Rahner's fundamental argument, "Remarks
on the Dogmatic Treatise "De Trinitate"," in Theological Investigations, trans. Kevin Smyth
(Baltimore: Helicon Press, 1966), 77-102, also 70. Theodore Jennings also sees this as
deleterious to Christian theology, Beyond Theism: A Grammar of God-Language (New
York: Oxford Univ. Press, 1985), 16-18. The distinctions between Eastern and Western
traditions found throughout this work are based primarily upon the differences in
trinitology, primarily seen in the work of the Cappadocians, in contrast to Augustine's
formulations, although we will emphasize some interesting similarities also.

[11]This differentiation between divine and human being is older than the discussion
about person, but is basic to it. Plato, Aristotle, Pseudo-Dionysius, Augustine, the Greek
Fathers all dealt with it in a variety of ways. Here see Paul Tillich, Systematic Theology,
vol. 1 (Chicago: Univ. of Chicago Press, 1951), 188-189, 235-241. From statements like the
above, Paul Edwards labels Tillich as a 'metaphysical' thinker in the sense that he abhorred
the opposite, an 'anthropormorphic' view of God. But he goes on to accuse Tillich of
unintelligibility in that he takes the via negativa to an extreme, when he says that the
absolute being of God means that one cannot even speak of the existence, only the actuality
of God; to do the former is to be atheistic. Ibid., 205. All language thus must be symbolic
or metaphorical with reference to God, yet, as Edwards points out, the symbols finally have
no meaning. Our view of analogical language coincides with Edwards ontology. Although
we cannot fully understand the Being of God, our language must, to be intelligible, refer to
something substantial, meaningful, or to use Tillich, it must not be an 'infinite emptiness'
or abyss. Paul Edwards, "Professor Tillich's Confusions," in Philosophy of Religion, ed.

human mind can expect to fully comprehend a transcendent category of this magnitude, but the ontological position taken affects every theological category which from it ineluctably issues.

Third, at other points a hermeneutical tack, formed by the modern interpretive tool of making the economic Trinity equal to the immanent, is employed which demands that all we can know of God must be explicitly supported by His 'acts in history'.[12] From this fundamentally existentialist interpretation any other thought about God is suspect. We shall discuss this at several points in what follows, but fundamentally what is a stake here, it seems to me, is an important connective element. If one is not circumspect the result of the 'economic' interpretation, can be that function (recorded acts in history) supercedes or, as in some cases, replaces ontology. In response to the characterizations of the 'ontological interpretation', which accuse it of mere speculation concerning the divine, I am advocating a strong complementarity between salvific acts and the interpersonal ontology of the God who performs those acts. Much remains to be divulged by a historically-based method, which attempts to interpret the events in such a way as to reflect on the nature of the God who has revealed Himself to Israel and the Church. The perennial debates about 'what' God has done and how that is to be interpreted in light of 'who' God is will continue. The concerns here are focused on that which is behind the actions. Has the Augustinian/Thomistic tradition of 'subsistent relations' most efficiently expressed the 'why' and the 'how' of the acts of God? Does the 'economic' Trinity form a demarcation line which cannot be crossed save for the merely speculative? I do not think so.

I. East and West Approach Trinitarian Language: The Possibility of Bridges

If one were to honestly chart the cherished values of the world today, almost assuredly one of the dearest could be subsumed under the category of relationality[13].

Steven M. Cahn (New York: Harper and Row, 1970), 209-235.

[12]Indicative of this trend is the enormous influence G. E. Wright's The God who Acts (London: SCM Press, 1952), has had not only on Biblical studies but on subsequent theology as well, often in ways that might grieve the author. Rahner's axiom, that the immanent Trinity is the economic and vice versa has also held great sway. See The Trinity, trans. Joseph Donceel (New York: Herder and Herder, 1970), 45ff. With specific regard to the influence this has had on doctrine of divine person see Catherine LaCugna's entire corpus, primarily in "Re-conceiving the Trinity as Mystery of Salvation," Scottish Journal of Theology 38:1 (1985): 1-23. Our tentative agreement and critique of the economic focus alone will follow.

[13]A short list indicates the direction in which relational categories are being interpreted. Mention is required of the influence of the nineteenth century Idealists who brought the idea of person as relation into vogue. Fichte, Hegel, Feuerbach, and Schelling all made reference to the transcendent individuality, or subjectivity, which required another in order to be real. This "I- You" paradigm was seized by personalistic philosophers and applied anthropologically.

When all is said and done, relations - often equated with persons and their constituent factors, are a major preoccupation with an history which reaches to the earliest thinkers. Even though the combined efforts of Scholasticism, Enlightenment thinkers and scientific materialism have sought to explain reality by tenets which promulgate philosophically impersonal monisms, the antithetical majority response has been that of affirming an interpersonal reality, an order that speaks of relations.[14] In spite of the difficulty in a

---

Initially it was the dialogical or intersubjective philosophers who applied the principle of interrelatedness to personhood. Martin Buber, I and Thou, trans. R. G. Smith (New York: Charles Scribner's Sons, 1958), or introduction to several in B. Casper, Das dialogische Denken, Eine Untersuchung der religionsphilosophischen Bedeutung Franz Rosenzweigs, Ferdinand Ebners und Martin Bubers (Freiburg: Herder Verlag, 1967). See also the emphasis here by Gabriel Marcel and Dietrich von Hilderbrand. A review of Personalisms is so diverse and even confusing that all we can offer are indicators of sources of the philosophy. From the Boston tradition; Brightman, Edgar Sheffield, Person and Reality: An Introduction to Metaphysics (New York: Ronald Press Co., 1958); and his Personalism in Theology (New York: AMS Press rep. 1943 ed., 1979); a more modern approach in the same vein, Peter A. Bertocci, The Person God Is (London: George Allen and Unwin Ltd., 1970). Alfred North Whitehead, the father of Process thought, redefined traditional categories of relationality, see Process and Reality (New York: The Free Press, 1957). For a more modern process application, Marjorie Hewitt Suchocki, God, Christ, Church (New York, Crossroad, 1988), see p. 35-45, 213-220. Also the intriguing twist of these emphases in the ethics of Norman Pittenger, The Meaning of Being Human (New York: Pilgrim Press, 1982.) Note also the French Personalists led by Maurice Nédoncelle, Intersubjectivité et ontologie: Le Defi personnalist (Louvain: Nauwelaerts, 1974); and Catholic existential Personalism is discussed in American Catholic Philosophical Association Proceedings, Existential Personalism, vol. 60, ed. Daniel O. Dahlstrom (Washington, Catholic Univ. of America, 1974). The social philosophers include Nicolas Berdyaev, Spirit and Reality (London: Geoffrey Bles: The Centenary Press, rep. 1946 ed.), Freedom and the Spirit (London: Centenary Press, 1935), The Destiny of Man (London: Geoffrey Bles, 1948); S.L. Franck Reality and Man, trans. Natalie Duddington (New York: Taplinger Pub. Co., 1966), John MacMurray, The Form of the Personal, Gifford Lectures 1953-54. 2 vols. 1969 (Atlantic Highlands, NJ: Humanities Press, rep. 1979), Frank G. Kirkpatrick, Community: A Trinity of Models (Washington: Georgetown Univ. Press, 1986). Max Scheler's thought permeates this discussion also. See his Formalism in Ethics and Non-Formal Ethics of Values, trans. by Manfred S. Frings and Roger L. Funk (Evanston: Northwestern Univ. Press, 1973).

[14]Cf. the "Unmoved Mover" of the cosmological proof, the influence of Cartesian principles or Leibnizian categories of individuation or Hegelian 'Absolute Subject". Douglas Hall has postulated that Luther broke the vice of the Athenian philosophical structures in positing relationality, instead of rationality in defining the imago dei, Imaging God: Dominion as Stewardship (Grand Rapids: Eerdmans Pub. Co., 1986), esp. ch. 4. C. Gunton's Enlightenment and Alienation (Grand Rapids: Eerdmans Pub. Co., 1985) is an excellent counterpart to Andrew Louth's Discerning the Mystery, in critiquing the Enlightenment categories. On Hegel see John O'Donnell's "The Trinity as Divine Community," Gregorianum (1988): 10-11 for helpful analysis. The Hegelian Trinity is seen as an expression of a fundamental individualism. He says, "In the last analysis, in this model, the other's being is functional." Ibid., 10. Cf. also the monumental multi-faceted task of the Erwin Schadel's ed. Bibliographia Trinitariorum 2 vols. (New York: K. G. Saur, 1984-1988, vol. 2, xii-xv, reviews of Vol. 1, 461-572), as a witness to the diachronic fascination with the "analogia trinitatis" compiled with specific interest in Comenius' assessment of universal triadism.

Text critique the Enlightenment

change in modern paradigmatic emphases, i.e., from the mind or the will as the bases of ontology to relationality, there is evidence of just such a shift in many sectors. There is a burgeoning commitment to study of the sources and implications of relationality in the world.[15] That which is of interest here are the philosophical, sociological, and theological discussions which tie that relationality to something beyond the tangible world. In short, for many this world 'reflects', 'images', or 'adumbrates' the existence of a loving, or relational God.[16] If that is the case it would behoove us to attempt to understand more fully the revealed categories which provide the source, the definition of relationality.[17]

Modernity has seen a groundswell of 'personalisms' that purport to be sources of redemption from the impersonal existence from which modern philosophies have been birthed. The problem is that these 'personalisms' themselves are, more often than not,

---

[15]Liberation theology in general has shown increasing interest in the issue of relationality, with differing commitments to consensual dogmatic formulations. Jürgen Moltmann and Elisabeth Moltmann-Wendel's Humanity in God (New York: Pilgrim Press, 1983) has had influence on some feminist approaches to this subject, especially in the recurrent critique of patriarchy and postulating of other options, including a look at the feminine within the triune reality, and the "social personalism" called for to image the Trinity. Other feminists are critiquing modernity's solipsistic tendencies, see Carol Gilligan, In a Different Voice: Psychological Theory and Women's Development (Cambridge: Harvard Univ. Press, 1982), esp. 151-174. Of course, both feminist interests and process theology's emphasis on relationality are joined, however spuriously, in Marjorie Hewitt Suchocki's God, Christ, Church: A Practical Guide to Process Theology (New York: Crossroad, 1988), 214-233.

[16]To save laborious footnoting here we will mention representatives from a variety of areas, most of whom we will refer to in the course of this paper. In Philosophy, M. Scheler, H. Arendt, M. Nedoncelle, John Macmurray, A. Shutte, D. Brown, C. Gunton, T. Torrance; Sociology, P. Berger, S. Hauerwas, A. MacIntyre, F.G. Kirkpatrick; Theology, F. D. Maurice, K. Barth, J. Moltmann, J. Segundo, H. Mühlen, C. Plantinga, W. Hill, J. Mouroux, J. Galot, B. de Margerie, J. Zizioulas, W. Kasper, L. Boff; and within this group specifically, the Social Analogists, R. C. Moberly, L. Hodgson, C.C.J. Webb, L. Thornton. Equally important is the critique of social theories of the Trinity like Richard's which states that there is a love possible between the Lover and the Loved that only requires one intersubjective reality. My response will be evident in what follows but to anticipate, my concern would focus on the kind of love that would entail and the question then whether it is of the highest notion of love.

[17]This has been the basis of one of the "proofs" for the existence of God. See Thomas Oden, "A divine person must be posited as the premise of human personhood," The Living God, 150, see also 87. Oden provides a consistently balanced view of the major themes in Christian theology because of his commitment to traditional, consensual postulations. The theme of this dissertation finds agreement in many of the early fathers, however, it does not take the same extreme Idealistic route of the Hegelian 'Geist' or the Boston Personalist's anthropomorphized monadism.

grounded in an individualistic world-view which negates the reality they propound.[18]

The connection between one's view of a relational reality and either the recognition or rejection of a divine being which is related within itself, appears to be inseparable. One strategic place where this has produced a marked difference is between the Eastern and Western traditions. On the relationship between the nature of Divine Unity or Essence and the resultant worldview, we find that they exist within opposing analogies which are difficult to reconcile; on the one hand there is God the Father as 'fons' or source of divine life and persons, which, in the West, advanced a hierarchical ordering within the Trinity, and on the other the analogy of persons in a divine community which, in the East mainly, left unanswered questions about the well-protected unity of the Godhead. The fundamental difference can be stated in the form of questions: Is there a concrete reality to the essence of God or must it be relegated to the sphere of abstraction?[19] What does one mean when speaking of that reality, the Latin 'substantia' or the Greek 'ousia'? Does 'person' indicate something that is constituent of the Trinitarian reality or is it merely a means of perceiving the ways in which God acts?

There are signs of amelioration. Intriguingly, it has been an arch-Thomist, E.L. Mascall, who, feeling that this discussion is far from peripheral, and in need of constant

---

[18]In La réciprocité des consciences, Maurice Nédoncelle surmised, "All the personalisms until now have been monadologies," quoted in Jean Galot, The Person of Christ: Covenant Between God and Man (Chicago: Franciscan Herald Press, 1984), 36. Louis Bouyer, says of modern personalism that it has:
"unfortunately been already debased. The opposed meanings of person (one living in interpersonal relationships) and individual (one essentially partitioned off and alienated from others) have been turned—by the same Christian thinkers who drew attention to the contrast in the first place—into a fawning and unseemly apologia for Marxism. The only one in this group to hold his own was Maurice Nédoncelle.... Far from holding that the person has the exclusive ability and duty to merge into the crowd, he developed with subtlety and depth the theme of reciprocity of consciousnesses as the leitmotif of his personalism."
Cosmos: The World and the Glory of God (Petersham, Mass.: St. Bede's Publications, 1988), 183.

[19]Christos Giannaras (sometimes seen as Yannaras) states strongly that this was the fundamental point of schism between East and West. He distinguishes between the Greek philosophical heritage of the West and the Hellenic forebears of the East's ontological starting point, who, in contradistinction to the rational interpretation of divine essence issuing in monarchial interpretations, based their theology on Biblical revelation, thus connecting "being" with "acting". This difference, he feels, issues in radically different views of God and of every other point of the order of salvation. "Consequences of an Erroneous Trinitology in the Modern World," in Les Études théologiques de Chambesy, Vol. 2 La Signification et l'actualité du IIe concile oecumenique pour le monde chretien d'aujourd'hui (Chambesy-Geneve: Editions du centre Orthodoxe du Patriarcat oecumenique, 1982), 499. See also his scathing critique of modern Catholic trinitology in, "The Distinction between Essence and Energies and its Importance for Theology," St. Vladimir's Theological Quarterly 19 (1975):232-245.

clarification, has proposed a point of rapprochement between the East and West at the place where the disagreement has most often been fueled. He wonders if theologians have not overstated the separation of the traditions. Reviewing the modern concept of 'subsistent relations', he focuses quite rightly on Augustine's original intention, dynamic relationality not abstract static origins.[20] Rather than an attempt to depersonalize the Godhead, Mascall sees the West as proffering helpful categories to the East, especially in its usage of 'relational being'.[21]

Nonetheless, the debate has caused deep rifts which will require tolerant deliberation if the healing of differences is to occur. The East does have supportable criticisms concerning the West's retrenchment in an understanding of the Godhead as an absolute unity defined philosophically apart from biblical foundation. The Eastern theologians continue to remind us of the 'non-personal' categories inherent in Platonic and Aristotelian logic upon which much of the West's theology has been constructed without recognition of important nuances. They contend that the Cappadocians were the source of a theological revolution, of Copernican proportion, in their ruminations on 'hypostasis' and 'prosopon'. In fact, John Zizioulas, feels that the world owes the concept of the person to the Greek fathers.[22] The attempt will be made here to show the strong similarities between the traditional viewpoints, parallel approaches which have been obscured until quite recently. Some in the western tradition are taking the advice of the East, as well as softening criticisms of Eastern epistemology.[23] Constructive planks, of theological and philosophical nature, are being erected in this renewed discourse.

II. Philosophical Functionalism and the Person

Another place where the notion of person has gathered new force in metaphysical discussion is in the philosophical arena. In criticism of the undue separation of the noumenal and the phenomenal there are those who are arguing for a reassessment of the implications behind the philosophical category of person. P.T. Geach finds it logically

---

[20]We will argue for this same point in chaps. Two and Three.

[21]E.L. Mascall, The Triune God: An Ecumenical Study (Allison Park, PA.: Pickwick Pub., 1986), 24-33. His use of J. Galot is commendable in this regard, as he attributes this phrase to the French theologian. We will also be using some of Galot's categories, especially his corollary to relational being which is "hypostatic relation." The Person of Christ: Covenant Between God and Man (Chicago: Franciscan Herald Press, 1984), 32.

[22]This viewpoint will be taken up again in chap. Three. John Zizioulas, Being as Communion: Studies in Personhood and the Church (Crestwood, New York: St. Vladimir's Seminary Press, 1985), 17, 65.

[23]We will discuss the interrelationship of 'via negativa' and 'via positiva' in the next section.

sound and theologically accurate where he ponders the origins of the term 'person' that:

> Here some will protest that I am equivocating between the normal use of the term 'person' and its technical theological use. I reject the protest. The concept of a person, which we find so familiar in its application to human beings, cannot be clearly and sharply expressed by any word in the vocabulary of Plato or Aristotle; it was wrought with the hammer and anvil of theological disputes about the Trinity and the Person of Christ.[24]

In response to the increase of interest in relationality and the place of personhood new questions are being raised about the categories of the person that have been made normative.

Interestingly, it has been the notion of "goodness" that has moved some philosophers to re-think the nature of reality and as a consequence their concept of God. There would be little disagreement that the will has been the mainstay of post-Enlightenment definition of person. Only recently have moral philosophers fully criticized that thesis. Iris Murdoch, though not arguing for a Trinitarian analysis by any means, has critiqued the Kantian paradigm.

> Stripped of the exiguous metaphysical background which Kant was prepared to allow him, this man is with us still, free, independent, lonely, powerful, rational...The raison d'être of this attractive but misleading creature is not far to seek. He is the offspring of the age of science, confidently rational and yet increasingly aware of his alienation from the material universe which his discoveries reveal.... In fact Kant's man had already received a glorious incarnation nearly a century earlier in the work of Milton: his proper name is Lucifer.[25]

In contradistinction to the preeminence of volitional categories she writes:

> The concept Good resists collapse into the selfish empirical consciousness. It is not a mere value tag of the choosing will.... The proper and serious use of the term refers us to a perfection which is perhaps never exemplified in the world we know...and which carries with it the ideas of hierarchy and transcendence.... The self, the place where we live, is a place of illusion. Goodness is connected with the attempt to see the unself...(it) means that virtue is the attempt to pierce the veil of selfish consciousness and join the world as it really is.[26]

Goodness, for Murdoch, is not dictatorial but freedom within right constraints. It is fundamentally an other-oriented concept which argues that Good, to be good, cannot fall into selfish absorption. What is implied here is a major philosophical shift where

---

[24]P.T. Geach, The Virtues, 75.

[25]Iris Murdoch, The Sovereignty of Good over Other Concepts, Leslie Stephen Lecture, 1967 (Cambridge: Cambridge Univ. Press, 1967), 5. A more complete discussion can be found in her The Sovereignty of the Good, 1970 (Boston, Ark Paperbacks, 1985 ed.,) of which the above lecture serves as the last chapter.

[26]Ibid., 22-23. I was first introduced to the insight of Ms. Murdoch by Colin Gunton's Enlightenment and Alienation, 71-76. His point, as here, is that Good, not an isoloated will, is transcendent, however his trinitarian basis for that claim offers the necessary backdrop for Murdoch's claims that, though provocative, can only point to the concepts of good and love but ultimately leaves them inaccessible. See Sovereignty of the Good, 1985, p.92, 94ff.

individualism is brought up against the judgment of reality and is found lacking in self-definition or in self-fulfillment. A new category is offered, not the Hegelian Other, but an other who gives meaning to the subject in a trans-subjective relationship. As David Braine summarizes:

> The two most common approaches have been to make either intellectuality or freedom of choice the hallmark of personhood. We must see why neither of such approaches is right and discover the richness of the concept of "person", involving an integration of intellect and will and an openness to rapture, creativity, and relationship.[27]

Though the focus on personhood is prima facie anthropocentric, it is often recognized that there must be something behind the conclusions, something which appeals to mystery or the transcendent as to the ultimate source of this other-orientation in defining person. Theologians would talk of vestigia, of analogies, but that in no way diminishes the value of this new genre of philosophical insight, rather it ought to encourage a mutual dialogue between the humanities and the sciences.

While it is not the intention or scope of this work to contest every facet of Kantian relativism or the prevalence of empiricism even within modern theology, it will be contended that in the final analysis a wholesale unreflective capitulation to scientific method is left without a framework with which to comprehend the relationality which has been universally intuited and attested or the God who orders and sustains that intersubjectivity.

The structure which traditional Christianity has posited upon scripture, experience, reason and tradition, is that the foundation and pattern for a relational view of reality is the Trinity. That eternal relatedness is reproduced in creation due to divine initiative.[28] Austin Farrer, is one of many who has, in this century, championed these premises from a philosophical vantage point. Speaking of this relational aspect of God as a "prior actuality" as the only real possibility, he surmises that:

> It is the defining form of our traditional faith and if you throw it over you have a different religion - a different understanding of God's love for us, of our present

---

[27]David Braine, The Reality of Time and the Existence of God: The Project of Proving God's Existence (Oxford: Clarendon Press, 1988), 268.

[28]Two examples of this thesis provide interesting analyses of creation imaging the Trinity. From a philosophical angle see R.C. Neville, "Creation and the Trinity," Theological Studies 30 (March 1969): 3-26. Neville's work is helpful in response to process categories and the challenge that creation does not speak to three modes of divine being. For a more audacious analysis see Nathan R. Wood, The Secret of the Universe: God, Man and Matter, (Grand Rapids: Eerdmans Pub. Co., 1955). On the analysis of creation these two authors are quite similar. See also J. E. Davey, "Lines of approach to a trinitarian ontology," Hibbert Journal 55 (1956/57):223-232, Nicol Cross in the article following Davey's, "The Blessed Trinity," Hibbert Journal, 233-240, disputes vehemently this line of reasoning.

existence in relation to him, and of our ultimate hopes.[29]

There are, no doubt, other worldviews than the one which presupposes a relational deity. The smorgasbord of cosmologies is replete with varieties of deisms and pantheisms and positivisms.[30] What is posited here is that a certain heuristic, or resonant element resides in the philosophy of traditional theism. Relatedness, if it is to be distinguished from mere organismic construction exampled everywhere but which manifests little mutual connectedness, finds a cogent source and explanation in a God who is himself related. Those who disagree, both the metaphysician and the positivist, must offer an equally cogent assessment along with the more prominent critiques of a trinitarian worldview. We will discuss further the place of analogical talk about God, but at this point its philosophical cogency is based on the presence of a God who ought in some way to be like that which he has made. Well aware of the modern post-Barthian anathema of the analogia entis the question still remains as to a correspondence between what sort of being the God who reveals is and the recipients of that revelation. Trinitarian inter-personal co-existence must find a true correspondence with the created order. "True" here does not imply exhaustive knowledge of the origin of that correspondence; but with that caveat, the opposite, no true knowledge at all of God, is not implied either. There is a place for "approximate" knowledge and talk about God as long as it meets the demands of reality as clearly as possible.[31] By that I mean that anyone can postulate something about God and say it is true, but it may be refuted by evidence and experience. The Christian claim has been impugned but never refuted in any final form, and as we have seen above it is both directly and indirectly finding attestation where the "dissociation of sensibility" paradigm has been catapulted and a more holistic approach, one that includes the notion of person as a part of the essence of reality, is proposed.

Though, as stated above, the Eastern Church has much to offer in support of the general thesis offered here, one of the basic Orthodox tenets is not accepted here without qualification, i.e., apophaticism. The term we have chosen, that of initiative, is an attempt to provide a ballast for the often ill-fated discussion between the via negativa and the via

---

[29]Austin Farrer, "The Prior Actuality of God," in Reflective Faith: Essays in Philosophical Theology, ed. Charles C. Conti (Grand Rapids: Eerdmans Pub. Co., 1972), 185.

[30]An extremely helpful volume here is Charles Hartshorne, and William L. Reese, Philosophers Speak of God. (Chicago: Univ. of Chicago Press, Midway Reprint, 1976).

[31]See Brian Hebblethwaite, "'True' and 'False' in Christology," in The Philosophical Frontiers of Christian Theology: Essays presented to D.M. Mackinnon ed. Brian Hebblethwaite and Stewart Sutherland (Cambridge: Cambridge Univ. Press, 1982), 227-238.

positiva.[32] An overemphasis on either transcendence or immanence destroys the Christian gospel. The twin doctrines of the creation and the incarnation reveal the delicate balance necessary, on the one hand, to protect the glory of God, and on the other, to express the full intentions of the love of that God. Care is required in explaining the two methods of approaching theology. Reverence for the transcendent holiness of God, in the East, produced a distinct vocabulary which clearly delineated the essence from the energies of God. All too often though, that reverence has been misinterpreted as restrictive, even speculative. As we shall see in our chapter concerning the Cappadocians, the result of this reverent hesitation towards over-familiarity, was not constricting but more creative and flourishing than many theologians in the West. It was first, the recognition that no term, prosopon, ousia, or hypostasis, could ever comprehend the mystery of God, and second, that this inscrutable God had not left himself without a witness. This second element set the Greek mind free to explore every vestige possible for signs of his revelatory energeia.[33] The Cappadocian negative theology was far different from the non-cognitive approach of modern philosophies' denial of any objective knowledge of absolutes. The earlier form was an expression of spirituality which encouraged worship, discovery, and relationship. For Kant knowledge has to be discarded in order to keep faith. Discovery of the nature of God in any form was made impossible.

The emphasis on relationality and persons has, in my mind, the possibility of further ecumenical discussion. Our traditions have been divided for too long, often over needless misinterpretations. Two other areas must be looked at in connection with our ability to talk about Triune persons and the philosophical structuring that facilitates rather than obfuscates that enterprise: the place of analogy or metaphor, and the function of

---

[32]Albinus, Didaskalos, ch. 10, which until recently had been wrongly attributed to Alcinous, was apparently the first to leave record of the the three ways of "describing" the unnameable; 1) kat' aphairesin - according to that which is taken away, later referred to as the via negationis, 2) kat' analogian - to become via analogiae, 3) anagôgê - leading upwards or eventually, via eminentiae. Bohn's Classical Library, The Works of Plato vol. 6, The Doubtful Works, trans. George Burges (London: George Bell and Sons, 1899), 264-266. Although we find these clearly here it is without doubt that the categories were already in use. See John Dillon, The Middle Platonists (Ithaca: Cornell Univ. Press, 1977), 284-285. This basic thrust towards the unspeakable-ness of the "beyond being" in some senses negates itself if taken literally. We shall see how it is not followed thus, and becomes the source of much discussion.

[33]In chap. Three we will take issue with the Eastern epistemology concerning their input on person. Here we are concerned more with the positive elements found within the entire enterprise. See Thomas C. Oden, Living God, 44-46. Don Cupitt, "Kant and Negative Theology, in Hebblethwaite's Philosophical Frontiers, 55-67 explains the difference in world-views which produced this epistemology which has been questioned by deists like John Toland up through the heirs of Kant. A world seen as the effects of a Cause as well as the hierarchical structure of all of reality presented the basis for the focus on "indirect knowledge" of God. Thus God does not reveal himself, he reveals his will, etc. Kant despised that talk as the "despotism of mystery," Ibid., 59, The difference is a crucial one.

mystery in theology.

A. Mystery as Inexorable Reality

As difficult as explaining a means of talking about God is, there is the equally taxing task of discerning mystery. "Mysterion" in the early Church did not carry the same absolute impenetrability or undiscernibilty which it connotes today.[34] Rather, it spoke of those realities which were specifically revealed and apprehended in an open-ended manner. The idea was of a purposeful uncovering of something which was intended to be communicated by God to humanity. Understood accordingly, mystery is not to be approached with reservation or with presumption, but with expectation.

Perhaps no more helpful analysis of that concept can be found than the one made by Gabriel Marcel, in the now famous first series of Gifford Lectures in 1949, The Mystery of Being. It is unique in that Marcel's phenomenology is balanced by an element of realism. For him, the act, by its very nature not complete in itself, must reflect an essence or being. His well-known distinction between the scientifically discernible object and the real encounter of that "presence" which elicits the awareness of an inner need for self-transcendence and the place of participation, a communion, is found where he says:

> A problem is something which I meet, which I find complete before me, but which I can therefore lay siege to and reduce. But a mystery is something in which I myself am involved....A genuine problem is subject to an appropriate technique by the exercise of which it is defined; whereas a mystery, by definition, transcends every conceivable technique. It is, no doubt, always possible (logically and psychologically) to degrade a mystery so as to turn it into a problem.
> We must carefully avoid all confusion between the mysterious and the unknowable. The unknowable is in fact only the limiting case of the problematic.[35]

---

[34]Musterion was nearly interchangeable with the kerygma and even at other points with apocalupsis and other revelatory terms. TDNT vol. 4, 819-827. The Eastern tradition, with its via negativa has applied Dionysian categories to the biblical view of revelation. After arguing that the Eastern Fathers all used theoria to speak of the vision which is beyond rational comprehension, Lossky concludes one of his arguments by stating that St. Anastasius the Sinaite distinguished between phusis and prosopon by advocating that the later meant a face to face vision with the Incarnate Lord. The Vision of God, trans. Asleigh Moorhouse (London: The Faith Press, 1963), 72, 107, 137. Both East and West have, in the main, interpreted mystery accordingly. See New Catholic Encyclopedia, 11th ed., s.v. "Mystery (in the Bible)," by Raymond Brown. And from the succeeding article, "Mystery (in Theology)" Avery Dulles notes:

> "If God wishes to reveal Himself and draw men into friendship, He must share with men His own inner mystery. The human relationship of personal communication therefore provides a fruitful analogy by which to approach the mystery of that communion." Ibid., 153.

[35]The Mystery of Being: Reflection and Mystery, vol. 1, Gifford Lectures 1949-1950 (London: Harvill Press, 1950), 211-212. Marcel goes on to elucidate that, "Every presence is mysterious and,...it is doubtful whether the word 'mystery' can really be properly used in the case where a presence is not, at the very least, making itself somehow felt." Ibid., 216. On this see also his Being and Having, trans. Katherine Farrer (Boston: Beacon Press, 1951).

In essence, Marcel's "mystery of being" is similar to the apophaticism of the Eastern Church. Though the divine mystery is seen as transcending reason, and thus non-objectifiable, it nevertheless confronts human subjectivity with ontological force. Divine mystery "engages" and informs all of reality, not as an objectification to be analyzed. There is a reality which informs and initiates the desire for communion, for "co-esse" in humankind. However, for thinkers like Berdyaev, this in no way threatens the foundation of actual reality. The only complete reality is that of Divine mystery which simply "is" as the fundament of all being. Applied epistemologically, this is often misinterpreted as pantheism by Western thinkers. The East, on the other hand, is quite right in its hesitation on the over-emphasis on psychological structuring of reality in the West.

> There is no gulf between the Creator and the creature such as exists in the Catholic and Protestant West. Theosis bridges this gulf. The sensible world is symbolical of the spiritual world....In the East the human element is permeated by the Divine, while in the West the human element ascends toward the Divine....Nature is made Divine by the real presence of the Deity.[36]

Rahner's view of mystery is foundational to his entire transcendental Thomistic systematic principle, and there are essential agreements with what is outlined above. God's absolute, holy illimitability coupled with the absolute concreteness of the Incarnation, forms the Rahnerian conception of mystery, or what George Vanderwelde calls his "monistic dynamic" or the "single ontological principle of explanation." He says that mystery is not the place where the mind can no longer go, rather it conditions any human reflection.[37]

> Mystery is not something still undisclosed....This would be to confuse mystery with the still undiscovered unknown. Mystery on the contrary is the impenetrable which already present and does not need to be fetched....It is the indomitable dominant horizon of all understanding, that which makes it possible to understand other things

---

Kenneth T. Gallagher in The Philosophy of Grabriel Marcel (New York: Fordham Univ. Press, 1975) ch. 3 "Problem and Mystery," 30-49, gives a helpful synopsis of this central theme of Marcel. See also the collection of essays with personal responses by Marcel in The Philosophy of Gabriel Marcel, ed. P.A. Schilpp and L.E. Hahn, Library of Living Philosophers, vol. 17 (La Salle, IL.: Open Court Pub, 1984.) The critique of Marcel might include the challenge that if a mystery is not verifiable is it then merely illusory. His response, Gallagher says, was to point to a "secondary reflection", the reunifying of that which the methodology of clever solution has divorced in a "primary reflection." We use Marcel here because he acknowledges a transcendent substance to mystery. His is not a modern nominalism. Our task will be to discuss that mystery in distinctly Christian terms, ones that must be personal to make sense of the mystery at all.

[36]Nicolas Berdyaev, Spirit and Reality (London: Geoffrey Bles, The Centenary Press, 1946), 140-141 see also 10-12.

[37]See "The Grammar of Grace: Karl Rahner as a Watershed in Contemporary Theology," Theological Studies 49 (1988): 445-459. There are those who are uneasy by this collusion of nature and grace; Moltmann sees it as monism, and Küng sees it as dualism. Cf. Karl Rahner, "The Concept of Mystery in Catholic Theology," Theological Investigations vol. 4, 36-73.

by the fact that it is silently there as the incomprehensible.[38]

For these influential thinkers, and for this work, the modern notion of the inaccessibility to meaningful discourse is countered not because of a lack of awareness of human inability to discern transcendent reality unilaterally but because of an ineluctable presence which has been revealed in Scripture and in the community.[39] Yet, in spite of this strong doctrine of the immanent energies of God, it is the Western theologians who have gone further than the East in actually probing the mystery of the inner-trinitarian life. We shall have reason later to talk of the relationship between the Cappadocian use of "perichoresis" and the steps that Richard and Aquinas took in the same direction but beyond their Eastern forebears in attempting to discern that mystery. A further intriguing factor is the wide acceptance of Pseudo-Dionysian theses, especially as the source of the concept of a dynamic divine nature which offered a new view of relational mediation that offset many of the more static theological trends of the Middle Ages. Yet when it came to the utter unknowability of God the West did not coalesce.

Theology which has stood the test of time has always acknowledged the mysteries of God and of the created order. In essence, the "problems" of Marcel's discussion are brought under the scrutiny of the "mysteries" and not vice versa as our scientific era would have us believe. Andrew Louth asks for a reconsideration, that "we realize the true character of mystery: mystery not just as the focus of our questioning and investigating, but

---

[38]Karl Rahner,"On the Theology of the Incarnation," Ibid., 108. The context here is the mystery of the self-transcendence of human nature. But the same thesis applies to the divine-human interrelatedness by the incarnation. When Rahner moves on to the mystery as fulfilled in the vision of God he indicates that,
"It is precisely the removal of the illusion that our lack of total comprehension is only provisional. For in this vision we shall see by God himself and not merely by the infinite poverty of our transcendence that he is incomprehensible. But the vision of the mystery in itself, accepted in love, is the bliss of the creature and really makes what is known as mystery the burning bush of the eternally unquenchable flame of love." Ibid., 108-109.

[39]We recognize the opposite viewpoint that is part of a strong attempt to couch everything that is known about God in terms of human cultural terms. The Feuerbachian heritage and the impact of the deconstructionism of Derrida, Foucault, et al., have produced a view of theology which regards any divine input as a basis of theological construction as "naïve". See for example, Gordon D. Kaufman, "Mystery, Critical Consciousness, and Faith," The Rationality of Religious Belief: Essays in honour of Basil Mitchell, ed. William J. Abraham and Steven W. Holtzer (Oxford: Clarendon Press, 1987), 53-69. The questions still remain however, in spite of the attractiveness of continual critiques of theological positions and the desire to not make a God in our own image, as to what is the Mystery that confronts us. Is it merely Otto's 'numinous' or is there more to be understood? One wonders if there is an option between "wooden" interpretations and the unknowable Mystery which is so arduously protected. Newman's use of 'mystery' is one of the pinions of his epistemology, since it is supra-rational not ir-rational. Clyde Nabe, Mystery and Religion: Newman's Epistemology of Religion (Lanham: Univ. Press of America, 1988), 14,15.

mystery as that which questions us, which calls us to account."[40] The engagement initiated by that mystery negates any predilection towards univocality and militates against equivocation. In true Thomistic fashion then we must consider the place of analogy in this argument.

B. Analogical Language and the Use of 'Person'

Built upon the structure of revelatory mystery, an initiating, ineluctable, yet inscrutable, downward movement of grace, the notion of analogy takes on an ontological complexion which some would claim reflects the character of a Triune God. Others are repulsed by the inference of a retroactive discernment of divine essence. Stated simply there are two main schools of analogical thinking. One is the 'below-above' approach, an ascending method of taking human attributes and applying them at various levels of subtlety to the divine nature so that "something" can be said about that transcendent order. The other, dependent upon the acceptance of creation and revelation, is an 'above-below' movement, a descending understanding of analogy. The difficulties arise from the fact that these respective movements slam into each other, according to interpreter, compounded further by the perennial quandary that nothing is ever tidy in theology. As with any systematic principle, the approach which is over-emphasized, to the exclusion of the other's qualifications, monopolizes conclusions and inexorably assures aberrant findings. The immediate application of these methods to our thesis elicits the question as to which personhood defines which. Do we anthropomorphize when we speak of divine persons or does that mystery in some way inform, "theomorphize" if you will, human personhood?

Though it is virtually self-defeating to attempt to categorize the various theological positions on this issue, a general schema like that of Janet Soskice may be of assistance. She would categorize the analogical movements we have articulated above as the "realist" camp over against the "instrumentalists". The latter entails the proposition that all talk about God is metaphorical in a more or less apophatic sense. This stance comprises "those who believe that religious language provides a useful, even uniquely useful, system of symbols which is action-guiding for the believer but not to be taken as making reference to

---

[40]Louth, Discerning the Mystery, 145. Interesting that Louth here ends with mystery of human personhood, which we would take as the penultimate mystery, informed and consistently brought into the sphere of wonder by the reality of the preeminent mystery of divine Personhood. Daniel Hardy and David F. Ford, Praising and Knowing God (Philadelphia: Westminster Press, 1985), chap. 7 contains an insightful discussion of Christian epistemology in response to the critique that talk of the Trinity is mere projection (contra modern Feuerbachian-based interpretations). Their apologetic, which includes an ecumenical awareness of both positive and negative ways of approach to the divine mystery, assumes that epistemology rightly understood ought to find its basis in divine knowledge and diffusive characteristics that devolve from that philosophical presupposition. A modern interpretation of the Russian Orthodox position on mystery can be found in Anthony Ugolnik, The Illuminating Icon (Grand Rapids: Eerdmans, 1989), 91-98.

a cosmos-transcending being in the traditional sense."[41]   Realists, on the other hand, reminded constantly of propositionalism, or of maintaining incorrigible theological conceptual categories, posit a distinctly independent reality. Some realists would claim a personal reality, which consistently provides epistemic continuity, a foundation, even, a presence that both enhances rational discourse and supports the cogency of the models and metaphors used in theology.

The instrumentalist position has enjoyed enthusiastic support given the modern philosopical-scientific propensities of our culture, but must catapult large chunks of the traditional theological depositum as a result.[42] On the other hand, accused of naivety, obscurantism or even idolatry, realist theologians must concertedly disallow inclinations toward insidious claims of capturing complete models or analogies of God.[43] For the instrumentalist, divine person is a manner of speaking and any other usage borders on projectionism.

In response, realists are quick to shout reductionism or skepticism. For them, the idea of a divine person then would be acknowledged as analogically heuristic, not idiosyncratic, but a product of a succession of cultures; not intransigent, but open to modification, not irreproachable, but an, as yet, irreplaceable theological term. Philosophically, it is based upon the assumption that being precedes action, verbs require subjects, no matter how different those subjects might be from human interpreters.

---

[41]Janet Martin Soskice, "Theological Realism," in William Abraham ed. The Rationality of Religious Belief, 105-119, here, 108. These distinctions are adumbrated in the work of two Gifford lecturers in our century, C.C.J. Webb's God and Personality (New York, Macmillan Co, 1919), 20-22, and John Baillie's The Sense of the Presence of God (Charles Scribner's and Sons, 1962), 113-129. They both confront the onslaught of interpretation of Christian symbols that divorces them from ontological content from what Soskice would call a "realist" perspective. On the other side one would find Lotze, Bosanquet, Tillich as examples of "instrumentalists". See James A. Doull, "Augustinian Trinitarianism and Existential Theology," Dionysius 3 (December, 1979):111-159 for a criticism of existentialists at this very point among other incisive discernments of that movement.

[42]Helpful here are the insights of T.V. Morris. He would call the instrumentalists, "anti-realists". He is quite right in noting that the supposed non-propositional stances of this camp merely replace a realist metaphysic with a materialistic one. He sees the critiques of a traditional, realistic view of reality as insufficient to bear the claim that they are rationally incoherent. He perspicuously concludes that,
"If Christian thinkers do not...seek to develop and refine suitable philosophical tools for the expression of their faith, they inevitably just inherit their philosophical assumptions and dispositions from the cultures around them....not all such cultural legacies are equally suitable to the expression of the Christian faith,"
from "Philosophers and Theologians at Odds," Asbury Journal of Theology 44:2 (Fall, 1989), 36.

[43]This is the tack that Sallie McFague continues to espouse to loud acclaim from the instrumentalist camp. See her, Metaphorical Theology: Models of God in Religious Language (Philadelphia: Fortress Press, 1982), 128-129, 144.

Realism, so understood, provides a "continuity of access" necessary to make sense of the world in spite of the beseiged concept of revelation and the excessive anthropocentricism of excavating human individuum in hopes of uncovering a meaningful personhood.[44]

While Claude Welch claims that in the present era of thought, one relatively free from "Hegelian despotism," or the usurpation of theology by philosophy, he also warns realists against the opposite error, that of a "confirming revelation."[45] Extrapolations result from evidence or analogy when it becomes in and of itself an argument independent of its reference and thus determinative of theological content. I think that moderate realists have no intention of "encompassing" the divine mystery within the contingent, finite structures of human reason. Rather than comprehension in an absolute sense, analogy allows an ever increasing possibility of apprehension, a heuristic stance which delineates the trajectory most informative for the position taken here. This is to say that there is an intelligible correspondence between the divine and the human realities. It is not suggested that 'person' is a divine idea that is epistemically implanted or bestowed in a philosophical sense. What is acknowledged is that there must be some logical connectedness between two referents in order for any symbolic, metaphorical or analogical predications to be meaningful.

David Brown has responded to the criticism of advocating a univocal ratio between the finite and the infinite by stating that:

> Unless we admit some connexion...then talk of God will no longer be possible at all....(Some) would respond that only talk about God in his effects is appropriate. That is where we can be most confident I would agree. But it seems to me that to talk about effects is to already offer some clues, however small, to what the cause of those

---

[44]Soskice concludes with a helpful reminder to the critics of this position that it is not "words which refer, but speakers using words who refer." Ibid., 118. This resembles the perspicuous correction, with regard to making worthless statements, of Richard Mitchell, in The Gift of Fire, (New York: Simon and Schuster Inc., 1987), esp. 49-59. Here there is an agreement with the place of experience but also an acknowledgement of the need for an underlying unity in which to meaningfully correlate the varieties of experiences. See also the discussion of functionalism and ontologism in Thomas A. Smail, The Forgotten Father (Grand Rapids: Eerdmans, 1980), 86-112.

[45]Claude Welch, In This Name: The Doctrine of the Trinity in Contemporary Theology, (New York: Charles Scribner's Sons, 1952)), 90. The premise upon which his investigation rests is the cruciality of the question, "What is the basis of the doctrine of the Trinity in revelation and faith, and further, how is the doctrine to be developed from that basis and what does the doctrine affirm?" Ibid., 91. Although I do not agree with Welch's conclusions, there is little doubt that the logic of his insights and criticisms of the social analogy specifically have been of great help in pointing out some of the weaknesses inherent in less rigorous interpretations. It is interesting that although that analogy is abhorrent to Welch, nearly two-thirds of his book is given to a critique of that conception of the Trinity.

effects might be like.[46]

If there is to be any human understanding of God then the terms we use must in some way reflect a literal descriptive knowledge of God. The interpretive battlefields produced by the thoughts of masters like Aquinas, are strewn with the remains of realists and instrumentalists struggling to assert their epistemology. Without the typical caveats to protect a philosophical flank, this author would side with Cajetan, Gilson, and Mascall who say that "the Angelic Doctor", "undoubtedly does allow us a certain knowledge of God" but that knowledge does not entail identification of essence but of its affirmation.[47]   Analogy, so viewed, is more than half-knowledge, more than nominalism, and allows theological reflection to inform agnosticism. As Hilary of Poitiers ably states, "Every analogy, therefore, is to be considered as more useful to man than as appropriate to God, because it hints at the meaning rather than explains it fully."[48]

Against the trend to bifurcate fact and value, it would follow that I also hesitate on a total separation of revealed truths about God and sensate knowledge of those truths.[49]

---

[46]From "Wittgenstein against the Wittgensteinians: A Reply to Kenneth Surin on The Divine Trinity," Modern Theology 2:3 (1986):257-276. See also John Thurmer's discussion of analogy where he states:
No doubt it is true that we can know the 'essential' Trinity only through the 'economic' Trinity. But what is so known and revealed is true of God's eternal being. That is what it means to call God 'faithful'. If this were not so, then analogy...could tell us nothing about God, and there would be no basis for theology.
From, A Detection of the Trinity, (Exeter, England: Paternoster Press, 1984), 72, 13-16.

[47]See E.L. Mascall, Existence and Analogy (New York: Longmans, Green and Co., 1949), 115-121. Mascall distinguishes between logical, epistemological, and ontological orders of thought which pertain to Aquinas' analogical usages. Also found in He Who Is (New York: Darton, Longman and Todd, 1962), 14-29, 198. David Burrell, has made this a focal point of his Thomistic expertise. Note the discussion in the context of an overview of Aquinas' theology in Aquinas: God and Action (Notre Dame: Univ. of Notre Dame Press, 1979), 55-67; see McInerny "Analogy and Foundationalism in Thomas Aquinas," in eds. Audi and Wainwright, Rationality, 271-288. There are, of course, detractors of the Thomistic enterprise. John Morreall, takes the whole analogical system to task in his Analogy and Talking about God: A Critique of the Thomistic Approach (Washington: University Press of America, 1979).

[48]The Trinity, trans. Stephen McKenna, (Washington: Catholic Univ. Press of America, 1954), 1.19,19.

[49]Austin Farrer, "Theology and Analogy 2" in Reflective Faith, 69-81, chooses to summarize Dorothy Emmet's profound point that, with regard to human knowledge of physical being, external reality acts upon or interacts with the "process of our existence," not on intellect alone; in other words, a reality comes to bear upon us. It is more of an ontological connection from which signs are given at the sensate level. However, he, like T. Torrance and T. Kuhn, would argue that to say that analogy signifies another ontic reality but that nothing is truly revealed in those signs is a logical fallacy. Emmet has made the same division that Kant would make between certain kinds of knowledge. If one were to separate these too far the only plausible statements about God would be, "God is an X to which we are related as children to father." The question would always remain,

As George Tavard says, "A denial of the Tri-unity of God on the ground that the classical analogies do not "prove" what they only adumbrate, could not be taken seriously. For it would misread at the start, the very purpose of analogical reflection."[50]

   We are not concerned here with the semantic debate surrounding the distinctions between metaphor and analogy.[51] Regardless of the extent of similarities implied by the latter and dissimilarities inherent in the former, both are seen as conveyances which bring insight into reality. They help us to get at reality while, if properly understood, not offering inchoate univocal definitions.[52] Richard Boyd investigates the capacity of metaphors to cut "the world at its joints."[53] Colin Gunton's metaphorical understanding builds on Boyd's in such a way as to project a relational view of reality is opened by metaphor. Gunton employs a distinctly Polanyian affirmation that metaphorical language is a way in which we "indwell" our world.[54]

---

what is an X? The realist tradition sees analogical language about God as a window into reflection upon the nature of the reality which bears upon us. To stop with talk of the relations alone causes the whole process to come into question. See also the preceding article, part one of Farrer's discussion for reservations concerning Barth's rejection of the Thomistic use of 'analogia entis.' Ibid., 64-68.

[50]George H. Tavard, A Way of Love (Maryknoll: Orbis Press, 1977), 130.

[51]See Ralph McInerny's "Analogy and Foundationalism" where analogy is primarily understood semantically and not metaphysically, and his "Metaphor and Analogy" in Inquiries into Medieval Philosophy: A Collection in Honor of Francis P. Clarke, ed. James F. Ross (Westport, Conn.: Greenwood Publishing Co., 1971), 90-96 which reveals the interconnectedness of the terms.

[52]John Cahalan, Causal Realism: An Essay on Philosophical Method and the Foundations of Knowledge (Lanham: University Press of America, 1985) makes this point in direct attack on the Humean heritage of modern empirical thought. His "reconstruction of philosophy" is based on the connection between events and cause. He does, however, distinguish between the analogical use of words and analogical reasoning. In basic agreement with Thomistic categories, Cahalan notes that terms like 'person' can be used to signify a perfect being even if the mode of signification is imperfect, because analogies refer to "extra-objective existents" not just to objects as objects of knowledge. (438-446) It is this epistemological and ontological position upon which this thesis takes its stance. The plethora of critics of this position have to bear the burden of proving that "descending" analogies are contradictory.

[53]Richard Boyd, "Metaphor and Theory Change: What is "Metaphor" a Metaphor for?" in Metaphor and Thought, ed. A Ortony (Cambridge: Cambridge Univ. Press, 1979), 356-408. However, T. Kuhn in the following article, "Metaphors and Science," Ibid., 409-419, critiques the joint metaphor due to its inherent resemblance to the principally unknowable Kantian category: "Ding-an-sich".

[54]See Colin Gunton's "Christ the Sacrifice: Aspects of the Language and Imagery of the Bible," in The Glory of Christ in the New Testament: Studies in Christology (Oxford: Clarendon Press, 1987), 228-238, and his yet unpublished article, "The Sacrifice and the Sacrifices: from Metaphor to Transcendental?". On "indwelling" see M. Polanyi, Personal Knowledge: Toward a Post-Critical Philosophy (Chicago: Univ. of Chicago Press, 1958), 199,

The insight brought about by analogy and metaphor is more than reflective; there is a creativity which forces, some say "shocks" the thinker into new perceptions.[55] There is a strong element of truth in the use of both which cannot be denied even by the most stringent linguistic literalism. In spite of the accusations inveighed against the truth-claims of analogical language, even the most precise language is essentially analogical. Judged within the context of prosopological exegesis, doxology, communal ecclesiology, and the traditional Christian understanding of revelation there is an elevation of language to which the literal, in comparison with the analogical, cannot aspire and which it cannot comprehend. The "truth" of an analogical statement such as "three Persons in One" is not dependent upon literal equivalence with philosophical or psychological or mathematical exegesis of the various parts of that statement. It is my argument that there is, at the present state of theological reflection, an irreducible truth conveyed by the notion of person, however imperfect the term, when used as an analogy for the Triune Godhead. 'Person' employs an irreplaceable precision in the "insight" that such a rich term brings to indwelling reality, which more literal ascriptions, (if that is possible) do not bestow.

Proper theological method then, if one hears the realist tradition properly, objects to any claim to exclusivity in an agnostic ascent and seeks the interpretation of a cataphatic descent, with the mutual qualifications of a recognized inability of human comprehension and a corresponding "continuity of access" provided by a revealing God. "If God had not revealed triune nature, we would never have suspected it, and all our attempts to grasp his

---

143, 279, 280, 283. Iris Murdoch agrees where she sees metaphors as "irreplaceable" to any critical thought. Metaphors supercede philosophy and models as a "mode of understanding" our condition as humans. Sovereignty of the Good Over Other Concepts, 23. For critiques of this position from a philosophic and scientific stance see Joseph Agassi, The Gentle Art of Philosophical Polemics: Selected Reviews and Comments (LaSalle, IL.: Open Court Pub., 1988),13-17.

[55]C.M. LaCugna, "Placing Some Trinitarian Locutions," Irish Theological Quarterly 51:1 (1985):17-37, outlines her understanding of theological language. With dependence upon Ramsey, Ricoeur, and D. Burrell, she advocates a "language of indirection" which frees one from "the troublesome analogia entis," (Ibid., 19) while disclosing the being of God without literalism and idolatry. Her 'model' approach would include analogy, symbol, metaphor and parable, but only under the aegis of the Rahnerian axiom replete within all of her works. She thus resides in Soskice's "instrumentalist" camp. Likewise, she and Burrell would see this endeavor as "naive realism". (Ibid., 19) In light of that charge if it is posited at all, it is one point where modern Thomists diverge from their medieval mentor. One wonders just what is communicated by revelation. If there is no real understanding of divine being, then what can be said with any assurance? "Jesus does not supply us with a metaphysics of divine being. He depicts the loving God in relation to him." (Ibid., 27) I think there is a middle ground between scholastic metaphysical presumption and non-ontological exemplarism. On "metaphor" see also Chester Gillis, A Question of Final Belief: John Hick's Pluralistic Theory of Salvation (New York: St. Martin's Press, 1989), 150-156.

triunity on the basis of finite experience are bound to be inadequate."[56] In all of the work of Augustine and Aquinas to ensure proper distinctions between creatures and Creator, there is never a glimmer of the modern existential proclivity to separate essence from existence. The "otherness" of God was not an intraversible abyss. Prevenient grace informed a Christian ontology which claimed that God did not equal all being, but that creatures, images, were called to participate in that being, a being that was different but not unapproachable. There is an intrinsic causality resident in this epistemological approach which, if not acknowledged, necessitates either a univocity or an equivocal basis for theology which is not acceptable in traditional Christian thought.[57]

Analogical or metaphorical language is by nature heuristic. The three trinitarian analogies with which the Church has continually grappled and which serve to categorize many subsidiary ones have been: 1) the Augustinian/Thomistic intra-subjective analysis of the essence of knowing, loving or willing, 2) the inter-subjective analogy of Love, Lover, and Loved proposed by Richard of St. Victor and, 3) closely corresponding to the second, the Franciscan analogy from ontological "fecundity" or the self-diffusiveness of the Good, found in Alexander of Hales and Bonaventure.[58] It is apparent that the Church has opted

---

[56]O'Donnell, "Trinity as Divine Community," 31-32. He is drawing from Balthasar's yet untranslated work Theologik II, Wahrheit Gottes, 61. He bases this realist epistemology on the belief that, "if creation has been brought forth in Christ and for him, if Christ is the center of reality, then must not there be a reflection of divine being in created reality?" O'Donnell, Ibid., 5, (cf. Balthasar, Ibid., 155.)

[57]See a good discussion of this in Norman Geisler and Winfried Corduan, Philosophy of Religion (Grand Rapids: Baker Book House, 1988), 252-291. They would have reservations about my use of "heuristic". For them it has been used by thinkers like Frederick Ferré duplicitously, or as they state, "quasicognitively". Ibid., 285, n.44. · I intend its meaning to carry that ontological similarity between Creator and creature which can only be predicated analogically.

[58]These distinctions are agreed upon by a number of thinkers, Cf. Ewert Cousins', "Models and the Future of Theology." Continuum 7:1 (1969): 78-92. George Tavard's Way of Love (Maryknoll: Orbis, 1977). The three categories which follow are more continuums in that the various thinkers may reflect their position through partial commitment to another. For modern assessment of the Augustinian position, King-Farlow's "Is the Concept of the Trinity Obviously Absurd?" Sophia (Melbourne) 22 (1983): 37-42. John Thurmer's "The Analogy of the Trinity." Scottish Journal of Theology 34:6 (1981): 509-515. See especially his emphasis on Dorothy Sayers' The Mind of the Maker. His article astutely discerns this position (which he more openly espouses elsewhere) latent even within its critics like John Macquarrie. The Ricardine position is represented by a wide spectrum of theologians as well; E. Jüngel's, [God As the Mystery of the World:, 318,] applauds Richard and then goes on to explicate a very similar paradigm without further reference, but C. Plantinga sees him as thoroughly Barthian, "The Threeness/Oneness Problem of the Trinity," Calvin Theological Journal 23:1 (Apr. 1988):39 n.9; See also W. J. Hill's Three Personed God, W. Kasper's God of Jesus Christ, 225-232; (although John Milbank's "On a Second Difference, A Trinitarianism Without Reserve," Modern Theology 2:3 (1986):212 ff., finds Kasper's personalism distinctly deficient, with its Kantian overtones,) and Y. Congar's I Believe in the Holy Spirit, vol. 1, trans. David Smith (New York: Seabury Press, 1979), 77-90. The

more for the idea of God as One in whom memory, intellect, and will reflects the Trinity. This, it seems, is insufficient with regard to the distinct divine threeness revealed in Scripture. On the other hand, the structural oneness of the Trinity is hard to express analogically when attempting to protect a notion of threeness that does justice to the evidence.[59] While the first of these analogies has been deeply engrained into the Church's thoughts about the Blessed Trinity, it will be argued that the analogy of love between divine persons is the highest analogy which accomodates the approach of a non-rationalistic, non-scientific demonstration of the Trinity.[60]

Once again, the analogical use of the term 'person' is to be understood, in contradistinction to any univocal tendencies. It is not a direct analogy as divine mystery, properly understood, vitiates. Instead the focus is the similarities, and likenesses to that inter-communal, co-inherent love. In light of the accusation that there is no consistency in this methodology, those likenesses are to be based first, on the relational statements found in Scripture, and then upon a high view of created 'vestigia' which signify a transcendent Reality. Cornelius Plantinga, in a similar analysis based on a theological reflection of Johannine data, puts it forthrightly from the perspective of a revelational ontology that "Father, Son and Spirit are not only in believers; they are also as believers. That is they are social beings who are compared with believers."[61] 'Person' applied to God here, will be done so in only the most rigorous sense. An analogical participation in this divine mystery results from an acknowledgement that no individual fully represents the Trinity. However, full, mature and productive love relationships between persons do bear living resemblances

---

Franciscan\Bonaventurian line is represented with distinct process theology inclinations in Cousin's Bonaventure and the Coincidence of Opposites (Chicago: Franciscan Herald Press, 1978), "The Coincidence of Opposites in the Christology of Saint Bonaventure." Franciscan Studies Annual 7 (1968): 27-45. "Fecundity and Trinity: An Appendix to Chapter Three of The Great Chain of Being," in Studies in Medieval Culture 11 ed. J.R. Sommerfeldt and Thomas H. Seiler. Medieval Institute. 103-108 Kalamazoo: Western Michigan Univ. Press, 1977). "God as Dynamic in Bonaventure and Contemporary Thought." In Proceedings of the American Philosophical Society 48 (1974):136-148. See also J. Bracken's The Triune Symbol: Persons, Process and Community. Lanham: Univ. Press of America, 1985).

[59]Cf. H. R. Niebuhr's classic statement of three Unitarianisms while warning against theological "snobbery" which produces strong trinitarian statements. "The Doctrine of the Trinity and the Unity of the Church," Theology Today 3:3 (Oct. 1946): 371-384.

[60]Tavard, Way of Love, 130. He adds "Analogies are meaningful only as they are freed from limits and imperfections that human experience fastens to them." Ibid., 130. This coincides with the assessment that the depth of a metaphor multiplies the difficulty in either discerning or expressing all the similarities that are being resident within the term. The key is the knowledge of the analogates. If one is secure there, one has hope of determining the relative worth of fruitful similarities and, if present, what effect the dissimilarities have on the results.

[61]Cornelius Plantinga, "The Hodgson-Welch Debate and the Social Analogy of the Trinity," (Ph. D. dissertation, Princeton Theological Seminary, 1982), 168.

to a primordial referent or model. It is we who are like the Original.

Bernard Lonergan's intriguing book The Way to Nicaea has helped sharpen one point in this thesis, even if by way of disagreement. He argues that the Fathers were concerned to offer no more than heuristic devices, rules of speech, rather than making ontological statements about the divine nature.[62] A proper reading of the Fathers indicates that much more was at stake than Lonergan allows. Semantic subtlety is required here. For the use of "heuristic" may imply a real connectedness between the primary and secondary analogates discoverable in reality. By heuristic, in the thrust of this work at least, more is intended than mere exploratory methodology alone. While holding a sufficient reservation with regard to human capacity for God-talk, inscrutable as it may be, the ontological content of the analogy used here is inexorable in light of Scripture, tradition and reason.[63]

A caveat is in order. Let there be no mistake, all talk of God is figurative and and what follows is couched in the same sort of awe and love which prompted Gregory of Nazianzus in a discussion of the mystery of the communicatio idiomatum to exclaim, "For if he condescended to Flesh, He will also endure such language."[64]

III. Hermeneutics, Soteriology and the Economic Trinity

The results of the dichotomy of objective fact and subjective value, of geschichte and historie on scriptural exegesis and hermeneutics have been cataloged extensively.

---

[62]Bernard Lonergan, The Way to Nicea, trans. Conn O'Donovan (Philadelphia: Westminster Press, 1976). Cf. also the influence of this approach to theology which is found throughout George Lindbeck's, The Nature of Doctrine: Religion and Theology in a Post-Liberal Age (Philadelphia: Wesminster Press, 1984).

[63]Barth's "Nein" was not adequate in renouncing Brunner's 'analogia entis'. The latter recognizes the inviolable character of the 'imago dei', however damaged by sin and the ubiquitous character of this method in theology. Using Barth he says, "Christian theology is not a negative one...but is a positive theology which rests upon the truth that there is a relation of similarity between God's being as Person and the being of man as human," The Christian Doctrine of Creation and Redemption, in Dogmatics vol. 2 (Philadelphia: Westminster Press, 1952), 23-24, 42-45. New appraisals of analogical meaning are appearing. Cf. what is said here with the Jewish scholar Jacob Neusner in From Description to Conviction: Essays on the History and Theology of Judaism, Brown Judaic Studies, vol. 86 (Atlanta: Scholars Press, 1987), 8. Neusner distinguishes between analogies of which God serves as the system and those for which God serves as system. In the first God, exists as premise and presence of reality. In the second, God "may act as a person for the system, with whom all other persons relate. In this sense God realizes and embodies the system in such a way that human beings may identify themselves and their traits with those required in the system." See Tad Dunne's "Trinity and History," Theological Studies 45 (1984): 151-152 for tentative support for this heuristic enterprise.

[64]"Oration 37.2, ANF 338C, PG 36: 285A

Perhaps there is no better example of the implications of modern interpretations concerning the scriptural evidence for a Triune God than Claude Welch's In This Name: The Doctrine of the Trinity in Contemporary Theology.[65] In a masterful synopsis of the major trends in trinitology, Welch's critical, if not fundamentally biased, approach was most dissatisfied with the "social trinitarians", those who saw the divine nature as constituted by three persons in community. Foundational to his criticisms, however, was a different view of revelation than the majority of theologians categorized as social analogists. The recurrent criticism of the obscurantism of trinitarian conservatism is revealed in questions like the following which sets up his epistemology, "Could the speculative Trinity be essentially and directly related to the economic Trinity, and if not, then was it of real value as buttress for faith?"[66] At first glance, this seems like a valid paradigm for critiquing over-speculation just as is the reservation against "understanding personality as essentially complementary and inclusive."[67] He quite rightly sees the fallacy of allowing that speculation to become more than a means of understanding the Trinity by being used as an argument for the necessity of a divine relationality. Welch further probes that approach by way of the ridicule of any "necessitation" arguments which propound that God, of necessity, could not create a mechanical universe, or that God could not love with a divine love any other than a divine person, or that to be self-satisfied in some way God would then be seen as imperfect, egoistical. The protection Welch and many others have found against this audacious interpretive model has been a commitment to the economic aspects of the Trinity, or so they say.

Though there is little disagreement with the fundamental approach of tying any theologizing to revealed categories, one wonders if latent here is yet another form of the fact/value dichotomy. Where the emphasis has been shifted to experience, the sensate and cognitive hermeneutical categories of the modern period follow suit with a corresponding

---

[65]Claude Welch, In This Name: The Doctrine of the Trinity in Contemporary Theology (New York: Charles Scribner's Sons, 1952).

[66]In This Name, 17. One has only to see the impact of George Lindbeck's The Nature of Doctrine: Religion and Theology in a Post-Liberal Age (Philadelphia: Westminster Press, 1984), to see the direction this type of thinking can take while sounding quite orthodox. His radical distinction between the regulative and the ontological claims of Christian doctrine are highly questionable. See an interesting critique of Lindbeck's position in David F. Ford's "'The Best Apologetics Is Good Systematics.' A Proposal about the Place of Narrative in Christian Systematic Theology," Anglican Theological Review 67:3 (1985): 247-251.

[67]In This Name, 96.

"functionalist" approach.[68] Oscar Cullmann is self-avowedly functionalistic in his Christology.[69] Karl Rahner, who has a distinctly different Christology from Cullmann, has been instrumental in solidifying the economic-immanent paradigm in modern trinitology.[70] The result of this hermeneutic has been the restriction of trinitarian emphases to the divine actions ad extra alone. As a logical corollary the inner life of God is either propounded as not discernible at all, or only as tangential to the divine operations.[71] Thus, the "threeness"

---

[68]Basic to our critique of modern philosophy, theology and Biblical studies is the position which many, like Fergus Kerr, make that the predominate paradigm is not social but solipsistic. In Theology after Wittgenstein (Oxford: Basil Blackwell, 1986) Kerr relates a fundamental phenomenological Wittgensteinian critique of modernity's view of the individual as, "the solitary self-communing self, radically independent of relationships with anyone or anything else in this world." Ibid., 72. He calls this the "metaphysics of solipsism" which Wittgenstein protested, that Cartesian principle of the autonomous self, an idealistic solipsism, which permeates every level of theological discourse. Cf. this critique with the earlier one of N.H.G. Robinson, "Trinitarianism and Post-Barthian Theology," Journal of Theological Studies 20 (1969): 186-201. His thesis, based on Barthian categories, is that undue intellectualism leads to the distinction between ad intra and ad extra which in turn leads to an excessive individualism.

[69]He writes, "It is only meaningful to speak of the Son in view of God's revelatory action, not in view of his being." The Christology of the New Testament, trans. Shirley Guthrie and Charles A. M. Hall (Philadelphia: Westminster Press, 1959), 293, 306-314 esp. 314. Speaking of the first Christians he writes, "for them it is his very nature that he can be known only in his work - fundamentally in the central work accomplished in the flesh. Therefore, in the light of the New Testament witness, all mere speculation about his natures is an absurdity. Functional Christology is the only kind which exists," 326. See H. Ridderbos' critique in Paul: An Outline of his Theology trans. John Richard De Witt (Grand Rapids: Eerdmans, 1975), 68-75. He does say that due to criticism Cullmann later attempted to join the functional Sonship with the ontological. Ibid., 68 n.81. D.M Mackinnon reminds us that the functional/ontological dichotomy in Cullmann is not a philosophically based argument, rather he is "concerned to distinguish concepts by means of which Christ's work is articulated from concepts purposing to capture what the One is, who in them is incarnate," from "The Relation of the Doctrines of the Incarnation and the Trinity," in Creation, Christ and Culture: Studies in honour of T.F. Torrance, ed. Richard W. A. McKinney (Edinburgh: T.& T. Clark, Ltd., 1976), 92-107, here, 94.

[70]See note 9. Another theologian who parallels Rahner's axiom for the most part is P.J.A.M. Schoonenberg. He attempts to ameliorate the modalistic and the personalistic vantage points but yields to the former.
The question whether God is trinitarian apart from his self-communication in salvation history could be answered if the relationship between God's immutability and his free self-determination were accessible to us. Because this is not the case, the question remains unanswered and unanswerable. It is thereby eliminated from theology as a meaningless question.
"Trinity - The consummated covenant: Theses on the doctrine of the trinitarian God," Studies in Religion 5 (Autumn/Fall, 1975-76): 112.

[71]One of the strongest arguments against "reading back" propositional and consequently ontological prescriptions into the Godhead is the critique that this line of reasoning tends toward Doceticism, and its horrendous implications for any real relationship with God, see J.A.T. Robinson The Priority of John, ed. J.F. Coakley (Oak Park, IL.: Meyer-Stone Books, 1987), 372-394. Conversely however, what is not recognized is the

of God is made to represent the way we think about God exclusively; it in no way can represent, due to its absolute, non-cognitive nature, the way in which God exists in se.

Leonard Hodgson's classic statement elicited a theological mêlée earlier in the century. He stated that the doctrine of the Trinity:

> Is a product of rational reflection on those particular manifestations of divine activity which centre in the birth, ministry, crucifixion, resurrection and ascension of Jesus Christ and the gift of the Holy Spirit to the Church....Derived from the special self-revelation of God, a doctrine which, so far as we can see, could not have been discovered by reason apart from revelation.[72]

Though Hodgson caught flak from both ends of the theological continuum it was the specifically propositional approach to the Trinity which he intended to confront here. Revelation in act and event must necessarily supercede any propositional formulations.[73] There have been those who would argue that even Hodgson's affirmation of a revealed Trinity is an impossibility, or rather "an arbitrary analysis of the activity of God, which, though of value in Christian thought and devotion, is not of essential significance."[74] Far closer to a traditional view of revelation and the opera ad extra is Edmund Hill's response to the above approaches. To the accusation that, in the formative periods, there was no logical or rational compulsion to conceive of a Trinity, that at most what was proposed was binitarian, Hill points to the ridiculousness of an "arbitrary analysis" resulting in a Trinity. He says:

> I find it quite incredible, and can see no value, but only a headache and an obstacle to any heartfelt devotion, in an arbitrary analysis that does not derive from, and throw light on God's revelation of himself....Give me the Jewish, or the Islamic monad every time - unless the Christian triad has a true reference to God's nature (which we could

---

inherent adoptionism within the anti-propositionalists who reason accordingly, no matter how eloquently they interpret Jesus as the "true Son of God."

[72]The Doctrine of the Trinity (New York: Charles Scribner's Sons, 1944), 25. Originally published London: James Nisbet and Co., 1943.

[73]The modern version of that same battle, between the so-called "foundationalists" and the more empirically based groups, such as the canonical criticism school out of Yale, has taken various forms. See Ronald Thiemann's critique of T. F. Torrance in Revelation and Theology: The Gospel as Narrated Promise (Notre Dame: Univ. of Notre Dame Press, 1985), 31-41.

[74]This is the third plausible stance according to Maurice Wiles and the one he chooses to take with regard to the Trinity, "Some Reflections on the Origins of the Doctrine of the Trinity," The Journal of Theological Studies n.s. 8 (April, 1957): 104. Cf. the conclusion of C. C. Richardson, The Doctrine of the Trinity (New York: Abingdon, 1958), 145, 148-149. For a more recent example of functional Christology gone amok and the theological implications we dispute here see Thomas Sheehan, The First Coming: How the Kingdom of God Became Christianity (New York: Random House, 1986).

only know by revelation.)[75]

But he also critiques Hodgson on what he refers to as "easy exegesis."[76] Like many today, Hodgson caricatures "propositional" theology as the belief by some, of a bestowal of chunks of philosophical theology directly into human minds. With that beginning point it is not too difficult to then say that Scripture is exactly the opposite of that, merely a recording of salvation history. Thus, in essence, nothing can be surmised from terms like Logos, Image, Firstborn, or even, as Hill postulates in his critique, Father and Son. As Hodgson concludes, "The divine revelation is given in acts rather than words."[77] The Triune God is a revealed category but that category is all too easily restricted to straight verbal correspondence.

What seems missing is an allowance of interpretive elements, even in the earliest records of the revelatum. We would neither agree with Hodgson that revelatory phenomena drove the Church Fathers to a doctrine of the Trinity nor would we agree with Wiles that it was an arbitrary analysis. Lampe's criticism of the doctrine of three persons as incoherent is also unconvincing. Speaking of the early fathers he openly states that theirs was a "wooden exegesis, which fastened on particular words without properly considering how the authors intended them to be used.[78] Of course, implied here is that Lampe does know what they intended by the words chosen. He also disparages the attempts of the Cappadocians and Athanasius in their formulation of a language of personal distinctions within the divine unity. For him the "personal distinctions have no content, and therefore are meaningless, so long as they are understood to consist solely in the relations themselves."[79]

There is much to be said for this recognition of the latent problems in relating a list of esoteric distinctions to any form of spirituality. But, when Lampe offers the social analogy as a response to "dry abstractions of Trinitarian orthodoxy by reinterpreting it," the

---

[75]Edmund Hill, "Our Knowledge of the Trinity," Scottish Journal of Theology 27 (1974): 3.

[76]E. Hill, "Knowledge of the Trinity," 4.

[77]Hodgson, Doctrine of the Trinity, 35. It is interesting to note the subjective element in Hodgson in all of this. In the preceding pages he is adamant that God reveals these themes to any seeker whose heart and mind are focused on the revelatum. One wonders if the doctrine of the Christian Trinity would surface that easily. It seems as if Hodgson will allow a personal illumination but not a canonical one or traditional, conciliar expression of that illumination. For a more adequate representation see Thomas Oden, Systematic Theology: Volume II, The Word of Life (San Francisco: Harper and Row, 1989), 17, passim.

[78]G.W.H. Lampe, God as Spirit, The Bampton Lectures, 1976 (Oxford: Clarendon Press, 1977), 224.

[79]God as Spirit, 226.

analogy is immediately declared tritheistic.[80] Going in the same direction as Hodgson, and Rahner, but stepping across traditional formulations into a cryptic modalism like Wiles and Cunliffe-Jones, Lampe attempts to elude meaninglessness, abstraction, incoherence or tritheism by a "return to our experience of Jesus and of the Spirit of God who operates in us," because, "the Trinitarian model is in the end less satisfactory for the articulation of our basic Christian experience than the unifying concept of God as Spirit."[81]

It may be profitable at this juncture to remember that these criticisms of relational trinitarian formulations are not novel. They share interesting comparisons with aberrant Christian concepts while having even at the foundation of their arguments rather insidious implications. John Calvin elucidates this in his discussion of the "hellenized" terms where he states that:

> If they call a foreign word one that cannot be shown to stand written syllable by syllable in Scripture, they are indeed imposing upon us an unjust law which condemns all interpretation not patched together out of fabric of Scripture...when it has been proved that the church is utterly compelled to make use of the words "Trinity" and "Persons"? If anyone, then, finds fault with the novelty of the words, does he not deserve to be judged as bearing the light of truth unworthily, since he is finding fault only with what renders the truth plain and clear?[82]

More complete responses to these renowned thinkers are access-ible.[83] What follows is included as apologetic and as fundamental to my expressed purpose. The "propositional" epithet, used denigratively has been quite useful in modern theology to discount any notion of inner-trinitarian life. Prior to any philosophical response, it is apparent to this author that any honest consensual appraisal of the thinkers who applied themselves to this mystery in the first five centuries, will reveal a distinct abhorrence of inscrutable or useless speculation. The tendency is to "proof-text" the "propositionalists" by choosing those elements of their work which seem obtuse. Theology for them equalled

---

[80]God as Spirit, 227.

[81]God as Spirit, 228. Cunliffe-Jones joins Wiles in referring to the latter's choices regarding the Trinity and says, "I have no doubt that some form of the third possibility (Trinity as arbitrary analysis) is the one which we must choose," "Two Questions Concerning the Holy Spirit," Theology 72 (1975):298. Following both Wiles and Cunliffe-Jones but with different vocabulary is Bernard M.G. Reardon, "A Comment," Ibid., 298-301. See also the responding letter by John Thurmer on p. 427. Each has a problem with "latent tritheism" and attempts to seek solace in the unity-model along the lines of Western human psychological analogies.

[82]John Calvin, Institutes of the Christian Religion, ed. John T. Macneill, trans. and indexed by Ford Lewis Battles, vols. 20 and 21 The Library of Christian Classics (Philadelphia: Westminster Press, 1960), Bk. 1: 13, 3.

[83]C.F.D. Moule, "The New Testament and the Doctrine of the Trinity: A Short Report on an Old Theme," Expository Times 88 (1976-77): 19; John Webster, "The Identity of the Holy Spirit: A Problem in Trinitarian Theology." Themelios 9:1 (1983): 4-7; C. Plantinga's "Hodgson-Welch Debate", passim.

worship - an ineluctable part of being Christian. A survey of any of the major texts will reveal that the "propositions" come out of a profound reverent awareness of the inadequacies of human language.[84]   Apparently they felt that to "know" a little of the Trinity was of infinitely more value than any other form of knowledge that could be mastered, because it was seen as the foundation of all other knowledge and being.

A. Scriptural Use of Analogical and Personal Language

Extended discussions of the biblical support for the social analogy have been amply provided elsewhere.[85]   The theological notion of person is primarily based on that analogical interpretation of scriptural evidence of a God who is referred to as Father, Son and Holy Spirit. Our defense against the prevalent modern view of interpretation is based upon the perceptions of a differentiation within the Godhead in the early Church, in worship and in reflection. Granted, there is not an articulated doctrine of the Trinity in the New Testament.[86] However, it is readily apparent that the early Church moved through a series of stages in the interpretation of the scriptural evidence and its own experience, which culminated in trinitarian formulations.

---

[84]Cf. Bk. 1, and Bk. 15 of Augustine's De Trinitate, any of Gregory Nazianzen's Orations, Richard of St Victor's De Trinitate, Bk. 1 or Anselm's prayer at the beginning of his Proslogion as examples.

[85]The basic texts and additions (though a far from complete listing) are: with regard to lineaments of trinitarian theology in Old Testament, G.A.F. Knight, A Biblical Approach to the Doctrine of the Trinity (Edinburgh: Oliver and Boyd, 1953), A.R. Johnson The One and the Many in the Israelite Conception of God, 2nd ed. (Cardiff: Univ. of Wales, 1961), see also B.B. Warfield's essay, "The Biblical Doctrine of the Trinity," in Biblical and Theological Studies ed. Samuel G. Craig (Phiadelphia: Presbyterian and Reformed Publishing Co., 1952), esp. 22-43; with regard for New Testament articulations, Arthur W. Wainwright, The Trinity in the New Testament (London: S.P.C.K., 1962), H.A. Wolfson, The Philosophy of the Church Fathers, vol. 1. Faith, Trinity and Incarnation (Cambridge: Harvard Univ. Press, 1956), esp. Pt. 2, 141-191. Also helpful is R.G. Crawford, "Is the Doctrine of the Trinity Scriptural?" Scottish Journal of Theology 20 (1967): 282-294, Christopher Kaiser, "The Discernment of Triunity," Scottish Theological Journal 28:5 (Oct. 1975): 449-460, F.J. Schierse, "Die neutestamentliche Trinitätsoffenbarung," in Johannes Feiner ed. Mysterium Salutis vol. 2 (Einsiedeln: Benzinger Verlag, 1967), 85-129, C.F.D. Moule, "The New Testament and the Doctrine of the Trinity: a short report on an old theme," Expository Times 88 (1976-77): 16-20; for recent discussions of trinitarian notions in the Gospel of John see, R.G. Greunler, The Trinity in the Gospel of John: A Thematic Commentary on the Fourth Gospel (Grand Rapids: Baker Book House, 1986); also see Cornelius Plantinga, "The Hodgson-Welch Debate," chap. 3, 96-176. More accessible and a summary of his position is his article "Images of God," found in Mark A. Noll and David F. Wells ed. Christian Faith and Practice in the Modern World (Grand Rapids: Eerdmans Pub. Co., 1988), esp. 59-63.

[86]Note Bruce Kaye's reservations on the relationship between usage of New Testament and theology, and the implications for "Scripture" if doctrinal developments are regarded as superceding the text, in his article, "The New Testament," in Peter Toon and James D. Spiceland ed. One God in Trinity (Westchester, Ill.: Cornerstone Books, 1980), 24-25.

The God of Israel was not perceived as "Other" in an absolute sense. Though the divine-human distinction was always clarified to prevent idolatry or pantheism, there was no doubt that Yahweh was a personal God and the Messiah was the ultimate expression of divine relationality.[87] From the earliest pages of Scripture the God who spoke, and called and then promised was understood as Another, who transcended the normal anthropomorphisms of pagan religion, yet who had no hesitation in revealing Himself in categories of friendship, love, covenant, even admitting the inference of inner distinction.[88] Though later theologians, in efforts to clarify a difficult topic, used philosophical categories at hand to provide analogies for understanding what Scripture revealed, the original point of exegetical departure was the relations revealed in the Incarnation. It was these which produced the paradigm and logic for the worship of the Triune God.

B. Doxological Theology

The pervading worldview of the early Christian community was revealed in the confession of a divine self-communication inclusive of three distinct persons. From a Biblical perspective, Jane Schaberg's analysis of the triadic phrase in Matt 28: 16-20 leads

---

[87]Oscar Cullman's illuminating monograph, Early Christian Worship, (London: SCM Press, 1953), accentuated the Christocentrism of the early Church. The expectant presence of a personal God was the formative experience behind all worship. See Jacob Neusner's fascinating article, "Story-Telling and the Incarnation of God in Formative Judaism," in The Incarnate Imagination: Essays in Theology, The Arts and Social Sciences: In Honor of Andrew Greeley, A Festschrift. ed. Ingrid H. Shafer (Bowling Green, Ohio: Bowling Green State Univ. Popular Press, 1988), 197-228. He shows the connection between the written and oral Torah, emphasizing the personification of the presence of God in the Mishnah. Although he expresses the expected antipathy for incarnational language, he does conclude that in the Mishnah:
"God appears as premise, presence, and person, but not as a fully exposed personality," Ibid., 228
and,
"When the founding intellects of both Judaism and Christianity wished to explore the meaning of the notion (in Christian language) of the word become flesh, they resorted to stories to say just what that could mean," Ibid., 228.

[88]It can be postulated that the anthropomorphisms of the OT are not the source of embarrassment they have been made out to be. Could it be that they are there to protect against the very idolatry that critics of such language usually lay against it? One is apt to consider spiritual categories as more clinically analogical, but then unwittingly to find that it also is a restrictive category. Ronald Thiemann has written of the traditional Christian understanding of the personhood of God as couched in promise. The promising agent, a God who speaks and who is faithful to his words, bears the identity of an intentional agent who acts. Rather than the causality theory of revelation (which "collapses into self-contradiction") Thiemann chooses the relational category of "narrated promise," focusing on the progressive revelation of the prevenient inter-relatedness implied by the God revealed in Jesus Christ. Revelation and Theology: The Gospel as Narrated Promise (Notre Dame: Univ. of Notre Dame Press, 1985), 107-109, 130-139. For a Biblical approach to this same theme, see Walter Brueggemann, Genesis: A Bible Commentary for teaching and preaching (Atlanta: John Knox Press, 1982).

her to conclude, "that there is not sufficient evidence to indicate that the triadic phrase, is trinitarian (and).... Whatever the idea of the Trinity became, in its triadic origins it was neither boring nor a contemplation of the inaccessible and irrelevant."[89] Though the first Christians did not immediately begin to ponder the mystery of the unity between the three persons, one still marvels at the general continuity of the New Testament with regard to the threeness, which is reflected especially in the doxological life of the Church.[90] Any study of trinitarian doctrine must begin with acknowledging that the preoccupation of the Church lay in relating experience to a basic trinitarian consciousness.

If worship tied the disparate fledgling churches together then the focus of worship, the Trinity, was the underlying connective tissue, the 'logic' of their praise."[91] The liturgy of the Church recognized the self-diffusive nature of the Holy One as "the work of the Trinity in its execution and content."[92] The New Testament has incorporated many liturgical elements into the text which, when recognized, reveal the distinctly personal categories with which the Triune persons were viewed. For many centuries the Church, in its liturgical prayer, has begun morning prayer with the Psalmist's petition, "Lord, open my lips, that my mouth may proclaim your praise." It is the tenet of many theologians that praise informs theology, that it is "theologia prima" which guides and informs "theologia secunda," or that more esoteric discipline of explanation and systematization.[93]

---

[89]Jane Schaberg, The Father, the Son and the Holy Spirit: the Triadic Phrase in Matthew 28:19b (Chico, CA: Scholars Press, 1982), 336-337. Schaberg is not hostile to trinitarian emphases, her work is not theological, but retains an openness to an elemental, or incipient trinitarianism, which was not fully refined. Recognizing the juxtaposition of various forms of referring to deity in the text, she is honest enough not to advocate the idea of a confused Church on this issue as in K. E. Kirk, "The Evolution of the Doctrine of the Trinity," in Essays on the Trinity and the Incarnation ed. A.E.J. Rawlinson (New York: Longmans, Green and Co. Ltd., 1928), 199-208.

[90]Note however the preponderance of 'trinitarian' appelations in the Odes of Solomon esp. 23:22, 36:3-8, 41:9,10,11, and 3:6-10, which some argue were produced in the decades immediately following the NT writings and were most likely hymnic in origin. Ed. and trans. with notes by James Hamilton Charlesworth, The Odes of Solomon: The Syriac Texts (Chico, CA.: Scholars Press, 1977).

[91]Daniel W. Hardy and David F. Ford, Praising and Knowing God (Philadelphia: Westminster Press, 1985), 56. This helpful book recognizes the "unstudied naturalness and simplicity" (Warfield's phrase) with which the Church began its trinitarian praise.

[92]Edward Kilmartin, Christian Liturgy vol.1 Systematic Theology of Liturgy (Kansas City, MO.: Sheed and Ward, 1988), 102.(authors emphasis) He is referring to a diachronic conception of liturgy which needs further articulation. Though I am uneasy with his continual emphasis on the Rahnerian axiom, this is an excellent analysis of the coinherent qualities of trinitarian thought and liturgy.

[93]See C. M. LaCugna and Kilian McDonnell, "Returning from 'The Far Country': Theses for a Contemporary Trinitarian Theology," Scottish Journal of Theology 41 (1988):191-215], for an application of this principle. Their thesis coincides with the

Worship, as a source for the self-understanding of the Church in relation to the Triad which was also One, constantly reminded these early thinkers that no philosophical or grammatical ascriptions were in and of themselves adequate to affix immutable categories to their understanding of God. It was, at once, protective of the openness of Christian experience and regulative in dealing with other claims of ultimate reality.[94] While there should never be a separation of worship and more rigorous theological pursuits, the question remains as to what elements of praise would be found lacking if it were not for formulations within the latter.[95] When the contexts of many of the theologians who have been regarded as destroying simple faith by scholastic rumination, have been uncovered, they resonate with prayer and worship. The concept of "person" then, is crucial to both sides of the Church's life. Without a strong element of interpersonal relationship, praise is weak. Without assisting the Church in how to properly understand that notion which illuminates every facet which can be truly termed relational theology will have done a great disservice to the worshipping community.

C. Prosopological Exegesis

Tertullian's hermeutical approach to inter-divine discourses of the Psalms in his critique of Praxeas appeared a decade after Hippolytus' diatribe against Noetus. Still unsettled as the issue remains regarding who actually influenced whom in the ensuing literary debate, the underlying agreement in fundament has caused those who are skeptical to reassess the origins of Trinitarian thought. There are strong evidences of an apperception of inter-trinitarian relationality in the early early form of exegesis which purported intra-communal discussions or other forms of communication between

---

"economic equals immanent" axiom spawned by Rahner and prevalent within trinitarian thought. They write that, "Talking about the immanent trinity is an oblique way of talking about God's activity in history," 205. While I do not disagree with the premise, as reflected above, I am wary of an over-emphasis on the category of what cannot be known about God, thereby eclipsing something of that revealed tri-unity which ought to be a basis for the rest of our "theologia secunda." For an even more extreme statement of this paradigm see Jean Ansaldi, "Approche Doxologique de la Trinité de Dieu: Dialogue avec J.-L. Marion," Études Théologiques et Religieuses 62 (1987):81-95.

[94]Robert M. Grant, Early Christian Doctrine of God (Charlottesville, Univ. of Virginia Press, 1966), 99-101. See also Jennings, Beyond Theism, 186-208.

[95]Hardy and Ford, Praising and Knowing, allude to this corrective relationship where they write that:
those three basic ways of absolutizing one dimension of the Christian God roughly correspond to the Father, Son, and Holy Spirit. Taken as a unity, the Trinity continually dispels illusions and fantasies about God. It applies a corrective to any one type of language, whether talk about the transcendence of God in analogies, or sacramental and historical accounts of God's character and presence, or subjective, experiential witness to the immediacy of God. So the Trinity is a comprehensive 'negative way', refusing to let one rest in any image of God. Ibid., 55.

differentiated prosopa in the Godhead.

The Father took pleasure evermore in Him, who equally rejoiced with a reciprocal gladness in the Father's presence; "Thou art my Son, to-day have I begotten Thee;" even before the morning star did I beget Thee. The Son likewise acknowledges the Father, speaking in his own person, under the name of Wisdom: "The Lord formed Me as the beginning of His own works; before all the hills did He beget Me.[96]

Michael Slusser has argued that prosopological exegesis "was the source of the use of persona/prosopon in Christian theology."[97] The earliest exegesis took special note of the texts that appeared to be dialogues between co-equal partners, and though they did not surmise on the ontology behind those statements they did discern differentiation within the Godhead.[98] This method of literary analysis was used by the majority of the Church fathers in the apologetic mode in which they often found themselves due to the encroachment of various heresies.

There is an agreement here between the early exegesis of the Church and the

---

[96]Tertullian, Ad Praxean 7, ANF 3, 601-602. Ch. 11, ANF 3, 606 states, "But almost all the Psalms which prophesy of the person of Christ, represent the Son as conversing with the Father - that is, represent Christ as speaking to God. Observe also the Spirit speaking of the Father and the Son in the character of a third Person:..," and here he quotes Ps.110:1. See also ch. 13, ANF 3, 607. For support of this understanding of early exegesis, see Hans Urs von Balthasar's "On the Concept of Person," Communio 13 (1986): 20-21.

[97]"The Exegetical Roots of Trinitarian Theology," Theological Studies 49 (1988): 463. Although his discussion mainly surrounds the relation of the Eastern and Western Fathers it may be relevant to include here the NT texts which repeatedly occur in contexts of Trinitarian discussion of the type Slusser acknowledges. Lists of texts supporting the various views on the Trinity normally comprise the early chapters of any text on this issue. A cursory approach might be to break down the evidence into categories with several scriptural examples for each. 1)Threefoldness of the One God: 1 Cor. 12:4-6, 2 Cor. 13:14, Eph. 4:4-6, 2:18, 2 Thes. 2:13 2)Threeness at Baptism of Jesus Mt. 3:11-17, Mk. 1:9-11, Lk. 3:21-22, Jn. 1:32 3)Three declared to be God: Father-(Rahner's 'ho theos') Jn. 6:27, Eph. 5:20, I Pt. 1:2; Son- Jn. 1:1, Heb. 1:8; Spirit- Acts 5:3,4, I Cor. 6:19 4)Three grouped together: Mt. 28:19, Lk. 1:35, Rom. 1:3,4, Eph. 3:14-17, 4:4-6, Heb. 2:3-4, 9:14, I Jn. 3:21-24, 5:5-7, Jude 20,21, II Cor. 13:14, I Pt. 1:2, Rev. 1:4,5, (the last two references are the only two NT salutations which possess trinitarian allusions, 16 others bear 'binitarian' construction) 5)Other distinctions between persons of the Trinity: Father-Son relationship, Heb. 1:3, 208 times. in NT Jesus is referred to as Son, Of over 1,000 references in all of Scripture God the Father is used 265 times, of which 77 times Jesus refers to him as Father; Jesus as Sent, Gal. 4:4, Acts 10:38, Phil. 2:6; Holy Spirit proceeds, Jn. 8:42, 15:26; Positional distinction, Mk. 16:19, Acts 2:33, Rom. 8:34, Eph. 1:20, Col. 3:1, Rev. 3:21.

[98]Slusser refers to Justin Martyr's (100-165) exegesis in his lengthy Dialogues with Trypho beginning in ch. 50, where he responds to the challenge to "prove that there is another God besides the Creator," and ch. 55 to "prove that the Prophetic Spirit ever admits the existence of another God, which he begins with in 56 with a discussion of the three angels in Gen 18., the discussion inferred between the 'Lord' and 'my lord' in messianic Ps 110:1, and its counterpart often intepreted as a messianic coronation, 44:6,7. Trans. here by Thomas B. Falls, Writings of Saint Justin Martyr in The Fathers of the Church (New York: Christian Heritage, Inc.) See also ANF vol 1. 220-230. Carl Andresen's "Zur Entstehung und Geschicte des Trinitarischen Person-begriffes," Zeitschrift für die Neutestamentliche Wissenschaft 52 (1961), is one of the major sources for Slusser's viewpoint, see esp. 9-14.

elements of Jewish monotheism which reveal a latent triadism in the Old Testament. The concept of 'corporate personality' and its theological implications in early Israel have often been traversed.[99] To the chagrin of much modern Biblical scholarship and even theologians this form of exegesis naturally issued in increasingly metaphysical constructs when the systematic questions were asked about how the evidence fit together. It is, of course, a difficult task to determine whether the exegesis and resultant ideologies influenced early Christian worship or vice versa.[100]

What is to be noted here is the place of personal language and the concomitant perception of a God who revealed himself as a transcendent, personal Being within an increasingly clearer context of triadic proportions. This must be remembered in connection with the prevalence of sources that speak of the mystery, the 'presence which confronts' in doxological contexts. The ontological interpretations can be seen as purely mythological or as redolent with revelatory implications that point to real triune distinctions. This point is clearly made by J.A.T. Robinson in his rejection of those thinkers who begin with the appropriated works of the Persons of the Trinity and work back from there to ontological formulation. One cannot start from the effects of 'power', 'wisdom' and 'goodness' or 'memory', 'will' and 'love' in trinitarian discernment. Instead the relationships indicated in the early chapters of the Gospel, added to what follows, form the only proper basis of the ontological inquiry affirmed here. Robinson has stated in an unpublished dissertation that:

> At the Incarnation, therefore, the Godhead is revealed for the first time as existing in three distinct relations. It is these differences of relation that make necessary a

---

[99]Primary figures in this discussion are H. Wheeler Robinson, The Corporate Personality in Ancient Israel (Philadelphia: Fortress Press, 1964); J. Pederson, Israel; Its Life and Culture 1-2 of 4 vols.(London: Oxford Univ. Press, 1964); both A.R. Johnson One and the Many, and G.A.F. Knight Biblical Approach to Trinity, have garnered from their findings to open up new ways of viewing the Yahweh of Israel. Johnson's notion of the 'extensions' of the personality, both human and divine, in the concepts of 'word' (dabar), 'spirit' (ruach), 'sons of the Gods' (bene elohim), 'messenger', or 'angel' (mal'ach) drive him to consider "whether a further step in consideration of the Godhead," with regard to those 'extensions' which might be seen as comprising a "social unit," 22, see also 37. Knight goes further, in discussing the above, but also the "anthropomorphic" references to God, i.e., face (panim), and sees him revealed as a person, Ibid., 10. His view of organic and dynamic and communitarian "oneness" ('echad) is a strong point in allowing an interpretation of unity of consciousness, a diversity within the unified God that Israel worshiped, Ibid., 16-17, 47-48. A fine example of latent categories of 'personhood' in the OT is O.R. Jones, The Concept of Holiness (London: George Allen and Unwin, Ltd., 1961).

[100]Slusser, "Exegetical Roots," 476, expresses reservation at this point, recognizing the mutuality of experience and exegesis. He leans toward the assumption that trinitarian preconceptions influenced this form of exegesis. The debate will continue. However, it should not be rejected outright, that we have here an example of the almost unselfconscious trinitarian attitude of the Church. It is hard to imagine a Church prior to the centuries of argumentation. But at face value, until the end of the first century there is an amazing cooperation, or oneness of interpretation with regard to a God consisting of Three, whatever those three might be.

doctrine of the Trinity, not differences of "character" or modes of working. The Old Testament, too, knew God in different "characters", but it was not forced to a Trinitarian Theology. It is only from this point, from the difference of relations, that a satisfactory doctrine of the Trinity can start. We cannot begin with God creating, God redeeming, God sanctifying, or any other such collocation of attributes, and then proceed to identify these with Father, Son and Holy Spirit. On that method there is no compelling reason for stopping at three Persons and no ground for any real differentiations. Rather, one must start with the three Persons, no more and no less, which are required by the three relations at the Incarnation. From there it is possible and necessary to go on to a doctrine of appropriations.[101]

D. Johannine Trinitology

The deeds and words of Jesus formed the basis of this unpacking of a hidden trinitology in the Old Testament.[102] In the spiritual and metaphysical revolution that ensued upon the claims of Jesus which were interpreted as being statements of equality with God, the writers of the first century noted with special interest the forms of speech which their Messiah used in discourse and in prayer. It was virtually impossible to circumvent a self-perception in the Nazarene which implied a unity of nature with the object of his prayers or with the "Father" of his parables. Though the one speaking was different than the referent, there was an underlying similarity, a symbiosis, that the Church initially and then

---

[101]Based on the hermeneutical principle that all non-incidental human factors in the Incarnation must necessarily be predicated of the Divine nature, Robinson's "Thou Who Art," Ph.D. dissertation, Cambridge University, 1946, 585, strongly advocates a biblical basis for trinitarian personhood, while challenging the traditional doctrine of the relations of origin which he finds quite unbiblical. He sees the "economic" Trinity as more than an index to the immanent, thus equating the two and truncating the latter. (Ibid., 581) However, he allows no subordinationism of any kind in stating that the dependence clauses in the Johannine material are merely references to the humanity of Jesus. (Ibid., 582-583) Originally this reference was found in C.F.D. Moule's "The New Testament and the Trinity," 19. This author is most grateful to Canon Eric James, literary executor of Dr. Robinsons' estate, and director of Christian Action, London for his assistance in placing this quote in its context. Cf. Reginald Fuller, Foundations of New Testament Christology (London: Lutterworth, 1965), 248, where he says that the triadic formulas were "not just a quirk of the Greek mind, but a universal apperception."

[102]Apparently Jesus was making claims which cut across a variety of ideological lines. With regard to the predominant concepts of God relating to the world, Hugo Odeberg, in The Fourth Gospel (Amsterdam: B. R. Grüner, 1968) makes a point of showing the similarities, possible fulfillments, and exceeding of themes which were prevalent in Rabbinic, Mystical, and Mandaean circles, among others. The Mandaean Great First Life (Manda dHayye) sent the Saur'el who delivers, or the Kusta or Messenger who communicates truth under direct order. Ibid., 190-198. The Gnostic Odes of Solomon have a clear emphasis on a Father who sends a Son who bears the Spirit in a life-bestowing and judgment-bringing ministry. Ibid., 199-202. The Jewish Mystical writings, such as 3 Enoch discuss the relationship of the Holy One and Metatron (the little Yahweh), the begotten one who serves and receives authority and delivers, due to the fact that he was once a terrestrial being. Ibid., 204-206. It may be that this system of ideas as well as the Old Testament either found their fulfillment in the triune implications of the New Testament or they were later eclectic incorporations of it. See also 313-336 for clear examples.

more systematically reassessed as allusions to the differentiation between divine persons.[103]

In retrospect, Christological formulations went through basically three stages, according to Reginald Fuller, the 'historical,' the 'mythological' and the 'metaphysical'.[104] Though other descriptions are used these generally represent the synopsis of modern scholarship with varying degrees of acceptance and accusations of metaphysical contamination of a 'pure' historicity.[105] What is of importance here is that the early Church appears to have had little difficulty with the gospels seen as a "self-articulation of filial deity."[106] Unencumbered by the modern focus of "act" as basic to personhood, the Church viewed the person, work and words of Christ as reflective of divine being. Though no rigorous statement of the Trinity is found in the New Testament, nonetheless, the actions of Christ were accepted as proceeding from, and logically preceded by divine being.[107]

The Gospel of John has been ransacked for support of the opinions of thinkers on both sides of the ontological question. It is here that the social analogy finds its clearest scriptural evidence. Explicitly and implicitly, there is an intriguing dialectic at work in the references of Jesus to his Father. Statements of dependence: "For he (the Father) has granted the Son also to have life in himself," (5:26) are juxtaposed with those of independence: "So also the Son gives life to whom he will." (5:21) Heteronomy is qualified by a distinct autonomy; statements of identity are found next to those that communicate

---

[103]Slusser, "Exegetical Roots," 468-469, lists antecedents of the form of distinguishing which culminated in Jesus. Philo recognized a plurality even in the fact that Moses spoke "in the person" of God, or in the much debated "us" and "our" of Gen. 1:26.

[104]Reginald H. Fuller, "On Demythologizing the Trinity," Anglican Theological Review 43:2 (April, 1961): 121-131, see 125. 'Mythological' is used here as the usurpation and transformation of pagan philosophical/mythological concepts and their attribution to Christ.

[105]The ambivalence with which many modern critics of a traditional conception of a social Trinity approach the historical question may indicate its own obscurantistic bias. While at one time emphasizing the 'ipsissima verba' of Jesus as revealing the extent to which any speculation regarding the Trinity might go, at another, the words of Jesus are claimed as unhistorical when they are revelatory of ontological categories. Rejection of the social analogy must, it seems to me, be done so logically. Hermeneutics are decisive at this point. Historicity of the texts is a vitally important issue but the question to be asked here is if there is truth in the statements of Jesus. If so, then the ontological question arises alongside the soteriological.

[106]Mascall, Triune God, 31. He agrees with J. Galot and L. Bouyer in finding the Trinity revealed in the Incarnation.

[107]Fuller, "Demythologizing," 130-131. Cf. the insight of Gerald Bray, "The Patristic Dogma," in Peter Toon's One God, that skirting the Charybdis of modalism and the Scylla of adoptionism promulgated by a solely economic interpretation forced the early fathers back to Scripture, in which they repeatedly defended an ontological interpretation of christology. "Unless one believes that the christology of the New Testament is fundamentally ontological, then it seems most unlikely that classical trinitarianism will ever make much sense," 56.

real distinctions or, an incommunicability of personal attributes.

Theologians have struggled with the implications of these dialectic (or supra-dialectic) indicators for centuries. Some conclude that they do not indicate any distinction between the persons of the Trinity.[108] Others follow the traditional interpretation that there are real ontological implications for the intriguing inter-personal nuances of the text as transmitted. There is a mutuality inherent in the texts which reveal inextricable relations between the persons; language which entails mutual glorification, sending and giving.[109] John does not proffer a deep ontological discussion at a philosophical level but what may be more profound is the actual communication of love and life revealed in the accounts of actions, prayers, and self-perception of the historical Jesus.[110] The result of this

---

[108]Cyril Richardson said that any notion of divine persons in dialogue with one another, "involves confusing paradoxical principles of the divine with persons," in "The Trinity and the Enhypostasia," Canadian Journal of Theology 5:2 (April 1959): 73-78. He deplored any discussion of an ontological and personal distinction within the Godhead; for him the prayer life of Jesus is merely a facet of the "conditions of finitude" which immediately reveals Richardson's christology. In a subtle article, "Person or Personification? A Patristic Debate about Logos," in The Glory of Christ in the New Testament: Studies in Christology, ed L. D. Hurst and N. T. Wright (Oxford: Clarendon Press, 1987), 281-289, Maurice Wiles, deploying the arguments of Eusebius and Marcellus in the 330's, cannot disguise his agreement with James Dunn's assessment that the prologue of John indicates a personification rather than ontologically discerned individual person.

[109]Again, for a clear analytic approach to this interpretation see Plantinga's "Hodgson-Welch Debate," 144-175. The 'other-orientation' of these themes though incipient at times is supported by other more overt references that taken at face value reveal a deep interpersonal intimacy. Exegetical examples are: **Mutual glorification**, 16:14 (Son by Spirit); 17:4-5 (Son and Father); **Sending**, 3:16-17 (uses 'give') 3:34, 4:34, 5:30,36-37, 8:29,(42) (Son by Father, never of Father); 13:16, 14:26, 15:26 (Spirit by Father and Son); **Giving**, 3:35, 5:22,26,27,36 17:8,22; Intricate interconnectedness is revealed in the sharing of function or roles in ministry to the world; **Bearing Truth**, normally in terms of 'words' 3:33-34, 8:26,(32), (of Son); 14:17,26,27, (of Spirit); **Bearing Life**, 5:26, 6:48,51,54,57, 10:28, (20:22)(Father and Son); 3:5-6, 6:63, 7:38-39 (Spirit). Plantinga's trilogy, Will, Works, Words (see esp. 170-173), are helpful in categorizing both the unity and the triunity when he points to the verses that indicate a oneness of each and the corresponding differentiation of each. See **diversity** within Godhead in Will 4:34, 5:30, 5:38, 8:29, 10:18, 12:49-50, 15:16 (Father and Son); 1:33, 20:22 (Spirit); **Works** 5:19-22, 5:36, 9:3-4, 14:10 (Father and Son); 14:16, 15:26, 16:8-11 (Spirit); **Words** 3:34, 7:16, 8:26, 12:49, 14:24 (Father and Son); 14:26, 16:14; for **unity** within the Godhead see Will 17:1,2,4,5,6,7,11,17,24, 16:13,14,15; Works 5:17, 8:16-18, 14:23, 10:36, 17:19; Words 6:63, 7:16,17,18, 16:13. Plantinga's four other categories which bespeak triunity are: mutual **knowing** 10:14-15, 17:25; **loving** which he says is "primarily unity's expression," (160); **glorifying** 5:41, 7:18, 8:50, 13:31-32, 17:5,22,24; and **co-inhering** (he uses John's 'hen' as 'inness', 10:38, 14:10-11, 17:21,23-24, and by inference the Spirit in 14:16-17. As an aside; Plantinga's horizontal categories with respect to divine unity are also applied vertically in good Barthian 'analogia relationis' fashion. Though he woudl differ from Barth as the the extent of analogical discernment as it points to the actual "personae" in the Trinity.

[110]Christopher Kaiser's interesting analysis from a phenomenological vector surmised that "the prayer life of Jesus, as observed by the disciples and the early church, is a suitable empirical basis for the apostolic discernment of triunity," see "Discernment of

interpretation is a discernment of inter-personal complementarity, a differentiated unity that at once mystifies and transcends our idea of unity and multiplicity. It reveals an inner dynamism based on a social or communitarian understanding of love.

In response to the charge that there is within this framework a subordinationistic undertone, one must deal with the effect of philosophical conclusions that derivation is, of necessity, secondary to source. John does not explain the problems inherent in the kenotic statements such as "I can do nothing of my own authority...because I seek not my own will but the will of him who sent me." (Jn. 5:30, see 8:28) Yet the silence here may also be constructive for there are elements which correspond to this "line-command" that, in themselves, do not in any way denigrate the self-perception of the Son of God as a divine person. The 'monogenes' debate that is now more often rendered as "uniqueness" as opposed to "only-begotten," still reveals the Father as the 'fons' of the Godhead. Jesus consistently acknowledges his procession from the Father. The Spirit also proceeds from the Father, while also being sent by the Son.[111] Juxtaposed with this recurrent emphasis of derivative life and authority is an awareness on the part of Jesus regarding the altruistic character of his Father.[112]

> The Father glorifies the Son and makes himself available to Him, the Son glorifies the Father and defers to him, and the Holy Spirit seems almost to make himself anonymous in serving the Father and the Son, while they in turn appear to refer to the Spirit with loving equality and deference.... The identity of Father, Son and Holy Spirit is seen to lie in the merging of personality in interpersonal communion. There is no

---

Triunity," 457. See also his discussion of Hilary's exegesis of John in "The Development of Johannine Motifs in Hilary's Doctrine of the Trinity," Scottish Journal of Theology 29:3 (June, 1976):234-247. On this same note see Oden's Living God where building on the "scandal of particularity" with regard to revelation, (Ibid., 20) his discussion of each portion of the NT supports a triune interpretation, Ibid., 202-208.

[111]Cf. 1:13,18, 3:16,18, 8:42, 13:3,16, 14:28, 16:28, 17:8. Plantiga discusses the terms ek, apo, and para, as used in these texts to reveal ontological distinctions, "Hodgson-Welch Debate," 154.

[112]Possibly reflecting the bibliographic bias of much modern trinitology is the absence of attention given to Royce Gruenler's The Trinity in the Gospel of John: A Thematic Commentary on the Fourth Gospel (Grand Rapids: Baker Book House, 1986). His recurrent term on this score is "disposability". Well aware of the weight of evidence for subordinationism (Plantinga quite frankly acknowledges this "general subordination," "Hodgson-Welch Debate," 147, 151-3) Gruenler is so strongly convinced of the reciprocity of divine love that he speaks of a "deference" of the Father to the Son. The Father gives all judgment to Jesus (5:22) and all authority (5:27). Ibid., 37. The Father is never "threatened" by the glory bestowed on the Son or the attribution of worship. Greunler interprets the Father's attention to the believer's petition as a deference to the Son. (16:23). Ibid., 119. His use of unique terminology here would offend the modalist but proffers the rudiments for further investigation into the social analogy. Built upon the principle of a Divine "Family", the Christian faith is conceived of as entering into that reciprocal love. The "home" motif is compelling. (xvi, 8, 54, passim). Terms such as "mutual sharing", "availability", "hospitality", "coordinate unity" adumbrate the traditional interpretation of the Divine Triunity in its perichoretic fullness.

claim to independent individuality (which would be tritheism), but an assertion of essential identification in loving communion.[113]

Thus, subordination of the Son to the Father must be placed within the context of mutual disposability - love that longs to serve, to glorify the Other. This is not to say the Father is not the source, the fons et origo of the Triunity. It is merely a guard against an overemphasis, since the Arian controversy to deny a full co-equality between the persons of the Trinity. It is a proper conception of 'person' that assists at this point. Inherent in the subordinationist arguments is a distinction between the essential unity of the Trinity and the 'oikonomia' of the Triune persons. John's gospel would indicate that any subordination is of a voluntary nature, a self-giving kenosis. A full sense of divine personhood then would allow no essential distinction between opera ad intra and opera ad extra.

E. The 'Person' of the Holy Spirit

Most difficult, in an already arduous endeavor, is the theological conflagration with regard to the Holy Spirit. There are diverse thinkers in the area of pneumatology who, despite other differences, fundamentally agree upon a rejection of the notion of person, as applied to the Holy Spirit. Rigorous studies of the etymological and exegetical milieu of pneuma have been used to support that conclusion. On at least one point they are correct, that the application of the modern philosophical/anthropological definition of the individual person to any of the divine Trinity is heretical. As Franz Schierse notes:

> One must be careful not to characterize the Holy Spirit as person in the usual sense, that means as a self-conscious spiritual center of act. Otherwise it can happen that the exegete, under an understandable fear of remaining behind dogmatic teaching, shoots far beyond the target and lands in the neighborhood of a tritheistic error.[114]

One wonders, however, if the ascription of modernity's primarily individualistic definition to the divine Spirit is the only proper recourse. Ought it not be possible to regain former historical distinctives regarding personhood in order to inform and transform the deficiencies inherent in these newer more narcissistic orders?

The basic front lines of this modern debate consist of distinguishing between the Holy Spirit as person or as mere personification; as personal in a sense which equals that of the other two persons of the Trinity, or personal in a manner which merely sees the

---

[113]Gruenler, Trinity in Gospel of John, 122.

[114]Franz Josef Schierse, "Trinitätsoffenbarung," 121. He prefaces this by stating that, "the new dogmatic research has taught us that the concept of the person found in the doctrine of the Trinity should not be identified with an understanding of a person as an independent spiritual center of acts (sich selbst stehenden geistigen Aktzentrum)," Ibid., 121-122. He does however acknowledge the shift from a notion of impersonal force to a more personified understanding of the Spirit in both Paul and John.

Paraclete as God's immanent revelation of himself to humanity.[115] Though often criticized at a content level, the early Church undoubtedly regarded the differentiation between the Spirit and the Son to be a distinct, real one.[116] Origen went beyond the Apologists' inability to philosophically reconcile the generation of the Son with the idea of pure Being, or in our terms, function with ontology. Origen's bequest to the Church was a progression in the direction the earlier thinkers were already headed; that of a conviction that the real issue was an ontological assessment of the internal relations between three divine persons.[117] Rather than being a mere element in the life of Son and Father, the Spirit was seen as having an active personal role in the economy of salvation. Though consubstantiality was not fully articulated until the Cappadocians took up the challenge, the Church, generally, and however rudimentarily, acknowledged the Spirit as a unique and equal member of the Trinity.

There are those who disagree with this conclusion, making the early references to the Spirit simply an expressive or existential modalism.[118] Yet, the question must be

---

[115]Wiles, "Person or Personification," 288, claims that these are two possible ways to read, for instance, the prologue of John regarding the pre-existence of the Son. H. Berkhof, The Doctrine of the Holy Spirit (Atlanta: John Knox Press, 1977), offers the same "functional" Christology and then pneumatology in his analysis and use of Marcellus of Ancyra, in critiquing the use of 'person' which he deems as anachronistic, misleading, and "useless." 118-119.

[116]W. Kasper, The God of Jesus Christ, trans. Matthew J. O'Connell (New York: Crossroads Pub. Co., 1986), 361, nn.28,29, notes the progression of thought from the confusion between Son and Spirit of earliest reflections on Scripture and experience of Shepherd of Hermas 41, 58, 59; Justin Apologia 1:39 to clarifying statements of Gregory of Nazianzus, Oration 31, NPNF2 vol.7, see ch.30-31 for conclusions, 317-318.

[117]Origen, De Principiis 1.2.8, ANF 4, 248-249; 1.3 ANF 4, 251D - 256A is an extended discussion on the Spirit. 1.3.2 mentions the person of the Holy Spirit specifically. ANF 4, 252C. Of course the detractors of this position find places where Origen equivocates. While strong distinctions and statements of equality are made in De Principiis, Origen's work on the Gospel of John indicates an "inferior" status to the Holy Spirit (Commentary on John 2.6 ANF 10, 328-329,) at least according to Edmund J. Fortman, The Triune God (Grand Rapids: Baker Book House, 1982), 57. Closer examination of the text however reveals, what we might call a "proto-filioque" tendency in that passage which attests to both Origen's brilliance and his philosophical milieu. Without the advantage of the later consensus on the appropriations of the persons and indivisibility Origen does a remarkable job. Writing on John 3:8, "He (Origen) says, "This shows that the Spirit is an Essence. He is not, as some suppose a Divine Energy, having (as they pretend) no distinctive personal existence." H. B. Swete, The Holy Spirit in the Ancient Church (London: Macmillan, 1912), 133.

[118]Martin Kähler, Dogmatische Zeitfragen, 2, 2nd ed. (Leipzig: A. Deichert, 1908), 214 as quoted in H. Berkhof, The Doctrine of the Holy Spirit, 128. n.16;
"To conceive of the Spirit as a person in relation to God, he says, would contradict the classical dogma of the Trinity (!) and "would express something which would have no importance for our faith in God." "On the other hand, of decisive importance for us and for our life in faith is the fact that God's Spirit is person toward us and that therefore in him God himself meets us in person." (Quoted and emphasized as in text).

answered as to exactly who this "agency" of God is and how it is realized. To say that these questions are "speculative" is to disparage the value of an entire group of affirmations regarding the Spirit which are essentially congruous to straightforward statements made about any other 'individual', divine or otherwise, in the New Testament.

At times, large gaps in reasoning appear in even the most rigorous critiques of the 'personhood' of the Spirit. H. Berkhof, within the context of ejecting centuries of theological thought in a few paragraphs, and based on the same radical distinction between revelation and divine essence which the "functionalists" continually acknowledge, concludes:

> This plurality and diversity of God have to do with his activity and with his condescendence. He is a moving God; he is a movement of love. Such a movement cannot be described in one word or in one name....They are not other Gods, nor are they other departments within one Godhead.[119]

What remains unclear is what a "movement" means. Ironically, one is left, it seems, with more of a sense of abstractness than is laid at the feet of the traditional distinctions. Large portions of Scripture which offer more than a personifying interpretation are glossed over. Congar's monumental work on the Holy Spirit lists the majority of texts within the New Testament which speak of the Holy Spirit, and in the book of John, specifically.[120] It is not presumptuous to inquire in what way epithets such as: "the other Paraclete," (Jn. 14:16), "sent," (Gal. 4:6 cf. "proceeding," Jn. 15:26), "given,"(Jn. 14:16), "does not speak of himself," (Jn. 16:13), "dwelling within," (Rom. 8:9, Jn. 14:17),[121] are to be interpreted. Are they not meant to indicate strong personal categories of the Spirit that comprise a form of progressive revelation of the 'ruach' of the Old Testament and the distinctly different notion of 'pneuma' in Greek thought which carries a satellite of personal refernces?[122]

---

[119]Berkhof, Doctrine of the Holy Spirit, 118. Catapulting persona, subsistentia, and modus entis, he chooses modi revelationis in agreement with the Rahnerian axiom. Ibid.

[120]Yves Congar, I Believe in the Holy Spirit, vol. 1, 15-62. His list for John is from F. Porsch's Pneuma und Wort (Frankfort am Main: J. Knecht, 1974.), 237ff.

[121]One need only chart the New Testament usage of the terms, "oikeo" - to dwell, live, and "enoikeo"- used exclusively (except Lk. 13:4 variant) - by Paul, of the divine-human relationship as indwelling, especially of the Holy Spirit. Every time the Spirit is the subject of the verb it indicates a personal literal indwelling, unless one insists on skewing the language to fit the modern proclivity towards depersonalizing the Spirit.

[122]J. L McKenzie, Dictionary of the Bible, s.v. "Spirit" (Milwaukee: Bruce Pub. Co., 1965), 844, "The occasional personifications which he (Paul) employs do not go beyond the personifications found in the Old Testament and Judaism." Ed. G.Kittel and G. Frederich, Theological Dictionary of the New Testament, trans. and ed. Geoffrey Bromiley, 9 vols. (Grand Rapids, Eerdmans Pub. Co., 1964-74) (hereafter, TDNT,) s.v. "pneuma," by Eduard Schweizer, vol. 6, 332-451, (359), "Profane Greek knows no hypostatic person of the Spirit understood as an independent divine entity. In the Greek world 'pneuma' is always regarded as a thing never as a person."

The 'hypostatization' of Wisdom, glory, Word and Spirit in Hellenic Judaism served as an apologetic in the face of encroaching Greek categories of immanentism. These distinctions not only from creation but within God himself stood in stark contrast to the elemental nature of Greek pantheism.[123] Though not descriptive of person specifically, the Spirit as transcendent and as holy was unknown in Hellenic thinking. A personal, living, active Spirit was conceived in two ways, Conzelmann states; at times an animistic or more personal notion was attached to the Spirit, but more predominant, he claims, was the dynamistic interpretation, or Spirit as impersonal power.[124] Important to note here is that whether one agrees with Conzelmann or not, the Spirit gained status as a 'substantial', personal being over against the rampant idealistic and pantheistic definitions pertaining to 'pneuma' which preceded early Christianity.

Crucial here as well is the distinction which the New Testament and the early Church made between Christ and the Spirit. Although Jesus bears the Spirit continually from the Baptism in Jordan onward, it is clear that the One who descended is other than the recipient. Jesus also bestows, and baptizes with the Spirit upon his Ascension, and it is that Triune Person who is at present empowering, convicting, witnessing to Christ, and making the full presence of God known.[125] It is not a coherent position which states that there is no real distinction between the Spirit and the other two persons of the Trinity. The parallels which Scripture draws between Christ and the Spirit are not to be conflated. Instead, they are indicative of the mutuality of the Trinity and personalness of a Triune ministry. Both give grace, peace, liberty, life, glory, and also offer adoption. Both intercede, call, and bring comfort.[126] The uniqueness of the Spirit is seen most dynamically

---

[123]TDNT, "pneuma," 338-339. Schaberg's Father, Son and the Holy Spirit, discusses the position that the Spirit is understood best in relation to the Hebrew concept of 'angel' (mal'ach), those "extensions of the power of God," 15, 62 n.30.

[124]Hans Conzelmann, An Outline of the Theology of the New Testament, trans. John Bowden (London: SCM Press, 1969), 38-39. Based on the use of 'anima' and 'dunamis'. He states, "The recognition that the spirit is thought of as a kind of substance can offer a safeguard against idealistic interpretation." Ibid., 39.

[125]E.g. Mt 3:16, Mk 1:10, Lk 3:16,22, 24:49, Jn 1:32,33, Jn 16:7,8-10, Jn 20:22, Jn 14:26, Jn 16:14. Acts 2:33, Rom 8:16,26, I Cor 2:11,13, 3:19, 12:11.

[126]Cf. Lucien Cerfaux, Christ in the Theology of St. Paul trans. Geoffrey Webb and Adrian Walker (New York: Herder and Herder, 1959), 285-293. Of those who reduce the persons to one he says:
"To conclude that equivalent effects must have the same cause (in this case to presume that Christ is identical with the Holy Spirit) is mistaken logic. The same reality, seen under two different aspects, may be connected with two causes....We shall see that this efficient causality is also a formal and exemplary causality which can be expressed by the idea of presence. But presence is only a vague word which covers in fact very different notions. For the Spirit is present by communication of himself." Ibid., 291-292.

in the acts of God after Pentecost. The early Church's comprehension deepens as they find the promise of "Another" true in every sense of the word. They respond to Him with the same sort of openness and obedience which is revealed in the relation to Father and Son, yet with a marked difference. In the tradition of the dialogical philosophers, John Robinson distinguishes the person of the Spirit where he points out that:

> In a real sense the Spirit too is revealed to stand in a "Thou" relation to the Godhead. For the "I" who makes the "Thou" response of faith is in fact the Holy Ghost informing, without superceding, the personality of the believer. Here also God is truly on both sides of the "I-Thou" relation, as He was in the response of the incarnate Christ. Thus, though the Spirit does not, like the Son, become man, He is capable of existing towards God through man, in the polarity of the "Thou" relationship.[127]

The problem of John's use of Paraclete (**parakletos**, Jn 14-16) in his discussion of the Spirit has been interpreted in numerous ways. Some maintain that this title does nothing to mitigate a distinct impersonality with regard to the Spirit, others vacillate between personal and impersonal attributions, and there are those who feel that the Comforter is a real personal being, the alter ego of Jesus.[128] The use of this masculine

---

Schierse disagrees with this methodology as proof-texting, and as insufficient evidence when compared with the 'personifying' of sin, Law, flesh, etc. Like many others, he feels this interpretation does not deal adequately with the impersonal characteristics of the 'pneuma'. "Trinitätsofferbarung," 120-121.

[127]Robinson, "Thou Who Art," 384-385.

[128]Stephen Smalley gives a good review in his John: Evangelist and Interpreter (Nashville: Thomas Nelson Pub., 1984), 228-232. In the non-person sector George Johnston has effectively stated, in The Spirit-Paraclete in the Gospel of John (Cambridge: Cambridge University Press, 1970), the arguments against the use of 'person' in relation to the Paraclete, though he does not go so far as to say that the Spirit is impersonal. But he does negate the presence of a third hypostasis. See 81-87, 122-123. One might add here; H.B. Swete The Holy Spirit in the Ancient Church (London: Macmillan, 1912), 376 ("mode of being"); Edmund Dobbin takes a similar tack as Johnston, personal but not person, in "Towards a Theology of the Holy Spirit, I" Heythrop Journal, 27:1 (1967):18-19. This stance is of course the basis of G.W.H. Lampe's God as Spirit, see 11, 91-92, 95. Following Bultmann's lead Ingo Hermann, Kyrios und Pneuma: Studien zur Christologie der paulischen Hauptbriefe, Studien zum Alten und Neuen Testament, vol.2 (Munich: Kösel-Verlag, 1961), 132-142, "Ein hypostatisches oder trinitarisches Pneuma-Verständnis ist nicht gerechtfertigt," Ibid., 138. Smalley presents Otto Betz as an example of the middle, "mediating" group, which sees the Paraclete as Person and impersonal power at the same time (Der Paraklet (Leiden, E.J. Brill, 1963). Emphasizing Spirit as gift, Georg Kretschmar, Studien zur Frühchristlichen Trinitätstheologie, in Beiträge zur historischen Theologie, vol. 21 (Tübingen: J.C.B. Mohr, 1956), 13-14, 121-122. Schierse's "Trinitätsofferbarung" belongs here also although he does not use person, he will say that the spirit "plays an indispensable role," 125. For more explicit "personification" references see Otto Kuss, Der Römerbrief vol. 2 (Regensburg, Pustet Verlag, 1963), 580-584. Raymond Brown has taken a position which would place him in the "Person" camp, ("The Paraclete in the Fourth Gospel," New Testament Studies 13 (1966-67):113-32. He does however, see this mainly in John; "divine agent" or "animating principle" suffices for him in the Synoptics and Paul, see The Birth of the Messiah (London: Geoffrey Chapman, 1977), 125. William Hill, The Three-Personed God: The Trinity as a Mystery of Salvation (Washington: The Catholic University of America Press, 1982) feels the NT is neutral concerning distinct 'hypostasis', 298. Yet, the

noun in references to the 'pneuma' (neuter) may be one indication of the beginning of a Triune differentiation of a personal Spirit which clarified what might have been previously interpreted as impersonal.[129] Speaking of the Paraclete, Edmund Fortman states forthrightly;

> There can be no real question of the personality of the Holy Spirit here. He is not merely a divine gift or power, nor is He a metaphor for Jesus Himself. He is as much a living person as Jesus Himself and one whose action is so divine that His presence will, for the disciples, advantageously replace the visible presence of Jesus. So clearly does John regard the Holy Spirit as a person that he uses a masculine pronoun for the Spirit, even though the Greek pneuma is neuter. What is even more decisive is the analogy between the Spirit and Jesus. The personality of Jesus is the measure of the personality of the Holy Spirit. They must both be denied or both be accepted.[130]

Distinction by no means implies independence, rather it is part and parcel of the divine unity. Any attempt to reduce the Spirit to christology or anthropology disregards the weight of evidence for a distinct pneumatic person and brings into question the divine unity which the Church has defended from its beginning.[131] Bernard Cooke is helpful in reminding that conflation of personal categories is a risky business when dealing with the Spirit.

> The Spirit is not identical with the faith consciousness of the early communities, yet as known in faith he is inseparable from that consciousness. Even to use the term "person" of the Spirit can be misleading, for there is the danger of using the category "person" generically and thinking of him as being a person like the Father or the Son is person.[132]

Spirit is nothing less than the immediate source of divine love as the "person of love", Ibid., 296. Walter Kasper, The God of Jesus Christ, 210-214; see also David Brown's unusual approach in The Divine Trinity (La Salle, IL.: Open Court Pub. Co., 1985), 185-215. Based on an analysis of "indwelling" Brown deflects the "impersonal" attribution adroitly.

[129]C.K. Barrett, The Gospel According to St. John (Philadelphia: Westminster Press, 1978), 91. Further illuminative "violations" of grammar can be seen in Jn 16:13-14; 14:16,17; 15:26; 16:7,8. Eph 1:14 uses the masculine article 'hos' instead of the neuter 'ho' in relation to the Spirit, which is debated by those who say the latter refers to 'arrhebon'. It is arguable that there is a doctrinal progression resident here along the same lines that one could argue about the dawning of a perception about the two natures in Christ. He says, "the materials are present out of which the doctrine grew," Ibid., 91. Cf. G.E. Ladd, A Theology of the New Testament (London: Lutterworth Press, 1974), 295.

[130]Edmund J. Fortman, The Triune God, 28. See also George T. Montague, The Holy Spirit: Growth in a Biblical Tradition (New York, Paulist Press, 1976), 364-365; "In the process of using this term (paracletos)...John has etched more clearly the traits of distinct personality in the Holy Spirit." For William Hill, (Paracletos) implies a personal agency that is lacking in the neuter name Pneuma. The Three-Personed God, 300.

[131]John Webster, "The Identity of the Holy Spirit,", 4-7.

[132]Bernard J. Cooke, Beyond Trinity, The Aquinas Lecture, 1969 (Milwaukee, Marquette Univ. Press, 1969), 52. In contradistinction to Lampe and others Cooke says, "We must refuse to reduce this concrete understanding (the experience of the Spirit in the early church) to categorized concepts." Ibid., 53. In support of the above statement he concludes his discussion of the distinctiveness of the Triune persons by saying,

The defense of the Spirit as person is not an obscurantistic one. We will, in our fifth chapter on modern theological views on trinitarian person, test the proposals made by Heribert Mühlen and David Coffey on this score. Exegetes and theologians who support that view are well aware of the differences between the Person of the Son and the Spirit. The critiques of the Spirit as **vinculum** or as 'gift' or as the triune 'self-love', or even of Richard's condilectus or 'co-loved' are often based upon the assumption that 'person' is a univocal term in the Trinity and in humanity. Louis Bouyer refers to this quandary where he claims that:

> The Spirit does not appear simply as a perfect reciprocity in a community of love; it becomes apparent that this reciprocity implies a communication of the very community established by love....It is in this sense that the Spirit is love, which is not to say that the Father and the Son are not already love, nor that the Spirit is not also, like them and with them....But it is in the Spirit that the fullness of love shows itself to be the plenitude not only of a mutual love, but also of a shared openness of this reciprocity of love to yet another person.[133]

How the Spirit is person will remain a mystery to the human mind, yet that does not demand denial of the assertion. While being careful not to attribute cognitive or volitional categories as the sole factors in that ascription, and while maintaining a strong sense of the relationships which provide the outlines of a divine person with the Trinity, it may be that our inability to fit the Holy Spirit into our strictures of apprehension actually serves as a corrective rather than as a problem. As Geoffrey Wainwright notes, "The presence of a less-easy-to-personalize Holy Spirit in the Trinity may have saved trinitarianism from developing into tritheism."[134]

Kilian McDonnell, sensing the modern difficulties with pneumatology, feels that although the personhood of the Spirit is a thorny issue, anything less than a trinitarian

---

"We have employed the term "person" and must unavoidably do so, but hopefully we have indicated that this word should be used of Father, Son and Spirit with full awareness of the analogous nature of this predication, therefore with stress on the radical distinctiveness of "person," not just differentiating divine from human personhood, but distinguishing the reality of personhood as it applies to Father, Son and Spirit." Ibid.,58.

[133]Louis Bouyer, Cosmos, 184. He clarifies the difference we have stated above with regard to the analogical use of 'person' as he continues that:
"The concept of personality, far from raising questions regarding how it applies to God, applies only to him in its most rigorous sense. It applies to us only because we carry within ourselves, as conscious and spiritual beings, an analogical participation in the divine mystery. But like all analogies between the creator and his creature, this analogy cannot be a direct one. Man, the human individual is not properly speaking an image of the Trinity; rather, it is the relationships between men which makes humanity a natural image of the Trinity." Ibid., 185.

[134]Geoffrey Wainwright, Doxology (New York: Oxford Univ. Press, 1980), 103. Applied liturgically this also may be a reminder that the Church is to "keep open the possibility of recognizing that the divine Spirit may be present in worship on a plane wider than historic Christianity." Ibid., 106.

understanding of God, would cause irreparable damage to Christian theology as a whole. He argues for a markedly economic trinity with a strong pneumatology which is the "contact point of entry into history and the Church in one direction, and, in another, into the Christological and Trinitarian mysteries."[135]

Thus, to be faithful to the exegetical, experiential and conciliar affirmations of the Church is to acknowledge a qualified "personhood" to the Spirit, so that instead of a pneumatic Christology, or a modalistic Godhead, there is evident a co-inherent self-giving which bespeaks freedom and dependence understood mutually and generatively.[136]

IV. Conclusion

It has been necessary to explain the presuppositions upon which this dissertation is built in order that what follows will not be construed as "an acrobatic display of a priori concepts" any more aggrediously than those of which its critics are guilty.[137] In fact, the weight of evidence from a scriptural and consensual standpoint places the burden of proof on those who negate the position taken here. Despite the fact that detractors of the relational definition of 'person' continue to disparage its validity and worth it remains a relevant task given the fundamental questions which underlie modern culture. To understand and critique the modern notion of person in Trinity, a relational interpretation is one which first, takes into account the effects of an East-West ecclesiological separation, and which hears and responds to the Eastern Church's critiques and formulations; second, adheres to a realistic epistemology, attempting to balance the mystery of the Trinity with a proper view of analogies as revelatory of important aspects of a transcendent referent; and, last, finds its foundation as conceivable from Scripture, properly understood and in continuity with the finest in traditional hermeneutics.

Before carefully considering the actual history of the notion of person another pinion of a relational definition must be traced. We turn to the ontology which is generative of a relational notion of person in the following chapter.

---

[135] Kilian McDonnell, "A Trinitarian Theology of the Holy Spirit," Although he and and Catherine LaCugna "applaud the motive" of the thinkers who pondered the immanent Trinity, they join Rahner in the critique of the separation of economic and immanent trinities, by beckoning any ("in a far country") who might delve too deeply in the inaccessible. Though they "affirm the tremendous spiritual and intellectual prowess" of their theological forebears, they discourage anything which smacks of "scientific ontology," C.M. LaCugna and Kilian McDonnell, "Returning from a Far Country: Theses for a Contemporary Trinitarian Theology," Scottish Journal of Theology, 41 (1988):212-215.

[136] See Rowan William, "Trinity and Revelation," Modern Theology 2:3 (1986):197-212.

[137] Nicol Cross, "The Blessed Trinity," Hibbert Journal, 55 (1956/57):237

If whatever is spoken of God
is spoken according to substance
then that which is said,
"The Father and I are One,"
is said according to substance.

Augustine, De Trinitate 5. 3,4

Chapter Two

Substance and Person

The cruciality of this chapter rests upon the necessity of appraising the major points of maturation represented in the progressive concept of 'person' in the earliest period of Christian tradition. The intent here will be: 1) to highlight the pivotal figures and issues regarding 'person', both philosophical and theological, up to the third century and, 2) to reveal the primacy of a relational over a rational understanding of the doctrine of personhood in the early Church.

We will center on the Aristotelian notion of substance and its relationship to the Patristic elements in this discussion which culminated in Tertullian's usage of 'persona'. It may be that Tertullian was not as far from Aristotle as he imagined. From that basis it is possible to see the ideological connectedness between the West and the East as Tertullian's paradigm is in many respects paralled by the Cappadocian understanding of divine personhood.

I. The Bases of Christian Ontology

God is substance. That ontological statement, germinating in Platonic and Aristotelian constructs, has spawned a maze of torturous options still unresolved. In the West, we have tended to over-simplify the problem by either equating 'ousia' with abstract, static denotations, or with a general appellation, such as 'stuff'. Whatever the case, divine nature, or substance, carries the notion of immutability, admitting no distinction or plurality which dilutes, if not abrogates, the essential qualities of 'ousia'. This philosophical stance has done much to delimit theological constructs and has had deleterious effects on the modern usage of 'person' in a trinitarian context.

It was pointed out in the preceding chapter that one of the Eastern Church's most troubling theological irritations caused by Western theology stems from, what is deemed, a fundamental ontological flaw pertaining to issues like substance. Empirical proof of truncated and obscurantistic theological positions ought to serve as a warning for either

East or West of the danger of unilateral position-taking. However, from a consensual standpoint, even in an age of attempted ecumenicity, the divisions remain unmitigated, the questions unanswered. What is the nature of the God who reveals Himself in creation, covenant, Christ and Church? If we agree that static definitions of 'nature' have been superceded, to what do we attribute the move to more dynamic delineations?[1] In our continued quest for analogies which are necessary, though self-avowedly inadequate, to retain a full expression of Scriptural evidence and tradition's legacy while maintaining vitality in modern theology and spirituality, does there exist an ontological connection between that nature and the analogies? If so, to what extent, does an analogical use of person further inform a proper view of the Divine nature?

The fundamental concern here is the definition of an ontology which either negates or produces the context for the analogical comprehension of a relational God who exists in three Persons. Though there are many who would tentatively assent to relational classifications, generally applied, in this inquiry, ours is to reconsider the cogency of person as an inexorable, maybe (at present) irreplaceable, component in that relationality. It is agreed that the "what" of God's essence is not exhaustible within the confines of the human 'intellectus'. However, based on the revelatory nature of the God of Israel, this accord does not disallow an investigation into the possibilty of an "altruistic" character within that nature.[2]

Rather than focusing exclusively on the 'opera ad extra', the controlling principle used in this argument is decidedly retrospective. The method employed here originates in revealed categories, takes direction from consensual and canonical standards, includes the importance of shared experience, and draws from the implications elicited by all of the above. It is insufficient, even where a semblance of the notion of person is allowed as a possible interpretation of biblical statements interpreted trinitologically, to then prevaricate on the issues regarding in what way or how that God is three persons. It is my

---

[1] Thorleif Boman's argument in Hebrew Thought Compared with Greek trans. Jules L. Moreau (Philadelphia: Westminster Press, 1960), is more irenic than ours. In his distinction between Hebraic dynamism and the more static Greek concepts, he redefines static notions by the terms "harmonic" or "resting." Though he mentions the energeia akinasias of Aristotle (Metaphysics 11.7, 1072a,) as an indicator of dynamism in the Greek concept of God, it still remains to be seen that the inheritance of unitarian/psychical categories predominant in Western theology has not been exacerbated by the original conception of being which originated in Plato and Aristotle. See Boman, 27, 189, 204. I agree that the original intent of the Greeks has been misinterpreted, to an extent, but also latent within it is a questionable ontology, of which the Hebraic mind was free.

[2] Jean Galot, The Person of Christ, 35, 65, passim. The distinction between the "that" and the "what" of the divine essence is discussed with solid Cappadocian support in Thomas Leo Anastos' "Essence, Energies, and Hypostasis: An Epistemological Analysis of the Eastern Orthodox Model of God," dissertation, Yale Univ., 1986, 50, n.1. This is to be discussed extensively in the following chapter.

presupposition that investigation of divine ontology is not only proper but crucial as one of several possible responses to revealed truth. Well aware of the accusations of "audacity," "speculation," even "idolatry," my thesis follows the general trend of theology, particularly in the East, up until the modern period, in methodology if not in ontology.

In a certain sense, ontology is the hidden factor which informs Christian life in worship and service, with the distinct possibility of illuminating 'leiturgia' and 'diakonia' while consistently reminding the philosophical theologian of the inherent fallacy of isolating ontology from them. "Fides quaerens intellectum," the basis for most sectors of Christian philosophizing and theologizing, by implication allows a humble approach to the borderlands of the "mysteries" of the Godhead.

The Incarnation, was for the early Church the "mid-point," the fulfillment of the divine intentions humanward, first revealed at Creation, and it has served over the century as the basis of Christian ontology.[3] The forays into this uncharted territory have been a consistent effort of the Church to know, primarily and as fully as possible, the person of Christ. In that endeavor the personhood of both the Father and the Spirit and the interrelationship between them also became the arena of ontological inquiry. Our postulate is seen as one facet of that holy labor, with full recognition of the state of the mirror (I Cor 13:12) into which we now peer.

To underscore the crucial place of historical realities in this work is to concomitantly acknowledge that the redemptive acts of God do reveal something of his nature. As Bernard Cooke has stated, "It is well-nigh impossible to read the N(ew)T(estament) and come away with the view of a God who in his creative work "ad extra" reveals nothing of his own immanent life. This seems to negate the very notion of a God who reveals himself in his salvific deeds."[4] Ontological assessments of some sort are what made possible the church's "universal apperception" of the Trinity.[5] The self-revelation of God at the Incarnation and at Pentecost was the foundation of the endeavor to understand the essentially relational nature of the Discloser. In Christ, the inner differentiations of the Godhead were revealed, and it was there that the wellsprings of Trinitarian personhood began to flow forth.

---

[3]Oscar Cullmann brought this term into vogue as he discerned the early Christian worldview in Christ and Time, trans. Floyd Filson (Philadelphia: Westminster Press, 1950), passim.

[4]Bernard J. Cooke, Beyond Trinity, The Aquinas Lecture, 1969 (Milwaukee: Marquette Univ. Press, 1969), 24-25, abbreviations and emphases are Cooke's.

[5]See chap. One, 40, n.87. Cf. Robert Grant, The Early Christian Doctrine of God (Charlottesville: University Press of Virginia, 1966), 97, "There are crucial religious realities, expressed not only in words but in events and in symbolic re-enactments of events, which lie behind the trinitarian terminology."

To speak of the 'differentiation' or 'equality' of the Son with the Father was to raise ontological questions which would challenge the highest conceptions of being. From a philosophical standpoint, to speak of the Son's individuality yet, at the same time to confess that He was of 'the same substance' with the Father, meant that new constructs had to be proffered for logical clarity. Of course, where Aristotle would reflect on a substance-accidents relationship in category distinctions, the Church had to stake out its claims and disavowals with regard to the that predominant structure. In the tenuous effort to reshape the philosophic tradition while maintaining intellectual respectability, Christian theologians refused to accept the concept of unity, divine or otherwise, in definitions that presented a bare reductionistic unit that demanded purely static, immutable connotations. It was in the Church's reflection on the Scriptural testimony of Christ, that the One and the many found their fundamental identification in a relatedness which transcended multiplicity while not altering its reality.[6]

This attempt to explore the divine nature was first brought into light in direct connection with the Greek philosophical discussion of 'ousia'. The difficulties arose when the fundamentally personal categories of Judeo-Christian religion began to use terms which originally reflected impersonal being. As stated in the first chapter, the earliest Christians discovered more than merely the functional interpretations of christology or pneumatology. C.F.D. Moule disagrees: he discerns that the first believing generations:

> Found themselves driven to say things of him which imply an estimate not only of his function but of his being; that is, an ontological estimate of the 'person' of Christ, not only a functional estimate of his 'work'.... The religious experiences reflected in the New Testament are not adequately described in terms simply of the noble example or lasting influence of a great, human leader. If and when it comes to attempting some definition of their implications, it is necessary to speak of Jesus as himself divinely creative, and to put him 'on the side of the Creator'; and that means indeed reaching the borderlands of ontology.[7]

---

[6]When D. M. Mackinnon discusses this issue he ends by claiming that the Trinity is the only place where the One and the many dilemma is ameliorated. The modern ontological speculation is, in his estimation, futile. The talk of pre-existent or quasi-substantival relatedness is meaningless. Only the Trinity offers a clue that is concretized because of the Incarnation. "Substance in Christology - A Cross-Bench View," in ed. S. W. Sykes and J. P. Clayton, Christ, Faith and History. Cambridge Studies in Christology (Cambridge: Cambridge Univ. Press, 1972), 288-289. Also R. M. Grant, Early Doctrine of God, 99.

[7]C.F.D. Moule, "The Borderlands of Ontology in the New Testament," in ed. Brian Hebblethwaite and Stewart Sutherland (Cambridge: Cambridge University Press, 1982), 9. He goes on to add, "However sparingly the New Testament borrows the language of that country beyond the frontier, students of the New Testament discover themselves to be in some sense its citizens. The New Testament is no island." Ibid., 10. Reginald Fuller's Foundation of New Testament Christology, 248, concludes with a recognition that an ontic christology pointed to the need for onto-logical formulations that were intelligible to the world. Thus, there is a continual need for NT scholars to defer to systematicians at this point.

The era following the formulation of the New Testament texts found it necessary to answer questions both from within and without the community of faith regarding the divinity of Christ. The language used was that which crossed a variety of frontiers. Christian thinkers were not intimidated by rigorous philosophical scrutiny. In fact, they saw ways in which those languages could be garnered as heuristic analogies for the revelation they had received. They had their own answer for the content of absolute reality, but in an effort to express and explain that reality they too used the categories bequeathed by the Greek philosophers. The notion of being was "dehellenized" in the sense that an immutable essence was redefined in relational terms. Both christological and trinitarian formulations took on a "covenantal" model with respect to the divine nature.[8] Divinity was seen as substance, but the 'ousia' of the Greeks was transformed from impersonal nature to personal reality. What is intriguing is that later interpreters of the Aristotelian conception of being may have been more at ease with absolutistic definitions than the originators of that philosophical distinction.

A. The Substance of the Divine Nature

Although a full investigation of 'substance' is out of the question given the parameters of this endeavor, a cursory introduction is required to lay the basis for the remaining postulations.[9] Even for the honest sceptic it will be acknowledged that the ontological issues evident here carry profound weight in any discussion of the basic nature of the Christian God. Similar to the absence of a rigorous articulation of a trinitarian doctrine, formulation of the idea of substance developed out of an understanding, informed by contemporary philosophical insight, of the original affirmations of the New Testament.[10]

---

[8]William Thompson, The Jesus Debate: A Survey and Synthesis (Mahwah, NJ: Paulist Press, 1985), 324-333. The Catholic Theological Society's 1988 Seminar on Christology reveals a warmer approach to the Chalcedonian view of Christological ontology than has been apparent in contemporary theology. A relational model "struggling through to expression," (Ibid., 329) such as that suggested co-constitution, personalistic and interrelationality, may not be completely orthodox in the way that Pannenberg, Bouyer and Rahner use it but the tendency to see divine substance in less than absolutistic terms is encouraging. Catholic Theological Society of America Proceedings vol. 43 (Washington: Catholic Theological Society, 1988), 134-137.

[9]For the interested reader it is readily apparent that there have been scholarly debates on these issues before and that the following can only take the form of summary. Though space will not allow a treatise on each, the concepts of substance, or nature, must be referred to in order to provide an horizon for the study of person in Trinity. The crucial notion of relations will be approached in chapter three.

[10]'Hypostasis', one of the misunderstood words of the Greek East, probably due to Augustine's uneasiness with it (cf. De Trinitate 5, 10), was used in the NT period to communicate that which 'stood under', or supported (from hupistemi). Used in Heb. 1:3, 3:14, 11:1, (in 2 Cor. 9:4, 11:17 as "confidence") it has been argued as carrying a notion of fundamental reality, in a dualism with the material world. Thus, the Son can be spoken of

This consensus formed along the lines of the tentative alliance of Scripture and Greek philosophy. Recent aspersions, originating in Europe, cast against that alignment have produced a healthy wariness against over-assimilation but have not undercut the advances brought about by the Church's "plundering of the Egyptians."[11] Harnack's, and then Dewart's cry to "de-hellenize" Christian theology did not enjoy unanimous support as Patristic scholars took a fresh look at the early Christians' use of pagan categories. Their research did not confirm the destructive philosophical usurpation of theology that had been so vigorously denounced.[12] It may be, that we have not credited our forebears with the subtlety for which they ought to be applauded. Rather than being unwittingly assimilated by the surrounding philosophical culture they may have quite astutely appropriated and converted the most profound categories of classical thought, thereby radically altering all

---

as the express image of that transcendent reality in Heb. 3:1. James W. Thompson, The Beginnings of Christian Philosophy: The Epistle to the Hebrews, Catholic Biblical Quarterly Monograph Series, vol.13 (Washington: Catholic Biblical Assoc. of America, 1982), 71-73, 94. Other terms which took on more philosophical connotations were 'ousia,' used in Lk 15:12,13 only meaning physical goods, and 'huparxis,' Acts 2:45 of goods, and in Heb. 10:34, of an enduring 'substance' or reality or existent, paralleling 'hypostasis'. This is confirmed by H. Köster where he states that there is "No straight line from this early Christian use of the employment of the term in the Christian doctrine of the Trinity. One has rather to consider at every step the corresponding philosophical usage in the period concerned," TDNT vol.8, 589.

[11]In fact there are those who see the union as a positive step in Christian self-understanding and articulation. Speaking of the Nicene formulations, John Courtney Murray, The Problem of God: Yesterday and Today (New Haven: Yale Univ. Press, 1964), 46, notes regarding the use of "homoousion" in the Church:
"the transition is from a mode of understanding that is descriptive, relational, interpersonal, historical-existential, to a mode of understanding that is definitive, explanatory, absolute, onto-logical. The alteration in the mode of understanding does not change the sense of the affirmation, but it does make the Nicene affirmation new in its form."
Murray's thesis finds resonance in the philosophical analysis of Nicea by B. Lonergan, The Way to Nicea, 14, 136.

[12]The reasoning of the "dehellenizers" may have been faulty but the effects of their charges are still being felt. This is not to say that their misplaced critiques do not carry import when seen in specific areas of use, as we shall see in Augustine's heavily neoplatonic view of divine substance. Yet, as in nearly every theological fray a middle ground might be the best solution. The emphasis on historical and phenomenological experience must be balanced, it seems to me, by the philosophical structuring of those experiences against the backdrop of consensual agreement, otherwise there is nothing to curtail myriad subjective interpretations. See Leslie Dewart, The Future of Belief: Theism in a World Come of Age (New York: Herder and Herder, 1966), 131-148. A collection of critiques, which also acknowledges the impact of his analysis by the caliber of respondents, is found in The Future of Belief Debate, ed. Gregory Baum (New York: Herder and Herder, 1967). While Harnack saw the influence of philosophy as corrupting, Dewart saw it as no longer applicable nor helpful. Cf. Jaroslav Pelikan, in the same work, "The Past of Belief," 29-30; and B. Lonergan's "The Dehellenization of Dogma," Ibid., 69-91.

subsequent ontology.[13]

B. Substance in Pre-personal Philosophy

Plato's and Aristotle's concept of the nature of being never dealt with personal being adequately, although it was they who first "sought to trace the veins and sinews" of that convoluted issue.[14] One of the reasons that substantiates this critique is, as we have said, that the early Greeks did not hold a perception of the person in any holistic sense.[15] The dualism, which freighted exclusive importance towards those objective, eternal and impersonal values, pervaded their world-views and thereby eclipsed the uniqueness of the particular and the individual.[16] It would be myopic not to see that the Greek philosophers

---

[13]Christian philosophy and theology were related to their milieu in a variety of ways. First, the Evangelistic mission of the Church revealed itself in the use of pagan categories in order to maintain connections. The Areopagus model (Acts 17:28) was followed quite naturally. Second, the Accomodative (or adaptive) approach in which truth, or the witness to truth, was recognized and employed without threat to the 'symbolon' of early Christianity. All truth was viewed as God's truth and could be used accordingly. Although, there was in this interaction a defensive stance contra over-assimilation which attempted to transcend by redefinition of secular insights with Christian content. Third, the Apologetic mode was definitely well-used. With strong aversion to rationalistic interpretations of reality, and consequent "heresies", the need arose for protective criteria. Vocabulary became very important in maintaining a unified front, and maintaining some form of harmony. Ironically, the terminology of the wider philosphico-religious environment became the language of interpretive theology. See Robert M. Grant, Early Christian Doctrine of God (Charlottesville: Univ. Press of Virginia, 1966), 2, 5, 96-97; same author, Gods and the One God, Library of Early Christianity, ed. Wayne Meeks (Philadelphia: Westminster Press, 1986), 150-175; Gerald Bray, "The Patristic Dogma," in Toon's One God in Trinity, 42-61, esp. 48-50, makes a helpful distinction between epistemology and historicity as the place of ultimate discernment about the veracity of trinitarian thought; Murray, Problem of God, 51-65; George Lindbeck, The Nature of Doctrine, 92-96, 104-108, offers a critique of the above categories focusing heavily on cultural /linguistic background.

[14]D.M. MacKinnon, "Aristotle's Concept of Substance," in Renford Bambrough, ed. New Essays on Plato and Aristotle (London: Routledge and Kegan Paul, 1967), 97-119. Cf. Sabbas Kilian, "The Holy Spirit in Christ and in Christians," American Benedictine Review 20 (1969):113.

[15]Allan Wolter, Life in God's Love (Chicago: Franciscan Herald Press, 1958), 12-14, begins by critiquing the Greek philosophers as singularly egoistic. Love was equated with perfection of purpose. In essence, it is the activity of preserving elements requisite to perfection and striving to gain those that are absent. Altruistic love was then a non-category, perfection is rational perfection as seen in Metaphysics Bk. 12.9,33-34, "Therefore it must be of itself that the divine thought thinks (since it is the most excellent of things), and its thinking is a thinking on thinking."

[16]The difference Christian philosophy brought to the discussion of the individual emerged out of incarnational discussions (cf. chap. One). The telic orientation of the person of Christ, desiring mutual response from humans established a personal value requiring personal development and self-understanding. Sears, "Spirit: Divine and Human," 10-11. See Sterling M. McMurrin, "Is God a Person?" in Great Issues Concerning Theism ed. Charles H. Monson, Jr. (Salt Lake City: University of Utah Press, 1965), 98, 105 where he argues that the tendency toward a metaphysics including a powerful monistic persuasion,

recognized that persons were social beings, though in actuality that meant only that they were attributes of the 'polis'.[17] Interiority was a category until the later Hellenistic philosphers acknowledged logical distinctions between the elite individual and the social ideal.[18] It may be best then to refer to this era of thought as "pre-personal" at least in the sense that the 'essence' of individuality was of far greater importance than the individual per se.[19]

Of the major Aristotelian inheritances of the Church, the distinctive forms of causality were not in themselves exhaustive enough to explain the dimensions of grace. A self-giving God was not even a remote possibility for Aristotle.[20] Upon closer examination it may be that in his disagreement with his mentor's dualism, Aristotle's 'realism' formed some categories which, rather than detracting from the possibility of three Persons in Trinity, actually made it a logical option for those who were to draw from his epistemological well.

Christopher Stead has produced a number of additions, some more helpful than others, to the discussion of the original Christian use of 'substance' as a theological category.[21] He recognizes that it is a concept removed from existential reality and therefore, normally, of little interest. One reason for this might be that the term 'ousia' is fundamentally a philosophical term while other terms such as 'hypostasis' come from

---

obliterated personal gods or creatures.

[17]de Vogel, C. J. "The Concept of Personality in Greek and Christian Thought." Studies in Philosophy and the History of Philosophy 2 (1963):20-60.

[18]A. Momigliano's "Marcel Mauss and the quest for the person in Greek Biography and Autobiography," in ed. Michael Carrithers and Steve Collins, The Category of the Person (Cambridge: Cambridge Univ. Press, 1985), 89-92.

[19]Sears, "Spirit: Divine and Human," 275-276 shows Mühlen's assessment that this pre-personal stance is nothing other than a "metaphysics of subjectivity" which is still the predominant philosophical presupposition. Neither era has offered any consistent explanation for personhood or inter-personal relations based upon this type of metaphysic.

[20]We shall see Mühlen's category of 'causa moralis personalis' is in direct opposition to this ontology, where direct relationship is possible but does not necessitate absorption into the divine to be effected, S. Kilian, "Holy Spirit in Christ," 112.

[21]Christopher Stead, "The Concept of Divine Substance," Vigilae Christianae 29 (1975):1-14; also Divine Substance (Oxford: Clarendon Press, 1977), and "The Origins of the Doctrine of the Trinity," Theology 77 (1974):508-17, 582-588. See also for Platonists after Plato, A. H. Armstrong's The Cambridge History of Later Greek and Early Medieval Philosophy (Cambridge: Cambridge Univ., 1967), 53ff. Stead's fundamental thesis is that the usage of 'prote/deutera ousia' is normally far afield from Aristotle's original intention. Both his article and his book advocate that 'ousia' was rarely used in a precise manner, especially among the early Christian thinkers. Though not accepted by all, Stead's argument must be laid against some of the more simplistic answers given to the problem by Zizioulas, Being as Communion, 28-35.

realms outside of philosophy and are inherently more palpable when understood lexicographically. In other words, we are inclined to be drawn to the subjective categories rather than the objective.[22] More often than not, 'ousia' is interpreted as that which exists of itself or "a perfect being (which) must be an absolute undifferentiated unity".[23]

Against what he deems is a monolithic conventionalization of the idea of divine simplicity, Stead probes the point from a etymological/contextual stance due to Aristotle's own apparent confusion concerning the original meaning of the term in question.[24] Based on his interest to maintain a connection between the concrete and the abstract, Aristotle delineated the term 'ousia' in two ways. First, as a particular category, his primary substance admits the idea of individual entity either human or deity. He begins by pushing everything back to substance; he views it is as fundamental to the promulgation of self-existence, which is the highest example of substance. Various interpretations have seen tautological implications in the summarization of primary substance as, "that which exists of itself."[25] Latent here may be a critique of the 'relational being' in Platonic thought, where 'relational' pertains to the idea that everything in nature is an instance of what it is in itself and some indiscernible subject. Aristotle draws a distinction between 'ousia' and an independent 'hupokeimenon'.

> Substance, (ousia) in the truest and primary and most definite sense of the word, is that which is neither predicable of a subject (hupokeimenon) nor present in a subject (hupokeimenon); for instance, the individual man or horse. But in a secondary sense those are called substances within which, as species, the primary substances are included; also those which, as genera, include the species.[26]

The Metaphysics extracts and expounds upon the implications of his Categories. Matter

---

[22]Stead, "The Concept of Divine Substance," 2.

[23]Stead, "The Concept of Divine Substance," 7. See Divine Substance, 57 for the quote from Aristotle's Categories 5, which reveals his basic paradigm.

[24]Stead, Divine Substance, 93.

[25]Aristotle, Metaphysics Bk. xii, 1069a, line 17-1071b, line 23. All reference to Metaphysics are from The Student's Oxford Aristotle, ed. W.D. Ross, vol.4 (Oxford: Oxford Univ. Press, 1942), unless otherwise indicated. The best comparison with the Greek is found in W. Jaeger, Aristotelis: Metaphysica (Oxford: Clarendon Press, 1957), whose numbers coincide with above. See Mackinnon, "Aristotle's Concept," 108.

[26]Categories 5. 2a11-16. What is not always clear here is what hupokeimenon represents. Its philosophical application in early Church theology was tainted by this lack of clarity. Apparently in his discussion on unity, Metaphysics 5.5-6 1015b-1016a, this distinction carries the notion of substratum and thus can be seen as a formal, and thus really undiscernable element in substance. It is both positive and negative in that it allows a numerical unity which in not necessarily monadic but on the other hand it implies a substratum that is, in effect, unknowable. When later thinkers applied this distinction to the Trinity it was not always clear what they intended by its usage either.

and form may be distinguishable in certain kinds of substances (i.e., works of art or craftsmanship), but there are other substances which do not allow the dichotomy. Being is primary, but not in Platonic form; rather a new form of relation is posited between the "this" and the "what." A mutual dependence, a union, between potentiality and actuality, defines the parameters of 'ousia'.[27]

This dynamic Being-Substance offers new vistas of possible meaning. Thus, Stead tenders that for Aristotle, despite latter attempts to simplify and calcify Aristotelian categories, the concept of substance does not always mean a particular object necessarily.[28] At other points substance was described as the genus of things that are, a mere subject or the counterpart to predicates.[29] It was, for him, capable of being in a class, accordingly, God could be seen as an individual in a class. He even went so far as to state that it admits of contrary determination, yet it can remain what it is.[30]

---

[27]L.A. Kosman, "Substance, Being and Energeia,' in Oxford Studies in Ancient Philosophy vol. 2 ed. Julia Annas (Oxford: Clarendon Press, 1984), 137-147. See also Leonard Eslick, "The Material Substrate in Plato," 39-54 and Ernan McMullin, "Four Senses of Potency," 290-319 in The Concept of Matter in Greek and Medieval Philosophy (Notre Dame: Univ. of Notre Dame Press, 1965). With a different perspective, from a more "relational" view of being as "what" and "that" in Plato, see Ivor Leclerc, "God and the Issue of Being," Religious Studies 20:1 (1978):70-71. He acknowledges the differences though and says, "It constituted a most significant break with the Parmenidean conception of 'being' as immutable."

[28]His Metaphysics esoterizes the delineations of the Categories. By a process of elimination Aristotle strives to clarify the meaning of substance. His is an overt attempt to re-evaluate the Platonic dichotomy of Forms and particulars. Although not consistent in his critique he does separate himself from the notion of a 'this' (eidos) which is the transcendent model of a resemblance or a likeness. This latter category is the place of the particulars in Plato's paradigm, a 'such' which corresponds to a 'this'. In Metaphysics 7, he rejects the notion of 'substantia' as: 1)Substrate (hupokeimenon) which was identified with matter (ule) [Note here the implicit disavowal of the caricature which Locke bestowed upon modernity equating substance with substratum, in Essay on Human Understanding ed. Peter Nidditch (Oxford: Clarendon Press, 1975), Bk. 2 ch. 13, par. 18-19, 175; Bk. 2 ch. 23, par. 1-4, 295-296.], or with shape (morphe) or a combination of the two (sunolon); 2)Genus,(genos); 3)Universal (katholou) and then deals with its definition as essence in a rather unique way. Stead, Divine Substance, 67-88.

[29]Stead, "The Concept of Divine Substance," 9. Stead lists no less than seven basic notions behind 'ousia' in his perusal of early thinkers; 1)mere existence, 2)kind or category, 3)substance, (vintage Aristotelianism), 4)stuff or matter, 5)form or species, 6)a thing defined, and 7)truth, Ibid., 11-12.

[30]Categories Ch. 5, or 4a line 11 in The Basic Works of Aristotle ed. Richard McKeon (New York: Random House, 1941), 13. Already the confusion dissuades further discussion, and Stead mentions that Aristotle himself was confused. In essence, he asked the wrong question: "What is ousia?" ought to have been "What is the ousia of 'X'?" If 'X' were specific forms that would have necessitated a species, and accordingly the answer could vary due to the nature of 'X'. Stead, Divine Substance, 97,103. Due to the pervasive influence of Aristotle, it becomes immediately apparent that to speak of the substance of God one must be a contextually aware of the usage intended by the specific author based

Stead argues that the Categories must have been written by an "'immature'" Aristotle. His Metaphysics shows more sophistication, amidst its profundities and its polemic against Platonism.[31] Despite the lack of a systematic statement within the Aristotelian corpus there is considerable agreement that the noun 'ousia' is roughly equivalent to 'something that is' in an absolute sense. Stead alludes again to the confusion in interpreting Aristotle where he states that 'ousia' could also roughly mean 'what something is'.[32] However, it is this latter interpretation of primary substance which gave rise to Sabellianism, and other modalistic interpretations which posited that the only differentiation possible had to reside within finite receivers of divine manifestations. It was the Aristotelian view of God as 'genikotatos' or 'pure being' with its counterpart the 'principle of individuation' residing within matter that fed the Scholastic distinctions, 'De Deo Uno' and 'De Deo Trino', which have since been vehemently denied.[33]

C. Uniqueness of the Divine Substance

In his discussion of substance, it is apparent that Aristotle acknowledged a distinction between divine substance and other substances. It is here that some new insights were interjected with regard to divine existence. Rather than being absolutely unknowable or unthinkable, for Aristotle the divine took on the essence of the truly individual, the concrete, the determinative, without necessitating imperfection within that nature.[34] This flies in the face of the tendency in much philosophical theology to exclusively posit an immaterial unity as a proper idea concerning God.[35]

Although Aristotle was unaware of the God of Israel, his insights can be seen as

---

on its 'fluidity' in early philosophical usage.

[31]Note especially here, Metaphysics, Bks. 7 and 8. Divine Substance, 63. L.A. Kosman, "Substance, Being and Energeia," 142.

[32]Divine Substance, 69. My emphasis. Mackinnon, commenting on Aristotle's rejection of Platonic dualism notes that his doctrine of categories leaves a tinge of remoteness in an otherwise realist context, "Aristotle's Concept," 110-111. The doctrine of substance then is a doctrine "of the relation of the self-existent to that which is existentially derivative," Ibid., 112.

[33]B. Lonergan is one who retains the distinction stating that its origin was misunderstood. See his De Deo Trino (Rome: Gregorianae, 1964); the English translation of the prolegomena of that work is found as The Way to Nicea.

[34]Metaphysics Bk. 11. 1071b-1072b. The concrete thing can be involved in change. Though the doctrine of Forms appeals to him, substantiality is still attributed to composites (with primacy over their parts acknowledged).

[35]Stead points to H.A. Wolfson's influential monograph The Philosophy of the Church Fathers. vol.1 (Cambridge, Mass.: Harvard Univ. Press, 1956), 308-309, 338. See Stead, Divine Substance, 97.

coinciding at interesting points with the Judeo-Christian claims regarding the being of God. Seen as neither dependent and utterly self-sufficient, God is not thus absolutely relegated to immutable Form. Instead, God is supremely free to determine the divine reality and that freedom allows the possibility of qualification. Apart from being a total abstraction, an inscrutable mystery there are, in Aristotle's mind, some apprehendable individuating characteristics within the nature of God. Existing as the highest in Being did not necessarily mean that God was equal to a 'universal'.[36] An immediate implication then follows that neither pantheistic or panentheistic attributions of being can be applied to God. The result of that notion, if conceded, is that God is free from human determinations of being. Aristotle challenges the descriptions of divinity as 'unqualified being' or 'immutable essence' bequeathed by the Platonic tradition, though he does so in a haphazard manner for there are places where he seems to vacillate.[37]

It may have been that Roman "realism" calcified the notion of 'substantia' which Aristotle had never meant to imply.[38] What the earliest Christian thinkers faced in building philosophically coherent theology may have included the difficulty in finding and using Greek categories which had not been tainted by numerical or material notions of substance.

D. The Possibility of Dynamism

What is fundamentally important for us at this point, in spite of the discussion of substance as it relates to material and sensible objects, is the 'dynamism' Aristotle infused into more static Platonic categories of matter. Forms, to use as a starting point for his discussion of his mentor's own language, were only such in that they bore a degree of actualization (entelecheia or energeia).[39] Being was not a concretized notion for Aristotle.

---

[36]Divine Substance, 88-104. In this chapter and the previous, Stead applies logic to critique Aristotle revealing a number of confusions. Instead of positing doubt, they, in fact, reveal that Aristotle was not as 'set in concrete' as he is often made out to be as our discussion of substance reveals. See also conclusion, Ibid., 273-274. Note here also that debate yet wages concerning the equation of the Good with God in either Plato or Aristotle. We use God here in the sense of a supreme being in the mind of the philosopher.

[37]Our assessment is only to show the change in thought which would allow further distinctions to be made about Divine Being, it is not to place a false construct over Aristotelian categories.

[38]It would be an interesting study to see how philosophers have repeatedly taken a material view for a concept originally intended to transcend 'materia'.

[39] Stead, Divine Substance, 75, 87. Aristotle came to the place of identifying the substance of a thing with its realization or actuality. Ibid.,88. Stead goes on to honestly admit that even these summations of Aristotle's thought are tentative based on the philosopher's own confused use of certain analogies (Ibid., 72, 86-87) or residual Platonic confusion (Ibid., 77) and even fallacious argument based on compound expressions (Ibid., 83 f.n.41). See also L.A. Kosman, "Substance, Being and Energeia," 145-149; D.M.

"The one and the simple are not the same; for 'one' means a measure, but 'simple' means that the thing itself has a certain nature."[40] For him, substance could carry a telic orientation that allowed growth and development without negating its essential characteristics. Oddly, this interpretation has not found its rightful place in the diachronic usage of the term. Though other differences between Aristotle and Plato are proposed there appears, all too often, a conflation of their ontologies, with consequential formalization of static models which have ubiquitously affected the modern view of God.[41]

Aristotle's second distinction 'secondary substance' admitted species, genera, and determination; the 'what' of a given entity, which distinguished it from the primary category. Problems arose in maintaining distinctions where Aristotle included various forms of 'accidentiae' within this category.[42] One of these, 'relation' or 'pros ti' was also pregnant with implications for the philosophical undergirding of trinitarian distinctions.[43] By nature every relative term implies a correlative, i.e. superior - inferior, knowledge - what is known, master - slave, double - half. Thus relationality cannot be predicated of a simple, individual essence.[44] Christian thought of a personal God took this logical analysis into account in its deliberations on the triune relations. Though still mysterious, one can see the implications in allowing distinction without division within the one God. It is important to note in light of this distinction that 'secondary substance', 'deutera ousia' was

---

Mackinnon, "Substance in Christology-A Cross-Bench View." in ed. S.W. Sykes and J.P. Clayton, Christ, Faith, and History, Cambridge Studies in Christology (Cambridge: Cambridge Univ. Press, 1972), 279-300.

[40]Metaphysics Bk.12. 7, line 34-36.

[41]In "Being and One Theologian," Thomist 52:4 (Oct 1988):654-655, Philip Clayton proposes that it was Hegel's strong critique of static notions within Greek ontology which was based upon eternal essences and devoid of reference to the temporal, that marked the modern re-conceptualization of the nature of God. Though Hegel himself was guilty of a "spiritualization" of the substance resulting in little if any connection with the temporal, he was still effective in transmitting the idea of Being as self-related dividedness.

[42]Stead Divine Substance, 58. Aristotle was not consistent in classificatory distinctions often allowing various definitions to apply to different substances and species without clarification. G.E.L. Owen has said that Aristotle developed the notion of 'focal meaning' regarding substance, whereby some of the confusion is alleviated, Ibid., 67.

[43]This is a seminal contention in Irénéé Chevalier's S. Augustine et la pensée grecque: les relations trinitaires (Fribourg en Suisse: Librairie de l'université and St. Paul of Fribourg, 1940), i.e., 110, 167-173. However, Edmund Hill The Mystery of the Trinity (London: Geoffrey Chapman, 1985), 82 n.1 regards Chevalier's interpretation as suspect, especially in its Augustinian dependencies.

[44]Categories 6a36-8b24. Cf. C.M. LaCugna, "The Relational God: Aquinas and Beyond," Theological Studies: 46 (1985): 654.

not used by Aristotle outside of the <u>Categories</u>.[45] The upshot of this is that the exclusive application of 'individual' to the primary and 'species' for the secondary is highly questionable. A desire for security in categories has resulted in deficient metaphysics.

A distinction which more closely follows Aristotle's may be drawn between the metaphysical interpretation, (i.e., God as possessor of attributes, and the empirical concept, God as light or spirit) is helpful in an application of the two notions of substance.[46] Yet, if strictly adhered to, the recurring idea of undifferentiated unity is fundamentally irreconcilable with Trinitarian thought. As we have seen though, it is possible for the metaphysical category to provide a general framework for inner-trinitarian discussions.

It ought not be interpreted from the preceding discussion that Aristotle knew anything but an impersonal, impassible God. It was only one faltering step away from Plato to state that God was not merely an ideal but a real Being. What is crucial is the possibility of interpreting the Christian tradition's view of God in light of an honest approach to Aristotle without the overlay of succeedingly restrictive views of substance.[47] It is also clear that most classical definitions of person continued to draw the fundamental Aristotelian equation of rationality, self-consciousness and will with discussions of the divine.[48] Hopefully, further Aristotelian studies will reveal more of what he had in mind with this infrequently-used dichotomy. The greater battle will be to find theologians willing to relinquish calcified notions of divine being solidified by usage and time rather

---

[45]Stead, <u>Divine Substance</u>, 114-115. Based on its infrequent use prior to its assumption by the Eastern Church, one is hard put to find classical philosophic support for the categories upon which much of the distinctions within God found in the 'via negativa' are based.

[46]Stead, "The Concept of Divine Substance," 13-14, he sees the problem as one with Platonic disagreement: the first, rationalistic; the second, more Stoicizing.

[47]There are some refreshing notes here. John Macquarrie's description of Chalcedon, for instance, reveals an understanding of substance which is close to the one here. See "The Chalcedonian Definition," in <u>Foundation Documents of the Faith</u>, ed. Cyril Rodd (Edinburgh: T. & T. Clark, 1987), 28-29. But also note that with this estimation comes the typical statement that **prosopon**, "did not mean 'person' in the full modern sense." Ibid., 30. The question remains for those who advocate a relational view of divine Being, What exactly did the early Church mean by **prosopon**? It is intriguing how bent modern scholarship is to deny the subtleties that surround 'person' to the early thinkers. How can we be so sure about a dynamic substance and then retract that dynamism when it comes to the persons?

[48]Aristotle uses **prosopon** in the same basic ways we will outline. His usage indicates that prior to its application as "mask" it had to do with the "part that lies under the skull" for humans only. <u>History of Animals</u> Bk. 1.8, 491b, <u>Aristotle: Vol. II</u> in <u>Great Books of the Western World</u> vol.9 (Chicago, Univ. of Chicago Press, 1952),13. See footnote 81.

than actual reality.⁴⁹ Geach points to a more open approach where he lays the parameters that:

> A Christian cannot indeed follow Aristotle in holding that the number of everlastingly moved heavenly spheres manifests the number of everlasting Divine Beings; but he must hold Aristotle to have been right in not *a priori* excluding plurality from the Divine, and even right in holding that this plurality is somehow manifested in the world.⁵⁰

In sum, substance has been used both philosophically and theologically in various and often contradictory ways. Most generally, it is used to describe a thing in itself, unattached, or unaffected by another thing. As difficult as that may be to clearly conceive from a temporal standpoint, it has played a major role in theological definitions. Another way 'ousia' has been discussed is as a complex of those properties which are essential to a thing being a thing. Ancillary to that usage, and from a different tack, a third possibility is substance as that which admits of certain properties, or modes which make up its unique reality. In this regard it is impossible to speak of substance apart from inherent, inseparable components which coalesce to constitute that certain substance. Although we cannot say that Aristotelian ontology would assent to a trinitarian reality, this third option, a substance which admits constituents, or better, inseparably comprises in itself those elements, is a distinctly possible interpretation and one which overtly or covertly fed the strains of Christian thinkers whose trinitarian discussions we have found the most satisfying from a relational perspective.⁵¹ For them God is substance, but that divine nature is 'sui generis,' neither unstructured nor fully comparable to tangible comparisons. There was a way of relating Scriptural indications with the concept of a transcendent substance which bore dynamic, personal properties. It was the discussion of these constituent elements which ultimately divided the Church but gave Christianity a means of cogently conjoining its primary text and reality.

E. Legacy of Substance in the Christian Tradition

Undoubtedly the marks of Greek metaphysics were found deeply embedded in the architectonic structuring of early Christian theology. The absolutizing of God's nature and character bore, at times, a disquieting resemblance to the transcendent values of the Greeks. Even the attempts to ameliorate the dichotomy between ideal and actual, as in Plato's

---

⁴⁹For example, note the pains to which Ray Dunning must go in order to clarify what he means by a relational model of ontology, his stated systematic principle, because of the regnant predisposition toward only one definition of substance. Grace, Faith, and Holiness: A Wesleyan Systematic Theology (Kansas City: Beacon Hill Press, 1988), 14-17.

⁵⁰Geach, The Virtues, 79.

⁵¹See the discussion by Laurence Wood, Pentecostal Grace (Wilmore, KY: Francis Asbury Press, 1980): 160-168.

theory of participation in an ideal form, has been referred to by some as a "magnificent failure," though its suggestiveness is still applicable at some points. There is no escaping the profound influence which it played in the Christian minds affected by Plotinus, and the Neoplatonic tradition.[52]

While the notions of an ideal or of unity were helpful, such as in discussing how God is love or is one, they lacked precision.[53] The early Christian response was to agree in essence that God was indeed the source of ideas. It was the ensuing doctrine of plurality or division of function requiring subordinationistic interpretations, as implied with the Platonic Ideal and subsequent discussions of the emanating Logos, which brought orthodox reservation.[54] It followed that some questioned the implications of added lists of predicates, i.e., absolute, immutable. However, it would not be until Augustine's day that the absolutization of these attributes would be shown to not logically deny the existence of a personal, interactive God.

---

[52]Gerald Watson, "The Theology of Plato and Aristotle," Irish Theological Quarterly 37:1 (1970): 56-64. Watson agrees with our position. He proposes that Plato was the origin of "negative language about God," (64) and by that he means the elements of immutability and utter simplicity. The lack of a concept of personalness and the focus on principles alone has produced an impotence in the Christian theology which followed that lead. G. Quispel disagrees, taking C. de Vogel to task for denigrating the Platonist (specifically Proclus') concept of love. She says, as I would, it is vacuous; he says there has to be something to it. As noble as his effort is, there is never an answer as to the source of the ideal. Granted, the Greeks did experience love, one might even argue a selfless love for each other to some extent. The difficulty appears in his questionable use of Johannine material. Comparison all too easily bleeds over into identity here, and at root one must recognize that the love in John is based upon a much higher order of self-abnegation than the cosmogonic Eros Quispel sees it evidencing. "God is Eros," in Early Christian Literature and the Classical Intellectual Tradition: In Honorem Robert M. Grant, ed. William R. Schoedel and Robert L. Wilken (Paris: Éditions Beauchesne, 1979), 189-205.

[53]Stephen Gersh, Middle Platonism and Neoplatonism. Publications in Medieval Studies, ed. Ralph McInerny, vols.13:1,2 (Notre Dame: Univ. of Notre Dame Press, 1986). Gersh's principle is that the later Neoplatonists provided "progressive elaborations of Plato's own notions of spiritual and material and of transcendent, immanent and transcendent-immanent," 47. Whether that is the case or not, it remains that in all reality is ultimately equated with a Unity that is absolutely simple. This also can be seen in the approach taken by the Gnostics, even though there is more time taken in the make-up of Ogdoad and Pleroma and Achamoth, before it all, at least according to Tertullian, is the monadic 'Pro Arche,' the Complete, Perfect 'Aion,' before the beginning, in absolute solitude. Tertullian, "Against the Valentinians" ANF 3, 503-520, esp. c.27

[54]The debate concerning similarities between Platonic triads and Christian Trinity has waged incessantly. Though it is arguable that a theological Trinity did evolve in Plotinus and Numinius, the foundation of those triads remained true to the general theory of the 'first principle'. There seemed to be an effort to transpose that which was essentially impersonal into the realm of the personal and thus accessible. Even Plato allowed this with his ideal and phenomenal orders of reality (later he added 'receptacle'). Yet behind it all was the creative Demiurge to complete his triad of principles. It should be noted that his seven orders of deity also fit into this schema.

The 'via negativa' resident in pure Neoplatonism was fundamentally illogical, because there had to be some way of connecting all that was with that source, the immutable 'One', upon which all was dependent. Iamblichus and Damascius could never adequately explain why that Unity, if self-sufficient, should ever diffuse itself.[55] The absence of personal categories in the Greek notion of the divine, apart from the concept of a living, thinking being produced an immutability and an incomprehensibility which reacted violently when met with the Christian conception of reality.

The Stoics believed that God was perfectly one and simple, yet could be given a number of distinct titles based on his different 'energies' directed toward the world. Though pre-Christian Stoicism would in turn be rejected by the Christian Church, the Eastern thinkers produced similar distinctions between essence and energies. The Aristotelian countermeasure to both the Platonists and the Stoics would be that God's substance is defined by his energy. Medieval theologians, for the most part, continued discussion in the Aristotelian line. Important to note for this thesis however is that the early Christian theologians never viewed 'energeia' as accidents. Whether they might be seen as eternal manifestations of God's power or as attributes, or 'opera ad extra' they remained essentially divine.

Substance remained fundamentally inaccessible.[56] Ironically though, it has never relinquished its centrality to trinitarian discussion. Without undue generalization, it may be said that this has been one of the major points of theological contention since the end of the New Testament period and the Apostolic Fathers. The attempts to relate prosopological exegesis and the phenomenology of the early Christian thinkers with the Greek concepts of nature often floundered due to the static notion of ultimate being inherent in the latter.[57] As the early preachers and writers of the Church continued to reflect upon the love of God

---

[55]Atherton, J. Patrick, "The Neoplatonic 'One' and the Trinitarian 'Arche'." in The Significance of Neoplatonism, ed. R. Baine Harris, 177-179. (Norfolk: International Society for Neoplatonic Studies, 1976).

[56]This indicates one of the strands of thought which has led to various levels of apophaticism in theology. The Orthodox position would find its roots here as we have intimated. The Middle Platonists (the author is well aware that Gersh has attempted to change the normal distinctions in his massive work) maintained the triadic distinction of Supreme Transcendent, immanent world soul, and assistant creators (cf. Plutarch, Albinius, Apuleius). See Stephen Gersh, Middle Platonism and Neoplatonism. Even the early interpreters were influenced here, Justin's First Apology relegates the Spirit to a fourth divine figure! Philo is discussion unto himself. He is obviously affected by the Greeks, without the tool of Hebrew, revealed triads. Cf. all of this with G.C. Stead's "The Origins of the Doctrine of the Trinity" Pt.2 in Theology 77 (1974):582-88.

[57]See above Slusser's insight, chap. One, 47-48.

expressed in Christ the notions of Fatherhood and Sonship were viewed relationally.[58] With the ensuing challenges due to theological attacks on the divinity of Christ (subordinationism) and the efficacy of a distinctly Triune God (modalism), theologians like Tertullian were forced to forage into new apologetic and explanatory fields of interpretation. The Arian controversy produced similar strides in the thought of Athanasius and in the East; Basil, Gregory of Nyssa and Gregory of Nazianzus produced their own unique defense which issued in new theological gains. Chalcedon summarized the best of orthodox thought on both person and substance. Yet throughout this doctrinal history the category of one single **absolutely immutable** divine nature prevailed. Not that this view of nature is illogical, but in order to meet the avalanche of philosophically-based attacks on orthodoxy a thorough investigation of the interrelationship between that divine nature and the three distinct persons was required by each theologian. More often than not the resulting formulations had been self-contradictory. It was to that task that the Cappadocians addressed themselves. But first we must lay the ground work for their revolutionary ontology.

II. The Concept of the Person

It will be apparent to the student of the history of theology that 'person' as we have come to know it, would not have occurred had it not been for the reification of a uniquely Christian concept of God. P. Henry has noted that even as late as Plotinus the Greeks had no word to express the self other than by pronoun even though there were long discussions of the 'psyche' and the 'nous'.[59]

There is little doubt that the term 'person' has remained as a Demosthenic pebble in the drive for lucid and relevant theological speech in modernity. Max Müller's epithet summarizes the response of anyone who ventures into this philological miasma, "Whoever

---

[58]Throughout this work, the Biblical terminology will be referred to with respect for the modern critique of patriarchal theology, but shall be maintained due to the historical nature of the investigation. It is also to be noted that these terms are not viewed in sexual or gender categories which may reflect in a finite way the transcendent quality of the divine inner-life but ought never to be equated with it.

[59]P. Henry, "Une comparaison chez Aristote, Alexandre, et Plotin," in Les Sources de Plotin, Entretiens vol.5 (Geneva: Fondation Hardt, 1960), 448. "Je vois dans le mot 'autós', employé par Plotin l'expression de la personne en grec. Le mot 'personne',...n'existe pas en grec et je crois que ce qui en approche le plus pour exprimer le 'moi', c'est le pronom autós tel qu'il est employé ici." Note also that Tertullian's treatise Adversus Praxean Liber was written in 213; Plotinus was eight at that time. G. Misch offers insight as to how the Greeks did view themselves, indicating that autobiography, in its rudimentary forms goes back to post-Homeric authors (700 BC and after), i.e; Hesiod, Heraclitus. He is clear though that the concept of individual was always seen in the relation bween the persons and the society of which they were a part. See A History of Autobiography in Antiquity, trans. E. W. Dickens, vol. 1 (London: Routledge and Kegan Paul, 1950), 67-95.

invented or started this word, whether a squinting actor or some maker of musical instruments at Rome, had certainly no idea of what would be the fate of it."[60] Terminological reservation, especially about non-biblical terms, like person, has long-standing status among theologians.[61] In the fourth century, Jerome, puzzled by the Greek equivalent for person, 'hypostases' in contradistinction from Arian perversions, recognized that, if not careful, such language could produce further difficulty since "poison is hidden within the honey."[62] Augustine's famous query in this regard is often cited out of context. In a section dealing with the inadequacy of all religious language not just the notion in question, and speaking about God relatively as opposed to attributing accidents to the divine nature, he wrote,

> Yet, when the question is asked, Three what? (quid tres) human language labors altogether under great poverty of speech. The answer, however is given, three "persons," not that it might be explained, but that it might not be left unspoken.[63]

Anselm, at the end of his Monologion and a discussion of the unity of divine essence, exclaims, "I do not know by virtue of what three (tres nescio quid) it is trine and a trinity....I cannot in a single word name that by virtue of which they are three."[64] And Calvin, at least according to Barth, castigates those who have the audacity to illustrate the Triune persons as "trois marmousets", like three grotesque ivory figurines on someone's mantle.[65] More recently, Heinrich Ott, who represents an increasing caste of metaphysical

---

[60]Biographies of Words and the Home of the Aryans (London: Longmans, Green and Co., 1888), 37. He refers here to the legend surrounding the actor with a facial defect, Roscius Gallus, who required a mask which would help him "sound through".

[61]I distinguish between non-biblical and un-biblical or anti-biblical. Orthodox systematization of Scriptural evidence has realized the tensions of importing "foreign" terminology but has chosen to do so for lucidity, comprehensiveness, and cultural accessibility.

[62]Aquinas, ST 1a, 29, art. 3, reply obj. 3. However, in Blackfriar's edition, 55, note d. Aquinas's use of Jerome and others is critiqued. Kasper, God of Jesus Christ, 286 referring to Jerome Epistle (Ad Damasum) 15,4. It needs to be remembered that Jerome's disposition upon writing this was of inquiry not didactic, to question his being forced at Antioch to profess belief in three hypostaseis. See text in Lettres, vol.1, ed. Jerome Labourt (Paris: Société d'Édition "Les Belles Lettres", 1949), 49. PL 22, 357.

[63]Augustine, De Trinitate 5, 9. De Trinitate: Libri XV, ed. M.J. Mountain. Corpus Christianorum, Series Latina, vol. 50 (Turnhout: Typographi Brepols Editores Pontificii, 1968), 217, (hereafter Corpus). PL 42, 918. NPNF1, vol. 3, 92. McKenna's trans., 187-188. This shall be further explored in chapter three.

[64]Anselm of Canterbury, Monologion 79, vol. 1 ed. and trans. Jasper Hopkins and Herbert Richardson (New York: Edwin Mellen Press, 1975), 84. PL 158:c.78(sic), 221C. Kasper, God of Jesus Christ, 286 translates the phrase "three something-or-others."

[65]Karl Barth, Church Dogmatics, (hereafter CD) Doctrine of the Word of God vol. I/1, 410.

sceptics, curtly consigns the metaphysical duo, person and substance, to the status of unintelligible albatrosses bequeathed to us and which need to be left behind.[66] Is there sufficient reason to keep such a term? What vested interest would the Church have over the centuries of disagreement of its usage? What did the idea mean for those who are a part of it?

A. History of Terms Related to Person

Philologists have assisted the theological enterprise concerning person. Yet, etymologically, the term in question has remained fascinatingly obscure.[67] Early in this century, archaeological investigation of Etruscan sepulchres resulted in the adscription 'phersu' beneath two figures bearing masks dating to the 6th century BC. The automatic response of scholars was to tie 'phersu' to the Latin "persona" but further investigation revealed that the Greek term for face, "prosopon", had antedated even **phersu**.[68] "Prosopon," it seems, had been taken over by the Etruscans and transformed into use for a masked man or mime who was present at funerals and games to display different roles. Only later, a derivative "phersuna" meaning "that which belongs to the mask" was brought

---

[66]God, (Edinburgh: St. Andrew Press, 1971), 60. Oddly, Ott argues for a personal God, seeing the radical worldview it connotes. He recognizes that the impersonal categories are just as replete with anthropomorphisms as their opposite. He advocates God as a Person, never as three persons, (Ibid., 60) but only in a transcendent sense, a "personal reality of a higher order." (Ibid., 57) My difficulty with Ott's approach is that he tries so hard not to advocate triune personhood that it almost seems that humans are more complete than his Transcendent. The reciprocity, the Buberian "between," (Ibid.,46-47) the responsibility, dignity, self-giving, capacity to say "Thou", (Ibid., 41-43, 60) are all predicated of human persons. One is to accept that these are present in the Divine Person but this begs the question, how can Ott know this? He ends his discussion of "personalistic thinking" of the social analogy (which he never names) by averring to the retrogression into child-like illusion which underlies that notion of divine personhood. Ibid., 64.

[67]G. W. Allport, claims that, "There is probably no single word of greater interest to philologists." Personality: A Psychological Interpretation (New York: Henry Holt and Co., 1937), 25. In English, I have found no other source with as helpful a skeletal outline of the options for the origin of "person" than Allport's though the subtleties of the issues are of necessity excluded in his focus which is the adjectival reality of person, or personality. His schema takes its root in the four-personae theory of Cicero that is based on the Stoic Panaetius's work. In the end he finds at least fifty definitions for "persona", under the categories: 1)Inner Nature - Theological, philosophical, ethical, 2)Outer Nature - Romantic, Juristic, Sociological, Bio-social, Ibid., 49. Of course for Allport, the psychological is the preeminent definition, but in quoting it there appears that absence of relationality which is the central theme in this work, "Personality is the dynamic organization within the individual of those psychophysical systems that determine his unique adjustments to his environment," Ibid., 48.

[68]For classic discussions of this perpective see Franz Altheim, "Persona," Archiv für Religionswissenschaft 27 (1929): 35-52, and F. Skutsch, "Persona," Archiv für lateinische Lexikographie 15 (1908) in Literaturbericht für das Jahr 1907: Italische Sprachen und lateinische Grammatik: Glotta 1 (1909):392-416.

to Rome and eventually found its way to the performance of Roman tragedies. If this is true, the conclusion is proposed that person is directly tied to the Greek word for face or mask and only tangentially related to the Etruscan phersu.[69]

- Prosopon and Persona

The elusive etymology of **prosopon** has, of course, been the source of different schools of interpretation, especially in its possible connection with the Latin **persona**.[70] The

---

[69]This etymological relationship and its attending problems have found international disagreement. A helpful introduction is found in O. Szemerényi, "The Origins of Roman Drama and Greek Tragedy," Hermes 103 (1975): 308-313. His is the minority stance but has some compelling evidence. From another viewpoint, see H.C. Dowdall, "The Word "Person"." The Church Quarterly Review 212 (July, 1928): 229-234. Maurice Nédoncelle, "Prosopon et persona dans l'antiquité classique: essai de bilan linguistic." Revue des Sciences Religeuses (Strassburg) 22 (1940), see 293 for summary. Suffice it to say that this is not a concluded study but it does question the derivation from "phersu" that has been uncritically accepted by many theologians, cf. H. urs von Balthasar, "On the Concept of Person," 20.

[70]Other etymological studies which reveal the gamut of opinions on origin are: Adolf Trendelenburg, "A Contribution to the History of the Word Person," Monist 20 (1910): 336-341; Rudolf Hirzel, Die Person: Begriff und Name derselben im Altertum. (rep. New York: Arno Press, 1976), 40-54; Hans Rheinfelder, Das Wort "Persona". in Beihefte zur Zeitschrift für Romanische Philologie. vol. 77 (Halle: H. Neimeyer, 1928); Siegmund Schlossmann, Persona und 'Prosopon': im Recht und im christlichen Dogma (Darmstadt: Wissenschaftliche Buchgesellschaft, 1968), 11-21. As indicated the options here are numerous. Mention of a few will reveal difficulties not soon to find amelioration:

I. Etruscan origin
1)Persu, Phersu, used at times where translation as "phersonian mask" formed the basis of the substantive, pers-una, pers-ona.
2)Phersu, (cf. to the changes in Phersepone, to Persipnei, or Proserpina) - all relating the mask motif to the religious dramas especially surrounding death rituals which pointed to the goddess. Skutsch's argument regarding the hardening of the first consonant as the word crossed over into Latin is challenged by many, (see Rheinfelder, "Das Wort "Persona," 23-25). Altheim recounts the arguments for the added "n" suffix, "Persona," 35-39.

II. Greek Origin
1)Prosopon - "face, mask" (Hirzel's main thrust, Die Person.) Of course the major critique of this is the radical change in the form of the words from Greek to Latin - persona.) See note 71 for more on this option as well as p. 88.
2)Peri Soma - "around the body" (or with zoma) around the waist, Scaliger's highly contested suggestion, came from the fact that he did not show how a name could derive from an attribute of, rather than the essential nature of, the mask itself.

III. Roman Origin
1)Personare - "to sound through", personando - "sounding through", a Roman-originated theory which has been long accepted. Aulus Gellius refers in his Noctes Atticae to Gabius Bassus' discussion of the source, "whence persona is derived, in books he has written on the origin of substances. For he conjectures this substantive to have been made from personando (sounding through).... Since, then, this mask (which he describes) makes the voice resound clearly, it is called persona for that reason, the letter o being lengthened on account of the form of the substantive," (quoted in Trendenlenburg, 339). Boethius accepts this etymological origin, Contra Eutychen, 3, in The Theological Tractates. trans. H.F.

major options oscillate between direct derivation from the Greek and a parallel development between the two. In the broad outline the classical Greek usage appears to be almost exclusively connected with facial connotations followed by its usage for theatrical masks.[71] As examples from the post-Classical era reveal, the anatomical service expanded into the idea or the role represented by the "mask" or the 'prosopeion'. From the Greek stage it was not long before diversification from "mask" was evidenced, in its use for both actor and the role played: as Nédoncelle puts it the mask became, "un second visage."[72]

In the Hellenistic period **prosopon** continued to express liquidity in usage and meaning. The move from the impersonal and the objective to that which pertains to expressive personality or level of subjectivity was made as the "rôle" metamorphosed into depictions not merely of characteristics of a certain player but the actual character of the

---

Stewart and E. K. Rand. Loeb Classical Library (Cambridge: Harvard Univ. Press, 1978), 87.

2)**Perzonare** - based on the Latinization of the Greek "zone" - "girdle" or "to gird or encircle." Bearing direct ties to actors known as **togatarii**, those who wore specific coverings to indicate characters as in the **togata** or national drama of the Romans.

3)**Personatus** - "clad in a mask", eventually leading to persona.

4)**Persam, Persas** - (This is Old Latin, and therefore also Etruscan probably) other words for "mask, head or face" which metonymously resulted in person.

5)**Per se una** - "self-containing" or "per se ona" taking "ona" as the Latin ending indicating fullness, thus "fullness in and of oneself", taken from Placidus' dictum, "persona eo quod per se una est." This served as a new derivation point separate from the others which are originally connected with the theater or sound. (Nédoncelle, "Prosopon et persona," 286).

6)**Persona** ("resounding instrument") Müller's idea, spawned from W. Corssen's projections based on the Sanskrit root "svan" to "son" in "per-son-u-s". There is not any real support, but Müller's critiques of the simpler ideas of others are strong.

7)**Per se sonat** - Papias in the 11th century wrote in a glossary, "persona dicitur quia per se sonat," but after discussing the connection of sound and sound making devices he states the evolution's end for most medieval thinkers, "Secundum vero substantiam persona est individua rei repraesentatio." (Rheinfelder, Das Wort "Persona", 21. We will take a closer look at Boethius' awareness of the Greek theater masks in chapter Three.

[71]Eduard Lohse, "Prosopon," TDNT, vol. 6 (Grand Rapids: Eerdmans, 1968): 768-770. A variety of options have been garnered from a plethora of classical sources on the original meanings. Apparently the first usage, or at least a concomitant to the theatrical definition of prosopon, was purely anatomical, referring to that area between top of head and neck, or as Nédoncelle surmises from Aristotle's usage, the face. "Prosopon et persona", 278. Other translations of Greek classical authors include; "The part below the skull," Aristotle Historia Animalium 1.8; "the part beside the eyes," or taking the prepositional thrust of "pros" it is rendered "over against the eyes,". Probably most intriguing for our discussion is the possible definition, "what is directed to the eyes (of another)," Lohse, "Prosopon", 768-769. We see here that Euripides did use prosopon in the sense of "personal presence" taking "face" and "figure" and deepening its literary usage, Ibid., 769.

[72]The delineations of Classical (inclusive of the Archaic and Homeric influence and 6th - 4th cent BC), and Post-Classical or for some Hellenistic are used guardedly here. They are not hard categories in any of the research I have explored. Nédoncelle, "Prosopon et Persona," 278-279. Polybius is a strong example of later Greek usage which reveals the shift from face, to rôle, to social personality, to that which approximates an individual. Schlossmann, Persona und Prosopon, 41-42.

individual. Perhaps the most radical shift was the replacement denotation of 'soma' or human body with the implementation of **prosopon** to denote externality or the figure of the individual person.[73]

However, in the Roman period the content of **prosopon** evolved into meaning either dramatic characterizations or that of one's bearing a particular character. The latter definition was the origin of Roman juridical constructs which, in turn, have often served since more uncritical works as the primary source for the understanding of person, apart from the context out of which it grew.[74] Notwithstanding the possible relationship between **prosopon** and persona, their meanings coincide as they pertained to histrionic figures and eventually to individual human beings.[75] Up to this point there appears to have been no philosophical content implied in either of the terms. Evidence indicates that especially in the midst of adjudication considerable importance was attached to the communal role played by a person. The slaves were considered persons but only in the most minimal sense, more a thing which belonged to an owner, because they did not possess a legal personality.[76] But the legal personality of the "personae" or free men was directly related to membership in the smallest social group, the family, at least in the community of a house.[77] Though there are glimmers of introspective analysis in the autobiographies of the

---

[73]Hirzel gives a graphic summary of this where he relates the speeches surrounding Plato's demise and notes that only one word appears in concurrence with soma and that was prosopon. Die Person, 40.

[74]It is also arguable that many of the classical scholars focus on the juridical as the main emphasis of Roman usage, i.e. Schlossman's, or von Carolsfeld's continual theme in Persona und 'Prosopon', but others, like Ivo Bruns have taken a different and corrective tack. See Bruns' Die Personlichkeit in der Geschictsschreibung der Alter, Reprint (n.p., 1896).

[75]Nédoncelle argues rather forcefully against the proposition that prosopon informed persona. Taking the route of the debated Etruscan connection in its phersu and a strong commitment to the cross-cultural impact of religious play, he sees the connection to Persephone as a more viable option. He does however confirm that the similarity of usage in the categories to which we have pointed is accurate. "Prosopon et Persona," 293-297.

[76]Gaius, Institutes II.15 indicates the tenuous position held by slaves in Rome. "Servus non habet personam." David Brown estimates that nearly 200,000, one-fifth of Rome were rendered without personal status of any kind by this dictum, from lecture given"Trinitarian Personhood and Individuality." Now published under same title in R. Feenstra and and C. Plantinga, eds. Trinity, Incarnation and Atonement: Philosophical and Theological Essays (Notre Dame: Univ. of Notre Dame Press, 1989), 48-78.

[77]Max Kaser, Roman Private Law, trans. Rolf Dannenberg (London: Butterworths, 1968), Pt.2, para. 13. I. 1, p.63-64, para 17. I, p.76-77. The eventual result that association could take on legal personality and thus, juristic personhood, was a result of nineteenth century legal distinctions and was not known in antiquity. This reflects one interpretation of the actual entity of the slave for Brown in "Trinitarian Personhood," quotes Gaius, Institutes, 2,15; "Servus non habet personam." based upon the inability of entering into

post-Homeric authors, for the most part, person remains defined in external, social contexts rather than in reflective consciousness or in ontological categories.[78]

Latin discussions of person continued to expand and deepen. Cicero took his pragmatically-inclined predecessor, Panaetius', approach to the individual but added to it, as Christopher Gill has shown, in his implications that to be a person meant more than Stoic utilitarianism insisted. Instructive here is the Ciceronian use of 'persona' in his discussion of the Stoic's 'prosopon'.[79] The paradigm is quintessentially Roman. Personae consist of four facets: the universal aspect of rational self-direction; the more particular category of decorum, or that character appropriate to harmonious existence; third, the circumstantial backdrop of social position which ought to finally result, fourth; in the persona making proper choices.[80] Panaetius altered the Stoic prosopa, which was for them merely a role played, in his distinct co-ordination of rational and social categories. However, Gill believes that de Officiis contains even a deeper element of moral commitment, one that outdistances the Panaetian baptism of Roman cultural mores as the highest an individual could reach. Beyond pre-determined roles, ingrained reiteration of social decorum and latent competitiveness, Cicero viewed the person as not only under the Stoic notion of social necessitas but inextricably and morally committed to his peers.[81]

---

social relationship constituent of being called a persona in Roman private law.

[78]"Roman thought, which is fundamentally organizational and social, concerns itself not with ontology, with the being of man, but with his relationship to others,...(thus, persona) does not have ontological content." Zizioulas, Being in Communion, 34.

[79]de Vogel, "Concept of Personality," 30-31. Here de Vogel argues that both the words and the concepts for 'person' and 'personality' are in usage as early as the second century BC. "Panaetius not only formally defined the concepts of person and personality; but by considering them under the aspect of the universal and particular *nature* of man, he also integrated them into a universal system of metaphysics." Ibid., 31. However, she pushes her argument back to Heraclitus or even to Pythagoras (sixth century BC). In the final analysis, there may be ruminations of self-reflection or even of metaphysics, but there is still nothing of the granduer given to individuality that the 'selem' of Genesis, or the 'eikon' of the New Testament indicated in terms of relationality and equality. Still less is said of the ontological basis for such self-reflection.

[80]Christopher Gill, "Personhood and Personality: The Four-personae Theory in Cicero, de Officiis I." in Oxford Studies in Ancient Philosophy. vol. 6, ed. Julia Annas, 169-199 (Oxford: Clarendon Press, 1988). In de Officiis 1.2 Cicero uses Cato to indicate the question by Epictetus which Panaetius answered. How is it that a person maintains his/her persona/prosopon? The answer came in the four personae theory, if a balance was found there then an individual was fully expressing humanness. Where Panaetius tended toward teleological constructs Gill discerns a "deontological" emphasis in Cicero, see Ibid., 187.

[81]Gill, "Personhood and Personality," 195-198. The author intimates some of the same interests of this work especially in his own use of sources. A. Macintyre's use of "character" and Rom Harré's psychological viewpoint on relationality are sources external but supportive to the theological task here, in much the same way they assist Gill.

Though unable to come to the same existential understanding of the Christian scriptures, nonetheless Cicero reveals at least the yearning for a logical personal connectedness beyond the ambit of the rational animal.[82]

There is then a tentative agreement that some relationality is present. According to Plato, Socrates is related to the state as a person. Aristotle can even discuss a person who is the subject of love, the concern for the well being of another. But Greek metaphysics could not develop the relational constitution of a person in an ontological sense. The difference which the Judeo-Christian heritage brought to the subject, Zizioulas concludes, was due to the difference in cosmology.[83] From a biblical perspective the person came to be seen as an entity that was not tied to the vicissitudes of 'fortuna' or of the secular order. The person as created was the recipient of a freedom to transcend deterministic social roles.[84] The reality which the 'mask' could only adumbrate, was found to have a perduring essential quality in each individual.

B. Person in the Biblical Tradition

Christian theology drew upon this multi-faceted semantic structuring and from Scriptural interpretation. In the early hermeneutical exercises of the Church the Old Testament use of "panim" or face was taken in the dynamic sense it was originally intended. Hebraic realism and vividness pertain in its derivation from "panah" which meant "to turn"; panim thus carried with it more than descriptive elements. Often it meant a countenance turned toward another, or of being face to face with one, even indicating at

---

[82]Aristotle's 'zoon logon ekhon'- humans as rational animals has been pervasively formative for definitions of person. Hannah Arendt articulates the later misuse of that Aristotle's 'zoon politikon' category, though even there his focus on the 'nous' or the 'logos' as central diminished a more complete understanding of personhood. The Human Condition (Garden City, N.Y.: Doubleday Anchor, 1959), 24-26. See Aristotle's Topics Bk. 5. ch. 3, 132a, 10-22, Nichomachean Ethics Bk. 1. ch. 7, 1098b, 5-10, On the Soul Bk. 3. ch. 3-8, 659c-664d. Charles Lefevre, "La personne comme être en relation chez Platon et Aristote," Mélanges de Science Réligieuse 30 (1973):161-183. He presents the opposite of de Vogel's perspective on the Greek philosophers. See Jean Galot, Who is Christ? (Chicago: Franciscan Herald Press, 1981), 288 n.11.

[83]Being as Communion, 33-35.

[84]The theme of Charles Norris Cochrane's Christianity and Christian Culture, Reprint (New York: Oxford, 1980) is similar to Zizioulas'. Tuke or fortuna permeated the Greek world as the expression of the fortuitousness of reality. Augustine's view, which he claimed as fundamentally Biblical, of the Logos and the Trinity met and countered that cosmology. The full integration of the person, in relation to reality, is made plausible by that radical shift. See, Ibid., 450-454, 482-486.

times the presence of a person.[85] Much like the Greek investigation of the psychology and individuality of the person, the Old Testament bears strong indications of the outlines of a progressive understanding of the person. 'Nephesh' carried the connotation of the whole self, a unity of flesh and spirit, even the actual life; 'lebab' denoted essential volitional characteristics.[86] Humans created in the image of God, were embodied spiritual beings responsible to the community and to God form the framework for the deepening conception of human and divine persons to come.[87] As representations of the Creator it is interesting to note the relationality inherent in each of the psychological categories. All of the human life was to represent dependence on another, whether God or human. Evil was the source of catastrophic alienation, from God, from fellow humanity and from the created order. If a Hebrew cannot be understood in isolation one might find basic assistance in defining the imago dei with ontological relatedness at its base.[88] I would argue that

---

[85]Francis Brown, S. R. Driver, Charles Briggs, A Hebrew and English Lexicon of the Old Testament (Oxford: Clarendon Press, 1976 (1907)): 815-817. Of interest here is the fact that prosopon is used over 850 times in the Septuagint, the majority of which translate panim. The latter occurs in root form 2,100 times in the OT. There is similar usage in Philo and Josephus and the Rabbinic Writings; intriguingly the Talmudic period saw some use of prosopon as a loan word. Lohse, TDNT, 774-775.

[86]Brown, Driver, and Briggs, Hebrew and English Lexicon, (nephesh): 659-661, (lebab):523-525, and in Deut 6:5 following the use of these, 'me'od'is used intriguingly which may also point to the will of an individual (me'od):547. A selected list of other terms which point to person include: the generic, 'adam', and other more specified gender specific, 'ish', 'anosh', 'ishah', 'neqevah'.

[87]'Ruach' and 'basar' are used as concomitant factors in the duality of nature represented in 'adam', which comprise an understanding of an inherent transcendence. That transcendence is only meaningful if the 'image' comprehends its origin. There is a radical dependence on God implied which surfaces in a study of any of these terms. Each individual bears moral responsibility for the use of that coincisive duality of spirit and flesh.

[88]Glenn E. Whitlock gives a summary form of the 'psychological' components of the 'imago dei' in "The Structure of Personality in Hebrew Psychology," Interpretation 14:1(1960):1-13. He refers, on p. 12, to G.E. Wright's conclusion regarding the covenantal basis of Israel's self-perception in his The Challenge of Israel's Faith, 75, that according to this understanding of imaging God, "the greatest curse which can befall a man is that he be alone." Of course, one immediately recognizes the influence in our century due to the Barthian emphasis on the 'imago' as relational in his CD 3:2, 203-324. Meredith Kline rejects that interpretation as a distortion of the text in, Images of the Spirit (Grand Rapids: Baker Book House, 1980) who emphasizes the functions of the image as primary and relation secondary. Ibid., 27,33-34. David T. Asselin emphasizes dominion as central to selem, "The Notion of Dominion in Gen. 1-3," Catholic Biblical Quarterly 51:3 (July 1954): 277-294. John Sawyer studies it in the context of Gen. 1-11 but circumvents relationality. See his "The Meaning of Beselem Ha'Elohim ('in the Image of God')in Gen. I-XI," Journal of Theological Studies n.s. 25 (1974):418-426. Closer to our interpretation is Frederich Horst, "Face to Face: The Biblical Doctrine of the Image of God," Interpretation 4:3 (July, 1950):259-270. A refreshing Afrikaaner voice on this can be found in Adrio König, Here Am I: A Believer's Reflection on God (London: Marshall, Morgan and Scott, 1982), 102-109.

relationship is at the root of the plethora of implications for the being created in the image of God. Without it, dominion or righteousness rendered anemic. It makes no sense to emphasize creation for the sake of ruling, working, or ethical choice-making if not humans were not primarily made for another, whether divine or human. If Israel had something unique to offer would it not be centered in a God who was neither polytheistic nor pantheistic, but one whose essential holiness precluded absolute or arbitrary determination?[89] The image of God finds heuristic definition and relevance in the progressive self-revelation of a God who is self-related.

The New Testament use of **prosopon** closely parallels the Hebrew **panim**. "Face," or "front side" are the most common meanings. There are also passages which denote a person's appearance or presence.[90] Again the indication is that, although not totally, a transition from objective to more subjective definitions is evidenced in the first century. 2 Co. 1:11 reveals that sort of linguisitic shift as does I Clement 1:1 where **prosopon** is used to refer to specific persons.[91] The face is what one looks at because it is the window of the personality, the indicator of the whole person (Col. 2:17, I Thess. 2:17.) Resident here, in germinal form, is one of the major differences between Christian anthropology and the ideologies in its milieu. The person, not only the community or the congregation, was of absolute importance.[92] And yet that importance was not conflated into rational or moral

---

[89]I have found no better assessment of the uniqueness of Israel's faith than Yehezkel Kaufmann's The Religion of Israel (New York: Schocken Books, 1972), 7-147.

[90]Of the 78 occurences of **prosopon** in the NT, 58 refer to "face" or "countenance" (both of God and human persons), seven specifically refer to a whole individual: Mt. 22:16, Mk. 12:14, Lk. 20:21, I Co. 1:11, 2:10, 2:6, Jude 16. Seven other references are indicative of the presence of an individual (equally of divine or human) or group. Six places it is used for other purposes, either temporally or prepositionally. The cognates **prosopoleteo**, **prosoleptes**, **prosolepsia** all refer to the idea of respect of or towards persons or carry the negative connotation of the LXX's **prosopon lambanein** to translate **nasa' panim**, "to lift up the face" and thus to show undue adulation of one and not of another. William F. Arndt and F. Wilbur Gingrich, A Greek-English Lexicon of the New Testament (Chicago: Univ. of Chicago Press, 1957): 728-729.

[91]J. B. Lightfoot, The Apostolic Fathers ed. J. R. Harmer (London: Macmillan and Co., 1907), 5. Arndt and Gingrich, 729a indicates the debate on this conclusion. See Lohse, "Prosopon," 774 for sources of usage in Josephus. His paragraph on Philo does not include much from De Vita Mosis where his use of **prosopon** may indicate the influence of Greek ideas. See the comment of J. J. Lynch, "Prosopon and the Dogma of the Trinity: A Study of the Background of Conciliar Use of the Word in the Writings of Cyril of Alexandria and Leontius of Byzantium," Ph. D. dissertation, Fordham Univ., 1974, 51.

[92]This results in one interesting use of **prosopon** which relates to the rejection of partiality between persons since all are equal. Based upon the OT warnings against such activity the NT reiterates the proscription with the use of **prosopon** in the same sense in which regard for the **panim** of another might be wrongly motivated (Dt. 16:19, cf. I Pet.1:17, James 2:9, Col 3:25, Acts 10:34. Note Rheinfelder's discussion, Das Wort 'Persona', 81-82.

categories alone. It was a nobility which found its roots in the possibility of being both the object and subject of self-giving love. To be a prosopon was to be of immeasurable value but that worth only found its fulfillment in disinterested other-orientation (I Jn. 4:7-12, Phil. 2:3-8,17,20,30, Mt. 5:48, Jn. 15:9-14). This view of persons was informed by the grandeur of the Incarnation, and its corollaries of 'ekklesia' which was the unified Body of Christ and the hope of a resurrection which superceded the immortality of the soul by involving the whole person in its scope.

The use of 'prosopon' or any other term indicating both human individuals and the divine Godhead did not enjoy immediate ecumenical agreement. The application of a histrionic, legal or social term in depicting the Triune mystery found much disagreement. It may be that one of the strengths of 'hypostasis' or 'prosopon' was their eclectic nature. They came to incorporate much more than their original meanings.

The early defenders of a triadic understanding of God came to scriptural interpretation with at least one consistent presupposition; the inexpressible nature of a transcendent God. Justin Martyr reveals something of the origin of the Christian apophatic tradition regarding the ineffable nature of God where he writes:

> For the ineffable (arrhetos) and Lord of all neither has come to any place, nor walks, nor sleeps, nor rises up, but remains in His own place,....and He is not moved (achoretos) or confined to a spot in the whole world, for He existed before the world was made.[93]

Yet this God was purported to have revealed Himself. The paradox was inescapable. The Unknowable had made Himself known and the only One who fully fit the description of God was second in relation to the first. The Uncircumscribable had chosen to delimit Himself in the revelation of a personal being which the Church recognized as the Messiah, Jesus Christ. The Logos of God was at once God and yet not identical with the Father.

Clement of Alexandria described this "individuality" of the Son with the term 'perigraphe'. Of course, he did not envision the identity of a distinct person; still the rational Logos was of one substance with God while exhibiting a differentiation from Him.[94] The divine self-limitation which made divine communication with creation possible indicated an important qualification in the study of God.

> The Logos became flesh, not only when He became man, but also when, in the beginning, the Word in identity, that is to say One with the Father, became the Son

---

[93]Justin, Dialogue with Trypho, 127 ANF vol.1, 263. We find already in Ignatius the use of 'silence' as a term equivalent to either the Father or the later 'ousia', which was quickly dropped from use because of the Gnostic re-application of it. See, Epistle to the Magnesians, 8 ANF vol.1, 62

[94]Robert P. Casey's The Excerpta Ex Theodoto of Clement of Alexandria, in Studies and Documents ed. by Kirsopp Lake and Silva Lake (London: Christophers, 1934), 30.

according to individuality (kata perigraphen) not according to essence.[95]
The upshot of this might seem to negate, at least superficially, the apophatic approach.
However, a continual element in the early centuries of hermeneutics stated that the
Unlimited could in no way be contained.[96]   As a result, it was in the distinction of the
Logos that the delimitation was found. The Father was seen not as a person, nor
circumscribed within Himself. The 'perigraphe' of the Son, was a distinction, of which the
Father was the source, and who was equal as the expression of the Unnameable. It would
not be until the fourth century that the concept of 'prosopa' as limitation would be
replaced. The Logos remained the full expression, the visage of the Father who revealed
himself. The element of distinctness came, not as result of Gnostic influence, rather it was
freedom from philosphical constructs which allowed equality in distinction.[97]

This is not to say that the determination of the divine persons was initiated in the
fourth century. Hippolytus and Tertullian are the first to specifically apply prosopon to
the persons of the Trinity, marking the beginning of a theological progression from
histrionic categories to interrelationship within the divine economy. The former speaks of
the Father and Son as persons and the latter all three.[98] The discussion in both of
'prosopa' and manifestations of the 'oikonomia' indicate the externality present in their
thinking without any of the subtle internal characteristics in later definitions of the Persons

---

[95]Clement of Alexandria, from the second-century Valentinian Gnostic fragments he
collected, referred to as Extracts of Theodotus, 19,1. Translated from "La notion de
personne chez les père grecs," in Problèmes de la Personne, ed. I. Meyerson (Paris: Mouton,
1973) 115-116. See the use of "circumscription" to translate 'kata perigraphen' in Robert P.
Casey's The Excerpta 55. Of course, there is disagreement here about who really authored
the passage. We would agree with Casey that it is Clementine. Cf. his desire for clear
distinction between 'pneuma' and 'psuche', The Excerpta, 17.3,4.

[96]Gregory of Nazianzus, Oration 28. 7, NPNF2 7, 291; PG 36: 33C.

[97]See for example Basil, Letter 262.2, NPNF2, vol.8, 301. John of Damascus,
Exposition of the Orthodox Faith 4.1, NPNF2, vol.9, 74.

[98]Hippolytus, Against the Heresy of One Noetus, 7, ANF vol.5, 226. In ch. 14 he
clarifies that the Father and Son are persons but the Spirit is a third "economy" or
"disposition". It is Tertullian who fully merits the Spirit with full personhood. Ad Praxeas
ch. 25, 31, ANF vol.3, 623, 627. A summary of Harnack's emphasis placed on the use of
this term by Tertullian and Hippolytus is found in Carl Andresen, "Zur Entstehung und
Geschicte des Trinitarischen Person-begriffes," Zeitschrift für die Neutestamentliche
Wissenschaft 52 (1961): 7-9. Andresen agrees with Slusser that "prosopographic exegesis"
was the basis of the early Church discussion of the prosopa. See chap. One, 47-48. Of
Tertullian's pneumatology, G. Kretschmar states that the juxtaposition of the Father and the
Son is:
"Complétée par l'introduction de l'Esprit qui pare comme une troisième personne
independante...Ce qui est nouveau et important, c'est l'emploi de la notion de personne,
déjà utilisée pour le Père et le Fils. C'est de cette manière que l'existence propre de
l'Esprit est fixeé...." "Le développement de la doctrine du Saint-Esprit du Nouveau
Testament à Nicée," Verbum Caro 22 (1968):36.

of the Trinity.[99]

Based upon prosopological exegesis, the intricate analysis of the divine inter-communication passages of the New Testament, it is not hard to see why the **prosopa** of the Roman stage were used to indicate the unique sources of speech within the Godhead.[100] It is no wonder then that the Early Christian Apologists, Irenaeus, and Tertullian, in the light of modern rational analyses, seem a bit crude in their discussions of the members of the Godhead; it is as if they were speaking about distinctly different persons.[101] But a deeper look at context reveals that as unsophisticated as it may appear, even the earliest of Church fathers did not intend a division of the unity of God, though their assimilation of histrionic language was rough-edged to say the least. Prestige posits that:

> No ancient Father until Basil uses the word **prosopon** in this sense of mask. When the word is employed to describe the Persons of the Trinity, it means not a transitory and superficial presentation, but simply an individual.[102]

The radical position implied here is easily missed. Not only were these thinkers revolutionizing the ancient concept of God as Impersonal Absolute, they were proposing a God who in God's self was to be understood socially.

C. Persona as a Theological Category[103]

It is well known that the Church's inability to come to clear consensual agreements on the terms we conflate in the one word 'person', has been the cause of untold debate and confusion. It is equally befuddling that a concept like '**homoousion**' found ecumenical acceptance much more readily than **prosopon** ever enjoyed. Of course, it was the gamut of meanings which inextricably surrounded **prosopon** which elicited the reaction it endured.

---

[99]Lynch agrees with J. N. D. Kelly and G. L. Prestige on the absence of philosophical implications in the use of '**prosopa**' at this stage of development. "Prosopon and the Dogma of the Trinity," 75.

[100]See von Balthasar's article for bibliographic help here, and see Mackey's article "On relativising the Trinity" for a scathing critique.

[101]I Clement, 42, Lightfoot, The Apostolic Fathers, 27, trans. 75. Ignatius, To the Ephesians, 9, Lightfoot, The Apostolic Fathers, 108, trans. 139, Athenagoras, Plea for the Christians, 10 and 12 ANF vol. 2, 133, 134, Irenaeus' Adversus Haereses Bk.3 chapters 9-12, ANF vol. 1, 414-436, are examples of the radical departure of the early Fathers from the heretical eclecticism of Valentinian Gnosticism, especially at the point of differentiating the persons of the Trinity. For indisputable examples of this use of prosopa see Tertullian Ad Praxean 22 and 23, ANF vol. 3, 617-620, and chapters 7-9, ANF 3, 601-604 reveal the same "asseveration" between the persons.

[102]G. L. Prestige, God in Patristic Thought, Reprint (London: S.P.C.K., 1964), 113. Speaking of the supposed Sabellian usage of **prosopon** as mask, or mere successive manifestations of divinity.

[103]We will deal with **prosopon** specifically in chap. Three.

It was the retention of earlier definitions which precluded its further ecumenical use. However, it would be fallacious to conclude that the eventual deferral to 'hypostasis' was more than a means to distinguish Christian trinitarian thought from heretical discourse. Modern thinkers have skewed the evidence with regards to prosopon. If anything the early Church erred in an overemphasis on individuality. There is no doubt that the Fathers' use of prosopon meant an object with a unique being of its own, not just the "manners" or "modes" we are so often told best interpret its usage.[104] After the purging fire of both the trinitarian and the christological debates the Church came to a partial consensus on 'persona', though it did so after a huge definitional schism between East and West had occurred, which has even yet has only seen provisional amelioration.[105] However, even in the beginning of the debate between traditions, the relational elements of the trinitarian discourse do not take precedence while the possible non-biblical extrusions possible in unguarded terminology are given the most attention. The challenge, for the modern theological mind, is to recapture the depth of the term in context, without the flattening, impersonal, non-relational trappings of later scholarly interpretations.

Where the Apologists and Origen had proposed primarily a "Logos-theology" with unforeseen yet distinct deficiencies pertaining to the equality of the persons, Tertullian produced a paradigm that more adequately comprehended the equality without denying the distinctions. It was he who gave so many crucial "firsts" in the Church's advance in trinitarian thought. 'Trinitas' was to replace 'trias', 'monarchia' and 'relatio' were to deepen the term 'oikonomia' which in itself was redolent with trinitarian possibilities.[106] His use of 'persona' proved pivotal in the advance beyond the era's dispensationally-motivated modalism that a predominantly economic trinitarianism had spawned.

If the Alexandrian Origen challenged the perception of God as ineffable absolute, thereby paving the way for God's perfection to be seen in His presence in the world,

---

[104]I am indebted to the thoroughly researched and compelling evidence compiled by J. Lynch here in his "Prosopon and the Dogma of the Trinity." Regrettably, this dissertation has not found its way into scholarly discourse, other than articular form, of which I am aware.

[105]It will be apparent that this discussion precludes inclusion of the overall history of the trinitarian and christological controversies, which have been well canvassed and reassessed. The intention here as stated is the unique role of the concept of person in those discussions, specifically as they impinge upon the inner reality of the Trinity as the Church has portrayed it.

[106]Theophilus apparently was the first to use 'triados'. It is used in To Autolycus 2, c. 15, ANF vol. 2, 101, in a manner which seems to be of common usage for him. 'Persona' appears also in the same section, To Autolycus 2, c. 22 ANF vol. 2, 103, but it is only in the symbolic sense. Tertullian adds theological insight to each of these terms. 'Monarchia' had already been perverted by Praxeas, see Ad Praxean 3, ANF vol. 3, 599, and Tertullian was to salvage it by re-informing it.

Tertullian's concomitant contribution was the conception of a revealing God with distinct "social" characteristics.[107] The Carthaginian evidently had observed 'substantia' in much the same way we have described 'ousia'. For him, there was no contradistinction inherent in a substance comprised of differentiated 'personae'.[108]

- Tertullian's Contribution

R. Braun's monumental work confirms this conclusion regarding the Carthaginian innovator. Tertullian's view of substance is equal on a philosophical level to the Greek 'ousia', that is, as nature, reality or essence. For him the divine substance consists of its inherent spiritual reality.[109] But his emphasis on substance as "constitutive matter" and "the matter of being" did not philosophically preclude reference to the substance of the Son. In his confrontation with Praxean modalism, substance was used in such a way as to emphasize the real being of Christ the Logos out of necessity. The Word was a real existent being, a particular reality.[110] And he did not see the two affirmations, a triune substance and a substantial person, as contradictory.[111] Yet this claim did not rest on insipid fideism; one instead finds Tertullian striving for logical and biblical clarity.

Some have said this double use of 'substantia' confuses the issue, but not if the

---

[107]We will explore Tertullian further. Note here Origen's approach to the idea of God in De Principiis, Bk. 1, 1-3, for a remarkable re-interpretation of Biblical truth in the face of the philosophic tyranny of Middle-Platonism. Noteworthy also, is the well-known fact that for Origen the Son was seen as a "second God". Tertullian's actual trinitarianism has been challenged as some would see a binitarianism before his conversion to Montanism. Robert Sider, "Approaches to Tertullian: A Study of Recent Scholarship," The Second Century 2:4 (1982): 252-253.

[108]Tertullian, Ad Praxean, 2. ANF 3, 598, is the source of his famous distinction statement which he then explicates further. Against those who conflate the Trinitarian persons, he wrote:
Three, however, not in condition (statu), but in degree (gradus); not in substance, but in form; not in power, but in aspect (specie); yet of one substance and of one condition, and of one power, inasmuch as He is one God.
See also Ad Praxean 3, ANF 3, 599; Ibid., 13, ANF 3, 609; Ibid., 19, ANF 3, 614.

[109]René Braun, Deus Christianorum: Récherche sur le vocabulaire doctrinal de Tertullian, 2nd ed.(Paris: Etudes Augustinniennes, 1977), focuses on the doctor's prosopological exegesis (much in agreement with Andrèsen's approach) but always in the context of the divine reality evidenced in John 4:24, "God is spirit." See Ad Praxean 7, ANF 3, 602.

[110]For a full discussion of this see Braun, Deus Christianorum, 179-192.

[111]Braun correctly states:
L'épaisseur sémantique de substantia explique á elle seule que Tertullian ait pu l'employer, sans avoir le sentiment de se contredire, pour affirmer, d'abord dan la doctrine de l'unité de substance, que le même tissu spirituel forme l'être des Trois divins, ensuite, dans la doctrine de la distinction personnelle, que le Fils est une réalité consistante et non un mode incorporel.
Deus Christianorum, 193. See also 194.

unity of the Godhead is seen in relational categories from the outset, which is the position I believe Tertullian took. One might say he is "Aristotelian" in his insistence that divine substance admits of individuating characteristics, or that it is comprised of different elements. He transforms the Stoic metaphysic, rids substantia of its material elements, and redefines divine unity to include three existants, three real substantial beings.[112] To speak of divine love or of the divine essence in terms of three persons was not to inject a "compositional" view of God. His view, as ours, depends upon a fundamental "incompositeness" which fully accords with an other-relatedness. Thus, individuality in any modern sense is denied in Tertullian. Instead, a concrete, real existant does not necessitate independent distinction. To be a divine existant is to exist in a ontological relationship which is inextricably conjoined without material compositedness.[113] As we have said, in the discussion of divine substance, if the "what" alone is the primary focus of substance, modalism soon enters. Tertullian's primary position was to start with "who" it was whose substance was being investigated. That is why there are consistent echoes of a deep relationality in his work over against the rationality of much Christian philosophizing.

The Son is viewed then as a concrete individual by Tertullian.[114] Though he should not be credited with a full explication of orthodox trinitology, Tertullian did assist in consolidating the needed distinctions between modalism and Christian monotheism that admitted differentiation. He writes of the relation between God and man in Christ:

> We see plainly the twofold state, which is not confounded, but conjoined in One Person.... Neither the flesh becomes Spirit, nor the Spirit flesh. In one Person they no doubt are well able to be co-existent.[115]

There is the undeniable accent of a permeative quality, a co-inherence of natures in Tertullian's christology, an idea which would be further explored on both christological and

---

[112]See above 13, n. 27.

[113]David Braine's excellent philosophical assessment of personhood and its implications has been helpful in the clarification of my language here. See his The Reality of Time and the Existence of God: The Project of Proving God's Existence (Oxford: Clarendon Press, 1988), 269-333. I find no disparity in the sort of subtle philosophical distinctions made by Braine and the attempts Tertullian makes in the third-century to protect both the unity and the triunity of God, although Braine is, of necessity, more reserved.

[114]Tertullian, Ad Praxean 25. ANF vol. 3, 610. Here Tertullian clearly distinguishes between the persons. In the previous chapter he discusses the unity/diversity theme, in that the Father is the face of the Son. Ibid., 24. ANF vol. 3, 610. In the context of discussion of the substance of the Father and anything which comes from him we find his first attempt at defining person in Ad Praxean 7. ANF vol. 3, 602.

[115]Tertullian, Ad Praxean, 27. ANF vol. 3, 624. It is here that the issue of a tertium quid is dispelled, and of interest to us is the use of substantia, that disallows a composite essence while admitting of a conjoining.

trinitological fronts.[116]

Though a full rendition of the christological debates will not be recounted in this work, we do recognize the clarifications they proposed with regard to the subjectivity of 'prosopon' and 'persona'. Tertullian, in essence, introduced the question by his rampant use of persona as well as by being the first to use relatio in dealing with the threeness/oneness issue.

The Spirit is also a person, a third person, who shares in the relational view of the Trinity which Tertullian finds primarily in Scripture with confirmation in reason. Against the Valentinian Gnostic heresy which conflated the biblical evidence for three persons, especially in relation to the Spirit as "Power of the Highest" he counters:

> Whereas these (ipsae, referring to Son and Spirit) are not themselves the same as He whose relations they are said to be, but they proceed from Him and appertain to Him.[117]

There is much evidence in Ad Praxean for the presence of new additions to the well-traversed arena of the unity of the Godhead. If his Christology allowed an incipient form of perichoresis, it is possible that he also saw its implications for the eternal generation of the Son, of which he was only partially aware.[118] As Origen, Tertullian saw trinitarian logic directly tied to the ontological implications of New Testament christology. In the midst of confrontations, which have modern counterparts, the functionalistic options of adoptionism or modalism were found to be untenable. But beyond that Tertullian explored intra-trinitarian relationships. In a series of refutations he delves into the

---

[116]Braun is right in correcting Prestige's oversight regarding Tertullian's uniqueness with regard to 'person'. He apparently missed the implications for 'oikonomia' which he does acknowlege as special, God in Patristic Thought, 111. But the reason it had the impact it did was because of the definition of person. Discussion of co-inherence is only possible if the members referred to are by nature, other-oriented. What one deduces from the incarnation points directly to the primary relationship which preceded Bethlehem.

[117]Tertullian, Ad Praxean 27, ANF vol. 3, 623. Note also ch. 12 where he is discussing the 'imago dei' texts in Gen. 1:

> It was because He had already His Son close at His side, as a second person, His own Word, and a third Person also, the Spirit in the Word, that He purposely adopted the plural phrase, "Let us make"...(Speaking again of the Son but also applicable to the Spirit he concludes,) "In what sense, however, you ought to understand Him to be another, I have already explained, on the ground of Personality, not Substance—in the way of distinction, not of division...I must everywhere hold one only substance in three coherent and inseparable (Persons).

Ad Praxean, ANF 3, 606-607.

[118]G. L. Bray, "The Patristic Dogma," in ed. P. Toon and J. Spiceland's, One God in Trinity, 54. Bray adequately deals with the perennial economic preoccupation of M. Wiles by contesting his usage of Ad Praxean. Tertullian was farther along than the Apologists but not a precursor to Athanasius for in the East his thought was virtually unknown. Ibid., 52. Tertullian's use of persona was broader than Harnack's attribution of legal definition. Although only an introduction to the deeper theological implications Schlossmann's Persona und Prosopon, 123-124, challenges the Harnackian influence.

"secondness" of the Son and then a third "coherent" person who with the Father comprise one essence, not one person.[119] He espoused a distinction of persons without separation, yet identical in substance.[120]

It was here that he also had to deflect accusations of tritheism. Depending heavily on his facility with both Old and New Testaments, a redefinition of divine economy and the use of Greek philosophical categories, Tertullian moved trinitarian discussion into a plausible ontological discourse. He subtly dispatched Pythagorean and Platonic questions of the relation of the One and the many by reassessing the One, or the "Arche." According to Tertullian, the One of the philosophers must confront the Biblical God who is not static, but self-revealing. It is consistent with the character of a God who is mutual love to send the Son and the Spirit. Choosing 'probole' or prolation, probably to distance himself from pervasive Plotinian emanationism, he presents a relational trinity based in the concept of an interpersonal and self-diffusive unity.[121]

We cannot force upon Tertullian what he does not intend. Harnack was wrong in purporting that the Western viewpoints of Hippolytus, who used prosopon and Tertullian, who redefined persona, were the formers of the Church's full understanding of person at this point in history.[122] We will see presently that the East had remarkable input into the idea of divine personhood. It is safe to say that at root the notion of person or substance in abstraction was not prevalent in the apologetic defense of the Trinity in the third century. Person is not represented by Tertullian as the "composite" entity which we find, say in Augustine, but the important thing to note is that at this point in theological history, there is a shift in its meaning and usage. The divine personae are dynamically related, and revelatory. The divine reality is not hidden in obscurity nor threatened by any form of necessitarianism. Self-giving is natural for God. The power and consistency of that

---

[119]Tertullian, Ad Praxean 19-25, ANF 3, 614-621.

[120]Prestige rightly interprets Tertullian's use of 'oikonomia' where he states: "The divine economy is not an economy of redemption, nor an economy of revelation, but an economy of divine being." God in Patristic Thought, 106.

[121]Tertullian, Ad Praxean 7, ANF vol. 3, 602-603. It is here where the problematic potentially subordinationistic analogies of root - tree, fountain - river, sun - ray appear. But any critique of them must give him the benefit of the context in which they reside and his remarkable situation in this early period of trinitarian thought. One would have to work hard to deny that Tertullian is not pointing to prolations that are intimately related before salvation history began.

[122]See Slusser's comment on this in "Exegetical Roots," 462. Prestige discusses the relationship between Hippolytus and Tertullian briefly but accurately it seems to me in God in Patristic Thought, 97, 159.

reality reside within the divine essence alone.[123]

If this interpretation is accurate in its representation of Tertullian, we must then use those findings to reflect on the questions raised at the beginning of the chapter. We have seen a progression in thought concerning the nature of God, from static to dynamic to an interrelatedness between divine persons as the best human description, however provisional, of the inner life of the Godhead. In early Church terms, that are still debated in trinitarian discussion — substantia, ousia, natura, essentia, relatio, or oikonomia — found deeper clarification and application in their connection with prosopon and persona. That relationship is not absolutely clear but it is heuristic, in the best sense. In the Christian tradition the ultimate source of and basis for a dynamic understanding of personhood resides within a Triune reality whose nature is willingly and "naturally" revealed in self-diffusive salvific acts. Thus, there is support for advocating strong connection between human analogical language and the divine nature with regard to the concept of 'person' and its concomitants, when placed in the context of relationality.

The problem with this interpretation is the tendency in theology to see unity or essential statements as more fundamental than the distinction or notional categories. Tertullian makes a marked advance on the essentialist position without contradicting its correct premises. It is intriquing that along with the relational categories we have mentioned Tertullian uses the more philosophical Logos constructions.[124] He did not see this "hellenistic" intrusion as detrimental. In fact, it is arguable that when properly interpreted in context he viewed it as a potential corrective to any propensity to extend the relational categories into tritheism. For it is evident that his discussion on human psychology as an analogy for the Trinity was in part the basis for nearly half of Augustine's De Trinitate.[125] What is of interest here is that Tertullian offers that analogy in the center of an attempt to redefine static conceptions of unity.[126] Triunity describes the reality of divine unity. The Eastern church was not the only place where this sort of dynamic Trinity was promulgated, although it did improve its logic considerably.

---

[123]Prestige's proclivity to disallow a dynamic relational Trinity is expressed in the way he treats Tertullian's use of 'prosopon'. It is a travesty to conclude from Ad Praxean that all Tertullian does with the notion is reapply the legal definition or: "the concrete presentation of an individual than, as is commonly alleged, the holder of the legal title to a hereditament." God in Patristic Thought, 159.

[124]See for example, Ad Praxean 5-8 passim, ANF 3, 600-603.

[125]I am in agreement with J. Quasten at this point, Patrology (Westminster, Maryland: Christian Classics, 1986) vol. 2, 285.

[126]One should note Tertullian's usage of 'dispositio' which is used in much the same way that we find 'oikonomia' utilized in Ad Praxean 5,6, ANF 3, 600-601, which has been interpreted as pertaining distinctly to mutual relations within the Godhead.

If my interpretation is accurate it would give reason for reticence in accepting the avalanche of modern propositions to the contrary. We are told that any use of 'person' inevitably requires a radical divergence between modern usages and trinitarian formulas. It is pervasively accepted that 'person' has always been a highly ambiguous term.[127] A look at the data, however, elicits reservations with regard to this modern assessment cast on early Church concepts. It would seem that there is more evidence of clear thinking mixed with proper reservation than ambiguous discernments with reckless results. The thinkers we have mentioned included transcendental categories that exceeded the dimensions suggested by those who would classify them as having limited plausibility structures or restrictive historical perspectives.

It is often forgotten that the discussion of person was hammered out on the anvil of encroaching modalism. Sabellius used 'prosopon' in its symbolic form, as mask or face of the divine monad, seeing a direct correspondence with the normal and original Greek usage. The three manifestations of God could carry a strong notion of equality. Sabellius would even use analogies similar to Tertullian's - a round sun which emitted heat and light, or the human construction of body, soul and spirit.[128] The orthodox thinkers disdained manifestation categories as inadequate, unbiblical and detrimental to the Christian faith. It is hard to see then why so many modern students of Christian tradition attempt to strip away any notion of triune person which would contain "modern" elements of understanding, volition, and especially mutuality. The unity of God was less abstract for Tertullian than it was for the Cappadocians. For the North African doctor the unity was best seen in light of the three divine persons in communion.

In sum, then there are certain stages in the progression of the use of 'prosopon' and then 'persona' which set the stage for the 'Cappadocian settlement'. There is the "symbolic" stage and its incorporation of funerary usages and literal histrionic applications. Second, we have located the "physical" stage which saw a broadening of the usage to include role, and external being, recognizing an individual. This stage was the most persistent of the early usages. Next came the "moral" stage, in which the roles played came to bear both characteristics and specific characters. It is with the "theological" stage

---

[127]For an example of this form of scholarship we refer again to Claude Welch, In This Name, cf. 272-273, passim. But this same sort of thinking is found in Barth, Rahner, Pittenger, Cobb and many others.

[128]Clear refutation of these and other misleading premises of the Sabellians in the West and the Arians in the East can be found in Athanasius' powerful De Decretis, NPNF2, 150-172. Interestingly we find a similar stand-off between the Arian Eusebius of Caesarea and the Sabellians, Paul of Samosata and Marcellus. The latter uses three prosopa and one hypostasis in God, which follows closely the Sabellian line of three names, or three faces. Eusebius gives glimpses of tri-personal categories in his responses, but his tendency toward subordinationism precludes anything of real help here. For a thorough discussion see Lynch, "Prosopon and the Dogma of the Trinity," 77-78.

that we are the most concerned. Tertullian laid the groundwork in both apologetic and anti-heretical writings for a conception of divine person which bore the burden of unity and differentiation. His thought is immature at points yet amazingly prophetic of the direction the term and its conceptual reality would take in the centuries to come. Concrete individuality coupled with dynamic interrelatedness were to be the bases for orthodox trinitarianism in both East and West.

In the period prior to Nicea **prosopon** was used with more than one meaning, which raised suspicion in theologically astute minds. Its usage was tested upon the clear evidence of Scripture interpreted by the earliest traditions of concrete otherness in the Christian Godhead. But as Braun points out **prosopon** and **persona** were to take different courses.[129] The Greeks found the use of **hypostasis** more conducive to trinitarian formulations, and retained **prosopon** for specific references to the "face" of God and similar expressions. The use of **prosopa** by the Sabellians precluded its further usage. While in the West **persona** retained wide usage. The terminological conflict which resulted from the two traditional usages will be alluded to in chapter Three.

III. Conclusion

Schleiermacher's rancor will suffice to encapsulate the modern misunderstanding of the relationship between divine substance and person which has eventuated in the loss of both as meaningful theological terms. He wrote:

> The term 'essence' is certainly more appropriate to the Godhead than the term 'nature,' yet the question inevitably arises what the relation is between what in Christ we call His divine nature and that unity of essence which is common to all three Persons of the Trinity, and whether each of the three Persons outside their participation in the Divine Essence, has also a nature of its own as well, or whether this is a peculiarity of the Second Person.[130]

We see here, and in others who follow suit in an attempt to discredit the intricacy of Christian thought by presenting the past as nothing but a miasma of confusion, a simple inability to discern what the orthodox early Church intended.[131]

To start, we would conclude from the evidence thus far that they did not radically

---

[129]R. Braun, Deus Christianorum, 241-242.

[130]Friedrich Schleiermacher, The Christian Faith vol. 2 (New York: Harper Torchbacks, 1963), 395.

[131]There is a corresponding criticism of "scholastic" trinitarianism in Process thought, which repeats the same sort of metaphysics seen in Schleiermacher. See for example, Ivor Leclerc, "God and the Issue of Being," Religious Studies 20:1 (1978):63-78. There God cannot be a being because he is immanent in the world. See a similar article "God and the Problem of Being," in Person and God, ed. George F. Maclean and Hugo Meynell (Lanham: University Press of America, 1988), 3-13, followed by a cogent criticism by Salvino Biolo, Ibid., 15-21.

separate person and essence. The two were seen as mutually related. Persons equalled divine essence, without producing a quaternity. Essence was comprised of persons, protecting against a monism. The same sort of permeation which was discerned from Scripture with regards to Christ's humanity and divinity, is clarified when one considers the inter-permeative characteristics of the Eternal Godhead. In essence, the God-man was not defined by his humanity; his humanity was seen to bear divine form, a form which incorporated mutual indwelling without confusion. At a point in time, the Eternal God took human form into permeative relationship with one Person of the Trinity.

Although we have more to add to our logic on this point, it is not premature to indicate the direction in which we are going. Modern theology has, for the most part, recapitulated the excesses of the aberrant viewpoints which surrounded early trinitarian discourse. Modalism and Adoptionism stem from obscurantistic views of divine substance. To demand philosophical absolutism either numerically or constituitively replays the mistakes of the Stoics and the Sabellians.

Modern rhetoric which claims to be couched in Scripture can be very misleading on this score. Take Rahner's statement, "there is only one real consciousness in God, which is shared by the Father, Son and Spirit, by each in his own proper way. Hence the threefold subsistency is not qualified by three consciousnesses."[132] He writes with a view to halt heresy but one wonders what presupposition rules here. Again, if nature is presupposed to be virtually non-relational, oneness must be the overarching paradigm. That oneness means that divine nature will not admit any constituents whatsoever. And 'person' must mean absolute individuality, or a consciousness that is in some way not allowed in the Godhead in any other sense than monadic. As Lynch points out in agreement with my interpretation of Rahner's own ambiguity regarding the consciousness of the divine "manners of subsisting." He concludes, "It is self-defeating for an author to cling to a single 'subjectivity' and 'one-consciousness' when he admits that three 'subjects' are 'conscious' or 'aware'."[133] But if person does not necessarily need to be equated with individuality then there may be the possibility of relational difference without ontological separateness. The continued use of personal terms indicates that the early trinitarians saw them as less abstract that other options which we define as "modes" or "subsistences" or "manners".

Hippolytus and Tertullian point us to the Cappadocians. But they do so with a rich notion of both divine person and substance, that all too often Eastern thinkers have denied the West. Traditionally, to be a divine Person does not necessitate the exclusion of

---

[132]Rahner, The Trinity, 10

[133]Lynch, "Prosopon and the Dogma of the Trinity," 281.

another divine Person, it is to be eternally open to Another and Another.[134] Divine essence is not exclusive but inclusive. It will not be a surprise then that the Eastern doctors would eventually use a term in defining the divine essence which anthropomorphically views the trinitarian life as a dance. The earliest orthodox Christians saw nothing stagnant about the life of God, nor did they intend any circumscription of divine nature by adding human analogies. In an attempt to clarify the dynamism they saw from scriptural interpretation with the use of Greek categories, they had to constantly be on guard to not allow ascendancy to monadic structural apparatuses. They rejected the absolutism and emanationism of their pagan counterparts but re-shaped elements in an attempt to express their religious consciousness in all of its aspects. Instead of an abstract self-identical unity, the notions of substance and then person offered a strict "unity whose identity consisted in the very act of self-diremption and which was just as much subject as it was object."[135]

There has never been a ready place for a personal God to be received. The idea just does not seem to fit our metaphysics. It was that realization which awakened a few to begin to ask questions about the kind of God it would require to make a sensible confession regarding the possibility of love, in God's self and toward creation. Those questions bore conclusions in both the West and the Each which would be recognized by the Church as sitting very close to reality. Both prosopon and persona were to serve as the crucial sources for what Jennings has called the "provocation of discourse."[136] Person, seen clearly as an analogical term was introduced cathechetically and heuristically, into the theoretical language of the early Church in a usage which was not previously known and which would alter all future conceptions of personhood.

.

---

[134]Note the excellent rendition of Biblical, traditional and practical applications of this understanding of personhood in Bernard Cooke, "The Theology of Person," Spiritual Life 7 (1961):11-20.

[135]Atherton, "The Neoplatonic 'One' and the Trinitarian 'Arche'," 181.

[136]Theodore Jennings, Beyond Theism, 83.

O blessed One,
to Thee I turn my gaze again
Thou art my strength,
the Lord of all,
The Unbegotten, the Beginning
and the Father of the
Beginning,
who is the immortal Son.
Thou art the Great Light
sprung from similar light,
circling in a manner that is
ineffable from One to One...
and Spirit
proceeding from the Father,
Light of my mind,
who comest to the pure
and makest God of man.

Gregory of Nazianzus

Chapter Three

Divine Person as Relation

It can prove infuriating that so much theological history and orthodoxy could come to rest, as Gibbon quipped, on a "single dipthong."[1] The way from Nicene and neo-Nicene orthodoxy to the Chalcedonian settlement revolved around extremely subtle theological distinctions.[2] The points of clarification were focused primarily on the issues raised by the Greek Fathers: **ousia, prosopon,** and **phusis** and their Latin counterparts;

---

[1]Edward Gibbon, The Decline and Fall of the Roman Empire, vol. 1 in The Great Books, ed. R. M. Hutchins (Chicago: Encyclopedia Britannica, 1952), 313. Harnack indicates that, as he sees it, **homoousion** was used so loosely, that even though it might have been held as "same substance" by Athanasius and a few others, it ought not be made the fulcrum of Nicene orthodoxy which was in reality a replacement of "true" religion with "knowledge" and a dessicated sense of mystery. A. Harnack, Outlines of the History of Dogma, trans. Edwin Knox Mitchell (Boston: Beacon Press, 1957), 252, 273. Cf. also his History of Dogma, vol. 4, 74-101. Note the conservative response of Bethune-Baker in The Meaning of the Homoousios in the Constantinopolitan Creed, in Texts and Studies: Contributions to Biblical and Patristic Literature, vol. 7. ed. J. Armitage Robinson (Cambridge: Cambridge Univ. Press, 1901, Reprint. Nendeln/ Liechenstein: Kraus Reprint Ltd., 1967) 6-11. A more modern approach is found in G. Stead's "The Significance of the 'Homoousios'," in Studia Patristica 3:1, ed. F. L. Cross, 397-412 (Berlin: Akademie-Verlag, 1961).

[2]We use "neo-Nicene" with the same reservations of De Halleux, contra Zahn and Harnack, see "'Hypostase' et 'Personne' dans la formation du dogme trinitaire (ca. 375-381)," Revue d'Histoire Ecclésiastique 29:2 (1984): 317.

substantia, persona, and natura, with their theological cognates. Athansius, unable to forsee the implications raised by the homoousion doctrine, was defended and expanded upon by the work of the Cappadocians, though in others the great defender retained superiority over his successors.[3] What is of interest is that these Christians spearheaded a new ontology, with personhood at its center, which shook both philosophical and theological worlds.[4]

Neither East nor West has been guiltless of disparaging the items which the opposing critic deems as an area of over-emphasis.[5] On the simplicity of the divine substance, Easterners argue that the West, following Augustine, has made too much of the unity of the Godhead, disallowing adequate attention to the distinctions of persons, while the West is uncomfortable with the apophatic "essence-energy" paradigm characteristic of Byzantine dualism which could tend, they say, to produce an abstract, impersonal, even quaternarian essence in God.[6] In relation to the triune Persons, the East is accused of

[3]E. R. Hardy correctly states that, "the years from 361 to 381 (1st Constantinopolitan Council)...are of great importance in the history of Christian doctrine." Christology of the Later Fathers, ed. Edward Rochie Hardy, in Library of Christian Classics (Philadelphia: Westminster Press, 1954), 23. T.F. Torrance, whose high opinion of Athanasius occurs in a number of his works, would agree with those who say that the difficulty of several centuries of theologizing was due to the attempt to "Christianize the terminology" which with myriad nuances involved meant disagreement and eventually schism. The Trinitarian Faith, 30.

[4]T.J. Horringe writes,
In general we may say that the period from 325 to 451, far from witnessing the 'acute Hellenization' of the Christian gospel, witnessed on the contrary the disintegration of many of the most cherished concepts of Greek philosophy and the beginning of a completely different metaphysical tradition.
"'Not Assumed is Not Healed': the Homoousion and Liberation Theology," Scottish Journal of Theology 38:4 (1985): 488.

[5]De Régnon's paradigm-setting treatise, Études de théologie positive sur la Sainte Trinité. 4 vols. Paris: Victor Retaux et Fils, 1892, produced its own form of intransigent followers of the theme which runs, "The Greeks are accustomed to see the person in recto and nature in obliquo. In other words, their thought falls first and foremost on the person...(The Latin scholastics') thought falls first and foremost on the substance and adds to it the idea of subsistence as a completing determination", Ibid., Vol. 1, 143-145. Bouyer says of this mindset that rather than looking at the possible complementary factors they are seen as diametrically opposed, Le Père Invisible: Approches du Mystère de la Divinité (Paris: Les Éditions du Cerf, 1976), 269. We have alluded to the East/West tensions and presuppositions in chap. One, pp. 16, 18-22, 25-26, 28. See Congar's compilation of caricaturizations in I Believe in the Holy Spirit vol. 3, xvi-xvii.

[6]Although the Stoics and Plotinus used an essence-energy formulation, the Cappadocian version is attributed to Gregory Palamas. See the extended discussion in Wolfson, The Philosophy of the Church Fathers, 305-363. Cf. P. Henry "The 'Adversus Arium' of Marius Victorinus, the First Systematic Exposition of the Doctrine of the Trinity," Journal of Theological Studies 6:1 n.s.(1950): 45-48. The main Cappadocian fathers made a distinction between knowing God in His essence, theologia and involvement in history, oikonomia. J. Mackey in his typical anti-traditional stance, critiques this paradigm in "The

tritheism, the West, in turn, of modalism.[7]

I will argue that the Cappadocians never intended divine persons as philosophical monadic abstractions hidden beneath a veil of agnostic mysticism, and that Augustine, as the fountainhead of the Western trinitarian tradition was favorable toward a relational trinity which carried a strong sense of person, even if reserved about the use of the terms pertaining to that distinction.[8] The Bishop of Hippo may have had indirect connection with the East but nonetheless his themes surrounding 'person' are strikingly similar, in spite of a decidedly different perspective.[9] The Cappadocians and subsequently Augustine would view the Trinity, neither haltingly or timidly, as a relational reality, though they jousted with terms couched in Greek philosophy that threatened the diminution or exaggeration of

---

Holy Spirit: Relativizing the Divergent Approaches of East and West," Irish Theological Quarterly 48:3/4 (1981): 256-267. From a more objective viewpoint see the critique of T.F. Torrance, The Trinitarian Faith, 14-17. The Orthodox position is ably defended by J. Zizioulas, "The Teaching of the 2nd Ecumenical Council on the Holy Spirit in Historical and Ecumenical Perspective," in Credo in Spiritum Sanctum: Atti del Congresso Teologico Internazionale di Pneumatologia (Vatican: Libreria Editrice Vatican, 1983), 51-52. For an interesting analysis of Nyssa's view of divine infinity see S. Gustafson, "Gregory of Nyssa's Reformulation of Christian Thought: Some Paradigmatic Implications of his Doctrine of Divine Infinity," Ph. D. dissertation, Drew University, 1985, esp. 123-134. Also C. Andresen, "The Integration of Platonism into Early Christian Theology." In Studia Patristica 15:1. ed. Elizabeth A. Livingstone, 399-413. Berlin: Akademie-Verlag, 1985.

[7]Basil, Letter 8 NPNF2 vol. 8, 116. See John Thompson for reverse criticism of the West. "The Holy Spirit and the Trinity in Ecumenical Perspective," Irish Theological Quarterly 47:4 (1980): 279.

[8]This is in contrast to the thesis that the Cappadocians were merely a recrudesence of Neoplatonic thought. See Harnack, Outlines of the History of Dogma, 261. It is also an attempt at ameliorating the contention that the West "flubbed" what the East had begun in toto. See Jensen, The Triune Identity (Philadelphia: Fortress Press, 1982), where one wonders whether he is accurate that trinitarian doctrine came to Augustine a "finished product" Ibid., 114, or if it is totally accurate to say that the West contributed the notion that "personal being is an ontological kind of its own." Ibid., 122.

[9]If space would permit one would trace the Eastern contacts from which Hilary profited during his Phrygian exile and their eventual impact on the West. One of his battles was with Auxentius the predecessor of Ambrose, Augustine's mentor. Alan Jacobs, "Hilary of Poitier and the Homoousians: A Study of the Eastern Roots of his Ecumenical Trinitarianism," Ph. D. dissertation, Emory Univ., 1968, 28-30. See De Synodis 5, (Jacobs sees this as a prolegomena to his De Trinitate, Ibid., 239) NPNF2 vol. 9, 5. Note his use of substantia in reflection of Eastern hypostasis in De Synodis 25 Ibid., 11. Meijering's Hilary of Poitiers on the Trinity (Leiden: E. J. Brill, 1982), 9-10. P. Löffler, "Die Trinitätslehre des Bischofs Hilarius von Poitiers zwischen Ost und West," Zeitschrift für Kirchengeschicte 71 (1960): 31-36. See also, C. Kaiser, "The Development of Johannine Motifs in Hilary's Doctrine of the Trinity," Scottish Journal of Theology 29:3 (June 1976): 237-247.

the Biblical witness, if unchecked.[10] A general outline of the factors which are evident in Athanasian and Cappadocian orthodoxy would include the emphases of **Monarchy, Unity, Derivation,** and eventually a notion of **Relational Personhood.**

I. The Cappadocians and Divine Personhood

It is the perspicuousness of Athanasius, not obtuseness, which is revealed by his silence with respect to a explicitly consubstantial Trinity.[11] **Homoousion** is not used in his theological writings with reference to all three Persons concomitantly, although it is used separately of both the Son and the Spirit in relation to the Father.[12] That theme alone would seem like the expedient and expeditious route he could have taken, locked as he was with the horns of Arianism. Here we find a stalwart commitment to a 'Monarchian' theme which continues in the Cappadocians. This tenet has fundamental similarity to Alexandrian Neoplatonic emanationism, with its concomitant subordinationistic Logos theology. It is debatable whether the theology of Athanasius and the Cappadocians are simply restatements of that influential school or represent major divergences from it.

What is unmistakable is their undeterred desire to protect the place of the Father as 'Origin' or 'Source' of the Godhead. Athanasius compared the Father to a light Source

---

[10]We have discussed in chap. One, 40-43, the "hellenization" argument. Influential thinkers such as Harnack originated the debate. See his What is Christianity? trans. T. B. Saunders, intro. R. Bultmann (New York: Harper Torchbooks, 1957), where, after an intriquing "demythologization" of the Christian faith, he states in a scathing rendition of the early Church's "intellectualism" that theology, "takes the form, not of a Christian product in Greek dress, but of a Greek product in Christian dress." Ibid., 221. A bit more irenic is Edwin Hatch's The Influence of Greek Ideas on Christianity (New York: Harper Torchbooks, 1957). He notes the historico-political elements as more abusive than philosophy but points out the growing effect of philosophical pressuppositions. Ibid., 250-282. Lossky in The Vision of God, trans. Asheleigh Moorhouse (London: The Faith Press, 1963), 61-62, challenges the claims to a neo-Origenism in the Cappadocians with strong arguments.

[11]Stead points out that of the nearly 150 references to **homoousion** in Athanasius, only half are of direct theological construct. A semantic analysis shows that Athanasius used "indivisible Godhead" rather than "consubstantial", for the context for his use of **homoousion** always protects the 'arche' of the Father. Stead, Divine Substance, 260-261.

[12]This in no way is intended to denigrate Athanasius' strong understanding of unity between the Persons. The point is that Athanasius used functional language. As Torrance puts it, "He preferred to speak concretely of the relations between Father, Son and Holy Spirit, avoiding as much as possible the employment of fixed terms." Theology in Reconciliation (Grand Rapids: Eerdmans, 1976), 242. See for example his Third Discourse against the Arians 15.15 NPNF2 vol. 4, 402. The Spirit is **homoousion** with the Father, Ad Serapion 1:27, 28, 33; 2:4, 3:1, 4, 6.

producing rays, the Fount of a stream, the Origin of the Triad.[13] Often these analogies are relegated to methodological inconsistency in theological construction, anthropomorphic embarrassments. In defense of this astute apologist let it be noted that he had no difficulty, at other points, in switching between intrapersonal and multipersonal terminology, which did not carry the same potential for misuse as the inanimate analogues.[14] The orthodox Church has had to defend the intentions of the distinctly asymmetrical approach in his dubious analogies from nature, but it is often missed that the most common analogy was familial as he compared the Trinity to a Father and Son relationship, where there is perfect symmetry and equality and inseparability, a "full unbroken continuation of being."[15] Of at least four specifically personal analogies in Athanasius' corpus, three concerned distinct individuals, and could be named familial. Of these, only one pertained to the mind of one individual. In spite of this fact, the rational analogy became the primary medium through which Augustine and eventually Aquinas expressed the trinitarian life.[16] Underneath all of these resemblances lies an emphasis on shared life, communicated love.

Athanasius did not display a preference for the philosophically-based terms that would cause so much rancor. He chose instead to use relational terms and analogies,

---

[13]Other terms include, arche, pege, and aitia. Fountain: Expositio Fidei, 2. NPNF2 vol. 4, 84; De Sententia Dionysii 24; Light Source: Ad Serapion, 2.3; De Decretis 23, 24 (Sun analogy) NPNF2 vol. 4, 165-166; Vine: De Sententia Dionysii 10 NPNF2 vol. 4, 180. Summary of several, De Sententia Dionysii 18 NPNF2 vol. 4, 183. Tertullian had mentioned the same analogies as Athanasius, with the addition of "prolation" in Ad Praxean ch. 8 ANF vol. 3, 602. It might be well to mention the use of "greater" here with respect to the Father and the Son (Jn. 14:28). The Cappadocians consider the term to refer to origin rather than nature. Basil Letter 8 NPNF2 vol. 8, 118-120. Gregory of Nazianzus, Fourth Theological Oration 7 NPNF2 vol. 7, 312. See also Third Theological Oration 15 Ibid., 306. T. Torrance feels that Cyril of Alexandria uses Athanasian categories here and refers meizon to the soteriological oikonomia. Theological Dialogue Between Orthodox and Reformed Churches (Edinburgh: Scottish Academic Press, 1985), 87-89.

[14]Family analogy: De Decretis 20, (Cf. Adam and Seth) NPNF2 vol. 4, 164; Ad Serapion 2.6; (Two Men analogy: Ad Serapion 2.3). See R.P.C Hanson's excellent exposition, "The Transformation of Images in the Trinitarian Theology of the Fourth Century." In Studia Patristica 17:1. ed. Elizabeth A. Livingstone, 97-115. Oxford: Pergamon Press Ltd., 1982. Found also in Studies in Christian Antiquity, 253-278.

[15]Ad Serapion, 1:28. See Stead's Divine Substance, 260-266.

[16]Tertullian also discussed the "inner word" motif; we shall examine Augustine's rigorous analysis of this analogy later in this chapter. Cf. the comment on this in Richard Swinburne, "Could there be more than one God?" Faith and Philosophy 5:3 (July, 1988): 240, n.18.

especially for the Father and the Son.[17] Braun may be terminologically correct, that for Clement, Origen, and Athanasius, "Rien dans leur usage ne pouvait rattacher à prosopon la notion de 'particularité distinctive et individuelle' qu'en latin persona portait avec netteté."[18] But it would be a distortion to imply that he only used the term adverbially.[19] He saw the Sabellian misuse and avoided its inherent pitfalls. What is clear is that he sees hypostasis as one way, though used with reservation, of referring to the interrelational subjects within the Godhead.[20] He defends the Triad and uses prosopon cautiously but there is little doubt that Athanasius was aware of a threeness that was deeper than manifestations, which his relational use of ousia indicates.[21] Gregory of Nazianzus contrasts the disorderliness of anarchy, and the latent sedition of 'polyarchia' with monarchic trinitarianism which reveals distinctions without diminution of perfect Being.[22]

The monarchic principle continued to be used in this crucial period of controversy in its advocation of the commensurability of the Persons of the Trinity. It was the threat of a sequential rather than the substantial Trinity in Dynamic Adoptionism which forced a deeper clarification of the relation of the Father to the Son and the Spirit. In order to logically buttress the unity of the Godhead, **homoousion** was introduced into the discussions of the mid-fourth century. Far from being an obscuring 'Hellenized' term , we find instead, it cuts cross-grain against the highest Greek metaphysics. Murray's note is instructive:

The only place where one cannot find Hellenism is in the **homoousion**. It would be impossible to find a conception more remote from, at odds with, all the ontologies of

---

[17]"Triados" we have noted is found earliest in To Autolycus, 15 by Theophilus, NPNF vol. 2, 101. "Trias" and "Monas" carry a concreteness that "Trinitas" and "Unitas" do not. Thus Greek theology combatted Arianism incessantly and the West, forms of Sabellianism. Thus "Father," "Son," and "Spirit" are named but often "One," and "Three" are used by Athanasius. These are recurrent throughout but examples are found in De Decretis, 11 NPNF2 vol. 4, 157. In a clarification on use of "hypostasis", Tomus ad Antiochenos, 5 NPNF2 vol. 4, 484. Cf. Ad Afros, 11, Ibid., 494. Third Discourse against the Arians, 25:15,16, Ibid. 402. De Sententia Dionysii, 17, Ibid., 182. In Gregory of Nyssa we find the same elements, Against Eunomius 2.6, NPNF2 vol. 5, 107. For identity of operation of the Three see Against Eunomius 2.15, in Ibid., 132. Identity of nature, On the Holy Trinity, Ibid., 328.

[18]R. Braun Deus Christianorum, 242.

[19]He uses prosopon in reference to humans, De Decretis 3.14 NPNF2 vol. 4, 159 and De Sententia Dionysii 4, Ibid., 177.

[20]He prefers the Father - Son language but also uses hypostasis at points, Statement of Faith 2 NPNF2 vol. 4, 84; In Illud Omnia 6 Ibid., 90; De Decretis 6.26 Ibid., 167.

[21]Cf. De Synodis, 35-37, NPNF2 vol. 4, 469-470.

[22]Gregory of Nazianzus, Third Theological Oration 2 NPNF2 vol. 7, 301. His similarity with Neoplatonism is shown in the same place with Unity - moving into Duality - and returning to rest in Trinity.

the Graeco-Roman world than the conception embodied in this word, which says that the Son is all that the Father is except for the name of the Father....It may be said that in the homoousion the Fathers of Nicaea christianized Hellenism in the single sense that they sanctioned the ontological mode of conception characteristic of the Hellenic mentality. But it may not be said, on peril of learned absurdity, that they hellenized Christianity.[23]

The unity emphasis must be seen not as advocating modalistic subordinationism but as viewing the intimate relation of the Spirit and the Son to the Father as originative source. The Athanasian/Cappadocian paradigm revealed at least one radical delineation from the Alexandrian Neoplatonism of Plotinus, Porphyry and Proclus; the "emanation" of the Logos, was a distinct Incarnate mediator not an impersonal inferior agency.[24] The interrelationship between essence and distinguishable properties within that ousia required the category of derivation which precluded any form of subordinationism. From the passages of Scripture that indicated a derived life by the Word or Son from the Father, the Cappadocians constructed a concept which held together monarchy and unity.[25] Within the idea of a Divine Source from which the eternal Son and co-equal Spirit drew their existence, the Cappadocians were careful to enumerate distinctions in the Persons. In this same Eastern thought-line Gregory the Theologian would say:

> Now, the name of that which has no beginning is the Father, and of the Beginning the Son, and of that which is with the Beginning, the Holy Ghost, and the three have one Nature - God. And the union is the Father from Whom and to Whom the order of Persons runs its course, not so as to be confounded, but so as to be possessed, without distinctions of time, of will, or of power. For these things in our case produce a plurality of individuals.[26]

Two important concepts are revealed here. First, the use of taxis, or order, for talking about the internal relations of the ineffable persons is clear; the Father is the aitia of a divine relationship which bespeaks harmony and orderliness.[27] Second, and more crucial,

---

[23]J. C. Murray, The Problem of God, 55.

[24]The theme of Mediator, and its cognates, **theandrike energeia** (the God-man action), **boule** (emphasizes His being the will of the Father, against Arian "from the will"), and **prototokos** (first-born), all pertain to clarifying the Christian position from heretical or Greek philosophical encroachments. They also indicate the epistemic and salvific tenets of the Eastern notion of deification centered on the topos, Christ, where God and humanity meet.

[25]Note for instance the use of Prov. 8:22, Ps. 110:1, John 1:14 etc. In each of the orthodox thinkers of the period, their conclusions on these verses and similar passages can be summarized by the term derivation.

[26]Oration 42.15, NPNF2 vol. 7, 390. PG, 476B. "Union" here is **henosis**, **unio** in Latin indicating a deepening view of monarchy from its Tertullianic background but also a divine mystery of divine interdependence.

[27]The West was at home with **arche** and **pege** but **aitia** was definitely an Eastern configuration which lent itself to criticism at points regarding the person of the Father.

although there is a definite derivation theme here, it in no way is meant to imply a second-class within the deity. Derivation, begottenness and procession, are logical categories which point to the intratrinitarian relations; they are not to be understood temporally or spatially. Basic to this was the Cappadocian understanding of divine substance.

A. The Eastern View of Substance

It is difficult for a western mind impressed by Augustinian dualism to collate Eastern epistemology and theology. The strong apophatic statements can be construed as thoroughly agnostic.[28] There is a clear theoretical distinction between talk about what God is not and the ineffable essence of the Godhead. However, in the Cappadocians, one soon finds that often even within the context of the via negativa there are statements which pertain to, if not comprehend, the being of God. Note Gregory of Nazianzus' statement that, "He who is eagerly pursuing the nature of the Self-existent will not stop at saying what He is not, and say what He is."[29] As part of the mystery of divine revelation, as perceived in the East, it must be remembered that for the early Church worship was response to a God who is at once utterly unknown and One that must be known. It was in His operations that God's essence was indirectly, or rather mediately, revealed by the illumination of faith and divine indwelling.[30]

---

[28]The mix of Biblical material, tradition, and mystical Platonism is as unique as the personalities of its Eastern proponents. It must be clear here that we do not include Athanasius with the Cappadocians on apophatic thought. He was more reserved than they, see Letter 52:2 as an example of the same tendency to awefulness when approaching God-talk. But, as Torrance argues forcefully, his conception of the internal relations of God and its impact on revelation precluded any divorcement of the energeia from the essentia. Torrance, Theology in Reconciliation, 220-221, 236-239.

[29]Second Theological Oration 9 NPNF2 vol. 7, 291. Jensen refers to this section as representative of the disavowal of distinction between cataphatic and apophatic terms in The Triune Identity (Philadelphia: Fortress Press, 1982), 150 n.30. Nyssa has a similar view where he wrote, "Man cannot know what God is, he only knows that God is." Against Eunomius PG 36, 32B.

[30]Gregory of Nyssa, Against Eunomius 3:4 NPNF2 vol. 5, 144-145, and Answer to Eunomius' Second Book, Ibid., 262-263. Gregory of Nazianzus, On the Great Athanasius, Oration 21:34 NPNF2 vol. 7, 279. Nazianzus comments elsewhere, "I say, that is it impossible to express Him, and yet more impossible to conceive Him." Oration 28:4 NPNF2 vol. 7, 289-290. Oden says of early Christian worship, "It did not desire to lay hold of the Trinity but only to behold God as triune." Living God, 217. The modern Eastern philosopher, Pavel Florensky draws some intriguing implications based upon this illuminationist epistemology. His view of a concrete unity between divine Persons produces a world-view which is based upon homoousion. Slesinski, in a critique of Florensky, says he divided all philosophies based on this premise, "In a personalist universe, accordingly, no 'self' is in abstraction from its 'other'. R. Slesinski, Pavel Florensky: A Metaphysics of Love (Crestwood, New York: St. Vladimir's Seminary Press, 1984), 137. In a metaphysic of participation, persons in relation then are heuristic realities

This antinomy of absolute otherness, the ineffable "whatness" of God, is paradoxically countered by an accessibility, a "thatness".[31] One can immediately see the paradox of language, in this distinction where Athanasius discusses the divine essence.[32] Substance, then, is God's very being. It is in no way incomplete, nor constructed. It is the eternal, unalterable divine existence which is progressively expounded by each subsequent Cappadocian.

> But if God be simple, as He is, it follows that in saying 'God' and naming 'Father' we name nothing as if about (peri) Him, but signify his essence itself....When Scripture says, 'God,' we understand nothing else by it but the intimation of His incomprehensible essence itself, and that He Is, who is spoken of.[33]

Simplicity of the divine being required this affirmation. However, this is a different view of substance than the Aristotelian-Stoic monad.[34] Ousia is used in the simplest sense, yet it

---

for interpreting reality only as they partake in divine love.

[31]The basis of John Zizioulas' masterful work, Being as Communion is found in a proper ecumenical perspective of "apophatic" theology. Rather than a negation, it is a transcendent affirmation of a divine "ekstasis", a self-giving, which is not based on the individuum of personality (i.e., will or act) but on the basis of divine nature itself an other-love which transcends all human conception of love and thereby fully reveals the incommunicable communing Persons that are that Being. Ibid., 27-65; 89-92; 105-107. For background see G. Watson, "The Theology of Plato and Aristotle," 56-64. For critique, D. Cupitt, "Kant and the Negative Theology," in B. Hebblethwaite, and S. Sutherland, The Philosophical Frontiers of Christian Theology: Essays Presented to D. M. Mackinnon (Cambridge: Cambridge Univ. Press, 1982), 55-67. Positive statements: for focus on evocative not descriptive language, P. Gregorios, "God - To What, if Anything, Does the Term Refer? An Eastern Christian Perspective." in G. McLean and H. Meynell, Person and God, 133-143; for tangential attempts at paradox, see D. M. Baillie, God was in Christ, 106-118.

[32]Discourses against the Arians 1: 20-22 NPNF2 vol. 4, 318-319; 2:2-4 Ibid., 348-349. The Cappadocian defense against the Arian camps included strict attention to terminology (as is the case in every era where lines must be drawn between what is orthodox and what is not). Epinoia, or roughly, conception is one such term. Where Eunomius critiqued the Fathers for their "fanciful" use of terms, the responders invoked Scripture as the data source for such conceptions. Athanasius preferred the term dianoia due to the objective connection with revelation it entailed as opposed to the more subjective elements of conceptual thinking in the literalistic Arian preconceptions. Even when it came to terms like agennetos, they sensed deep biblical support for its use and meaning. The point here is that some approximation of truth is possible for the human mind which takes in account the ineffability of the Godhead. They are heuristic terms in the sense we have used it. See Torrance, Theology in Reconstruction (Grand Rapids: Eerdmans, 1965), 46-52.

[33]De Decretis, 5.22 NPNF2 vol. 4, 165. See also De Synodis 34 Ibid., 469. Basil, Letter 189:3, NPNF2 vol. 8, 229. Letter 234, Ibid., 274.

[34]Here we are in agreement with Zizioulas, who echoes Stead, and Mackinnon on the Greeks and Aristotelian 'ousia.' It is fallacious to attribute strict adherence to 'prote' and 'deutera'. Through its connection with hypokeimenon, hypostasis took on a more concrete individual meaning while the former was referred to more often with more

is formed by the witness of Scripture and experience. The divine nature is active in its essential being, incorporating both change and constancy.[35] However in refuting Arians, like Aetius and Eunomius, the issue had to be handled in such a way that the substance of the Father and the Son could be almost seen as in contradistinction. "If we confess," Athanasius wrote, "that He is not a work but a genuine offspring (gennema) of the Father's essence, it would follow that He is inseparable from the Father, being connatural, because He is begotten from Him."[36] But note how he continues to argue for the absolute divinity of the Word, "Next, if the Son be not such from participation, but is in His essence the Father's Word and Wisdom, and this essence is the offspring of the Father's essence...how must we understand these words?"[37] The Arians also emphasized an absolute simplicity but from a different tack.[38] They opposed any distinction as an automatic denigration of divinity under the guise of an attempted protection of the self-sufficient Unbegotten Monad. Instead of static notions of ousia, the Cappadocian writers offer triadic discussions which are replete with inherent activity, movement which we shall see is based upon the idea of divine self-giving which only serves to intensify the concept of divine unity.

---

general or more inclusive categories. Being in Communion, 38 n.30. What we are tracing is the eventual identification of hypostasis with prosopon and its implications. B. Krivocheine, "Simplicité de la nature divine et les distinctions en Dieu selon S. Grégoire de Nysse," in Studia Patristica 16:2. ed. Elizabeth A. Livingstone, 389-399, (Berlin: Akademie-Verlag, 1985).

[35]D. Balas, "Christian Transformation of Greek Philosophy Illustrated by Gregory of Nyssa's Use of the Notion of Participation," in Scholasticism in the Modern World, ed. George McLean, 152-157, Proceedings of the American Catholic Philosophical Association. vol. 40, (Washington: American Catholic Philosophical Association, 1966).

[36]Athanasius, De Synodis 48 NPNF2 vol. 4, 475. Athanasius uses the term "offspring" often. Newman indicates this in a note on De Decretis 21, Ibid., 164. It apparently fell into disuse because of the Arian interpretations surrounding that theme. In referring to the Father as agennetos, or the Unoriginate, the term was not made to express more than God as Source. Though it did not suffer the same demise as other "conscripted" terms it did endure equal abuse at the hands of the Anomoeans. It was the implications of de-divinizing the Spirit in the Arian use of agennetos of the Father which spurred on the Cappadocian clarifications which became the strongest statements on the personal divinity of the Third Person in the history of the Church up to that point. See Gregory Nazianzus Oration 42:15 for use of anarchos, without beginning. But he also used Unoriginate. Wace clarifies usage in a helpful note, NPNF2 vol. 5, 100.

[37]Athanasius, De Synodis 48 NPNF2 vol. 4, 476. Emphasis mine.

[38]Plantinga is helpful here regarding Nyssa, who he considers, "the fullest and most technical of the Cappadocians," "Gregory of Nyssa and the Social Analogy of the Trinity," Thomist 50:3 (July, 1986): 328. He confronts the modern distortion of the Cappadocian idea of ousia and hypostasis. R.D Richardson, "The Doctrine of the Trinity: Its Development, Difficulties, and Value." Harvard Theological Review 36 (1943): 129, is an example of the thought-line of Baillie, Prestige and Kelly refuted by Plantinga. To "Augustinize" the Cappadocian social analogy is both an historical and a theological impropriety.

Foundational to theological reformulation, were the terminological distinctions of the Eastern Fathers. Ousia in the East had found counterparts, at times replacements, in the terms, hypostasis and huparxis.[39] Athanasius could write, "Subsistence, (hypostasis) and essence (ousia) is existence (huparxis): for it is, or in other words exists."[40] This fluidity between substance and subsistence caused consternation as it was applied to the trinitarian discussion. One reason the Latins were hesitant with the East was due to the dual use of hypostasis, (in Latin, substantia), and ousia.

It was the Cappadocians, following Athanasius' paradigm, who altered the use of the term ousia which came to mean more exclusively the essential nature of divine existence.[41] Tertullian had used substantia in the West but the East chose a term not fraught with as much misunderstanding. Both hypostasis and prosopon became the referents for the specific concrete nature, the hupokeimenon, of the divine persons.[42] This distinction of meaning found its first step in a different view of substance from either the Greek philosophers or from the heretics in Fourth century Christianity. Basil wrote, "The distinction between the ousia and hypostasis is the same as that between the general and the specific."[43]

---

[39]Hypostasis is a conjugate of the the verb, hupistanai; both terms carried the meaning of essential nature in Platonic sense and substantial nature in the phenomenological category.

[40]Ad Afros Epistola Synodica, 4. NPNF vol. 4, 490. The anathemas of the Nicene Symbol include the equation of hypostases and ousia, Denzinger, 53.

[41]See Gregory of Nazianzus on this, Fifth Theological Oration, 9 vol. 7, NPNF2, 320; Ibid., 32, p. 328.

[42]Hatch refers to a text which is now questioned as belonging to Athanasius, Dialogi de Sancta Trinitate, 2, "Ousia signifies community, hypostasis has property which is not common to the hypostases of the same ousia." Influence of Greek Ideas, 277. Quasten, Patrology, vol. 3, 31 attributes this work to Didymus, which still reflects Eastern usage. The terminological conflict East-West is well known. As ousia became more and more distinct from hypostasis, the Latin counterpart of substantia had to also be clarified. Eventually, substantia came to equal ousia and persona (whose etymology we have traced in relation to prosopa) was used as a counterpart to hypostasis. Nonetheless it took a long time for the East to stop accusing the West of Sabellianism and the West the East of tritheism. The Greek term phusis with its Latin counterpart natura had their own christological history, but in the main that did not affect the trinitarian distinctions in the way that others did.

[43]Letter 236, NPNF2 vol. 8, 278; Letter 214, NPNF2 vol. 8, 254.
Congar uses common (koinon) for general, in distinguishing for instance, the common class of animals or mammals from a particular person. I Believe in the Holy Spirit, vol. 3, 31. Harnack says,
> Ousia now received the middle sense between the abstract idea of 'being' and the concrete idea of 'individual being'; so, however, that it very strongly inclined to the the former. Hypostasis received the middle sense between person and attribute (accident, i.e. modality), in such a way, however, that the conception of person was the stronger.

This important difference is fundamental to the Cappadocian view of divine person, but it has not been unanimously recognized for its uniqueness. In his summation of the Cappadocian view of substance, Kelly echoes Prestige's comment by quoting him that, "The whole unvaried substance, being incomposite, is identical with the whole unvaried being of each Person...the individuality is only the manner in which the identical substance is objectively presented in each several Person."[44] The gaps in this prima facie reasoning reflects inattention to at least two major Cappadocian themes. The first is a fundamental misunderstanding of the strides the Eastern fathers made to critique and supercede inadequate Greek philosophical categories, especially the notion of substance. It reflects little of the dynamic love which was the Cappadocian approach to the divine nature. Second, is the negation of the realistic interpretation of Biblical language which might be referred to as "familial" and the relational analogies which each thinker in question most definitely employed. Substance, for the Cappadocian mind, was more than an "objective presentation."

The Cappadocians are not merely philosophizing. They are adamant on substantial equality and the incomposite nature of the divine persons but are careful not to imply that the divine substance is absolutely identical in the Persons, which would be to deny the Trinity outright. Divine ousia was painstakingly distinguished, in terms of a transcendent class, different from other substances.[45] The Cappadocian separation of essence and energies is based upon this premise. But more, this divine genus is not interpreted as a "single concrete entity" capable of various presentations.[46]

There are passages which do emphasize a view of divine substance as inaccessible. "Monad and Unity...signify the nature which is simple and incomprehensible."[47] The

---

Prosopon, since it sounded Sabellian-like, was avoided but not rejected. Outlines of the History of Dogma, 260

[44]Kelly, Early Christian Doctrines, 266. See Prestige's God in Patristic Thought, 244, and 169, 300-301, where it is clear that "objects of presentation" is the best way to interpret trinitarian language.

[45]Gregory of Nazianzus, Oration 38:7-9 NPNF2 vol. 7, 346-347. PG 36, 318-322. Zizioulas points to Gregory as the source of this distinction which, he says, culminated in Maximus the Confessor. Being in Communion, 91 n.75. Stead points to the costly usage of genus for God in these thinkers to emphasize the unique class they discerned when discussing divinity. Divine Substance, 164.

[46]Stead defies Prestige's conclusions and shows the un-Aristotelian (at least as his interpreters have conveyed him) way in which Athanasius uses ousia. Whatever his ambiguities may be there is not a hint of modalism in him. "The Significance of the "Homoousios"." In Studia Patristica 3:1. ed. F. L. Cross (Berlin: Akademie-Verlag, 1961), 402, 408-411.

[47]Basil, Letter 8, NPNF2 vol. 8, 116.

plethora of negative terms, "ineffable," "simplicity," and "uncircumscribable" among others, are a result of the Cappadocian epistemology.[48] Athanasius, in his defense against the Arians wrote:

> There is one Beginning and therefore one God, so one is that Essence and Subsistence which indeed and truly and really is, and which said 'I am that I am,'....For were He not essential, God will be speaking into the air, and having a body, in nothing differently from men; but since he is not man, neither is His Word according to the infirmity of man. For as the Beginning is one essence, so Its Word is one, essential, and subsisting, and Its Wisdom.[49]

And John of Damascus would begin his exposition on The Orthodox Faith with a representative statement of this Eastern epistemology,

> The Divinity, then, is limitless and incomprehensible, and thus His limitlessness and incomprehensibility is all that can be understood about Him. All that we state affirmatively about God does not show His nature, but only what relates to His nature.[50]

A commitment to the absolute otherness of God does not necessitate that anything positive or of logical content cannot be said, especially if that transcendent Being is desirous to communicate an understanding of the ineffable. The Word, as the exact Image of the Father, perfectly expressed all that the human mind was created to receive.

Athanasius, at once, both leads the Cappadocians and paves the way for them theologically on this score. It is through the Spirit who is in the Son and thereby in the Father that divine illumination in the heart and mind is made possible. This mutual indwelling is the basis for Eastern epistemology although the Cappadocians do not seem to expand on the insight of Athanasius as they did at other points.[51]

B. Divine Persons as Relations: Substantial or Subsistent?

---

[48]Examples abound in each of the Cappadocians. Tied to our discussion of incircumscribability in God, we include: Basil, Letter 8, NPNF2 vol. 8, 116 and Gregory of Nyssa Answer to Eunomius' Second Book, NPNF2 vol. 5, 309.

[49]Against the Arians, Discourse IV 1, NPNF2 vol. 4, 433.

[50]John of Damascus, Exposition of the Orthodox Faith NPNF2 vol. 9, 4. Trans. from FC edition, Writings, trans. Frederic Chase, vol. 37, 1958, 172. He concludes his On Heresies, with a series of statements that sum up the Eastern view of Unity and Trinity discerned by the human mind. He also uses the "questionable" analogies of sun, ray, heat in his discussion of conceiving God's reality, then he adds, "The Holy Trinity transcends by far every similitude and figure," but then states, "For the concept of the Creator is arrived at by analogy from His creatures." FC, 162-163.

[51]Torrance writes concerning Athanasius' concept of,
"The mutual relation of the Son and the Father as constituting the epistemic ground for all our knowledge of God, for that mutual relation included the relation of the Spirit to the Son and to the Father and therefore the inseparable place of the Spirit in the triune God."
Theology in Reconciliation, 232.

In order to see the uniqueness of the Cappadocian view of person the theological context must be clear. Between Nicea and Constantinple II (AD 553) the East was forced by a variety of factors, mainly heretical, to tighten the usage of hypostasis and prosopon in both trinitology and christology.[52] The former had been used in Aristotelian and in Neoplatonic paradigms but never carried the individuated characteristics that it came to possess in the Cappadocians.[53] Against that Greek and Alexandrian background it would take several councils and myriad opinions to come to a consensus on a definition for person. What was clear to the Cappadocians was that a fundamental distinction had to be made between the divine nature and the prosopa. But that distinction was only for clarification and not the positing of an ontological chasm between ousia and prosopon. The question here pertains to both definition and application. Did either hypostasis or prosopon ever reach a level tantamount to the subjective understanding of person in modernity or did it remain merely a "verbal and descriptive" distinction until Boethius' deliberations?[54]

On the one hand, the Eastern thinkers follow Origen in an area crucial to our concern. The primary focus is the perfections of God based on biblical data, not an absolutism that is philosophical.[55] This set a different trajectory for theology. It allows a conception of God which is interactive with creation. That relationality had to be based in a God who was discontinuous from His creation, requiring a prior relational being which finds evidence in the Cappadocians. In contrasting Augustine with the Greeks fathers, Chevalier says that the Cappadocian idea of relation "se présente sous une forme plus

---

[52]There had been attempts at the issue of person in other parts of the East. A survey of Syriac theologians on the person of the Spirit is somewhat revealing. Cramer shows how it is more than translation technicalities but a tendency to personify pneuma in Mt. 27:50, "His Spirit rose on high." Der Geist Gottes und des Menschen in frühsyrischer Theologie in Münsterische Beiträge zur Theologie, vol. 46 (Aschendorff: Münster, 1979), 19. He says that the tendency to make an independent being of the Spirit of Holiness carried distinct notions of personal character. Ibid., 21. Aphrahat's contribution is not conclusive and Cramer feels it is ill-advised to push the personality issue too far in Syriac theologians. Ibid., 67. Other scholars feel that the tables should be turned. H. B. Swete notes that "the only Catholic writer of the first four centuries who is charged with it (rejecting the personal character of the Holy Spirit) is Lactantius," the lay theologian whose theology smacked of deism. The Holy Spirit in the Ancient Church (London: Macmillan, 1912), 374.

[53]Gregory of Nyssa, Great Cathechism 1 NPNF2 vol. 5, 475-476. John Meyendorff, says that the "agency" and possession of a nature that admits a "unique subject" who acts, was definitely a theme not found in Greek philosophy. Byzantine Theology: Historical Trends and Doctrinal Themes (New York: Fordham Univ. Press, 1974), 182.

[54]R.T. Sears, "Spirit: Divine and Human," 12.

[55]Missing this point has caused many to disparage the Cappadocians as being as impersonal in their theology as the West. L. Bouyer, Le Consolateur: Esprit-Saint et la vie de grace (Paris: Les Éditions du Cerf, 1980), 306-307, says only Nyssa was immune from an impersonal Trinity.

réaliste, plus vitale. Il importe de souligner que la skesis (relation) n'est pas envisagée d'un point de vue statique, comme principe constitutif de l'hypostase divine."[56]

On the other hand, the differences from Origenism pertain to the Cappadocian rejection of the impersonal implications of Greek philosophical ontology. That relational divinity is discerned primarily by the revelation of the Eternal Son as the "prosopon" of the Father.[57] It is the incarnate Person who most often is referred to as either possessing or is being identified as a prosopon. The anathemas of Nicea had temporarily precluded the use of hypostasis for the Three so Athanasius took both biblical terms and prosopon as his mainstays.[58] What remained to be done was the separation of the actual identity of the co-eternal Son from latent residual implications of 'logos endiathetos' and 'logos prophorikos' in Origenism, where the "role" motif for prosopon could not be logically altered to coincide with the deepening desire for the attribution of full personhood to the Logos.[59] In this sense, Greek philosophy was inadequate to interpret the hypostatic union of the Son or the inner life of the Trinity. What was required was a relational approach which incorporated both ousia and hypostasis.

Basil had reservations on the use of prosopon, in large part due to his battle against the modalistic inducements of Sabellianism.[60] He agreed to its use as long as it did

---

[56]This has been noted as a major development in the contra-Eunomian battle of Nazianzen. It is a view of substance as relational. Skesis, carries the idea of essential constitution or relational nature. Nazianzus, Third Theological Oration 16, NPNF2 vol. 7, 307. Chevalier, Augustin et la pensée grecque, 169. We agree in part with this analysis as shall be seen in part two of this chapter.

[57]Clement of Alexandria, The Instructor 1.7 ANF vol. 2, 223. Gregory of Nyssa most likely or Basil Letter 38:8 NPNF2 vol. 8, 141.

[58]Denzinger, 53. Hypostasis and ousia are identified in the first anathema.

[59]Athanasius and Basil are vigilant Niceans. See Basil, Letter 125 NPNF2 vol. 8, 194-196. Lynch notes the need for this in comparing the "immature" concepts in Theophilus in the 2nd century with Athanasius in the fourth. "Prosopon and the Dogma of the Trinity," 68. He notes that due to the successive terminological clarifications and political intrigue of the Synods of Antioch (AD 345), Sirmium (AD 351)) and Alexandria (AD 362), Athanasius preferred "one hypostasis in God," and the Cappadocians chose three hypostaseis. Ibid., 276. Athanasius uses treis hypostasis as early as 10 years after Nicea in Statement of Faith 2 NPNF2 vol. 4, 84 and In Illud Omnia 6 Ibid., 90. Ziziuolas maintains it was Maximus the Confessor who put the finishing touches on this reconciliation of Judaic, Christian and Greek phlosophy and ontology, with concomitant rejection of incongruencies. Being in Communion, 92-98. See Bourassa, "Théologie trinitaire chez saint Augustin." Gregorianum 58 (1977): 692, for a list of other early usage of hypostaseis in the Church.

[60]Letter 189:2 NPNF2 vol. 8, 228. Prestige, God in Patristic Thought, 113, defines Sabellianism as the denial of full individuality but confessed a distinct type of deity in the Son.

not serve as a synonym for **hypostasis**.[61] He definitely had a desire to clarify the person of the Son where he wrote:

> Sabellianism is Judaism imported into the preaching of the Gospel under the guise of Christianity. For if a man calls Father, Son and Holy Ghost one thing of many faces (or many names) and makes the **hypostasis** of the three one, what is this but to deny the everlasting pre-existence of the Only begotten?[62]

It is too early in the progression of doctrine to find a clear conception, a **definitio** or the limits and boundaries, of the person or of selfhood in the Son, but both Athanasius and Basil lay the groundwork for its eventual debut. It was Basil who first labored on the personal properties of the **hypostaseis**.[63] The careful distinction between the essence of God and the **hypostaseis** bore a radically different approach to theology. Each **hypostasis** possessed identifiable **idiotetes**, **idiomata**, or distinguishing characteristics, and was seen as a unique subject whose absolute identity could not be duplicated.[64] The Cappadocians foresaw the intrinsic possibilities of tritheism in this discussion as is seen in Gregory of

---

[61]Letter, 214:3-4 NPNF2 vol. 8, 254. He argues here that ousia is common to the Triad while hypostasis pertains to particular "special properties." Those who contend that the Persons are "without hypostasis" (anupostata) are absurd and destructive to the Triune reality. See here also the disputed letter, attributed to Ps. Basil or to Nyssa by some, Letter, 38:2 Ibid., 137. Lynch, "Prosopon and the Dogma of the Trinity," 119, 250, 275.

[62]Letter 210:3 NPNF2 vol. 8, 249. For his discussion of the Spirit see a surprisingly short excursus in On the Holy Spirit 18:45 Ibid., 28; Letter 52 Ibid., 156.

[63]Grillmeier ties the distinctions to follow in Basil and especially in Letter 38, with Stoic distinctions between ousia ule or undetermined matter and hupokeimenon which admits characterization. Ps. Basil's (?) use of koinon and idion as the distinguishing factors in the "community of substance", that were to find more common expression as "community" and "person" (hypostasis and prosopa) or "individuating characteristics" does bear Stoic outlines. I find the comparison correct, while I disagree with the author's overweening economic assessment. Grillmeier, Christ in Christian Tradition, 372-373. William Thompson in his, The Jesus Debate says, "Hypostasis was a quite original way in which the Cappadocian broke through to the personal and dialogical view of the Divine characteristic of the New Testament," 308.

[64]Noting again the questioned authorship of that crucial interpretation of unmistakeable Cappadocian elements, Letter 38 NPNF2 vol. 8, 137-141, (in 38:5 they are rendered, gnoristike idiotetes) it is clear that the author, probably Gregory of Nyssa, was fully aware of the "peculiarities" and the "particulars", or "signs of indication," that serve as the "under-standing" (hypostasis) of that which has no discernible "standing" of its own. Nazianzus, Oration 42:16 NPNF2 vol. 7, 391; Oration 43:30 Ibid., 405. Oration 21:35 Ibid., 279. The idiotetes circumscribe the Godhead. The author goes on to list what those "special marks" are which of course revolve around Ungenerateness, (agennesia), Begottenness, (gennesis), and Procession (ekpempsis or ekporeusis). Due to origin language, the term hyparxis was used, or "mode of existence. The Trinity as source of life and existence was revealed in three possessors or instances of that life, tropos hyparxeos. What is important to note is the relational language which accompanies the distinctions. He speaks of "intercommunion," "mutual harmony", "concrete relations," as foundational to the idiomatum of the persons. We shall see this distinction again in the Latin theologians as notiones, proprietas, and relationes.

Nyssa's On "Not Three Gods". Based upon the relational view of indivisible nature of Theos the tropos hyparxeos, or "modes of existence" do not admit numerical interpretation, as detractors scoffed using Peter, James and John as hypostaseis of human essence.[65] In defense of the inseparable Trinity the response was two-fold. First, as a result of the essence-energies paradigm the Cappadocians proffered a distinction between God in his essence and the Godhead in opera ad extra. The Theotes or Godhead is "not significant of nature but of operation."[66] Although this viewpoint is vulnerable to being interpreted as advocating a God beyond God, that is not the intention of the paradigm.[67] It is a reflection of the solid conception of divine discontinuity with creation and the contemplative theoria so often missing in scholastic theologies.[68] Second, the perception of the divine nature as an interpersonal communion which pervades the Cappadocian view of the divine nature has to be completely overturned to intimate they espoused tritheism. As a bottom line Gregory of Nazianzus would say, "It is better to take a meagre view of the Unity than to venture on a complete impiety," meaning a conception which overemphasized threeness over oneness.[69] Gregory of Nyssa used a community notion to describe the union of the Three, while Nazianzus discussed the consubstantial nature using the familial analogy of Adam, Eve and Seth.[70] For both Gregory's three prosopa do not make three Gods. "God" is seen as a communal ousia, and the "manners of presentation" of that divine nature carry strong personal indications expressing the Being-in-love.[71] They were aware of the weaknesses of human analogies and approached the language circumspectly. To repeat, the

---

[65]Gregory of Nyssa, On "Not Three Gods" NPNF vol. 5, 331.

[66]Gregory of Nyssa, On "Not Three Gods" NPNF vol. 5, 334.

[67]The Pseudo-Dionysian strain however did evolve in this sort of apophatic transcendentalism, in the form of John Scotus Erigena, Meister Eckhart, and even in Paul Tillich.

[68]Torrance feels this is the magisterial Cappadocians' major downfall, taking Athanasius' approach as far clearer a representation of the divine-human encounter, Theology in Reconciliation, 217-219. His appreciation for these same thinkers is evident here and in Theology in Reconstruction, 30-45, 260-263.

[69]Fifth Theological Oration, On the Holy Spirit, 12 NPNF2 vol. 7, 322.

[70]Gregory of Nyssa, On the Holy Trinity NPNF2 vol. 5, 327; Gregory of Nazianzus On the Holy Spirit NPNF2 vol. 7, 321. J. P. Mackey says that Gregory was the one who abused language, see "The Holy Spirit: Relativizing the Divergent Approaches of East and West," Irish Theological Quarterly 48:3/4 (1981): 256-267.

[71]Lynch feels that the prosopa of the Son is used abstractly and statically. The Son is a "totally adequate presentation of the Father," in such a way that He is "not how...God reveals himself in space and time...but how the knowledge of the 'hypostasis' of the Father occurs." "Prosopon and the Dogma of the Trinity," 69-70, 119.

Cappadocian advance over Greek philosophy and even Athanasius' thought was the distinction of the **ousia** from its **hypostaseis**.

Gregory of Nazianas used **prosopon** as a revelatory mode and as an equivalent term for **hypostasis**, which was used ubiquitously in the East.[72] His conflicts with Apollinarianism forced him to clarify his understanding of the person of Jesus, while the battle against the Arians in Constantinople resulted in **prosopa** being used for the Trinity. Gregory's importance lies in the historical progression of meaning in the usage of **prosopa** to refer to the "One Nature in Three Personalities (**proprietatibus**), intellectual, perfect, Self-existent, numerically separate but not separate in Godhead."[73] The addition of these adjectives was to distinguish the use of **prosopa** from the Arian subordinationism and Sabellian distortions of "modal" implications.[74] Its usage as real objective differentiations with **idiotetes** in the context of the Unity of God effectively negated the use of **prosopon** in any one-dimensional histrionic capacity. The philosophical background of **hypostasis** ("support" or "that which underlies"), made for a reticent transition from the self-evidently more apprehendable **prosopon**. Though every **prosopa** in a theological or anthropological

---

[72]Oration 21:35 NPNF2 vol. 7, 279. Gregory reveals this in a tongue-in-cheek ecumenism as he pummels the heretics where he says, "What is the meaning of the Hypostases of the one party, of the Persons of the other, to ask this further question? That They are three, Who are distinguished not by natures, but by properties. Excellent." Oration 42:16 NPNF2 vol. 7, 391.

[73]Oration 33:16 NPNF2 vol. 7, 334; PG, 36, 229D-232A. Oration 39:11 Ibid., 355. Lynch discusses the documentary investigation of the historical disagreement concerning Constantinople from the release of Meletius in 379 to the Council of 381. "Prosopon and the Dogma of the Trinity," 98, 274. It is quite clear that Gregory of Nyssa's writing had great influence on Constantinople I but it is not until Constantinople II (AD 553) that we find "a consubstantial Triad, one Godhead in three hypostaseis or prosopa." Bettenson, Documents of the Christian Church, 91. We focus on Gregory here but it is true that the impact of all the Cappadocians was felt in this general council. Amphilochius of Iconium, relative of Nazianzus, used prosopa with a recurring impersonal hint as "form of presentation," according to Lynch, Ibid., 119-120, 152. Remembering that he wrote in a pre-Macedonian era, Cyril of Jerusalem's cathechetical lectures include prosopon as revelatory mode (Lecture 10:7 NPNF2 vol. 7, 59). One would question the conclusion of reservation of personhood of the Spirit in this cathechesis advanced by some. See Documents in Early Church Thought eds. M. Wiles and Mark Santer (Cambridge: Cambridge Univ. Press, 1975), 76. Contrast that with Cyril's Lectures 17:5 NPNF2 vol. 7, 125, 16:3 Ibid., 115.

[74]It was the synodical and conciliar efforts surrounding Constantinople I which possibly for the first time brought the christological usage of the term as "personal subject" into the ecumenical sphere while concomitantly broadening the meaning of prosopon to indicate three persons in relation, who are self-determinative in inseparable union. Lynch deftly incorporates the synodical data succeeding Constantinople I and posits the existence of a now non-extant writing the year before, which may have formed the basis for the Council's reaffirmation of Nicea in a letter of AD 382 (for text see NPNF2 vol. 14, 189) while also expressing the use of prosopon as we have noted here. "Prosopon and the Dogma of the Trinity," 88, 274, 382. Its ecumenical status is questioned due to the absence of a Western contingency. Later Cappadocian usage forces Lynch to define both prosopon and hypostasis as "permanent and objective modes."

sense is a hypostasis, not every hypostasis is a person by strict definition.[75]   Eastern thinkers have attempted to correct the economic interpretation that has often distorted the original intent of hypostasis.[76]   Accentuating the oneness of God and the Biblical terms, "begotten" and "proceeding" served to conjoin the paradoxical notions of homoousion and derivation together. This properly began the refutation of the Anomeans, Homoeans, Arianism and Apollinarian modalism. The eventual reference to the 'Subsistents', huparxis, and the ousia possessing treis hypostasis as self-identifying personal realities was related to other developments, one of them being the Eastern view of divine relations.

Of course, there have been those who feel that the Cappadocians did not intend a relational view of the Persons in any full sense.[77] These reservations provoke the question, are the Persons only relatively distinct in Cappadocian thought? From monarchian, unity and derivative elements the Cappadocians proffered a unique view of divine relations. It is here that the intricacies of divine personhood were worked out. Nicea had left many aspects of the unity of God unattended. Athanasius would attribute divine function to each of the Persons. Their activity was not exercised in individual isolation as indicated by the external operation being presented as undivided energeia.[78] These were articulated by a number of "properties", the distinguishing relations that are characteristic of each person of the Trinity.

The tying together of substance and person is informed for the most part by the Cappadocians' use of relational analogies which are complementary to the West's Aristotelian-based, and subsequently Thomistic, categories to which we have referred. De

---

[75]J. Burnaby makes this point and states that "The Latin persona on the other hand, is more specific in meaning than hypostasis, and in ordinary use is only applicable to human beings." The Belief of Christendom: A Commentary on the Nicene Creed (London: SPCK, 1959), 202.

[76]On personality, F.W. Green is more than a bit confusing, though he does say that the Cappadocians "were the first to develop such an idea as a possibility," even though they revealed no "serious interest in personality. And yet they came very near it," in Rawlinson's Essays on the Trinity, 289.   He points to the activity of God as the basis of their thought. Dorothea Wendebourg has missed the fundamentals of Cappadocian thought in her critique of Palamite theology, by her over- emphasis on economic trinitarianism. See "From the Cappadocian Fathers to Gregory Palamas: The Defeat of Trinitarian Theology." In Studia Patristica 17:1. ed. Elizabeth A. Livingstone, 194-198. Oxford: Pergamon Press Ltd., 1982. Anastos critiques her interpretation of Palamas also, "Essence, Energies, and Hypostasis," 240-241.

[77]We list briefly; Welch, Prestige, Kelly, Wiles, and Grillmeier.

[78] Ad Serapion, 1:28; Prestige, God in Patristic Thought, 258.

Margerie refers to them as "familial intersubjectivity" or "family" analogies.[79] Augustine was to proffer an analogy of this sort as early as Bk. 8 of his De Trinitate but then would return to the relative safety of the so-called "psychological" analogies until his closing arguments in Bk. 15.[80] It is intriguing how unabashed the Cappadocians are in presenting an analogy which they knew would be attacked by their opponents. It gives the impression that they desired to use it for more than polemic reasons.

Against a Sabellian backdrop, the relational models of the Cappadocians must be assessed as carrying strong apologetic as well as constructive content. Their trinitarian analogies of family, military hierarchy, and others are well beyond a mere "manner of appearance"; rather they are centered on the social relationships inherent in them. Though divine unity is never compromised intentionally the understanding of that unity is tied to its basis, intra-trinitarian love. John Lynch has provided strong evidence that along with differentiated existents, prosopon, by implication included a "note of rationality," a form of consciousness, in that each trinitarian person was seen as a distinct actor and willer.[81] This follows the emphasis in christological questions. Zizioulas points out that person, not natures was the primary interest of Cyril of Alexandria.[82] When applied to trinitology the same emphasis appears.

---

[79]See Trinity in History, 274ff. De Margerie uses Augustine as an example of "personal intrasubjectivity" which I feel is closer to the overall picture of Augustine, see below. He would add the categories also of "ecclesial intersubjectivity" and the analogy of Spirit as bond or mutual love. Ibid., 292.

[80]See Hibbert's contention that love and the metaphysical understanding of its inherent reflexivity was foundational to both Augustine and Aquinas. "Mystery and Metaphysics," p. 199 n.36.

[81]Cf. On "Not Three Gods", NPNF vol. 5, 333-334. John J. Lynch, "'Prosopon' in Gregory of Nyssa: A Theological Word in Transition," Theological Studies 40:4 (1979): 728-738.

[82]Zizioulas, Being in Communion, 109 n.107. This we interpret to apply in various forms of progression to the other magisterial Cappadocians. Cyril uses hypostasis primarily in christological context as the trinitarian usage had been sufficiently outlined at Antioch (AD 379) and Constantinople (AD 381 and 382). When Theodore of Mopsuestia uses of hypostasis as referent to nature, it "has" a prosopon. When used for distinct Person, hypostasis equals prosopon. Lynch notes that he did not enjoy the mature reflection which was to follow, nonetheless, he laid groundwork for his successors through his own pilgrimage of thought. This is especially true on the relationship of hypostasis and prosopon, which was finalized only after considerable christological reflection in later periods. "Prosopon and the Dogma of the Trinity," 111, 117. Leonard Hogdson has shown that Nestorius' metaphysics precluded a full understanding of prosopon in, "The Metaphysics of Nestorius." Journal of Theological Studies 19:1 (1918): 46-55. Roberta Chestnut, "The Two Prosopa in Nestorius." Journal of Theological Studies n.s. 29 (1978): 392-409, reveals the anachronistic tendency of much modern theology in her rendition of the volitional and agency-oriented definitions of prosopon in Nestorius. She says "we live in a world of 'will' more than in a world of 'hypostases'. Ibid., 409.

Aware of the Aristotelian categories at work despite the absence of fine distinction, it would be safe to summarize the use of **hypostasis** and **prosopon** as "entities" adequate to and undiscernible apart from communion. Athanasius and the Cappadocians did not stop with the substantival relation of the Son to the Father.[83] The ecumenical consensus entailed in the formulation "three consubstantial subsistences in one single divine nature" led to further deliberations as to the distinctions within the Triunity pertaining to 'relation'.[84] Originally a Dionysian construct, the connection between person and relation came through the Cappadocians and subsequently by way of Augustine, the concept was solidified at the Second Constantinopolitan Conference (AD 553).[85] There is a paradigmatic shift away from the aegis of Aristotelian distinctions. The Cappadocian input allows agreement with Mascall's view of divine personhood as "three subjects of a concrete triadic relation by which God exists as supreme reality in trinitarian being."[86] Gregory of Nazianzus is the clearest of the three as to the divinity and consubstantiality of the Spirit.[87] His stance is based however in the reclamation of **ousia** from Arian distortion. It was he who argued that the divine essence need not be seen as denigrated by the presence of a begotten hypostasis or a proceeding one. Nyssa's ineffable essence was differentiated by the inner relations of the Trinity.[88] Nazianzus stressed the incorporeality of the Son's generation in that begottenness was an absolute rather than a relative term.[89] It was the divine unity

---

[83]Tertullian was the first to make this substantival derivation clear. Ad Praxean 7, ANF vol. 3, 602.

[84]Constantinople II (553). Literally, "Father, Son and Holy Spirit, are one nature (physis) or essence (ousia), one might and power, a Trinity one in being (hoomousios), one Godhead to be worshipped in three hypostases (hypostaseis) or persons (prosopon). Neuner and Dupuis, 152; Denzinger, 421, p.145.

[85]We refer here of course to Dionysius of Alexandria. The fifth ecumenical council documents pertained to christological issues primarily but the matter-of-fact attitude concerning the consubstantiality of the Three shows the impact of orthodox thought. Denzinger, 145.

[86]Mascall, The Triune God, 79.

[87]Oration 39:12 NPNF2 vol. 7, 356. Fifth Theological Oration 26-27 Ibid., 326. Oration 12:1, 6 Ibid., 245, 247. George Kretschmar feels that the monastic movement of the 4th century rejected polytheism and therefore settled for the impersonal "gift" (Gabe) motif over the person. Studien zur frühchristlichen Trinitätstheologie in Beiträge zur historischen Theologie vol. 21 (Tübingen: J.C.B. Mohr, 1956), 15. Note however Niceta of Remesiana, "We know that the Spirit is a Person in the proper and true sense of the word." The Power of the Holy Spirit FC vol. 7, 28. Mary Clark says of Gregory that he is first to shed light on the intimate life of God. Augustinian Personalism, 36 n.2.

[88]Gregory of Nyssa, Answer to Eunomius' Second Book NPNF2 vol. 5, 253, 298-302, 306.

[89]Gregory of Nazianzus, Third Theological Oration 4 NPNF2 vol. 7, 302.

which possessed both relativeness in the intercommunication of co-equal prosopa and concomitantly, absolute quality. The relationships of origin, Unbegotten, Begotten, and Procession, are how Gregory saw the idiotetes expressed within the divine unity.[90] The distinctive character of each prosopon is viewed as incommunicable to the others.[91]

> A prosopon is an entity, identifiable both as a participant in an ousia (God; man) and as an individual (the Father; Paul) separate from others (the Son and the Spirit; Peter, Barnabas, and all other human beings) which shares the same ousia but not the same differentiating qualities.[92]

The shift from the equation of 'God' as ousia is a subtle but devastating move if not presupposed as admitting the Three as God.[93] Any other approach leaves one with quaternarian or tritheistic quandries.[94] Nonetheless, the properties are mutual relationships which, Congar argues, never makes the step to subsistent relationships.[95] It is correct that Nazianzus never advocated a "mob of gods" but neither did he court a "poverty-stricken" view of God.[96] The issue becomes confused if one remains with the majority report on persons as relations. The clarity and the forthrightness of the Cappadocians, especially Gregory of Nazianzus, must face a bias that circumvents repeated connotations to maintain

---

[90]Cf. Basil Letters 189:7 NPNF2 vol. 8, 231 and De Spiritu Sancto 17:43-18:44 Ibid., 27-28. John of Damascus, De Fide Orthodoxa, 8 NPNF2 vol. 9, 6-11. Congar notes that Gregory of Nazianzus recognized the inflexibility of the Latin language distorted clear comprehension. Greek allows a breadth and a precision not commonplace in Latin. I Believe in the Holy Spirit, vol. 3, 87-88. K. Holl has critiqued Nazianzus for imprecise use of idiotetes but C. Stead counters rightly that if that sort of precision is required of all ancients then little could be said of any. "Individual Personality in Origen and the Cappadocian Fathers," in Substance and Illusion in the Christian Fathers (London: Variorum Reprints, 1985), art. 13, 181.

[91]Gregory of Nazianzus is said to be the first to use "relatio" to refer to the intercommunication of the hypostatseis. An abbreviated list includes, Orations 20:7, 25:16, 26:19, 29:16, 31:7, 34:14, 41:9.

[92]Lynch, "Prosopon in Gregory of Nyssa," 737. Lynch recognizes that some of the evidence for this assessment of prosopon as atomon, (cf. Ad Graecos, PG 45, 179, he uses prosopon 31 times in first three paragraphs) or individual is tied to the anti-Sabellian apologetic of Ad Graecos or Ex Communibus Notionibus PG 45 176-185; Gregorii Nysseni Opera Dogmatica Minora, Part 1, ed. Frederich Mueller, 19-33 (Leiden: E.J. Brill, 1958). Gregory does not attempt any defenses againts tri-theistic interpretation there as that was not the issue.

[93]Ad Graecos PG 176, Opera Dogmatica Minora, 19.

[94]Gregory repeats this for emphasis in an extended sentence for effect as well as polemic. The orthdox are careful to distinguish ousia from prosopon, "all' hosper ousia ho pater, ousia ho huius, ousia to hagion pneuma kai ou treis ousiai." Ad Graecos PG 177, Opera Dogmatica Minora, 20.

[95]Congar, I Believer in the Holy Spirit, vol. 3, 92 n.13.

[96]Gregory of Nazianzus, Oration 39:7 NPNF2 vol. 7, 347

this flat definition.[97]   Take, for instance, the anti-Arian statement of Nazianzus that the divine names indicate a differentiation within the substance, a "relationship (scheseos) in which the Father stands to the Son, and the Son to the Father. For as with us, these names make known a genuine and intimate relation."[98]   Lossky would add, "the relations only serve to express the hypostatic diversity of the Three; they are not the basis of it. It is the absolute diversity of the three hypostases which determines their differing relations to each other."[99]   More often than not, it is not a foregone conclusion that Gregory determines a relative being without meaning that the hypostaseis themselves are relational beings. If we accept the "person as relation" schema without discernment we are very close to requiring that the prosopa are accidental to divine essence.[100]   This latter option begs the question as to why a nature would admit a personhood at all. In its defense, would the category of relation be reason enough? That apologia alone does injustice to what we have seen regarding hypostasis. Instead, the distinctions are made to emphasize incommunicability of characteristics, to preclude any chance of identity with the substance.

Prosopon, we have seen, withstood repeated attacks that it was a deficient trinitarian term in its reflection of internal qualities, i.e., rationality and consciousness. Hypostasis helped to further delineate the person from more of a substantial perspective. Due to the philosophical undergirding of the latter, it was imperative that the Cappadocians place it in the context of relation, an ontic explanation which deepens philosophical analysis. It would not be till Chalcedon that the distinctions between prosopon and hypostasis would be ratified, but it is clear that the egocentricity latent in psychological aspects of prosopon is not present in the self-transcending elements of hypostasis.[101]   The problem for hypostasis was that its background offered no fundamental connection with personhood. Its qualified usage drew upon the surplus elements of "support," or "self-supported presentation," but there also was an element of identity which

---

[97]Welch chooses only the narrow view of tropoi, in Trinity in Christian Tradition, 190. Sears points out that tropos actually carries the meaning of "turning" so that the hypiostaseis are presented as turning from self and "resting in another." "Spirit: Divine and Human," 298. Plantinga, "Gregory of Nyssa and the Social Analogy of the Trinity," 329-330.

[98]Third Theological Oration 16 NPNF2 vol. 7, 307; PG 96A.

[99]Lossky, In the Image and Likeness of God, 79. Cf. Gregory of Nazianzus, Orations 31:14 NPNF2 vol. 7, 322; PG 148D-149A.

[100]It will be apparent here that I am indebted to Jean Galot, Who is Christ? (Chicago: Franciscan Herald Press, 1981), 279-300. His ubiquitous category of "hypostatic relation" may be a proper correction, (as Mascall has seen also in his The Divine Trinity), to person as "substantial relation". He argues cogently for a distinction of person from nature, hypostasis from ousia.

[101]Paul Evdokimov, "Mystère de la Personne Humaine." Contacts 21 (1969): 284-285.

saved divine Being from Sabellian modalism.[102] Nature is the content of the person, rather than a mere presentation of it. That substantial content includes a strong sense of origination or derivation, and is ontic in orientation. The perspective throughout the Cappadocian period is best understood as "being-for-another."

In sum, the Cappadocians baptized the term prosopon and secured its place in Christian deliberation and thought until today. Fearing persona as making too great a distinction, and prosopon as possibly saying too little, hypostasis was more often than not the preferred choice of the Cappadocians. It was however, based on a different metaphysic than its Greek philosophical origin. Divine Persons are, in the Cappadocian framework, not just relations, but equally substantial subsistents.[103]

Further definition will be required to offset anthropomorphic excesses but nonetheless the essential elements are laid for a personal distinctiveness which closely approximates person as relational subject. It never garnered a rigid definition, as most theological terms do not. We have seen that context, intent and at points outright statements indicate more of a sense of personal qualities to the "modes" than most modern scholarship is willing to credit to the Eastern fathers.[104] In a crucial period in the pilgrimage of the term, person and its attendant implications, the hypostaseis are discerned as standing outside of oneself, circumscribed but not in any diminutive way from the essence, in a logical and personal "ekstasis" from the substance.[105] One is not left with a

---

[102]Here we would disagree with G.L. Prestige Fathers and Heretics (London: SPCK, 1940), 93, that the difference between prosopon (which is a mere "embodiment" or "presentation") and the ousia is one "not of content but of manner." See Lynch's critique of Seller's, "Prosopon and the Dogma of the Trinity," 274.

[103]R. Swinburne, in an apparent shift from other statements, recognizes the Cappadocian element, though not acknowledged, of the divinity of the Persons who "form" the substance we call "Deus,". "Could there be more than One God?" Faith and Philosophy 5:3 (July, 1988): 240 n.19. Plantinga says of Nyssa, "Surely Gregory did not see Father, Son and Spirit as separate or autonomous persons along the lines of Cartesian individualism....But neither, on the other side can Gregory be charged (with obfuscating) his theory with perichoretic, modalist, and simplicity concepts as to render it paradoxical along the lines suggested by Baillie and Prestige." "Gregory of Nyssa and the Social Analogy of the Trinity," 352.

[104]It is a credit to the scholarship of John Lynch, although he follows the majority line of "modes of revelation", that he allows the flexibility of the term's usage from the Hellenistic era through to Cyril of Alexandria and Theodore of Mopsuestia to qualify his conclusions. He acknowledges where other scholars do not, the inexplicable passages which indicate a strong selfhood in the Persons. "Prosopon and the Dogma of the Trinity," 121.

[105]Daniélou, "La Personne chez les Pères Grecs," speaks of the determination of the person as a key factor in the fourth century response to the impasse of holding the "Boundless" together with individual concrete subsistents. The Eastern approach to infinite personal reality, he calls "l'évolution actuelle du concept de la personne, avoir une importance très grande. On peut dire qu'avec cette prise de conscience par la pensée

fragmentation of the substance, the essence, but neither does one need to interpret "mode", or *energeia*, as anything but the highest of personal attributions.[106] The most telling category for this analysis is found in the notion of the mutual indwelling of the individual subsistents which was a resilient, highly heuristic theme tried and perfected from Basil to John of Damascus.

C. Perichoresis: God as Reciprocal Love

It was the Eastern emphasis on 'perichoresis' or the mutual indwelling of divine persons, which provided new groundwork for theologizing about the inner life of the Trinity.[107] In many ways this theme and its cognates are characteristic of the dynamism in Eastern theology.[108] The history of the term is nearly as elusive as 'prosopon,' however, it is another example of the heuristic depth of analogical terms which assisted the Church in its attempt to worshipfully and cogently approach divine reality.

The Stoic Anaxagoras perceived the dynamic participation between the transcendental Nous and the material cosmos as perichoresis.[109] Of course Christian views

---

chrétienne de ses implications, le "personnel" prend pied, si je peux dire, dans l'être absolu." Ibid., 117.

[106]C. Giannaras, "The Distinction between Essence and Energies," 325. Rowan Williams is very clear in the discussion of this relation,
> As to whether the Son, being begotten (gennetos) can rightly be said to share the same and self-sufficient (agenetos) nature as the Father, who is both unbegotten (agennetos from gennao) and self-sufficient (agenetos, from ginomai). The answer of developed orthodoxy is that the life of the Father and the Son is equally agenetos, but it is a life they share precisely in their mutual relations - i.e. neither is agenetos qua person, but only by nature.
"Trinity and Revelation," 211 n. 24.

[107]Plantinga, lists perichoresis along with "opera ad extra sunt indivisa," essential equality and the simplicity doctrine as corrections to the possible misuse of the social analogies. "Gregory of Nyssa and the Social Analogy of the Trinity," 325.

[108]C. A. Disandro makes this point in "Historia semántica de 'perikhóresis'," in Studia Patristica 15:1. ed. Elizbeth A. Livingstone, (Berlin: Akademie-Verlag, 1985), 447. Another theme is the theological "disjunction" which resulted from the usage of this term. Judaism and Hellenism abhorred the christological and trinitological implications of the term, of course, but the concept proved to be a standard against a variety of syncretistic reinterpretations of patristic theology. Ibid., 444.

[109]Disandro notes that the classical Greek elegiac-lyric literature and the tradgedies do not use either the verbal or nominal forms. Herodotus uses the verb to indicate dynastic succession. Neither Plato nor Aristotle use the noun. Aristophanes includes the verb (perichorein) in parodying an ancestral rite. Anaxagoras' milieu might be a factor in his sole use of the noun in ancient Greek philosophical history. Klazomene on the Gulf of Smyrna provided an undulating ocean background for his critique of Parmenidian static views of reality, "Historia Semantica," 443. Little did Anaxagoras realize how he would effect future theology with the use of the term.

of creation altered the Stoic interpretation of reality but perichoresis came to be more directly applied to the nature of God. Athenagoras, in the second century, gave elements conducive to a conception of mutual interrelationship in the Trinity.[110] Dionysius the Areopagite also, incorporating Neoplatonic structuring, wrote of the Oneness of God that, "It possesses the mutual Abiding and Indwelling (as it were) of Its indivisibly supreme Persons (hypostaseis) in an utterly Undifferentiated and Transcendent Unity, and yet without any confusion."[111] The philosophical background of the term made it as appealing as hypostasis to Eastern minds as well as offering a new direction for thought devolving from interpretations of homoousion. Perichoresis offered a concept which could contain oneness of nature and the biblical witness to a mutual "inness" between the Persons.

Discussions of Christological personhood incorporated the theme, but were eclipsed when it became evident that the usage was distinctly different with respect to trinitarian deliberation. Preliminarily it was used to articulate the dynamism between the natures of Christ. No usage of the noun occurs before Maximus the Confessor, according to Prestige.[112] Those who disparage the translation of perichoresis as mutual inexistence again reveal the modalistic oneness bias that has pervaded much of Christian thought.

Although Basil and both Gregorys' explored the idea of mutual inexistence its full explication was to follow them. The Eastern thinkers reveal four general tendencies in usage; 1)faith was construed as a unifying element in the process of deification, 2)the believer's union with the Triune God is a mutual indwelling, 3)christological paradigms included this idea with regard to the natures in the one Person, and 4)Trinitarian (or triadological) contexts.

---

[110]Athenagoras, A Plea for Christians, ch. 10, 12 ANF vol.2, 133, 134. Fortman says he gives "more than a hint of the later doctrine of circumincession." The Triune God, 94.

[111]Henosis (Union) and diakrisis (differentiation) are just two of the terms which Dionysius uses to describe the ineffable (paradox !) communion within the Godhead. Dionysius the Areopagite, On the Divine Names 2:4. On the Divine Names and The Mystical Theology, trans. C.E. Rolt, Translations of Christian Literature, Series I, Greek Texts (New York: Macmillan, 1920), 70. A. Louth points to the Proclian background of Dionysius' language as well as the similarity with the Cappadocians in the discussion of the "source of the Godhead" being in the Father. These themes are precursors to Damascene articulation of the Trinity. Most scholars place this work toward the end of the fifth century AD.

[112]G.L. Prestige, "'Perichoreo' and 'Perichoresis' in the Fathers." Journal of Theological Studies 29 (1928): 243. True to his modalistic tendencies Prestige argues that "reciprocity" is the best definition of perichoresis rather than interpenetration. In the line from Dionysius, through Nazianzus, to Maximus, Prestige argues that the Damascene "entirely missed" the true meaning of the term due to a misreading of the uncompounded chorein (hold, contain). Ibid., 243-244. (Disandro also points to the possibility that chorein could mean pneuma or psyche. "Historia semantica," 443). While this may be true in christology it is not as convincing with regard to the contexts of the Cappadocian writings to which he refers. "Perichoreo and Perichoresis," 247.

Faith is described, with Neoplatonic adumbrations, as return to the arche, the "turning half-circle from appearance to reality."[113] This reveals the teleogical dynamism inherent in Eastern notions of reformation of the image of God and deification. The "return" is based upon the prior movement of a self-revealing God who has directed the overflow of inner-trinitarian love toward creation.[114] To miss this underlying metaphysic distorts the trinitarian conception basic to it. No absorption or annihilation of one entity by another is intended. The reason that anthropological and even christological usages do not compare with the trinitarian is due to the difference of substance, or **genus**, under discussion. The permanent and inviolable communication of the two natures in Christ is something quite different from the all-encompassing union of the **hypostaseis**.[115]

In defense against tritheism and modalism, the language of mutual inexistence, in Latin **circumincessio** (**circuminsessio** was to come into use later in scholastic thought), and in Greek, **perichoresis** and **emperichoresis**, grew out of prosopological exegesis, mainly concerning the "in" references from John 10:38, 14:10, 11, 20 and 17:21.[116] Apart from Hilary it would appear that the Eastern thinkers adopted and elaborated reasoning pertaining to the permeability of divine personhood. As usual in the Church's approach much more evidence is explored in terms of the dynamic dyadic relation, Father and Son, but is

---

[113]Prestige's interpretation of Maximus the Confessor, "Perichoreo and Perichoresis," 245. See Disandro, "Historia Semantica," 446.

[114]Within the context of a discussion regarding the incomposite divine nature as foundational to Cappadocian theology and anthropology (Orations 28:7, 40:7, 29:2, 23:8, 42:15, 31:14, 23:8) A. Ellverson astutely comments that Nazianzus reflects two forms of dynamism, a "kind of movement from the Father within the Trinity as such, and on the other hand, with a more or less certainty, even a kind of movement "back" to the Father. The Dual Nature of Man: A Study in the Theological Anthropology of Gregory of Nazianzus (Uppsala: Almqvist and Wiksell International, 1981), 39-40, 94-95. Mascall states that perichoresis saves triadic relations frrom meaninglessness by expressing the very meaning of the relationship in which the hypostatic Persons stand. The Triune God, 82-84. The noetic of Cappadocian theological metaphysic has a distinct relational ontic foundation.

[115]See Oden, The Word of Life, 182-183 as an excellent response to Prestige's argumentation.

[116]Athanasius, Third Discourse Against the Arians 32:1,1-1:4 NPNF2 vol. 4, 393-395; cf. 3:24.21-25 for implications of faith in believer and indwelling. Second Discourse 25:15 Ibid., 402; 25:25 Ibid., 407. Multiplied references could be garnered from Athanasius, First Discourse 1:26-27; Basil On the Holy Spirit, 47; Cyril of Alexandria, Commentary on John 1:5 "reciprocal irruption" of Persons; Cyril of Jerusalem, Catechetical Orations 16:4; Hilary, De Trinitate 3:4. Prestige says that sunaloiphes (coalescence) is an opposite term used in contradistinction to perichoresis. The key to this theology is found in the early Church's discussion of the immanence of God in Himself, an 'inexistence', but in the East it was "hen allelais" or "in one another" and other similar forms.

completed by the Holy Spirit in an eternal mutual interpenetrative self-giving.[117] The East discerned an ontology of reciprocity that produced a framework for existence. Perichoresis, had strong christological connections, and was not used in a specific trinitarian reference until Pseudo-Cyril, and subsequently John of Damascus in the sixth century; the Cappadocians are noted for establishing its cogency.[118] Nyssa, speaking of the mutual glorifying of the Persons wrote:

> "You see the revolving circle of the glory moving from Like to Like. The Son is glorified by the Spirit; the Father is glorified by the Son....In like manner, again, Faith completes the circle, and glorifies the Son by means of the Spirit, and the Father by means of the Son.[119]

This reflects the basis of profane usage, "cyclical movement" or "rotation."[120] But it also illumines the approach to distinct personhood in relationship which the East explored however self-effacingly. The giving of glory is meaningless without a subjective donor or sharer. If we join the usage of three men as an analogy, the ubiquitous indirect witness of personal attributions to each of the divine Persons, and the dynamic view of substance in the Cappadocians, with these explicit statements of threeness, it is quite clear that the tropoi hyparxeos are meant as compenetrating, self-identifying subjects.[121] The idea of three

---

[117]It ought to be noted that there is no explicit statement of "inness" with regard to the Spirit and the other Persons; that understanding is tied to the homoousion and the total deity of the Spirit.

[118]Pseudo-Cyril's work is probably De Sacrosanta Trinitate, often attributed to Cyril of Alexandria. John of Damascus, The Orthodox Faith 1:4,8 ("the hypostases are in each other"),14 NPNF2 vol. 10, 3-4, 6, 17. The monophysite Joannes Philoponus held a relational view of God but apparently was far too close to tritheism for later Eastern tastes. Prestige, God in Patristic Thought, 282; Torrance, Theology in Reconciliation, 12, 249. See the Council of Toledo's (675 AD) pronouncement on relation of persons, Denzinger, 531-532.

[119]On the Holy Spirit NPNF2 vol. 5, 324.

[120]H.G. Liddell and Robert Scott, A Greek-English Lexicon s.v. "Perichoresis," (New York: Harper and Brothers, 1878). Stephen Ford argues that Coleridge was the transmitter of "interpenetration" as a definition of perichoresis into English. "Perichoresis and Interpenetration: Samuel Taylor Coleridge's Trinitarian Conception of Unity." Theology 89:727 (1986): 20-24. Cf. the insights of Bishop Bull in his Defensio Fidei Nicaenae (Oxford: John Henry Parker, 1851-1858) at 2:9 discussing Dionysius of Rome (239), 2:10-2:11 (303-305) and his conclusion at 4:14 (652-653) for a strong determination of the early meaning of 'perichoresis'. Note also that Prestige seems to have changed his position between God in Patristic Thought and his article on the subject in Lampe's Lexicon which finds him using "interpenetration" in much the same way as found in Bull's Defensio.

[121]This might have something to do with the statement, "the Son is begotten from the womb of the Father (de patris utero), that is from His substance." Eleventh Council of Toledo (675 AD), Denzinger, 526, Neuner and Dupuis, 308. Plantinga has similar arguments in his "Gregory of Nyssa and the Social Analogy of the Trinity," 333-352. Note especially his critique of modern thinking which over-Platonizes substance and our similar statements regarding rigid categories on Aristotelian substance. Opposed to this in a rigid Augustinian position is the remarkably obscurantistic statements by B.M.G. Reardon, who

is in the end meaningless if a cordon of philosophical monadism is imposed to protect a numeric understanding of divine oneness. The divine love evidenced by this other-consciousness which is interexistent in its "circularity" without either commixture of the persons or of separability.[122] Not only are the **hypostaseis** inconceivable apart from co-inherent triadicity, there would not be divine love without the Three.[123]

Another clue to the dynamism of divine personhood is tied to the theme **"ekstasis"** found in the Easter Fathers. The category of the diffusion of the Good (**bonum diffusivum sui**) is one way which philosophers and theologians have posited as a cosmology.[124] It is debated whether Pseudo-Dionysius used the Neoplatonic idea of divine bestowment in a hierarchical fashion as one way of viewing the divine-human relationship throughout <u>On the Divine Names</u>.[125] He wrote of the connection of all things to the Supra-Divine, "Their rest is in the Divine Goodness, wherein they are grounded, and This Goodness maintains

---

quotes Bull's famous "perichoretic" statement in <u>Defensio Fidei Nicaenae</u> 2:9, and then concludes it is obviously a view of personhood far removed from anything that "personality" means to us today. "A Comment," <u>Theology</u> 72 (1975): 299. More irenic is the position of H.M. Relton, <u>Studies in Christian Doctrine</u> (London: Macmillan, 1960), 47.

[122]Just one look at Nyssa's anti-Sabellian <u>Ad Graecos</u> reveals the Cappadocian tendency to view the persons as distinguishable (**diaphora**) from each other yet intimately disposed to one another. Note the terms; **sundesmos** (bond, union, used repeatedly) versus **sumpleketai** (twined without distinction), **sunaptomen** (joined), **koinon** (commonness). <u>Ad Graecos</u> PG 45, 176-179, <u>Opera Dogmatica Minora</u>, 21-23.

[123]Note the consistent Eastern preoccupation with this theme, especially as it relates to the holistic worldview in **sobornost**. N. Berdyaev, <u>Freedom and the Spirit</u> (London: Geoffrey Bles: The Centenary Press, 1935), 199-200. N. Berdyaev, <u>The Destiny of Man</u> (London: Geoffrey Bles, 1948), 57-58. S.L. Frank, <u>The Unknowable</u>, trans. Boris Jakim (Athens, Ohio: Ohio University Press, 1983), 173-179. Lossky, <u>In the Image and Likeness</u>, 183-192.

[124]A modern interpretation of this "principle of plenitude" is found in Arthur Lovejoy, <u>The Great Chain of Being: A Study of the History of an Idea</u> (Cambridge: Harvard Univ. Press, 1936). He shows a connection with the presuppositions of Process Theology, see Ibid., 332-333. Cf. A.N. Whitehead, <u>Process and Reality</u> (New York: The Free Press, 1957), 41-42, 403-413. C. Hartshorne, <u>The Divine Relativity</u> (New Haven: Yale Univ. Press, 1964), 142-147, 156-157. More recently Ewert Cousins of Fordham has directly attributed the dynamism in God overagainst the "Pure Act" tradition, to the East. His process presuppositions are evident throughout; nonetheless his insight especially on Bonaventure's application is helpful. "St. Bonaventure, St. Thomas, and the Movement of Thought in the 13th Century," in <u>Bonaventure and Aquinas: Enduring Philosophers</u>, R.W. Shahan and Frances J. Kovach eds., 5-23 (Norman, Ok.: Univ. of Oklahoma Press, 1976).

[125]See C. Giannaras' discussion, <u>Person und Eros: Eine Gegenüberstellung der Ontologie der griechieschen Kirchenväter und der Existenzphilosophie des Westens</u>. Göttingen: Vandenhoeck and Ruprecht, 1982, 207-211.

them and protects them and feasts them with Its good things."[126] Of course, Christian thinkers had to reinterpret Plotinian categories at every sector. Dionysius did not use "hierarchy" as a reductionistic cosmology. Existence, for the precursors to the Cappadocians, Dionysius and Maximus, was unified in a creation context not a dissolution of multiplicity through emanation or panentheism.[127] Nazianzus wrote:

> Since this movement of self-contemplation alone could not satisfy Goodness, but Good must be poured out and go forth beyond Itself to multiply the objects of Its beneficence, for this was essential to the highest Goodness.[128]

Lossky is right to distinguish necessitarian views of diffusion with the "eternal mode" of self-giving which pertains to divine reality.[129] Nazianzus gives remonstration of the Plotinian categories of the One and the many when applied to God that indicates any necessity of many substances in the One.[130] Nonetheless, the Eastern view of God included a dynamic divine inter-communication which found its source in "ec-static", "out-of-one's self" love.[131]

With a radically different view of the Originator of reality one can quickly see that personal love in all of its fullness and implications pertains both to theology and anthropology. Where rational categories had gained preeminence, now inter-subjective love was posited as a way of perceiving reality. In terms of divine essence, the particular and unique Persons are the Trinity. The Cappadocians used diverse tactics which altered ontology. Zizioulas states it succinctly in reviewing the paradigmatic shift in hypostasis as the Cappadocians applied to personhood and less to ousia with ekstasis at its fundament:

> If the notion of hypostasis, no longer in the sense of 'substance' but of 'person', points to that which makes a being itself, then we are indeed confronted with a revolution with regard to Greek and especially Aristotelian ontology....(It) means that the

---

[126]This is just one of scores of similar statements in On the Divine Name example, ch. 4:1ff., Rolt's trans., 87ff. Ibid., 5:7-5:8, 138-141.

[127]Dionysius the Areopagite, On the Divine Names 5:5, Rolt's trans., 136-137; 7:1, 146-148; C. Lock, in a review of Being as Communion (St. Vladimir's Theologicial Quarterly 30:1 (1980): 91-94) states that Lossky differs from Zizioulas' interpretation of Maximus attributing a rather negative understanding of "ekstasis". Whether he uses the term or not, however, Lossky is in general agreement with the sentiments of "being in relationship." See In the Image and Likeness of God, 28-29, 76-86, 111-123.

[128]Gregory of Nazianzus, Oration 39:9 NPNF2 vol. 7, 347.

[129]Lossky, In the Image and Likeness of God, 86.

[130]Oration 29:12 NPNF2 vol. 7, 307. See Kasper, The God of Jesus Christ, 293-294. Here is an early Church refutation of the necessitarianism so rampant in modern process-tinted theology.

[131]We resonate here with Zizioulas' reasoning that basic to his theme of discerning the relation between truth and ontology, or communion, is the cosmology of both the essence-energy antinomy and "ekstasis". Being in Communion, 91-92.

ontological question is not answered by pointing to the 'self-existent', to a being as it is determined by its own boundaries, but to a being which in its ekstasis breaks through these boundaries in a movement of communion.[132]

The energies then express, but more importantly, are the divine other-orientation which issues from, the distinct hypostatic reality of the trinitarian persons. God "ek-sists" toward his Creation in the divine "ek-sistences". There is no division at the fundamental level between the acts and being of the Triune God.[133] Divine Otherness has no meaning unless there are enhypostatic Persons, both rational and relational entities, who are ordered (taxis) according to origin alone, without regard any priority, except perhaps logical.[134] The hypostaseis are dynamically related in that each possess the same enhypostatic energeia in their own incommunicable personhood, as Ungenerate, Generate, and Procession.[135] Without this understanding of divine Personhood there is no way to comprehend Eastern view of ousia.[136] Where the Cappadocians redefined hypostaseis they altered the philosophical notion that there could only be one hypostasis in one essence. The continuums of Trinity-unity, subject-object, and person-substance find their paradoxical resolution in such a conception. In spite of the radical antinomies resident in Eastern thought there is a strong strain of tri-personalism which feeds the architectonic structuring of their entire theological

---

[132]J. Zizioulas repeats the basic themes of Being as Communion in "Human Capacity and Human Incapacity: A Theological Exploration of Personhood," Scottish Journal of Theology 28:5 (1975): 409. I have found the modern Orthodox thinkers the most satisfying in a modern approach to person that takes into account philosophy and theology in the context of the faith of the Church. See the themes discussed here in C Giannaras, "Consequences of an Erroneous Trinitology in the Human World," in Les Études Theologiques de Chambesy. vol. 2, 497-502, La signification et l'actualité du IIe Concile Oecumenique pour le monde Chrètien d'aujourd'hui (Chambesy-Geneve: Éditions du Centre Orthodoxe du Patriarcat Oecumenique, 1982), and his "The Distinction between Essence and Energies and its Importance for Theology," St. Vladimir's Theological Quarterly 19 (1975): 232-245, it also permeates The Freedom of Morality, trans. Elizabeth Briere (Crestwood: St. Vladimir's Seminary Press, 1984), esp. chapters 1 and 11.

[133]M. Aghiorgoussis, "Christian Existentialism of the Greek Fathers: Persons, Essence and Energies in God," The Greek Orthodox Theological Review 22:1 (1978): 39-41.

[134]Note this theme in Nazianzus, Letter to Cledonius, NPNF2 vol. 7, 440. Also conciliar/synodical statements which drew from this tradition. The Faith in Damasus, (382 AD) in The Christian Faith, Neuner and Dupuis, 10-11, 100-101. Psuedo-Athanasian Creed: Quicumque, (end of 5th c. AD) Ibid., 11-12. Eleventh Council of Toledo: Symbol of Faith, (675 AD) Neuner and Dupuis, 102-106, Denzinger, 525-532. Fourth Lateran General Council: Symbol of Lateran (1215 AD) Neuner and Dupuis, 107-109, Denzinger, 804-805. The last includes almost a direct quote from Nazianzus. Cf. also the Bull Auctorem fidei (1794), where the clarification is helpful, "Deus unum quidem "in tribus personis distinctis" dicitur, non "in tribus personis distinctus." Denzinger, 2697.

[135]Gregory of Nazianzus, Fifth Theological Oration 9 NPNF2 vol. 7, 320.

[136]See Anastos, "Essence, Energies and Hypostasis," 97-118.

enterprise.[137]

II. Augustine: Persons as Relations in De Trinitate

The Western Church benefited from the insights of Tertullian during the two centuries that followed his apogee. The fifth century provided a respite from the heated christological debates prior to the Chalcedonian proclamations. It was during this "hiatus" that Augustine was able to complete what is debatably his magnum opus, De Trinitate.[138] In a sense the heresies and conflagrations of three centuries of argumentation assisted in the production of the architectonic structure of this work. An immediate contrast is evident when the tone of Tertullian's necessary apologetic style is placed beside the via contemplativa method in this mature work of Augustine's. But more, it is arguable that those contentions and formulations allowed Augustine to break new ground in trinitarian contemplation.[139]

A. Sources and Theological Method in De Trinitate

It has been the assessment of some that due to the Western proclivity towards a 'unity model' of theology Augustine naturally represents the preeminent example of static notions of the Trinity. The assimilation of Greek metaphysics into his systematic endeavor

---

[137]See the astute philosophico-theological undertaking of C. Giannaras, Person und Eros, 35ff, 238-240. His argument parallels Heidegger's (one can sense the impact of G. Marcel as well) at some strategic points but also strongly criticizes that tradition in the West, derives from the thesis that the ontological-existential understanding of essence or nature is a radically different world-view than the noetic-ontological. As close as Robert Jenson appears to this type of conclusion, I am uneasy with the language of "identities" which is not continually couched in terms of divine love. "Three Identities of One Action." Scottish Journal of Theology 28 (1975): 1-15 as well as his The Triune Identity. In spite of the awareness of problem, see Nyssa where he says, "If I try to refute Sabellianism I am accused of tritheism; when I try to refute tritheism, I am accused of Sabellianism." Letter 189:2 PG 32, 685.

[138]Various speculations have been offered as to the dates of completion of portions of this massive work. The most sound scholars advocate a twenty year reflection period (ca. 399-420), interrupted by a clandestine stealing and publishing of an unfinished portion which was filled with corrections to the central theses and a progression of ideas based upon earlier notions. Space will not allow a discussion of Augustine's own psychology but it is interesting to note that in terms of self-awareness, the Confessions are pre-dated by Nazianzus' Carmi de Vita Sua. It is intriguing connection to see how these two minds gave so much to the world in terms of personhood. The effort to honestly explain oneself is a decisive contribution to our understanding of person. If one compares the self-awareness of Isocrates, Demosthenes or even Josephus, the general tone is self-defensive not self-revealing. See Momigliano's article, "Marcel Mauss and the quest for the person in Greek biography and autobiography," in M. Carrithers and Steve Collins. eds., The Category of the Person (New York: Cambridge Univ. Press, 1985), 90.

[139]Any foray into the mind of Augustine is a torturous task. The elements chosen carefully here bear directly on his notion of divine person.

is pointed to disdainfully for this tendency.[140] Rahner implies that the methods of Augustinian-inspired Scholastics have irreparably divorced the Trinity from "real" Christian thinking.[141] Upon close perusal however, it would appear that Augustine is not the "hellenizing" culprit he has been made out to be. The "unity" model or "simplicity" theme was not original with Augustine or the West alone. Clement of Rome indicated a first century understanding of the relationships within the framework of a firm commitment to the oneness of God.[142] Justin Martyr, with a definite Platonic background, strove to protect a type of "oneness" of the scripturally revealed Three even if in rudimentary fashion.[143] Irenaeus defended the one God against the Marcionite dualists and the Gnostics while alluding to the Trinity.[144]

---

[140]F. Bourassa gives an insightful response to the detractors of Augustine's methodological moorings in "Theologie trinitaire chez saint Augustin," Gregorianum 58 (1977): 679-684. His two-part analysis of Augustine's method is helpful in responding to the accusation that Augustine was destructive to true Christian theology in his incorporation of Platonic principles. Paul Tillich's overstatement of the case is an example of this influential but deeply flawed assessment. See his History of Christian Thought (New York: Simon and Schuster, 1967), 116. Edmund Hill castigates Hodgson and Wiles for their misunderstanding of Augustine's methodology in "Our Knowledge of the Trinity," Scottish Journal of Theology 27 (1974): 1-11. I find Wiles far more misleading than Hodgson although I think Hill is correct in his critique of their bewildering view of the relationship between revelation and early trinitarian thought. See M. Wiles "Psychological Analogies of the Fathers," in Studia Patristica vol. 11. ed. F. L. Cross, 264-267. Berlin: Akademie Verlag, 1972.

[141]Rahner's famous essay, "Remarks on the Dogmatic Treatise 'De Trinitate'. Theological Investigations. vol. 4. 77-102. trans. Kevin Smyth (Baltimore: Helicon Press, 1966), was written in 1960 just prior to the first meeting of the Vatican Council. Its influence, as we have indicated, has been remarkable. The Dominican, Edmund Hill, has responded to that influence with equally remarkable clarity. He found that the Early Church thinkers had already responded to the immanent (Hill feels "transcendent" is a better understood distinction)/economic issues which Rahner raises. It was the modern Church which was at fault for not making known to its members the everyday implications of trinitarian reality. According to Hill, Augustine did incorporate the economic features of Justin, Irenaeus and Tertullian but superceded their inherent subordinationism with a sound transcendental approach to the processions/missions of the Godhead. See E. Hill, Mystery of the Trinity, 45-46, 65-72, and his "Karl Rahner's "Remarks on the Dogmatic Treatise 'De Trinitate' and St. Augustine." In Augustinian Studies 2. 67-80. Villanova: Villanova Univ. Press, 1971.

[142]To the Corinthians, Lightfoot, Apostolic Fathers, 27; trans. 75. For a more "earthy" pastoral conception see Ignatius, To the Ephesians, Lightfoot, Apostolic Fathers, 108; trans. 139.

[143]First Apology, 6. ANF vol. 1, 164; Ibid., 22. ANF vol. 1, 170; Ibid., 37-39. ANF vol. 1, 175-176. These statements are among some of the strongest statements which reveal that "universal apperception" of the Trinity in the early Church.

[144]One finds both a Oneness theme and concomitant binitarianism in Against Heresies, 2.30.9. ANF vol. 1, 406 both are used in defense against Valentinianism in Ibid., 3.25. ANF vol. 1, 439-440. See his Trinity emerging in Ibid., 3.27.3. ANF vol. 1, 445.

Granted, Augustine had profound ties with Plotinian Neoplatonism.[145] Ambrose's Hexameron led him to Plotinus' Enneads and to the other libri Platonicorum with which he became acquainted through contact with the thought of a previous convert to Catholicism and astute philosopher, Marius Victorinus.[146] The Neoplatonic 'hypostaseis' which Victorinus had reformed as an analogy of the Trinity were also used by Augustine, some fifty years later, in both referring to the Trinity and for understanding the imago dei in his "psychological" or rather, "mental" trinities.[147] In all of this however, Augustine remained stalwartly committed to a Christian understanding of revelation and of creation which clearly demarcated the lines between Greek philosophy and his Christian epistemology.

If recognized as part of the framework rather than representing a total philosophical capitulation, the Neoplatonic underpinnings of Augustine's theological method give assistance to one's understanding of the concept of 'person' in De Trinitate. Leaving behind the materialism of Manicheanism, Stoicism and Epicureanism, Augustine was freed

---

[145]Augustine reveals his ties to Platonism and Neoplatonism in De Trinitate from Bk 8 on. E.G.T. Booth points out that this may have been written at the same time as The City of God, where we find the same sorts of revelations beginning in Bk. 9 and in much that follows. Consult "Augustine's 'de Trinitate' and Aristotelian and neo-Platonist Noetic," in Studia Patristica 16:2. ed. Elizabeth A. Livingstone, 487-490 (Berlin: Akademie-Verlag, 1985). See specifically City of God 9.16, 10.23-24, 30-32, 12.21, 19.23 in the edition trans. by Henry Bettenson with intro. by David Knowles (New York: Penguin Books, 1972). Cf. the distinctions he saw between the Neoplatonists and Christian doctrine in Confessions 7:9,10,20. T. Wassmer gives indication of the clarity of Augustine's use of Neoplatonic thought in "The Trinitarian Theology of Augustine and His Debt to Plotinus," Scottish Journal of Theology 13 (1961): 248-255.

[146]Apparently Marius Victorinus Afer had a strong understanding of Greek philosophy, but his relative obscurity in the modern discussion is due to his inscrutable, primarily philosophical, approach which Augustine translated into more tangible terms. This philosophical pilgrimage is well documented in Gerald A. McCool, "The Ambrosian Origin of St. Augustine's Theology of the Image of God in Man," Theological Studies 20:1 (March, 1959): 62-81. Also G. Maertens' "Augustine's Image of Man," in F. Bossier, Images of Man in Ancient and Medieval Thought: Studia Gerardo Verbeke Ab Amicis et Collegis dicata, 175-198; in Symbolae: facultatis Litterarum et Philosophiae Lovaniensis. vol. 1. Louvain: Louvain Univ. Press, 1976. Proclus and Dionysius the Areopagite use the triad which enamored Victorinus. See On the Divine Names ch. 5, trans. C. E. Rolt (New York: Macmillan, 1920), 68-81. Like Hilary, if we took the space needed we would see that dynamism, or tridynamos, (i.e. esse, vivere, and intelligere, is essential to the theology of Victorinus. Against Arius 4 FC, 284-285. Paul Henry, "The 'Adversus Arium' of Marius Victorinus, the First Systematic Exposition of the Doctrine of the Trinity," Journal of Theological Studies 6:1 n.s.(1950): 42-53. Mary T. Clark, "The NeoPlatonism of Marius Victorinus the Christian." In NeoPlatonism and Early Christian Thought: Essays in honor of A.H. Armstrong. eds. H.J. Blumenthal and R.A. Markus, 153-159. London: Variorum Publications Ltd., 1981.

[147]It is well attested that Augustine had contact with Plotinus' Ennead 5.1 The Enneads, trans. Stephen MacKenna and B.S. Page, ed. R.M. Hutchins in Great Books of the Western World (Chicago: Univ. of Chicago and Encyclopaedia Britannica, 1952), 208-214.

to see the spiritual reality of divinity. However, he discerned that spiritual essence had not left itself without a witness in the creation. In a refutation of the dualism inherent in Greek philosophy, Augustine pondered the epistemological inseparability of God and creation.[148] Simply stated, eternal truths are, for Augustine, exemplified in every particular here and now.[149] From what we have called the "realist" position, Augustine maintained that the outer world referred to the inner realities; the lower images signified the higher truths.[150] The fabric of his thought was woven by this method of signification, or "referencing" similar to the implications of the natural order as the "changing image of eternity" espoused by the Greek Neoplatonists.[151]

Plato dared to distinguish between the world known by sense and the one known by intellect, and suggested that the latter was better and more real. Plotinus drew upon the distinction and internalized it. For him the chief object of knowledge became the individual mind. Augustine reflects a similar understanding where he prays, "Then indeed I saw intellectually Thy invisible things, through those things which are made...."[152] 'Fides' both confronted 'ratio' and assimilated it, according to Augustine. Augustine definitely laid the foundation for the theologizing we advocated in chapter one. His realism is an "above-below" method with the Trinity revealing itself as the center of reality and the source of

---

[148]See Anton Pegis, "Augustinian Man: Between God and Matter," in V. Bourke, Readings in Ancient Medieval Philosophy, ed. James D. Collins, 143-155 (Westminster, Maryland: Neuma Press, 1960).

[149]See John S. Dunne's interesting commentary in A Search for God in Time and Memory (Notre Dame: Univ. of Notre Dame Press, 1977), 101. We hasten to add that Augustine's "imaging" method had within it certain hierarchies of acceptability. It was the more rational and esoteric which won out over the lower and more physical images.

[150]Note: Reference to the Latin are found in De Trinitate: Libri XV. ed. W.J. Mountain. Corpus Christianorum, Series Latina, vols. 50, 50A. Turnhout: Typographi Brepols Editores Pontificii, 1968. Hereafter, CC. Only those references which are of integral importance will bear full citation both in NPNF and CC. See 4.1.3, 8.3.4, 13.20.26. For an exquisite discussion of Augustine's debt and concomitant disavowal of Neoplatonic (and Enlightenment) dualistic presuppositions, see Thomas Torrance's "Theological Realism." In The Philosophical Frontiers of Christian Theology: Essays presented to D.M. Mackinnon. eds. Brian Hebbelthwaite and Stewart Sutherland, 169-190. Cambridge: Cambridge Univ. Press, 1982. See discussion in chap. One, 30-35.

[151]The use of 'referencing' is tied to Augustine's summary and interpretive passage 15.20.39. NPNF vol. 3, 221; CC, 517, that one, "ought to refer (referre) the whole of his life to the remembering, seeing, loving that highest Trinity, in order that he may recollect, contemplate and be delighted by it." Emphasis mine. McKenna has "direct all that lives in him to..." On the Trinity, 506.

[152]Confessions 7.17. Note also the reference in ch. 17 ff. to memory, reason, and the mind which is the place where this revelation of God makes its strongest impression. See also 20-23. One immediately sees hint of Rom 1:20 which was a mainstay for Augustine in this epistemology.

everything good, especially that which images it the most effectively, human rational capacity. It was from the triune God that Augustine ascertained the triune character of human personhood and thereby demanded a phenomenology of the the human mind as foundational to human understanding. Cochrane, however, is quick to elucidate that Augustine went beyond Greek philosophical categories:

> By thus recommending faith, not as a substitute for, but as a condition of understanding, Augustine formulates, in terms which recall and reinforce the language of Athanasius, the true issue between Classicism and Christianity.[153]

What we find is Augustine's theological and pastoral acumen intermixed. He still serves as a paradigmatic example of the relationship between faith and reason. The experiential and the ethereal find themselves based in faith that is both a bestowed gift and a personal response.[154]

Wisdom, then, is a journey within led by a Guide who is beyond the subject. "Hence, 'that which was made' was already 'life in Him,' (Christ) and not any kind of life, but that life which was the 'light of men,' the light certainly of rational minds."[155] The One who supercedes the "brute givenness" of human teachers was the indwelling Christ. Here Augustine's doctrine of illumination becomes the basis of all knowing and believing.[156] The soul cannot receive or apprehend intellectual truth without the "mysterious influence" of God. In reaction to panentheistic or ontologistic interpretations, Augustine sees divine truth producing an indelible image upon the mind which determines rational capability. God is

---

[153]Cochrane, Christianity and Classical Culture, 402.

[154]Of course, this is an arena of continued discourse. We have mentionned Lindbeck's attempts relating 'regulative' and 'expressivistic' modes of Christian thought processes. For an attempt to do the same from a process orientation yet with an adequate appraisal of Augustine is Ewert Cousins', "Models and the Future of Theology," 88-91 and from a psychological perspective there are some cogent insights that parallel Augustine's methodology in Fraser Watts and Mark Williams, The Psychology of Religious Knowing (New York: Cambridge, 1988), 145-146. It is becoming apparent to more and more thinkers that reality, even scientific reality, reflects divine or triune existence and that its "over-againstness" is ineliminable and inexorable. See for example; William G. Pollard, "Rumors of transcendence in physics," American Journal of Physics 52:10 (October, 1984): 877-881; W. Jim Neidhardt, "The Creative Dialogue Between Human Intelligibility and Reality - Relational Aspects of Natural Science and Theology," Asbury Theological Journal 41:2 (Fall, 1986): 59-83. Neidhardt reflects the same emphases one finds in M. Polanyi and T. F. Torrance on this score. See also Margaret Masterman, "Theism as a scientific hypothesis, III, Icons: The nature of scientific revelation," Theoria to Theory 1 (1967): 232-250. (Watts and Williams refer to her also.)

[155]4.1.3. translation from McKenna, De Trinitate, 132-133; CC, 163.

[156]Torrance asserts that the Thomistic return to Aristotelian categories is the negation of the illuminationist approach to Augustine. We shall see. Thomas Torrance, Theology in Reconstruction, 262.

the One who imprints the representations of eternal truths.[157] Metaphors became tools which took the rational creature outside himself in telic fashion.

Augustine advocated a reflective hermeneutic that was dialectic in nature, as seen in his definition of things that "are to be enjoyed, others to be used, and there are others which are to be enjoyed and used."[158] Things were determined, defined, given significance in relation to signs. "All doctrine concerns either things or signs, but things are learned by signs."[159] Things for Augustine were the meaning, or the actualization of a sign. A sign is the potential which is informed by the thing. Symbols and their corresponding ascendant reality require an Inner Teacher for proper referencing to occur. This informed interiorism reflects Augustine's epistemology and theology. The significance for our purposes is that foundational to this epistemology is the reality of perfect love channeled to the believer through the Word of God and the Holy Spirit and its requirement of a growing love in the illumined believer for the God who is to be enjoyed. This fusion of knowledge and love precludes excessive rationalistic interpretations of Augustine's method. In the movement from external vestigia by perception toward the internal powers of memory, understanding and will, there is the consistent undergirding of the ineluctable love that is God's essential nature. To be the image of God is to love one's self, but in order for that to be pure love it must be rightly referenced in love for God.[160] Ordinata dilectio, is that love which does not "love what should not be loved nor fails to love what should be loved."[161] Disorder at that point results in the most insidious form of idolatry.

This dyadic movement of 'signa naturalia' and the things to which they refer is built upon in De Trinitate to reveal numerous inherent triadic relations. A trinitarian epistemology surfaces out of which subsequent analogies are drawn. A three-term relation is presented: of the object for which the sign stands, the sign proper, and the subject who

---

[157]Augustine's conversation with his son Adeodatus in De Magistro bears directly on this discussion, see 11.38-12.39, 14.46. See Earlier Writing, in Library of Christian Classics, selected and trans. with intro. John H.S. Burleigh (Philadelphia: Westminster Press, 1953), 95-96, 100-101. But note how it also forms the basis of his trinitarian discussion in De Trinitate 4.2 NPNF vol. 3. 71; 4. 20 NPNF vol. 3. 84-86, where the connection between revelation, intelligibility and trinity is distilled.

[158]On Christian Doctrine 1.3, trans. D.W. Robertson (Indianapolis: Bobbs-Merrill Educational Publishers, 1981), 9. See De Trinitate 9.8, 14.17.23.

[159]On Christian Doctrine 1.2.

[160]See an exacting critique of the logical implications without careful qualification of Augustine on pure love of God in Robert Merrihew Adams, "The Problem of Total Devotion," in Rationality, Religious Belief and Moral Commitment: Essays in the Philosophy of Religion, eds. Robert Audi, and William J. Wainwright, 169-194 (Ithaca: Cornell Univ. Press, 1986).

[161]Augustine, On Christian Doctrine 1.27.28, trans. Robertson, 23.

is the end or purposed recipient of the sign signified, as in Lover, Love, and Loved. However, it is apparent that throughout this treatise Augustine is more concerned with the Inner Teacher's activity than with external signs, "whose participation is our illumination, the Word who is the life which is the light of men."[162]

For Augustine the triune God is the only 'thing' that is to be enjoyed supremely.[163] All signification is to be used toward that goal. The creation and creatures all refer to God in some distinct way though the world is fallen.[164] Natural revelation as a right use of the world thus opened the door for deriving aspects of the God to be enjoyed. This 'analogia entis' of course could be misused, producing an idolatrizing of the signs rather than maintaing proper referencing, as the Barthians have aptly and continually reminded us. "He is a slave to a sign who uses or worships a significant thing without knowing what it signifies."[165] Thus, he builds an epistemology upon the dialectic between a formal principle, the relation between things and signs, and his material principle, the revelation of the triune God in the rational faculties of the creature with the resultant self-love activated by faith. Self-love is only proper in its intimate dependence upon love for God which issues in love for others. If these stages do not occur then a person rejects wisdom and settles for stupidity.[166]

One is liable to misinterpretation however if with this analogical method there is not also mention of the distinction Augustine continually draws between creation and the

---

[162]De Trinitate 4.2.4 NPNF vol. 3. 71. Here quoted however from a smoother translation from R.A. Markus, "St. Augustine on Signs," in Readings in Ancient Medieval Philosophy, ed. James D. Collins (Maryland: Neuman Press, 1960), 157.

[163]On Christian Doctrine, 1.10,22

[164]Note here that our contention that relationality is finding renewed interest in modern theology is supported by the work of a variety of Catholic theologians. See an excellent treatment of the French philosopher/theologian Mouroux by T. Gerard Connelly, "Perichoresis and the Faith That Personalizes according to Jean Mouroux," Ephemerides Theologicae Lovaniensis 62:4 (1986): 362 passim. Connelly mentions Rahner at this point in more glowing terms than we would endorse. Ibid., 357-358. Balthasar's "Creation and Trinity," Communio (US) 15 (Fall, 1988): 288-290, is redolent with Augustinian illuminationism based on the Trinity and is similar in import to Mühlen in this regard.

[165]On Christian Doctrine 3.9, see also 3.13. On Barth's disqualification which was his continual response to Brunner see CD 3:2, 220. But here we also have his intriguing use of the 'analogia relationis' which smacks of that which he has just denied.

[166]'Stulta' in 14.12.15. NPNF vol. 3, 191; CC, 443. 14.14.18. NPNF vol. 3, 192-194; CC, 445-447. Sullivan explains this accurately in The Image of God: The Doctrine of St. Augustine and its Influence (Dubuque, Iowa: Priory Press, 1963), 137-138; its results are "self-forgetfulness, self-ignorance, and self-hate." Ibid, 138.

Creator.[167] The theme of discontinuity is unmistakeable in this treatise. Thus, at the end of his discussion the employment of the Pauline metaphor of a "dim glass" represents the enigma which the Trinity will always be, even to illumined human reason.[168] No human intellection can carry the depths of simple unity inherent in the Triune relationship. Augustine is aware that knowledge and will, conception and perception, mind and the object remembered, are different in ways that the persons of the Trinity are not.[169] Beginning or source, generation and procession are essentially realities based in Scripture, informed by an Inner Teacher, and grasped by divinely-bestowed faith. This ancient thinker never allowed intimations of the Trinity to become more than heuristic symbols but they were also not less than that. It was this biblical notion of discontinuity which was one of the major marks in Augustine's repudiation of the the implications of Plotinian immanentism.[170] Greek philosophical notions of personhood were doomed to individual isolationism based upon their cosmology and epistemology. The Cappadocians and Augustine re-affirm a trinitarian world-view which gives meaning to individuals by referencing them to a higher order of Person, one where communal interrelationship is the major consistence.

Also basic to Augustine's relational intention is the intriguing structure of this monumental treatise. Donald Daniels disagrees with a majority of interpretations which typically deflate the grandeur of De Trinitate by standard chronological or dramatic interpretations of its content. He suggests a holistic approach which fits both the style and the personality of the author. He contends that the relationship of reason and faith is

---

[167]There are, of course, criticisms of this distinction in its application beyond the fundamental distinctness of Creator and creature. Both Torrance and Gunton feel it is extremely dualistic and thus part of the reason for the West's inability to comprehend the true implications of trinitarian reality. See Torrance, Theology in Reconciliation, 12, 30-31. Gunton, "Augustine, the Trinity and the Theological Crisis in the West," Scottish Journal of Theology 43:1 (1990): 33-58.

[168]Cf. 14.17. 23, NPNF vol. 3, 196; CC, 455. 15.23.43, NPNF vol. 3, 223; CC, 522.

[169]15.21.40-15.27.50, these caveats immediately precede Augustine's benediction. That positioning, in itself, is reason to approach the "psychological" analogies with extreme care. For instance, the mind is substance in a way that understanding and will can never be. There are implicit inequalities in every one of the "trinities" when compared to the profound, inscrutable oneness and threeness of the Triune God.

[170]Oliver O'Donovan, makes this point clearly,
In this phrase, transcende et te ipsum, we see what the unambiguous theism of Christianity has made of the Plotinian ecstasis. Any suggestion that the soul is itself an extension of the divinity has to be undercut...."Return to yourself!" he will say; and then adjusting the cliché to the point of destroying it, "But don't stay there!".
The Problem of Self-Love in St. Augustine (New Haven: Yale Univ. Press, 1980), 73-74.

central to Augustine's systematic approach.[171] Faith precedes understanding as its suprarational counterpart. "We begin in faith, and are made perfect by sight."[172] Daniels maintains that Books 1-15 are demonstrative of the desire to glean from the "signs" of both scripture and creation the perichoretic mystery of the Trinity. This process of signification culminates in Book 15 taking the believer from the 'vestigia' of creation to the contemplation of the Creator by way of the 'imago dei'. Rather than a separation of faith and reason, Daniels sees in Augustine a synergistic mirroring which is available to the one who would love God for God's sake.[173]

In order for this movement to occur Augustine discussed two trinities within man that can be used to enjoy God. To support this notion he distinguishes the conventions and rules of human language in his discussion of signs and things from the third level of discourse, contemplation, which is the "Divine Art" or "Language" as it is seen in nature. His focus is upon the signs inherently implemented in significative creation. Books 1-14 are artistically constructed to bring the reader to belief.[174] The final book, in a crescendo of contemplative thought, points the entire discourse to the things to be enjoyed most. The Trinity is presented as the only true bestower and worthy recipient of pure love and illumined faith. The natural theory of signs in De Trinitate is an ordering principle of the topics of faith, rather than scattered sets of data.[175] The structure of this pivotal treatise is purposive, relationally constructed, coherent and formulated upon a principle which we shall see is remarkably person-centered.

---

[171]Donald E. Daniels, "The Argument of the De Trinitate and Augustine's Theory of Signs," in Augustinian Studies vol. 8 (Villanova: Villanova Univ., 1977), 33-54. Bourassa's response to the detractors of Augustine along the "hellenization" argument includes a rigorous defense of Augustine's method. He aptly defends the same bipartite movement of Scripture and reason. "Theologie trinitaire chez saint Augustin," pt.1 688-702, and pt. 2, 379-383.

[172]Augustine, Enchiridion 6. NPNF 3, 238. Cf. statements like De Trinitate 8.5.8. which is a crucial passage in the thought flow of the work.

[173]Daniels, "The Argument of the De Trinitate," 43-44. See for one example Augustine's discussion of achorista, inseparability in the relation of accidents and substance in De Trinitate 5.2.3-5.5.6. NPNF vol. 3, 88-89; CC, 207-210.

[174]The same point is made from another tack than Daniel's by Hill, in his Mystery of the Trinity, 80-82. Hill feels that De Trinitate is constructed chiastically with Bk. 8 being the center. This is very appealing given the modern interest in structural analysis. Some of his correspondences are persuasive. His suggestions that Bks. 5-7 are artificially constructed to meet this over-arching schema is problematic given the time and effort Augustine put into this work. If it is correct that Bk. 9 is to critique Bk. 8 and the analogy of love, then that also questions Hill's centrality of the latter in connection with Bks. 1 and 15. See O. Du Roy, L'Intelligence de la foi en la Trinité selon Saint Augustin (Paris: Études Augustiniennes, 1966), 437.

[175]Daniels, "The Argument of the De Trinitate, 46, 51.

Supportive of the larger structuring of De Trinitate are its major components. Books 1-8 reason that trinitarian thought is securely placed first and foremost in Scripture. Augustine is not unique in this biblical hermeneutic but his breadth is remarkable.[176] On the other hand, reason as a means of apprehending and expressing spiritual truth is used in the second half of the work. It is myopic to conclude that this method is speculative in the strictly scholastic sense. Instead it is a contemplative method which elicits the best form of worship and and intellectual rumination in co-existent harmony.

B. Augustine and Substantial Relations

Roughly the first half of his work treats the doctrine of the Trinity as inseparable from the unity of God, a theme well attested to in the orthodox formulations of the West. It is the unity of the Godhead which sets the tone of the discourse. Yet, to overemphasize the oneness motif is to miss the constant appearance of references to the distinctions in the Godhead with respect to the divine missions. Repeatedly he insists in terms similar to the following that:

> Whatever, therefore is spoken of God in respect to Himself is both spoken singly of each person, that is of the Father, and the Son, and the Holy Spirit; and together of the Trinity itself, not plurally but in the singular.[177]

As others who stood in opposition to the Arians, Augustine argued that unity of substance or essence was crucial to any human apprehension of the divine inner life.[178] It is immediately apparent that Augustine, while intransigently maintaining a commitment to unity, is well aware of the subtleties of a philosophical notion of substance.

> But because the Father is not called the Father except that he has a Son, and the Son is not called Son except in that He has a Father, these things are not said according to substance; because each of them is not so called in relation to Himself, but the terms are used reciprocally and in relation each to the other; nor yet according to accident, because both being called the Father, and being called the Son, is eternal and unchangeable to them.[179]

---

[176]We have mentionned Bourassa's, "Théologie trinitaire," Pt. 1. 696-713, as a defense of Augustine's biblical moorings prior to any "psychologizing." J. Pelikan asserts that, "the quality that marked Augustine and the other orthodox Fathers was their loyalty to the received tradition." The Christian Tradition: A History of the Development of Doctrine. vol. 3. The Growth of Medieval Theology. (Chicago: Univ. of Chicago Press, 1978), 17. E. Hill is correct in advancing that Augustine deplored the theophanic interpretations which forced the argument that only the Son could be incarnated. Mystery of the Trinity, 68.

[177]De Trin 3.11.27, NPNF vol. 3, 68; CC 158. De Trin 4.21, NPNF vol.3, 85: CC, 202 (work inseparably,inseparabiliter operari). De Trin 5.8.9, NPNF vol. 3, 91; CC 215. De Trin 7.3.5, NPNF vol. 3, 109; CC 254.

[178]A fundamental passage on substance is 5.2.3-5.6.7, NPNF vol. 3, 88-90; CC 207-212.

[179]5.5.6. NPNF vol. 3, 89; CC, 210-211.

Substance was not a static reality for Augustine just as it had not been for Tertullian or the Cappadocians. But it is correct that we do not find the freedom to deal with distinctions in the divine substance due to the Arian ploys to twist differentiations into accidentia. It was the semantic abuses of Arianism on that topic which forced him to place extreme emphasis on the Son's oneness with the Father in every respect.[180]

Is it possible that Augustine, who never completely divorced himself from Greek philosophically-based apologetics, gave more indication of a relational trinity than he is given credit? It could be that the Church's response to discussions of personhood due to Augustine's reservation about the word 'person' is an over-reaction which disregards the major themes in Augustine's mature work.[181] If the word irritated him it did not keep him from the use of dynamic relational language in theologically interpreting the divine unity.

Distinction was to be seen in the reciprocal relation of the various persons. Scholars who have attempted to align Augustine with Ambrosian concepts on the one hand or Plotinian absolutes on the other mar a proper interpretation of Augustine's doctrine of the person as relation. While both strains assisted his discussion, they do not exhaust his genius.[182] It has been suggested that Tertullian's Adversus Praxean 5 was the basis of De Trinitate Books 8-15.[183] Whatever the source, Augustine's eclectic mind was fed by a

---

[180]Note the same emphasis even when Augustine refers to the spiritual incorporation of believers in 5.16.17 "simul et ille pater noster esse incipit, sed nulla suae commutatione substantiae", "at the same time He becomes our Father, but nothing of his own substance is altered." NPNF vol. 3, 96; CC, 227. It was in his discussion of the persons, based upon this simplicity doctrine, that he confronted the Sabellian doctrine of his period.

[181]We recall the caveat Augustine maintains in De Trinitate 5.9, "Dictum est tamen tres personae non ut illud diceretur sed ne taceretur." The approach taken here is not opposed to that of Colin Gunton, but is more irenic. The insights he offers in "Augustine, the Trinity and the Theological Crisis of the West," Scottish Journal of Theology 43:1 (1990): 33-58, are profound in their implication. As much as I agree with the wrong usage of Augustinian presuppositions in the West, I am here presenting the De Trinitate having given Augustine the benefit of the doubt, which Gunton definitely questions. Note how Gunton critiques McKenna's translation of the above quote. Ibid., 43.

[182]Mary Clark's Augustinian Personalism is an excellent treatment of the Plotinian and Porphyrian backdrop to Augustine's view of trinity. But she is also astute in recognized his "Pauline Platonism" (p. 34) that is informed by the preponderance of Johannine themes with regard to love. She sees clearly the demarcation lines between philosophy and Christian faith especially as it pertains to persons, both divine and human, in community.

[183]Quasten, Patrology, 285. It is an alluring idea. Tertullian writes, "Thus, in a certain sense, the word is a second person within you, through which in thinking you utter speech, and through which also, (by reciprocity of process), in uttering speech you generate thought. The word is itself a different thing from yourself."
Ad. Praxean, 5. ANF vol. 3, 601. However, CC does not give any indication of reference to Ad. Praxean 5, only the statements concerning una essentia, tres persona which we have seen appear in chapters 2, and 26 of the same. Ibid., 465. Note that Porphyry, Didymus

vibrant pastoral heart so that mere philosophical gesticulations never appear in this discussion.[184] Preceding councils, with Cappadocian elements which Augustine knew at least indirectly, had laid a framework that was now being plumbed for deeper understanding. If the allegation is true that Augustine did not have scholarly facility with Greek, it would serve indirectly to confirm our acknowledgement that this prodigious mind came to conclusions that find uncanny essential, if not particular agreement with the Eastern Fathers.[185]   The contention that Augustine stands over against the Cappadocians in defending the coequality of the Trinity disregards the amount of space he gives to the roles of the members of the Godhead. The economic trinity must be seen with the context of his distinction between relation and substance. A perfect, unconfused, substantial unity which precludes "three gods" is fundamental. These three are not separate individuals in the way that men are of the genus "man". Therefore, Augustine is adamant in the expression of a unique and singular supernatural nature:

> But the Father and the Son together are not more truly than the Father singly, or the Son singly. And since also the Holy Spirit equally is truly, the Father and the Son together are not anything greater than He.[186]

It would seem that one must choose to misread Augustine to find Hellenistic static notions of unity, or to find an illegitimate usage of those categories in promulgating orthodox trinitarianism.

---

the Blind, Cyril of Alexandria, and Basil make the same sort of distinction.

[184]See Letter 169. 1.2, NPNF vol. 1, 539, for a glimpse of Augustine's priorities in relation to the completion of this demanding work.

[185]CC has in the appendix of sources reference to only three citations of Gregory of Nazianzen, seventeen of Basil's, none of Nyssa's, and twenty-three references to the Graeci, most of which come in his discussion of prosopa. Those that refer to Nazianzus as a possible source in AD 413-414 for the new use of relatio is Augustine's works, include 15.20.38, NPNF vol. 3, 220 and Oration 29:6, NPNF2 vol. 7, 302-303; PG 36: col. 80-81. Irénée Chevalier has been the source of this new chronology and source interpretation though he did not clarify in what manner Augustine became acquainted with Nazianzus where he says, "Il est donc certain que saint Augustin a connu l'enseignment de Grégoire de Nazianze." in S. Augustin et le pensée grecque: les relations trinitaires, 142. Chevalier then lists the doctrines he see as a direct Cappadocian bestowment on Augustine. Altaner, though reserved in his acceptance of Chevalier's insights does agree that Nazianzus' Oration 29 is a crucial source for the concept of the Son's personal bestowal of love in Augustine. The problem is how he had access because a Rufinian translation of that text is not known. Augustine apparently had access to Didymus through Rufinus' translations. See, E. TeSelle, Augustine the Theologian (New York: Herder & Herder, 1970), 295. Mary T. Clark, agrees especially in regard to relatio in Augustinian Personalism: The Saint Augustine Lecture, 1969, The Saint Augustine Lecture Series (Villanova, Pennsylvania: Villanova Univ. Press, 1970), 36. n.2. See also, Michel Schmaus, Die psychologische Trinitätslehre des heiligen Augustinus (Münster: Aschendorffsche Verlagsbuchhandlung, 1967), 5-9.

[186]De Trin 8.1.2, NPNF vol. 3, 116; CC, 269.

Augustine conceives of God, not as a Person, but as personal, meaning that the divine unity is an orchestration of a unity of operation between three mutually co-inherent distinctions.[187] Where Augustine differs from his Eastern counterparts is in the terminology surrounding those distinctions. His doctrine of the 'homoousion' might be summarized in this way; the Trinity is primarily the nature of God considered in various revealed aspects. That revelation however indicates an unique mode of interrelationship. Each person is the other two and the entire Trinity, for each possesses the totality of the nature while comprehending the other persons. From his perspective, philosophically and apologetically, Augustine speaks, as the Cappadocians did, of the incommunicability of persons from the corrective standpoint of relations.[188] This subtle but radical reformulation of Aristotelian categories has affected Western trinitology since the fourth century.

We have noted that relation was different from the other categories spelled out by Aristotle. I would contend that Augustine saw in relations a means of keeping substance and individuation separate. He viewed divine substance dynamically with the protections that the persons can neither be equated with it nor are they accidents of it. There is little here that would indicate a separation from the Athanasian emphasis on Unity in Trinity and Trinity in Unity. It is the subtle explication of that orthodox statement which sets Augustine apart.

F. W. Green, in Rawlinson's deeply influential compilation, is an example of the proclivity of most modern scholarship to preclude the possibility of co-inherence language in Augustine, reserving that for Athanasius and the Cappadocians.[189] There would appear

---

[187]R.P.C. Hanson reads 7.4.7-4.8 wrongly as basis for the comment that "God should only be regarded as one persona." in Studies in Christian Antiquity (Edinburgh: T. & T. Clark, 1985), 289. His critique of Augustine is typical and misleading. It is true, that Augustine does not confront person as a modern mind might be able to but he was not as negative as he is made out to be on the notion of a "objective reality capable of acting" Ibid., 289 (attributed to Bray by Hanson). Hanson contends that the category of subsistent relations is meaningless, and that may be true if left by itself. It is odd that Hanson does not say much about the scripture Augustine and the Cappadocians used in defense of the personhood of the Spirit; he emphasizes the nexus amoris and the donum/donatum traditions that the West took from Augustine. One wonders if Augustine botched the job handed him by the Cappadocians as much as Hanson or Gunton feel he did.

[188]9.1.1."Sed trinitatem relataru ad inuicem personarum et unitatem aequalis essentiae." CC, 293; "There is a trinity of inter-related persons, and the unity of an equal substance." McKenna, De Trinitate, 270; find "persons mutually interrelated." NPNF vol. 3, 125

[189]Rev. F.W. Green, "Later Doctrine of the Trinity," in ed. A.E.J. Rawlinson, Essays on the Trinity and the Incarnation, 291. He clearly states that the Cappadocian "vagueness and incoherence," referring to perichoretic analyses was brushed away by the psychological analogies of Augustine, Ibid., 290. Prestige, God in Patristic Thought, 236-237, follows the same sort of radical separation. He, like Green, points out that the West did know that the East was different, but no allowance is given for the similarity which we see. On the other hand, Hanson castigates Augustine for not building upon the Cappadocian bequeathal, see

to be in these renditions an obscurantism, or at least a restriction, of the roles of the Trinity as Augustine articulates them. In terms of Christian exegesis, both Scriptural and experiential, there was by Augustine's era an understanding that the monarchic and unity models were inadequate in themselves without further explication.

Monarchy, as discussed in De Trinitate, correctly asserts that, based upon the scriptural schema of co-equality in every sphere, the Son lives from the Father's ousia, the divine essence. That derivation of life from the fons of the Father does not imply any reduction of "Godness" in the Son, or by comparison, in the Spirit. Tavard points accurately to this Augustinian perspective on the homoousion where he acknowledges:

> As attributes of God are no other than God, the Father is the 'that' of God as yet unrelated, though filled with potentialities for relationships. The Son is the same 'that' as emerging in relationship. As soon as one understands the divine ousia as self-giving love, one perceives something of the Father and the Son. Total love giving itself, yearning for an object to be given to, for a subject in which to inhere....[190]

This is what lies behind Augustine's firm monarchical unity; there is no static approach to the life of love within the Godhead. For him the Trinity is personal in its self-consciousness and in its social essence. In spite of his reservation regarding 'persona' it would not be over-stated to claim that anything which pertains to personhood according to Augustine ultimately depends upon this mutual understanding of the divine reality.

In the prosopological tradition of the early Church, Augustine weaves a tapestry of argumentation which reveals clearly a departure from the Plotinian 'One'. The modern notion of proof for the Trinity in Scripture must meet Augustine at the point of his method. The only ground for belief in the Trinity is faith informed by revelation. For instance:

> That which is written, "Hear, O Israel: the Lord our God is one Lord," ought certainly not be understood as if the Son were excepted, or the Holy Spirit were excepted; which one Lord our God we rightly call also our Father.[191]

Studies in Christian Antiquity, 290. See the same in Gunton's article where repeatedly he accuses Augustine of not having adequate "conceptual equipment" for advancing three actual divine persons. He focuses on the Bishop's platonic dualism, blindness to the Cappadocian advances on explaining divine substance, over-rationalized "trinities," and the inadequacy of the 'vinculum' motif for applying personhood to the Spirit. "Augustine, the Trinity and Theological Crisis," 33-58.

[190]George Tavard, The Vision of the Trinity (Washington: Univ. Press of America, 1981), 69.

[191]5.11.12. NPNF vol. 3, 93; CC, 218. One has to look carefully for Augustine's theological exegesis. Portions of sentences are formed from scriptural quotation both indirectly and directly. Augustine's love for the subject is such that "rambling" is often an excursus of worshipful intellection spawned by awe of the topic at hand. Cochrane is right when he notes that the doctrine held Augustine in such fascination that he is never more himself than when he contemplated the Trinity. It was an exercise that held profound emotion for him. Christianity and Classical Culture, 411.

Only if the author discerned a dynamic Godhead would this interpretation make sense. He does not refer to an economic Trinity alone; there is something antecedent to salvific works which captured his attention.

The derivation of the Son from the Father is most pronounced in his exegesis of John's Gospel. As the Apostle renders the mystery it is clear that the Father is greater than the Son.[192] In the role of servant Christ is metaphorically referred to as "less".[193] The comparisons are made with a view to the human comprehension of divine reality but they also incorporate the fact of the Son's "begottenness".[194] The Son derives his life, is begotten, essentially and relationally. The person of the Son kenotically divulges the Father, as the self-expressive Word of the Trinity.

The Father is not exhausted by the Son but there is a second movement in the Godhead, a procession according to both the Eastern Fathers and Augustine. The Beginning, the Generation, and the Procession are but one way Augustine approaches the mutual relations of the Godhead. His doctrine of the Spirit is fundamental to the Western 'filioque' doctrine.[195] The mutual relations of the Persons is the source of distinction between them. The Father is distinguished because He begets the Son; the Son is derivative from that originative Source as begotten, yet co-essential; the Spirit is differentiated from both in that he is bestowed by them in mutual love.[196] In all of the

---

[192]Augustine refers to it as subjection of the Son to the Father, but that is to be seen only in light of his rejection of Arianism. See 1.8.15. NPNF vol.3, 24-25. CC, 46-47.

[193]He refers to these biblical indications of derivation as "apparently contradictory and mutually repugnant." See 1.11.22. NPNF vol. 3, 29; CC, 60. He prefaces this chapter with the statement "Wherefore, having mastered this rule for interpreting the Scriptures concerning the Son of God, that we are to distinguish in them what relates to the form of God, in which he is equal to the Father, and what to the form of the servant he took." Ibid. That this method extended throughout the centuries in orthodoxy both East and West can be seen by the helpful distillation of John of Damascus. Nearly three centuries later than Augustine he laid out the orthodox hermeneutic for interpreting the kenotic and theandric passages. Exposition of the Orthodox Faith, 18. NPNF2 vol. 9, 90-92. E. Hill distinguishes Augustine's approach from Tertullian's "tangle" of economic subordinationism in Mystery of the Trinity, 65-67.

[194]1.12. 26. NPNF vol.3, 32; CC, 66. (Latin incommutabilem, for unchangeable). Cf. 4.20.28-29. NPNF vol. 3, 84; CC, 198-199.

[195]4. 20.29. NPNF vol. 3, 84; CC, 199-200. He says of the Spirit, "That he was given twice was certainly a significant economy (dispensatio)." Ibid. The 'double procession' of course was to be an irritant between East and West for centuries, eventually becoming a part of the reason for the ecumenical split.

[196]It should be noted here that there is direct affinity to the progression of thought in the East with regard to the Spirit's deity and incommunicability. Basil, the Gregories, Athanasius, and Epiphanius laid the groundwork, at least in a conciliar mode, (Nicea, Constantinople) if not actually seen by Augustine, in order for him to come to some of his conclusions. Of course, Augustine's lead in what was to become the filioque doctrine has

trinities which arise this fundamental understanding of divine love in interrelatedness is at work. It is the adhesive factor in Augustine's method and theology.

At points he comes close to equating the Spirit with the actual relationship between the Father and the Son.[197] It would seem that Augustine came short of attributing aspects of personhood to the Spirit which he places on the Son and the Father, but that must be kept in tandem with the recurrence of claims to the absolute co-equality of the three. He describes the Spirit in terms similar to the perichoretic love between the Father and the Son claimed by the Eastern tradition. Like the Son, however, the Spirit is co-equal in every respect with the Father.[198] Divine substance is not discerned however as 'triplex' but as the intimate, inscrutable loving co-inherence of three personal relations.[199] It was the Spirit's place in that tri-unity which mesmerized Augustine.

> Therefore the Holy Spirit, whatever it is, is something common both to the Father and Son. But that communion itself is consubstantial and co-eternal; and if it may fitly be called friendship, let it be so called; but it is more aptly called love.[200]

'Friendship', amicitia, is an intriguing word to choose at this juncture. In a context in which the author consistently attempts to elude sacrilegious comparisons, there are several points at which the rational examples fall short and the relational take preeminence. This word and its counterpart reveal the ambiguity in Augustine's mind regarding 'person' while at the same time illuminating the issue which orthodox minds constantly confronted: how is it that one can be three and if so, what are the best analogical terms to use in relating that truth. It is becoming more apparent that in spite of Augustine's sporadic

---

had negative commentary. See R.P.C. Hanson, Studies in Christian Antiquity (Edinburgh: T. & T. Clark, 1985), 290-292. John Zizioulas, Being as Communion, 41 n. 35, but his critique on the West and substantia permeates his entire argument.

[197]5.11.12. NPNF vol.3, 93; CC, 219. McKenna's translation is clearer it seems to me, "Hence, the Holy Spirit is in a certain sense the ineffable communion of the Father and the Son (Ergo spritius santus ineffabilis quaedam patris filiique communio)." De Trin. 190. Shedd's has "the Holy Spirit is a certain unutterable communion of the Father." Ibid., 93.

[198]5.11.12 - 5.15.16, NPNF vol. 3, 93-95; CC, 218-224. The implications of this for the doctrine of appropriations is buttressed by the argument that any difference one finds in the Persons must be in the realm of substantial relations and never in an ontological accidence, which was a major pinion in the Arian polemic.

[199]6.7.9, NPNF vol. 3, 101; CC, 237. In a clear distinction from the implications of speaking of triplicity in the Godhead. Of all Gunton's criticisms, it is this one regarding the Spirit which carries the most weight. Apart from the contentions here, a defense might also include a reservation in demanding that one thinker in the early fifth century, given the philosophical history and historical situation which informed Augustine by his own admission, must of necessity have all the answers to questions which were relatively new to the West. What Gunton does not provide is a rendition of the connections between the advanced Cappadocians and the "occasional" writings of this Western bishop.

[200]6.5.7, NPNF vol. 3, 100; CC, 235.

statements to the contrary, the elements of interpersonal love described in terms of actual relationship are central to his thinking. Augustine employs a theomorphic, not an anthropomorphic, method.[201] The beauty of loving relationships find its source in a transcendent oneness of mutual co-inexistence. It is that divine community which is the model for earthly friendships, not vice versa.[202]

The debated issue remains that Augustine's lack of proficiency in Greek kept him from completely understanding the treasures of the Cappadocians; conversely, it can be shown that the theological consensus, in spite of truncated communication, still produced fundamental similarities. Rather than revealing an intimate awareness of perichoresis or hypostasis, Augustine does indicate a strong lines of connection with Hilary's De Trinitate and the elements of co-inherence resident there.[203]

Meyendorff castigates Augustine for setting the Western status on the divine manifestation.[204] He feels that there is no distinction between 'essence' and 'energy' in the discussion of the different roles within the Trinity in Augustine.[205] This is a

---

[201]O'Donovan says on this the "ectype reflects the archetype." The Problem of Self-Love, 134.

[202]In my graduate work, one colleague in particular helped me to get a grasp of this theme in Augustine. Joseph Murphy and I worked on separate occasions on this specific topic in the De Trinitate and I owe him a debt of gratitude for the insights which he so graciously shared with me.

[203]See 6.10.11 for altered quote from Hilary's De Trinitate 2.1.1. Augustine has "Aeternitas, inquit, in patre, species in imagine, usus in munere." CC, 241. Hilary wrote, "Infinity in the Eternal, the form in the Image, and the use in the Gift." The Trinity. trans. Stephen McKenna, 212. See Meijering's, Hilary of Poitiers on the Trinity (Leiden: E. J. Brill, 1982), 67. Note also discussion of the Father's being "greater" indicated his ungenerated character not an indication of another substance from the Son, 2.1.3, CC, 84 and Hilary, De Trinitate 9.54-56. Also a refutation of Arian inequality with implications for perichoresis in 6.1.1. uses a quote allegedly of the heretic from Hilary, 12.21. There are of course, more appropriate passages in Hilary for perichoretic language, see De Trinitate 2.11, 3.2-4, 9.69. The major difference between Hilary and the Cappadocians is his view that the Word is caused by the Will of God while the latter held that the Word is the will of God, disallowing any hint of inequality.

[204]Vladimir Lossky also has not much good to say about Augustine and the West on this point. In fact, the filioque of Augustine is an extremely sensitive point for Vladimir Lossky, In the Image and Likeness of God (Crestwood, New York: St. Vladimir's Seminary Press, 1985), 70-96. He notes that the Eastern critics of Augustine have yet to work through De Trinitate before they can really conjoin him with their disagreement with the West. Ibid., 95-96. We note here that Congar sees as one of the purposes of his monumental, if not fully satisfying work, I Believe in the Holy Spirit, the rectification of calcified categories according to de Regnon concerning East and West on the Trinity. Ibid., vol. 3, xv.

[205]John Meyendorff, Byzantine Theology: Historical Trends and Doctrinal Themes (New York: Fordham Univ. Press, 1974), 186-187.

misunderstanding of the North African doctor's thinking. He accepts full well the absolute transcendence and immutability of God. It is his concept of participation in the divine nature which converges in the person of Christ that causes him to discern the divine nature differently. De Trinitate reveals no inherent difference between the essential and the economic aspects that the East maintains the West, following Augustine, bifurcated irreparably.

Taken from a christological viewpoint the relational aspects of the essential connection between Father and Son and their economic results are the main pinion of Augustine's trinitology.[206] Early in De Trinitate, Augustine expresses this general commitment which is then worked out in the remainder of his section of scriptural evidence to support orthodox trinitarian thought where he discusses equality of essence, or substance, in relation to texts of distinct economic import.

> ...Because the life of the Son is unchangeable as that of the Father is and yet He is of the Father; and the working of the Father of the Son is indivisible, and yet so to work is given to the Son from Him of whom He Himself is, that is, from the Father; and the Son so sees the Father, as that He is the Son in the very seeing Him....Hence the working of both the Father and the Son is indivisible and equal, but it is from the Father to the Son. Therefore the Son cannot do anything of Himself, except what He seeth the Father do.[207]

This equality of essence and work is supported by the co-eternality of the two persons in differentiation. It is here that the analogy of Father and Son is seen as integral to the dynamism of the Trinity. Tavard warns us rightly that the divine Fatherhood is not adequately represented in its human corollary.[208] Clear lines are drawn concerning the use of analogy in discussing paternal themes. As we have argued, analogies as heuristic tools are instructive of the mystery of the divine life if only as "dim mirrors." The 'homoousion' of Augustine is founded in the biblical expressions of co-inherent divine love. The Father-Son analogy is based on the fact that the Father is different from the Son, yet uniquely One due to perfect divine giving and receiving. Person defined as relation must be qualified by the contexts in which we find Augustine's excurses on interpretation of trinitarian texts:

> For it is said in relation to something, as the Father in relation to something, and the Son in relation to the Father, which is not accident; because both the one is always Father, and the other is always Son; yet not always meaning from the time when the Son was born, so that the Father ceases not to be the Father because the Son never ceases to be the Son, but because the Son was always born, and never began to be the

---

[206]This is one of the crucial differences between Marius Victorinus' triadism and Augustinian trinitarianism.

[207]2.1.3, NPNF vol.3, 38; CC, 83. Augustine rightly equates "seeing" the Father with being "born of" the Father, and to see the Father's work with actually doing that work with Him to correctly address any issue of fundamental separation.

[208]Tavard, Vision of the Trinity, 69.

Son.[209]

The dynamism of the intra-trinitarian life, comes from more than economic expressions, it issues from the completeness of love that is the central divine nature.

God is complete only as Trinity. The plenitude of that co-inherence is found in the analogy of Lover, Beloved and the uniting bond of Love.[210] The principle of personhood is integral here in the economic inter-relationship in the Trinity. He realizes that 'person' is not a univocal term, it is what specifies each person; it is not modalistic in intention, rather it is the relation that negates any concept of independence within the Trinity. In Augustine's Trinity there is always the consciousness of the self in relationship. There is no hint of succession, only simultaneity.[211] Oneness is Threeness.

> A thing certainly wonderfully ineffable, or ineffably wonderful, that while this image of the Trinity is one person, but the Highest Trinity itself is three persons, yet that Trinity of three persons is more indivisible than this of one.[212]

Augustine warns that to think of a Trinity in God is fallacious, the Triune reality is God.[213] The 'Persons' are defined by their reference to the others while retaining distinctness by means of the incommunicable properties that are appropriated by each.

Here we see the dialectic that permeates the reasoning of De Trinitate. The Trinity is only explainable as One in Three. That which is predicated severally to each person as being relative to each of the other persons of the Trinity is that which intensifies our understanding of the unity of the Godhead. As he writes in his discussion of 'persons':

> For the Father, the Son, and the Holy Spirit together is not a greater essence than the Father alone or the Son alone; but these three substances or persons, if they must be so called, together are equal to each singly....When we are told that the Son also is the only God, we must needs take it without separation of the Father and the Holy Spirit. And let him so say one essence, as not to think one to be either greater or better than, or in any respect differing from, another.[214]

---

[209]5.5.6, NPNF vol. 3, 89; CC, 210.

[210]The use of the Apostle John's dictum, "God is love" is crucial to Augustine's systematic principle in De Trinitate. The discussion begins, of course, in the early books relating to the Father and Son, but its usage intesifies after the Holy Spirit is presented as the intra-trinitarian 'communio'. Cf. 6.5.7, 8.8.12 (note the interesting discussion on love as substance in 9.4.6,) 15.17.27-15.19.37 for more of this central theme that is often neglected in modern assessments.

[211]One example of many, see the Doctor of Hippo's, On Christian Doctrine, 1.5.5, trans. Robertson, 10.

[212]15.23.43, NPNF vol. 3, 222; CC, 521.

[213]15.23.43, NPNF vol. 3, 222; CC, 520.

[214]7.6.11,12, NPNF vol.3, 113; CC, 265-266. In 7.1.2 he previews his conclusion. He uses properly understood Aristotelian categories to respond to the question how it is, that the Father, in respect to Himself, is neither His own essence, nor is at all in

In order to circumvent quaternarian inclinations, Augustine defines divine substance in terms of relations. It is not a material substance with which the believer must contend. The unity of co-equal relations is the divine substance. He does not intend to intimate a God behind the Triune God although his use of the Aristotelian category of huperkeimenon has been interpreted as such.[215] Based upon an awareness of the development of doctrine it is more probably accurate to say that Augustine did not consider the material effect his formal elements were to have. We are concerned here with as fair an assessment as is possible of his own notion of divine person which was definitively heuristic.

C. Relational Christology in De Trinitate

From this emphasis on co-inherent unity, in which the Persons are relatively differentiated, comes a strong affirmation on the uniqueness of Christ.

> Therefore the Father and the Son together are one essence, and one greatness, and one truth, and one wisdom. But the Father and the Son both together are not one Word, because both together are not one Son. For as the Son referred to the Father, and is not so called in respect to Himself, so also the Word is referred to Him whose Word it is, when it is called the Word.[216]

One of Augustine's strongest lines of argumentation for trinitarian reality is his subtle awareness of the indivisibility of the attributes of the Persons from their essence. To call the Son the Word, is the same as calling the Word the Son. Here again we see his strict rule of incorporating economic and essential categories.

The dynamism of this construct ought not be missed. It is not some inner divine "stuff" which brings salvation. It is the Incarnation that is the humanly accessible dynamic which reveals the heart of the Triune God. Here we then can distinguish relation from person without, what Mascall refers to as "chasing our own tails in a ballet of bloodless abstraction."[217] Possessing co-essential unity with the Father and the Spirit, the Son in substantial predication is differentiated relatively as the Begotten of God. The Word came

---

respect to Himself, but even His essence is, in relation to the Son?" Augustine says, "Much more is He of one and the same essence, since the Father and Son are one and the same essence; seeing that the Father has his own being itself not in respect to Himself, but to the Son, which essence He begat, and by which essence He is whatever He is. Therefore neither is in respect to Himself alone; and both exist relatively the one to the other.
(trans. emphasis.) NPNF vol. 3, 105. By proper understanding I mean the close agreement with Aristotle while transposing those Greek elements for the most part those ideas for the community of faith.

[215]Gunton, "Augustine, the Trinity and the Theological Crisis of the West," 57-58.

[216]7.2.3, NPNF vol. 3, 107; CC, 249-250.

[217]The Triune God, 30.

to make God visible and salvation appropriatable. It is the self-consciousness of the Son of God revealed in Scripture that solidifies all that Augustine says about the three Persons. Sonship is not merely ascriptive, it is a real relation. "What we see on the created level, is the filiality of the eternally begotten Son....Dependence does not involve inferiority, since what the Father communicates to the Son in eternally begetting him is nothing less than the fullness of his own being."[218] The eternality and immutability of the person of Christ is protected in the continual refrain concerning the co-inherent activity of the Trinity, from the theophanic manifestations to the Cross.

The roles of the Father and the Son are differentiated in the midst of the ousia. This dynamic relationship is bi-directional. Christ is the Mediator between humanity and God, the Priest that effectuates redemption.[219] Incarnation and Atonement are closely connected. "It was necessary that He should be both man and God. For unless He had been man, He could not have been slain."[220] An interesting implication of the relationality for which we are arguing on Augustine's behalf is seen in the subtle distinction between the righteousness of God and His power. The devil is defeated by the inherent righteousness of the suffering Servant. Power followed righteousness in redemption.[221] It may be that Augustine's personalism served the transformative elements of his soteriology more than the impersonal elements residing in power language. He was committed to the

---

[218]Mascall, The Triune God, 32-33. What follows pertains to our argument to come, where he writes,
I think it is by emphasizing the completeness of the Father's giving of himself that we can see that the difference between the two Persons consists, not in any difference in their several natures (for each possesses the one nature of God), but simply in their mutual and reciprocal relatedness, it being equally stressed that this relatedness is not a merely logical or schematic comparability but a metaphysical and existential reality. Ibid., 33

[219]Christ as Mediator, 4.7.11, NPNF vol. 3, 75; CC, 176. As Priest, 1.10.20-21, NPNF vol. 3, 28-29; CC, 56-58. Augustine seems to have had difficulty with the hypostatic union at points. He questions the omniscience of the Son (1.12.23). His explanation of Mk. 13:32 is that Christ was ignorant to deal with our ignorance. While extreme subordination is not evident there are still hints at uneasiness with several NT paradoxes. He never admits a nature in the humanity of Christ. His recourse is to constantly return to the indivisible working of the Father and the Son. The Word is Creator (1.11.22), the Head of the Body, Lord of Glory and Bridegroom (1.8.15). The Servant (1.8.15) is both Son of Man (1.13.28) and Son of God (1.13.28). He also strongly advocated the assumption of humanity into the Godhead in Christ's ascension (1.8.15).

[220]13.14.18, NPNF vol. 3, 1771; CC, 406. Augustine accepted the substitutionary atonement theory (13.11.15) The ransom theory is also present (13.12.16).

[221]13.13.17-13.14.18, NPNF vol. 3, 176-177; CC, 404-407.

reformation of the imago dei in much the same way as the Cappadocians.[222] It is essential to incorporate this insight with the catena of relational 'trinities' that explore self-differentiation in the unity of the person. For it is not merely self-remembering that is reflective of divine love, but a remembering of God that is foundational to the Christian life.[223]

The Incarnation was the supreme mission of the Son. He was the revelation of the power, wisdom, image and Word of God.[224] That disclosure was the crucial means by which humanity, according to Augustine, became inexcusably aware of God's love for the human race, but also it revealed the co-inherent love of the Triune God. Perichoretic relationship 'imaged' on the divine level was offered as a gift of love to those made in the imago dei.[225]

Of the myriad advantages bestowed as a result of the Incarnation, one which pertains to the overall concept of justification is the application of dignity of the human person due to the reality of divine personhood and the restoration offered by grace.[226] The mutual love of the Trinity does not preclude, through the Incarnation, the joining of the divine and the human. The same perichoresis evident in the Trinity, now meant that the

---

[222]Gerhardt B. Ladner, The Idea of Reform (Cambridge, Massachusetts: Harvard Univ. Press, 1959), ch. 5, esp. 195-203. "May I remember you; may I understand you; may I love you. Increase in me these (actions) until you reform (renew) me through and through (donec me reformes ad integrum)." 15.28.51. NPNF vol. 3, CC, 534.

[223]14.15.21. NPNF vol. 3, 194; CC, 449-450. Augustine also discusses the progress of the imago in time and eternity. Note the confluence of redemption and the proper 'referencing' discussed here in a pivotal passage, 14.17.23.
He, then, who is day by day renewed by making progress in the knowledge of God, and in righteousness and true holiness, transfers his love from things temporal to things eternal, from things visible to things intelligible, from things carnal to things spiritual.

[224]7.1.2, NPNF vol. 3, 104; CC, 246.

[225]Book 4 comprises Augustine's ordo salutis. The Word is eternally God (1.2). This Word came to enlighten hearts for the purpose of humbling them in order to deal with the pride (or wrong referencing) basic to sin (2.4). As an example of humility God poured out Himself to cleanse mankind from sin, to win them for restoration, to bring them from division to unity through incorporation wrought by the one Mediator (2.4). Augustine speaks of a 'double redemption' of soul and body, by which the ungodly and the incorruptible are by faith renewed and justified (7.11). O'Donovan draws some excellent conclusions concerning amicitia and the "neighbor-love" which the Trinity intends for the redeemed. The Problem of Self-Love, 120-127. He says, "Of a love which has no interest at all in establishing friendship Augustine has no knowledge." Ibid., 127.

[226]Augustine writes in 13.17.22, NPNF vol. 3, 179; CC, 412.
"It has been demonstrated to man what place he has in the things which God has created; since human nature could be so joined to God, that one person could be made two substances, and thereby indeed of three, - God, soul, and flesh."

individual might fully partake of the divine nature, a reformation reminiscent of the Cappadocian theme. Against the grain of his Neoplatonic foundations, Augustine offers a physical God-man and a "return" that included both soul and body.

D. Relational 'Trinities'

As we have seen there is ample evidence for a relational interpretation for the 'opera ad intra' and the 'opera ad extra' of the Trinity according to Augustine. Using categories which resonate with properly-understood Aristotelian categories, biblical and experiential data, and sound criticisms of Neoplatonic thought, in the second half of his treatise Augustine launches into what has been erroneously called the "psychological" or "philosophical" trinities within human existence. These are misnamed in that the titles tend to ignore the biblical basis laid in the first eight books, and they imply that the self-relatedness is a virtually solipsistic enterprise. Augustine's dynamic view of the creating and regenerating life of the Trinity disallows an independent view of personhood, even in one's consciousness.[27] His trinitarian metaphysic is now explored in the interior of the unified self while constantly referring to its own inherent inadequacies. Augustine asks, "From what likeness or comparison of known things can we believe, in order that we may love God, whom we do not yet know?"[28] It is from the foundation of the mapping of the human consciousness that Augustine sees one of the clearest vestiges of the co-inherent Trinity. "I am, I know, and I will," provides the architectonic structure for this remarkable paradigm shift.[29] This is not a pre-Enlightenment Cartesian construction.[30] W. Principe has forcefully argued against the majority opinion on Augustine's semantics. Instead of accepting the short-hand form of "memoria, intelligentia, and amor" he notes that in almost every instance Augustine uses the verbal rather than the nominal forms.[31] It is the act of remembering, understanding and loving which reflects the Trinity, not mere psychologizing. These living trinities are plumbed to open the believer to actual participation in the life of the Trinity of which that one is the created image.

---

[27]One striking example is 14.14.20. NPNF vol. 3, 194; CC, 448. The "image of God in itself is so powerful that it is able to cleave (inhaerere) to Him whose image it is." This is a recurrent theme that must be kept in mind throughout the discussion.

[28]8.5.8. NPNF vol. 3, 120; CC, 279.

[29]Confessions, 13.11, For an extended personal discussion of memoria which aids in discerning what Augustine means in De Trinitate see Confessions 10.8-20.

[30]Mary Clark, Augustinian Personalism, 9-10.

[31]Walter Principe, "The Dynamism of Augustine's Terms for Describing the Highest Trinitarian Image in the Human Person." In Studia Patristica 17:3. ed. Elizabeth A. Livingstone, 1291-1299 (Oxford: Pergamon Press Ltd., 1982). He found no texts in Bks. 14 and 15 in which the typical triads of noun forms were used.

In a series of intricately devised triplicities Plotinian Neoplatonism offered the analogical starting-point for Augustine's method. Much has been written about the Neoplatonic prototypes for this thought line. For instance, the relationship between the knowing hypostases and the Transcendent One involved a plethora of triads imaged in ratiocination.[232] Ambrose bequeathed a strong philosophical heritage of 'imago' and its inherent grappling with created likenesses to the divine as a theological undertaking to Augustine.[233] The 'mirror' found in the human mind and soul is reflective of the unity and co-equality of divinity. He reveals an exasperation at stopping with attempts at offering cogent examples of intra-trinitarian equality through biblical terminology and other physical comparisons.[234] That which yet may not be clear to the intellect must, in faith and humility, be excavated merely because the nature of truth is revealed to the seeking mind and heart.[235]

To know the Trinity one must know the nature of love, a love that rests on love of God as supreme Love in Unity. It again supports our contention in that as he begins this arduous task, it is imaging with an analysis of human love.[236] He leaves the "physical"

---

[232] Plotinus, Enneads 5.1.6-7, 6.7.35, 5.3.1., 5.4.2, 5.7. The last reference uses ocular vision as an example, much in the same way Augustine does, to illustrate the interrelatedness of First Principle (Nous), Intellectual (eikon) Principle and Object as they are reflected in the image of the soul or in the world (eidolon). Shedd has an intriguing footnote in his corrective translation comparing the Neoplatonic kinesis kuklikai, (which was the transformation of the noesis noeseos concept in Aristotle, made cosmic in import) or the reflective circularity of the human psyche with the perichoretic ternaries of Augustine that he finds in the Cappadocians. De Trinitate, NPNF vol. 3, 129 n. 1. I like what Booth says on this, "Is it more likely that we have here an eirenic if critical treatment of neo-Platonist themes with an apologetic intent?" E.G.T. Booth, "St Augustine's 'de Trinitate' and Aristotelian and neo-Platonist Noetic," In Studia Patristica 16:2. ed. Elizabeth A. Livingstone, (Berlin: Akademie-Verlag, 1985), 489.

[233] Gerald A. McCool, "The Ambrosian Origin of St. Augustine's Theology of the Image of God in Man," Theological Studies 20:1 (March, 1959): 62-81.

[234] One can sense the emotion of this in his On the Gospel of John 39:1-5 NPNF vol. 7, 222-223 and 14:9 Ibid., 97-98. Both indicate that Augustine did not completely divest himself of interpersonal relationships as a vestige of the Trinity. In this sense, Richard of St. Victor remained an Augustinian.

[235] 8.1.pref. NPNF vol. 3, 115; CC, 268-269.

[236] 8.10.14 "Ecce tria sunt, amans et quod amatur et amor." CC, 290. His progression of increasingly subtle theological interpretation is as follows:
Bk. 9 Mind, the mind's self-knowledge, the minds's self love. "quaedam trinitas..., id est mens et notitia, qua se novit, et amor, quo se notitiamque suam diligit" (See 9.4.4, 9.5.8, cf. 15.3.5) John Sullivan, calls it the "first image", The Image of God, 117-123.
Bk. 10 Memory (which replaces mind in his structure of subjectivity, understanding, or thought, will. "memoria... intelligentia... voluntas" (See 10.11.17-18 memoria sui, notitia sui, amor sui). Sullivan's "second image," Image of God, 124-136.
Bk. 11 Sense perception analyzed as the object seen, the external vision, and the

discussions with his section on prosopa, but in a sense he does not eschew the ideas involved in the discussion of person. The likeness of the divine Word is rigorously sought in the inner and the mental. Here Augstine separates himself from the Academics whose speculative rationalism produced an agnosticism. The "word" of the human mind, and the Word of God challenge the limits of any monadism that saw reason as the highest reality.

There is in all of this discussion the radical dynamism of interrelatedness that points back to the Three in One. Rather than the abstract notion of a memory bank, God's inner being is radically "personalized". God's knowledge is based on its motivation, love. That intentional triune love is reflected in creation.[237] Substance is not staticized, it is attributed to Lover, Beloved and Love in the Trinity. The substantial unity of the mind is basic to Augustine's argument as it bespeaks the co-inherent perichoretic relationship of the triunity of God. The 'images' that Augustine has tentatively proffered are all in themselves "dynamically developing" realities which point to the reflexive in-beingness of their rightful object, the Trinity.[238] Again let it be said that these "mirrors" are only reflections in that

---

attention of the mind. "ex corpore scilicet quod videtur, et forma quae inde in acie cernentis imprimitur, et utrumque copulantis intentione voluntatis" (11.1, cf. 15.3.5) Augustine compares this with memoria, informatio, intentio voluntatis.

Bk. 12 Trinitarian explorations of scientia are promised but only mentioned at end of the book (12.20.26, hints given at 12.1.4). See possible reason for this in O'Donovan's suggestion that it is the "most important retraction Augustine ever wrote." The Problem of Self-Love, 87.

Bk. 13 fides, but he uses memory, understanding and love; Idea in memory, contemplation, and the will/love that unites both the former.

Bk. 14 Memory, wisdom, (Sapientia) love, (memoria Dei, intelligentia Dei, amor Dei is Sullivan's third image, Image of God, 136-148. O'Donovan has sapientia, notitia sui, dilectio sui, in The Problem of Self-Love, 135. True human wisdom, or understanding, is the most adequate analogy in the restored imago dei and is distinguished from knowledge. That is a mind that rightly references because of the participation of the mind in the life of the Triune God. See 14.14.18, 15.6.10, 15.16.30-15.19.37.

[237]Augustine's self-critique of the rational "trinities" as insufficient is remarkable. For he can claim that the human mind is the image in 14.8.11 (NPNF vol. 3, 189; CC, 436), and in 14.12.15, with equal clarity state that "this trinity, then, of the mind is not therefore the image of God," (NPNF vol. 3, 191;). In both places, Augustine is clear that the imaging is only as strong as the relationship between the mind and its Creator, that is in participation and in shared love (both texts use capax and particeps potest.) Cf. 14.14.20. 15.27.49. (NPNF vol. 3, 226; CC, 530-531) is the apex of this denial in the face of the glory of God. The rational notion is without foundation without the relational. Real love must be apprehendable in intellection or it is "dull and infirm." Ibid. Cf. Torrance's view of this apparent "ambiguity" in Reality and Scientific Theology (Edinburgh: Scottish Academic Press, 1985), 170.

[238]A.K. Squire, "Personal Integration in the Latter Books of Augustine's 'De Trinitate'," In Studia Patristica 16:2. ed. Elizabeth A. Livingstone, (Berlin: Akademie-Verlag, 1985), 566. In the same place Squire offers the insight that the threeness spoken of is in no way to be interpreted quantitatively. We must mention, that these "trinities" produced problems as well, for evil as well as good could be applied to all these examples. The role of faith was yet obscure until Bk. 13. We have alluded to the "idolatry" possible when the

their ultimate object is knowing, loving, and becoming like God. The being of God provides ontologically the true being for human existence, the **imago trinitatis**.[239]

E. Person in Augustine's Theology

We have seen that Augustine's distinction or particularity of divine Persons is seen in the relations by which they subsist. But we have also argued that Augustine does not stop there. It is true that the simplicity model from which he draws his general framework, precludes a relationality of three "beings" in Trinity. The question comes however as to what Augustine meant in his usage of person in light of the fact that he presents a somewhat ambiguous stance. Does he maintain a philosophical unity or does he go beyond it into a personal, relational onenness?

There is little doubt that Augustine was not attempting an entirely new approach to the concept of person. His usage is not uniform and includes the histrionic-based concept of "role" or "character" along with the later incorporation of "office," and "function." The philosophical clarity of Boethius was adumbrated a century earlier, though not exclusively, in Augustine's understanding of the individual rational nature. What is unmistakable is that he saw 'person', as Tertullian did, when applied to God as a specific term denoting "what three?"[240] Reflecting his awareness and reservations regarding the Eastern use of 'hypostasis' Augustine still distinguishes between three persons in one substance and three substances. "Here, when there is no difference of essence, it is necesary that these three should have a specific name."[241] There are not three persons who comprise a divine substance, but rather, one essence, one substance which is three

---

mind too intimately attaches itself with the images. 10.5.7, 10.6.8. If the mind "con-fuses" with unmitigated adhesiveness to the vestige then God is not rightly enjoyed. "But when the will leaves better things and greedily wallows in these things (images, sensible things) then it becomes unclean..." 10.6.8, CC, 321.

[239]Thomas Fay, "Imago Dei: Augustine's Metaphysics of Man," Antonianum 49 (1974): 186-187.

[240]7.6.11. NPNF vol. 3, 112; CC, 262, the terminology used here is similar to the reservation we see in 5.9.10, "That we mínght not be altogether silent, when asked, what three, while we confessed that they are three."

[241]Found in 7.4.7 but whole discussion is in 7.4.7-7.6.11. NPNF vol. 3, 109-113; CC, 255-265. R. Boigelot, writes, "Augustin semblerait souhaiter qu'on inventât pour qualifier les Trois divins un nom spécial qui les différencierait en leur individualité de tous les êtres doués d'intelligence." "Le mot "personne" dans les écrits trinitaires de saint Augustin." Nouvelle Revue Théologique 57:1 (1930): 11-12. Boigelot states that the normal terms, "Father," "Son" and "Spirit" are chosen on a 50:1 ratio in Augustine's treatises that have to do with the Trinity. Ibid., 6. He says that in De Trinitate "il considère le nom personne comme un nom absolu," an absolute which is "predicated plurally." Ibid., 15. We agree in part with his assessment, but want to go beyond his Thomistic conclusions.

persons.[242]   As the Cappadocians did, Augustine does not see divine substance as a hypostatic monad.[243]

His attempt to clarify the "enigma" projects another paradox for the modern mind. For all the passages which can be taken to support the contention that it was he who first internalized spiritual reflection with the strong simplicity resident in the analogy of memory, understanding and will, there are other corresponding passages which propose an equally dynamic relationality. Nonetheless, it is primarily within the individual mind, that internal order, that we see his images of the Trinitarian life expanded. It may be that here, as in the Cappadocians there is an underlying assessment of the relationality of the person, whose mind is reflecting the Trinity.

From the standpoint of missions or the opera ad extra, the place of loudest complaint by the critics of intra-trinitarian discussions surrounds its supposed gaps, Augustine's view of person is distinctively comprehensive. In his denunciation of the summation of Wiles and Hodgson that the doctrine of the Trinity is a product of rational reflection, E. Hill postulates that the concept of relationships was a "logico-metaphysical instrument" used to assist in discerning the transcendent Trinity.[244] He is correct in the view of revelation that Augustine espoused but I would question his view of divine persons and the missions. The bishop of Hippo discerned real divine persons in active relationship to believers. Though this dynamic relation is in no way reciprocal as between equals it carries a "filial" content. The biblical doctrine of Christ's "Lordship" is always in tandem with "adoptive sonship".[245]   The eternal godhead is not altered in any way by these relationships but that does not mean that within the Trinity itself there is no distinguishability which has direct bearing on the "inseparable" opera ad extra.[246] The Three are One in essence; the One is Three in both divine being and economic expression.[247]

---

[242]This is the origin of the Thomistic category of subsistent relations. See. ST 1a.40.3 (Blackfriar's edition), 149-155; 1a.41.6, 181.

[243]This is a theme in E. Bailleux's, "Le personalisme trinitaire des pères grecs," Mélanges de Science Religieuse 27 (1970): 3-25, although he is strong to distinguish the Augustinian "psychological" approach from the personalism of the Eastern Fathers.

[244]Hill, "Our Knowledge of the Trinity," 9.

[245]Ex. Jn. 14:10-24; Gal. 3:23-4:7.

[246]Augustine refers to the external manifestations of the Son in relation to the immutable Godhead in 15.3.5. NPNF vol. 1, 200; CC, 462.

[247]This may assist in the translation of that difficult phrase, "person Trinitatis." 2.10.18., NPNF vol. 3, 46; CC, 104 and 2.13.23. NPNF vol. 3, 48; CC, 111. Rather than negating all that Augustine purports about the trinitarian distinctions, this is merely another way of saying "aspect" of the Trinity. See Boigelot, "Le mot, "personne," 8-9.

This view of person has, as Mascall indicates with regard to **perichoresis**, "not only metaphysical but also **noetic** significance; that is that it provides not only a **de facto** description but expresses the very meaning of the triadic relation."[248]

It is apparent at this point that what we have discerned in Augustine concerning 'person' is inferred from the entire work, and is more than adequately supported.[249] We have attempted to elude eisegetical affirmations while trying to discern the intentions of this strong mind of another era. Relationality is evident throughout Augustine's mature writing, but one looks in vain, if one seeks a succinct definition of personhood from that perspective. We have seen the achievements of the Cappadocians in their usage of relational language for the Trinity but have also noted the difficulties of the early ecumenical Church in agreeing upon the proper terminology to use with reference to the Father, Son and Holy Spirit.

The Rahnerian axiom has held sway far too long. He finds resonance with Lonergan as well in the proposition that the three only comprehend themselves as relations. Augustine is often brought in as support for this contention. I would argue, that to do so is illegitimate. De Trinitate does not give an unequivocal defense of that position. It has been shown that relation, based in and configured by divine love, is the **leitmotiv** that propels the intensive thought structure of this masterpiece. In relation to that proposal there are three major responses regarding Augustine's view of person.

First, is the stance that overemphasizes Augustine's sound reservations in use of 'persona' because of its automatic abuse by the Sabellians. He is also aware of the tendency to extrapolate grossly anthropomorphic applications that disparage the oneness which he diligently seeks to protect.[250] Of "person", Hill can say that, "When applied to the divine mystery they lose (or should be deprived of) practically all their own proper content or signification, and should be treated as simply the least inconvenient of labels."[251] The odd thing about this sort of critique is that there is no satisfying alternative given. To say 'person' is a concession and then to state that 'subsistent relation' is better leaves one bewildered. Relations are important but they do not constitute all the evidence which 'person' necessitates. That is why Mascall attempts a correction of emphasis on "three

---

[248]E. L. Mascall, The Triune God, 82.

[249]"Formal" definitions of person carry a typical philosophical feel. "Man, then, as viewed by his fellow man, is a rational soul with a mortal and earthly body in its service." On the Morals of the Catholic Church 27.52. NPNF vol. 4, 55. See also De Ordine libri II 2.2.31, "Homo est animal rationale mortale." PL 32, 1009. And De quantitate animae 25.47-49 PL 32, 1062-1063.

[250]9.4.6-7. NPNF vol. 1, 128; CC, 298-300. 12.5.5. NPNF vol. 1, 156-157; CC, 359-360.

[251]E. Hill, Mystery of the Trinity, 59.

subjects of a concrete triadic relation" in trinitarian unity.[252] Relations do not constitute the persons; the mutual relationship of three Persons constitutes the divine Being.

Second, is the position which focuses on the non-relational aspects of personhood. We have discussed the rational vestiges in creation and in the 'imago dei'. Margaret Miles has suggested the use of vision in Augustine as the clearest indication of what 'person' means.[253] She contends that the 'other-orientedness' which marks the person is not relational but rather object-directed. Vision is the connector between subject and object. It is the soul's chosen focus on that determines the depth of the individual, for that object retroactively forms the viewer in its image. Thus, the soul or self is seen as, "not primarily a separated entity for whom the problem is the formation of "relationships"; rather it is a "partially centered energy... which comes to be cumulatively distinguished and defined by the objects of its attention and affection."[254] She echoes the misperceptions of theological interpreters where she states that the "pressing problem of human existence is not relationship, the building of bridges between separate entities, but differentiation, the construction of a center which defines itself and determines the direction of its investment of energy."[255] There is no doubt that Augustine does present a view of the soul that is unable to properly focus on meaningful objects without illuminatory grace. The question unanswered here is the reason for the "differentiation". The kind of world Miles projects is the modern utopia, whole individuals who make right choices, and who choose to relate to others, because it is advantageous. Augustine is not a whit interested in that sort of world or to its imaging of the divine Trinity. It is a truncated, misguided view of personhood. This idiosyncratic interpretation disregards the connection between knowledge and love in Augustine's epistemology.

The other two positions are often confused because of the definitions behind similar words. L. Bouyer is accurate when he notes the primarily philosophical trajectory out of which this stance emerges.[256] There is a second facet of the modern tendency toward economic trinitarianism which all but eclipses the opera ad intra. It is probable

---

[252]Find Mascall's ecumenical attempt and insight in, The Triune God, 79-82. We would prefer "relational being", or "hypostatic relation", J. Galot's offerings which Mascall also likes, see Ibid., 11,12,74,75. His critique of Augustine's categories may be attributed to their normal static interpretation.

[253]Margaret Miles, "Vision: The Eye of the Body and the Eye of the Mind in Saint Augustine's De trinitate and Confessions," Journal of Religion 63 (April, 1983): 125-142.

[254]She says the soul is an "object-oriented or intentional entity." Miles, "Vision," 129.

[255]Miles, Vision, 130.

[256]Dictionary of Theology. S.v. "Person," Louis Bouyer. trans. Charles Underhill Quinn (New York: Desclee Co., 1965), 347.

that Augustine would respond to this view of divine person as relation with his ubiquitous realism. To speak of *caritas* necessitates a true signification, not a nominalism. Augustine does not adequately define all the elements of the relational subsistents but he does not take the rationalistic lines of a rehashed Plotinianism, which is as far as Lonergan, Rahner, Wiles, and many others have been able to go.[257] It is possible that Rahner's own gauntlet can be thrown back. He says that it must be with embarrassment that one attempts to approach divine personhood in any manner other than by the salvific acts of God. Yet, even after he has castigated the latent "tritheism" he states with resignation, "However, there it ('person') is, sanctioned by the usage of more than fifteen hundred years, and there is no other word which would be really better, more generally understandable and less exposed to misconceptions."[258] To advocate "modes" or "relations" is to proffer nothing if those actualities do not carry the full weight of the scriptural witness. To then say that a "mode" became incarnate is equally baffling, just as the "mode" of the Spirit descended and remained on the "mode" of the Son. We do not equate the temporal mission with the eternal mutuality of the Godhead. Relations between persons are not ancillary to divine personhood, it is predicated upon the essential nature of God, which is the co-inherent existence of Three inseparable and non-diffusible Persons.[259]

The third perspective is the one chosen here. Given the history of 'persona' and Augustine's awareness of the difficulties surrounding it, nonetheless, his view of the relationship between the three persons as intimate love and self-giving overshadows all his other attempts at explaining the unity of the Godhead. He had a strong grasp of the individual human person.[260] The person is a rational, mortal animal with an underlying

---

[257]See Illtyd Trethowan's, "In Defence of Traditional Trinitarianism," Monastic Studies 17 (Christmas, 1986): 143-154, for an excellent critique of Hill, Lonergan, and Rahner in light of a relational perspective on Augustine's personalism. For him the concept of subsistent relations, "turns mystery, to which we should expect some clue, into an enigma." Ibid., 151. He agrees with us that "interdependence" between the persons is the missing factor in these modern viewpoints.

[258]Rahner, "Remarks on the Dogmatic Treatise 'De Trinitate'", 101. One wonders how far from modalism his offer of triune "personality" is in this regard. Ibid., 102

[259]J.A.T. Robinson agrees with this contention by noting that to disallow this predication "introduces a fatal distinction between nature and will in God, between the essential and the economic. 'Thou Who Art," 581. He also finds the doctrine of the relations of origin as "insufficiently grounded in Scripture." Ibid., 583. His analysis is very similar to G. Marcel's discernment concerning humans that the "'I-Thou' relationship is valid only if it posits a Supreme God from Whom 'I' and 'Thou' derive their very being, depth and dynamism." Quoted in P. Henry, St. Augustine on Personality, 17.

[260]Drobner gives a rigorous analysis of Augustine's concept of human person. As of 411, Augustine had examined the interrelationship of soul and body on numerous occasions, revealing a distinct Neoplatonic tint. H. Drobner, Person-Exegese und Christologie bei Augustinus: zur herkunft der formal "una persona" (Leiden: E.J. Brill) 1986.

unity of body and soul. Drobner repeatedly emphasizes the personal nature of that body/soul unity and at points draws the comparison with marriage, both physical and spiritual.[261] There even seem to be stronger lines of influence from the Cappadocian's "hypostasis" than the Neoplatonic psychology.[262]

He was able to converse concerning the Christological use of 'person' because of his commitment in human personhood to the hypostatic relation between body and soul. The well-defined doctrine of **communicatio idiomatum** is another of the bequeathals of Augustine.[263] Human psychosomatic unity is an image of the divine co-incision in Christ of Logos and man.[264] Before Chalcedon and feeding its eventual conclusions, Augustine was able to discern the problems presented by the confusion of the two natures, the vitalistic dynamism of Apollinarians and may have even circumvented the inherent lacunae in Cappadocian Christology.[265] Likewise, he related his christological findings to the trinitarian applications of personhood. He emphasized the unity of the Father and the Son, explored the implications of the filioque and defended against the commom criticism of a quaternity in relating the Incarnation with the eternal Trinity.[266] This departure from his Plotinian

---

[261]Augustine says of the relationship of Christ and His Church in proclaiming the Word of God in Expositions on the Psalms 75:4 (74:4 in Latin texts) NPNF vol. 8, 351. , "There shall be two in one flesh....For in order that ye may know these in a manner to be two persons, and again one by the bond of marriage...He is preaching Himself even in his members now existing." See also, Homilies on the Gospel of John, Tractate II.14. NPNF vol. 7, 18.

[262]Drobner writes,
"Vom menschlichen Willen ...als "Grundsubstanz und copula des intelligiblen Vermogens und des Bewußtseinsinhaltes, das eigentliche personbildende Element" bei Augustinus analysiert, spricht Augustinus im Kontext des Menschen als una persona nicht, zumindest nicht explizit. Er mag implizit im Begriff der persona enthalten sein, wie auch die griechische hypostasis ihn mit umfaßt."
Person-Exegese, 124.

[263]Grillmeier gives an exhaustive historical analysis of this theological construct in the West in his Christ in Christian Tradition, trans. John Bowden. 2nd rev. ed. (London: Mowbrays, 1975), 392-413.

[264]See A. Outler's excellent article, "The Person and Work of Christ," in R. Battenhouse ed., A Companion Guide to the Study of St. Augustine. Reprint. (Grand Rapids: Baker Book House, 1955), 343-355. He says, "He was a Chalcedonian before Chalcedon." Ibid., 345.

[265]Grillmeier, Christ in Christian Tradition, 147-149, 337, 365-368.

[266]Drobner, Person-Exegese, 258-270. He summarizes his research that according to Augustine,
Die Trinität sind tres personae, nicht una, sodern unum. Christus jedoch ist una persona geminae substantiae. Aber auch heir kann Gott nicht ein Teil der Person

background was also a defense against modalism and tritheism. Divine Persons that are not identical to their substance in any other way than by their communion, are not accidents because they are essential to the very nature of that co-existence.[267] Each of the persons is distinct, but their distinguishability is only as discernible as the inseparability of the three is held tenaciously.

The modern critics caricature the doctrine of relational tri-personhood as advocating the subjective experience of the individual, or the splintering of the Trinity in person as experiencing mind, conscious subject and individual reality. They settle for 'relation' as 'relationship', so that each of the persons is equated with those relations. It is amazing how much in Augustine is missed if that tack is adhered to indiscriminately. He would find resonance with modern reinterpretations such as: 'deep interconnectedness,' a 'mutuality which transcends human understanding of unity,' and 'reciprocal dependence' which distill the tenor of his trinitology and his larger theological schema. Love in De Trinitate is based in divine giving and receiving of three co-equal, co-bestowing Persons.[268]

Important to note is that Augustine did not equate the persons with the substance of the Godhead in any identical sense as the Arians argued.[269] That would have been to promulgate three distinct gods. Only as one incorporates Augustine's awareness of the uniqueness of the divine substance does this make sense. It was never viewed by him as composed by three entities; instead, the divine nature expressed its unalterable simplicity in the interdependent reality of the three.[270] A place where we see a major area of weakness

---

genannt werden, sonst wäre der Sohn vor seiner Menshwerdung nicht vollständig gewesen. In beiden Fällen zeigt sich also, daß Gott immer einer und unteilbar ist, nie nur ein Teil einer Person. Ibid., 262.

[267]T. Wassmer, "Platonic Thought in Christian Revelation as seen in the Trinitarian Theology of Augustine," American Ecclesiastical Review 139 (1958): 294. A. Trapè, emphasizes De Trinitate 7.6.11 in this regard, "I termini "natura" e "persona" nella teologia trinitaria di S. Agostino." Augustinianum 13 (1973): 577-587.

[268]See Augustine's Letter, 169, 2.6 "although their existence in inseparable union is at every moment simultaneous..., they are by certain created things presented to us distinctively and in mutual relations to each other...- these things presenting the Three to our apprehension separately, indeed, but in no wise separated." NPNF vol. 1, 540. This is echoed by Cairns when he sees the difference between Plotinus and Augustine. Speaking of the ultimate source of agape he says "What a difference the doctrine of Trinity...has made to our understanding of God! For the Persons of the Holy Trinity love one another with a pure and selfless love of which Plato and Aristotle and Plotinus seem to have no knowledge. The Image of God in Man (London: SCM Press, 1953), 97.

[269]15.3.5. NPNF vol. 1, 200; CC, 462.

[270]Here we take exception to Lossky's inference regarding Augustine, though I am sure it has been true in the West, in The Image and the Likeness of God, 78-80. Also we reject Lloyd's extremely limited philosophical approach, "Augustine's Concept of Person." in Augustine: A Collection of Critical Essays, ed. Markus, R. A. (Garden City, NY: Anchor

concerns Augustine's view of the Holy Spirit. No matter how the modern mind attempts a reconciliation it is difficult to comprehend a "gift" or a "communion" as a person. Only if Augustine's larger intention is kept in mind is this "giveable" person comprehendable.

It is possible that Augustine exceeded the Cappadocians in the doctrine of divine indwelling.[271] This relationship between the believer and God is profoundly trinitarian. The Holy Spirit is not an amorphous "gift" but the vital contact 'person' for the infusion of divine love.[272] It is through the Holy Spirit that the 'viator' is introduced to the charity of God and is inhabited by the God who is that love. "He who cleaves to the Lord is one spirit."[273] This habitational presence is not universal, it is an effective presence which originates with baptismal grace. Augustine saw an incorporation in this relationship that issued in a variety of graces. The individual believer was ushered into a new life within the 'communio sanctorum'. Within that new familial structure, knit together by the reconciling work of Christ and the reforming work of the Holy Spirit, an intimacy was formed by which the believer was to be constantly challenged to take on a greater likeness to the divine love made known to him by the Holy Spirit.[274] The unity of the Spirit is union with God. It is this person of the Trinity which provides the culminative entry into full participation in the Godhead.

When this active sanctifying work of the Holy Spirit is discussed there is no question Augustine is referring to a Person which is the alter ego of the dynamic Christ he confesses. Thus, we conclude with Teselle that "The purpose of Augustine's investigation is not to get an exact terminology - too much effort has often been devoted to repeating his numerous triadic formulas - but to understand the nature of substance and relation in the

---

Books, 1972): 191-205. To not put Augustine in context is to conclude as the Moltmanns in Humanity in God (New York: Pilgrim Press, 1983), 100-101, that his thinking is "spiritless"; or as T. R. Martland says, from a markedly Eastern polemic position Augustine "failed", in "A Study of Cappadocian and Augustinian Trinitarian Methodology." Anglican Theological Review 47 (1965): 252-263.

[271]Peter Brown, Augustine of Hippo, 155 notes that the indwelling of God in the Incarnate Word and of humans by Jesus Christ is "the actual character" of Augustine's christology. Fortman makes this point and then punctuates it with an analysis of Letter 187, which is more a doctrinal treatise than an epistle. The Triune God, 147-148. See Augustine, Letters Vol. 4, trans. Sr. Wilfrid Parsons, FC vol. 30, 1955.

[272]An excellent historical survey of the views on the Holy Spirit and a strong argument for his "contact" function is found in K. McDonnell, "A Trinitarian Theology of the Holy Spirit." Theological Studies 46 (1985): 191-227. Another perspective which indicates the importance of selectivity of data to draw conclusions from is found in William Menzies' "The Holy Spirit in Christian Theology," in Perspectives in Evangelical Theology, eds. K. Kantzer and S. Gundry (Grand Rapids: Baker Book House, 1979), 67-79.

[273]De Trinitate 14.14.20. NPNF vol. 3, 194; CC, 448.

[274]Augustine, Letter 187, chaps. 25-29, 38, 41. FC vol. 30.

mind.[275] The interrelational communion of distinct entities is an inherent premise in Augustine's view of salvation. In order for his analogies to be comprehensible in that framework they must carry a concomitant, if not ascendant, emphasis with that pertaining to "psychological" substance. It is that triune based interdependence and self-giving that informs Augustine's view of both divine and human persons. As Heron indicates in his attempted amelioration between East and West:

> Augustine's whole approach to the question is relational; in trying to discover the images and analogies to explain the doctrine of the Trinity he concentrates on those models, taken from the human experience, which help to reveal the interplay between the three Persons while maintaining their unity.[276]

It is because this relationality has not been taken seriously, that the schism between traditions still exists and that most theology at present is stymied in stagnant views of God and the bewildering individualism spawned by solipsistic definitions of person.

III. Conclusion

Augustine is definitely person-centered. His reservations about "person" as a viable symbol for the Triune God are at once, perspicuous and obscurantistic. If he could have drawn more heavily upon the Greeks whom he could not read but of whom he was definitely aware, he might have deepened his insights considerably. Even if by modern standards his personalistic emphasis is indirectly presented, it remains foundational to his premises and conclusions. His trinitarian dogma is relational, based on his concept of the person. Apart from the Neoplatonic carryover of an aversion to biological metaphors he posits an ascending scale of analogies which are based on a relational view of reality. We have said that due to his revelational realism, he abhorred materialistic anthropomorphisms and at that point may have rejected the full implications of his own commitment to the doctrine of creation. Out of a desire to protect the divine from misuse he may have squelched an area that would have given even more grist to his relational argument. Gen. 1:27 is deeply embedded in Augustine, but its relational implications for the imago dei,

---

[275]E. TeSelle, Augustine the Theologian, 303.

[276]A. I. C. Heron, "Who Proceedeth from the Father and the Son: The Problem of the Filioque," Scottish Journal of Theology 24 (1971): 164. Examples of the tendency toward a blindness to Augustine's relationality are J.Bligh, "Richard of St. Victor's De Trinitate: Augustinian or Abelardian?" Heythrop Journal 1 (1960): 118-139 and Olin Curtis, The Christian Faith (New York: Eaton and Mains, 1905). On page 495 the latter chooses "not Augustine, but Athanasius. For this choice I have two reasons. First, Augustine seems to me never to have caught the Christian view of God. In fact much that he says about God and the ways of God is Christianity so tampered with as to lose the spirit of the New Testament altogether."

indicated by 27b, so recently expressed by Barth, are neglected beyond mere mention.[277] Nonetheless, the Person who is the self-donation of the Father and the Son, the Holy Spirit is the Illuminator who joins the signs to the things to be enjoyed. He is the muscillage of a communal religious life by which believer is conjoined to believer as well as the Triune God.[278]

Having noted that love is the basis of the first half of De Trinitate and that it is the underlying adhesive to the rigorous scrutinies of the second major segment, one could argue that the love of God is Augustine's systematic principle, and that a relational interpretation would be the theological method which ties his later writings together.[279] The City of God is only fully comprehendable if one has understood the communality Augustine sees as the leitmotiv of Christian existence. The Trinity infuses the Church with the reality of its purpose, the communion totally dependent upon Divine Love and in which Love has absolute and purposeful freedom in recreation. In the Trinity the persons stand in a relation of love that is supra-rational and supra-volitional. Love between the Father and the Son is, (not, "results in") a third "subsistent", the Holy Spirit.[280] At the apex of the Reformation, the Augsburg Confession affirmed Constantinople (AD 381) at this point in its first article. The reformed believers, "understand the word 'person' in the sense in which the ecclesiastical writers on this subject have used it, not, therefore, as a part or

---

[277]Example, 12.7.9-10, NPNF vol. 1, 158-159; CC, 363-365. Franz Mayr has presented some interesting and questionable analyses of the intra-trinitarian relationship in terms of the family motif. He strains the philosophical background of Augustine unnecessarily and has a tendency to overemphasize the "matriarchal" understanding of God. See his "Trinitätstheologie und Theologische Anthropologie." Zeitschrift für Theologie und Kirche 68 (1971): 427-477 and "Trinitat und Familie in De Trin. XII." Revue des études Augustinniennes 18 (1972): 51-86.

[278]15.17.27, NPNF vol. 3, 215, CC, 501-502. 15.17.31, NPNF vol. 3, 216-217, CC, 505-507.

[279]6.5.7, 15.17.27, 15.17.31 outlines the place of the Holy Spirit as the reciprocal love of the Father and the Son. See also 8.8.12 for exposition of I Jn 4:8,16. We have shown that the inner and outer trinities have as their third element most often the term love or will which means the connective element which serves to conjoin the first two or more specifically the volitional choice to perceive, or contemplate or to go out beyond one's self. See also 15.18.32, 15.19-15.23.44.

[280]O'Donovan, The Problem of Self-Love, 127-136 is a good summary of the points we have seen here. The difficulty I see in most of these modern discussions is a circumventing of the central issue, that of personhood. Without it we must state with Hanson, "Augustine's doctrine leaves us in an impossible situation: God in one mode of subsistence loves himself in another mode of subsistence and in a third mode of subsistence is the love with which he loves himself!" in Studies in Christian Antiquity, 290.

quality of something else, but as something which exists for itself."[281] This other-oriented love, of necessity is a mutual relationship. The image of that relationship is found in the human person within the context of the believing community.[282] Burnaby puts it succinctly:

> For Augustine the earnest of the Spirit is a unity which is 'unity because it is love, and love because it is holiness'. (6.5.7) And this unity is not Plotinus' flight of the alone to the Alone....The solitary soul cannot be in Christ. It is not the individual who is called to be 'in Christ', to imitate or reproduce the union of human nature with the Word. For the love of God cannot exist apart from the love of the Brethren. But in the Communion of Saints love is a 'theandric activity', Emmanuel, God with us -- unus Christus amans se ipsum."[283]

We concur then with Paul Henry's comment that Augustine's "doctrine of the person has had an incalculable influence on the development of the Christian idea of God and man and the relations of man to God."[284] Although, the doctrine of substance remained clouded by the commitment to apophatic antinomies in the East, there have been signs of attempted ameliorations without capitulation of stance for ecumenical reasons.[285] The suggestions and implications of both the Cappadocian "ec-static" hypostaseis and Augustine 'anagogical' trinitarian images, however, lead the sincere thinker to no other conclusion but that divine personhood is grounded in a mutuality that transcends either numeric unity or individual personality.[286] In both camps, though the East appears to have

---

[281]"Et nomine personae utuntur ea significatione, qua usi sunt in hac causa Scriptores Ecclesiastici [die Väter], ut significet non partem aut qualitatem in alio, sed quod proprie subsistit. Augsburg Confession 1530, Article 1, P. Schaff, Creeds of Christendom, vol. 3, reprint (Grand Rapids: Baker Book House, 1977), 7. One can sense the similarity with Athanasius' comment that the Son is of the Father's substance, uncompounded, and yet he is not a part of division of the Father. De Decretis, 11 NPNF2 vol. 4, 157.

[282]I am indebted to Joseph Murphy for pointing me to 14.14.18 where the distinction between humans and other creatures is clearly delineated. Love is a rational, volitional capacity, not merely affectional. It is of course important to emphasize again that love is not accidental to God's essence, He is Love.

[283]Burnaby, Amor Dei, 177.

[284]Paul Henry, Saint Augustine on Personality: The Saint Augustine Lecture, 1959. The Saint Augustine Lecture Series (New York: Macmillan Co., 1960), 18.

[285]C. Stead states the criticism and softens it with a true reading of ekstatic background, Divine Substance, 280. See E.L. Mascall, The Triune God, 71.

[286]See O. Du Roy, L'Intelligence de la foi en la Trinité selon Saint Augustin (Paris: Études Augustiniennes, 1966), 420-466 for an incisive, if not myopic consideration of the topic at hand. In the discernment of the relation between intellect and faith, Augustine's trinitarianism is an essential element. He, as other commentators we have seen, takes the "rational" route in interpretation. He refers to Malet's Thomistic interpretation of Augustine and critique of Richard of St. Victor in that it "safeguards" the personal love of the Son and the Father. He writes,"Il ait été possible à saint Thomas de corriger les risques inhérent à la théorie augustinienne par l'apport de Richard de Saint-Victor et par un sens théologique

been more free of philosophical restriction, each of the persons possess distinctiveness and real content as "proper personalities."[287]

The Cyrilline paradigm that is being recognized in recent discussions did not occur *sui generis*. Hypostasis from its original usage as a support or buttress and its convenient distance from ousia offered both the relationality and individuation required by prosopon, but had to give way to personae for ecumenical considerations. The ensuing objectification of hypostasis, in whatever term it is intended by classical Christian thinkers, reflected a relational theology which affected trinitology and christology but also altered a worldview.[288] The concept of divine Person then in the fourth century is a more aptly delineated heuristic category than in the preceding two centuries of Church history. A comprehensive reflection of reality included a conception of a divine alterity independent of creation yet deeply affecting its meaning and purpose.[289] Subsistent relations ought not to be seen from a truncated Aristotelian-Augustinian framework in the West alone.[290] Neither should these "relations" be thought of, as some critique the East, as impersonal modalistic constructions or materialistic and thus, subordinationistic.[291] This is not to say that the West has ever fully explained its commitment to Augustinian simplicity theory while at the

---

très aigu." Ibid., 450. Note in contrast, P. Henry's statement that after (both temporally and ideologically) Augustine, "in the days of Richard of St. Victor, Saint Thomas, and the great Council of Florence in 1439, when for one brief, wonderful, marvelous moment, East and West were more fully united around this doctrine (of the person)." Saint Augustine on Personality, 18.

[287]Dictionnaire de Spiritualité, s.v. "Esprit Saint chez les Pères, Pères Latins," Pierre Smulders. 1278-1279. He indicates that Ambrose excised subordination of the Spirit in Latin theology but that the Latins were nominalistic in their approach to the coequal distinctions. Ibid.

[288]Cf. the deliberations of the 1988 Catholic Theological Society Proceedings 43, Seminar on Christology, 137. Zizioulas, Being as Communion, 55-56. Grillmeier is extremely critical of the Cappadocians on the lack of a distinction between nature and person in Christ, but softens in their "steps toward a conceptual distinction" in trinitology. Grillmeier, Christ in Christian Tradition, 370.

[289]This is meant as a response to Welch's ubiquitous critique of the social analogists, which is, to posit finite individuality as a "positive and necessary factor in defense of trinitarian concept and in the determination of its form." Doctrine of the Trinity in Contemporary Theology, 85.

[290]Rahner notes this and says that the "West too over the formal portion of the theology of the Trinity from the Greeks and made it the (whole) doctrine of the Trinity....Giving it more substance and content from the 'psychological' doctrine of the Trinity as developed by St. Augustine." "Remarks on the Dogmatic Treatise 'De Trinitate'. Theological Investigations, vol. 4, trans. Kevin Smyth (Baltimore: Helicon Press, 1966), 85.

[291]Material distinctions is Grillmeier's constant critique of the Cappadocians. Christ in Christian Tradition, 375-376

same time holding to subsistent "relations", could be both relative and eternal.[292] Nonetheless, the evidence indicates that persons are neither accidents nor equal to substance, they are hypostaseis, relational entities. We have seen that even Augustine, the fons of Western categories, carried "Eastern" characteristics of persona which, when missed, have caused a diminution in the way the Church is able to perceive reality, however inadequately.[293] The analogical perception of this heuristic component is deeply tied with the analogical and real participation of persons in the Divine, through the inexorable connection we find to the person of Christ, God incarnate. Neither the Cappadocians nor Augustine played with the idea of a "group mind", a collection of divine entities, but they did not preclude a view of divine substance which was relational prior to economic discussion.[294] The two approaches are very different. Modern modalism often throws up the smoke-screen of well-articulated statements about salvation-history and the audacity of discussion about the essential Trinity. Both East and West recognize the audacious nature of God-talk and approach it with extreme caution and honor. They radically confront an absolutistic ontology that by its very nature rendered paradoxical the possibility of many in the One.[295] Divine Being and Act are not separated in these thinkers. Although they differ in philosophical commitment, emphases and analogies the impact of their combined influence must find re-affirmation in modernity which longs for a basis for the relationality it discerns but cannot fathom.[296] We will find a similar coincidence of viewpoints in the Medieval period between Richard of St. Victor and St. Thomas. The latter drew heavily

---

[292]See Jenson's critique, The Triune Identity, 123. He also rephrases the complaint we have made that it is not obvious, as we are often coaxed to believe, that there "must first be things that in the second place may be variously related." Ibid. Prestige feels Augustine "possess(es) less philosophical cogency," than the Greeks. God in Patristic Thought, xi.

[293]M. Orphanos is a bit misleading in his "The Procession of the Holy Spirit According to Certain Later Greek Fathers," in Vischer ed., Spirit of God, Spirit of Christ: Ecumenical Reflections on the "Filioque" Controversy, Faith and Order Paper No. 103. (London: SPCK/ Geneva: W.C.C., 1981), where he states that the notion of 'love' was started by Augustine in the West, and that Palamas is the first to use it, even though it "is strange to the eastern tradition," 33-34. Mascall questions this also in The Triune Mystery, 60-61.

[294]Wheeler Robinson is an example of this typically uninformed criticism. The Christian Experience of the Holy Spirit (London: Nisbet and Co.), 271.

[295]Cyril Richardson uses Parmenides' recognition and eventual sidestepping of the paradox as the basis for his rather weak critique of divine diffusion, derivation and the medieval Christian concept of trinitarian persons. "The Trinity and the Enhypostasia," 75.

[296]Chevalier speaks of Nazianzus' thought as "a sort of immanentist dynamism" and of Augustine as one who formed a conceptualistic dialectic." S. Augustin et la Pensée Greque, 150.

upon Augustine and Boethius for his personalism while Richard shows some indirect affinities with the Eastern viewpoint. It is to that more concentrated debate which we must now turn.

Vedi oltre fiammeggiar l'ardent spiro
D'Isidoro, di Beda, e di Riccardo
Che a considerar fu più che viro

Dante, Paradisio, Canto X. 130-132

Chapter Four

Divine Person: Origin and Individuation in Relationship

The contributions related to divine personhood of the Cappadocians and Augustine assisted in bolstering Christian philosophy in the distinction between God as Being and God as a Being. However, the question which still remained as inadequately answered pertained to the cogency of advocating three in one substance. Were divine Persons substances? The medieval period produced the first scholastic definitions for human personhood. It was in light of those discussions that further delimitations were made in clarifying the intended meaning of divine Persons. Amid the rise and fall of numerous religious groups, two major strains of thought are representative within the philosophical-theological realm that directly pertain to the development of a notion of divine Personhood: the Augustinian-Boethian tradition and the often misunderstood Victorine school. The later drew heavily upon Augustinian spirituality but offered a variety of interpretations of his epistemology and theological considerations.

I. The Abbey of St. Victor and the Twelfth Century Renaissance

A careful study of the millenium prior to what we call the renaissance period reveals a series of renascent periods which lay the groundwork for, and which culminated in, the humanistic cry of the sixteenth century, "ad fontes."[1] The Carolingian regime, the twelfth and the fifteenth century each possessed the characteristics of noteworthy rebirth from which radical alterations emerged in nearly every level of society. If one were to imagine a moving map of societal and political influences, there could be a metaphorical resemblance to a variety of helium balloons in constant contact and motion. With the expansion of each influence - at one point military might, at another the shift in feudal structure, or the re-organization of the concept of hierarchy - there was a resultant

---

[1]One example of such a viewpoint is Sidney Packard's 12th Century Europe: An Interpretive Essay (Amherst: Univ. of Massachusetts Press, 1973) a delightful summary of this outstanding but often forgotten era.

172

displacement which radically altered the face of the continent of Europe. As each influence expanded those in proximity either waned or were expunged.

During the proliferation of the Germanic tribes which came to dominate central Europe, pushing theology and philosophy to the margin, there was in places like the Irish monasteries, the residual repository of a more powerful nature in places like the Irish monasteries which, when unleashed, countermoved Eastward with the Frankish establishment of monastic schools in Germany and France. The Germanic worldview was forced to give way to the more pervasive and permanent invasions of thought and social process. Feudal society began experimentation with various forms of group cooperation while dispensing with monolithic social orders. Thus by the dawn of the twelfth century Otto of Freising could say, "To Italy the Papacy, to Germany the Empire, and to France learning."[2]

Upon the entrance of that strange and wonderful creature, the university, it was the schools fostered by the monasteries like the one named after St. Victor (d.554), founded by William of Champeaux, that were all too quickly forgotten for their service in laying the philosophical ground work for the eventual ascendancy of the emerging universities.[3] Compared to the other great schools of the era, the abbey of St. Victor reveals a less than glorious inception. Nonetheless, when William retreated to the left bank of the Seine in 1108 little could he realize the prominence that abbey would enjoy in that century and beyond.[4]

---

[2]Quoted in Maurice De Wulf's Philosophy and Civilization in the Middle Ages (Princeton: Princeton Univ. Press, 1922), 43-44. See the appendix for more historical background to this chapter. It attempts to trace the sociological factors that dovetail with the theological strides made by the Victorines in the twelfth century.

[3]Stephen C. Ferruolo, The Origins of the University: The Schools of Paris (Stanford: Stanford University Press), 27-44, makes the helpful distinction between the school "at" St. Victor and that "of" St. Victor. The former had little impact on either university or theology; it was the latter's intellectual tradition which pertains to its lasting importance. The origins of the Victorine monastery can be found in John C. Dickinson, The Origins of the Austin Canons and Their Introduction into England (London: S.P.C.K., 1950), esp. 85ff. Another voluminous if not ponderous work (Dickinson refers to it as "useful but irritating,") that focuses on Paris particularly is Fourier Bonnard's Historie de l'abbaye royale et de l'ordre des chanoines réguliers de Saint-Victor de Paris, 2 vols. (Paris: Arthur Savaète Éditeur, 1904-1907). PL 175, xv.- c. also provides a cursory introduction to the school by a later Abbot, Hugonin.

[4]And "retreat" is exactly what any teacher would have done (or may have wished to) if a student, of the calibre of an Abelard, had vehemently disagreed with one's most fundamental philosphical conclusions, specifically pertaining to universals, and then both surreptitiously, and worse, publicly ridiculed that position. The stormy relationship is recounted in Leif Grane's, Peter Abelard, trans. Frederick and Christina Crowley (London: George Allen and Unwin Ltd., 1970), 37-42. Abelard says that the establishment of the school was a shrewd political move on the part of William who was seeking a bishopric by means of a short-cut. Dickinson mitigates that thesis by placing the school within the

The ambiance which was Paris was its own implicit drawing card. Made the capital of France at the turn of the twelfth century by Philip Augustus, this burgeoning city sported a freshly-built protective wall which quite intentionally encircled the be-scholared Left Bank while producing a city twice the size of any French competitor.[5] The de-institutionalization of the tradition-laden schola saw the shift of prestige from place of study to person studied under. With the ensuing attachment to individual masters a type of "bush-telegraph" disseminated the names of the theological 'prima donnas,' which in turn produced many avid seekers at the doorsteps of Parisian houses of learning. It has been estimated that during the first decades of the twelfth century, with a population between 25,000 and 50,000, ten percent of the population was composed of masters and their students.[6] By 1140 Paris had out-distanced the other European schools in number and name.

But there were internal differences, as in educational philosophy, which complemented the external milieu. One finds a new spirit of creativity, liberality, and consequently independent thinking, in Paris which was to eventuate first in the more traditional schools like St. Victor but would then culminate in the advancement of scholastic thought in the thirteenth century. Philip's patronage brought hitherto unknown privileges to the scholares. Colleges were formed which were to provide the monies to support what would become the universities.[7] Protection from any aggressor or censorship which

---

context of the impact of the Gregorian Reform instigated by the Lateran Council of 1059. Apparently William was urged by Hildebert of Louvardin not to completely withdraw from theological discourse for the safer realm of contemplation, the result being the ascendancy of an cadre of "contemplative" scholars for the next century. Dickinson, Origins, 26, 60-61, 85-87. See also Hastings Rashdall, The Universities of Europe in the Middle Ages, ed. F.M. Powicke and A.B. Emden, vol. 1 (London: Oxford University Press, 1936), 50-55, 276-277. For an indication of the influence of the School see Dickinson's Origins, 284-285 for a manuscript chronicle leading up through the Third Lateran Council and Pope Alexander III (d.1181).

[5]Interestingly, the Abbey of St. Victor stood outside the city wall maintaining an air of isolation which may have fed its independent thought. Carl Richard Brühl, Palatium und Civitas: Studien zur Profantopographie spantiker Civitates vom 3 bis zum 13 Jahrhundert, vol. 1, (Cologne: Gallien, 1975), 17-19, establishes that by 1210 Paris was 252 hectares in size with a population of ca. 25,000, 2,500 of which were outside the walls.

[6]R.W. Southern, "The Schools of Paris and the School of Chartres," in Renaissance and Renewal in the Twelfth Century, ed. Robert L. Benson and Giles Constable with Carl D. Lanham (Cambridge: Harvard Univ. Press, 1982), 113-137. In the same volume see John W. Baldwin, "Masters at Paris from 1179 to 1215," 138-172.

[7]Hastings Rashdall, Universities of Europe, 344-351, outlines the changes endured by the monasteries as society sought education elsewhere. The split between clerics and secular canons has been rehearsed too often to be reproduced here but the Victorines were to be different than most in their spiritual commitments to the Rule and to the vows they took; thus the response of that particular school to the changes in Europe were quite similar to that of the monasteries.

questioned the "freedom and special rights" of the scholars was personally vowed by the king, birthing a unique liberal arts mentality. With such a security and the unmistakable international flavor of Paris the Victorine abbey was soon staffed by top Regent masters whose lecturing and disputing was among the most respected of the estimated twenty-four masters of theology expounding in Paris at the time.[8]

A. The "Self" in the Twelfth Century

Of the many factors which fed into this twelfth century renaissance, the most intriguing is the shift in views regarding the individual. It is here that "for the first time the lineaments of modern man appear."[9] Colin Morris has been both criticized and supported for his contention that this period marked the beginning of a new form of subjective content within the individual.[10] It is undeniable, however, that not since the self-

---

[8]Hastings Rashdall, Universities of Europe, 278-281, 504-505. Baldwin, "Masters at Paris," 143. Southern's "Schools of Paris," 114-119, summarizes these findings under the categories of: 1) De-institutionalization of the "Schola", 2) Attachment to individual masters, 3) Convenience of place over importance of institution. When these factors were coupled with the resurgence of vigilant spirituality within the Church as a whole as well as within canonical circles, St. Victor's prominence among Parisian schools was solidified. Ferrulo, Origins of the University, 29-30, alludes to the proof of lay education that was a distinct form of communication of ideas that had germinated in the abbey with the outside world. Due to misgovernment however, this practice had probably come to a halt during Richard's apogee.

[9]R.R. Bolgar, The Classical Heritage and its Beneficiaries (Cambridge: Cambridge University Press, 1963), 188. Bolgar's delineations of the main themes within the Carolingian period, 91-129, and what he calls the "Pre-scholastic Age", 130-201, are helpful in understanding the broad history of ideas within these periods which we do not have time to outline. The quote here was pointed out to me by Colin Morris' response to C. Bynum's critique, "Individualism in Twelfth-Century Religion: Some Further Reflections," Journal of Ecclesiastical History 31 (1980):195. There are those who would argue that Augustine was the first "modern man", but I think, that this era bears the epithet more exhaustively due to the intense interest across the board in discerning the meaning of individuality.

[10]Colin Morris, The Discovery of the Individual 1050-1200 (London: SPCK, 1972). See also Giles Constable, "Twelfth-Century Spirituality and the Late Middle Ages," in Religious Life and Thought (11th-12th Centuries) Art. 15 (London: Variorum Reprints, 1979), reprint of "Twelfth-Century Spirituality and the Late Middle Ages," Medieval and Renaissance Studies, 5, ed. O. B. Hardison (Chapel Hill, N.C.: Univ. of North Carolina Press, 1971), 27-60. Taking the opposing position is Caroline Bynum, Jesus as Mother: Studies in the Spirituality of the High Middle Ages (Berkeley: Univ. of California Press, 1982) esp. ch. 3, 82-109. Her argument is well-reasoned though may have missed the point made by Morris and others. Realizing the strong tendency in the Middle Ages to think in terms of structure and community, Bynum wishes to distance herself from those who claim an individualizing movement in the twelfth century. See her helpful bibliography of that position on pp. 83-84. She replaces "self" with "individual," recognizing the evidence of a preoccupation with inwardness but always with the proviso that this "soul" was never detached from the larger group. While we may agree that this shift was not of the atomistic revolution of the sixteenth century nonetheless it was radical enough to merit our

revelation of Nazianzus' <u>Carmen de vita sua</u> and especially the rigorous self-examination of Augustine had there been anything quite like the twelfth century's absorption to understand the self, the soul, the anima. Abelard's dictum, "Scito te ipsum" exemplifies the spirit of the age, both individually and corporately. The means of this examination included forms of extremely candid rather than pious autobiography, the rise of interest in portraiture; even names began to reflect an individual's specific character.[11] A new sense of worth permeated the writings about humanity made in the image of God.[12] The Pseudo-Dionysian heritage of hierarchy as constituent of a world-view, while not being ejected outright, was reformulated to meet the demands of this emerging personal awareness.[13] Granted, this was not a total recapitulation of the architectonic structure of the world for the medieval mind, where everyone was assigned a place and filled it unquestioningly.

---

attention regardless of the term chosen to represent its subject matter. It should be noted that we find her focus on the new realization of relational categories redolent with implications for our thesis.

[11]This statement is made with an awareness of what has been said about Gregory of Nazianzus in chap. Three, which may be an unwitting bias in the West towards Latin thinkers rather than the Greeks. John F. Benton, "Consciousness of Self and Perceptions of Individuality," in Robert Benson's <u>Renaissance and Renewal,</u> 263-295. Like Bynum, Benton disagrees with Morris, "Although the way in which one 'knew oneself' in the 13th century differed greatly fron Antiquity, it cannot be said that they understood subjectivity more clearly," Ibid., 264. For Richard's approach see <u>Benjamin Minor</u> ch. 78, Kirchberger, <u>Selected Writings on Contemplation,</u> trans. Clare Kirchberger (New York: Harper, 1957), 116-117.

[12]Richard of St. Victor, <u>Benjamin Major,</u> <u>PL</u> 196, 3:13, 123A.
"A man's own experience can easily teach anyone, I think, how greatly this speculation (what we might call psychology) has power to arouse the soul both against sin and towards good. Recognize your dignity, oh man, I beg; consider the excellent nature of your soul, how God made it in His image and likeness, how He raised it above all bodily creatures."
(interpolation mine) trans. by Giles Constable, "Twelfth-Century Spirituality and the Late Middle Ages," 36. He says there also that the Augustinian maxim referring to rightly-ordered love, "Love and do what you will," was of distinct prominence, in these new attempts at understanding intersubjectivity.

[13]Dionysius the Areopagite, <u>On the Divine Names</u>, trans. C.E. Rolt, passim (see specifically, 1.1, 51-52; 4:2, 88; 4.7, 95; 4.9, 98). It would be difficult to estimate the influence of the Areopagite in medieval theology. For the hierarchical world-view it was his <u>The Celestial Hierarchies</u> which radically affected the Catholic Church's cosmology. Dante reiterates the paradigm in his highly influential works. Diffusion of the Good, transmission of Aristotelian causality, and the 'positive' aspects of the via negativa, are but a few of the Dionysian themes ubiquitous in this period. His source idea was, of course, the huperousios thearchia, the Super-Essential Godhead which admits revelation and diakrises or titles of differentiation, but for the most part disallows either a Personal God or a view of divine personhood which is adequate. It is important to note the deep Augustinian and Dionysian background of the Victorines before critiquing them on the social analogy of the Trinity. Their appreciation for the apophatic tradition and 'unity' model ought not be overlooked when assessing the merits of 'familial' analogies.

What we can say is that increased external societal stability provided breathing room for an internal journey, the examination of the inner life.

The 'communio sanctorum' was regarded at this juncture as best exemplified within the cloister, the place that was acknowledged, even envied as the seat of contemplative, communal, and personal growth.[14] The monastery however began to produce a revolution which was to have both a pervasive and perduring effect. It was within the environs of the the religious houses that several new approachs to the concept of personhood appeared. Though the idea of 'persona' was etymologically similar to its Greek forebear, the mask or role played by its bearer, there was an undercurrent of challenge of accepted descriptions in this period. Though not univocally equal with personality, which we must be careful not to presuppose here, now there was a sense that the mask had an individual history, an accumulation of experiences, an import not known before. Benton has rightly discerned this new conceptualization by retaining the strong medieval sense of orders where he says that personhood was increasingly understood as "directionally-put...a journey inward was a journey toward self for the sake of God, rather than for the sake of the self."[15]

One indication of this shift comes in the burgeoning anticipative interest in elements of psychology, especially among the clerics. A vigorous discussion arose around the study of mens, its place in relation to theology and its significance as an image of the Trinity.[16] The innovative emphasis on subjectivity in religious expression found its focus on the will and the mind. Inwardness and decision were integral parts, sometimes even ascendant over obedience and conformity. This produced a new stress on a personal relation with Christ. The life of Christ was meditated upon, and adoration of his body and person was frequent if not predominant. Not only the life of Christ, but His physical body became predominantly an object of intense adoration.[17] Caroline Bynum reveals the

---

[14]The earliest this phrase is found is in Niceta of Remesiana's (d. c. 414 AD) De Symbolo, 10, FC vol. 7. The shift here is in the context. The community of the saints is now seen as preserved in a pristine sense behind cloister walls.

[15]Benton, "Consciousness of Self," 285.

[16]Pierre Michaud-Quantin, "La psychologie dans l'enseignement au XIIe siècle," in Actes du premier congrès internationale de philosophie médiévale, Louvain, Brussels, 28 August - 4 September, 1958. L'Homme et son destin d'apres les penseurs du moyen âge (Louvain: Éditions Nauwelaerts, 1960), 407-415. He says, with regard to this new form of studying humanity, the Cistercians at first had an aversion to this apparently questionable anthropocentrism (the question of using Aristotelian categories arose also), but the Victorines were instrumental in bringing the complexity of "l'observation intime" (Ibid., 414) of the imago and the place accorded to it theologically into discussions beyond the moral sphere to which it had been relegated previously.

[17]Constable, "Twelfth Century Spirituality and the Late Middle Ages," 35-45.

revolutionary aspects resident in being able to make oneself a subject of conversation, to stand outside of oneself and discern emotions, defenses and motives. It was this century which saw the revelation of the inner landscape of the soul.[18]

Again we must be careful not to read too much into this period of awareness. Self-actualization was constrained by the desire to find the 'imago dei' within the human soul. This psychology was telic in orientation, self-development within an over-arching pursuit of God. The outline of the self was defined as one drew into fellowship with God. Though the alienation of sin might be expiated it was immediately replaced by another estrangement, that of a 'peregrinus' or stranger to this world. A phenomenological awareness which might have resulted, in modernity, in antinomianistic hedonism or existential despair, was countered effectively in the twelfth century acceptance of a ordered universe. The temporal orders of clerics, monks, and laity, subsisted within a larger 'ordo'. What we might call "existential alienation" was checked within the sacred communion of a divinely-based order. Any negative elements of life were considered divisive, and were excised by immersion in one's specific order. What had been accepted for millenia as merely functional human existence now was given new meaning for those who sought it. Granted, the abuses of such a world-view are self-evident, yet the underlying intent was to lay supreme authority and disposition of personal life in the hands and heart of God.[19] One cannot understand the emphases of the Victorines without including this feature of the twelfth century.

B. Victorine Personalism

David Knowles examines three strains which help to summarize this discussion of the twelfth century. He says first, that the creative energies of the period were due to a broad literary culture. The writings of Augustine and Aristotle were extensively disseminated; second, figures of the past were revered with deep devotion as originators of a 'golden age'; and third, a high value was placed on the individual with an emphasis on emotions and opinions which was original to this era.[20]

The tenor of the scholarship of the Abbey of St. Victor was that of rigorous

---

[18]Caroline Bynum, Jesus as Mother, 85-88. Note that she refers to the rise of friendship as a focal point, and the use of that category in Trinitarian discussion, though no mention of Richard appears, 88.

[19]Gerhart Ladner summarizes this concept of self-understanding in his sensitive lecture printed as "Homo Viator: Medieval Ideas on Alienation and Order," Speculum 40:2 (April 1967): 233-259.

[20]David Knowles, "Humanism of the Twelfth Century," The Historian and Character (Cambridge: Cambridge Univ. Press, 1963), 16ff.

intellection based upon a fervent spiritual hunger.[21] The result was an intriguing mix of cognitive elements and ecstatic mysticism, the former arising out of the latter, but at the same time guarding the latter from excess.

The battle between the claustrales and the scholares during this period adumbrates the continual conflict which arises when the ideals of contemplation and ratiocination are brought into proximity. Rather than accept Bernard's pressure to evangelize with ascetic fervor, the Parisian Augustinians chose to serve the cause of Christ by remaining secluded in study so that contemplation could be brought to bear on the thought-life of the age.[22] Fundamental to the unique contributions of the Victorines was their view of ratio. Drawing from the distinction between superior and inferior ratio first delineated by Augustine, Hugh and others were able to look at the world with a vibrancy that fed both worship and scientia. The ratio divina was the source of all other forms of ratiocination. With telic force, the will of God directed and empowered all of reality. The superiority of the human soul was found in its participatory relationship with the Divine will. The soul, being created, came to awareness of the divine will by two means. For arrival at any form of true knowledge or apprehension, speculative reason was required; to intuit the meaning of action, or the inferior faculties, practical reason was acknowledged. Both forms of reason partook of one principle, divine ratio. This divine law was profoundly reflected in the imago dei. Both aspects had to be kept in tandem for a proper, ordered human existence.[23]

---

[21]Ludo Milis, gives excellent thematic background to this period of struggle between the eremitical centers like Cluny and the so-called "heretical" new houses like St. Victor. What was common to both, however, was an increasing criticism of the spiritually defunct structures of the Church, so that whether by intellectual correction or ascetic/evangelistic spirit they both served in a general reform movement. See Milis' "The Regular Canons and Some Socio-Religious Aspects about the Year 1100," in Étude de civilisation Médiévale (IXe-XIIe) siècles: Mélanges offerts á Edmond-René Labande, B. Janneau, et al.(Poitiers: C.E.S.C.M., 1975), 553-561.

[22]This is not to say that the Victorines were reclusive to the point of irrelevancy. A sermon of Richard's, apparently given on the day commemorating Gregory the Great, who was of immense importance to the Victorine tradition, reveals a distinctly different approach to asceticism. Jean Chatillon says that Richard places contemplation at the forefront but insists "sur la nécessité de ne point négliger l'action, qui procure à la contemplation....C'est spiritualité qui reste orientée, sans aucun doute, vers l'éternite et la vision de gloire, mais qui mesure aussi le prix du temps et celui de l'histoire humaine." "Contemplation, Action et Prédication d'après un sermon inédit de Richard de Saint-Victor en l'honneur de saint Grégoire-le-Grand," in J. Guillet, et al., L'Homme Devant Dieu: Mélanges offerts au Père Henri de Lubac (Paris: Aubier, 1963), 97.

[23]G.-Ed. Demers, "Les divers sens du mot 'ratio' au moyen age. Autour d'un texte de Maitre Ferrier de Catalogne (1275)", in Études d'histoire littéraire et doctrinale du XIIIe siècle, Premiere série 1, 105-139 (Montreal: Publications de l'Institute des études médiévales, 1931), notes the variety of meanings within the fourth to the thirteenth centuries. The origin however of the concept of ratio is most like the Greek concept of logos in its

In Victorine spirituality all intellectual pursuit was for the greater purpose of leading people to God. The desire to see God "facie ad facien" was the impetus behind Hugh's and Richard's systems. Natural theology was a result of the emphasis on abstraction inherent in the Victorine view on universals. Consciousness and experience bore witness to the spiritual framework of creation. The interiority of the period was harnessed philosophically and systematized into theories of causation. Conversely, that speculation was subsumed under faith categories and the "oculus contemplationis", which were both needed in the pursuit of knowledge.[24] Direct knowledge of God, for the Victorines, resided in a "knowing love," a mystical experience pervaded with the use of the mind and the heart.

This method was to serve as a unifying factor within the larger medieval discussions on the Trinity. Fundamentally, there were two pervasive categories of thought which were at odds during this period. The Cistercian influence championed the affective concept of mystical adoration and union with the ineffable Trinity. On the other side, the Anselmian and Abelardian schools had attempted more cognitive approaches. Though it would be a misunderstanding to leave either category without some element of the other, the latter was a distinct effort to give Christian claims a viability withing larger philosophical spheres. The Victorines were crucial in drawing the two strains together.[25]

C. Divine Goodness and Personal Love in the Twelfth Century

Concomitant with this personalistic paradigm shift, the Victorines took part, however unwittingly, in a fundamental metaphysical question. Arthur Lovejoy's chapter on the medieval period, in his monumental work, The Great Chain of Being, discerns two distinct, if general, strains of thought also crucial for an understanding of Hugh of St. Victor's, and subsequently Richard's, theologizing. He terms one strain the "rationalist" school, grounded in Neoplatonic background, as represented by Abelard and the Victorines. The "anti-rationalists" or the Scotists and Ockham may be better understood as standing in a nominalistic line of thought. Generally, this second group gave an ascendancy to the will

---

illuminative role. Ibid., 105. The double function of reason then led upward, towards speculative wisdom of the apprehension of divine things, and downward, by the procuring of the "représentations sensibles que nous en donnent les choses extérieures, contingentes, historiques." Ibid., 128. Augustinian exemplarism is basic to the theologizing of the Victorines.

[24]George Tavard, Vision of the Trinity (Washington: Univ. Press of America, 1981), 74. Leclercq, et al., Spirituality of the Middle Ages, 225-227.

[25]This is unmistakable from surveys such as J. Ebner's, Die Erkenntnislehre Richards von St. Viktor, in Beiträge zur Geschichte du Philosophie des Mittelalters: texte und untersuchungen, vol. 19:4 (Münster: Aschendorff, 1917). See Salet, La Trin., 24-45; Ribaillier, De Trin., 20-33.

in relation to the intellect.[26]

The latter school, as Lovejoy understands it, would understand the idea of Absolute as arbitrary and inscrutable, and thus the inevitable conclusion that whatever might be known must come through experience or revelation, not reason alone. On the other extreme, there were those who desired to see an essential, self-giving 'goodness' behind the discussions about a God who was called 'good'. In short, it was an argument on the perennial dialectic of the acceptance or rejection of the principles of plenitude and continuity. Following Augustine and Abelard, Hugh and Richard accepted the burden of defending against the misguided accusation of an inherent 'necessitarian optimism' as 'rationalists' so as not to reject the notion of the self-diffusive nature of the goodness of God. In spite of the determinism which could be attributed to this position, they maintained there was a 'necessary reason', a definite cause behind all of reality.[27] As expected, the anti-rationalist camp emphasized the freedom of God, a will not dependent upon any sort of coercion. Thus the dilemma arose between choosing a self-diffusive goodness which found itself saddled with rationalistic necessitarianism or advocating an arbitrary voluntarism which redefined the Good so that it was seen as a final and not an efficient cause, passive _ad_ _extra_.[28]

As with any theologian who attempts to systematize a sector of Christian thought, Richard could not be, nor was he, oblivious to the major ideas that formed the world outside his cloister walls. Thus we want to present him as an eclectic theologian; as one of the 'communio sanctorum', one who had drunk deeply at the mystical and exegetical fountains of Hugh, as one acquainted with the psychological construction upon which that mysticism rested, and as one who experienced a societal personalistic revolution. There remains lttle room for wondering from where the major sources, which Richard used to

---

[26]Arthur Lovejoy, The Great Chain of Being (Cambridge, Mass.: Harvard University Press, 1936), 67-98.

[27]Barth describes Anselm's usage of the tension between auctoritas and ratio and the relationship of both to faith. Necessitas, in both Anselm and Richard, is inextricably connected with ratio. The ontic necessity which precedes the noetic in both thinkers is based upon what the divine being cannot be, thus the term chosen was 'necessity' to describe the object of faith in reason which is derived from a self-revealing God. K. Barth, Anselm: Fides Quaerens Intellectum, (London: SCM Press, 1958), 47-53.

[28]I am indebted to Kevin Keane's intriguing article "Ordo Bonitatis: The Summa Fratris Alexandri and Lovejoy's Dilemma," in Marion Leather Kuntz and Paul Grimley Kuntz, Jacob's Ladder and the Tree of Life: Concepts of Hierarchy and the Great Chain of Being (New York: Peter Lang, 1986), 55-71, see esp. 57-58.

construct his magisterial De Trinitate, were elicited.[29]

The debate continues concerning the origin of the logic of self-diffusion in creation which found its medieval expression in the "rationalist" school. Evidently Bonaventure of Clairvaux felt there was a strong connection where he paints rather broadly, "Augustin est suivi par Anselm, Gregoire par Bernard, Richard a suivi Denys; car Anselm s'occupe de dogme, Bernard de predication, et Richard de contemplation."[30] On the other hand, there are those who do not accept that source criticism. "Dionisio no ha influido nada en el De Trinitate."[31] Just how this fundamental Greek tradition of a perfect and actual diffusion between the persons of the Trinity finds its way into Victorine thought is not clear. Regardless of direct textual transmission, the resemblance adumbrates that earlier tradition. Mutual self-giving, was for Richard, the central construct upon which the systematic principle for his mysticism, his metaphysic, and his theology was built. Speaking of the concept of "ex-sistence" in the Dionysian-Cappadocian tradition J. Pikaza says of Richard, "Esta postura es claramente griega."[32] These are examples of the diverse opinions on this point, but in the main Richard's view of divine plenitude reflects the East in ways that most Western trinitarians of the period rejected.

The position taken here is that the influence is unmistakable with regards to the tradition of an intentionally non-necessitarian, self-diffusive good whether Richard gives direct reference to it in De Trinitate or not. Consistently throughout what follows the concept of a self-diffusive good will be evident, an expression of mutual love which is 'reasoned' by means of the 'via eminentiae'. It is the "plenitude of glory" which is at the root of Richard's argument for the necessity of a divine Person to both receive and give

---

[29]Ribaillier, De Trin., 20-33, is far more exhaustive here than Salet, La Trin., 10-13 at this point. Both emphasize Achard's De Trintate as a crucial source. The abbey in Richard's day was caught in the foment of the perennial struggle between contemplatio and ratio. The canon regulars were well aware of the need for a synthesis. It was a constant struggle to be at once claustrales and scholares. Criticism from the Cistercians centered on the "dalliance" of these canons who interpreted the lectio divina in broader, more inclusive, categories. The philosophy of education expounded in Hugh's Didascalion apparently found expression in Richard as his disciple. For an excellent translation see Jerome Taylor's The Didascalion: A Medieval Guide to the Arts (New York: Columbia Univ. Press, 1961). The studium sacrae scripturae that had been the strong suit of the abbey scholars was distinguished from the other forms of knowledge, theology, etc. The supposed incompatibility of this educational structure brought about the waning of the school "at" St. Victor much sooner than necessary, see S. Ferruolo, Origins of the University, 35-36.

[30] Quoted in Bonnard, Historie de l'abbaye, 115.

[31] Olegario Gonzalez, "Sobre las fuentes de Ricardo de San Victor y su influjo en San Buenaventura," La Ciudad de Dios 176, no. 3-4 (1963):601.

[32]"Notas sobre la Trinidad en Ricardo de San Victor," Estudios Trinitarios 6:1 (1972):87.

divine love.[33] The plenitude of generosity is only comprehended if the Trinity is perceived as mutually self-bestowing and that without any hint of personal reserve.[34] The highest good cannot lack any goodness and thus fundamental to the idea of good is the idea of mutual bestowal or free, rationally directed love. The personalistic approach to reality then, based on a coherent view of inner-trinitarian self-giving, became the 'order' in which these particular medieval minds described the continuity between a rationally free Creator and a corresponding, imaging creation.

It is also important to see in this century a synergistic interaction of society and the academy which has not always been the case in the centuries to follow. C. S. Lewis is rarely regarded adequately for his primary expertise, medieval literature. It is his arresting statement concerning the Troubadours and Provençal poetry that summarizes the actualization of this personalistic evolution. Speaking of these poets he says:

> They effected a change which has left no corner of our ethics, our imagination, or our daily life untouched, and they erected impassible barriers between us and the classical past or the Orient present. Compared with this revolution the Renaissance is a mere ripple on the surface of literature.[35]

While the concept of romantic love flooded the secular sphere there was no less an influence in this realm even among those who had come under rule and cloister. An example is the preponderance of commentaries on the Song of Songs, one of which was produced by Richard, or other works more speculative in nature which dealt with love, which were produced in the first decades of the twelfth century.[36] The exploration of the self culminated in the the philosophical and theological excavation of the deepest of relationships; it is no wonder that even yet scholars and dilettantes alike are enamoured with the escapades of Abelard and his Heloise.[37] Divine love was seen as given and, in

---

[33]PL 196, 3:4, 918C-D. The same argument is applied to the effulgence of sovereign light, PL, 5:6, 956C.

[34]PL 196, 5:17, 962B.

[35]The Allegory of Love (New York: Oxford University Press, 1958), p. 54.

[36] Refers to list by C. Spicq, Equisse d'une histoire de l'exégèse latine au Moyen Age (Paris: Vrin, 1944), 397. Richard also produced a commentary on the Song, In Cantica Canticorum Explicatio, PL 196, cols. 405a-524a.

[37]The beauty of the friendships between monks becomes a sensitive topic due to the prejudices against expressions of love between males which time and place have produced concerning that lifestyle. The vision of the monastic life was that the cloister "est l'école de l'amour, le dispensaire de la Charité," in Jean Déchanet's assessment of William of St. Thierry's Lettre aux frères du Mont-Dieu (Lettre d'or) Sources Chrétiennes, vol. 223 (Paris: Les Éditions du Cerf, 1975), 385. Under the aegis of divine love there arose an entire system of practical works and expressions of love between clerics and canons Both C. Morris, Discovery, 96-107 and C. Bynum, Jesus as Mother, ch. 4, refer to the intimacy of relationality found there. For the concomitant issue of love between a man and woman,

spite of its perversions, human love was also to be given. A new view of the individual subject paved the way for some troublesome but, I believe, helpful insights into the doctrine of the Trinity.

Before we discuss Richard's method it is important to keep this milieu in mind, political security, philosophic liberality, a dynamic reasserted in metaphysics, and the close ties between a new personalism and the dawning of Romantic love.[38] These elements combined with Augustinian illuminationism and an epistemology which resembled Aristotle's produced one of most unique and profitable approaches to the Triune reality that the Church has received. Its response to Richard went the way of most relationalists but, for a short period, a clear line was drawn between tritheism and philosophic oneness. The method Richard applied to this rigorous task drew first Hugh of St. Victor's theological worldview.

II. Richard of St. Victor's Concept of Person in De Trinitate

It is an intriguing relationship between Richard of St. Victor and the Church, or maybe more precisely, between Richard and the theologians who disagreed with his social analogy of the Trinity. In the rise of relational categories in the last century his trinitology has become central to some arguments while remaining a foil for the proposals of others. While Richard's argumentation has not seemed to satisfy many rigorous assessments it has not been completely expunged from theological discourse. The reasons for the perennial influence of this Augustinian canon's view of the Godhead rests upon; 1) the realism upon which his doctrine was based, 2) the conception of divine goodness as the highest and most fruitful symbol of the Triune reality, and 3) the notion of love as central to an understanding of divine personhood. His De Trinitate has had impact due to its clarity, existential appeal, and possibly because it does not set out to prove its thesis in an apologetic manner. What one finds when Richard is compared to trinitarians from another perspective is that a theological hermeneutic reveals its power immediately. When one starts with the ontic notion of a self-diffusive Good the results are extremely different than the position that holds divinity as best understood in absolutes that exude from an epistemological ontology. To measure the worth of Richard's contribution it is crucial that one understand the worldview and the theological sources which produced the heuristic notion of 'person' in Trinity.

---

specifically Abelard and Heloïse, recognizing the uniqueness of that relationship see Leif Grane, Peter Abelard, trans. Frederick and Christine Crowley (London: George Allen and Unwin, Ltd.), ch. 4, 47-70.

[38]See Appendix, where the spirituality of the regular canons is also shown to play a distinct role in this strong tendency toward personalism.

A. Individual and Trinitarian "simulacra"

Not only by its title but also by its inclusiveness, Hugh of St. Victor's monumental treatise, De Sacramentis, was an explication of a symbolic interpretation of Scripture revealing a close connection with the Augustinian metaphysical hermeneutic.[39] It represented the significative epistemology which credited a realistic connection between created nature and its source, the Triune God. Conceived in accordance with the prevalent hierarchical components discussed above, coupled with a conception of revelation of God in nature, Hugh builds this "summa", which was to be the fountainhead for the summae to appear during the ensuing century, upon the systematic principle of an "oikonomia."[40] One key then to uncover Hugh's agenda must be his "restorative" design. Redemption pervaded creation for Hugh, and its effects are all reparative. The "opus conditionis," or the created constitutive elements of the "imago" is clearly separated for the "opus reparationis," those recapitulative elements within the Atonement that are pointed to and prepared for by the conditional works but have been hindered by sin.[41] This "reparatio" means the disclosing of the sacramental nature of history, philosophy, the arts, tradition, Scripture, and nature. In a Christocentric mystical theology Hugh christened philosophy as "sapientia inferior" and speculation as the stage by which theology is completed as "sapientia superior." Above all, Hugh sought to bring all of the order created in the image of the Triune God into the realm of "contemplatio."

A triadic structure explicit throughout this work at various levels bears formal witness to the underlying philosophy of Trinitarian imprinting on all of nature.

> And there are in these things certain representations, (simulacra) as it were, signifying from afar and having likeness in part. Certain things, in truth, marked by a clear image and perfect imitation produce a clear demonstration (claram demonstrationem).... Now this is the rational creature itself, which is made excellently and properly according to His likeness,...In this, therefore, was found the first trace of the Trinity, when the rational creature itself began to recognize what was in itself, and from this considered what was above itself....Three things, as it were, appear in one - mind, wisdom and love; mind and wisdom are of mind, and of mind and wisdom love.[42]

Hugh risked the inevitable accusations of over-rationalizing, as he builds his anthropology upon this triad of mind, wisdom and love. Reminiscent of Augustinian vestigia the imago dei is reflective, a likeness or "simulacrum," a demonstration mirroring the infinite Trinity.

---

[39]See chap. Three, 133-142

[40]PL, 176, 1:3,1-2, 217AB; On the Sacraments, 41-42, "Therefore in truth, God from the beginning wished neither to be entirely manifest to human consciousness not [sic] entirely hidden."

[41]This recurrent element originates in PL 176, Prologue, c.4, 184C-185A.

[42]PL 176, 1:3,21, 225C-D, On the Sacraments, 50-51. One can see the immediate dependency upon the so-called psychological trinities of Augustine's De Trinitate.

Hugh does not trust human cognition alone to accomplish a "clara demonstratio" of the Trinity. Divine illumination is required as an epistemological source, to reveal the power within the mind out of which wisdom is born and love which proceeds from that loving fecundity. In order to distinguish truth one follows a hierarchical order of revealed and rational lines to discern from simulacra the reality of the Trinity. Hugh does not focus on persons of the Trinity other than to affirm what is believed about their distinction. His purpose, which is Richard's also, is to draw pilgrims to an understanding of the perfection of God through the image of the soul, which is the most perfect likeness in creation.[43] Nevertheless, it is clear that Hugh's method of "sacramentalizing" all of creation assisted Richard in his method of drawing a strong reflective comparison between human love and divine love.

In all of this Hugh, and the Victorines in general, held a fairly conservative theological stance. The use of Augustinian paradigms did not serve a license to head off in a direction other than that set by the major core of tradition. The Victorine abbey itself was known for its strong criticism of some of the results of the dialectical method.[44]

Hugh does not belabor the philosophical attribution of person in Trinity, although he does make distinctions between the divine and the human. In a comparison of the human mind and the divine nature he says:

> Reason asks itself why those three things (tria illa) which are found in the Godhead are called persons, since in that Trinity which the mind first finds in itself three things are likewise found...since man himself is a person, but these (internal distinctions) are found to be only affections, as it were, adhering to the person and existing in relation to it, to be a person is not at all proper to these, but only to be present in the person.[45]

In God however, he continues,

> But since those things which are in God can not be different from Himself as if neither accidents nor affections changeable according to time nor separable on account of the incommutable nature of essence... the three things are truly predicated to come together in Him...The three things are called three persons, not three essences, because the nature of the three individually is perfect and undivided in the three. And so they are called persons individually.[46]

---

[43]Hugh does not reside in rational alone for his theory of likeness. The corporeal qualities of power, knowledge and will correspond to the rational distinctions he has made. PL 176, 1:3,28, 230D, On the Sacraments, 57.

[44]Ferruolo, The Origins of the University, 37-41, discusses the reactions within the Victorine order to the rise in academic specialization within the other major orders and the resulting isolation from the other schools that eventually took it out of the main conversations of Parisian theologians. Ferruolo marks the end of Victorine influence there at the exile of Godfrey.

[45]PL 176, 1:3,25, 227AB, On the Sacraments, 52-53

[46]Ibid., col.227BC, On the Sacraments, 53.

For Hugh only the soul is properly the individual because it reflects unitivity, whereas the body implies multiplicity. Boethius' definition is the source of Hugh's notion of person in his Christological discussion.

> They may ask what is person and then they adduce a definition of person as it has been made and proved by certain people, that person is the individual element of rational substance. (Persona est individuum rationalis substantiae)[47]

Hugh maintained the Boethian line because of a commitment to a certain Christology, but he was also aware that there was not an exact definitional correlation. "What person is has been well defined on our part. We cannot by any means express what is above us. It is something that cannot be expressed since it is incomprehensible."[48] It will be evident that Richard did not agree with his confrère at this point. He saw a connection that was deeper than Hugh's analysis of personhood.

Hugh reveals his orthodoxy on the subjects of unity and diversity, the generation and the procession within the Godhead at various points.[49] His emphasis on rational substance differed from the machinations of Abelard and Gilbert Porreta. Their interest lay not so much in the substance of the person as it did in the numerical unity.[50] It may be said that Hugh marks a transition point in our analysis of the medieval concept of the person. Richard was to outdistance his mentor with regard to philosophical analysis and application of the imago in its relational definition, but he did so because of the epistemological foundation he found in Hugh. It ought not be missed that Hugh's work on interpersonal relationship reflected the personalism of the day as well as provided grist for his pupil's discussion of friendship. One example would be Hugh's view of

---

[47]PL 176: 2:1,11, 406A, On the Sacraments, 406. See Lauge Olaf Nielsen, Theology and Philosophy in the Twelfth Century (Leiden: E.J. Brill, 1982), 193-213 for a complete analysis of Hugh's incarnational theology. Nielsen makes the point that Hugh attempted to counter several disparate views of the incarnation but that in good medieval fashion he does not give actual names. It is clear however that he disavowed any Christology which did not affirm the unity of Word and man per se. Contrast Abelard, who could not accept "person" as applicable to both God and man, thus he allowed a distinction between Word and the assumed man, 219-220.

[48]PL 176, 2:1,11, 406A, On the Sacraments, 243. Hugh is distinctly Augustinian here as he refers directly to De Trinitate, PL 42: 7:4,7, 940. He says,
"What are the three? Indeed human speech labours with great deficiency. It is called three persons not that that may be said but that it may not be passed over in silence...On this account we say three persons, not that any diversity of essence may be understood, but that indeed by one word an answer can be given when it is said: "What three persons?"
PL 176, 2:1,4, 379B; On the Sacraments, 214

[49]PL 176, 2:1,1-13, 371C-416A, On the Sacraments, 205-253. Hugh is thoroughly Augustinian and Chalcedonian in his Christology.

[50]Nielsen, Theology and Philosophy, 216ff. They did not take Boethius as their departure for the discussion of person.

matrimony. In the reformative line of the Cappadocians and Augustine, he saw conjugal love as integral to the restoration of humanity. Ordained before the Fall it was a sacrament of the kind of society which was to be reflected in the "marriage" of Christ the Bridegroom and the Church, the bride.[51] In a radical break from the tendency to misinterpret the Father's view of sexuality as inherently evil, it becomes commonplace to find the Victorines employing the most intimate of human relationship's reflecting the heart of God.[52] It would be for Richard to take the analogy of inter-personal love further. What we do see in Hugh is an intensification of the concept of person, although fundamentally orthodox and Augustinian, which, along with his symbolistic method prepared for the advances of Richard.

B. Method in De Trinitate: Rationes Necessariae

This relationality is compounded by the importance of experience in the theological synthesis in Richard.[53] In order to counter some of the initial reservations about Richard's epistemology one has to understand the relationship he advocates between reason and faith and experience. In Bk. 1.1 Richard states these three as means of knowing. Experience records temporal reality and interior psychological states. Though it is argued whether Richard had actual contact with Hugh or not, it is without a doubt that this 'concrete' basis for knowing is fundamental to understanding Richard. The place of support to which Richard consistently returns is love between persons. In one of De Trinitate's most famous quotes he says;

> "Let each one examine his consciousness and without doubt or contradiction he will discover that as there is nothing better than charity so there is nothing more pleasing than charity. Nature itself teaches this and so does varied experience.[54]

---

[51]PL 176, 1:8,13, 314D-315B; On the Sacraments, 151-152. See also PL 176, 2:11,8, 495D; On the Sacraments, 341. The intriguing switch here is that marriage is deemed as the first sacrament instituted by God. The imago was intended for relationship according to the divine will, see 2.11.2-11.8, On the Sacraments, 325-340. There are relational themes throughout the discourse which reflect the implications of the twelfth century renaissance.

[52]See introduction and treatise, Augustine, On the Good of Marriage NPNF vol. 3, 397-413. Though Augustine and the majority of the Fathers lauded virginity, they still viewed marriage as a "good." See chaps. 9, 21, 24. It is also is a sign for a greater thing. Nonetheless it is unmistakable that Hugh and Richard have a more open view to the positive features of marriage than Augustine.

[53]Throughout this section my dependence upon the work of Ewert Cousins' "The Notion of the Person in the 'De Trinitate' of Richard of St. Victor," Ph.D. dissertation, Fordham University, 1966, will be evident. References to his 1966 doctoral thesis will be noted as "Notion." For his discussion of experience see, "Notion," 81-126, esp. 82-101.

[54]There is no complete published translation of Richard's De Trinitate in English. (Hereafter, PL 196 with Bk. and ch. delineations). References will be made to the Patrologiae Cursus Completus, Series Latina, ed. J. P. Migne, vol. 196 of 220 vols. (Paris:

At every level of his treatise this focus on a measure of certainty within experience is drawn upon, reflecting the sacramental worldview found in his mentor's On the Sacraments. Revealing an Aristotelian framework a century before it became common, and on the other hand his preoccupying faithfulness to an examination of the interior life, Richard is one of the clearest theological representatives of a "Christian Socratism".[55] In Augustinian fashion, this experiential element is never divorced from faith.[56] Continuing the dialectical tradition which William of Champeaux had fumbled, Abelard had championed and Hugh had transmitted, Richard constantly used experience as the first step in an epistemological ladder of ascent. The visible was a constant signpost towards the invisible. Unlike the Neoplatonic tradition however, the concreteness of the temporal was not disparaged; the symbol was sacramental, not superfluous to reality. In fact, Richard is

---

Migne–Garnier, 1855), thus, with the above quotation, hereafter as PL 196, 3:3; 917C. Any other text within that volume will be noted accordingly. Other helpful translations of portions of the text in English will be referenced. The best critical edition of De Trin. in this century is Jean Ribaillier's edition, Richard de Saint Victor, De Trinitate, texte critique avec introduction, notes et tables (Paris: Vrin, 1958), hereafter Ribaillier, De Trin. He refers to the Migne translation as defective, our use of it is for the sake of accessibility for the reader although any translation work done here will interact with Ribaillier's text with necessary differences noted. Careful comparison will show immediately differences in spelling, as well as in transmission of the text. Ribaillier mentions the English manuscript translation and commentary of Richard by John Bligh. See Ribaillier, De Trin. 11 n. 1. In Bligh's critical article of Richard he castigates Ribaillier for improper use of source citations. See "Richard of St. Victor's De Trinitate; Augustinian or Abelardian," Heythrop Journal 1 (1960): 136, n. 1. In extensive correspondence I have been unable to locate such a translation. It would appear that one ought to be pursued given the modern interest in Richard. In French, Gaston Salet has edited and translated Richard de Saint-Victor, la Trinité, texte latin, introduction, traduction et notes. vol. 63, Sources Chrétiennes (Paris: Éditions du Cerf,1959), hereafter Salet, La Trin. Bk. 3 has been translated by Grover Zinn in his Richard of St. Victor: The Twelve Patriarchs, The Mystical Ark, Book Three of the Trinity, in The Classics of Western Spirituality (New York: Paulist Press, 1979), hereafter Zinn, Book Three, except where the mystical works are used. Other portions have been gathered from the text of Cousins, "Notion," and from John F. Wippel and Allan B. Wolter, Medieval Philosophy: From Augustine to Nicholas of Cusa (New York: Free Press, 1969).

[55]Cf. just one of many allusions to this epistemology in De Sacramentis by Hugh of Saint Victor:
   "Certain things, in truth, marked by a clear image and perfect imitation produce a clear demonstration. That of God which is invisible is more quickly recognized, therefore, in those in which it is more clearly demonstrated through manifest evidence."
On the Sacraments of the Christian Faith, English version by Roy J. Deferrari (Cambridge, Mass.: Medieval Academy of America, 1951) Bk. 1, pt.3, c.21, p. 50-51. See Cousins, "Notion," 86-87.

[56]The literature is enormous with regard to the two major strains of spirituality that came out of the 12th century. An introduction to it can be found in Cambridge Medieval History, vol. 7, Decline of Empire and Papacy (Cambridge: Cambridge Univ. Press, 1932), 783-784. The Cistercian strain is often cited as "anti-intellectual," but the Victorines for all their "rationalism" were just as angered by the encroachment of pure philosophizing within the ambit of theology.

known for a unique 'proof' for the existence of God at the outset of his treatise on the Trinity.[57] Based on the law of contradiction, he proposes that from the existence of contingent objects known by experience, beings which cannot exist of themselves, it is logical to assume the existence of an immutable, non-contingent Being.[58]

This method of dialectic ascent is most unique where Richard draws upon the experience of inter-personal relationships which mirrors the inner-life of the Godhead. His desire is to go beyond the esoteric conceptions of God and to ground them in created reality. He expresses his aspiration in introductory statements concerning the 'proofs' he employs, in terms which echo Gregory of Nazianzus:

> I hear of the three that they are not three almighties but one Almighty. I hear further that they are not three gods, but one God, not three lords, but one Lord. I find the Father to be neither made nor begotten,.....All these things I often hear or read, but I do not remember having read how these points are proved. In these matters statements from authorities abound, but they are not matched by arguments. Empirical knowledge of such things is wanting and arguments for them are rare.[59]

However, and this is where most critics of Richard's method do not give proper allowance for a significant difference of meaning to the term "proof," Richard never attempts "proofs" of eternal reality based on experience in any modern rationalistic or scientific sense. Faith precedes reason and experience in his schema; it informs the latter, deepens and enriches it.[60] With a distinct nod in the direction of Anselm, he states in his epilogue, "Let us strive, in so far as it is right and possible, to understand with our reason what we believe by faith."[61] It is here that the concept of 'necessary reasons' must be explored for cogency or correction.[62] Though Anselm is often accused of being an originator of the rationalistic epistemology which influenced thinkers like Richard, he did follow the Augustinian inheritance of person as "relation," which has been shown to be only a partial application

---

[57]PL 196, 1:6-1:25, 893D-902B. Wolters has translated this in Medieval Philosophy, 212-223. Fairweather's Scholastic Miscellany carries a portion, 1:1-1:5, 324-328.

[58]Cousins, "Notion," 75, 91. Copleston, Medieval Philosophy, 2:1, 200-201.

[59]Quote from Medieval Philosophy, ed. John F. Wipple and Allan B. Wolters, 214. Richard, PL 196, 1:5, 893C. See also Cousins, "Notion," 102 where he quotes Richard's statement regarding not having seen proofs, only propositional arguments for the Trinity. PL 196, 1:5, 893A-B.

[60]Cousins, "Notion," 97.

[61]Richard, PL 196 prologue 889C, trans. Cousins, "Notion," 101. See also, Ibid., 1:4, 892C, "In so far, therefore, as God grants it to us, it will be our intention in this work to adduce reasons which are necessary and not merely probable, for the things we believe." trans. Wolter, Medieval Philosophy, 326. "L'influence de s. Anselme sur Richard est certaine." Richard de St. Victor: Opuscules Theologique: intro., notes, and tables, J. Ribaillier, Textes philosophique de Moyen âge 15 (Paris, J. Vrin, 1967), 241.

[62] Richard, PL 196, 1:4, 892C. See Wolters' trans. Medieval Philosophy, 213.

of a broader approach in Augustine.[63]

There has been distinct reservation about this line of reasoning in both Richard and Anselm. Chenu states:

> Richard of Saint-Victor, like Anselm, was not especially concerned with scriptural citation, and the fathers were far from satisfying to him. Intellectually intoxicated by his faith, he gave himself over to speculation which, even in its conceptual framework, its **sobria ebrietas** (sober intoxication), strikes one as deriving from the pressures of his mystical life.[64]

This reveals a bias which does not match up with the most recent analyses of Richard's work. His dependence upon Hugh, methodologically and scripturally, has been thoroughly revealed. Though, as we will find, he did cross over prescribed Augustinian lines of Trinitology, nonetheless, he does not step outside the pale of orthodoxy at any point. More central to our concern here, the question remains, can the recurrent critique of philosophical inexactitude be persuasively laid against Richard?[65] To argue this way is to miss the "symbolistic" methodology of the Victorine as well as the intention of the "proofs" of the Trinity. Richard was not so mystically "inebriated" as to negate the fundamental awareness of the inadequacy of human reasoning with regard to trinitarian speculation. Rather:

> The demonstrations which he proposes, evoking the "necessary reasons" of which Anselm of Canterbury had spoken before him, is that of a contemplative whose meditation has so familiarized him with the three divine persons that they have become more present to him than he is to himself.[66]

---

[63]Anselm, On the Procession of the Holy Spirit, 1, in Trinity, Incarnation, and Redemption. ed. with intro. Jasper Hopkins and Herbert Richardson, 83 (New York: Harper and Row, Pub., 1970). For a comparison of epistemological approach with the Victorine note Proslogion 1, in The Prayers and Meditations of Saint Anselm, trans. Sr. Benedicta Ward, 239-240 (New York: Penquin, 1973). Cf. also Monologion 60-64, Anselm of Canterbury: Monologion vol.1. ed. and trans. Jasper Hopkins and Herbert Richardson. New York: Edwin Mellen Press, 1974.. Barth concurs with the assessment of an Augustinian heritage in his Anselm: Fides Quaerens Intellectum ((London: SCM Press, 1958), 58-59. Gersh indicates that Boethius drew from the Alexandrian school of Platonic thought of the fifth century. He declared the desire to translate and transmit both the Aristotelian and Platonic corpora as in essential agreement. Middle Platonism and Neoplatonism, 512-513.

[64]M. D. Chenu, Nature, Man and Society, Midway Reprint, 1968, selected, ed., and trans., by Jerome Taylor and Lester K. Little (Chicago: Univ. of Chicago Press, 1983), 290.

[65]Chenu speaking of "arguments of convenience" during this period of various uses of Scripture, says that Richard did not, "in the ecstasy of his trinitarian speculation, reflect(ed) on the quality and epistemological limits of the demonstrationes they presented, any more than St. Anslem had calculated the formulation of his necessary reason," Nature, Man, and Society, 296. I concur with Cousin's rebuttal of Bligh's attack upon Richard's supposed rationalism. He summarizes this point of Richard's methodology as a rational reflection upon "faith-permeated experience." "Notion," 125.

[66]J. Chatillon's preface to Zinn's Book Three, xv, reveals the insights of one who has spent a lifetime with the Victorines in nearly every aspect of research. One need only to look at the indices of his edition of Richard's Liber Exceptionum, critical text, intro., notes and tables, Jean Chatillon, Textes Philosophique du Moyen âge 5 (Paris: J. Vrin, 1958), or

Though soon to be eclipsed by the stature and Aristotelian prowess of Aquinas and the Scholastics, nonetheless, this epistemology served to underscore the immanence-with-discontinuity of the Creator's relation to creation. It allowed a heuristic approach to divine Mysteries by excavating analogies at every level, and to conjoin the two highest elements of human existence, reason and love, whose commingling produced a type of epistemological "perichoresis" from which issued Richard's theology in De Trinitate.[67]

So strong is Richard's view of the relationship of Creator and creation, though fully aware of the residual effects in the perceptive capacities in the imago due to sin, that he regards experience as reflective of the order and rationality of a transcendent order. Convinced of what necessarily exists Richard sets out to show the necessary arguments for their existence.[68] Here Richard would respond to the Eastern tradition's apophaticism with a profound respect for the inscrutability of mystery, but also with a corresponding delight in discovery. In the epistemological line traceable from Anselm to William, and then to Hugh's high view of reason as constituent of the imago dei, "necessary reasons" are never meant to pass judgment on revelation; they are the tools by which that revelation ineluctably proffers deeper participation.[69] The ratio aeterna always dictates, limits, and

---

Ribaillier's edition of the Opuscules théologiques, to see the preponderance of scriptural texts used by Richard and the references, when he steps outside of the fashion of his day which was seldom to mention sources, to the Fathers and other theologians of his day.

[67]One also wonders if it is accurate to say that Anselm and Richard were in need of a "more modest and mature self-assessment of their own efforts at ratiocination." Jean-Marc Laporte, "Christology in the Middle Ages," in The Christological Foundation for Contemporary Theological Education, ed. Joseph D. Ban, 111 (Macon, Ga.: Mercer Univ. Press, 1988). Approaching these thinkers without the biases imposed for centuries upon them is difficult but revealing. See Ribaillier, De Trin. 20ff; Ethier Le "De Trinitate" de Richard de Saint-Victor (Paris: Vrin, 1939), 69-71; Dumeige, Richard de Saint-Victor et l'Idee Chretienne de l'Amour (Paris: Presses Universitaires de France, 1952), 77 n.80 and 85; A. Stohr, "Die Hauptrichtungen der Spekulativen Trinitätslehre in der Theologie der 13. Jahrhunderts." Theologische Quartalschrift 106: 1-2 (1925): 121-126.

[68]Cousin's lucidness is commendable here. The category of necessity was not unique to Richard. It carried the idea of a "quality of an idea by which it is universal and eternal." "Notion," 121. Those who misunderstand Anselm and Richard do so from a scientific definitio of necessity.

[69]Ribaillier makes the point with regard to "Ad me clamat ex Seir" but with which we would agree here as well that although there is a distinct line of connection between Anselm and Richard, the Victorine was in no way an unthinking disciple of the archbishop, "Il lui emprunte son esprit, s'inspire de sa méthode dialectique, lui prend quelques formules. Le plan du traité (De Trinitate) est en gros celui du Monologion. Mais le Victorin reste toute à fait original," Opuscules Theologiques, 242. He enumerates the differences between them, since often "Ad me clamat" is compared with Cur Deus Homo, concerning sovereignty and free will. In response to a deterministic Anselm, Richard sees it as a "personne á personne" relationship; and concerning anthropology, Richard does not see humans as a mere "remplacement," but as "nature créé pour elle-même." Ibid.

informs the **rationes necessariae**. As he says, "...we should always hasten to the more interior depths of understanding and press on with all eager diligence to advance daily to an understanding of those things we know by faith."[70] This co-inherence of a primary factor, faith, accompanied by a dauntless and illuminated reason, mirrored in coherent experience images a systematic principle which feeds out of and into his view of a relational Trinity.

Basic to this discussion of reason is an illuminationist epistemology.[71] Though this Augustinian canon is not in perfect agreement with his tradition's founder at this point, he does maintain the strong commitment to a participative relationship between the creature and creator. The light of the mind of God illumines the human mind, bringing about an interiorization of truth.[72] This Augustinian strain blended with Aristotelian elements is evident in both Hugh and Richard.[73] What is different from the Aristotelian/Augustinian tradition is the extent to which Richard applies his realism. The God who reveals Himself in the world, actually compels as He informs. The inner coherence continually draws productive implications. Richard is not bound to a dualistic epistemology, nor is he an advocate of panentheism. In this "ascending" methodology, visible reality signifies the invisible. Each step in the contemplative process includes looking beyond signs to things.[74] Eternal truths are paradoxically inaccessible and inviting, mysterious and heuristic.

---

[70]Richard, PL 196, 1:3, 892A-B, trans. Cousins, "Notion," 104.

[71]Hugh of St. Victor, Didascalion Bk. 6, see Jerome Taylor's edition, 141-142. The mystery of the Trinity is the foundation of an eight course mysterious ascent. It however is to be thought through, not just accepted at face value. Here again is the Eastern flavor of the Victorines. Reason was not antithetical to faith; it was to be used as an part of an "intellectus fidei." Congar, I Believe in the Holy Spirit, vol. 3, xviii.

[72]Cousins refers to this element repeatedly, see "Notion," 113-119.

[73]A distinction most likely a residual influence of High Medieval Scholasticism, is sometimes made in theology between revealed truths that are of the immutable nature and those that are free decrees of God (salvation history events, etc.). Some have seen "rationes necessariae" as a reflection of an awareness of the Aristotelian categories for demonstrative knowledge. i.e., knowledge based on intuitive induction which grasps "necessary connections" within the forms that provide deductions from which demonstrative knowledge is gained. Wippel and Wolters, Medieval Philosophy, 226. This sort of analysis may both help and take away. For instance, to focus on Richard's argument for the existence of God in De Trinitate to the exclusion of his highly organized trinitarian ruminations is to miss the connection between "necessary reasons" and contemplation. Ibid., 11, 210.

[74]Zinn, Book Three, 174-75. This method of transference is an Augustinian inheritance but as we shall see Richard is far more at ease with using insights reflected in human relationships to point to the Trinity than was Augustine, at least overtly. Ribaillier indicates that at the time of writing De Trinitate Richard had at least read Augustine's De Trinitate, Contra Maximinum, De Doctrina Christiana, and In Ioannis Evangelium. De Trin., 23.

One key to understanding this crucial notion of reason is to look at Richard as a contemplative mystic; as one enthralled with Divine love. Though we cannot divert here to a full exposition of Richard's main contribution as a doctor of contemplation, some broad strokes will help to illuminate his method in De Trinitate. Among the luminaries, whose active intellect Dante no doubt admired, and which Aquinas introduces in Paradisio, Richard's work as a contemplative is summarized poetically, "Che a considerar fu più che viro."[75] Dorothy Sayers points out that the use of considerar is of importance here since it should not be translated as contemplation, an experience reserved for the spheres including Saturn and above.[76] While Richard may not have acknowledged this highest of experiences for himself, it has been often attributed to him in varying degrees.

Richard's concept of Person is inextricably connected with his discussion of the Trinity. The structure of his text may help in placing his distinct emphases.[77] De Trinitate is comprised of six books, each containing twenty-five chapter divisions. Book 1 deals with God's existence, with proofs that are unique twists on Anselmian propositions, but it is here that he clarifies the perichoretic nature of reason and faith, in "necessary reasons."3 Book 2 is a study of the attributes of God. Book 3 places his thrust concerning Person in interpersonal union. His concern here is relatedness, the plurality requisite for true love to transpire. Book 4 views the Person in terms of individuation. Here the categories are: distinctness, individuality, incommunicability. Books 5 and 6 focus again on the notion of the inherent diffusiveness of the Good, especially with regard to fecundity, or creativity. Cousins quite rightly refers to this section as a discussion of the "Person as Dynamic."[78]

As our focus will pertain to Books 3 and 4 for the most part, we will begin with Richard's discussion of the highest in God and in humanity - love. We have recognized above that beginning in the hidden life of the Godhead may prove troublesome in our era

---

[75]"Who in his contemplation was more than man." Canto 10: 130-132. in The Divine Comedy of Dante Alighieri, intro. and comm. Allen Mandelbaum (Berkeley: Univ. of California, 1982). In the ascent to the fourth heaven, the list of personages include: in order: Aquinas, Albert Magnus, Gratian, Peter Lombard, Solomon, Dionysius, Orosius, Boethius, Isidore, Bede, Richard, and Siger of Brabant. Here Dante reveals many of the sources for his monumental works.

[76]Dorothy L. Sayers, Introductory Papers on Dante (New York: Harper and Brothers Pub., 1954), 119.

[77]Salet mentions the impact which this work had across the ensuing centuries. "Les Chemins de Dieu d'après Richard de Saint-Victor," in L'Homme devant Dieu, vol. 2, 74. Apart from an apparent lull in the 19th century Richard's De Trinitate has been used repeatedly as a cornerstone of the social analogy of the Trinity.

[78]Cousins realizes a shift in Richard's thinking beginning in Bk. 4 continuing through Bk. 6. It seems to him that Richard retreats into a more scholastic Aristotelian approach, which he would deem as a flaw. "Notion," 194-195, 215. "Yet the dynamism is latent in the text and is sensed under the abstract structure." "Notion," 218.

of theologizing. Richard did not have to contend with the bifurcation of reality implicit within our modern critique of knowledge of or speech about God and the essential nature of God. The continuum between divine revelation and human knowledge was not an epistemological difficulty for the Victorines. This Augustinian realism must be kept in tandem with the Victorine purpose of contemplative worship as a lifestyle. Richard is most concerned with the significant characteristics of the perichoretic relationship of the Trinity and their implications for spiritual transformation; one is not dealing here with scholasticism. If we divorce this treatise because of stylistic differences from Richard's mystical texts we have done him an injustice.[79] There the notion of "that which is beyond reason and contradicts it" is explicit but it is also one of the fundamentally accepted ideas resident in this text. Richard considers the supra-rational, super-substantial essence of the Godhead in light of his contemplative paradigm. It is not so esoteric, however, that vestiges are not discernible. The heuristic category of human love is one such revelational remnant.

C. Richard and Consummate Love

Richard's argument then follows that if God's inner life informs in any way our own "reflective" relationships then it is logically requisite that God love another besides himself. "But where fullness of goodness exists, true and supreme charity cannot be lacking."[80] For love to exist there is the necessity of another, yet in order to be perfect this love requires a person of equal worth to receive that love. This caritas ordinata is Augustinian in background and well may have been channeled to Richard through Achard.[81]

> However, as long as anyone loves no one else as much as he loves himself, that private love which he has for himself shows clearly that he has not yet reached the supreme level of charity. But a divine person certainly would not have anyone to love as worthily (digne diligeret) as Himself if He did not have a person of equal worth (condignam personam). However a person who is not God would not be equal in worth to a divine person. Therefore, so that fullness of charity might have a place in that true Divinity, it is necessary that a divine person not lack a relationship (consortio non carere) with an equally worthy person.[82]

Self-transcendent love is superior to self-love in Richard's mind. Constitutive of true being

---

[79]See Appendix for an extended explication of this contention.

[80]See Richard, PL 196, 3:2, 916C-D.

[81]Augustine, On Christian Doctrine, 1:27. See John Bligh's argument concerning Richard's use of the Augustinian concept of self-love which Bligh says Richard uses in a negative sense quite out of synch with its original meaning. In "Richard of St. Victor's De Trinitate," 118-139. Ribaillier lists the terms and phrases which indicate Richard's Augustinianism. De Trin., 22.

[82]Quoted from Zinn, Book Three, 375 (Latin added).

is a love that is not turned in on itself. Since the Triune God is the core of reality there must be a self-transcendent love within that Godhead. Thus, Richard sees plurality, an Other in distinction from each of the Persons of the Trinity, as the revealed categories in which to speak about God.

By the organic principle articulated above we can see how a doctrine of exemplarism is foundational to Richard's argument. Limited perfection participates in absolute perfection. Therefore as a human is open to God, who is the archetype of humanity, this self-transcendent love ought to be evident in actual life in order for there to be an individual authenticity, a true being as that individual is in relationship. It is self-evident, Richard says, that a perfect love is more than love curved in on itself. If that were the case there would be a 'lack' within that which is highest. The "amor privatus", which is regarded in this work as descriptive of the nature of the Father, the source of divine love and creativity, requires by its nature an "amor mutuus", or the mutual love of another.[83] This love must be a condign love, requiring an object of equal worth, a love which "proves" to Richard the perfection of divine love within the Trinity.

> Therefore, love cannot be pleasing if it is not also mutual. Therefore, in that true and supreme happiness, just as pleasing love cannot be lacking, so mutual love cannot be lacking. However, in mutual love it is absolutely necessary that there be both one who gives love and one who returns love. Therefore one will be the offerer of love and the other the returner of love. Now, where the one and the other are clearly shown to exist, true plurality is discovered. In that fullness of true happiness, a plurality of persons cannot be lacking. However it is agreed that supreme happiness is nothing other than Divinity itself. Therefore, the showing of love freely given and the repayment of love that is due prove without any doubt that in true Divinity a plurality of persons cannot be lacking.[84]

Cousins has perspicaciously interpreted a substantiatory outline for this argument. At each stage of Richard's logic there are substantiations drawn from experience and logic to confirm his claims regarding the supreme Good.[85]

---

[83]One would expect Richard to draw immediate implications from Scripture and tradition to a co-inherent Trinity but he does not. His argument continues along the line of reasoning with regard to supreme Goodness.

[84]Richard, PL 196, 3:3, 917D. "Prove without any doubt" here is Zinns's rendering of "indubitanter convincit". Book Three, 376. Cousins has "without a doubt leads us to the conclusion," "Notion," 96.

[85]Though mentioned above, let it be said that for the English reader, there is no more helpful outline of Richard's work than Ewert Cousins' 1966 Fordham dissertation. His insights have been extremely helpful in my assessment of the place of Richard in the history of trinitarian personhood. A summation of his pioneering work is accessible in "A Theology of Interpersonal Relations," Thought 45 (1970): 56-82, hereafter "Interpersonal Relations." It is a travesty that no other substantial work in English on this aspect of Richard's thought has been produced in the subsequent twenty years. For Cousins' analysis of experiential substantiations on the two planes he describes as vertical and horizontal see "Interpersonal Relations," 70-80 and his "Notion," 149-158, 236-243. One of the hopes of this present work is to meet Cousins' acknowledged need for a more

First, is the aspect of self-transcendent love. **Caritas** as the supreme good must include a loved one, an object or recipient of the proffered love. Second, in order for that resulting love to be perfect is must in turn be reciprocal, or the aspect of happiness. This category of course must be understood in the Patristic sense of happiness which is dissimilar to the modern notion of personal gratification. Third, this mutual love exhibits its perfection in its creative or beatific essence, the aspect of generosity.

To substantiate these categories Richard uses first their opposites. One can almost imagine a humorous streak in the Victorine as he ironically draws pictures of a God who displays characteristics contradictory to those resident within the supreme Good.[86] In De Trinitate 3:4, Richard gives two illustrations close together. He calls us to try to imagine a God who would be "lonely", as well as one whose desire might be not to share his fullness with another. With an ever-present air of incredulity at the possibility of such an occurrence within divine love Richard guides his reader through possible reservations using a series of anthropormorphisms:

> But if He would be absolutely unwilling to have one to share with Him when He really could if He wanted, then observe, I ask you, what a defect of benevolence this would be in a divine person (in **divina persona benevolentiae defectus**) and how great it would be. Certainly, as has been said nothing is sweeter than charity; nothing more pleasing than the delights of charity...He would lack these delights in eternity if He remains all alone on the throne of majesty because He lacks fellowship.
> And so from these points we can realize what kind and how great the defect of such benevolence would be if He should prefer to keep for Himself alone in a miserly fashion the abundance of His fullness.[87]

To have a God who is a transcendent monad, alone on a throne, is utterly ludicrous to Richard. If it were the case, he goes even farther to say that that God would have to hide in shame, "If He were like this, He should quite rightly hide from the gaze of angels and of everyone. If such a great defect of benevolence were in Him, quite rightly He should blush with shame to be seen or to be recognized."[88] Divine glory by its very nature is perfect; accordingly a full comprehension of that consummate glory would include a God who is not narcissictic but self-giving. For Richard the essential nature of divine glory is relational.

Thus, there are two major lines of thought converging to make Richard's fundamental point. A God who is love, in himself must reveal a self-love which is defined

---

thorough theological discussion of the horizontal elements of individuality and union and creativity as they reflect the inner life of the Trinitarian Persons. "Notion," 243.

[86]PL 196, 3:2-3, 917A-918A, make the point that a perfect Love, or supreme charity, is one that is reciprocal in donation and receiving.

[87]Richard, PL 196, 3:4, 918B, Zinn's translation, Book Three, 377, (Latin added).

[88]Richard, PL 196, 3:4, 918B-C. Zinn, Book Three, 377.

by mutual and then consummate love. Concomitantly, first by way of negation, he ponders the human categories of loneliness, selfish, and narcissistic love which implicitly destroy love. Then in affirmation, his use of the **via eminentiae** as revealed in the vestige of true love resident within human friendship or love, corrects a flawed conception of love, with the companionship, happiness and glory evident in the fullness of divine love. Though not always laid out together or in sequence, these 'proofs' re-occur at crucial junctures of this treatise. See the accompanying diagram A for a schematic view of Richard's theological method involving his method of confirmation by experience.[89]

The third major section of Richard's thought which proves to be equally unique in its formulation is a discussion of the procession of the Holy Spirit. Here again Richard explores caritas with the sort of "proofs" delineated above.

> Behold how the fullness of divine goodness and the fullness of happiness and glory come together in one witness to truth. They clearly demonstrate what ought to be thought concerning the fullness of divine charity in that plurality of persons. Together, they condemn suspicion of any defect in that supreme charity; in accord they proclaim the fullness of all perfection. In order for charity to be true, it demands a plurality of persons; in order for charity to be perfected, it requires a Trinity of persons.[90]

Supreme love is not exhausted with a binitarian love; it necessitates a trinitarian completion. The **dilectio** of the Father and the Son is only perfect as the **condilectio** of the three persons is manifest.

> A plurality of divine persons has been established but not yet a Trinity of persons. For plurality can exist even where there is no Trinity. Indeed duality itself is plurality....Now, it is necessary that supreme charity (**charitatem summam**) be altogether perfect....For just as in supreme charity what is greatest cannot be lacking, so what is clearly excellent (**quod constat esse praecipuum**) cannot be lacking either....Certainly in mutual and very fervent love nothing is rarer or more magnificent than to wish that another be loved equally by the one whom you love supremely and by whom you are supremely loved. And so the proof of perfected charity is a willing sharing of the love that has been shown to you.[91]

Just as self-love, which can run the danger of a solipsism if not superceded by a charity which is other-oriented, that **amor mutuus** is fulfilled in **caritas consummata** which is the revelation of a clearly excellent love, one marked by absolute integrity.[92]

---

[89]Cousin's calls Richard's method dialectic and notes as we have the confirmations that occur at different levels to support his claim about a relational view of divine Person. "Notion," ch. 4, 127-170.

[90]Richard, PL 196, 3:13, 924B, Zinn, Book Three, 387.

[91]PL 196, 3:11, 922C, Zinn, Book Three, 384.

[92]The first stage is made clear as we have said in Bk. 3:2, 916CD-917AB, and is argued through chap. 7, 919D-920B where the discussion then turns to substantial equality within the Trinity; however, this second level of consummate love, in the person of the Holy Spirit is only specifically addressed from 3:11-19, 922B-927C.

Diagram A
Richard of St. Victor's De Trinitate: Theological Method*

Faith

Experience   Reason

Ratio Necessaria ——— Ratio Aeterna

Aristotelian Epistemology
Augustinian Illuminationism
Dionysian Ontology

Via Eminentia
Self-Diffusive Good

Caritas
Amor sui
Amor privatus

Condignus
Amor mutuus

Confirmation: Pre-eminence of Self-transcendent love
1. Via Eminentia
2. Happiness in Other-Orientation
-loneliness-
3. Happiness in Generosity
-shame-

Condilectus
Caritas consummata

Confirmation: Consummate love - Shared Love
1.Via Eminentia
-jealousy-
2.Pleasantness of Complete love
ability/willingly/desire
-sadness due to lack-
3.Glory of Supreme Charity
-shame for defect-

---

*This diagram reveals my dependence upon Cousin's excellent analysis and my own confirmation of his interpretation from the original text. Any deviation from Cousin I might have found was too insignificant to mention. The diagram is to be read from top to bottom indicating methodological bases and thematic progression in De Trinitate.

Therefore it is necessary that each of those loved supremely (**dilectorum**) and loving supremely should search with equal desire for some who would be mutually loved (**condilectum**) and with equal concord (**concordia**) willingly possess him. Thus you see how the perfection of charity (**charitatis consummatio**) requires a Trinity of persons, without which it is wholly unable to subsist in the integrity of its fullness.[93]

The second person of the Trinity becomes the receiver and returner of the ordinate love of the Father while the Spirit originates within the eternal common desire of the Father and the Son. Richard followed the West with regard to the Filioque question, but as we have stated, there may lie here some hope for a mutual understanding on that question between East and West. Our purpose is to emphasize the epistemological presuppositions, not ecumenical implications. Richard's entire argument rests on the "ransacking" of human relationships for every vestige of the eternal "Community" and the formulation of a trinitarian argument from love as experience mirrors revelation, rather than the starting points of the substantialist or intellectualist positions.

The fullness of the life of the Godhead and human life must include an analysis of self-love, mutual love and shared love. This creative dynamism was Richard's greatest contribution but as yet very few have recognized the power of its implications.

III. Richard and the Medieval View of Personhood

The Augustinian 'oneness strain', or unity of the Trinity as the controlling systematic principle for trinitology, deeply influenced the Middle Ages as is seen in Boethius' definition of person. The resemblance to earlier static notions in his choice of rationality as definitive of the person is clear.

One distinctive voice, in many ways similar to the Cappadocian's role in the development of doctrine, which reminded the church of a relational conception of trinitarian personhood based upon the coinherent alterity of the divine persons was Richard. His De Trinitate was unique in its emphasis on the Trinity in communal terminology, a theme established by his religious order's founder, Augustine, who had alluded to love as foundational to comprehension of the Trinity in Bk. 8 and 15 of his own De Trinitate. As we have noted Augustine, for whatever reason, did not extrude implications from the ontology of goodness and love which his disciple did seven hundred years later.

Drawing upon earlier methodology but then charting a different course away from

---

[93]PL 196, 3:11, 923A, Zinn, Book Three, 385. See his summary statement:
Shared love is properly said to exist when a third person is loved by two persons harmoniously and in community, and the affection of the two person is fused into one affection by the flame of love for the third. From these things it is evident that shared love would have no place in Divinity itself if a third person were lacking to the other two persons.
3:19, 927B, Zinn, Book Three, 392.

the Aristotelian/Augustinian category of unity, the view of persons which Richard
introduced was dissimilar from the major thinkers who set the trinitarian course for the
Church in the middle ages. In order to extract the unique contributions of Richard in the
discussion of inter-trinitarian love as the basis of his definition of person we must put him
in the context of the major formulators of the medieval and modern views of personhood.

A. Boethius, Richard and Thomas Aquinas on Person

The trinitarian statements of the Pseudo-Athanasian creed, which bore strong
Augustinian concepts, provided the fifth century with the basic consensus of the Latin
approach to the Trinity.[94] But it was the Council of Chalcedon (AD 451) which radically
confronted, if not altered, the Church's conception of divine Persons. In sum, the Council
threw down the philosophical gauntlet regarding the relationship between 'person' and
'nature'. If divine persons are viewed as radically independent beings then tritheism is the
result. If to be a divine person is to only be a property of nature, then the former soon
loses any real connection with the evidence of Scripture regarding the individual
characteristics of the three Persons. Chalcedon stretched the existing argument in
advocating two co-existing natures in Christ.[95] To be a person is more than mere
"existence"; it implies more than modalism. Chalcedon confirmed the definite need of a
clarification of categories, for:

> To see the person as a modality of nature, even while taking care to call this modality
> substantial and not accidental, is to suggest that it is a reality accessory to nature, and
> fail to give proper consideration to its fundamental originality. The person must be
> defined as a basic principle, endowed with no less intrinsic value or ontological content
> than nature, profoundly distinct from nature although intimately united to it.[96]

The connection between the Tome of Leo the Great (AD 449) was firmly established. Read
as a preparatory element of the conference, Leo's letter to Flavian paved the way for the
'via media' taken between Antiochene and Alexandrian christologies at Chalcedon. What is

---

[94]Lynch points to the distinct shift to more personal categories relating to the use of
'prosopon' in the East through the christological statements of Council of Ephesus in 431,
and the anathemas of Theodoret's Symbolum, and the formulations of Cyril of Alexandria.
"Prosopon and the Dogma of the Trinity," 178, 203. Lynch believes that Cyril's usage of
'prosopon' as the subject of predicates which imply voluntary action and rational
communication is the factor which "isolated" 'prosopon', so that in the eighteen years from
Ephesus to Chalcedon (AD 451) the term came to be used in the way the modern mind
generally understands the concept of person. The four stages he delineates coincide
generally with the outline in this thesis: face, mask, mode of presentation or appearance,
subjects of predicates which imply voluntary action and rational communication. Ibid., 218.

[95]Neuner and Dupuis, 23, (17). I have been assisted in this section by the excellent
work by Jean Galot, The Person of Christ: Covenant Between God and Man (Chicago:
Franciscan Herald Press, 1984).

[96]Galot, The Person of Christ, 22.

intriguing is that 'persona' and the inherent elements of subjectivity revealed in the Latin of the Tome is used in the conciliar statement with unquestionable dependence upon Leo and is translated in the Chalcedonian text as 'prosopa' and 'hypostasis'.[97] It is evident that 'person' admits a meaning which construes rational individuality and a permeative quality that allows the perichoretic interrelationship of two natures. The tenor of the Chalcedonian statement gave to the term person an "unmistakable – and permanent– concrete meaning."[98] Constantinople II (AD 553) further solidified this reformation of modalistic usages into distinctly subjective terms. It is clear from these ecclesiastical formulations that the selfhood of the Word is described as a 'prosopon'.[99]

- Boethius and the Rational Definition

In the period immediately following Chalcedon the figure most often named as the one who assisted in the philosophical clarification within this progression of doctrine was Ancius Manlius Troquatus Severinus Boethius. Dissatisfied with what he perceived as a lack of clarity on divine personhood present in the church, Boethius offered some extremely cogent delineations based upon Alexandrian Neoplatonism.[100] He attempted to clarify the central christological confrontation of Nestorian and Eutychean complementarily heretical views stemming from the identification of person as nature, but the implications also were applied to his view of the Trinity as a whole.[101] The difference between natura and persona, he rightly judges as a "hard knot to unravel" but the hinge of his argument-by-

---

[97]Denzinger, 302; Neuner and Dupuis, 615 (155). Lynch sees this as a definite progression in the meaning of 'person'. In the quotations he cites the evidence is undeniable that 'prosopon' is employed as denoting the substantial unity of a single concrete being so that what is conjoined in Christ is not just a fusion of wills but of 'hypostaseis' in a direct inheritance from Cyril in the context of Nestorian and Eutychean onslaughts. "Prosopon and the Dogma of the Trinity," 209-216, 277.

[98]Lynch, "Prosopon and the Dogma of the Trinity," 217. Leontius of Byzantium also is of importance due to the use of 'enhypostasis' and the "in-existence" which correlates well with 'perichoresis', but his thought was not nearly as influential as Cyril's. Lynch, Ibid., 258-278. Kasper, Jesus the Christ, 241.

[99]Anathemas 1-5, 12 of the Second General Council of Constantinople, Denzinger, 421-426, 434; Neuner and Dupuis, 620/1-5 (158-160), 621, (162).

[100]Sears states that Boethius was the first influential thinker to come to "grips with the phenomenon of person." "Spirit: Divine and Human," 12.

[101]Welch thinks this christological approach is the redemptive factor in Boethius' orthodoxy especially when compared to the "ambiguity" of Tertullian. Instead of proposing individual subsistents Boethius' definition fed the psychological analogy of the medieval period clarified and perpetuated by Aquinas. C. Welch, In this Name, 269. While Boethius certainly advocated an internal distinction of the Persons, Welch's assessment flattens his conceptions markedly to fit the Boethius' agenda.

elimination rests on a definition which still holds large sway on modern philosophical notions of person. His summation is instructive of the themes he argues, in that:

> Wherefore if person belongs to substances alone, and these rational, and if every substance is a nature, and exists not in universals but in individuals, we have found the definition of person: The **naturae rationabilis individua substantia**."[102]

It is quickly evident that this definition was for the most part logically derived, out of a distinctly metaphysical context, in a way that did not include the Chalcedonian method.[103] **Ousia**, nature or essence is that which bestows form to anything.[104] By individual substance Boethius intended that which cannot be further divided, a concrete living particular such as Cicero or Plato.[105] For him person could not be predicated of universals or of non-living things, but only of either created or uncreated rational substances, clearly

---

[102]Boethius, Contra Eutychen et Nestorium 3,1-5 in The Theological Tractates trans. H. F. Stewart, E. K. Rand and S.J. Tester, Loeb Classical Library, reprint (Cambridge, Mass.: Harvard Univ. Press, 1978), 84. Hereafter, other references to his theological treatises refer to this volume also; page numbers will appear in parentheses. See also 4,8 and 4,21 (92). The first three chapters are given to the distinction between the Greek concepts of **ousia** and **hypostasis**. The date of this statement is projected near 512 AD.

[103]Rheinfelder, Das Wort 'Persona', 169-170. Note here that he subscribes a direct line between Tertullian's "juridic" categories and the medieval philosophical "abschluss" of Boethian definitions of person. In more recent scholarship both the basis of Tertullian's conception and the connection between the two thinkers has been challenged. Gersh indicates the philosophical heritage of fifth-century Alexandrian Platonism and its Aristotelian proclivities as that which fed Boethius' philosophy. His Platonism did not dissuade him from the attempt to show the essential agreement, as he saw it, in both Aristotle and Plato. S. Gersh, Middle Platonism and Neoplatonism, 512-513. J. Auer, Person: Ein Schlüssel zum christologische Mysterium (Regensburg: Pustet, 1979), 18. Auer, Person, 18. Rheinfelder, Das Wort 'Persona', 170.

[104]Boethius, Contra Eutychen 1,57-58 (80). He has said earlier, 1,8-9, that "nature belongs to those things which, since they exist, can in some way be apprehended by the intellect." And "Nature is either that which can act or that which can be acted upon." Ibid., 1,25-26.

[105]Boethius, Contra Eutychen, 2,50-52 (84). Jorge Garcia presents evidence for the Boethian usage of the concept of "incommunicability", which played a major role in the discussion of persons in the twelfth and thirteenth centuries. Boethius' two editions of the Commentary on the "Isagoge" present a view of individuality which is less than clear. It is interesting to see the same fundamental difficulty we have discussed in chap. Two regarding "first" and "second" substance in Boethius. J. Garcia, "Boethius and the Problem of Individuation in the Commentaries on the "Isagoge," in Congresso Internazionale di studi boeziani, Atti, ed. L. Obertello, Pavia 5-8, Oct., 1980 (Rome: Editrice Herder, 1981), 176-181. Boethius' Porphyrian background did not help in the comprehension of divine substance or number in substance. The fundamental equation of mind and individual is as far as Boethius can go logically although he appears to maintain a trinitarianism throughout. Wayne Hankey firmly connects Boethius and Aquinas with Proclan Neoplatonism in "The Place of the Psychological Image of the Trinity in the Arguments of Augustine's De Trinitate, Anselm's Monologion, and Aquinas' Summa Theologiae," Dionysius 3 (1979): 99-100.

distinguishable from essence generally conceived.[106] The 'person' is indicated by an unrepeatable possession of nature; thus, general essences are not seen as persons. What is not satisfied in this pervasively influential definition is an explanation as to why "individual" and "rational" are factors in distinguishing 'person' from 'nature', since the latter can be predicated of both just as the former. Classical trinitarian thought necessitates that "nature" must be seen as clearly different from "person" if one is to evade tautological statements.[107] His famous definition, "Nature is the specific difference that gives form to anything," promised to indicate the specific quality of the divine nature.[108] But it becomes evident that for the Boethian strain in Christian theology a philosophical 'ousia' or 'substantia' does not provide the safest starting point for trinitarian thought unless one differentiates nature from person at the outset. It is at this point that Richard reveals a deep perspicacity while still honoring his Augustinian heritage.

Distinguishing between general substances and the divine substance, Boethius reflects the same theme of Pseudo-Dionysius in terms of an "ultra substantiam," to distinguish the supersubstantial nature.[109] By noting the difference between divine essence and any other type of universal, Boethius defends the ecclesiastical apologia regarding the absence of three substances in God or two persons in Christ.[110] The confusing factor is not that he rejects three 'substantias' but that he uses terms so subtly distinguishable that the ground he might have gained in defining the uniqueness of personhood was disabled. He

---

[106]The point being that both universals and particulars are in one sense essences or substances, but since universal essence cannot be known in itself, the individual rational substance is what reveals the universal. Therefore, subsistences are not identical to substances. Contra Eutychen, 3,33-41 (86,88).

[107]This is Richard's basic disagreement with Boethius. See PL 196, 4:21, 945A. Thomas's discussion and agreement with Boethius is found at ST 1. q. 29, aa 1-2. See an extended discussion of Boethian categories clearly laid out and critiqued by A. Milano, Persona In Teologia: Alle Origini del Significato di Persona nel Cristianesimo Antico, Universita Degli Studi Della Basilicata-Potenza, Saggi e Recherche, vol. 1 (Naples: Edizone Dehoniane, 1984), 359-373. Milano presents a schematic (p. 360) which is helpful for understanding the Aristotelian/Porphyrian/Boethian strains of philosophical theology. It would seem possible that most of the castigation of Augustine for "hellenizing" the gospel might be more accurately placed at the feet of Boethius.

[108]Boethius, Contra Eutychen 1, 57-58 (80).

[109]Boethius, De Trinitate 3,14-15 (16-18).

[110]Boethius, De Trinitate, 3,1-55 (12-16), Utrum Pater et Filius, 48-65 (36), Contra Eutychen, 3,92-97 (90). It is informative to see the orthodox approach to the theandric perichoresis of Christ in Boethius. Taking 'kata parathesin' or 'juxtaposition' as his point of contact with the Greeks, he uses Latin terms that mirror its meaning. Contra Eutychen, 4,27 (94) 'Coniunctio', Contra Eutychen, 4,32 (94) and copulatione, Contra Eutychen, 4,67 (96). Of ninety-five references to 'persona' and its derivatives in Boethius' theological tractates, eighty-nine occur in Contra Eutychen.

agrees with the Church's anti-tritheistic stance, but then he articulates the divine being as one "'ousia' or 'hosiosis', i.e. one essence or subsistence of the Godhead, but three 'hypostaseis', that is three substances."[111] It is little wonder that the Latin thinkers following Boethius struggled through the quandry of terminology repeatedly.

Boethius ties himself to the Augustinian tradition in the argument that 'relation' indicates the sole differing predication possible regarding the Persons.[112] In trinitarian categories the 'pros te' relation of accidents in Aristotle is used by Boethius as an 'ad aliquid' category of absolutely equal subsistences in one substance. However, in order to preclude the use of "objective accidents" in defining personal relations, the effort is made to indicate 'otherness' as a relation not tied to an objective other thing spatially conceived but to, as he states, "an otherness of persons."[113] The distinguishing characteristics of the "otherness" of the Persons is only that which is relative to the Others. According to Boethius, divine relations disallow any diminishing of the actual personhood of the Persons. Any other addition would convey accidents which cannot constitute personhood.[114]

Boethius' knowledge of the Roman theater is indicated by his view of the term 'person'. He says, referring to the histrionic application, that person "seems to be borrowed from a different source, namely from the masks (personis) which in comedies and tragedies used to represent the people concerned. Now persona...is derived from personare."[115] The

---

[111]Boethius, Contra Eutychen 3, 91-93 (90), emphasis mine.

[112]Boethius, De Trinitate 5, 33-45 (26-28), Utrum Pater et Filius, 58-65 (36). The translators have put "relatively" for "ad aliquid" which makes the passage lose some of its force. Ibid., 65 (36). In the preface to De Trinitate Boethius points to the "seeds of argument" through which Augustine's rational interpretation of the Trinity apparently caught this enigmatic thinker's attention. Ibid., Preface, 32-33 (4). Lossky quips in his incessant critique of the West that through Boethius, "the philosopher's 'persona' bcomes the theologian's 'relatio'." The Image and the Likeness, 116. Wayne Hankey argues persuasively that it was neither Aquinas nor Augustine who bequeathed the de deo uno and de deo trino bifurcation lamented by Rahner, Lossky and others. If its origin is to be found it is Boethius who is to blame. Aquinas, in his commentary on Boethius's De Trinitate states that methodologically Boethius chooses the rational route (secundum rationes) alone where, as we have seen, Augustine couples reason with scriptural and traditional authority (per auctoritates). The Trinity and the Unicity of the Intellect, trans. Sister Rose Emmanuella Brennan (London: B. Herder Book Co., 1946), 11. W. Hankey, "The De Trinitate of St. Boethius and the Structure of the Summa Theologiae of St. Thomas Aquinas, in Congresso Internazionale di studi boeziani, Atti, ed. L. Obertello, Pavia 5-8, Oct., 1980, (Rome: Editrice Herder, 1981), 367-368.

[113]Boethius, De Trinitate 5,40 (28).

[114]Boethius, Contra Eutychen 2,15-16 (82)

[115]Boethius, Contra Eutychen 3,7-11 (86). Thomas refers to this section in discussion of etymology of persona, ST 1a, 29, 3. The figures who refer to Boethius in the eras immediately surrounding Richard's interpret his meaning of 'person' in Contra Eutychen in ways which reveal the 'ad fontes' historiography of the twelfth century as well as the

background of sounds, the masks which project those sounds, and the character roles which eventually carried the original term serve as etymological connections with **prosopon**. However, he understood that hypostasis was a far more explicit and evocative term than its histrionic forebear. In this way he notes the relationship of persona with **hypostasis**, or individual subsistent, but he chooses **prosopon** as the best indicator of rational individuality in order to avoid the confusion which similar terms might induce.[116]

The individual person is a singular substance among other substances (**supposita**) which may or may not possess rationality. When applied to the Trinity however there are evident problems. Individuality in the Godhead cannot carry the connotations of radical singularity in **hypostasis** which Boethius may not have intended but nonetheless offered without necessary qualification. The end result is that the divine Persons really are nothing other than the divine essence itself. In an effort to combat the confusion of nature and person in Eutyches and Nestorian there is an inadvertent re-statement of just such a problem by Boethius. While it may be said that the Trinity is protected against any quaternitarian import, the notion of relationality, which either incorporates or supercedes the rational in terms of a complete view of person, remains absent.[117]   Though we have

---

waning understanding of the Roman theater in that era. **"Persona a personando"** is echoed in Gilbert Porreta's De Duabus Naturis; the anonymous De diversitate Naturae et Personae which carries strong Gilbertine overtones; the Gilbertine yet individualistic, Alan of Lille; Simon of Tournai; and possibly the Victorine predecessor of Richard, Achard in In Titulo. See Rheinfelder, Das Wort 'Persona', 19, 109 (see also his astounding compilation of medieval sources which reveal the same basic meanings which evolved into "body" and "being," instead of role). Ibid., 30-80. Congar accepts Ribaillier's thesis that Richard is absolutely dependent upon his abbot Achard, I Believe in the Holy Spirit, 103. The theatrical allusions in Boethius and sources which utilized his definition are presented succinctly in Mary Marshall's "Boethius' Definition of 'Persona' and Medieval Understanding of the Roman Theater" Speculum 25:3 (1950): 471-482.

[116]He supports other connections between Greek and Latin. Einai and husiosis with **subsistentia**, husiosthai is translated **subsistere**, huphistasthai carries similar meaning to **substare**. Contra Eutychen 3,42-78. He reflects the same confusion on substance we found in Augustine, and thus has to clarify the dual usage of hypostasis as substance and as subsistence. John Veerhaar questions Boethius' usage of **substare** as a "gratuitously" constructed deviation from Aristotle's substantia." "Theism Today and Tomorrow," in The Future of Belief Debate, ed. G. Baum (New York: Herder and Herder, 1967), 182. This reflects the confusion we have discussed in chap. Two regarding **substantia prima** and **secunda**.

[117]Lynch's otherwise commendable work to which we have appealed reveals an overdependence on Boethian categories of definition. The continual absence of relational categories gives the impression that it was only after Boethius that the issue was ever raised. One wonders if the agenda set by the more metaphysically-oriented scholastics overshadowed the indications of relationality in the earlier fathers. It is also intriguing to consider the Greek background for "rational" since 'logon' has at its core the essence of speech which is fundamentally relational. Demers mentions this source but makes nothing of it in "Les divers sens du mot 'ratio' au moyen âge. Autour d'un texte de Maître Ferrier de Catalogne (1275)," in Études d'histoire littéraire et doctrinale du XIIIe siècle, I (Montreal:

already dealt with Augustine's view of substance, it is apparent how easily the interpretation of the Bishop's work became philosophically-centered. Whether that is a true reading of Augustine's intentions by Boethius or not, its presence in Boethius and his philosophical lineage inevitably leads to a diminution in the concept of trinitarian personhood. Boethius' ought not to be castigated for adhering to his own stated purpose which did not include the scriptural exegesis as Augustine displayed, though somewhat strained at points, in his thesis. From this standpoint, if divine substance preserves the unity, then it is that "the relation makes up the Trinity."[118] So it must follow that the Father "never began to be Father, since the begetting of the Son belongs to his very substance; however, the predication of father, as such, is relative."[119] This is a distinct step backward from the advances of Chalcedon in the arena of trinitarian personhood.[120] To apply Boethius' definition either christologically or trinitologically disallows either a true enhypostasis in Christ or a perichoretic nature in the Godhead.[121]

His discussions regarding individual distinction and its implications for individuality further verify this criticism. Based upon "types" of numbers, Boethius' view renders two options: 1) numbers by which we count, which necessitates plurality if more than one, and 2) that which occurs in countable objects, where no plurality exists.[122] So he concludes that the Three Persons are in no way different things but are the reiteration of

Publications de l'Institute des études médièvales, 1932), 112, 118-119.

[118]See the progression of Boethius' Augustinianism and Neoplatonism in De Trinitate 3-6 (12-30). Quote is from chap. 6, 9-10 (28,30). Thomas repeats this argument often. Relation multiplicat personarum Trinitatem, ST 1a, 39, 1 reply. The basis of Augustine's discussion of the same issue, the substance/relation leitmotif, is found in De Trinitate 5.5-5.12, NPNF vol. 3, 89-94; CC, 209-220. If Augustine did not alter the impact of his statements in this section by the means we have indicated in chap. Three he also would be guilty of the same sort of philosophical conundrum which Boethius presents. C. Gunton has argued strongly that this is just the case in Augustine and in the West's truncated view of God. See his "Augustine, The Trinity and the Theological Crisis in the West," 44-45.

[119]Boethius, De Trinitate 5, 43-45 (28).

[120]A. Lloyd's rather vitriolic article on Augustinian personhood includes Boethius as one who followed the Bishop in the mistaken use of "relation". See his "Augustine's Concept of Person," in ed. R. A. Markus Augustine: A Collection of Critical Essays (Garden City, NY: Anchor Books, 1972), 202.

[121]There are, of course, a variety of opinions on this issue. A. Milano critiques Boethius' pneumatology but seems to agree with his 'subsistentia-substantia' paradigm. Persona In Teologia, 373-377. M. Schmaus feels that Boethius' concepts "can be freed from this danger," (disallowing three persons) and that Richard's view "would be less a correction than a continuation of Boethius." Dogma vol. 3: God and His Christ (New York: Sheed and Ward, 1971), 155. Logically, then, it flows that both Milano and Schmaus have strong reservations about relational views of personhood.

[122]Boethius, De Trinitate 3, 19-28 (15).

the same thing.[123] Again, the way around the conundrum of collating simple substance and plurality of persons is the relations of the unique divine substance, a sui generis category. The unity of the Godhead is preeminent in his mind and therefore it is explained negatively as the absence of plurality. Divine individuality was not an issue because divine nature was of a different sort of substance. He is intent upon affirming that number is insufficient as a predicate of God but in the process the articulation of the distinctions is all but lost.[124] Both J. Garcia and M. Nédoncelle have enumerated the logical difficulties in Boethius' rather disjointed conception of individuality and the impact it had on later medieval thinkers until Abelard critiqued it.[125] It is the latter identification of individuality with numerical difference which Boethius never denied, though never clearly articulated, that affected the view of divine Personhood throughout the middle ages. It is that problem which Richard attempted to overcome.

The seventh century gave the church an intriguingly perspicacious summary of trinitarian dogma in the statement of faith of a local council. Seventeen bishops constructed this orthodox statement at the Eleventh Council of Toledo (675). The use of person coincides with the Western view of the filioque but also indicates that at that time the individual characteristics of the divine Persons were carefully thought out and widely accepted.[126]

Lest it be thought that our critique of Boethius indicates a blindness to other attempts at approaching 'person' from a tack besides the rational alone, brief mention must be made of Alcuin of York (ca. 735-804). Alcuin, who played such an important role in the Carolingian renaissance, was far more forthright on the idea of person than Augustine,

---

[123]Boethius, De Trinitate 3, 36 (14).

[124]Boethius writes in De Trinitate 3,1-4 (12),
Now God differs from God in no respect, for there cannot be divine essences distinguished either by accidents or by substantial differences belonging to the substrate (in subiecto positis distent). But where there is no difference, there is no sort of plurality and accordingly no number; here, therefore, is unity alone.

[125]Jorge Gracia, Introduction to the Problem of Individuation in the Early Middle Ages (Washington: Catholic Univ. of America Press, 1984), 97-111. M. Nédoncelle, "Les variations de Boèce sur la personne," Revue des Sciences Religieuses 29 (1955): 201-38. The personalist writes of Boethius who he accuses of a monadism, "Il est obligé de supprimer toute trace d'accident en Dieu et de concevoir les trois personnes comme les émanations éternelle de la supra-substance divine." Ibid., 234.

[126]See the Statement of Faith, Eleventh Council of Toledo, Neuner and Dupuis, 308-320. Cassiodorus (d. ca. 580) gives a definition which nearly equals that of Boethius in an exposition of Ps. 8:2,1 ("substantia rationalis individua") Expositio Psalmorum I-LXX from Magni Aurelii Cassiodore Senatoris Opera, in Corpus Christianorum Series Latina (Turnhout: Typographi Brepols Editores Pontificii, 1968). We have mentioned John of Damascus' contribution to the support of the Eastern view of triune persons in the 8th century.

according to V. Serralda.[127] As Alcuin interpreted the creation texts he focused on the substantial quality of the soul in tandem with its "juridical power" drawn from the divine imperative to take dominion of the earth. Though there is a tripartite similarity between Alcuin and Augustine in anthropology, the facets they each choose to emphasize are different. In a unique shift from the main theological tradition in the West, Alcuin chose a holistic interpretation of the human soul as a spiritual substance revealed in the 'imago' passages of Genesis. His own version of substantia was explored as a basis for understanding personhood from a perspective outside the trend normal to the West, begun with Augustine, i.e., to focus on the mind and rational analogies of the imago.

Late in the career of Abbot Alcuin, the concept of person possessing "juridical power", the trait above all others in the complex of human personality, began to crystallize in his thinking. What transpired appears to have been a type of breakthrough in medieval theology which is little known. Substance and act are conjoined in a dynamic way for Alcuin. The power to choose, to reflect, to have dominion were not ancillary elements to personhood, but they were the very matrix through which true persons could be recognized. The implications in both theological and anthropological directions were remarkable examples of a Western thinker who in many ways was identifying the same characteristics of personhood which the Cappadocians had related four centuries earlier. Divine personhood found emphasis in the category of divine incommunicability, but that was inclusive of certain aspects of independence of intellect and will, even elements of autonomy.[128]

There was an openness to his paradigm which appears to be absent in Boethius. He did not reduce the discussion to questions of substance alone. He argued for personhood being seen as the principle, the matrix, of the unifying of the human soul Alcuin's exceptional theory was preceded, in the West, by Tertullian's approach to substance which admitted individuation; in the East, by the Cappadocian view of individuation in relationship, which in turn was adumbrated in Gennadius' and Leontius of Byzantium's dealings with incommunicability as underlying factors in both divine and human personhood.[129] It is continually intriguing how this line, the relational model, and

---

[127]Vincent Serralda, La Philosophie de la Personne chez Alcuin (Paris: Nouvelles Éditions Latines, 1978), 254.

[128]Serralda, La Philosophie de la Personne chez Alcuin, 17, 172, 228-229, 253-254, 342-343. The "creationist" approach of Alcuin demarcated him from Boethius by whom he is not assisted at all, though he is aware of the latter's definitions. Ibid, 82.

[129]Serralda also mentions Rufinus' "subsistent substance." Ibid., 344. The semi-Pelagian, Faustus of Riez (ca. 408-ca. 490) spoke of a juridical power, St. Fulgentius dealt with the "sovereignty of juridical power; but Pope John II directly confronted Boethian categories in confirming that the Eastern 'hypostasis' and the 'subsistentia' of the Latins did not deal with the volitional element which concerned Alcuin. Ibid., 345. It is

its philosophical supports are consistently left out of scholarly discussion.

The unity model, ratified in the West by Aquinas' assimilation of Boethian categories, is a concerted effort to protect the substantial nature, which is "super-substantial" in his mind, from differentiations which would threaten the oneness of the Trinity.[130] Among other cogent criticisms of this tradition, one of the strongest is laid to the root of this tendency to produce what Aquinas was to name a "transcendental." Whether it is Augustine's **'relation'**, Boethius' **'substantia rationalis naturae'**, or Thomas' **'subsistent relation'**, there is within each the latent possibility of advocating an essence "beyond" the Trinity. In an attempt to transcend philosophy while seeking to retain trinitarian commitments each is vulnerable to the criticism that there might be a quality or **'fons'** beyond revealed categories.[131]

- Richard: Origins and Exsistentia

Richard's definition of person was at once critical of the philosophical suppositions of Boethius and, on the other hand, a creative insertion into the dogma of the Trinity which was seldom the case in the Augustinian lineage.[132] Similarity of form ought not lead to a misunderstanding of the difference in content in Boethius and Richard. The Victorine quotes the Boethian definition, **"rationalis naturae individua substantia"** and offers his

---

disconcerting that as thorough a job as Serralda has done he does not mention a further support for the basic element of his argumentation, Richard of St. Victor, though both Hugh and Thomas are given space.

[130]"ultra substantium," Boethius, De Trinitate 4,11. One can see here the Dionysian influence also. The impact of Boethius was seen in several important thinkers of the twelfth century. One important example is Thierry of Chartres (or a disciple of his), who authored Librum Hunc, a commentary on Boethius' De Trinitate. Stephen Gersh compares and contrasts Thierry's Commentum with Boethian background and source material in "Platonism, Neo-Platonism and Aristotelianism in the Twelfth Century," in Renaissance and Renewal in the Twelfth Century, ed. Robert Benson, et al., 512-534 (Cambridge, Mass.: Harvard Univ. Press, 1982). Gersh helps to clarify the syncretism of both Platonic and Aristotelian systems concerning the Western trinitarian concept of "self-reflective hypostasis of intellect," begun with Augustine and Macrobius and transmitted into the twelfth century by Theirry. Ibid, 530-532. Of course his most famous expositor was Aquinas whose Commentary on De Trinitate (1258 AD), though more comment on questions raised than on actual exposition, served to secure Boethius' place in Western thought.

[131]Richard is vulnerable at the place of positing either a Dionysian conception of the Good or at his usage of the 'origo' for discerning the persons but we shall see how he eschews this substance beyond the actual Trinity. See Cousins on Augustine and 'relation', "Notion," 192.

[132]Duns Scotus, Bonaventure and Alexander of Hales also reflect the same dynamism which Richard infused during the twelfth century. Each acknowledges Ricardine influence. See Duns Scotus, Opus Oxeniense 1. 23, 1, and Ordinato 1. d.2 q.1-4 for definitions of person that indicate the transference of ideas directly from the Victorine.

correction, "**divinae naturae incommunicabilis exsistentia,**" in the following chapters.[133]

It is imperative to keep Richard's systematic principles in tact at this point. His ensuing explanation of divine personhood by an "ontological exemplarism" is based on the scriptural statement of the essence of God as love, and the experiential evidence of the highest good. The idea of *ratio* is different from the rational categories of Boethius or Aquinas.[134] Implicit in Victorine-Augustinian spirituality is a realistic reciprocity between Revealer and that which is revealed. The vestiges of divinity are recognized and explored throughout.

Thus the starting point for Richard's epistemology is triune love. Cognition for Richard is purposeful and worshipful, most of all relational, so that when Richard uses the Boethian category he includes what was meant philosophically but by applying supra-rational 'cogitatio' he goes beyond, not inductively but contemplatively. **Intellectualis** is the object of pure contemplation; faith then 'mirrors' ultimate reality, similar to Augustine's 'unmediated truth'. It is the revelation of a divine love in the heart and mind.

The Victorine confronts the majority position on the divine substance from several tacks. Richard is well aware of the Western/Eastern confusion on use of the terms substance and subsistence.[135] Nature, if we maintain the contextual emphases, is not static substance but existence of perfect love shared in communion. It is here that Richard criticizes the Boethian categories which had come to be unquestionably accepted and promulgated.

> Boethius' definition of the person is as follows: an individual substance of a rational nature. For this definition to be universal and perfect, every individual substance of a rational nature must be a person and every person must be an individual substance of a rational nature.[136]

Richard's critique of Boethius actually begins with a logic question. If 'person' is to be applied universally then it must be a univocal concept. He saw in Boethius the equation of substance and persons which resulted in a tautology. Either one or the other is a particular rational nature but both cannot be since 'person' then would lose any real meaning.[137] Neither noetic nor ontic explanations of personhood suffice for Richard. He

---

[133]Taken from Boethius' Contra Eutychen 3. 4-5 an exact quote being, "naturae rationabilis individua substantia." Cf. Ibid., 4. 8-9. Richard, PL 196, 4:22, 945C,D.

[134]This difference is also basic to the definition in PL 196, 4:24, 946D, "Person is an existant in itself, possessing a particular mode of rational "exsistence." Author's emphasis.

[135]PL 196, 4:20, 944B-C. He challenges the West to find a better term than 'person' at the end of this discussion.

[136]Cousin's translation, "Notion," 173.

[137]PL 196, 4:21, 945A.

begins his argumentation from a point similar to the Greeks and possibly Hilary.[138] Personal being, an interrelated nature, is the source of the trinitarian distinctions. Without a clear element of difference in origin, the Persons become nominalistic 'voces'.

To continue with the traditional definition, for Richard, is destructive to the constitution of what it means to be a person; he sees it as restrictive and atomistic. Adroitly Richard applies the Boethian definition to the divine substance. If one is to remain orthodox then the maintenance of unity of the divine nature is necessary, as is the attribution of rationality to it. Thus the definition already crosses the boundary of applicability to persons alone. Whether one accepts the divine nature as an individual or not, the present definition is no longer universally applicable.[139]

The argumentation shifts and Richard embarks on an audacious journey here, which reflects the milieu discussed above. He engages not only Boethius but the Aristotelian reasoning upon which the former's definition is based. Specifically, the mode of defining an object within a class is accomplished by recognizing the unifying generic quality while distinguishing with regard to specific difference. Thus the Boethian person is of the genus of animal, the species of man, with the specificity of rationality.[140] In light of what we have already said Richard recoils; for him to be a person is to be in relationship, an exsistence that is not submerged in the being of another without distinctiveness.[141] Cousins writes concerning Richard's opposition to the theological consensus pertaining to 'substantia':

> Man belongs to the genus of animal and to the human species, whose differentiating quality is that of rationality. Thus the definition of man is rational animal.
> The very technique of defining the person is immediately involved in two difficulties: (1) The distinguishing mark of the person is individuality and not the quality of belonging to a class. Therefore it would seem that a definition of a person would be impossible. (2) The whole purpose of the definition is to separate and distinguish the object from all others. In accord with Richard's analysis in Book III, the characteristic of the person is not to be separated but related—related, however, not in a logical way by being a member of a class, but in a dynamic, experiential way by being united to another person in a relation of love.[142]

---

[138]Congar notes Richard's separation from the Greek tradition on the filioque issue. I Believe in the Holy Spirit, vol. 3, 105. Although Richard does not negate the idea of the Holy Spirit as mutual love, he does proffer a pneumatology which constitutes a stronger conception of the Spirit's personhood than either Augustine's vinculum or Aquinas' donum. Richard does use the latter but primarily in economic contexts. Cf. PL 196, 6:14, 978C.

[139]Cousins, "Notion," 176.

[140]PL 196, 4:22, 945C-D.

[141]PL 196, 5:18, 962B.

[142]Cousins, "Notion," 174-175.

In this method of approaching the Godhead, Richard is not so audacious as to
discuss the divine essence but rather to explore the crucial points which distinguish the
Persons from each other. Equating person with nature does not suffice because generic
qualities tend to excise the elements of relational individuation and the dynamism inherent
in that approach. So he explores the category of "origin". Where nature refers to generic
categories, it is the origins of the Persons. Richard states that once the nature of
something, the "what", is known the next step is to investigate the "whence" of a distinct
thing.[143] There is a ubiquitous interest in De Trinitate to explore the differentiations
indicated by the Church's reflection on the Triune life.

Richard's carefully chosen correctives of the Boethian line are two; the first is the
concept of incommunicability, which may be implicit in Boethius but needed specific
clarification. There must be unique characteristics which set one individual apart from
another lest one is willing to identify two as one. He distinguishes between common
substance and "incommunicable exsistent."[144] Each subsistent person possesses distinct
personal properties.[145]. He is aware of the need to steer clear of modalism. Thus, as
George Tavard summarizes, the Father's personal property is that which communicates all
of himself to the Son, but for being the Father; and all of himself to the Spirit, but for
being the originator of both the Son and the Spirit."[146] Mutatis mutandis, this applies to
each of the persons in relation to the others.

Second, a divine person is an incommunicable exsistentia.[147] Here two
characteristics interest him. One is definitional regarding the mode of being or quality of
such a distinction; the other pertains to their individual origins or the process of the divine
nature. In the continuation of exploring relational categories, he breaks the word down to
its logical components. Looking at the verbal counterpart to the noun, sistere implies that
which stands 'in' something else; it points to that which 'stands under'. A divine person
who is 'existere' stands-from, is oriented 'ex aliquo' and thereby is not an isolated entity.
The uniqueness of the individual is tied to origin.[148] In a human individual the
differentiation would be in both quality and origin while in the divine nature it would

---

[143]PL 196, 4:11, 937A; Cousins, "Notion," 180.

[144]PL 196, 4:20, 944C.

[145]PL 196, 4:17, 941B

[146]G. Tavard, The Vision of the Trinity, 77.

[147]PL 196, 4:17, 941C - 4:18, 941D-942B.

[148]Ribaillier points to the reference in Gilbert of Porreta and Boethius for 'existens per
se solum'. Note on De Trin. 4:24, 189.

apply to origin alone.

Richard is striving for a precision which has been overlooked as just another view of individuality. This definition carries what Cousins says is "a richer connotation than individua since it hints at the paradox and mystery of interpersonal communication."[149] In order to communicate subjectively there must be a logical base of objective non-communication. The logicians resonate with the critique of de Regnon; Richard is on shaky ground but that faux pas has all too often meant the catapulting of the positive addition his definition brings to the philosophy of personhood. From the static notion of substance, Richard moves toward a dynamic, existential mode of origin as delimiting the person. The triune God is thus three 'existants'. There is here not a whit of self-sufficiency in independence or separation intended. The Cappadocian "mode" has found clearer expression in this Western theologian. The divine persons are not merely relations nor are they individuals, rather they are incommunicable other-oriented entities that are only definable in relationship.[150]

Cousins feels that it as at the point of the person of the Father where Richard's analogy founders initially. It is insufficient to say that based upon this relational model one of the members has his being from Himself.[151] When viewed from another direction it is not so apparent that Richard is blind to this issue. If we follow carefully the dialectic of mutuality in love, glory, generosity and goodness it is implicit that the Father receives these just as the other persons. Coupled with the attributed traditional element of 'fons' or 'origo' distinguishing the Father from the Son and the Spirit it is not at all surprising that Richard expresses his triad as "giving," "giving and receiving," and "receiving."[152] His stress on the equality demanded of the divine persons would be meaningless if there were a source who did not receive anything from that which generated and that which proceeded. What is also presupposed in the criticism is that the revealed property of "giving" is to be defined univocally. Innascibility is the "proprietatibus incommunicabiles"

---

[149]Cousins, 183.

[150]This approach is probably the reason why Cousins did not produce much more on Richard. He disagrees with my interpretation and moves into Bonaventurian studies which his personal bibliography indicates. My contention is that Richard properly understood is saying all that Bonaventure and Alexander of Hales eventually produced on this particular issue minus, of course, their vantage points being successors to the relational tradition. It may also be that the Teilhardian and then Process proclivities of Cousins found adumbration in Bonaventure where Richard did not reveal those similarities.

[151]Cousins, "Notion," 186.

[152]It seems that the same conceptions of the Godhead that formed the Johannine trinitarian statements as well as the Church's discernment of the divine essence are foundational to the relatedness Richard explains in PL 3:3, 917D, see also the clarification of this mutual total self-giving in PL 5:17, 962A-962B, Salet, La Trin, 346-347.

of the Father.[153] But that cannot be divorced from the matrix of mutual themes within which discussion of the incommunicability of the Persons must be placed.

He does purport the properties of the Persons first but that does not mean that reciprocity is not also present, even toward the Father. It is fallacious to posit that Richard did not "situate individuality within the sphere of relationship."[154] This is an obscurantistic perception given Richard's uses of exsistentia. He incorporates what the Augustinian tradition did not do by its elevation of relation over substance. In the final analysis it is Richard who promises a dynamic view of the Trinity and not the rational categories of his better-known critics. Against Boethius Richard makes it clear that the Persons do not equal the divine nature. Instead the categories are mutually defining; without the Persons there is not unity. Richard's emphasis on origins is a cogent means of providing a check for any misuse of his relational categories. Exsistentia, then, follows the outline of Richard's 'ecstatic' mysticism. The Trinity of love, the Persons exist or subsist in that which is outside, or confronts, their incommunicability. There is no One outside of the other two. The 'dilectio' of the Father and the Son is only perfect as the 'condilection' of the three persons is manifest.[155] To separate exsistence from origin defaces Richard's method and conclusions and opens up the Trinitarian doctrine to the typical heresies. To "stand from" is to "stand toward" in each of the Existants. To not comprehend that is to miss the entire intent of Richard's De Trinitate.

- Thomas Aquinas and Subsistent Relation[156]

The impact of the Augustinian-Boethian tradition of relation is seen in an intriguing proximity with the Ricardine period in Adam of St. Victor's statements in lyrical

---

[153]PL 196, 5:13, 959C.

[154]Cousins, "Notion," 212. See his Thomistically-based criticism of the lack of proper use of relation by Richard on page 201.

[155]Congar puts it succinctly, "There is the love which is received (debitus or due to another) and which gives (gratuitus). That love is the Son. The love that is purely received (debitus) is the Spirit." I Believe in the Holy Spirit, 104. PL 196, 5:16, 5:18, 960D-961A, 962C-962D.

[156]The use of Aquinas in this work is based as entirely as possible upon the Leonine edition of the Summa. All references are from the Blackfriars edition primarily; vol. 6, The Trinity: Ia. 27-32, trans. Ceslaus Velecky (McGraw-Hill Book Co., 1965); and vol. 7, Father, Son and Holy Ghost Ia. 33-43, trans. T.C. O'Brien (Ibid., 1976). Hereafter, only the appropriate citing in the ST will suffice. If another translation or volume is used it will be duly noted.

form of trinitarian personhood. There the persons are spoken of only relatively.[157] However, it is without doubt that Aquinas' stature and theological prowess were factors which led to the majority decision that Richard's definition of person was dissatisfying. Aquinas took up the concept and veritably entrenched it in the Western mind that distinction within the Godhead must be analogically referred to as real relations, subsistent however in a Being much like the philosophical mentor of the Angelic doctor, Aristotle himself, a being-in-itself.[158] Whether Aquinas intended it or not, the use of 'subsistent relations' became, without dispute, the formulation which has provided the framework upon which any orthodox trinitology has been based up to this century. Thomas postulated further the Augustinian categories concerning the relations of origin, or the processions in God.

E. Hill speaks of Thomas' early awareness and usage of Victorine categories, especially that of diffusion of the Good, which in turn Aquinas recast and subsequently divorced himself from through a fundamental rational epistemology.[159] Torrance postulates that methodologically Thomas rejected Augustinian illuminationism and replaced it with Aristotelian categories.[160] In a general sense then, the Eastern critique of Western concepts might find cogency in this paradigm shift. Is the issue of Trinitarian persons one of the places where the West took a wrong turn following Aquinas' lead?

St. Thomas saw, as did both Hugh and Richard, all of creation as replete with vestiges that indirectly reflect the "Exemplar".[161] The human intellectual capacity became a

---

[157]Rheinfelder presents the original text of a hymn attributed to Adam from 1192AD, "tres personas asserentes/ personali differentia./ Hae dicuntur relative". Das Wort 'Persona', 177. In an otherwise exhaustive study it is incomprehensible how so thorough an attempt at excavating the material on person could be done without a single reference to Richard.

[158]de Margerie comments to this effect in Christian Trinity in History p.140-141. Cf. Aquinas, I Sent. dist.23, a.3, in fine corp; De Potentia q.9, a.4; Summa Ia q.29, a.4.

[159]E. Hill, Three-Personed God, 79. N. Kretzmann sees in the Sentences more of an openness to Dionysian categories which is not evident in the Summa and Contra Gentiles. "Goodness, Knowledge, and Indeterminacy in the Philosophy of Thomas Aquinas," Journal of Philosophy 80 (1983): 632-634.

[160]Theology in Reconstruction, 262. C. Welch points out that the emphasis in Aquinas of received tradition as a theological source where Augustine used historical evidences is a bit far-fetched given Aquinas' keen interest in Scripture as a deposit of truth. However, his warnings against producing doctrine out of finite reflection ought to be heeded. In This Name, 119.

[161]Summa Contra Gentiles I, 49; II, 21, 9; ST 1a, 45, art. 6-7; Farrell says that according to Aquinas the creation was " to communicate the divine goodness so on every side of us we see something of the family likeness of God." Companion to the Summa, vol. 1 (New York: Sheed and Ward, 1941), 181. Mascall sees the purpose of this vestigial emphasis being the connecting link between Deo Uno and Deo Trino as relationally

crucial pinion of Aquinas' epistemological structure in its role of apprehending the imprints left by the Creator.[162] The 'sacra doctrina' included revelation as its starting point but it made room for a participative view of reality. Analogies which partook of ultimate reality retained a "form" of the divine essence they reflected. This modus significandi was perpetually protected in Aquinas' writings from the abuse of "exteriorizing" that which was meant to pertain only to the immanent and intellectual.[163] It is important to recall the place of the will and love in the formation of a systematic principle in Aquinas which closely aligns itself with Augustine. Above all Aquinas advocates a knowledge permeated with love. In fact the intellect is not superior to either will or love in spite of the primary position given to it by St. Thomas. To know God is to love Him. Love therefore possesses a unitive quality which motivates the will.[164] This created intelligence cannot know God through pure form as that is only possible in God himself. Thus, the human mind depends upon abstractions from phantasms. Through the created order, especially within the interrelated triad of intellect, volition and will, it is possible to know "that" God is, but with strong apophatic tendencies Aquinas disallows knowledge of the "what" of God's nature.[165] Robert Richard disagrees strongly with the claim that Aquinas followed the apodictic reasoning process of Anselm and Richard. Instead he sees employed an apologetic method which deductively moves from processions to eternal mysteries.[166] It is true that Thomas begins his discussion of processions with an analysis of biblical terms, but these are placed in the larger context of the theological order drawn from Augustine and

---

reflected in creation. The Triune God, 55.

[162]Summa Contra Gentiles III, 78; III, 113.

[163]Giles Hibbert, "Mystery and Metaphysics in the Trinitarian Theology of St. Thomas," Irish Theological Quarterly 31 (1964): 195. Hibbert views Thomas' method as synthetic of Platonic apophaticism and the Aristotelian metaphysical affirmations which assist in the discussion of otherwise ineffable mysteries. Ibid, 191.

[164]Summa Contra Gentiles III, 26; ST 1a, 8, art. 3 - art. 5; ST 1a, 19, art. 10.

[165]ST 1a, 27, art. 3, reply. See also R. L. Richard, The Problem of an Apologetical Perspective in the Trinitarian Theology of St. Thomas Aquinas, vol. 131, Series Facultatis Theologicae: sectio B. n.43 (Rome: Gregorian University Press, 1963), 131, 218.

[166]Richard, The Problem of an Apologetical Perspective, 120, 312. He does recognize that there are some passages which might indicate the use of "ratio necessariae" in Richard and Anselm. He does not see the same sort of rationalism we have attributed to him. Ibid., 210, 216, 223, 226, 230, 256. By "apologetic" Richard argues that for St. Thomas the Trinity was not based on reason but upon revelation. Possibly Richard follows Aquinas in a misunderstanding of the Victorine use of reason.

Boethius.[167] The Thomistic recapitulation of the major Western thinkers includes a theological methodology which moves from unity to plurality, from knowledge and love to relation and person, and thereby from divine substance to divine processions.

To know God then requires elements of similitude between Creator and creature in an analogical likeness. Aquinas sees the intellect as representative of divine being in a proper way for it is in intellection that the elements of consubstantial distinction and equality are evidenced.[168] The 'imago trinitatis' reflected most adequately in human understanding finds adumbration in the Augustinian "trinities." The rational process inclusive of memory, intellect and will is based upon Aquinas' notion of the "inner word" as generated and the terminus ad quem as "spiration" of the Divine love in rational reflection.[169] These three, or similar concomitants, were the 'real relations' that formed the basis of Thomistic trinitology. This may serve as ancillary support for Przywara's generalization that, "Nach Augustinus ist eine 'transzendierende Immanenz' zwischen Gott und Mensch anzunehmen, nach Thomas V. Aquin eine 'immanent Transzendenz'."[170]

The "verbum cordis" or inner word, became the root of the divine analogy. The divine intellect first understands itself, from which the "Word" then proceeds essentially rather than necessarily. This word is founded upon the known but unexplainable presence of the inner word in human intellection. It was within that vestige that Thomas placed his trinitological discussion. W. Hankey reveals the Neoplatonic thrust of Augustine's and Thomas' dynamic view of the intellect.[171] The 'exitus-reditus' motif is completed in both thinkers' view of the Holy Spirit as the "return", or as Hankey puts it, a "certain gathering-in of the distinguished persons," to unity without which the opposition of Father and Son

---

[167]ST 1a, 27, 1 reply. Richard's argument put simply is that one cannot understand the methodology of the Summa unless the heavy revelational categories of previous works are accepted as "understood" behind Thomas' most subtle reasoning. The Problem of an Apologetical Perspective, passim. W. Hankey, "The Place of the Psychological Image of the Trinity," 103.

[168]ST 1a, 27, 4, reply; 1a, 30, 2, reply. Cf. Richard, Problem of an Apologetical Perspective, 74-79, 148.

[169]ST 1a, 27, 4, 4 and reply; 1a, 28, 4, reply. Richard's approach is quite convincing due to the diachronic method he uses. He sees the early Aquinas dealing with these issues across all of his writing career. Problem of an Apologetical Perspective, 82, 220. Where Richard and others dealt with the divine nature and will, Aquinas later shifted from that line of argumentation back to the Augustinian formula of intellect and will.

[170]E. Pryzwara, Schriften vol. 3 (Johannes-Verlag: Eiseideln, 1962), 322.

[171]W. J. Hankey, God in Himself: Aquinas' Doctrine of God as Expounded in the Summa Theologiae (New York: Oxford Univ. Press, 1987), 123-125.

would not find personal union.[172] This helps to explain both the 'will' and the 'vinculum' language in these trinitarian theologians. What is intriguing is that the category of love is relegated most often to the 'relation' of the Spirit while the 'verbum' as irreducible distinction carries less of an overt emphasis on 'caritas'.[173]

Where Anselm and Richard had been hesitant to equate the person of the Spirit with the mutual love of the Father and the Son, Aquinas saw him as the end of the act of divine knowledge. If the Son proceeded from the mind of God, as inner Word, then the Spirit was a person through the the will of God, or love.[174] Generation and procession reflect the absolute perfection of the divine reality in intellectual and volitional procession as the first issues from the Father, or 'principium quod' and the second through the Son.[175] However, it is clear that 'relation' is not used with any element of distinction within Aquinas' view of Godness per se. This stems from his view of primary substance.[176] In an effort to eschew any claims of individualizing the Persons of the Trinity, Aquinas disavows any accidental qualities in the divine nature. Divine substance is a "self-grounded existence."[177] The logic of his argument necessitates that the 'hypostaseis' are equal to the term 'relations' which signify the divine nature indirectly. What is at play here is Aquinas' use of Aristotle's primary substance as interpreted by Boethius' 'individua substantia'.[178] Absolute divine essence cannot admit anything but the accidental nature of relations. The term 'Persons' is used to clarify these accidents. Although the distinction represented by persons is real, as opposed to rational, it is a "minimal distinction" in that the Person is

---

[172]Hankey, God in Himself, 124.

[173]Hibbert, in "Mystery and Metaphysics," 199, admits that little can be found to connect caritas to the verbum in a necessary rather than an accidental capacity.

[174]ST 1a, 27, 4, reply; ST 1a, 30, 2, reply. The latter reference also carries Thomas' defense against quaternarian attributions. The same logic is used which we have seen above. Nothing can be attributed as excessive or external to the perfect divine nature, thus the presence of any other procession in God is unnecessary, superfluous, and contradictory to the evidence.

[175]Richard, Problem of an Apologetical Perspective, 91, 97, 237.

[176]In 1a, 29, Thomas shows facility with both Eastern and Western traditions in the use of the terms hypostasis, substantia, subsistentia, and ousia. However, the recurrent theme is a recapitulation of the unity model of the Godhead.

[177]ST 1a, 29, 3, ad 4. Of course, it is here as well that Richard alludes to Richard of St. Victor's distinctive assessment of Boethian categories.

[178]ST 1a. 29, ad. 1, and reply. See Dowdall, "The Word Person," 252. "Persona is called a subsistence because it exists per se and not in alio, a res naturae because it supports a common nature, and substance or hypostasis because it supprts accidents."

"used with respect to the thing itself, not to another."[179] Thus, the distinction between nature and person, though real for Aquinas, finds rational clarification at the expense of relationality.[180]

As we have argued regarding Augustine's use of 'substance' and 'person' there is a distinct dynamism in the Thomistic view of substance.[181] Both thinkers reveal a dynamic view of reality. However, both are reticent to apply strong relational characteristics to the notion of 'person' and thereby lose much of the illuminating power of a relational concept of God that had been gained by previous orthodox thinkers.[182] Aquinas had only second-hand knowledge of Plato. Thus, the essentialism latent in that approach coinciding with his Aristotelian commitments never allowed him to fully elude an appraisal of divine persons that produced its own unique form of substantialism. The impact of both Augustine's and Aquinas' work has continued to guide the course of most Western trinitology in spite of this rationally-based, and to a large extent rationally-dictated, view of relation.[183]

Divinity, seen from the perspective of a consummate intellectual nature, permits relations as 'res' which are subsistent. 'Personae' immediately signify subsistent hypostatic relations grounded in the distinction of origins.[184] Origins, however, do not play as large a

---

[179]ST 1a. 40, 2 reply 1; 1a. 29, 4, reply 1. Hankey is of great assistance on this point, God in Himself, 118-120. There is a striking resemblance here with J. H. Hoban's analysis of Thomistic personhood understood in humans. The 'individuum' or unified nature finds expression in the 'persona' or rationally endowed self-subsistent nature. See his The Thomistic Concept of Person and Some of its Social Implications. In The Catholic University of America Philosophical Studies, vol. 43 (Washington: Catholic Univ. Press, 1939).

[180]Richard explains that the personal properties or the relations distinguishing the Persons are identical to the divine essence and are only rationally distinct from it, yet they can be real distinctions according to Aquinas. The Problem of an Apologetical Perspective, 70-71.

[181]Mascall's Thomism directs his argument toward this conclusion in The Triune God. I remain more reserved than he as to the possibility of rapprochement with the East using Thomas. Richard may be of more common interest.

[182]L. Wood agrees with R.G. Collingwood's assessment that Aquinas "altogether eliminated" the static Greek notions of substance in defining God as "Actus purus". In "substantial relations", Wood sees Thomas as an existential theologian as opposed to an essentialist. See Laurence Wood, "The Panentheism of Charles Hartshorne: A Critique." The Asburian Seminarian 37:2 (1982): 28-29.

[183]Welch says the Augustinian-Thomistic rational analogy became a "supplemental basis" for interpreting Scriptures and reality in the West. In This Name, 105.

[184]ST 1a, 28, ad 3. Richard, The Problem of an Apologetical Perspective, 106-108, relates the clarifications made of these distinctions in the Sentences, throughout the Doctor's later writings. Drawing upon the intentions behind Vagaginni's "illusion esthetique," Richard argues that Thomas was not seeking certitude but rather, understanding. The 'ordo doctrinae' meant that the order: procession, relation, persons was the order of revealed categories leading to the practical understanding of the divine reality by means of

role as relations in this construction. The divine relations, paternity, filiation, spiration and procession are seen as real relations within the "utter simplicity" of the Godhead.[185] These relations are person-constituting according to Aquinas. It is here that Boethius and Aquinas agree wholeheartedly. The plurality of the Trinity is not found in persons but in relations. Arduously defined, relations are identical with the divine essence yet do not exhaust it due to its perfection and absolute simplicity.[186] Schmaus says relations are a "special type of accident."[187] In spite of these questionable elements dauntless Thomists have continually maintained that the view of divine relations must be recovered. "Being-related is at the very heart of what it means for God to be God."[188] As attractive as this thesis is for explicating sacred doctrine it remains to be seen if true relationality can be discerned within the Thomistic method.

After defining relation and subsequently "real relations" Aquinas comes to a definition of person. Following both Boethius on rational nature and Augustine on divine simplicity (as Thomas interprets him), divine Person "signifies what is distinct" in the nature of God.[189] Person, then, is a subsistent relation, distinguished by origination, incommunicability and procession. Drawing from Richard, and deepening Boethian categories of individual nature, Thomas focuses on the uniqueness of the Persons while constantly avoiding any individuation which would slight the absolute unity of the Godhead.[190] "'Person' means that which is most perfect in the whole of nature, namely what subsists in rational nature."[191] This perfection, thoroughly explored by Thomas,

---

"approximate" demonstration. Ibid., 224-235.

[185]ST 1a, 27, 1; 1a, 28, 4. Thomas mentions five characteristics which are unique only in the addition of 'unbegottenness' of the Father which is different from the 'relations'. ST 1a. 32, ad 4; 1a, 33, ad 4.

[186]ST 1a. 28, ad. 2.

[187]M. Schmaus, Dogma, vol. 3: God and His Christ (New York: Sheed and Ward, 1971), 147. He may be correct here in distinguishing between the 'inesse' or "being-in" which determines the character of accident, and the 'adesse' which determines type. But this tends toward a hidden/revealed God paradigm with its own concomitant problems which we have seen already in the Eastern Fathers and in the critique of the de deo uno and de deo trino split.

[188]C. M. LaCugna, "The Relational God," 649. She says that Aquinas' simplicity was a relational simplicity. Ibid., 652. We would disagree with her argument which includes the critique that to miss Thomas' Aristotelianism is to miss his dynamism. It is precisely at the point of his tie to Greek philosophy that any relationality he possesses is restrained.

[189]ST 1a, 29, 4, reply.

[190]ST 1a, 29, 3,ad 4; 1a, 29, 4; 1a, 30, 4 and reply.

[191]ST 1a, 29, 3, reply.

terminates in a view of divine nature that is fundamentally static. The emphasis on subsistence and real relations never moves beyond the basis of a rational ontology. Person, then, is an accomodation within the larger discussion of the divine nature.[192] Thomas insists that 'individual' must include the idea of incommunicability.[193] This does not mean that Thomas incorporates Richard's viewpoint uncritically. He discerns an internal distinction that differentiates only at the point of origin and relation. Individuation is a way of subsisting, **modum subsistendi**, proper to particular substances.[194] The epistemological starting-point which Aquinas posits permeates all the active characteristics of the inner-trinitarian life. The aspect of love, though discussed, is definitely secondary in importance while contemplating the divine nature.

Aquinas' critique of Richard is first, methodological. It is a wrong use of reason and analogy which posits that the Trinity can be logically discerned from a basis of divine goodness.[195] Natural reason cannot proffer trinitarian vestiges, according to Thomas. Even the attractiveness of discerning persons within the components of the highest human experience - love, does not sanctify its use as the basis of comprehending the Trinity. He also states that "The analogy from our intellect also does not establish anything about God conclusively because it is not in the same sense that we speak of intellect in God and in us."[196] What is intriguing here is the time Aquinas spends uncovering the intellectual analogy in spite of its inconclusive nature. Though he disagreed with Richard, Hill is adamant that Aquinas did not disavow the basic truths inherent within the analogy though it has to be "purged" of its excesses if it is ever to "function analogously" within Aquinas' trinitarian epistemology.[197]

---

[192]Hibbert, "Mystery and Metaphysics," 205 In his effort to shore up the unity of God Aquinas propounds a "transcendentalized use of the Aristotelian category of relation." Ibid., 205.

[193]ST 1a. 29, 4, ad 3; 30, 4, ad 2

[194]ST 1a. 29, 4. See also De Potentia 9, 4-5. Sears finds the active principle in Thomas at this point. The modus subsistendi is an active ontological reality in which the divine essence diffuses itself and "returns to itself inasmuch as it has being in itself." ST 1a. 14, 2. See Sears, "Spirit: Divine and Human," 16. (He quotes here from Pegis' translation in Basic Writings of Thomas Aquinas, vol. 1, 138.)

[195]ST 1a. 32, 1. He, of course, is castigating the entire Ricardine tradition, including Bonaventure and Alexander of Hales. It is good to remember that in earlier works Aquinas agreed with the Ricardine paradigm. See De Veritate, 14, 9, ad. 1. Marsiello says of Aquinas, he "more often utilized the arguments of Richard to support his own position than he was in opposition to him." "Reason and Faith in Richard of St. Victor," New Scholasticism 48 (1974): 236.

[196]ST 1a. 32, 2 ad 1, reply.

[197]Hill, Three Personed God, 230.

In Thomas' rejection of Richard's definition which some have called an improvement, I would note one glaring omission. While Thomas may accurately rectify Richard's use of incommunicability, by drawing attention to the long tradition of substance and relation and their use with regards to divine persons, something is lost in the exchange. Returning to the definition of person as the special name among other substances, that is, as a rational nature, there is a question as to how the intellectual analogy can be more adequate than the relational.[198] Is it the mind that is the more basic and philosophically unsullied category? There were critics in the thirteenth century, Duns Scotus for example, who saw this rational approach as fallacious and thus saw no real progressiveness in the Angelic Doctor's view of person.[199] Scotus argued that the rational differentiations were illogical unless they proceeded from a predicating diffusion within the Godhead. Showing affinity with Bonaventure, Duns Scotus advocated a "virtual difference" between the Persons.[200] By this he drew a fine distinction between real and rational distinctions. He saw Thomas' rational distinctions as a reiteration of identicals without positing the distinguishing "quiddity" respective to them.

Thomas found 'incommunicability' enlightening but says nothing about the relational categories latent within the term 'exsistentia', which was without a doubt Richard's most unique contribution. It is thus the more intriguing that when Thomas comes to his conclusion on divine persons, relation is central. He says that it is "better to say that the persons or hypostases are distinguished rather by relations than by origin."[201]

One can immediately see the impact of Thomas on modern concepts, in his descriptions of the persons as those who has "dominion over their own actions," and as " act of themselves". The West has never been able to eschew the rationalistic implications of these concepts. Personhood is yet defined as an isolated being, separate from all others, self-determinative and self-reflective. It has been argued that neither Boethius nor Aquinas intended this definition. It seems to me that whether or not that is the case in the original the Church soon perverted the 'psychological' or cognitive analogies and unwittingly

---

[198]Cousins, "Notion," 196. ST Ia. 29, ad.1; 29, ad. 2.

[199]Sears, "Spirit: Divine and Human," 16.

[200]Gelber, "Logic and the Trinity," 75. She notes the shift from epistemology to "metalogic" regarding the relation of essence to relations in Duns Scotus. Welch oversimplifies the issue in his statement that Durandus posited 'modal' distinction, Scotus proffered 'formal' and Aquinas, 'virtual'. In this Name, 120. Even if Scotus and Aquinas used the same term, Duns Scotus used it in a definitely different way for he accepted the presence of real distinction alongside real relations. He join the Ricardine-Bonaventurian line of relating person to person in Trinity instead of following the person to nature relationship of the Augustinian Thomas.

[201]ST I, q. 40, a. 2, corp.

transmitted impersonal concepts.

Granted, Thomas goes on to describe divine persons as subsistent relations, which while sounding relational is in reality not. is. But there is the constant return to the oneness strain of the West, as a sort of protective reflex. In sum, relation is prior to substance for the Aristotelian/Thomistic tradition.

Aquinas' stature and work overshadowed that of Richard, and in line with the dialectic proposed in our thesis, his Summa served to re-direct medieval trinitarian thought back to the security of its more rationalistic/essentialistic Augustinian roots. However, there needs to be an objective criticism in approaching his notion of person.
Hill says he was aware of crypto-modalism so much so as to make the Trinity almost undecipherable in its practical application to real life and worship.[202]

B. Critiques of the Ricardine Social Analogy

A defense of Richard's thought on divine personhood must confront two major areas of criticism, one philosophical and the other theological. Each of these is composed of a variety of specified complaints but, in the main, these reservations can be subsumed under more general differences. The first arena pertains generally to the method which the Victorine employs. Often the term 'rationalistic' is used derogatively of this approach.[203] We need not repeat what has been said above concerning necessary reason.[204] Even a cursory perusal of De Trinitate indicates that he means nothing more of 'necessity' than his own systematic principle claims. Richard is covinced that the Exemplar of humanity reflects self-transcendent love, necessarily.[205] He is stating from his interpretation of revelation and experience that the Goodness of God, properly understood, requires a notion of self-donation. Other analogical perceptions may also assist in discerning trinitarian reality but the rejection of the social analogy requires either a capitulation of scriptural themes or a diminution of the character of God. "God is love" necessitates an ontological

---

[202]E. Hill, Three-Personed God, 78.

[203]Cousins feels that although Richard is deeply sensitive to spiritual reality nonetheless he "falls into extreme rationalism." "A Theology of Interpersonal Relations," 61. This is intriguing based upon comments made in the dissertation Cousins produced earlier. He defends Richard there, see "Notion," 103-123.

[204]Ralph Masiello traces the Augustinian background for 'necessary reasons' in "Reason and Faith in Richard of St. Victor and St. Thomas," New Scholasticism 48 (1974): 233-242.

[205]As above we intend the use of 'necessary' in much the same way Aristotle intended it, the condition: without which a being is not viable or explicable; that must be present in order for full good to be realized; that is contrary to impulse and purpose; (and most closely related to the usage here) "that which cannot be otherwise." Metaphysics 5:5, 1015a-1015b. One might qualify this term by stating that it is a sort of necessity.

reality which Richard felt was productively discernible. Richard, no doubt, knew full well the implications of an attribution which smacked of necessitarianism. His use must have carried another meaning. With subtle polemicism Richard is using a term, which had already begun to be used by scholastics, in such a way as to redefine the speculation inherent within it.

As we have seen, the necessary reasons of Richard for positing a Triune community are always informed by 'eternal reasons'. Richard would agree with the analysis that reason cannot be a source for 'threeness'.[206] His contention is that reason and revelation are not contradicted by the co-inherent divine reality that the self-love of the Godhead is other-love.[207] In fact, as Marsiello indicates, at the dawn of the "philosophization of religion and faith" Richard is one who believes so strongly in the revelation of the Creator that cogent philosophical arguments can be proffered for every truth of faith.[208] Richard does not abuse Augustine's categories, he reinterprets the evidence by intimating that it is inappropriate to separate the two concepts, for in God both are co-existent.[209]

Conversely, there appears a critique which accuses Richard of not being "rational" where he approaches his social analogy. This reservation is an undercurrent in several of the following criticisms. It would seem that the Western philosophical tradition, finding its source basically in the Neoplatonic background of Augustine, has made a nearly intractable commitment to substance as undifferentiated and static reality. We have argued that Augustine shows more openness to a relational view of substance but that has not always

---

[206]Note the view of 'proofs' Richard conveys in Benjamin Major 4:3, PL 196, 136B-138A. Selected Writings, 151-152.

[207]This type of reasoning permeates his discussion. See, for instance, De Trin., 5.9.

[208]Marsiello, "Reason and Faith in Richard of St. Victor," 234. This premise is specifically applied to trinitarian deliberations. It is wise to remember that it is not approached by Richard with a cavalier attitude. Henry of Ghent is guilty of overrationalizing Richard's method which may be the source of some of the misperception here. Summa quaestionum ordinariarum art. 22, q. 4. found in Wippel, Medieval Philosophy, 386. Marsiello's article directed me to this source.

[209]John Bligh, in spite of his facility with ancient and medieval sources, skews the issue when he accuses Richard of overrationalizing, just as he does by accepting the majority opinion that Augustine found the interpersonal relation analogy unequivocally repugnant. (See chap. Three.) I believe the Ricardine response to his challenge would be that there is no greater love than self-love, but that self-love is inseparable from other-love in the Trinity. Bligh's analysis is typical of the proclivity toward the 'unity' model which radically affects the hermeneutics of Scripture and tradition. "Richard of St. Victor's De Trinitate," 138-139.

been the case in the traditions which arose after him.[210] Richard is unique in that he represents a Western (and Augustinian) mind who is attempting to bring his tradition into direct contact with a similar approach found much earlier in the East. In his writing we find the coincisive application of reason and creational vestiges within human relationships. The text of De Trinitate reveals a theologian who strove for a personalistic ontology which fitted the consensual Christian understanding of God apart from the anachronistic overlay of a tyrranous philosophical monadism. As we have said, he approaches this discussion of divine interrelatedness with a proper amount of humility, but recognizing the quandry of a latent agnosticism he is willing to risk the possibility of misunderstanding in order to point to an ontology which is the basis of all personhood.

Another point of contention methodologically concerns how Richard is able to avoid binitarian or quaternitarian conclusions. On one hand, Richard is accused by the Thomistic tradition of assimilating the Dionysian tradition with a concomitant implication of emanationistic subordinationism. On the other hand, it is claimed that regardless of the veracity of Richard's premise that personhood is the basic expression of the divine reality, he does not sufficiently explain the origin of the three Persons.[211]

If one states that to be God means to be in self-relationship then where is the line drawn on what is a self-sufficient limit of relating 'entities'? This is a recurring criticism of the social analogy in general. One of Thomas' reactions to Richard came along this line which will be plumbed further. In modern critiques, however, it is apparent that this restraint is often an anachronistic imposition of problems.

There is both an immediate and a tacit response to this accusation. Richard goes to considerable lengths to dissuade the notion of another entity or source behind the Godhead. Bk 5:9 to 5:16 carries the overt disavowal of the necessity of only three within the Godhead. His view of generation and procession coincides with the orthodox delineations on this score.

A tacit proof resides in the tenor of the work itself. Richard was surely not given to gross misconstruction of thought and the primacy of scripture which, in spite of some intriguing exegetical conclusions related to his mysticism, is apparent in all of his writings. He accepts the traditional interpretation of the Church that there are three Persons. His theses then do not start with the human mind but rather are formulated with the stated

---

[210]Note the extreme agnostic position of Durrant, Theology and Intelligibility, passim. To even speak of God as "One" is logically inadmissable for Durrant. He does allow its "heuristic" use in a phenomenological way only. Ibid., 86. His is a classic example of a myopic interpretation of Aristotle which thinkers like Stead in Divine Substance have challenged. A more approachable text, yet similar to Durrant in obscurantism, is John Macquarrie, Principles of Christian Theology (New York: Charles Scribner's Sons, 1966), 176-177.

[211]This is Hill's main contention, Three Personed God, 78, 231.

preconceptions. If his ideas had been confronted as philosophically inadequate he would have without a doubt attempted a sufficient answer. He does respond at one point by using Adam, Eve and Seth as an example of the immediate relationship of the Trinity. Enosh, as grandson, is posited as a mediate existent, one who did not share in the face-to-face relationship of the perfect love of the aforementioned triad.[212] The point of this effort is that the notion of a dyad is altogether incomplete and illogical while positing more than three is meaningless. We have seen from a consensual perspective how prosopological exegesis formed the empirical basis for maintaining a trinitarian framework.[213] In light of that backdrop, Richard's response would likely be to ask what fourth or fifth 'entity' would be posited and, if so, how would that fit both traditional exegesis and interpretation of Christian experience.

Another tack to this critique is to question how Richard, or any social analogist, finds reason to stop with three 'Others'. If goodness naturally donates itself then why is it not given to an infinite number of recipients? The question of the possibility of a limit to the effusion of an eternally self-diffusive Good is met by Richard's view of personal relationship in relation to revelation and to the character of God. The "principle of plenitude" carries a "principle of parsimony."[214] Concomitant with this inherent restraint is the belief that the true nature of love incorporates perfect purpose and will which reflects on the perfect self-limitation of the Good. The possibility that the divine hypostatic relationship which Richard attempts to explicate includes reference to any possible "non-subjects" is disallowed through the same reasoning. For Richard, perfection of being or subjectivity precludes the presence of a non-subjective "ex-sistent." The hypostaseis, those who "stand under," find both origin for or from the other Persons.[215] In the Godhead equality of love and 'friendship' involves the full realization of all possibilities. A fullness of love, if unsurpassable, must be shared by equally giving and receiving persons, though each does so in distinct ways.

With regard to the question of origins and along this same line of critique is the

---

[212]PL 196, 3:14, 924C-925A; 5:8-5:13, 954A-959C address binitarian and quateritarian arguments as the logical backdrop for his conclusion in 5:14, 959D-960D, which is based upon the 'reasonable' evidence of proportionality, and the exhaustion of divine plenitude. There is for Richard no superfluity in the divine. See Sears, "Spirit: Divine and Human, 81. It is interesting to note that de Margerie aligns Gregory of Nazianzus, Aquinas (!) and Mühlen in a discussion of the family analogy. the Christian Trinity in History, 274-286.

[213]Kaiser, "Discernment of Triunity," 456.

[214]This is the basic response of Keane in "Ordo Bonitatis," 62-64.

[215]De Trin., 5:12, 937D-938A. Bear in mind that Richard does not adequately delineate the characteristics of the Father as Ungenerate. The tradition of the Father as arche permeates Richard's discussion. I do not see this approach as an oversight but as an accepted method of referring to the divine Fatherhood in light of the mystery of generation.

complaint that Richard gives no indication of an order to the processions. The category of love in itself, so it is stated, does not provide the same sort of inherent delimitations which the rational model contains in intellect and will. In response, Richard must be viewed from the vantage point of consensual agreement on the Father as 'fons et origo' of the Persons. He indicates there must be One who is Beginningless Beginning otherwise there would be infinite procession.[216] The approach which Richard takes is a bold one. He is stepping outside the Augustinian-Boethian-Thomistic line of divine 'Relation' and positing a view of 'Person' that, though at some points inadequate for modern sensitivities regarding psychological comprehensiveness, radically alters the intelligibility of the Triune mystery. For the first time, there is a clear and unapologetic connection given between human existence and the transcendent Trinity. Relation is resident in the construction, as is intellect and will, but the focus is love, an other-orientation which is mirrored in human life on a number of levels.

In terms of procession, this analogy, it is claimed, provides no consistent conception of the person of the Holy Spirit.[217] The Augustinian tradition did regard the Spirit as vinculum or as donum but it was not until after Richard's period that attempts were made to provide a more complete answer to that question and when others helped to clarify the Spirit's personhood in later constructions.[218]

One response might be to question whether the Thomistic analogy does any better in clarifying that mystery. Later scholasticism debated the two processions vociferously. The Thomistic strain adhered to the basic 'rational' commitment of the first procession as intellectual, thus natural, and the second as volitional.[219] There is a strong tendency implicit in these categories to advocate a pneumatology which denigrates the personhood of

---

[216]Richard bases his argument on the ontological 'proofs' of Bk. 1 here when he turns to one who "non habeat aliunde quam a se originem trahere," but that of necessity there is a "esse aliquam quae non sit ab alia," PL 196, 5:11, 958A. At this point Cousins has misgivings concerning the overall philosophical cogency of Richard's analysis. He sees the inequality of having one person 'ab aliquo' while the other two are 'ab alio'. As with Bligh, one wonders if this is not straining at a gnat. Richard evidently is attempting to traverse the precarious line of maintaining the traditional emphasis on the Father's ungenerateness. That does not preclude His "ex-sistential" being if grounded in what has come before concerning goodness, love and glory. "Notion," 185-186. I do think that Cousins is correct in noting that the experiential evidence in Bks. 3 and 6, does not appear in Bk. 5, which may lend itself to more criticism by any "Ockhamistic" philosophical assessment of De Trinitate.

[217]John Cowburn, The Person and Love (New York: Alba House, 1967), 273. See his fair, even if abbreviated, appraisal of the issue of the Spirit's personhood. Ibid., 259-297.

[218]In Gunton's "Augustine, the Trinity and the Theological Crisis in the West," 55, he states that Augustine's 'vinculum' gave the Spirit, "inadequate economic hypostatic weight."

[219]Aquinas De Potentia. 12, 2, c.

the Spirit.

Of many examples Cowburn's criticism in The Person and Love is representative of categorical misinterpretation of Richard. Even the place where he feels Richard can be appropriated without too much damage is mistaken. He writes, "(Richard) maintained that the love involved in spiration is a mutual love of the first two persons for each other." [220] We have shown that it is not amor mutuus but amor condilectus which completes Richard's argument. The Holy Spirit is a Person in that he receives love, not that he is the love between the Father and the Son.

The theological notion of love within Richard's analogy has produced a plethora of negative opinions. Discerning the possibility of self-love, Richard chooses to plumb the depths of ecstatic love. For that caritas to be authentic he discerns as a principle the self-love of the Triune Persons. It would not be condign love if the divine Other had some sort of inferior self-perception. [221] The coincision of self-love and other-love is not unique to Richard. [222] But he separates himself from the larger tradition of preoccupation with discerning differentiations within self-love by the overarching interest with other-orientedness. The clarification of the connection of the two types might assist some critics to re-think the position that the social analogists are bifurcating Trinity and unity. Richard repeatedly emphasizes the continuum of Trinity, or plurality, in unity, thereby pointing to the importance of relating person and nature without conflating the categories. [223]

---

[220]The Person and Love, 296.

[221]Bligh, "Richard of St. Victor's De Trinitate," 134-138; Cousins, "Notion," 186. Cowburn's final point of rejection pertains to Richard's assessment of self-love. We would agree, as would Richard, that divine self-love must be good, but the opposite side requires the burden of proof be placed on Cowburn and the tradition he represents. It is one thing to assert that God is love, but another to discuss that fact cogently. When the reaction subsides it does not remain clear at all from the Thomistic tradition just how one says God is love. This raises the spectre that Neibuhr posits in his radical monotheism theme. The oneness tradition in the Church must offer more than pontification and condescension on the point of discussing divine love. It is not that Richard says divine self-love is wrong; he is questioning the logic of that notion as a possible basis of even comprehending God. His dialectic method includes this point as confirmatory not as essential dogma, though its implications might pertain to the latter.

[222]Aristotle, Nichomachean Ethics, 9:4, 1166a; 9:9, 1169b. See the insights of Stanley Hauerwas, "Happiness, the Life of Virtue and Friendship: Theological Reflections on Aristotelian Themes, Pt. III: Companions on the Way: The Necessity of Friendship," Asbury Theological Journal (Spring, 1990): 35-48. Although slight differences on the relationship between the two types of love can be ferreted out of each medieval theologian, there is a general similarity here between Anselm and Richard. See Anselm, On the Procession of the Holy Spirit, 14-16, in Trinity, Incarnation, and Redemption. eds. Hopkins and Richardson (NY: Harper and Row, 1970), 125-134.

[223]This claim against a relation view of the Trinity is made repeatedly by C. Welch, In this Name, 157-158, 178.

Tangentially, however, this condign love is questioned. To some it appears not so much as disinterested love as it does a form of divine "imposition." What of love for that which is not condign? There is no doubt that Richard saw the need and possiblity of the communication of transcendent love. He had a strong view of grace but in De Trinitate is undeterred in its reference to the Trinity and maintaining the theme of co-equality. This emphasis was necessary for fidelity to the Biblical witness and protecting against an incipient quaternitarianism. He deals thoroughly with divine love for humans in his Benjamin Major and Minor.[24]

Another approach queries condign divine love in its consummate state and asks for an explanation of the existence of any other being, or more generally the purpose of the world. While it is true that in Richard's cosmology all things find their origin in the Triune God, caritas ordinata employs a proportionalism to divine love that delineates clearly the Creator and the creation. God does not need the world, nor is the world an adequate counterpart to God. Process panentheism is unable to confront thinking like that of Richard's because of the inherent discontinuity underlying his theology.

The 'objectivity' of the Ricardine social analogy has concerned some. Combined with the rational methodological approach Richard's advocation that love must have an object inevitably eventuates in what Warfield calls theological "artificialities."[225] The presupposition at play here is that abstract terms are the closest to revelation categories. There may be wisdom resident in Richard's use of this "embarassing" metaphor, which coincides with the use of anthropomorphisms found in Scripture. Since, as we have argued above, all God-language is analogical, even "spiritual" terms can be absolutized to a point where the threat of idolatry of those concepts is a distinct possibility. Any idea can be used wrongly, as Augustine has warned, thus becoming an "artificiality." There is a type of safety, often overlooked, involved in the use of tangible analogies. The realism of the Cappadocians and Richard supports a heuristic connectedness, properly adherent to scriptural delineations, between Trinity and imago.

An ancillary position which disparages the social analogy surrounds the numeric identity of the One while attempting to consider any form of threeness. Apparently, from this perspective it is proper to attribute numeric and monadic oneness to the divine nature but any intrusion of personhood is suspect because it is numerical. For these critics, even

---

[24]For example, Benjamin Minor, ch. 71-76, Kirchberger, Selected Writings, 109-114. Benjamin Major, ch. 18-23, Ibid., 172-180.

[225]Warfield, "The Biblical Doctrine of the Trinity," 25. Warfield's critique comes from a strict respect for revelation, but he, as many others, disallow that same commitment in the Victorines. It is not at all clear, he says, that God could not supply a satisfying object of his all-perfect love without that meaning a second trinitarian figure. Ibid., 26. To equate love and self-communication to an other "seems an abuse of figurative language." Ibid., 26.

if a form of threeness is admitted in a self-conscious manner, that immediately indicates some type of limitation in God.[226] Richard was not deterred by this argument either, it would seem. It is intriguing that after this "logical" approach is taken, the author must immediately refer to the applicability of the "paradox" to the Christian experience. Inevitably, there is a statement which follows the line that even though it is ludicrous to speak of God as three Persons we must still comprehend God as personal or as a Person.[227] In these instances the rigorous logic applied to Richard gives way to an illogical relevancy. If God is not three Persons, then one has no basis for reference to a personal God or even a relational God, at least according to the early Christian thinkers surveyed in this work. It is the contention here that it is with the heart of a mystic and a deeply religious canon regular that Richard approaches the reality of the spiritual life and the logical results of its foundational documents and distillations. At the root of spiritual reality Richard discerned the outline of an infinite love, the source of all being, intellect and volition. That love was most clearly apprehended by the heart and mind through its nearest human analogue, interpersonal relationship.

Last, the accusation is made that the social analogy in general is not plausible in modernity.[228] Two interconnected tacks are used: 1) There is only one possible definition of person, the modern notion of individualistic self-determination, 2) Due to the fact that there is no circumventing tritheism in the social analogy, it is of no use in theological discourse. The indications of possible retorts to this approach are rather striking in De Trinitate. Richard was not only aware of the possibility of abusing the relational category but was also willing to take the risk in order to bring a point of dynamism into a doctrine which was soon, if not already, bereft of scholastic analysis. In response to the moderns we see that the medieval definition of person does not by its nature reject the implications of personality but is not bound to that definition as the only plausible meaning. We find in Richard a more adequate understanding of divine substance, one that allows more than monadic status to divine reality. On the other hand, the mutuality of that divine life did not necessarily admit self-determinative entities somehow able to mutiny, if you will, and exit the Triune life. While we cannot argue that Richard met all the criteria for an

---

[226]Of any attempt to discern a numerical threeness, C. Richardson says: "He ceases to be one God who confronts us in an "I-Thou" relation, and who cannot be set over against another....Every attempt to find an underlying essence or unity in the three ends up either by really denying the three or dividing the essence. The Doctrine of the Trinity, 94-95.

[227]C. Richardson, The Doctrine of the Trinity, 95; A. Richardson, Creeds in the Making, 65.

[228]A. Richardson, Creeds in the Making (Philadelphia: Fortress Press, 1981), 58. Also Ott, God, 63-64.

exhaustive personalism we can state with confidence that the questions of divine personhood were placed on a new plane of contention. If one insists that Richard is a modern in the definition of person, then he is a tritheist. But if one is able to place him in a proper context and allow his explication to determine the meaning of 'person' rather than submitting it to a retroactive individualistic interpretation, he offers a provocative approach to personhood which modernity has fundamentally rejected.[29]   Modalism was not an option for Richard. The Triune Persons were used as distinguishable, if not separable, entities, as real differentiated exsistences without differing existences.

IV. Conclusion

    Richard, as any theologian, does not give a comprehensive philosophical nor theological treatise. His approach, though couched in the philosophical jargon of the day, is nonetheless pastoral and catechetical. It is no accident that it was the major trinitarian treatise between Augustine and Aquinas. Its approach, however, was different enough to raise some rather inappropriate reservations. In criticizing the Cappadocians, the relational model or social analogy of the Trinity has often been relegated to a variety of Eastern theological idiosyncracies. Richard is characterized as the exponent of illogical or infantile theology while his mysticism is lauded. The facts do not speak to a lack of logic or a desire to project something on the Deity which is in any way delimiting of the Unity revealed. Though misinterpretations abound but the profundity of Richard's insights is still bearing fruit even in arenas where he is given no credit. Person as incommunicable existent both producing and receiving the love which is the substance of the Godhead is an inexorable category in the Church. The "category of exchange" resident at Nicea and Chalcedon, in the Cappadocians and even provisionally in Augustine find its locus classicus in Richard's De Trinitate.[230] As Evdokimov summarizes the Cappadocians he does so with an implicit avowal of Richard's work where he states, "Chaque personne divine est une donation subsistante dans la circumincession des Trois. Chacune est vers l'Autre, c'est le co-esse: la Personne est pour las communion tri-une, elle est par elle essentiellement. Strictement parlant, il n'y a qu'en Dieu que la Personne existe."[231]

    Richard unwittingly challenged the Western ontological structures seven centuries old. Theology has never been the same. No matter how hard the struggle to once again

---

[29]Cousins, "Theology of Interpersonal Relations," 69.

[230]Phrase borrowed from the modern author who best explains the Ricardine social analogy in similar metaphors throughout his corpus, Charles Williams, The Descent of the Dove (London: Faber and Faber, Ltd., 1950), 52-53.

[231]Paul Evdokimov, "Mystère de la Personne Humaine," Contacts 21 (1969): 283. His criticism of Boethius is identical to the one outlined here also, see Ibid., 273.

equate person and nature, Richard's relational being curtails the philosophical closure the West has so often demanded. If Boethius reintroduced the Aristotelian distinction between primary and secondary substance, which Thomas usurped and maintained in his subsistent relations, then Richard must be posited as one who did not accept the logical conclusion of that separation.[232]

As with many theological mentors, often the reservations of later onlookers are based upon the misappropriations of an individual thinker's disciples. One wonders with many of the aforementioned criticisms if it is not Richard who should receive the reproof but rather an uninformed attempt at the repristination of his categories without the soundness he evidences in methodology nor the humility he exemplifies in the midst of his critique of other positions.

---

[232]A figure we have not mentioned, William of Auxerre, followed Richard but differed from him. Here again we see the impact of philosophy. The first procession was 'natural' and the second 'personal' and 'gratuitous,' which is quite different from the Ricardine assessment. See Cowburn's criticism of the entire "mutual-love" tradition, The Person and Love, 258-275, 296-297, as simply another example of rudimentary misunderstanding and presuppositions which alter the meaning of Richard's text.

Dicebat Bernardus Carnotensis nos
esse quasi nanos giganticum humeris
insidentes, ut possimus plura eis et
remotiora videre.

John of Salisbury[1]

Chapter Five

Towards a Modern Theological Notion of Person:
Relatedness and Personal Causality

Both implicitly and explicitly it has been argued in this work that one of the most
important doctrines of the Church as well as one of its major bequeathals to the world is
the notion of person. Even if we acknowledge the evidence for claiming that fact for the
past, are we able to say so now? Or has the Church lost the original intentions of its
usage? On the other hand, ought we return to that highly suspect Golden Age in an
attempt to reclaim a conception which was clear to former minds but it is obscure in our
generation, or should we relegate the concept of trinitarian person to the discard pile?
Some very influential thinkers in our time are sending mixed signals. Our analysis of this
current state of theological affairs may be exemplified in the discussions of two of the
twentieth century's most influential thinkers.

I. 'Person' in Modern German Trinitology

Karl Barth can state that, "In view of the history of the concept of Person in the
doctrine of the Trinity one may well ask whether dogmatics is wise in further availing
itself of it."[2] Rahner is a bit more politic, probably due to his relationship with the

---

[1]John of Salisbury, Metalogicon 3:4, "Bernard of Chartres said that we are like
dwarfs standing on the shoulders of giants, so that we are able to see more and farther
than they."

[2]Karl Barth, Church Dogmatics, eds. Geoffrey W. Bromiley and Thomas F. Torrance,
Various trans. 4 vols (Edinburgh: T. & T. Clark, 1936-1969), 1975 edition. Hereafter, CD
with volume and part. CD I/1, 359, or G.T. Thomson's trans., 412. Cf. CD II/1: 296-297,
"What we can describe as personality is indeed the whole divine Trinity as such", Ibid.,
297. Yet cf. II/1: 317 "But God himself becomes Another in the person of his Son"; See
III/1:196, and II/1:284, "In the light of the definition of His being as a being in act we
describe God as person...is the person (Barth's emphasis)); and IV/1: 203-205.

Magisterium as well as his profound respect for some former theological constructs.[3] 'Person,' for Rahner:

> has acquired shades of meaning to which our concept may not be tied within this dogmatic formula. Thus ...when nowadays we hear of "three persons," we connect, almost necessarily, with this expression the idea of three centers of consciousness and activity, which leads to a heretical understanding of the dogma.[4]

Barth is quick to offer his solution, by advising a return to the Eastern notion (at least by his interpretation) of "modes of being" which he says is "not absolutely but relatively better."[5] Rahner's God "subsists in three distinct manners of subsisting", manners which are distinct as relations of opposition, and manners that are real through identity with the divine essence.[6]

However, unlike Barth, Rahner seeks a pedagogical amelioration with the tradition in that, "This concept intends to be nothing more than an explanation of the concept of person as...legitimated by the truly Thomistic definition of the 'person' - (and) should not induce us to give up the use of the concept of person."[7] He would like to see 'manners' and 'persons' used together, considering his proposal "better, simpler, and more in harmony with the traditional language of theology and the Church than the phrase suggested by Karl Barth."[8]

Barth prevaricates, maybe due to a momentary recognition of the capitulation of tradition, by claiming that, "We have, indeed, no cause to wish to outlaw the concept of

---

[3]See his comments on trinitological methodology and relation to tradition in "Remarks on the Dogmatic Treatise 'De Trinitate'," 102.

[4]Karl Rahner, The Trinity, trans. Joseph Donceel (New York: Herder and Herder, 1970), 56-57 (author's emphasis). See also 40, 73ff., 103-108, where he vacillates between keeping the term rightly understood, though it is dubious that that is possible, and choosing another means of expression which might unburden dogma of unnecessary continual explication.

[5]CD 1/1, ed Bromiley, 359 or 412 ed. Thomson. 'Manner' is also a possible translation for, Seinsweise and tropos huparxeos.

[6]The Trinity, 113-114, is a summation of his argument.

[7]Ibid., 115. By "truly Thomistic" he means "subsistens distinctum in natura rationali" See ST 1a. 29, 3, reply, "'Person' means that which is most perfect in the whole of nature, namely what subsists in rational nature." He acknowledges the insight of "incommunicability" of person from Richard, Ibid., 1a. 29, 3, reply 4; 29, 4, reply 3, cf. challenge of 30, 4, q. 2.

[8]The Trinity, 110.

Person outright or to withdraw it from circulation."[9] However, several volumes later, he will say, "By Father, Son and Holy Spirit we do not mean what is commonly suggested to us by the word 'persons'...(but rather) the one active and speaking divine ego, is Father, Son and Holy Spirit."[10] And we begin to suspect that Rahner is not fully consistent either when he adds, almost under his breath, that it is only "a manner of speaking" which keeps 'person' in the center of modern trinitology.

In one way, Rahner's influence on trinitarian thought can be seen as building upon the apologetic prowess of Barthian trinitology even though they have distinctly different worldviews. Their emphasis on the indivisibility of the economic and the immanent trinities is similar at least in implication.[11] Since Rahner's theology has been in vogue more recently than Barth's, it will be advantageous to understand certain elements of his conception of divine reality before encountering Mühlen's contributions.

Rahner provides an interesting etymological note on 'person' where he says we must recognize:

> that the development of the word 'person' outside the theology of the Trinity, after the definitions of the fourth century took a very different direction from its originally near-Sabellian tone. It developed the existential meaning (as in Hermes) of the ego which is opposed to every other person in independent, proper and distinctive freedom.[12]

Rahner does not mention the strong relational categories evident in the theological symbol 'person' before and after the fourth century. The modern mind, if not informed, accepts this historiography as if Descartes were a fourth century figure. In one sense he is right, as Rheinfelder has indicated in the evolution of the enigmatic term in question. Within the theater, there was a shift from portrayal to actor, from role to essential substance. Outside of histrionic usage, 'person' shifted from being a functional idea to representing a fundamental property of humanity, including in its ambit contemplation, reflection and

---

[9]CD 1/1, 359. This is apparently the reason why we find the use of person in a large amount of his passage on the intra-trinitarian life. One wonders how the use of that term could assist in consistency with his neo-modalistic approach, other than to possibly be understood as speaking within the tradition. See an extended discussion of this issue in Z. Trítik, "Der Personbegriff im dogmatischen Denken Karl Barths: eine kritische Untersuchung," Neue Zeitschrift für Systematische Theologie und Religionsphilosophie 5 (1963): 263-295.

[10]CD IV/1, 204-205.

[11]No matter how hard Barth attempted to stay on the functional side of trinitarian understanding, it was more difficult for him to remain focused on that interest. Rahner is truer to his systematic principle at this point.

[12]Rahner, "Remarks on the Dogmatic Treatise 'De Trinitate'," 101-102.

subjective being.[13]   On the other hand, a point we have made and uncommon to modern discussion is that the growing understanding of individuality Rahner attributes to 'person' may be seen as a result of the "personification" implicit in a relational interpretation of the incommunicable existants of Trinity. Reflection on the Triune reality is, as Torrance puts it, the only means of "personalizing" persons.[14] True, there were abuses of the term but it did not carry the immediate negative connotations for trinitarian discussion which, the Rahnerian camp has purported, enabled certain 'irrelevant myths' in theology.[15] It is from this standpoint that he posits "distinct manners of subsistence" as a viable option, in order to counteract the prevailing individuality implied in the use of 'person' as a theological category. The "manners" apparently do not carry the subjectivistic baggage which the earlier term ineluctably does. Though it is meritorious to qualify 'person' in trinitology, it is unclear why Rahner completely passes over the positive ontological implications of the offending term.

In light of this stance on the category of 'person' it is a bit mystifying how Rahner can justify his transcendental anthropology. He claims that the history of salvation draws upon eternal realities but transcendence is only applicable if it relates to God's act of redemption. "Onto-logy is Onto-logy."[16] Therefore, 'person' is fundamentally misleading if not viewed from an anthropological standpoint which explains the economic focus in Rahner's construction. Using an 'ad fontes' approach with regard to Scripture as the starting point for determining the meaning of 'person', he justifies the immediate interpretation of the text to repudiate talk of 'God in himself' and advocates instead a "three-fold quality of God in himself which may be called a triune 'personality'."[17] He discerns in biblical data a triune structuring to existence which is inseparably tied to history.[18] All of this reflects his principle of the relationship of grace to nature which

---

[13]Rheinfelder, Das Worte 'Persona', 17. This page sets the stage for his entire work which, as we have said, pertains more to secular culture than ecclesiological determinations.

[14]T.F. Torrance, "The Goodness and Dignity of Man in the Christian Tradition," 318.

[15]Rahner, "Theology and Anthropology," in The Word in History, ed. T.P. Burke (New York: Sheed and Ward, 1966), 2.

[16]Rahner, "Theology and Anthropology," 9.

[17]Rahner, "Remarks on the Dogmatic Treatise 'De Trinitate'," 102.

[18]What is already suspected is acknowledged by Rahner, that is, a strong Hegelian undergirding for his systematic. German Idealism's 'Historicality' is central to all that transpires theologically because it re-asserts what scholastic theology excised, personal experience. "Theology and Anthropology," 20, 18. C. Plantinga points to Pannenberg's suggestion that Barth's "modes of being," was also influenced by Hegel through I.A. Dorner. "The Threeness/Oneness Problem of the Trinity," Calvin Theological Journal 23:1 (April, 1988), 39 n.6.

fundamentally disavows 'extrinsicism', or transcendent notions which, supposedly, have little to do with reality.

The criticism of Rahner here focuses on the viability of terms used ubiquitously but, based upon his presuppositions, rather nominalistically. 'Relations,' or an 'ontology of relation', 'relatedness,' 'self-relating activity,' 'intrinsic dynamism,' an 'onto-theology of divine relationality,' the 'distinction between real and logical (or relative) relation,' and 'distinction without division,' are cast as the basis of a proper understanding of anthropology grounded in God's 'self-communication'[19] In the light of these ideas it is no surprise that from the unlikely source of the Process theologian, J. A. Bracken we find a resonance in responding to Rahner. Bracken states,

> (The) manner of subsisting (such as the Father) is "somebody else" (ein anderer) than God subsisting in another manner of subsisting, but he is not something else (etwas anderes).
> The criticism that can be urged against Rahner here is then that, if interpersonal categories are used to illuminate the relations between God and man in the doctrine of the economic Trinity, the same interpersonal categories should be employed in his exposition of the immanent Trinity.[20]

His vocabulary of theological anthropology: 'humanity as subject, or person,' and humans as 'object of experience,' which incorporates a hint of the Neoplatonic or the Augustinian ideas of 'returning to the self' in knowing, freedom or willing, reflects a dynamic psychologically-based view of personhood. Self as 'self-reflecting' and 'being' open to all reality comprise the two major facets of Rahner's experiential anthropology. The human is a 'material spirit' with a distinct "receptive and intercommunicative character."[21]

For Rahner, love

> is the free self-bestowal of a person who possesses himself, who therefore can refuse himself, whose giving away of self, therefore is always an event of wonder and grace...Love is an abandoning and opening of one's innermost self to and for the other, who is loved.[22]

However, in the Godhead, "There is properly not mutual love between Father and Son, for

---

[19]These are used throughout Rahner's corpus. An example of the effect of this on a Rahnerian disciple can be found in C.M. LaCugna's "The Relational God: Aquinas and Beyond," Theological Studies 46 (1985): 647-663.

[20]J. Bracken, "The Holy Trinity as a Community of Divine Persons," II, Heythrop Journal 15:3 (1974): 258. Piet Schoonenberg points out the differences beteen Mühlen and Rahner in, "Zur Trinitätslehre Karl Rahners," in Glaube in Prozess, eds. Klinger and Wittstadt (Freiburg: Herder Verlag, 1984), 490.

[21]These are discussed lucidly by Mark Taylor, God is Love: A Study in the Theology of Karl Rahner, American Academy of Religion Academy Series, ed. Carl A. Raschke, no. 50 (Atlanta: Scholars Press, 1986), 52-67.

[22]Rahner, "Theos in the New Testament," Theological Investigations, 1, 123. Quoted in Taylor, God is Love, 69.

this would suppose two acts."²³ It is mysterious how modern theology built upon framework similar to Rahner can equivocate on this issue. For love to be, as Rahner indicates it is, 'ecstasis' in self-diremption and total trust there must be an ontological explanation other than self-perception or redemption. There is noticeable scholarly critical agreement that this inner contradiction is pervasive in Rahner.²⁴ As Taylor argues, the cogency of any indication of internal distinctions in the Trinity is a condition of the possibility of the ad extra communications of God in three distinct ways.²⁵ Rahner has no category for 'passivity' in God.²⁶ The opera ad extra are the place where divinity abandons itself. The predominant schema then is of a giving, saving God in history but whose inner being is undiscernible and relatively unimportant to the historical subject.

This stance produces a conundrum which is evident at many points of modern theology.²⁷ Interpersonal relationality is promoted at many junctures but without an ontological basis other than the perception of divine providence, or liberation, or process.²⁸ However, Rahner can say God is love but cannot say what that means in God's self, which

---

²³Rahner, The Trinity, 106.

²⁴G. Vanderwelde, "The Grammar of Grace: Karl Rahner as a Watershed in Contemporary Theology," Theological Studies 49 (1988): 445-459, mentions the critiques of Rahner by Moltmann (Monism) and Küng (Dualism) in his own discussion of the mystery of self-bestowal in Rahner without cogent moorings. M. Taylor, God is Love, 98, says Rahner is "ambiguous" here in the three modalities of divine self-communication and the fact that "the distinctions are real but only relative, not absolute." Ibid., 118. Cf. Theological Investigations, 4, 70. Fergus Kerr states that Rahner's theology is "embedded in an extremely mentalist-individualist epistemology and unmistakably Cartesian provenance." Theology After Wittgenstein (New York: Basil Blackwell, 1986), 14.

²⁵Taylor, God is Love, 119. Taylor sees the possibility of gnosticism in the continual stance that the 'why' of God or his love is inexplicable for Rahner. Carl Peter's friendly refutation of Rahner's position is unique in challenging the modern proclivity to define personhood by subjectivity without taking into account the effect on both the mind and will by evil in, "A Shift to the Human Subject in Roman Catholic Theology," Communio (US) 6 (1979): 72.

²⁶LaCugna reveals this fear where she states, "If theology starts with the divine unity, there is a danger it will remain only a speculation about God's inner being." "The Relational God: Aquinas and Beyond," 650. It is difficult to see why the fear of over-scholasticizing must of necessity preclude the notion of intra-trinitarian love.

²⁷We have mentioned C. Welch's In this Name above. It is worth noting how little truly creative trinitology has been produced by this desire to make personhood accidental to the Godhead in the twentieth century. Monadism can only be packaged in a certain number of ways.

²⁸LaCugna indicates that the cornerstone of theological feminism is a community based upon interdependence, mutuality, reciprocity and the absence of hierarchy. "Baptists, Feminists and Trinitarian Theology." Ecumenical Trends 17:5 (May 1988): 65-68. She along with Rahner advocate a transcendantal Thomism which proposes relatedness in relations. The bulk of chap. Four was centered on refuting the ontology latent within that approach.

would be arrogant to attempt. Is it accurate to say that God is personal because God is relational, meaning that God relates to us on a personal basis in the economy of salvation? What is required to be able to say God is personal?[29] It would appear that Rahner is positing the same 'lonely' God which Richard parodied while drawing upon the implications which the social analogy provides at an ontological rather than a notional level. No matter how accurate the economic presuppositions and hermeneutic is, there is still no circumventing the essence statements of Scripture, "God is Holy" and "God is Love." There will never be agreement on what these mean but both elicit the questions "Who"? and "Why"? Rahner would agree with many orthodox statements but Taylor notes that he never speaks of love between the Persons of the Trinity; to do so would be to abandon the economic emphasis and settle for a delimitation of the Trinity by the elements of consciousness and the projection of human love relationships.[30]

This influential position has been challenged in recent days.

> Certainly love is not an abstract notion. As an ensemble of openness of a person in view of an ultimate accomplishment it is an indispensable point for the expression of God. But that which is concrete in love is the event of love itself, the fact of loving and of being loved. The love as a "subsisting mode of existing" is scarcely helpful.[31]

Love by definition includes both giving and receiving. Simply stating that in order to experience full personhood humans ought to receive and give love and then to negate the possibility of that interrelatedness in God is highly suspect. Either one is saying that God is so beyond relatedness that it is only a human category or that humans experience something which God does not. The social analogists have never advocated a "humanized" God in relation, rather, they have acknowledged the transcendent quality of that divine

---

[29]I find this the most tedious of modern criticisms of the relational definition, in some ways more so than the "ineffabilist" camp. K. Surin, M. Durrant, A. Thatcher are among those who claim a personal God in Christ devoid of the "crude supernaturalism" of three Persons. "The Personal God and a God who is a Person," Religious Studies 21:1 (1985): 61-73. Cf. Macquarrie's Primordial, Expressive and Unitive Beings as options over divine persons, Principles of Christian Theology, 182-185. Cf. Rowan Williams' Ricouerian analysis of "Generativity," "Dependency," and "Re-presentation" triad. "Trinity and Revelation," Modern Theology 2:3 (1986): 197-212. Mackey, in his critique of modern trinitarian trends, especially Rahner and Moltmann, advocates a binitarianism, because it is really less bothersome for him to do so. The Christian Experience of God as Trinity (London: SCM Press Ltd., 1983), 209. Others in this vein of relational critics who assert a new form of relationalism or dynamism without three 'persons' are P. Schoonenberg, I. Leclerc, M. Wiles, N. Pittenger, C. Richardson, G. Lampe. The "Process" theologians are a non-descript group on this issue. J. Bracken speaks of community but incorporates the evolution of divinity inherent in his stance. E. Cousins also relflects a Process view of God in his Bonaventurian approach.

[30]Taylor, God is Love, 313-314. Taylor claims that nowhere does Rahner clarify the cryptic statements regarding divine love in Godself. Ibid., 314.

[31]W. Breuning, "Pneumatologie," Bilan de la Théologie du XXe siècle, eds. Robert Vander Gucht and Herbert Vorgrimler (Paris: Casterman, 1970), 345.

relatedness which does not necessarily preclude the presence of three divine Persons.

If Rahner's position on the knowledge of divine love is reviewed it elicits the question whether love can be perfect if it is only perceived as active? This is a bifurcation of reality which the relational definition will not allow. To say God is loving is far different from saying that God is love. Arguing for the absolute freedom of God by separating the immanent Trinity from his self-revelation is problematic also. For, Rahner's analysis would leave open the possibility that the God who is symbolized in redemptive acts for us might in himself be one who is capricious or arbitrary.

There is also a strong sense of the necessity of creation in these modern suggestions we have noted here as well. To posit that we know that God is love not ontologically but through what has happened in salvation history is to tie God to the created order in a most unsatisfactory manner. If we compare this position with modern forms of personalism as simply re-defined monadisms it is not difficult to see the same possibility within the intricately woven fabric of the Rahnerian axiom and its trinitological implications. Does any theologian have the right to posit that human creatures are the sufficient "others" toward which the love of God is made manifest? It is this assertion, I believe, which provided Richard with the impetus to express the aseity of the divine "community" in condign love. Basic to the orthodox trinitarian formulations, both cataphatic and apophatic traditions, is the enforcement of the absolute self-sufficiency of the Triune God. God's love is not explained by redemption it is revealed in it.

The fall-out from these dicta is still being felt; the result being a polarization of theological circles.[32] "Person" is more often than not on the one hand, transmitted unreflectively (cf. creedal formulations and recitation), and on the other, it is viewed as anachronistic, problematic and discardable. In the camp of "cultured despisers" we find valiant attempts to deal with this "troublesome terminology" by re-defining triune Persons. A survey of these efforts merits the critique of an overabundance of idiosyncratic expressions which, in the end, threaten to obfuscate the dynamic which propels what we call Christian.[31]

Barth was right, the last thing needed is a rehearsal of terminological intricacies, but if one were to compare the subtle shifts of emphasis resident in every sector of

---

[32]Donald Baillie, God Was in Christ, (New York: Charles Scribner's Sons, 1948), 134-144; and Claude Welch, In This Name; Berkhof's The Christian Faith, for Barthian line. See the entire emphasis of Cathering LaCugna's work for further extent of Rahnerian viewpoint. Note also Robert Jenson's The Triune Identity, For a critique of both Barth's and Rahner's position see J. Galot, "Valeur de la notion de personne dans l'expression du mystère du Christ," Gregorianum 55:1 (1974): 69-82.

[31]Catherine LaCugna, "Current Trends in Trinitarian Theology," in Religious Studies Review 13:2 (April,1987), 147, refers to the need to work through "the "troublesome terminology" of person used of God in the plural."

trinitology with the last minute surreptitious fine-print additions to bills on the floor of the Senate which often are passed unwittingly along with the first motion, we cannot accept the implication that Boethius or Descartes defined personhood adequately.[32] We need to look at the results of the detractors of the relational definition and ask if their alternatives meet the logical requirements beyond cogency to the modern mind. Maybe in meeting the criteria of psychology something is lost which could retrospectively inform the logic it claims to adhere to so vigorously. Scientia, or real knowledge might regain some ground from the science which has usurped it's position. Likewise, the stress on an economic Trinity can also carry extremely problematic consequences if not checked.[33]

Rahner and Barth represent two impressive trinitarian constructions in the twentieth century.[34] Neither find the social view of the Trinity acceptable. It is no wonder then that in a period of intensifying interest in the the 'person' there has been some reassessment in the categories delineated by these magisterial theologians. There is a fundamental agreement between Moltmann's critique of the impact of Aristotelian ontology and the position taken in this work. He attributes a philosophically-based "apatheia" in theology to the immutable notion of deity which we have found elemental in Stoicism and Neoplatonism and which, Moltmann critically notes, has extended into modern forms of

[32]We have dealt extensively with Boethius in chap. Four. Note the intriguing analysis of R. Descartes, in letter 219 to Mersenne where he refers to Augustine and the similarity he finds in the former's view of the imago with his view of individuality. He exults that, "qu'il y a en nous quelque image de la Trinité, en ce que nous sommes, nous sçauonsque nous sommes, & nous aymons cét estre & cette science qui est en nous; au lieu que ie m'en sers pur faire connoistre que ce moy, qui pense, est une substance immaterielle. (Emphasis his). Oeuvres de Descartes, vol. 3, Correspondence: Jan 1640-Jan 1643 (Paris: Charles Adam and Paul Tannery, 1956), 247.

[33]Refer here to chap. One, 38-43. C. Kaiser follows his mentor, T. F. Torrance in concluding that the economic axiom, if pushed to an extreme, alters the Biblical worldview. The disavowal of a distinction between transcendant and immanent latent in Rahnerian categories signifies grave consequences. "The Ontological Trinity in the Context of Historical Religions." Scottish Journal of Theology 29 (1976): 308. Coincidentally, Torrance, in an ecumenical gesture, posits Richard's Trinity as really "one" rather than a bifurcated reality as the "economic" school often finds repulsive. He says Richard's is the truly economic Trinity.

[34]It is intriguing that Barth and Rahner are comparable in their methodology. It is possible, as John O'Donnell confirms that the evident commitment to rational categories in both Rahner and Barth within a overarching structure of a modalistic trinitarianism to could "give the idea that the triunity of God could be deduced from the idea of revelation as such rather than from the concrete revelatory event of Jesus of Nazareth as it is witnessed in the New Testatment." J.J. O'Donnell, "The Doctrine of the Trinity in Recent German Theology," Heythrop Journal 23 (1982): 154-155.

Christian monotheism.[35] Remarkably, Moltmann disavows the monolithic conflation of immanent and economic Trinity. He affirms what is correct in Rahner's axiom and departs from it in a distinctly relational perspective. He states:

> From the foundation of the world, the opera trinitatis ad extra correspond to the passiones trinitatis ad intra. God as love would otherwise not be comprehensible at all.
>
> The relationship of the triune God to himself and the relationship of the triune God to his world is not to be understood as a one-way relationship - the relation of image to reflection, idea to appearance, essence to manifestation - but as a mutual one.[36]

Moltmann views divine Persons as realized and defined within a communal, perichoretic reality. He is clear on the essential being of the Persons which precedes and informs their incommunicability. Moltmann comprehends the essential contribution of Richard's exsistentia and the concept of mutual self-giving implicit in that circumincession.[37] We do not find anything specifically unique to the discussion of divine Person but his method is a radical statement given the propensity of much modern theology to construct a trinitarian structure upon Enlightenment subjectivism. He distinguishes the Persons from modalistic and rationalistic determinations. He uses 'fellowship', 'circulation', 'exchange of energies', and 'process of most perfect and intense empathy' to express the inner trinitarian relationship.[38] His addition to the nature - person discussion is that of divine self-surrender.[39] It should be noted that this is not a new insight. Richard's view of love carries this same sort of divine mutual 'disposition'.

---

[35]J. Moltmann, The Trinity and the Kingdom, trans. Margaret Köhl (San Francisco: Harper & Row, Pub., 1981), 10-12 is the beginning of the recurrent critique of the trinity of "substance", the affirmative inclusion of Unamuno's similar critique supports this, 37-39), and also see 129-150, where he confronts those who view the Trinity as "subjectivity" (Barth and Rahner are specified here.) Similar themes are to be found in "The Fellowship of the Holy Spirit - Trinitarian Pneumatology," Scottish Journal of Theology 37:3 (1984): 288-289. He advocates a third category, the trinity of "communion." Ibid., 289. See also "Gedanken zur "trinitarischen Geschicte Gottes"," Evangelische Theologie 35:3 (1975): 208-223. "The Trinitarian History of God." Theology 78 (1975): 632-646. "The Unity of the Triune God," St. Vladimir's Theological Quarterly 28:3 (1984): 157-171. The joint effort with his wife, Elisabeth in Humanity in God (New York: Pilgrim Press, 1983), also carries strong relational themes. These have all served to alter the idiosyncratic trinitarian presentation of his influential work, The Crucified God: The Cross of Christ as the Foundation and Criticism of Christian Theology, trans. R. A. Wilson and John Bowden (New York: Harper & Row, Pub., 1974).

[36]Moltmann, The Trinity and the Kingdom, 160-161.

[37]Moltmann, The Trinity and the Kingdom, 173-174.

[38]Moltmann, The Trinity and the Kingdom, 174-176.

[39]Moltmann, The Trinity and the Kingdom, 174.

It is a bit disconcerting to see "history" applied to the inner life of God.[40] But, on the whole the relational emphasis found in Moltmann further clarifies the orthodox content of the recurrent relational themes in trinitology. Although Moltmann's "historicizing" approach to the Trinity is problematic, nonetheless, his efforts have brought the discussion of the divine relationality as a cogent articulation back into the most recent theological scholarship.[41]

Eberhard Jüngel, Moltmann's colleague at Tübingen, also conjoins the immanent and economic Trinity in an effort to reassert a dynamic Trinity. With the use of terms similar to the Process theologians but qualifying their categories with distinct Barthian characteristics, Jüngel speaks of God's Being in Becoming.[42] Since God is not Pure Act, as is made known through his self-revelation, He must be dynamic and thereby self-differentiating. Over against modern atheism's claim that God is a non-entity, which was the logical result of monadistic classical theology, Jüngel presents the Christ of the Cross.

---

[40]Moltmann, The Trinity and the Kingdom, 94-96 serves as summation of this Hegelian-Rahnerian element in Moltmann's thought, see also 174, 178. There is a bit of monopatrism in Moltmann even though he notes its weaknesses, cf.189.

[41]Wolfhart Pannenberg indicates a strong triune relationality as the basis of human interpersonal communality in "Person and Subjekt: Zur Überwindung des Subjektivismus im Menschenbild und im Gottesverständnis," Neue Zeitschrift für Systematische Theologie und Religionsphilosophie 18 (1976): 133-148, esp. 145-148. This is confirmed by R. Jenson, who disagrees with Pannenberg that the three Persons are meant to be understood in the modern sense of 'person'. "Jesus in the Trinity: Wolfhart Pannenberg's Christology and the Doctrine of the Trinity," in C. Braaten and Philip Clayton, eds. The Theology of Wolfhart Pannenberg: Twelve American Critiques with an Autobiographical Essay and Response, (Minneapolis: Augsburg Publishing House, 1988), 192-193, 200. The Teutonic interest in God's relation to history from a predominantly eschatological perspective, propels the trinitarianism of W. Pannenberg. The "ontological priority of the future" is the key to interpreting the relationship between the immanent and economic Trinity. It is the future which dialectically reveals the God who is at work in history. See some of these themes in "The God of History," trans. M.B. Jackson. Cumberland Seminarian 19:2,3 (1981): 35-41. This revealed Trinity is not a modalism but, as Roger Olsen has noticed, there is an implicit subordinationism in the way Pannenberg deals with the monarchia of the Father. "Wolfhart Pannenberg's Doctrine of the Trinity," Scottish Journal of Theology 43:2 (1990): 203.

[42]There is a distinct Barthian flavor to E. Jüngel in The Doctrine of the Trinity (Grand Rapids: Eerdmans Pub. Co., 1976), 101-103. See also God's Being is in Becoming, trans. Horton Harris (Edinburgh: Scottish Academic Press, 1976) for this theme."The Relationship Between 'Economic' and 'Immanent' Trinity," Theology Digest 24 (Summer, 1976): 179-184. His major work is God As the Mystery of the World: On the Foundation of the Theology of the Crucified One in the Dispute between Theism and Atheism (Grand Rapids: Eerdmans Pub. Co., 1983). For a discussion of Divine Love as 'Becoming' based upon 'Being' as a viable notion in critique of the God of the Philosophers see, God as Mystery, 213-222, 371-373. Cf. the German edition, Gott als Geheimnis der Welt: Zur Begründing der Theologie des Gekreuzigten im Streit zwischen Theismus und Atheismus (Tübingen: J. C. B. Mohr, 1977).

The revealed, not naturally discerned, Word is the revelation of the triune reality.[43] It is this inner reality of three "modes of being" which is reminiscent of Barth's perichoretic understanding of Divine subjectivity.[44] It is the movement within the act of self-revelation, the outward orientation implicit in generation, procession and the election of Jesus, which constitutes the divine essence. God's Being then is Event, existent in three modes.[45] Jüngel serves as an example of the Barthian-Rahnerian camp with the modern emphasis on suffering, which Moltmann clearly excels in explicating. However, the advances of Moltmann are not found in Jüngel due to his maintenance of rigorous Barthian epistemological categories.

The impact of Enlightenment categories on the notion of 'person' have deeply influence theology. If 'person' can only be regarded as a rational or volitional self-determinative individual then trinitarian theology must divorce itself from both the term and the notion of divine Persons. But if there is a corrective to the modern understanding of person in its trinitarian use then its retention might serve more purpose than the anachronistic function it is too often attributed. From Barth to Rahner, Moltmann, Jüngel, Pannenberg and Mühlen, the Teutonic theological minds have explored yet again the notion of divine Person with differing emphases. The modern German theologians have led the way in defining and correcting the crucial categories pertaining to divine personhood which the Social Analogists did not delineate accurately.[46] 'Distinct manners of subsisting' or 'modes of existing', are apparently relational, but the further investigation of more recent thinkers has incorporated personal elements which have brought the discussion of 'person' back into acceptable God-talk. The relation of a unified substance with the coinciding factor of mutual personhood has not only clarified Heilsgeschichte but also pertains to the

---

[43]See W. Waite Willis' intriguing interaction between the Bartians and the Enlightenment-based subjectivists: Fichte, Feuerbach,, Theism, Atheism and the Doctrine of the Trinity: The Trinitarian Theologies of Karl Barth and Jürgen Moltmann in Response to Protest Atheism (Atlanta: Scholars Press, 1987). Although Jüngel does not play a part in the argument his Bartianism with the addition of his unique view of suffering makes him a bridge point which Willis did not make much use of, if any.

[44]Jüngel, The Doctrine of the Trinity, 32-33. See his explication of the Triune revelation and reality in light of the Spirit as donum in order that humanity might share in the historical love of God. The Mystery of the World, 379. Cf. R. Zimany's assessment of the interrelation of divine agape and human relationality in "Human Love and the Trinity: Jüngel's Perception," Dialog 21:3 (1982): 220-223.

[45]Jüngel, The Mystery of the World, 222-223, 374-390.

[46]Both American and British specialists are letting their voices be heard in keeping the Germans accountable for their epistemological and methodological considerations with regard to divine personhood. See the helpful bibliographical essay with sound interpretation by A.L.G.E. Joos, "Lineas sobresalientas del itinerario trinitario en la teologia "Protestant" de los ultimos decenios," in Bibliographia Trinitaria of Estudios Trinitarios 11:2-3 (1977): 443-507.

Being of God which is not absolutistic but primordially active in mutual self-giving. It is within this general context that Heribert Mühlen has forged a repristination of the relational categories within the Godhead.

II. Heribert Mühlen and Personal Causality

Though Heribert Mühlen has found wide acclaim as a trinitarian theologian in Europe, the relative paucity of translations of his works has resulted in insufficient attention to his unique contributions, at least on the American theological scene. He has served for twenty-five years on the theological faculty of Paderborn. His strong pastoral interests and vibrant spirituality mixed with a keen philosophical and theological mind have formed a stream of intelligent and practical pieces which have benefited those fortunate enough to be able to delve into them.[47]

Immediately prior to his appointment to Paderborn, Mühlen published two watershed texts, which remain his most important statements regarding trinitarian personhood and the impact of the personhood of the Spirit within the life of the Church.[48] These works have place Mühlen at the forefront of the resurgence of the social analogy of the Trinity amongst European theologians. W. Hill says that Mühlen's trinitarian theology of is "probably the best available development to date of the social model of the Trinity."[49]

A. Critique of the Tradition

---

[47]Mühlen was ordained in 1955. See the structure and content of his A Charismatic Theology: Initiation in the Spirit (London: Burns and Oates, 1978). Another indication of Mühlen's diversity is his leadership within the Charismatiche Gemeinde Erneuerung in Germany and service as co-deitor of Erneuerung in Kirche und Gesellschaft. A personal testimony of the impact of the Holy Spirit upon his life is recounted in Ralph Martin, comp. Spirit and the Church (New York: Paulist Press, 1976), 174-181. In the American milieu, little attention is given to charismatic scholars, but one finds a different response in Europe. Kilian McDonnell's major contribution, besides his pnuematological prowess, has been to chart the relationship between the Vatican and the renewal movements across the world. Since John XXIII (1961) to the present (cf. the Sixth International Leaders Conference, 1987) the pontifical response has been quite favorable to the charismatic element of which Mühlen has played a key role. See McDonnell ed. Open the Windows: The Popes and Charismatic Renewal (South Bend: Greenlawn, 1989).

[48]In 1963 Mühlen released Der heilige Geist als Person: Beitrag zur Frage nach der dem heiligen Geiste eigentümlichen Funktion in der Trinität, bei der Inkarnation und im Gnadenbund, Münsterische Beiträge zur Theologie, vol. 26 (Münster: Aschendorff). Hereafter, HGP. There has been a second edition produced in 1980 which includes some of the ecumenical spirit of Vatican II The following year Una Mystica Persona: Eine Person in vielen Personen (Munich: Verlag Ferdinand Schöningh, 1968), appeared. Hereafter UMP. The second work can be found in Frence translation as L'Esprit dans L'Église trans. A. Liefooghe, M. Massart and R. Virrion, 2 vols. (Paris: Les Éditions du Cerf, 1969). Research has indicated that no substantial portion of either work has been translated into English.

[49]W. Hill, The Three-Personed God, 233.

Where Aristotelian categories found use in the West to assist in a cogent explanation of the generation of the Logos, Mühlen critiques the absence of a solid ontological basis for the procession of the Spirit.[50] He lays a historical basis for his relational argument by indicating certain deficiencies in the traditional definition of 'person'. Boethius' contribution did not allow a view of substance other than individual which necessitated the "korrektur" of Richard's relational 'exsistentia'.[51] He indicates that the traditional ontology whether in Boethius, Augustine or Aquinas offered a relational logic which gave equal weight to the person of the Spirit.[52] Richard of St. Victor's analogy of inter-personal love becomes a mainstay for Mühlen's project. One finds an irenic element here as Mühlen views the two traditions we have outlined in chapter Four as complementary.[53] Even in this objective stance, however, the implications are clear that a static view of substance debilitates the notion of divine and human 'person'.

Mühlen sees Aquinas's "intentional" use of person as an ontological category which favored the Boethian over the Ricardine paradigm.[54] However, at the same time he acknowledges the unique contribution which "exsistentia" brought to the medieval notion of person[55] Since, his doctoral dissertation concerned this particular discussion in the work of Duns Scotus, it is from that vantage point that Mühlen approaches medieval categories of

---

[50]After commenting on Aquinas' use in ST 1a, 27, 2 and 1a, 42, 5 with references to Aristotle Physics 4:3 210a14-24, Mühlen critiques the absence of categories both to sufficiently account for the "inness" revealed in John 17:21ff, and for a equal category to be applied to the Spirit, HGP, 13-14. Cf. UMP, 193.

[51]HGP, 33-37.

[52]He begins his critique of Augustine earlier at HGP, 3-4.

[53]HGP, 42-44. B. Rey criticizes Mühlen here in that he yielded "á cette tentation pour atténuer les differences qui existent entre la position de Richard et celle de S. Thomas." "Trinité," 529. Banawiratma, "Heilige Geist in der Theologie von Heribert Mühlen," 26-27, speaks of the synthesis of the psychological and the social trinities in Richard. Coffey does not see this as a problem. Grace: The Gift of the Holy Spirit, 35.

[54]Building upon Richard's introductory comments in PL 196, 1,10, 895D, regarding the "intention" (ex intentione vs. ex occasione) of that work in relation to God-talk, Mühlen finds Aquinas making proper adjustments to Richard's definition. HGP, 28-29. This is a debatable point as we have seen. Cf. Aquinas' ontological statement at ST 1a, 30, 4, reply. The distinction between 'first' and 'second' intention is carried over in the realism of Duns Scotus. A third definition of the era following Richard was that of the Franciscan, Alexander of Hales and incorporated into Bonaventure's trinitology is "hypostasis proprietate distincta ad dignitatem pertinente," (distinct hypostatic propriety pertaining to dignity). HGP, 33.

[55]HGP, 37-40.

'person' which he feels are still efficacious.[56]

Scotus' keen philosophical and theological perception was employed in the clarification of earlier statements regarding 'person'. Respecting the category of 'intellectual nature', Scotus clarified the distinction between nature and relation. The positing of a 'formal' distinction between these two categories altered the course of medieval trinitology.[57] Aquinas' 'subsistent relations' simply did not suffice for Scotus and thereby taking Richard's lead, Scotus discussed generation and procession in terms of real persons as origins rather than mere relations as had the Angelic Doctor. Scotus wrote concerning origin and person:

> The Father possesses every operation according to all possible manner of Himself, insofar as He is prior to the Son, and this He has, both objectively and elicitely, so as the Son is in nowise the principle for the Father's eliciting any act, so likewise is He neither the objective reason necessarily required for any action of His, for the Father necessarily possesses both the object as well as the elicitative principle of every operation of His, both in Himself and of Himself.[58]

He clearly held to the 'monarchia' principle but we also see the indications of a clear formal distinction, (a philosophical mid-point between real and logical distinctions) where origin and volition are distinct within the Trinity itself. Where knowledge and reason fed Aquinas' structure, love and will fund the thought of the 'Doctor Subtilis'. Scotus' Trinity indicated that the Father loves himself and the Son in the Spirit, the Breath of God, with a perfect essential love. Unlike Thomas then, perfection of essence allows the clear ontological distinction of the three Persons without an equivocation regarding 'persona'.[59]

---

[56]Published as Sein und Person nach Johannes Duns Scotus: Beitrage zur Grundlegung einer Metephysik der Person. Franziskan Forschungen Vol. 47. Werl: Dietrich - Coelde - Verlag, 1954. Sears says that he wrote Sein und Person (abbreviated thus hereafter) in an effort to develop relationality as a category for personhood in contradistinction from the the spirituality emphasis of Boethius and Aquinas. "Spirit: Divine and Human," 16.

[57]Scotus' concept of the univocity of Being is at work here. For Aquinas there was a distinct duality to being as such, the natural and the supernatural conjoined by grace and analogical epistemology. Scotus, on the other hand envisioned one order. We know God's being because he is like our being and vice versa. See for instance his realist perception of truth in Opus Oxoniense ad IV Libros Magistri Sententiarum Bk. 1, Dist. 3, Q. 4, McKeon ed. Selections from Medieval Philosophers vol. 2, 313-350. He makes allusion to Richard's "proof" for the existence of God (De Trinitate 1, 8) in a Treatise On God as First Principle Q. 1, reply in Medieval Philosophy, Wippel and Wolters eds., 404.

[58]Duns Scotus from the Sentences, Reportationes d. 45, q.2, n.5. Quoted in K. Vasilj, Trinitarian Theories: As Judged by Reason (Chicago: Croatioan Franciscan Press, 1987), 49.

[59]Schmaus writes, "According to Scotus, it cannot, however, be denied that by the word "nature" we mean something other than by the word "relation." Dogma vol. 3, 164. A dissenting voice from this position can be found in a critique of Mühlen's Heilige Geist als Person in A. Hayen,"L'etre de la personne selon B. Jean Duns Scot." Revue philosphes de Louvain 53 (1955): 525-541. He does not criticize Aquinas at all but rather shows the continuum upon which the Angelic Doctor and Duns Scotus stand. Milbank follows the

For Scotus, divine perfection was a category drawn from Anselm and the Victorines. As perfect in will and love, God is absolute freedom and thus must be Trinity.[60] Perfect love desires that the object of love be loved by another.[61]

For Scotus if essence is communicable then person cannot be univocally so also. He did not view spirituality as a characteristic as sufficient to delineate divine personhood. Based upon his dynamic view of Being Duns Scotus saw divine Being as transcendental relation which admits, according to Mühlen, the category of divine 'selbständiger Gegenüberstand', or real, substantial opposition as definitive of personhood.[62] As Sears points out, a person is the co-existence of common nature and individuality.[63] It is here that Scotus presents the notion of 'personalitas' which gives concrete existence to what otherwise is an empty philosophical category.[64]

Fundamental to Mühlen's interpretation of Scotus and his own thought is the emphasis on person rather than exclusively on nature. He finds in both Boethius and Aquinas the framework of natura inadequate in itself to offer a holistic definition of person. Divine substance is unique in its unity-trinity reality. It is a different sort of substance than any other and can thus admit differentiation.[65] He views the definition which both Richard and Duns Scotus used, intellectualis naturae incommunicabilis existentia, as an approach which, along with the merits of the Boethian-Thomistic paradigm, convergently

---

criticism of Duns Scotus that attributes the displacement of the Trinity, despite his relational categories, from the center of Christian thought due to his emphasis on divine infinity. John Milbank, "The Second Difference: For a Trinitarianism Without Reserve," Modern Theology 2:3 (1986): 219.

[60]This is a repristination of the 'necessitarianism' in both Anselm and Richard we have dealt with in chap. Four, 188-193.

[61]See the excellent overview of medieval trinitarians in Dictionary of the Middle Ages. S.v. "Trinitarian Doctrine," by Kenan Osborne, ed. Joseph R. Strayer, vol. 12 (New York: Charles Scribner's Sons, 1989), 189-198.

[62]Sein und Person, 77, 87. In contrast with the Greek philosophical tradition and its impact of Aquinas contrasted with Duns Scotus, "Das unbegrenzte Du: Auf dem Wege zu einer Personology," in Wahrheit und Verkundigung: Michael Schmaus zum 70 Geburstag, ed. Leo Scheffczyk, et. al., Munchen, Paderborn, Wien: Schoningh, 1967), 1263-1265. It is odd that we find a silence with regard to Richard in this article.

[63]Sears, "Spirit: Divine and Human." 25. He notes on p. 27 that thought a divine nature may have a 'structured interior' it possesses such a differentiated reality in relation to a unified divine reality.

[64]HGP, 43.

[65]Sein und Person, 85-86. Duns Scotus uses the phrase, "res ad alterum" which Mühlen makes 'gegenüberstand'. Sein und Person, 87. HGP, 55.

offers important qualifications regarding divine personhood.[66] His affirmation of Richard follows the interpretation given in chapter Four concerning the intellectual aspect by stating that it does not refer to a "thisness" but rather to a 'there-being' (Dasein).[67]

The distinction between 'haecceitas' and the Aristotelian 'entitas singularis' made by Scotus is also resident in the language Mühlen chooses as 'first intention' usage. There is an underlying realism here which Scotus initiated in the face of predominant analogical theology which denied an ontological connectedness between analogy and referent. The concreteness of the 'haecceitas' of the divine Persons, was alluded to in Richard's 'exsistentia', elaborated by Scotus' contrast between intuitive and abstract cognition (indicating positive modality and common nature respectively) both of which are present in the realism of Mühlen.[68] Person is present where an actual incommunicable existant dwelling within a communicably divine relationship is, as Scotus posits, formally present.[69] The relationship of existant to existant is far different than one between substances or distinctions which posit no concrete difference between persons and relations.[70]

Mühlen follows the Ricardine-Scotian theses which would point from the "what" of person (nature) to the "by what" or the "where from" which informs the opposite relations indicated in the Christian tradition. With that move he posits, much like the Cappadocians, Richard and the later Duns Scotus, that the notion of divine 'Person' arises out of existing relationships. The relationship of real, substantial "existants" is the place where talk of the divine origins takes on meaning. Though not clearly separated from Thomistic 'relations' there is still much to commend the Scotian transmission of the 'incommunicability' of persons as entities in opposition, revealing a face-to-face overagainstness an 'In-Beziehung-Stehen', rather than a solipsistic view of divine and human personhood.[71] Relation is meaningless if not a result of volitional love from one Person to another Person.

---

[66]HGP, 42-44. Sein und Person, 68-75.

[67]Sears, "Spirit: Divine and Human," 29.

[68]de Vogel points to this paradigm shift in analogical discussion by Scotus over against the Aristotelian-Thomistic position in "The Concept of Personality in Greek and Christian Thought," 21-22. H. Arendt provides a deeper criticism of the Thomistic view of volition as the principium individuationis in contrast to the and the Scotian concept of the will that takes on much more profound individual 'active' commitment to a discernible divine entity. The Life of the Mind: Vol. Two/ Willing (New York: Harcourt Brace and Jovanovich, 1978), 120-141.

[69]Remeber that Scotus is using 'formal' distinction in such a way as to indicated concrete distinction. See Sears, "Spirit: Human and Divine," 29-35 for a good summary of Mühlen's use of Duns Scotus.

[70]HGP, 56-57.

[71]Sein und Person, 84, 94

It is not just from a philosophical basis that Mühlen argues for a relational Trinity; he delves into the Scriptural evidence taking as his point of embarkation the use of "I" by the Father and the Son.[72] The "we" statements of Jesus in the Johannine literatures, Mühlen concludes, point to the inclusion of the co-equal Spirit.[73] Mühlen stands in the same critical line as has been indicated in this work against the modern pneumatological interpretation of the Spirit as a personification, an element of expressive modalism, or as an impersonal power.[74]

B. The Trinity as Dialogue in Love

The use of the dialogical philosophers has marked Mühlen's methodology as distinctly unique in the composition of his personalistic theology. W. von Humboldt's linguistic analysis pursued the use of personal pronouns in the ontology of language as indicators of the fundamental relationality of existence. Buber's famous 'I-Thou' construct was preceded by a succession of thinkers who excavated the phenomenology of language for relational categories.[75]

Mühlen draws upon the phenomenology of the dialogical philosophers as an analogically heuristic source for his perception of the interrelationship of the divine Persons. He finds in them a strong support for the co-equality of the Persons, as well as analogical undergirding for a differentiated unity.[76] Under their influence he introduces the highly provocative and criticized 'ich - du - wir' or, 'I - thou - we' paradigm. The method whereby these pronouns indicate the reality of persons Mühlen calls 'personology'.[77] For

---

[72]HGP, 45-48, 83-100. See chap. One, 48. See the helpful notation of S. Kilian, "The Holy Spirit in Christ and in Christians," American Benedictine Review 20 (1969): 101-102, n.8.

[73]HGP, 95-99. He focuses on Jn. 14:23.

[74]See chap. One, 55-65. Cf. Mühlen's statements in HGP, 98-99.

[75]Mühlen refers to Grimm, von Humboldt, Ebner, and von Hildebrand.

[76]Space does not allow a tracing of the history of modern philosophy but it is interesting to note the concomitant rise of the linguistically based philosophy of the dialogical thinkers and the existential shift found in philosophers in the lineage of Heidegger which challenged Greek categories as insufficient. The idea of 'Being with' in philosophy took on a whole different perspective in the modern period, purportedly devoid of esotericism. One can also trace the rise of personalism from Royce to Brightman along this same critical trajectory. One possible contemporary theological source for Mühlen possibly was the work of Juan Alfaro, "Persona y Gracia," Gregorianum 41 (1960): 5-29; trans. "Person and grace," Theology Digest 14:1 (1966): 3-7.

[77]See his philosophical approach in criticism of the "absolutistic" systems both ancient and modern which are unable to deal adequately with the subject-object distinction in "Das unbegrenzte Du: Auf dem Wege zu einer Personology," in Wahrheit und

him "Da-sein ist Du-sein."[78] This mixture of scriptural exegesis, Scotian ontology with dialogical philosophy results in a centripetal effect of communication and self-donation in contrast with the perennial centrifugal determinations on divine nature.[79]

The personhood of the Spirit as the divine "We" is based upon Mühlen's view of the divine 'I'. In his thought the 'I' is never singular, rather it presupposes an 'opposite' relation.[80] Appropriation or propriety, is used to indicate the characteristics which set one Person of the Trinity apart from the other Persons, but it is 'relationis oppositis' which froms a clearer image of the relationship within which individual delineations find their source.[81] The 'I' must retain its incommunicability in order to produce a concrete entity so the Father is best viewed as the 'I' of the triune reality.[82] Although Mühlen never attributes the 'I' literally to any other person but the Father, the 'Thou' of the Son is the reciprocal 'Other' which alters the concept of divine substance as monadic to interpersonal communication and donation.

Thus, the perennial issue of the One and the Many are engaged here. The foundational or primordial one, or 'Urmodi' is not, as Richard quipped, in solitude, there is an eternally co-existent 'thou' who dialogues as an equal to the 'I' and yet retains its

---

Verkundigung: Michael Schmaus zum 70 Geburstag, ed. Leo Scheffczyk, et. al., (Munchen, Paderborn, Wien: Schoningh, 1967), 1259-1285.

[78]"Das unbegrenzte Du," 1285.

[79]Hill, The Three-Personed God, 234. We will be unable to trace all the sources for Mühlen's paradigm. M.J. Scheeben had a great influence on his thought regarding the analogy of the family and its implications for trinitarian thought. HGP, 76-77.

[80]HGP, 61. This is a recurrent theme based upon the Council of Florence's qualifications of Thomistic categories and in its defense of the Filioque. See HGP, 231-232; "Person und Appropriation - Zum Verständnis des Axioms: In Deo omnia sunt unum, ubi non obviat relationis oppositio," Münchener Theologische Zeitschrift 16 (1965): 43-47. For the most part this article is a further explication of points already made in HGP, 306-329. Anselm, De Processione Spiritus Sancti 1, seems to be one of the earliest statements along this line; see Trinity, Incarnation, and Redemption, ed. with intro. Jasper Hopkins and Herbert Richardson, 85-86. Cf. Florence's Decree for the Jacobites, Denzinger, 1330 (similarly to the Greeks, Ibid, 1300); Neuner and Dupuis, 325 (111). Cf. Pannenberg's "Person and Subjekt: Zur Überwindung des Subjektivismus im Menschenbild und im Gottesverständnis," Neue Zeitschrift für Systematische Theologie und Religionsphilosophie 18 (1976): 133-148.

[81]David Coffey, assists in noting the Augustinian and Cappadocian elements in the Florentine pronouncements in Grace: The Gift of the Holy Spirit (Sydney: Catholic Institute of Sydney, 1979), 8.

[82]Note how much Mühlen looks to Richard St. Victor in conjunction with dialogical philosophy in this section of his argument. HGP, 116-143.

unique distinction.⁸³MPSJE.PRSqual participation in the third person.⁸⁴ Again it is the "personen facie ad faciem" relationship of Richard which supercedes while incorporating the "psychological" categories of knowing and willing of the Augustinian-Thomistic interpretation.⁸⁵

Asserting full divine personhood to the Spirit is central to Mühlen's theological and ecumenical enterprise.⁸⁶ With a critical eye, Mühlen assesses the relative merits of the 'vinculum' tradition from Augustine to the present. There is no doubt that the themes of vivification and the unitive function are included in referring to the 'donum' of the Spirit.⁸⁷ However, the ecclesiological implications of this 'Gift' orientation often mirrors the static elements of absolutized substance and thereby negates full personal characteristics in its pneumatology.⁸⁸ Mühlen indicates that within the Trinity, concomitant with the 'I' and 'Thou', there is resident a personal 'We' which meets the exclusive-inclusive criteria for formal divine personhood.⁸⁹ The perichoretic characteristics abound in Mühlen's attribution of "one Person in two Persons."⁹⁰ He does not seek to eschew the donation language of the

---

⁸³See HGP, 54, 60, 121. Note here the emphasis on 'condilectus' which is based upon co-equal orQMS PS Jet+/800II/810/2200/JetScri

⁸⁴HGP, 54-57, 59-60. As Kilian notes,
"It is, then, evident that while the 'I'-"Thou" relationship brings about a new mode of personal relational behavior, this latter is completely missing in the "I'-"he" relationship (Ibid., 3.23) Consequently, there are only two primordial forms of personal relationship or personal involvement: the "I'-"thou" and the "we".
"The Holy Spirit in Christ and in Christians," 104.

⁸⁵HGP, 121.

⁸⁶Mühlen says the NT language regarding the Spirit provides an Ansätze for discerning personal particularity (Eigentümlichkeit) of the Spirit. HGP, 171. On OT and Rabbinic views see HGP, 2. Congar quotes Mühlen in connection with political monotheism where the latter emphasizes the need for an adequate pneumatology without which the Church is left with "a pre-trinitarian monotheism." "Classical Political Monotheism and the Trinity," in J. Metz and E. Schillebeeckx, eds. God as Father? Concilium 143:3 (1981): 35.

⁸⁷UMP, 33-34.

⁸⁸This is not to say that Mühlen has anything but an orthodox view of divine substance. One divine substance with one center of act with Persons constituted by oppositio relationis. HGP, 2-3.

⁸⁹Kilian assists in translating the 'Gross-Ich' as the 'singular-plural' I, in "Holy Spirit in Christ and Christians," 101. Congar makes it clear that the Mühlen's 'Great I' of the Spirit is that of Christ. See I Believe in the Holy Ghost, vol.1, 23. Sears notes that Ludwig Binzwanger postulated that ontologically the 'we' precedes the concept of 'I', in "Spirit: Divine and Human," 3.

⁹⁰HGP, 168; UMP, 199.

early Scholastics but does attempt to clarify its usage.[91]   The medieval categories of 'active' and 'passive' spiration pertaining to the Father and the Son in relation to the Spirit are not separable for Mühlen. They each are involved in the existence of the Spirit who is likewise a participant in the uniting of the other two Persons.[92] The Spirit is, to use Ricardine terminology, a 'condign' partner, or as Mühlen ascertains, an 'Ant-wort' in the divine 'I'-'Thou' dialogue.[93] The Spirit is a subsistent 'We-person' or 'Person-Wort'.[94] This is integrally related to the 'Gross-Ich' concept Mühlen interprets from the 'corporate personality' of Old Testament passages and the 'incorporation' New Testament texts. What is astounding here is that Mühlen is challenging the apophatic tradition within the Western thinkers with regard to the naming of the relationship between the Father and the Son to the Spirit. Neither Augustine nor Aquinas attempted such a naming, which for Mühlen is an 'Ich-Du' relation.[95]

Mühlen's emphasis on the anointing of the Jesus by the Spirit is a nexus for explicating the uniqueness and the unity of both the Spirit and the Son. The incarnation is a distinct constituitive reality for the Son. The Spirit did not become man. But the anointing of the Son, the property of the Spirit, proved to be the point where the Spirit was revealed in the economy of God as the binding of Christ to his own and the indwelling of those Christians is only a reality of the 'We' in Christ through the Spirit.[96] Where it is the property of the Son to personally make a human nature the Spirit is

---

[91]See the extensive interpretation of this theme in J. Banawiratma, "Der Heilige Geist in der Theologie von Heribert Mühlen: Versuch einer Darstellung und Würdigung," Ph.D. dissertation, Univ. of Innsbruck, 1980, 49-82.

[92]The indications of mutuality in Mühlen are so distinct that he joins the family analogy tradition of Nazianzus, Aquinas and Richard. See his statement in L'Esprit dans L'Église, trans. A. Liefooghe, M. Massart and R. Virrion, 272,
> Nous pouvons mieux dire quelle n'est pas la relation mutuelle des personnes divines, qu'énoncer positivement le mode de leur relation. C'est pourquoi le rapport père-mère-enfant est peut-être encore le plus apte à évoquer le mystère de la Trinité.
Cf. HGP, 150.

[93]HGP, 132-136.

[94]HGP, 51-59; This 'wir' in person is the particular (Eigentümliche) function of the Spirit in both the immanent and economic Trinity, HGP, 240; for a complete argument on the 'Person-Wort' of each person of the Trinity. See here the difference between a 'Person-Wort','Er' and 'Wir'. HGP, 57-58.

[95]HGP, 131-143. Coffey is correct in noting this claim of Mühlen's, Grace: The Gift of the Holy Spirit, 34.

[96]HGP, 195-196.

distinguishably the Person who binds Christ to the Church and to Christians.[97] Mühlen is clear regarding the doctrine of appropriations that any time a certain action: i.e., creation, incarnation or Pentecost, is seen only as the work of one divine Person then the point has been missed.[98] The Spirit's incommunicable characteristics are revealed at the baptism of Jesus but the entire Trinity is at work there concomitantly.

Similar to the thinkers we have chosen to represent the relational definition of Person in Trinity, Mühlen also lays much of the blame on static elements within trinitarian theology upon the assimilation of Greek philosophical constructs.[99] The question of essence or substance, seen through Platonic or Aristotelian constructs imports an absolutism which when worked out theologically either results in a form of agnosticism or conversely an excessive immanentism.[100] Ontology founded on natura rather than on relational being never suffices in answering the dilemma of the One and the Many. Thus, Mühlen critiques Aquinas for his inability to move beyond abstraction when referring to 'person' in Trinity and in the end constructing a theology which clearly points to a quaternity.[101]

---

[97]HGP, 196. UMP, 74-172; The Spirit is the "Prinzip der Einheit," Ibid., 168. Kilian is correct in his interpretation of the difference between the continuation of the Incarnation and the radical place that Mühlen feels the Scripture indicates for which the Spirit as Person ought to recognized. "The Holy Spirit in Christ and Christians," 105-106.

[98]Cf. David Coffey's assessment and critique of Scheeben and his disciple, Mühlen in Grace: The Gift of the Holy Spirit (Sydney: Catholic Institute of Sydney, 1979), 91-119.

[99]Space prohibits a full rendition of the impact of Greek philosophical constructs in precluding relationality in the Trinity in any way which admits a communal view of the Trinity. Locke's emphasis on the personality as continued consciousness as the only formal note of personality was meant as a refutation of the hypostatic union and tangentially trinitarian personhood. See Welch, In This Name, 110. Kant's insurmountable wall of practical reason disallowed the attempt at discerning God in himself and solidified the Enlightenment cQMS PS Jet+/800II/810/2200/JetScriptQMPSJE.PRSm for the Christian faith did not effect the impact of Hegel's Phenomenology of the Mind transmitted the philosophical dialectic of Greek thought into modern theology. A Trinity of the mind was transmitted to Rahner, Metz, Pannenberg, and Moltmann in varying levels but unmistakably shunted toward a notion of unity which precludes fundamental relationality in the divine. Harnack's view of the Trinity as an unacceptable Hellenization of essential Christianity was countered by the prowess of Barth. But even Barth saw fit to qualify the Augsburg Confession by bracketing "(quod) proprie subsistit," so that the three which subsist is made to reflect a static view of God subsisting in a three-fold way. Cf. Welch, In this Name, 111. The Boston 'personalists' repristinated the Greek 'Idea' of a living absolute intelligence behind all things. Tillich taught that God cannot be thought of a being who is a person since that would posit individuality to the unlimited Ground, which was a nineteenth century innovation and thus posited a "finitizing anthropomorphism" which "robs God of Ultimacy and absoluteness. Systematic Theology, vol. 1, 245.

[100]Mühlen, "Das Unbegrenzte Du," 1263-1264. Note his reference to Nichomachean Ethics, Bk. 7, ch. 14, 1153b, 32. "All things have by nature something divine in them."

[101]Mühlen, "Person und Appropriation," 48-50. See a similar critique of Augustine in HGP, 116.

Mühlen posits a personal causality in contradistinction to formal or efficient causality.[102] This relational emphasis is an application of his trinitarian discussion which precedes but is a substantiation for what has been argued. Unlike the theologians whose logic suffers in connecting a rational definition of God and relational elements in anthropology and ecclesiology, Mühlen makes the connection clear and cogent. Mühlen concludes that in light of a God who is in Himself a communion of personal differentiations, the Biblical material regarding personal, marital and national covenants and texts which merit prosopological exegesis, it is plausible to consider the relationship between human persons and the Trinity as a causa moralis personalis.[103] If the self-concious 'I' donates himself to the 'Thou', and with that Other gives himself to Another it would seem that every graced relationship issuing from that communion should reflect it mutatis mutandis. Personal causality effects an interpersonal relationship, one divine Person effecting another but in such a way as to evoke from the other the capacity for free, concious, self-donation in the mutuality of love. Where efficient causality focuses primarily on an external act; on the restoration of the Creator's intention, and where formal causality offers "the principle of the substantial being of the thing whose form it is," but does not necessitate a unity of essence, Mühlen posits a personal causality.[104]

This causality is an intimate all-inclusive act between persons whihc establishes a interpersonal relationship. The Holy Spirit is the triune Person who is the "inter-person", the "hypostasized We" who brings this Triune communion and uncreated grace in the verbindung of human hearts with the source of perfect love. Grace is, as Alfaro wrote, "God's personal communication and self-gift - an internal call to an immediate personal union with God."[105] The Church has long struggled with the proper way to understand the "Life of God in the Soul of Man." P. Chirico has outlined four classical ways this relationship has been viewed.[106] He also critiques the efficient cause and adds to it the exemplary and the objective causality. These are insufficient in that the union is not

---

[102]HGP, 264-280; Sabbas, "Holy Spirit in Christ and Christians," 112.

[103]HGP, 274.

[104]HGP, 264-267; Kilian, "The Holy Spirit in Christ and Christians," 112; Quote from Aquinas, Contra Gentiles Bk. 2, 68, 3. D. Coffey points to the connection Mühlen makes between efficient and personal causality, the latter is the "last species of the genus of efficient causes." Grace: The Gift of the Holy Spirit, 45. Cf. HGP, 279.

[105]Alfaro, "Person and Grace," Theology Digest, 3. Mühlen refers to this article HGP, 267.

[106]Pietro F. Chiricos, "The Divine Indwelling and Distinct Relations to the Indwelling Persons in Modern Theological Discussion," Ph.D. dissertation ad lauream, Rome, 1960.

ontological.[107] To say that God, in his Triune reality, is present in the believer is to say that the human person participates in the life of the Trinity. Where Chirico proposes the category of "final causality" with an "already-not yet" ambiance, Mühlen offers a personal causality which is based on a theologically articulated personology.[108] The free (Duns Scotus) self-giving (Richard St. Victor) to another intellectual being (Aquinas) is the trinitarian center of all reality.

Personal causality then is the gracious call for a personal response which finds its nexus in the person of the Spirit both in self-bestowing and uniting so that each recipient of grace can be indwelt and indwell within each Person of the Trinity. The personal action of God the Father is mediated by the Son and the Spirit. Rather than terminating within the Triune reality, personal causality brings about the personal union between the believer and the Trinity. [109] This causality is moral in that it neither forces reception of grace nor truncates the reality of either divine nor human personhood.[110]

This personalistic paradigm does not negate the statements of immanent and economic unity in orthodox trinitarianism.[111] The distinct theological advancement in

---

[107]He points out that the discussion did not even begin until Petavius (1583-1652) began to ask the questions. "Divine Indwelling," 10. The place of the Spirit as more than accidentally related to the Trinity is the issue in both Chirico and Mühlen's work. They are interested in plumbing the category of the the person in an effort to describe the relation of God and humanity by grace. Chirico may not have been acquainted with Alfaro and probably not with Mühlen whose major works surfaced three years after Chirico's dissertation. It should be said that Chirico is not simplistic in his critique, nor is Mühlen. Each of the theories have relative merit and "partial failure." "Divine Indwelling," 119.

[108]Chirico, "Divine Indwelling," 120-131.

[109]B. Rey, "Trinité," 532.

[110]HGP, 273. See also his, "'Gottesbeweis' heute: Überlegungen zu einem personologischen Aufweis der Existenz Gottes," in Martyria, Leiturgia, Diakonia: Feschrift für Hermann Volk, ed. Otto Semmelroth (Mainz: Matthias-Grünewald Verlag, 1968), 48-53. The paradigm shift present in his thought on the theology is presented in outline form in; his disparagement of the loss of a holistic triune concept of grace in the Church since the Reformation in "Das Vorverständis von Person und die Evangelisch-Katholisch Differenz," Catholica 18 (1964): 108-142; his, "Soziale Geisterfahrung als Antwort auf eine einseitige Gotteslehre." in Erfahrung und Theologie des Heiligen Geistes (Munich: Kosel Verlag, 1974), esp. 260-272; and christologically presented in Die Veränderlichkeit Gottes als Horizont einer zukunftigen Christologie: Auf dem Wege zu einer Kreuzestheologie in Auseinandersetzung mit der altkirchlichen Christologie (Münster: Aschendorff, 1969). Found also in "Christologie in Horizont der Traditionelle Seinsfrage?" In Catholica 23 (1969): 205-279; of his many articles on the implications of the Triune 'Wir-akt' perhaps most impressive is "Charismatiches und Sakramentales Verständnis der Kirch: Dogmatische Aspekte der Charismatischen Erneuerung," Catholica 28:3 (1974): 169-187.

[111]Mühlen, "Person und Appropriation," 57. Mühlen is offering a differentiation of the traditional 'taxis'. The Spirit in his "contact function" (K. McDonnell) is the person of the Trinity which introduces humanity to God. Of course, the Father as aitia or pege is

modern times one must attribute to Mühlen's perspicuous construction is that he places at the center of salvation-history and the innertrinitarian existence, the person of the Spirit.[112] The 'Gross-Ich', as self-revealing means that there One Person in two Persons, is the same Person in many Persons.

In criticizing Mühlen one must keep in mind the service he is attempting to offer to the modern Church. He does not claim to have solved the intense problems resident in the theological notion of 'Person'. It is immediately evident that even though he adroitly ascertains the effect of Greek absolutistic categories he begins his discussion with a caveat that quite possibly undermines what follows. It would appear that in an effort to eschew the typical reaction of the Church to social analogies as tritheism Mühlen reveals his own form of the simplicity theory. In defining his view of 'oppositio relationis' Mühlen says, "One should use Person in a trinitarian framework as though 'Person' here is a substance of a spiritual center of the Act. In God there is only one substance and only one center of the act. Terminologically this would be conceived as "Nature."[113] Elsewhere the 'I' of the Father is closely related to the divine nature itself. Mühlen does not fully connect these ideas with the relational ontology which follows. It must be a reason for the compounds found later in Heilige Geist als Person; 'I-relation' and 'Thou-relation'.[114] However inconsistent Mühlen may be at this point it is to obfuscate the impact of his analogy to disallow the plethora of relational motifs which presuppose a radical individuation in the divine Persons. No one thinker has ever been able to exhaustively handle the paradox of unity and trinity. His emphasis on one divine consciousness does not completely undermine what follows rather, it is the typical recourse to escape the attack of

---

not challenged but the place and the work of the Spirit is less susceptible to dispensational interpretation. See the insightful review in Irenikon 54 (1981): 587-588.

[112]He refers to the Spirit as the 'causa personalis' but also as the 'Bundesgemässe sich-selbst-verhalten. See discussion GHP, 278-280.

[113]HGP, 2-3; 127-128. Bracken points to both these passages in his critique that Mühlen's "difficulties with the strict application of interpersonal categories to the members of the Trinity is due to his assumption that there is only one conciousness or self (selbst) within the Trinity. "The Holy Trinity as a Community of Divine Persons, II," 268. Of course, the vested interest in Bracken is the evolving notion of divinity implied by his process orientation, so that 'interpersonal' takes on a different meaning for him than a Ricardine or Nazianzen formulation.

[114]In a section dealing with the notional aspects of divine relations in Aquinas, Mühlen posits an 'Ich-relation' and in a discussion of Richard's 'amor mutuus' he gives an 'Du-relation' epithet to the Son. I would say the second term is an attempt to protect divine love from being "sourced" from more than one person, rather than its being eternal and perfect.

'tritheism'.[115] There are very few modern scholars who are willing to risk being misunderstood as promoting tritheistic claims in an effort to alter the radical solipsism of modernity's definition of nature and person. A possible response at this point might be to reconsider divine consciousness in terms other than the radical individualism of modernity. Three inseparable centers of love and knowledge and will might be a way of looking at the 'Gross-Ich' rather than self-donation in three related way. It is consistently asked of the social analogists if the category of community is possible in God. For Mühlen, the burden of proof lies on his view of one Person of the Trinity as community.[116]

Although there are reservations to be expressed regarding a methodology which relies so heavily on phenomenology and its implications for the understanding of the person of the Spirit, there is much to be be commended as well. Coffey refers to the "pronominalization" of the Trinity as problematic.[117] It is questionable whether the use of 'We' or 'We-Act is, in fact, sufficient to delineate the true personhood of the Spirit. Even though the 'Du' is a double category applying to both the Spirit and the Son the consistent lack of clarity on the personhood of the Spirit in aspects other than the divine Bond merely repeats the unclear direction offered by former thinkers.[118] It would appear that the principle of intertrinitarian love from Richard funds Mühlen's project only at certain points. The proclivity to excavate the dialogical "communication" analogy precludes full apprehension of the communitarian aspects in Richard especially pneumatologically.[119] If

---

[115]Hill, The Three-Personed God, 237

[116]Walter Siebel is another example of the modern reaction and response to the social analogy understood other than by relation. See his Der Heilige Geist als Relation: Eine Soziale Trintätslehre (Münster: Aschendorff, 1986). He approaches the idea of other-love as an expression of the primary, or "Urbild", self-love. Ibid., quoting J. Pieper. He questions Mühlen's use of 'relation' as importing something the Fathers did not intend. Ibid., 24. Siebel spends a considerable portion of his book on Mühlen, in fact, his presentation is a recapitulation of Mühlen's theses. Siebel feels that Richard is too anthropomorphic and thus loses its persuasive power, yet in his conclusion he disagrees with Mühlen's 'We-akt' for as he says, "Auch Vater und Sohn sind als Personen in den beiden anderen Personen." Ibid., 86, which sounds much like the Victorine's comments he negated just previously. Siebel's answer to a relational Trinity is 'perichoresis', but it is again a relatively empty concept if the Persons discussed are merely one in substance. Ibid., 86-98.

[117]Coffey, Grace: The Gift of the Holy Spirit, 34-35.

[118]John Milbank, "The Second Difference," 220. In a rather vitriolic critique of Mühlen, A. Patfoort questions whether he has read some of the Fathers correctly at all. See A. Patfoort, "La 'fonction personnelle' du Saint-Esprit." Angelicum 45 (1968): 325. He claims that the personalism of Mühlen, Richard et al. is "terribly ambiguous." Ibid., 318, 326.

[119]Schmaus may have Mühlen in mind where he writes,
Frequently personhood is identified with a relationality, with the ordering of the one to the other, thus with dialogue or the capacity for dialogue. As important as the capacity

one is to follow through with consummate love then the third Person must be more than a principle or a vinculum. Even if the appropriation of the Spirit indicates a conjoining of the Father and the Son that does not necessitate that the Spirit be less than the other Persons.

A thrust which is critical of Mühlen's and claims to offer new insight, is found in David Coffey, S.J., who has offered a supposedly complementary formulation to the traditional 'processional' model of the Trinity.[120] He, like Mühlen, is convinced that it demands a Trinity to explain Grace. In conjunction with the "outgoing" aspects of the traditional model Coffey's "circular" or "bestowal" model promises a more complete view of the trinitarian reality.[121] The former approach has tended toward subordinationism, even though Nicea and Athanasius sealed the identity of each person of the Trinity. In response to what Coffey deems as an inadequate model in itself and in the lineage of W. Kaspar and K. Rahner, he posits a methodology which posits an 'ascending' christology to coincide

---

for dialogue is for the understanding of the personal, still it is one-sided to allow the personal to be merged in the capacity for dialogue. It must be stressed that man, or the person, stands in himself and in his own initiative opens himself in relation to the other, in relation to the Thou. A man can open himself to another only when he is deeply founded in Being.

Dogma vol. 3, 156. Conversely, Sears feels that Richard does not do as adequate a job as Mühlen does in explaining communality. "Spirit: Divine and Human," 6.

[120]In "A Proper Mission of the Holy Spirit," Theological Studies 45 (1986): 227-250 he advocates a replacing of the model he seeks to complement in earlier works. His argument in "The Gift of the Holy Spirit," Irish Theological Quarterly 38:3 (1971): 202-223, is expanded in Grace: The Gift of the Holy Spirit (Sydney: Catholic Institute of Sydney, 1979). "The Incarnation of the Holy Spirit in Christ"," Theological Studies 45:3 (1984): 466-480. "The Palamite Doctrine of God: A New Perspective," St. Vladimir's Theological Quarterly 32:4 (1988): 329-358. "The Proper Mission of the Holy Spirit," Theological Studies 47 (1986): 227-250. Coffey is from St. Patrick's Seminary in Sydney, Australia. His views on the physical resurrection have caused investigation by the Holy See. Coffey is one of the few English-speaking scholars to adequately deal with Mühlen, even if critically.

[121]There is in Coffey a double movement in the Trinity: From the Father to the Son in the Spirit back to the Father and From the Father to the Spirit through the Son to the Father. See the summary the two models in Grace: The Gift of the Holy Spirit, 31. Summaries of the bestowal model can be found in Vincent Martin, "Reciprocal Relationships in Trinitarian Theology," Monastic Studies 17 (Christmas, 1986): 25. Edward Kilmartin, Christian Liturgy, vol. 1 Systematic Theology of Liturgy (Kansas City: Sheed & Ward, 1988), 124-134, also his extensive application of the bestowal model 170-176. See Coffey in the context of modern Catholic pneumatology and theology of worship in T. F. Koernke, "The Pneumatological Dimension of the Eucharist: The Contribution of Modern Catholicism on the Relationship Between Office, Eucharist, and Holy Spirit," Ph.D. dissertation, Univ. of Notre Dame, 1983, 54-71 (Mühlen, 72ff.); and Barbara Ann Finan, "The Mission of the Holy Spirit in the Theology of Karl Rahner," Ph.D. dissertation, Marquette Univ., 1986, 29-31, (Mühlen,10-11), 137-140.

with the traditional 'descending' doctrine of the Son.[122] The 'procession' model is critiqued for its inability to adequately deal with the personal differentiations of the Trinity since it tends toward Christocentrism.[123] The problem Coffey notes is that the essentialist position of the procession model places the trinitarian notional categories on a secondary plane, Coffey seeks to reverse the methodology. Yet, within the magisterial tradition there are hints that a bestowal concept is resident, though hidden by the overarching model. Coffey refers to Augustine's use of the Spirit as 'common' love where 'mutual' would have better described what he deems a contradiction in the Mühlen's logic.[124] Coffey does not agree with the position that the Spirit is a term of the mutual love of the Father and the Son, which results in a 'closed' view of the purpose for the spiration, so it is the loving itself between them that best indicates the Spirit's personhood.[125] Other than new terminology there is really little difference between Coffey's proposition and the 'psychological' and 'processional' traditions he disparages. Taking the basis that the Trinity is absolutely self-sufficient, he appropriates the theme of divine self-communication from Rahner which is a single self-bestowal in two modalities.[126] The Spirit is presented as the Gift of the Love of God, Father for Son, Son for Father, and God for humans.[127] There is still no sufficient answer for how that absolute notion of God's self-sufficient nature actually participates in mutual love. Coffey has not progressed beyond the processional model apparently. It would be quite fair to use the statement made in critique of Mühlen to assess Coffey's own work. "While it is not without merit, its value is considerably less than is claimed by the author."[128]

---

[122]He has incorporated the Rahnerian axiom, the unity of the immanent and economic Trinity as the basis of his claim that the proper theological method is from the world to God and never the other way around. Grace: The Gift of the Holy Spirit, 2-3. Contrast this with the presuppositions in chap. One of this work and the thought of von Balthasar, Theologik, vol. 2, 61.

[123]Kilmartin, Christian Liturgy, vol. 1, 108.

[124]Coffey, Grace: The Gift of the Holy Spirit, 6. We have attempted to explain some ways of approaching Augustine on these 'contradictions' in chap. Three. We agree with Coffey, that the unity model is threatened with contradiction when the manner of procession is broached in the psychological analogies, or procession model. He critiques Mühlen's use of common, in the 'Wir-akt' of the Spirit. He says 'mutual' is the best way to comprehend that relationship. Ibid., 36.

[125]Coffey, Grace: The Gift of the Holy Spirit, 36-37, 142-143.

[126]Coffey, Grace: The Gift of the Holy Spirit, 41.

[127]Coffey, Grace: The Gift of the Holy Spirit, 148-149.

[128]Coffey, Grace: The Gift of the Holy Spirit, 37.

III. Conclusion

Mühlen issues a call to re-examine the traditional philosophical reservations about the three Persons. He sees the need in present theology to allow the opera ad intra and the opera ad extra to mutually inform one another. It is his fundamental agreement with the Cappadocian and Ricardine concepts of divine Person in contradistinction from the philosophical ontologies of their day, which intriques us the most. In each, the disposition of self-bestowal, of immanent Other-orientation, determines the intra-trinitarian reality. The incommunicability of divine 'opposition' is not egocentric but 'exocentric', or better, a coinherent personal self-determination. As we have seen in each of the the three eras, the social analogy of the Trinity, despite all detractions from the magisterial theologians, is based upon the notion of 'person' in Trinity which includes a radical unity of three self-conscious inter-existent subjects. The oneness is comprised of the threeness and the trinal categories are always related to the mystery of the unity of the divine substance. Recently, Gunton has written:

> To be a person is to exist in mutually constitutive relations with other persons. Father, Son, and Spirit are what they are because they constitute and are constituted by each other by virtue of their free relatedness. It is sometimes suggested that their relatedness may be construed as a kind of conversation, due allowance being made for the metaphorical character of the language. The suggestion finds some support in Scripture. "The Word was with God, and the Word was God. He was in the beginning with God." This sounds very much like a kind of eternal, albeit metaphorical, conversation.[129]

---

[129]Colin Gunton, "Using and Being Used: Scripture and Systematic Theology," Theology Today 47:3 (October, 1990): 256. One immediately notes the similarity in this "conversation" metaphor and Mühlen's inter-trinitarian dialogue.

The response to self-existent love is
self-abnegating love. The refusal of
Himself is that in Jesus which
corresponds to the creation in
God...When he died on the cross,
He did that, in the wild weather of
His outlying provinces, in the
torture of the body of His
revelation, which He had done at
home in glory and gladness.

George MacDonald

Conclusion

From a variety of sources we have heard that modern thought is near bankrupt
regarding 'person' due to the prevalence of egocentric categories. It has been my hope in
this endeavor to accomplish a balanced appraisal of former theological discussion in a
comprehensive manner while dealing with the difficult questions which have been raised
by opponents of a relational thesis in the past and present. There is no doubt that there is
mystery behind the meaning of person. However, in a significant period demanding an
ethical and theological creativity surrounding personhood it would be wise to note the
continuities as well as the differences bequeathed to modernity by forebears whose interests
parallel our deepest longings.

It is quite common to find predicates of personhood such as 'rational individuality'
or 'psychological experience and consciousness'. Although these may be partially adequate,
theology and philosophy, primarily in the West have come to equate notions of intellectual,
psychological and moral qualities centered on the axis of consciousness with what it means
to be a person.[1] The end result is unavoidably a notion of self-determination which stems
from a fundamental isolationism. Personality is made the complex of a variety of human
individuum to the exclusion of the "Other" at an ontological, if not a politico-ethical level.[2]

It is my belief that the 'unity model' of the Trinity, with all of its much needed
reiteration in pointing to the absolute indivisibility of the Godhead, is at present in

---

[1] J. Zizioulas, "Human Capacity and Human Incapacity: A Theological Exploration of
Personhood," 406.

[2] A. Shutte from South Africa has produced some intriguing thoughts on this issue
in a critique of modern solipsism based upon J. Macmurray's personalistic philosophy:
"Indwelling, Intersubjectivity and God," Scottish Journal of Theology 32:2 (1979): 201-216; "A
Philosophy of the Human Person for Contemporary Theology," Journal of Theology for
Southern Africa 41 (Dec.1983): 70-77; "What Makes Us Persons," Modern Theology. 1:1
(1984): 67-79.

desparate need of the qualification, and embellishment possible in the sort of plurality model of which Richard of St. Victor is the 'locus classicus'. Instead of acknowledging the heuristic categories for a relational Trinity in the social analogy the Church has consistently denied its ontological reality while at another level advocating unfounded and unexplained relational characteristics in the Godhead (at a notional level) and in humanity. The premise in this work is that the discernment is skewed in comments such as Robinson's that "We cannot possibly make sense of the classical doctrine of the Trinity without deliberately eliminating the full and rich content of the term 'person' which fifteen centuries have bequeathed us."[3] The subsequent scholarship has perpetuated the misinformation that 'prosopon' and 'persona' carried absolutely no remnant of self-consciousness which is patently false. It was long before Descartes, in fact, it was prior to Boethius' day that the themes of relationality and self-conscious divine Persons were plausible analogies to point toward the mystery of the Trinity.

There is little doubt that the society in which we live is looking for answers to the problems of narcissistic and even solipsistic particularity, solutions to the cul-de-sac of private individuality, that 'incurvatum se' which shuts an individual up in oneself.[4] Self-help and self-actualization or fulfillment have not paid what they promised and never will. I do not agree with Pannenberg, with whom we started.[5] His statement reflects the unwitting assimilation of de Chardin's Impersonal God, although it is couched in the safety of the cognitive model. The theological commitment of many is that the issue of trinitarian distinction resides in neither person nor nature but in relation. A variety of terms point to the same ultimately monadic concept: Siebel's modal perichoresis, Bracken's 'occasions' of an evolving Trinity, Schoonenberg's Rahnerian statement that the Three, "face one another as persons in the history of salvation", A. Kelly's "sheer Being-in-Love" without any hint of community, or specified relationality, are all statements couched in a radical monotheism

---

[3]H. Wheeler Robinson, The Christian Doctrine of the Holy Spirit, 216-217; see also The Christian Experience of the Holy Spirit (London: Nisbet and Co., 1930), 246-266. Lynch notes that Robinson does not even mention prosopon "Prosopon and the Dogma of the Trinity," 128.

[4]Prophetic voices have been ignored at this point. I find Hannah Arendt's work particularly incisive on our culture. I was she who first pointed me to the context of the Cartesian axiom "I think, therefore, I am" which occurs in the context of doubt which casts new light on the "enlightenment" promised and praised in modernity. Rather than self-certainty modern persons have little more hope in themselves than "dubito ergo sum." The Human Condition, 279. See also William Barrett's Death of the Soul: From Descartes to the Computer (Garden City, New York: Anchor Press/ Doubleday, 1986).

[5]Chap. One, 1, 5.

but a questionable trinitarianism.*

Traditional trinitarianism saw that much more was a stake in capitulating to veiled modalisms or surreptitious subordinationisms. The early Church always bore in mind the analogical elements of prosopon and persona. Augustine did not illegally cross the line between exegesis and analogical thinking. Analogy was primarily for contemplation. Like the Cappadocians, the relationship of the three Persons produced logike latriae, reasoned worship. Yet that worship was centered on an ontological reality. They discerned the self-revealing, self-abnegating love of the perichoretic Godhead which brought to the alienated the visible expression of divine self-donation, a God-man. The co-inherent One continues to indwell the Church through the 'donum', the Holy Spirit who is the completion of the fullness of divine Love.[7] These energeia are nothing other than emanations apart from a relational source which clearly points to a single divinity in three whose basic nature is alterity.[8] It would not be too far-fetched to retroactively apply the words of John Macmurray in his philosophy of human personhood whose dynamic carries, though unspoken, the adumbration of a Christian view of relational reality if not an incipient triune form:

> We need one another to be ourselves. This complete and unlimited dependence of each of us upon the others is the central and crucial fact of personal existence. Individual independence is an illusion; and the independent individual, the isolated self, is a nonentity. Being nothing in ourselves, we have no value in ourselves....It is only in relation to others that we exist as persons.[9]

Athanasius, the Cappadocians, Hilary and Augustine would have agreed from both a divine and a human standpoint.

We have traced the major steps of this relational theme in the middle ages where it became immediately apparent that the Church chose categories which originally were not

---

[6]P. Schoonenberg, "Trinity - The Consummated Covenant: Theses on the Doctrine of the Trinitarian God," Studies in Religion 5 (1975-1976): 114. Siebel, Heilige Geist als Relation, 97; Bracken, "Subsistent Relation: Mediating Concept for a New Synthesis?" Journal of Religion 64:2 (1984): 198. A. Kelly, The Trinity of Love: A Theology of the Christian God, (Wilmington: Michael Glazier, 1989), 182.

[7]The Holy Spirit is often spoken of in these contexts in ways which curtails the impact of defending his co-equal personhood. It is difficult to perceive of three on the same plane when one is referred to as 'bond' or 'Love of the Father for the Son.' However, I believe that these early thinkers had the consubstantiality of the Three as a foundational principle.

[8]L. Rougier, "Le sens des termes 'Ousia', 'Hypostasis' et 'Prosopon' dans les controverses trinitaires Post-Nicéenes," Revue de l'Histoire des Religions 73 (1916): 183.

[9]John MacMurray, Persons in Relation, 211. My comment on the trinitarian basis is not verifiable externally. He reveals however, a world-view which is decidedly Christian in form and the basis of his concept of person is found at the only source of absolute relationality, the Trinity, or it is nothing more than a rehashing of egocentric modern theology.

exclusively unity focused. One finds there were strong relational elements interspersed with the metaphysical and philosophical definitions which were produced. However, an individual rational interpretation of person, both divine and human soon took on more static notions than the original thinkers ever intended. Except for a few key theologians, the paradigm set by Boethius and Thomas Aquinas has remained in force till today.

In a bold step outside of the Boethian line in which theologians would find themselves entrenched for centuries, Richard of St. Victor, moved from the predominant schema of a cognitive ordering of the Trinity to the analogy of a rational yet, interpersonal, communion, in which each member was ontologically grounded in an incommunicable existence (i.e. that which is distinctly attributable to each: Fatherhood, Sonship, Spirit. That incommunicability did not exist by delineation but came from the divine center of a mutuality in one another within divinity. At no point could one Person of the Trinity be "touched" without the other Two being inseparably and necessarily related.

Within a quarter of a century, Thomas, while deepening Boethius's definition and maintaining Richard's view of differentiation, dispelled the social view of divine persons as easily as the Church had squelched the historically prior relational implications of both Gilbert of Poitiers and Joachim of Fiora. Although this century has seen the arrival of an upsurgence of relational discussions about God, they have been and are yet perceived as less than adequate analogies. There is a distinct bias in higher theological circles against entertaining the social analogy.

It seems that the time is right to take some risks here, of the same nature of the self-giving reflected upon in Richard. We appear to be at an Archimedean point in our generation concerning God-talk and the cogency of personal analogies. The Church is reacting to the implications of monolithic interpretation of divine reality. If God is personal, and is so not merely as a projection of our values or ideals then what do we mean by propositions such as, God is Love? One modern possibility that offers the most cogent coincision of Scripture, reason, tradition and experience is the position which discerns between talk about a God who is a person, or personal and the radical differences implied by positing a God who is three persons in, analogically-speaking, a "communal" reality. Whatever terms are used to describe that divine relationship, this position continually points to the indications from revelation and tradition on the inseparable all-consuming love of three distinct Persons.

If the determinative element of existence is divine interpersonal love, then reality takes on a new face. Colin Gunton has shown the transforming impact this position has on our concept of power and knowledge.[10] Process, Liberation, Black, and Feminist

---

[10]C. Gunton, Enlightenment and Alienation (Grand Rapids: Eerdmans, 1985), 76-77, 88-89, 96-97, 100-101. From this thesis another theme has surfaced in Gunton's work, quite similar to the recapitulatio of the early Church. He views sacrifice as a way to view divine

theologies are replete with the concept of relationality. However, when pushed to the corner very few of them base that inclination within the context of orthodox trinitarianism. Our world is far too critical to accept half a truth, so it is always a risk to point to a past delineation of interrelatedness in divine personhood. Richard's insights carry what Torrance calls, "onto-relational" aspects which provide a substantial basis for human interdependence and for disallowing an insidious dualism to which the notion of an undifferentiated God ultimately descends.[11] Unlike the scholastics he saw no division between real life and the mystery of divine love. Divine personhood was an metaphysical statement. If we do not at least look at these insights it would occur to me that the question still remains as to which is the darker age.

The lack of clarity on this subject directly impinges upon the viability and value of the term 'person' in theological contexts. In light of the present stalemate between the threat to de-personalize God which, if historically researched might coincide directly with a concomitant de-humanization, and the equal danger resident in advocating a tri-theism which conversely feeds a rampant individualism on the human side, there is a need to combat these trends.[12] It is encouraging, as de Margerie has pointed out that some recent discussions on the Trinity have produced analogies in the areas of familial intersubjectivity, ecclesial intersubjectivity and personal intrasubjectivity.[13]

The modern categories of person find expression in the practical spheres, the

---

reality as well as giving meaning to the entire plan of redemption. See "Christ the Sacrifice: Aspects of the Language and Imagery of the Bible," in L.D. Hurst and N.T Wright, eds. The Glory of Christ in the New Testament: Studies in Christology (Oxford: Clarendon Press, 1987), 228-238. See also his The Actuality of Atonement (Grand Rapids: Zondervan, 1991).

[11]Torrance feels Richard is a pivotal figure in much the same way we have supported here. See Reality and Evangelical Theology (Philadelphia: Westminster Press, 1982), 42-43. Reality and Scientific Theology (Edinburgh: Scottish Academic Press, 1985), 174-178.

[12]Louis Dumont, Essays on Individualism: Modern Ideology in Anthropological Perspective (Chicago: Univ. of Chicago Press, 1986), 60-103. Or see his perspicacious diachronic assessment in "A Modified View of our Origins: the Christian Beginnings of Modern Individualism," in M. Carrithers and Steve Collins. eds, The Category of the Person (New York: Cambridge Univ. Press, 1985), 93-121. Louis Dupré has made similar comments on the relationship betwee a view of divine reality and humanity's view of itself.

[13]These terms are found in Bertrand de Margerie's The Christian Trinity in History trans. by Edmund J. Fortman (Still River, Massachusetts: St. Bede's Publication, 1982) 274-324, where they are clearly explained. They are based upon the analogical application of the love between members of a family, the intense unity of the Body of Christ and the personal bond which de Margerie sees in the 'psychological' analogies. His view of Aquinas is apparent, Richard is given little notice.

histrionic, the physical, the juridical as well as in the ethical domain.[14] But these are based on the other esoteric delineations which interest us here. Depending upon the discernible components of personhood, the metaphysical notion of person has been seen in two ways, which are closely aligned with what has preceded, the substantial, comprised of rationality and free will and the relational, which views knowing and willing in a self related to other selves.[15] Although, the latter is found in various forms among dialogical philosophers, existentialist, phenomenologists and some theologians, there is little doubt that self-consciousness is a, if not the, fundamental vehicle for indentifying personhood in our time. In the crush of modern philosophical debates the relational has been pushed to the margin. The question remains, based on linguistic and historical analysis, does person automatically necessitate a modern notion of self-consciousness?

David Brown has pointed to part of the problem as a linguistic deficiency which both feeds and reveals other inadequacies. It is important to note the internal distinctions languages can or cannot make. For instance, the French, **individualisme** does reflect the Enlightenment categories that our term individual most often does, but the German **individualität** was developed in a way that reflected the need for a social unit in order for a proper understanding of the individual to transpire. Our term "self-consciousness" admits of autonomous psychological reflection, while the similar German **selbstbewußt**, self-recognition, even in its use by the German transcendentalists can only result in positive self-worth if grounded in a social context.[16] It is a related problem when we look at the rigid subjectivism which is applied to 'person' where the Church chose 'persona', 'prosopon', 'subsistentia', and 'exsistentia' because they include individuated characteristics within a larger framework of relationality.

The linguistic and philosophical results from the Cartesian period's re-definition of 'person' has been that modern Western culture defines personhood as pre-eminently

---

[14]One might add zoological and grammatical to this list. For current discussions from a philosophical standpoint see Jenny Teichman, "The Definition of Person," Philosophy 60 (1985): 175-185. David Braine's The Reality of Time and the Existence of God: The Project of Proving God's Existence (Oxford: Clarendon Press, 1988), argues for relationality as being the hallmark of personhood. David Grant, "Personal and Impersonal Concepts of God: A Tension Within Contemporary Christian Theology," Encounter 49:2 (Spring, 1988): 79-91. Grant outlines five basic uses of person in modern theology. A list of the major players in this discussions reveals how crucial an issue personhood has been: I. Kant, G.W.F. Hegel, J. Locke, G. W. Leibniz, Thomas Reid, J. Fichte, M. Scheler, M. Heidegger, Wilhelm Dilthey, E. Durkheim, G. Marcel, Marcel Mauss, Renouvier, F.R. Tennant, A.N. Whitehead, E. Levinas, M. Nédoncelle, R. Strawson, D. Parfit

[15]W.R. O'Connor's helpful analysis is found in "The Concept of the Person in St. Augustine's De Trinitate, Augustinian Studies 13 (1982), 134.

[16]David Brown, "Trinitarian Personhood and Individuality," in Feenstra and Plantinga eds. Trinity, Incarnation and Atonement (Notre Dame: Univ. of Notre Dame Press, 1989), 48-78.

exemplified in self-reflective consciousness. Until very recently this modern preoccupation with the self has gone virtually unchallenged. In a variety of fields there are glimmers of a refutation of this thesis. While some of these take the opposite pole, i.e., the deconstruction of the unity of the self altogether, there is a strong counteractive force in the those for whom the "other", or the relational is no longer foreordained to a peripheral status. It is taking Western theology a long time to shed its assimilation of individualistic categories which were not a part of its original birthright. Thus, by way of example, in spite of passages which would seem to claim the opposite, this century's leading exponent of a return to trinitarianism reflects a culture's bias; Barth's transcendent Ego is virtually a self-reflective unity whose logical connection with the world as self-revelation is threatened by consequence of its inherent self-enclosure.

If the basis of the Christian doctrine of the Trinity is an overflow of love, an other-orientation, that foundation challenges at least four centuries of solipsistic proclivity. We cannot, in reaction, deny the power of self-understanding, but it must be placed in a "perichoretic" context. Personal agency, potentiality and self-reflection may be argued as prefatory to community, but if it is to maintain its highest value, it must also issue from its indwelling that community.

Last, we have confronted in our historical-theological analysis the tendency to settle for a unity rather than a tri-unity. The creeds have affirmed perpetually that the Father is God, the Son is God, the Holy Spirit is God, yet they are not three Gods but one God. Since Augustine, western trinitology has been obsessed with the unity of God. Whether drawn from Platonic simplicity theory or from a questionable view of the Aristotelian substance, the implication has been that differentiation in the highest being or form equalled imperfection in that being. This onenness element has wound its way so tightly around the core of Western theology that it is nearly non-extractable. Any deviation in the affirmation of the absolute philosophically-based oneness of the Trinity has become suspect. With this has come a plethora of theological attempts to make human personhood meaningful apart from a notion of divine Persons.

In exploring the coherence of this claim or lack of it Cornelius Plantinga has presented a list of analogies, which outline the three major ways in which the Church has endeavored to circumvent contradiction, each of which tie into the argument of this thesis.[17]

---

[17]I am borrowing the themes from Plantinga's analogies found in "The Threeness/Oneness Problem of the Trinity," Calvin Theological Journal 23:1 (April, 1988): 37-53. He suggests the analogies of: 1) three persons who claim they are one - paradoxical, 2)one person with three roles - modalism, 3)three persons in one family - tritheist. Of course, he transforms the third into the idea of a social Trinity. See this even more strongly put in his, "The Perfect Family." Christianity Today (March 4, 1988): 24-27. I find Plantinga one of the most refreshing of a new cadre of trinitarians who are making great strides toward a modern apologia for the possible contemporary cogency of traditional views of the Three-in-One. Hans Urs von Balthasar, T.F. Torrance, David Brown and Colin

The first, is an attempt to make sense out of equivocation. What does the Church mean by One who is three Persons but not Three as we know three. We really mean a new sort of One. Plantinga calls this the "Incoherent analogy."[18] Our discussion of substance in chapter Two has formed the basis of much of this difficulty.[19] It is very difficult to release a notion of undifferentiated oneness no matter what the implications are for theological interpretation. If divine substance does admit the inclusion of persons then the incoherent argument is diffused.

The second analogy critiques the Modal viewpoint. I have tried to show the variety of ways this analogy has been used in the major junctures of Church history in subtly destructive ways. Anywhere that one finds it ascendancy there appears a concomitant loss of the meaning of human personhood or a distortion which results in radical individualism. No matter how it is packaged and or how many caveats to the contrary, the claim that God is one Person who plays three roles, or reveals in three modes, falls very close to the ancient heresy of modalism. Mühlen's work is an attempt to regain what was lost when personhood lost its appeal and rational qualities alone defined the Persons of the Trinity.

This chapter has pointed to several exquisite expositions or adumbrations of this philosophically cogent, if otherwise flawed interpretation. Divine Person is thus understood as a solitary consciousness, eternally existing in three expressions, modes, or manners, or relations. While I am sure it can be argued that my preference for the term person is a bit obscurantistic and that "modes" and "manners" can refer to instances, particularizations of the Trinity, my concern is that even if these manifestations are allowed, all too often, they find their ground in the existence of a primordial unitary Person. What is lost in the dust, are the communitarian indications which are evident in Scripture and which tradition has viewed as a meaningful inheritance in spite of its evident problems.

Gunton have been mentioned as thinkers who, in the main, are attempting the same sort of reinvestigation of the relational analogy of trinitarian personhood. Interestingly, a number of these defenders are philosophers and not theologians. L. Howe,"Ontology, Belief and the Doctrine of the Trinity," Sophia (Melbourne) 20 (1981): 5-16; C. Stephen Layman, "Tritheism and Trinity," Faith and Philosophy 5:3 (July, 1988), 291-298; A.P. Martinich, "Identity and Trinity," Journal of Religion 58 (April, 1978): 169-181; R. Swinburne, "Could there be more than One God?" Faith and Philosophy 5:3 (July, 1988): 225-241; L. Zagzebski, "Christian Monotheism," Faith and Philosophy 6:1 (January, 1989): 3-18; and P. Van Inwagen, "And Yet They are Not Three Gods but One God," in Philosophy and the Christian Faith, ed. Thomas V. Morris, University of Notre Dame Studies in the Philosophy of Religion: 5 (Notre Dame: Univ. of Notre Dame Press, 1988).

[18]Nineteenth century unitarians and modern Rahnerians, among others, suggest that what is at stake here basically is a contradiction in mathematics.

[19]See pages 62-81.

One indication of foul play in the present notion of God resistent to the relational definition, is immediately evident from a survey of the structure of recent theological works. Normally, after chapter upon chapter of different levels of modalism, the implication or praxis chapters, which are the places in which the author's normally forge the Church's self-definition as unmistakably social, advocating and pontificating on mutuality, advocating intersubjectivity, and covenant fellowship. It will be argued, that these truths are based on a perichoresis of supra-personal perfect cognition or divine volition but the theologians presented in this work do not see that as a viable explanation of the Christian worldview.[20]

If it is the case that a mode is both the object and subject of co-equal divine love then it seems that 'mode' is a modern word for 'person', and thus we really have not bettered the earliest tradition that we accuse so quickly of "cryptic tritheism". Even after regarding all the drawbacks the term "person" may have, "modes" and "manners" have equally been socially conditioned by some rather disturbing modern accoutrements. Or we are basing this high notion of human relationships as criteria in themselves and not drawing them out as an implication of a perfect Creator? In a real sense, modalism posits a God that is less than the creatures who in their relationships we so often claim are a reflection of the Trinity. Even within all the subtle interjections concerning the mode of the Father loving himself in the subsistence of the Son, it is incumbent upon those who advocate "modes" and "manners" advocates to show how one can cogently speak of both an active and a passive love in God which supports both the notions of self-love and alterity.

The third analogy Plantinga discerns is the Social. It is for him, as for me, the most cogent choice given the facts we now have.[21] This is the stance which we have seen

---

[20]See King-Farlow's article "Is the Trinity a Logical Absurdity," Sophia (Melbourne) 22 (1983): 37-42. John Thurmer's "The Analogy of the Trinity," Scottish Journal of Theology 34:6 (1981): 509-515, and Detection of the Trinity (Exeter: Paternoster Press, 1984). Plantinga is perspicacious in his confrontation with the modalism of modern Christianity. He questions whether modes, from Barth or Rahner, can love themselves much less love each other, "Threeness/Oneness Problem," 49.

[21]Plantinga's Princeton dissertation was focused on this analogy. The major modern thinkers from this school came out of Britain. Originally their concepts were formed to counteract a resurgent modalism which emulated the 'emanationism' of earlier centuries. April Armstrong, has produced a helpful introduction and critique of C.C.J. Webb, L. Thornton, L. Hodgson and C. Lowry in, "The Social Analogy of the Trinity in Four Twentieth-Century Anglican Theologians," Ph. D. dissertation, Fordham Univ., 1973. Proper as it may have been to confront the arid implications of British Idealism, the Social Analogists grounded much of their data on experience. Here we see a similarity to the way Richard of St. Victor has been percieved. (Most Social Analogists draw upon Richard, but choose to find their support in more well known thinkers.) The place of most misunderstanding pertains to the conflation of 'persona' in tradition and the modern understanding of "subjective consciousness." In a effort to make trinitarianism relevant the elements of extreme individualization were incorporated hastily.

throughout Church history and in some of the major figures, to certain degrees, of this work. As we have seen in chapter One, the early Church discerned a unique relationship between the rabbi Jesus and "Abba", Father. The Paraclete was no longer offered for particular national needs but was offered freely to every believer; a distinct entity whose ministry was a reminder of the physical presence of Christ and the meticulous grace of the Father, now in ubiquitous and immediately accessible spiritual form. Early in the doxologies, baptismal formulations and discussions of the Church the Three were recognized as co-equal members of the Godhead, while maintaining an intractable monotheism. The Church could not elude the implication that in God, the Three are One, at least since the work of the Cappadocian Fathers and Augustine The problem came in maintaining a coherent notion of oneness.

We have discussed the ambiguity of Augustine, long acknowledged as the source of the dubiously named "psychological analogies" but who is not often quoted from the climactic Bk. 15 of his De Trinitate. After the herculean effort in explaining the oneness of the three; he, quite unlike most scholars, ending twenty years of reflection, critiques his own methodology as inadequate, and then using the term which he said was only to keep him from total silence, [22] We have viewed this type of text in Augustine from several directions recognizing that part of the problem lies in the fact that he carried with him an excessive Neoplatonic background which did not allow the notion of a differentiaed substance. Our work in chapter Two was designed to bring into question the monolithic interpretation of 'substance' in the Greek philosophers. There are even indications now that Aristotle never intended "primary substance" to be the undifferentiated Absolute which has been promulgated as the highest interpretation possible for ousia.[23] The question is far from being settled but it is safe to say that Augustine, and subsequently the Western Church through the Boethian-Thomistic influence was nearly irreparably marred by this myopic interpretation. The unity model became the spectacles through which the Church viewed scriptural indications of tri-unity and the doctrine of God. Not only was the world outside the Church confused but the majority of Christians were mystified as well.

If, as Augustine, Boethius, Aquinas, Barth and Rahner claim, persons and attributes are identical with the divine essence, then the Church ought not to claim to be trinitarian. Niebuhr is right, Christians are only a peculiar sort of monotheists. The challenge to this

---

[22]This reflects Plantinga's fundamental agreement with the evidence presented in chap. Three, 146-166. He uses the same passage in Bk. 15 we looked at in chap. Three, where Augustine acknowledges that each of the "persons is a rememberer, a thinker, a lover, a willer." Plantinga, "The Threeness/Oneness Problem," 44. It is refuted emphatically by C. Gunton in "Augustine, The Trinity, and the Theological Crisis," 41-58, who feels that Augustine's ontology was fallacious and therefore disallowed any true rendering of trinitarian 'Person'.

[23]Chap. Two, 68-76.

perennial monadic tendency in the Church always lies in a reassertion of the "plain meaning" of the claims the authors of the New Testament made regarding Christ and the person of the Holy Spirit. The councils do not indicate God as simple object. Despite the apophatic dualistic tendencies of the Eastern Fathers, they reveal a dynamic Trinity that continues to threaten the West's incipient static theology. It is clear that the Western Church did not appropriate the insights of 'perichoresis' adumbrated in the Cappadocians and explicated later.[24]

Aquinas reveals the same sort of difficulty, promoting an intimate Trinity, yet Thomas claims adamantly that each person is the whole divine essence. Following Augustine as he was interpreted by Boethius, any incoherence is subsumed under the category of "relation" among the persons. Each person is identical with a divine relation. Thus follows the construct of five notions, four real relations, three persons, two processions, one God. In Aquinas, Divine differentiation can be neither accidental, nor substantial, thus only relative differences suffice for Western trinitology.[25] To advocate three Persons while maintaining this undifferentiated view of the divine essence makes it inevitable that one must advocate some sort of God beyond God, or a quaternity. This has profoundly negative consequences for Biblical interpretation and Christian ontology.

Thomas strives to maintain a logical distinction, and "relations of opposition" but in the end his relations, paternity and filiation are really the same as the divine essence. Fundamentally it is the proposal of one person, unless he means that the three are distinct instances of Godness, which is what the social trinitarians have said all along.[26] If relation, alone is the fundamental ontological category, it can "end up as an undialectical notion of original hierarchy."[27] The category of 'Person' saves that emphasis from obscure polarities.

---

[24]Cf. Boethius's analysis of Augustinian categories in the former's De Trinitate for as example of this.

[25]Even more strongly stated at the Fourth Lateran Council, (1215) "tres simul personae, ac singillatim quaelibet earundem: et ideo in Deo solummodo Trinitas est, non quaternitas; quia quaelibet trium personarum est illa res, videlicet substantia, essentia seu natura divina: quae sola est universorum principium." Denzinger, 804. Neuner and Dupuis, 805 (319) The second half of this can be rendered, "each of the three persons are that one thing (or, one simple thing), namely essence, substance or nature, is that thing; that is the divine substance, which alone is source of all things."

[26]Cf. Lonergan's "three centers of one consciousness," which might be compared to the tapping of three terminals into a mainframe. The problem here is the denial of the Church's understanding of the Persons. Would the Father know himself as Father? This option is does not incorporate the data properly. The relationship of a believer to the Trinity then must ultimately be directed to that original "trans-personal" or "super-personal" being.

[27]J. Milbank's critique of Kasper in The Second Difference: For a Trinitarianism Without Reserve," Modern Theology 2:3 (1986), 219.

The Christian tradition has understood Jesus is more than God's loving self-revelation. He is a person who reflects that love. Incorporating what we have seen from Mühlen, the Spirit is also a viable distinct member of the Trinity. The relationship of the Son and the Spirit to the Father merits the recognition of more than a relatedness in God, but also a necessary knowledge-through-this-relatedness.[28] A relational conception of the Trinity in this view is the intimate interpenetrating, the co-inexisting of three fully divine incommunicable entities, unified by love and will, and by their mutual and individual possession of the whole divine nature.[29] This Oneness reveals the same sort of dynamism possible in the Hebrew concept of unity. It is not a Stoic solitude but a perichoretic compenetration. As Mühlen enforces this he emphasizes the inter-personal communication of each to the other. Each partakes and possesses the divine nature without extinguishing their own personal exsistence, the 'proprieties' which distinguishes that person from the other two. Thus each person can say I and yet that I is intimately constituted by the other "I's". Each "I" is eternally divine and is not an "I" without that essential relationship which defines the Person.

Part of the problem in modern theologian's inability to comprehend the intent of the Social analogy seems to be a recurrent tendency to underestimate the minds of our forebears, they knew the viscissitudes of tritheism yet retained talk of persons for more than expediency. Yet, the intention of both Barth and Rahner and their theological disciples is quite clear, despite claim to the contrary, that the early fathers were modalistic, since they did not have the sort of Enlightenment and modern philosophical categories that we do, especially concerning individuality. To claim that the relationalists are guilty of tritheism is a gross historical generalization.

Tertullian's flamboyant style and fiery wit may have not offered a systematic approach to the problem but at least in one place as he raked Praxeas over the coals, he says that one divine monarchy does not necessitate one monarch, just as several persons administrate a human monarchy, like a king and his son, so in God the administration is

---

[28]J. Milbank, "The Second Difference: For a Trinitarianism Without Reserve," 219.

[29]Plantinga writes,
Each member is a person, a distinct person, but scarcely an individual or separate person. For in the divine life there is no isolation, no insulation, no secretiveness, no fear of being transparent to another. Hence there may be penetrating, inside knowledge of the other as other, but as co-other, loved other, fellow.
"Threeness/Oneness Problem," 50. He uses some jarring terms to carry his point. He speaks of the sharing the divine, or "generic," nature, or deriving life from the Father as a "quasi-genetic" reality. Ibid., 50,51.

shared.[30] It was modalistic and dynamistic monarchians had to face Novation; the Arians were force to confront the Cappadocians and Hilary. According to the orthodox thinkers, the Triune Persons were the same in kind, and were attributed full deity, without reserve. That is why the Cappadocians hesitated on the use of the Latin "persona", even if Jesus could be spoken of in some way as the one who, "forth" (per) - "sounded" (sonare) the divine and the human in some perfect way, they were concerned about its lack of ontological content. They saw the tendency in Latin thought to equate character with individual idiosyncracies, and to suppose that this is what distinguishes the three persons. The Cappadocian view of person is a corrective at that point, character and role were not to be viewed as distinct for the divine essence but rather as the revelation of a mutual indwelling.

What transpired was an ontic revolution, person (prosopon) is the means by which divine being is realized. Real Persons constitute the divine nature, they participate as individuated sharers in a unity which they "compose". In opposing an implied hierarchy of divine nature somehow comprising three persons, the Cappadocians distinguished that a divine Person was not an adjunct category, one that was second in priority, but was the substance of substance, the very expression of being, personal being. Thus the three persons made up what up to that point had been being quâ being. The three Persons, no more and no less, constituted the source of all being, and inversely, all being is traced back to the three.[31] Yet, without a hint of volitionally advocated tritheism in any text we possess.

If we follow the course directed by the Cappadocians and Richard of St. Victor, Divine substance is redefined. Substance is not a complex of essential properties, three who share a group of attributes or properties. Both of these opinion end up in modalistic interpretation.[32] On the other hand, we have argued that the idea of absolute oneness of substance existing as a concrete particular is counter-productive to aligning oneself with the consensual theology of the Church. We are left with Richard's "lonely God" in some sort

---

[30]Ad Praxean 3. Plantinga, "Threeness/Oneness Problem, 13, Harnack's claim of a univocal use of 'person' is fallacious if Tertullian's usage is contextualized. He makes the term do some very unique things in Ad Praxean. See E. Evans introduction to Ad Praxean for Tertullian's use of person. Tertullian's Treatise Against Praxeas, ed. with an intro., trans., and comm. Ernest Evans (London: S. P. C. K., 1948), 47.

[31]Zizioulas, Being as Communion, 36ff, 40ff, esp n. 37 for summary of ontological priority of person over substance. See also "Human Capacity and Human Incapacity," 404ff.

[32]In correspondence with C. Plantinga I was directed to Stephen Layman's work. From a less than orthodox approach he succeeds in cogently defending a dynamic view of divine substance. See his, "An Ontology for Trinitarian Theories." Los Angeles (1978). (Mimeographed) "Tritheism and the Trinity." Faith and Philosophy. 5:3 (July 1988): 291-299. One will notice at once the similarity between these two thinkers.

of monistic aloofness. In contrast, the classical theologians had in their purview a Being comprised, for lack of a better symbol, of persons in relation. Compare Basil's statement:

> He who receives the Father virtually receives at the same time both the Son and the Spirit; for it is in no wise possible to entertain the ideas of severance or division, in such a way as that the Son should be thought of apart from the Father, or the Spirit disjoined from the Son. But the communion and the distinction apprehended in Them are, in a certain sense, ineffable and inconceivable, the continuity of nature being never rent asunder by the distinction of the hypostases, nor the notes of prior distinction confounded in the community of essence.[33]

This may be one reason why the magisterial theologians traditions have found the analogy of marriage stimulating for beginning to comprehend the intention within a revealed Trinity, as well as the understanding of all relationships. For marriages are not just relations, and they are not just concrete entities, but they are as Layman notes, "metaphysically composite," a special sort of relation which transcends other approximate forms.[34] So the Divine persons exist in a special sort of relationship, conceived on analogies with intimate personal relationships present in the best of human relationships. What intimate relationships provide for analogically is the maintenance of the central element of relationality does not abrogate the profound unity of the Trinity. The differences of course, pertain to all the factors known and unknown in any relationship between the infinite and finite. But, at base it must be as clearly stated as in J. A. T. Robertson's "Thou Who Art," "Even the Divine personality is unthinkable in isolation; God can only be conceived as a person if He has from all eternity made His counterpart as free as Himself."[35]

Mutual self-giving and interdependence, perichoretic prosopa, incommunicable existents, these are all heuristic categories in the theology of divine personhood.[36] These divine 'stances' include total freedom, absolute equality, a will that is inseparable but which is a part of the coinherent reality of the Three. There is a radical self-disposition, an interexistence that admits of no autonomy due to the foundation of perfect intersubjective love. Autonomy is not found in the Trinity.

Dealing with the charges of a tritheistic division in the social relation model is the constant fare of its adherents. David Brown offers the analogy of conscious yet unself-

---

[33]Basil, Letters, 38:4, NPNF2 vol. 8, 139.

[34]C. Stephen Layman, "Tritheism and Trinity," 295.

[35]Quoted in Alistair Kee, The Roots of Christian Freedom, 59, from Robertson's dissertation, p. 24.

[36]In reiteration, 'heuristic' is used in this work as a term to indicate a relationalistic epistemology. It is not used in the way that Bernard Lonergan or Nicholas Lash do indicating "rules of speech" only. See David Brown's critique in "Wittgenstein against the Wittgensteinians: A Reply to Kenneth Surin on The Divine Trinity." Modern Theology 2:3 (1986): 266.

conscious activities, those which we engage in constantly that involve our action without prior reflection. There are things that we do that come naturally, as a member of a specific society, without prior thought. Or from another tack, the immediate response of the human when another is endangered is a critique of the entire modern notion of person, and in a finite way expressive of the deepest communality we know, the Trinity. I am at my most deeply committed when I am concentrating on the needs of another, on one who now constitutes, in a large measure, my own self-perception, and at the same time I am at my least self-reflective stage.[37]

Could these be ruminations, or what Peter Berger has called "signals of Transcendence"?[38] Of a divine "society" conscious of logically distinct individuals yet whose self-consciousness is comprised as a whole only in their co-inherence, their perfect unity? This is not what Rahner means by "three centers of self-consciousness," but rather the consciousness of three persons mutually mediating that unity which is a result of their perichoretic, and perfect love. Only in the Triune God is the notion of individuality transcended. It is in the Trinity that the One and the Many question is satisfied.

"Coinherence," Torrance writes, "applies fully to the three divine persons as conscious of one another in their distinctive otherness and oneness."[39] 'Person', and the satellite of qualifying terms, incommunicable, individuated, ex-sisting, and rational nature, is not only the best possible heuristic symbol to date for referring to the divine mystery of the Triune Godhead, it speaks to the center of reality in a coherent fashion if understood from an historical and a theological position.

Soren Kierkegaard, once penned this criticism, "To me the theological world is like the road along the coast on a Sunday afternoon during the races - they storm past one another, shouting and yelling, and when at last they arrive, covered with dust and out of

---

[37]Brown, "Trinitarian Personhood and Individuality," 48-78.

[38]This is the phrase that Berger uses as a basis for his book "A Rumor of Angels: Modern Society and the Rediscovery of the Supernatural," (Garden City, NY: Doubleday Anchor Books, 1970), 52ff. I am again indebted to David Brown for pointing me to a sociological study of an Eskimo sub-culture by Rom Harré, Personal Being: A Theory for Individual Psychology (Cambridge: Harvard Univ. Press, 1984), 85-89. The group he studied revealed a more mature attitude to personhood in their language; a perception quite unlike our own. Harré found that of two pronominal suffixes, "I" and "not-I," the "I" suffix was not an indicator of personal identity but was primarily locative. Thus personhood in that subculture was understood in terms of substantialized relations, with the result in an extraordinary degree, the "Eskimos seem to be influenced by their fellows. When one weeps, they all weep: when one laughs they all laugh." They may have something to say to more "civilized" cultures who regard self-reflection as fundamental to enlightened societies and whose philosophy of solisistic personhood has only seen the de-personalization of numerous sectors of modern culture.

[39]Torrance, "Ecumenical Consensus on the Trinity," 347.

breath - they look at each other and go home."⁴⁰ There is too much at stake here it seems to merely re-enact, like some mythic rite, that all-too-typical scenario. I do not feel it is possible to overestimate the importance of a proper understanding of the Trinity. The particular approach taken will affect every theological and ethical adjudication. "It is liguistically demonstrable that no one meaning of the word "person" ever entirely replaces or eclipses other attendant meanings."⁴¹ Although the modern notion of self-consciousness may be difficult to handle in trinitarian theology we have no warrant in ejecting a proximate suggestion which might deepen our understanding of the cogency of the Perfect Love based upon the doctrine of the Trinity. Thus, to maintain that trinitarian persons are just that without equivocation we must first acknowledge that they are so, not in the sense of modern self-consciousness, autonomous agency, or potency bearing substances, but with the conscious, co-inherent, perfect sociality intended by the term since its inception, conservatively speaking, in the third century if not before.

So St. Teresa of Avila reveals a perspicacity that supercedes the keenest of minds where she accentuated that the unity of the Trinity is infinitely more in its oneness that any other subjective, individual reality and likewise, the distinctions within the Trinity are insuperably more real than any human threesome.⁴² Love and relatedness are most perfectly defined by the inner life of the Trinity and all of creation can serve, in limited ways, in the expression of that reality. The Church is absolutely dependent upon God, for it is only characterized by love but the source of that love is a God who in God's self is love.

If personal love is the key to understanding the purpose and the extent to which Augustine delves into the meaning of the the Trinity then it must be said that God alone is truly personal. Brunner has said:

We are to believe in God as Love; this means we are to have unity in duality, in a duality which has to be constantly overcome by faith. God is not simply love. He **defines** himself as love....Only in this way can we think the personality of God. Only the God in Three Persons is truly personal. The non-Trinitarian God is simply the

---

⁴⁰The Journal of Soren Kierkegaard, ed. and trans. by A. Dru (London: 1938) entry 16, p. 9, quoted in Louth's Discerning the Mystery, 4.

⁴¹Porter, "On Keeping 'Persons' in the Trinity," 541.

⁴²E. Hill refers to Teresa but does not quote her, Mystery of the Trinity, 103; In her "Spiritual Relations" she discusses the Vision of the Trinity at several points, of mutual love she in her enlightened avowed apophatic way which carries a cataphatic tint,
"These Persons have mutual love, communication and knowledge, each in relation to the rest. If, then, each Person is One by Himself, how do we say, and believe, that all Three are one Essence - and this is a very profound truth: I would die a thousand deaths in defence of it? In all Three Persons there is not more than one will and one power and one dominion, so that none of Them can do anything without Another." Complete Works of St. Theresa, trans. and ed. E. Allison Peers, vol. 1 (New York: Sheed and Ward, 1944), 350.

rigid idea of God.[43]

This 'personality' does not subsist in God having intellect and will, for these are common to each of the three Persons; it consists in there being a triunal, not triple, or a tri-personal nature consisting of substantial relations. The Greeks would insist on a clear connection between 'persona' and 'hypostasis' in defining this tri-unity.

Mary McDermott Shideler indicates that Charles Williams comes to a similar conclusion in his writing on co-inherence (which is arguably his theological principle) in a discussion of the barrenness of radical individuality:

> Co-inherence depends upon individuality, as much as individuality on co-inherence....The three do not cohere, "stick to each other", but they co-inhere, 'abide in' each other. As the unborn child abides in its mother, the lover in his beloved, the spirit in body, the Word in flesh....Relationship, like separation is an ultimate metaphysical reality, and the substantial basis of being, and in William's phrase, this substance is Love, who is not a quality but a person who loved and can be loved without "confounding the Persons nor dividing the Substance."[44]

There are at least three major areas of interest that the relational definition of trinitarian person can clarify and inform that are crucial in the contemporary world: First, the dynamic reciprocity entailed in a relational definition encompasses an important challenge to the predominance of the philosophy that posits different theological notions of God as Actus purus which all too often is applied rationalistically and results in a staticization, or a passivity in one or more of the persons of the Trinity.[45] Being and Act are inseparable as the Eastern Church has reminded the West so often. The unity focus or essentialist position, though often seen as more orthodox, is equally vulnerable to the assertion of a type of 'idolatry' in its strict notions of what and what is not to be predicated of God.

---

[43]E. Brunner, The Mediator (London: Lutterworth Press, 1934), 282. Here Brunner both agrees and disagrees with my premise. I take strong exception to his bifurcation of the love of God originating from his will and not from the divine nature. And to his statement that the Son "becomes" a Person. Ibid., 279. He states in Man in Revolt: A Christian Anthropology (Philadelphia: Westminster Press, 1947), 221 that to be a,
> person is to be in relation to someone; the Divine Being is in relation to himself; man's being is a relation to himself based on his relation to God. This concept of personality can only be gained from love and not from the subject of the processes of knowledge.

[44]Mary M. Shideler, The Theology of Romantic Love (Grand Rapids: Eerdmans, 1962), 80-81. William's consistent use of "co-inherence" or of "exchange" indicates a deep comprehension of the Greek doctrine of perichoresis and Latin circumincessio. See his The Descent of the Dove (London: Faber and Faber, Ltd., 1950) 39,54,69,79, passim. The Forgiveness of Sins (Grand Rapids: Eerdmans Pub. Co., 1984) 1,2,10,11,23-26, passim. He Came Down From Heaven (Grand Rapids: Eerdmans, 1984), 24,25,26,39,50,90,104. The Figure of Beatrice: A Study in Dante (New YorK: Octagon Books, 1978), 92,172,195,204,210.

[45]Perhaps one of the deepest need in responding to the criticism of traditional trinitology by the process theologians, is the discussion of a God who is active, not impassible, or unconcerned. Even if they cannot hear the consensual statements regarding the Trinity then maybe they will be encouraged to look again at its dynamic claims.

Second, in a relational definition of person there resides the premise that for both divine and human spheres to be personal- they must be interpersonal. By its very nature the relational definition critiques the modern viewpoint of sociality; that of a collection of individuals who do not really have anything to do with one another but a mere truce of co-existence, hopefully peacefully. The modern sense of person is a bankrupt view of personhood. Tradition has shown that with each rise in the interest of personhood there has been a corresponding denial of it presuppositions and a continual return to monistic or rationalistic concepts. I feel this is due mainly to inadequate theological definitions of, and applications to, personhood.[46]

Finally, to view the Trinity and human relationships as analogically fecund instantiations of that Divine society means a different view of power, and of will than has been promulgated for a long while. The power of God is found in deference, in seeking the other's glory, in bestowing honor on another. I find that across the theological spectrum ruminations of this altered perspective are being expressed.[47] It seems to me that there is a hope resident here than transcends the notion of monadic omnipotence. God's existing in God's self and for us in an enduring relationship, as hard as it is to understand, is required if we are to take seriously the activity of Father, Son and Holy Spirit. In this case, human life is conceived of as not just an interchange of impersonal and mechanistic forces, not as the impotent assertion of a false deity, not as a collection of isolated atomic individuals, but as a community where the implications of our personhood is worked out, however stumblingly and inadequately. It would seem the relational trinitarian tradition, yet again, requires ecclesial response to the claim that there is an ineluctable personal, perfectly loving Presence which constrains us to look at each other, and then to welcome each other home, dust and all.

---

[46]If I am understanding the ecclesiology of Kilian McDonnell and Edward Kilmartin aright we must base our relationships within the Church and between faith communities on something higher than ourselves. See McDonnell's "A Trinitarian Theology of the Holy Spirit," Theological Studies 46 (1985): 191-227 and Kilmartin's Christian Liturgy, vol. 1 of Systematic Theology of Liturgy. Kansas City: Sheed & Ward, 1988.

[47]See for instance the recent work of any of the following: Jürgen Moltmann, David Brown, Colin Gunton, R. G. Greunler, T. F. Torrance, John Zizioulas, Thomas Oden and Dennis Kinlaw.

Appendix

The Milieu of Victorine Personalism

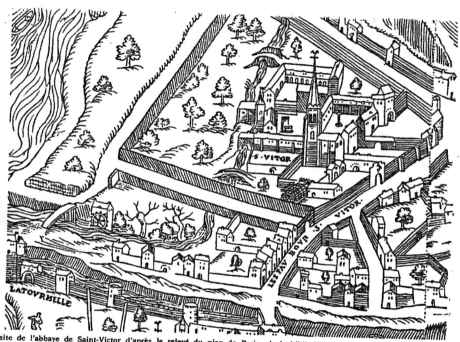

Le site de l'abbaye de Saint-Victor d'après le relevé du plan de Paris de la bibliothèque de Bâle (1552) *(Musée Carnavalet)*
Le faubourg Saint-Victor, visible sur ce plan, correspond au tracé actuel du début de la rue Jussieu et de la rue Linné. La cour d'entrée du monastère, entre le porche et l'église abbatiale, recouvrait approximativement l'emplacement de la place Jussieu. Les discontinuités qu'on peut observer à l'extrême droite du dessin, et qui figurent sur l'original, sont dues à un ajustement maladroit des bois gravés primitifs.
Cliché Giraudon.

A late medieval map indicating the Abbey of St. Victor and its situation on the left bank of the Seine outside the Parisian wall. Taken from Jean Chatillon's <u>Theologie, Spirituality, et Métaphysique dan l'oeuvre oratoire d'Achard de Saint-Victor</u> (Paris: Librarie Philosophique, 1969).

I. Medieval Background for Victorine Thought

Out of the bellicose background of the fifth through the eighth centuries, arose a new, constructive atmosphere, fostered by the Carolingian regime, and with it a desire to reorder society. It is possible to say that with that social reconstruction came an concomitant result, one through which the world was to be viewed from a new perspective. More central to the thrust of this work - a difference was initiated by a new relationship between individual persons and the world due to what, I believe, was a new self-awareness of the person. The foundation of this paradigm shift was to be found in the relative peace, economic equilibrium and the personal influence of the advisors closest to Charlemagne.[1] The transformation came to a culture which had suffered the loss of a cohesive initiative or originality, especially in the theological and philosophical arena. Learning was confined to the monasteries for the most part and even that had a sporadic nature. Currents of humanism were stirred further by the decentralization of the Carolingian structures of government which sounded the peals of sectional rule and eventual nationalism. The shift in governing power, however, was to spell the decline of the Carolingian line, and the concomitant rise of the German tribal chieftains destroyed the advancements society had been experiencing. These incursions undermined attempts at consolidating intellectual thought. Monasteries were evacuated and their inhabitants scattered.[2]

The Carolingian line did not fade out entirely until the end of the tenth century but it had long since lost any effective rulership. Feudalism was soon to take the place of the monarchy. It is important to note that the transmission of the Christian message in a world where the individual was of little or no account took on the Germanic 'earthiness' in

---

[1]Colin Morris, The Discovery of the Individual: 1050-1200 (London: S.P.C.K., 1972), 21. Morris charts the development of the medieval world from 500-1500 in the light of three 'renaissance' periods; the Carolingian regime, the twelfth and the fifteenth centuries. He is aware of oversimplification here but would maintain that these were the culminative periods of change that are most pervasive in their overall impact on medieval culture.

[2]Frederick Artz contrasts the societal effects of the Gothic invasions in 'barbaricizing' the West with the urbanized East and the ascendancy of Islamic philosophic thought as a result. The Mind of the Middle Ages (New York: Alfred A. Knopf, 1953), 443-445. An example of the 'dehumanizing' character of the Gothic invasions can be seen in the loss of a view of history as a storehouse of knowledge. The effect was a fundamental break with the past and a preoccupation with the present alone. Glimmers of advancement, for instance, in the area of linguistics were virtually eliminated. Jan Walgrave gives an example of the Radbertus/Ratramnus Eucharistic debate. Charles the Bald inquired of both the meaning of the phrase, "In verita...non in figura". Their linquistic analysis in response reveals the direction of thinking which was curtailed for nearly two centuries. Unfolding Revelation: The Nature of Doctrinal Development. (Philadelphia: Westminster Press, 1972), 92-93.

content as well as transmission. This was not a period of theological subtlety. The German mind could grasp the cult of relics much more clearly than linguistic analysis of the sacraments.

On the borders of this Gothic functionalistic empire there were glimmers of hope. The Irish monasteries were repositories, apparently because of their distance from the fray, of some of the important advances in theology and thought made in the centuries prior to Gothic usurpation. It was, ironically, the missionary thrust of the Irish monks toward Germanic tribes that provided the impetus for re-establishment of the monasteries and resulting theological communication. The highly-ordered ascetic monks carried with them a concentration of morality and hierarchical structure which were to influence European culture to the core.[3]

The tenth century saw the consolidation of the feudal system. One can see that both Church and State were structured according to strict class distinctions. Subinfeudation brought the question of the rights of lordship.[4] The result was a pyramid effect that permeated ecclesiastical and social institutions alike. The king was divested of real power, which devolved upon the liege lords whose armies were often more poerful than the royal forces in a given area.

This century also experienced a form of spiritual revival in the West. This is seen most clearly in the flourishing of the Cluniac, Cistercian, and Carthusian orders. Their presence elicited a form of consolidation under papal authority which mirrored the hierarchical nature of the new ordering within society.[5] Again the tie between the advancement of thought and the monastery produced new trends. The theological discussion of the period took on a 'proto-scholastic' tone in its intensity.[6]

It would be impossible within the parameters of our discussion to trace the influence of this period of consolidation upon the totality of society. Some general statements, though, about the medieval view of the individual are cogent to our thesis. It is widely accepted, that the place of the individual was seen as a functional position in this

---

[3] Albert Miregeler's intriguing chapter on the Irish monastic influence on the mainland, points to the rise of Benedictinism as a direct result of this form of spiritual invasion which proved more powerful than the barbarian hordes. Mutations of Western Christianity. trans. Edward Quinn (Montreal: Palm Publishers, 1964), esp. Ch.6, 79ff.

[4] Norman Cantor, Medieval History (New York: Macmillan Co., 1967), 238-247.

[5] Artz, Mind of the Middle Ages, 446. This hierarchical theme was usually presented triadically. The ternary approach is found in the Greek philosphers, but its Christian appropriation appears for example in Pseudo-Dionysius, John Scotus Erigena, Basil the Great, and Gregory the Great. Richard's usage of the hierarchical triadism was most likely learned from Hugh (not his commentary on The Celestial Hierarchy) and Achard.

[6] Francis Oakley, The Medieval Experience (New York: Chas. Scribner's and Sons, 1974), 175-176.

century of order and growth. At least externally, Boethius' concept of the individual person within the Trinity as a self-subsistent individual did not affect the notion of the human person amidst the prevailing communal orientation, which in its usual way produced some de-humanizing factors. Prior to the eleventh century the concern of the personal relationship between the soul and God was submerged in the rhythms of devotion which was collective rather than personal, external rather than internal, public rather than private.[7] The mediatorial role of the priesthood replaced the need for personal pursuits for holiness. Monks became powerful allies, backed by God, with whomever could pay the price for their intercessory favors. Religion turned outward, public, impersonal, structured, communal and heroic.[8]

The anonymity of corporate ritual and routine behind the facade of a corrupt papacy brought about the reforms of the eleventh century. It is not an accident that the cleavage between a highly objective, structured West and a more relational, subjective East took place: At the risk of overstatement, it is at least feasible that one of the factors of division with regard to the Filioque question could be based in the difference of opinion on the worth, the meaning of the person. The subjective emphasis of the Eastern trinitology was a threat to more than the place of the Son in the spiration of the Spirit. Underlying that point was a whole new way of looking at reality. Essentially, the division still remains due to the same reasons, in my estimation.

On the other hand, a major humanizing element in the eleventh century was the

---

[7] Our emphasis here is on the emergence of a need for clarification on the definition of person, as it is worked out anthropologically. This statement might be misinterpreted by those who have been influenced by the modern discussion on the need for a return to the collective and the enculturated. See George Lindbeck's The Nature of Doctrine: Religion and Theology in a Postliberal Age (Philadelphia: Westminster Press, 1984), ch. 2, 30-45, passim. The influence of Robert Bellah et al., Habits of the Heart: Individualism and Commitment in American Life (Berkeley: Univ. of California Press, 1985), also might produce a reaction to my thesis. The argument here is from the other end of the spectrum. We are examining a world that had never dealt fully with the specifically individual characteristics of humans, at least in a pervasive sense. These two seminal works are prophetic in an era which has fallen into individualistic narcissism, or as Bellah's work delineates, "expressive" and "utilitarian" individualism.

[8] Colin Morris, in The Discovery of the Individual, 2-26, deals with various eleventh century activities which reveal this tendency to focus on the 'order', the 'hierarchy' in opposition to personal faith or an understanding of volition. Oakley, Medieval Experience, 179. R.W. Southern says, "In the impersonal society of the early Middle Ages one man's penance was as good as another's. It was not a question of individual effort but of the payment of a supernatural debt," in Western Society and the Church in the Middle Ages (Grand Rapids: Eerdmans Pub. Co., 1970), 227. Cantor, Medieval History, 226ff., describes the impersonal, vicarious religiosity of the noble class who had no personal relationship with God but merely used the orders to assuage their guilty consciences by paying for prayers and dying dressed in habits.

Benedictine call to purity and the exploration of the inner man.' The individual was reintroduced to personal encounter with the divine. Cluny was the center of this Benedictine revival. There was to come the inevitable perennial struggle, sometimes resulting in division, on the relationship of the 'via contemplativa' and the 'via activa'. Spirituality took on new depths and objects. Personal devotion as a form of relation with Jesus Christ characterized the emotive eleventh century, often to excess.[10] Tenderness and compassion unseated the entrenched previous centuries' value of militant passion as proof of faithfulness and love.

However, both the papacy and the individual monasteries reacted with a 'fortress' mentality evoked by the conflicting worldviews manifested in the encounter of the 'personal' and the 'intentional' with the 'pyramidic' and the 'institutional' status quo. It was during this period that the Pope gained universal authority with the right to excommunicate as he pleased. This divine ordering of society, colored by the renunciation of the world in spiritual sectors, eclipsed any real concern for the individual. Alienation from the world was raised as a virtue yet strict adherence to the 'ordo' was demanded. Liturgy, ecclesiastical pomp, and feasts were built on hierarchical premises. Ordo was to manifest itself in the 'stabilitas' of faithful monks and laity. What that meant usually was an unquestioning adherence to the norm. Persons were caught in a maze of loyalties, to kin, king and friend, that were based on formal obligations not on relational intimacy.[11]

This is not to say that structure was solely negative in influence. The doctrine of the Trinity, as the basis of order, found attempted repristination in the buildings, literature,

---

[9]Cantor, Medieval History, 226, states that the "interpenetration of 'ecclesia' and 'munio'...heavily depended on the resources and activities of the Benedictine Order."

[10]Giles Constable, "Twelfth-Century Spirituality and the Late Middle Ages," 27-60, see 27-31, 35-45. Personal devotion to Christ realized an anthropomorphic change. Instead of the kingly motif, crosses depicted a suffering servant. The attributes of tenderness and acceptance were emphasized. The cult of the Virgin was a direct result of these trends which reflect a desire for intimacy within the monolith of the ordo. When one found an avenue of expression a characteristic flamboyance of affection often followed. Mariology, the rise of courtly love, along with angelology and demonology formed one side of a more creative selfhood in relation to the spirituality of the period. The hermetic movements, and some heretics such as Catharism and Lombardism, formed the most liberal camps in terms of voluntarism of the era. Jean Leclerq, Francois Vandenbroucke and Louis Bouyer, The Spirituality of the Middle Ages (New York: Desclee Co., 1968), 282.

[11]"Even the architecture of the period reveals the preoccupation with equilibrium and structure. Aquinas' Summa found architectonic counterparts in the Gothic cathedrals of Amiens and Riems. The 'monastic look' was replaced by ornamentation which was fundamentally structural. "The main effect comes from the right proportions and dispositions of such essential and necessary features as doors, windows, arches, and pillars." G.C. Coulton, Medieval Faith and Symbolism (New York: Harper Torchbooks, 1958), 11-12.

and self-understanding of the medieval minds.[12] The ordo was, for the most part, both a protective and instructive concept. In the dawning of the notion of the individual person, whether one prefers self or individual is really of no account here; the institutions provided guidelines for understanding reality. Incorporation into the ordo meant an absorption into the structure of the communion of the saints, or the 'fidelis'. The original intent was not to locate power in any of the structures, which interestingly, almost always took on ternary form. Rather, the goal was to recognize the supreme creative and judicial authority of a Triune God whose reflective image permeated all of existence. As we have noted, it was hard to keep that original intent in focus but nonetheless the ideal served as the reason for the existence of the structures, as abusive as they may have become. There were a few prophetic voices heard calling for a deeper understanding of themselves as persons even within the structure.[13]

The twelfth century saw the collapse the Benedictine influence which had marked the previous era. Rapid growth in the middle classes produced a nationalism that saw the entrance of representative governments. The renaissance of this century began with cultural diversification and development. In the growth of towns and cities, the monastery was to meet its intellectual counterpart in the more independent secularized catherdral schools. The papacy also experienced a waning supremacy. Religion, art, literature, philosophy and economy were challenged by innovative creative expansion. Implicit within this humanism was a deep sense of order and achievement.[14]

Several factors fed into the ascendancy of the monasteries as places marked by a converging paradigm shift. Due to the breakthrough of Erigena's Latin translations and transmissions to the Continent, in the centuries which followed Greek thought was assessed and assimilated in an increasingly philosophically-oriented theology as Aristotle's corpus became available. The Augustinian order with its rigor, both spiritually and academically came to the fore, claiming a heritage preceding Benedict and a rule founded in Scripture rather than a human source primarily. Within religion various ordinances took on a new style of subjectivity.

Marriage was interpreted in spiritual and relational qualities never before possessed. An appreciation of the sacredness of the bond between a couple and God, of

---

[12]Robert Lopez, The Birth of Europe (New York: M. Evans and Co., 1966), 190-194. G. Coulton, Medieval Faith and Symbolism, 252.

[13]Morris, The Discovery of the Individual, 31-32, quotes Peter Damiani among others who sounded the need for a return to the subjective:
Let it cease then; let sterile attention to business cease. To indulge in fruitless labour is pointless. Let the mind return within itself, with all its resources collected.
from his De contemptu saeculi, 30, PL 145. 286B.

[14]Artz, Mind of the Middle Ages, 447. Cantor, Medieval History, 288-289.

the covenant made, was legitimated and became a sacrament of the Church. A debate exists concerning whether there was actual personal awareness of a development in equality between the sexes. While there is evidence for women having major responsibilities in both business and politics, another side of the issue asks whether women were actually regarded as possessing higher worth than in the previous centuries?[15] Bynum, who does not feel that women did enjoy heightened estimation, says that the problem in interpreting this question is a historiographical one. The primary sources, of course, were mostly written by men. The egalitarian thrusts of our time in women has caused some to look for feminine aspects of the spirituality of the twelfth century, but Bynum would remind us to distinguish 'feminine' from 'female'. The usages of feminine categories in discussions of affectivity in religion and in communal life did not always signal an improved status among women.[16]

On the religious front, there are indications of an attempted, even if unwitting, balance of emphases which reflects a new view of the impact of sexuality in Spirituality. The Cistercian concept of hierarchical authority was interwoven with a strong emphasis on nurture. What might be called the 'feminine' aspects of Jesus were emphasized in the abbot's leadership. The imago dei was nurtured within the context of order. The whole person, affective and volitional, was brought into the light of this care.[17] With an ambivalence bordering on deep mistrust of authority outside the monastery, Cistercian spirituality advocated strict independence from the world while promoting an intricate matrix of interdependency within ecclesial hierarchies. It would be fallacious to place all these changes at the feet of a comprehension of the person. However, our point is that the milieu in which Richard contemplated the Triune Persons was one that allowed images of relationality and worth which up to that historical juncture had only been exceptions within society at large.

---

[15]Of the many sources regarding changing attitudes toward relationships, Jean Leclerq's Monks and Love in Twelfth Century France (New York: Oxford Univ. Press, 1979) focuses on Bernard and Cistercian uses of the Song of Songs at many different applicational levels. Ovid, as a influence on twelfth century romantic love, is also explored. His conclusion is that love in this period must of necessity be personified whether it be Mary, the Bride and Bridegroom motif or Dante's Beatrice. This feminization of love directly impacted the theology of marriage.

[16]The bibliography of this discussion is present in the notes of Bynum, Jesus as Mother, 135-146. She does not however negate the fact that the twelfth century did allow new rights to women and saw several institutional changes which benefited them. In contrast to the twelfth century, there is a decline of equality, however it is defined in the generations to follow. "There is little evidence," she says, "that the popularity of feminine and maternal imagery in the high Middle Ages relfects an increased respect for actual women by men." Jesus as Mother, 143.

[17]Caroline Bynum, Jesus as Mother, 154-168.

II. Victorine Mysticism: Relational Intuition

As we have noted in Chapter 4, practical divinity and mysticism was for the Victorines an invigorating counterpart of speculative abstraction if the active discipleship was aimed at true knowledge of the love of God. It was Platonic idealism which laid the groundwork for this mystical spirituality and intellection at St. Victor. Deductive reasoning, drawn from careful recapitulation of Augustine, Pseudo-Dionysius, Gregory the Great and Erigena, was applied within the context of an affective spirituality.[18] Though they preferred direct intercourse between divinity and the soul, reason was given a place of authority close to Scripture.[19] True knowledge of God did not come through reason or speculation but by grace. The mystical was definitely seen as greater than the pure philosophizing which was to mark the high medieval period.

The mystical was that which was hidden from immediate perception within the symbol. Under material realities lay the reality to which symbolism was a pointer and for which mysticism was employed as a means of apprehending spiritually and cognitively. Intuitive signification, for the mystic meant that God could be found in the sensible. By the incarnation, God had ordained that all of creation be redeemed and thereby transformed into "mirrors" of God's glory. Contemplation on those reflections revealed the transcendent truth of their Origin and Creator. This form of relational intuition took on gradations of purgation, illumination and ecstasy.

Revealing an amazing perspicacity with regard to the employment of ratio in both speculation and the natural sciences, Hugh's Didascalion outlined a comprehensive curriculum meant for cathechesis of monastic students but whose impact was felt far beyond the cloister. His use of the 'quadrivium' and the 'trivium' incorporated the basic Aristotelian components with the Augustinian mode of signification found in On Christian

---

[18]J. Chatillon adds to De Lubac's contribution regarding the connection between Hugh and Gregory by offering an analysis of Richard's debt to, and differences from the former thinkers (especially in the relationship of contemplativa and activa) in "Contemplation, Action, et Prédication d'après un sermon inedit de Richard de Saint-Victor en l'honneur de saint Grégoire-le-Grand," from J. Guillet et al., L'Homme Devant Dieu: Mélanges offerts au Père Henri de Lubac (Paris: Aubier, 1963), 89-98. The similarities between Richard and Thomas Gallus are found in the following article by R. Javelet, "Thomas Gallus ou les Écritures dans une dialectique Mystique," Ibid., 99-110. Gaston Salet's "Les chemins de Dieu d'après Richard de Saint-Victor," Ibid., 73-88, confirms our thesis that Richard was cataphatic in his theological and mystical approach. Although a mystic, Richard was neither an anti-intellectual, nor a rationalist.

[19]Pierre Pourrat, Christian Spirituality in the Middle Ages (Westminster: The Newman Press, 1953), 100-132 and Jean Leclerq, et al. The Spirituality of the Middle Ages, 223-242, give good summaries of Victorine mysticism in relation to other schools.

Doctrine to produce a new philosophy of education.[20] What had previously been seen as secular was now brought under the aegis of signs and things. The arts and sciences were included in the uncovering of divine symbols. In distinctly Boethian categories, Hugh gave theology preeminence among the arts, within the stricture of speculation of God alone, specifically concerning the Trinity. For Hugh the primacy of Love demanded the service of philosophy and theology in the endeavor to achieve union with God by affective faith within a relationship marked by caritas.[21] Thus, St. Victor became a vital center for the 'vita communis' by which the spirituality and thinking of Hugh and Richard began to be disseminated.

The emphasis of this work, relational personhood as foundational to a proper understanding of the Trinity, was symbolized in the exemplaristic mysticism of the Victorines and the Franciscans which followed them. The Augustinian paradigm, imago dei as locus of speculation of the trinitarian reality, was integrally tied to the mystical theology of the Victorines. Love, not reason, became the center of the stream of spiritual speculative mysticism at St. Victor and for Bonaventure's lineage.[22] This is not to say that reason became superfluous. R. Javelet notes in an interesting article on the confluence of love and ratio in the twelfth century that, according to Richard and Bonaventure:

> Ce qui est amour, c'est la relation interpersonnelle mais la raison d'image est fonction d'une donation qui procède du Père des lumières, de celui qui est l'Origine.[23]

---

[20]Augustine, De Doctrina Christiana, PL 34, 15-122; NPNF 2, 519-597.   Though not exclusively Hugh's in origin (see William of Conches, a contemporary d. 1154), Hugh divided his work in half, first dealing with the arts and the second with Scripture. By altering the original Aristotelian list, he distinguished four major branches with twenty-one disciplines divided between them. The impetus for this construction came from a pastoral desire to inform the areas required to restore the imago dei that had been defaced by the Fall. He placed the theoretical first, which guided the reason in search of wisdom (here he encompassed the quadrivium); the practical which assisted in reorienting the will; the mechanical which dealt with necessities; and the logical which provided the rules for cogent discussion of the other three. S. Ferruolo, The Origins of the University, 31-40; Michael Haren, Medieval Thought: The Western Intellectual Tradition from Antiquity to the Thirteenth Century (New York: St. Martin's Press, 1985), 111-114.

[21]Leclerq, et al., Spirituality of the Middle Ages, 229-234.

[22]G. Dumeige, offers an introduction to the gradations of love, from insatiable to insurpassable, in Ives Épitre a Séverin sur la charité Richard de Saint-Victor, Les Quatre degrés de la violente charité, vol 3, Textes Philosophiques du Moyen Age, (Paris: Librarie phiolosophique J. Vrin, 1955). Salet has an excellent bibliographic reference on the perplexing attempt to interpret Richard at this point in "Les chemins de Dieu," 83 n. 69. The impact of Richard's spiritual writings extends well into the fifteenth century. See G. Constable, "The Popularity of 12th Century Spiritual Writers in the Late Middle Ages," in Religious Life and Thought (11th and 12th centuries) (London: Variorum Reprints, 1979), 8, 19, 22.

[23]Robert Javelet, "Réflections sur l'exemplarisme Bonaventurien," in ed. W. Dettloff's S. Bonaventura: 1274-1974, vol. 4, (Rome: Collégio S. Bonaventura Grottaferrata, 1974), 351.

This synthesis of monastic mysticism, austere regulation and unity within the created order produced a diversity and inclusiveness unique within medieval culture. Lyrical poetry, sequences, philosophy and speculative theology are examples of the wide range of disciplines which reflected the mystery of the Creator.

III. Scripture and the Victorines

Scripture undeniably formed the basis of the Victorine enterprise. All instruction was referred to as the "lectio divina" or the "sacra pagina."[24] The canons attempted to draw upon both historical and allegorical interpretations. While they are most remembered for their investigations by use of the latter hermeneutic, it is evident that it would have had no basis without a clear understanding of historical background.

> Since, therefore I previously composed a compendium on the initial instruction in Holy Scripture, which consists in their historical reading, I have prepared the present work for those who are to be introduced to the second stage of instruction, which is allegory.[25]

Andrew Louth makes a strong argument for the reliance of the allegorical method upon the literal method as a diachronic interpretive tool of the Church. As he sees it, the fundamental category within its use is an appreciation of the mystery revealed in the literal but not exhausted there.[26] This is of highest importance for our discussion as it pertains to the methodology of Victorines. In light of modern interest in historical-critical method or even canonical criticism to an extent, an inner battle is waged between spiritual

---

[24]Ferruolo, Origins of the University, 34–41, described the difficulty in maintaining a commitment to the encyclopedia of knowledge bequeathed by Hugh in light of the inclusion of other disciplines within the pale of theology adopted by other schools with which the Victorines were forced to dialogue. The differing views on study of Scripture itself also forged divisions. Henri de Lubac disagrees with a major tenet of Beryl Smalley's The Study of the Bible (New York: Philosophical Library, 1952), 111, 149, that the Victorines were noted in their literal exposition of Scripture. His Exégèse Médiévale: Les Quatre Sens de l'Écriture Pt.2:1 (Aubier: Éditions Montaigne, 1961), states; "Décidément, il n'est pas possible de trouver chez nos Victorins, Hugues ou même Richard, ni chez Adam Scot qui leur ressemble tant, un exégèse 'littérale' en réaction généralisée contre 'l'allégorisme' des ancien âges." 418.

[25]De Sacramentis christianae fidei, PL 176: 173-618; English version by Roy J. Deferrari, Hugh of Saint Victor on the Sacraments of the Christian Faith (Cambridge, Mass.: Medieval Academy of America, 1951). Prologue, De Sacramentis, (hereafter cited as) PL 176: Prologue, 183; trans. Deferrari,(hereafter cited as) On the Sacraments, 3.

[26]Discerning the Mystery, Ch. 5, passim. In this excellent critique of Enlightenment thought which has cast its shadow over all of the humanities, Louth shows distinct dependence upon Henri de Lubac's Exégèse Médiévale (see below) for an understanding of the order of interpretive techniques, with which we agree. (Discerning, 115-121) He also views mystery in much the same way as Marcel did (Ibid., 68-70, 121,) "A problem can be solved, a puzzle can be unravelled: but a mystery, if it is truly a mystery, remains.", Ibid., 144. See Colin Gunton's critique of this in Enlightenment and Alienation: An Essay towards a Trinitarian Theology (Grand Rapids: Eerdmans Pub. Co., 1985), ix.

interpretation and cognitive hermeneutic. There is no question, but that the latter "scientific" approach has won individually and corporately. Thus, any foray into medieval exegesis produces immediate reservations in the post-Enlightenment mind. One must constantly keep in mind the synergism between the literal and the spiritual implied in this period of sacramental symbolism. Symbolic procedure, for the Victorines, to the dismay of the growing number of adherents to Aristotelian categories in exegesis, was often merited with typological interpretations. Though the format at first appears to be proof-texting or worse, the intent behind the tomes of typology is only understood in light to the heuristic tendency of the Victorine design: the desire to explore all of the mysteries of God.

The "symbolist" theory, what we refer to as typology or allegorical interpretation, whose initial construction and use is fundamentally attributed to Hugh was to be dismissed by Aquinas outright. The "lectio", an extended explication of Biblical texts, often on seemingly obscure portions of Scripture, found expression at every level of biblical theologizing.[27] Richard can be used as an example of a disciple of Hugh's method. His theological treatise, Ad me clamat ex Seir, is an example of the use of "littera" (literal/historical) level of interpretation, which was the basis of the "sensus" (fundamental sense) and of the "sententia" (or deeper meaning).[28] Each phrase of Isaiah 21:11 is exhaustively excavated for possible theological application. The "intellectus fidei" was applied to every area of the spiritual life, not in a proud or even definitive sense but in conjunction with the life of pilgrimage to see the face of God.[29] Thus, there is an immediate connection between the Victorine use of Scripture and the significative

---

[27]M.-D. Chenu, Nature, Man and Society, 279-300. Gregory of Nazianzus and Basil the Great were instrumental in transmitting the "organic" quadrilateral of interpretation proffered by Origen, in their Philokalia. He systematized what the Church followed up to the Enlightenment in the four ways approaching Scripture ; 1)literal, 2)moral/tropological, 3)mystical/allegorical and 4)the anagogical. The last is best understood as subsumed under the mystical. See Louth, Discerning, 115-117.

[28]Richard, Super Ysaiam exponens illud: Ad me clamat ex Seyr, PL 196:995-1010; see also in Jean Ribaillier's, Opuscules théologiques, 256-280. Ribaillier summarizes the use of Hugh's method in this treatise; 1)literal, the stranger cries to God; 2)mystical sense, the Gentiles await the Messiah; 3)tropological, the carnal makes penitence and asks for pardon. (235)   He shows how Richard is true to the method outlined in the prologue of In visionem Ezechielis, PL 196: 527BC. There Richard says the spiritual interpretation must rest on the literal sense of Scripture, the mystical must draw its likenesses from that proposed by the literal, and he shows a deep respect for the interpretations of the Fathers, not wanting to correct only to apply a more rigorous method.(232) English trans. A Scholastic Miscellany: Anselm to Ockham, ed. and trans. Eugene Fairweather (New York: Macmillan Co., 1970), 321-323.

[29]Chenu, Nature, Man and Society, 287 says, "...it was not a matter of establishing or even discussing an orthodoxy, but of theological inquiry where options and conclusions were unfixed and debatable." He gives excellent examples of this symbolist approach, 288-289.

epistemology explored above. To use the Anselmian categories of "**rationes necessariae**" can only be rightly understood and applied within the framework of a strong literalistic basis in Scripture, coupled with a "freedom" to explore all truth fecund with revelatory possibilities. The use of reason in that sense is more aptly defined as spiritually applying the mind to the immanent presence of a revealing God who makes himself known in ways that can be categorized for human understanding.[30]

The Victorines, specifically Hugh and Richard, come on the scene just prior to the "dissolution" of the medieval synthesis as Gordon Leff and others have articulated it. The shift from a necessitarian epistemology to a probabilism based on contingency, was to cast every accepted doctrine into immediate question. The Victorines were able to maintain the category of mystery, but within several decades the onslaught of Aristotelian principles within theology would greatly reduce its unqualified usage, almost expunging mystery amid quodlibets and syllogisms. The logical contradiction of a Trinity and a God who is simple, meant the "shelving" of earlier mystical ventures in lieu of more scholastic approaches.[31]

IV. Richard: The Intellectual Context for De Trinitate

We have suggested that Richard, who may never have been the actual physical confrère of Hugh, was nevertheless a loyal disciple who, to use a constant metaphor of the period, saw himself as a dwarf hunched on the shoulder of a giant in order to see beyond that forebear, and thus together with fresh insight brought new life to the medieval concept of divine personhood. In order to set his De Trinitate in proper historical context we will mention three areas: educational philosophy, mysticism, and literary production.

Using a theological stance hammered out by Hugh, Richard formulated a spiritual humanism in the midst of rigorous contemplative paradigm. His encyclopedic mind afforded him more originality than we have discovered in Hugh; however, his esteem for his master never waned. Little is known of this intriguing figure, one of the outstanding

---

[30]Chenu, Man, Nature and Society, 297. In contradistinction with the Thomistic interpretive method to follow, Chenu says, "...one must see in them the means of approaching mystery through exploration of its time-bound analogies." Affective spirituality was never devoid of scriptural connection although it is not to be surmised here that there was any less confusion as to what was the bottom-line interpretation of Scripture than we have today.

[31]Gordon Leff, The Dissolution of the Medieval Outlook (New York: Harper and Row, 1976), 29. See also Hester Goodenough Gelber, "Logic and the Trinity: A Clash of Values in Scholastic Thought, 1300-1335," Ph.D. diss. Univ. of Wisconsin-Madison, 1974.

minds of the Middle Ages, prior to his arrival in Paris under the abbacy of Gilduin.[32]
Richard, it is surmised, was a Scotsman, born probably in the 1120's. As was mentioned
(see chap. Four, 178-181) the Parisian schools drew students from all over Europe.
Apparently as a young man Richard made his way to the bastion of Parisian
Augustinianism.[33] It has been verified that in 1159 he became sub-prior and from 1162-
1173, held the office of prior. He died on March 10, 1173.

Apparently the Abbey was not without its share of intrigue, as Marvin Colker
suggests if one is to read with understanding the passages concerning stability which both
open and close Richard's Quaestiones. The abbot Ervisius, under whom Richard served,
was a horrendous administrator and a decrepit spiritual leader. This may have greatly
impacted Richard with the need to explicate the Augustinian rule by which the Victorines
were commanded to live. If this historical analysis is correct, Richard's work as prior would
have doubled as a result of his superior's incompetence.[34] As most administrative positions,
his seems to have been a sanctifying experience.

-Victorine Educational Theory

More than his mysticism was affected by the deep strain of spirituality that is
evident throughout the works of Richard. The Augustinian regular canons were, for the
most part, desirous of a life lived under strict obedience and sacrifice. Taking into account
the differences between the original authors of the respective Rules and the clerics, nuns,
canons and religious which attempted to follow them, it is quite apparent that, at least in
spirit, Richard desired to hold to the basic tenets of the Augustinian rule. Chastity,
poverty, prayer, fasting, Scripture reading, in the context of a shared life with a desire to
serve the larger Church, and conjoined with a definite love for learning, were evident in

---

[32]Dumeige, L'Idée Chretienne de l'Amour, 165-167, gives a thorough briefing on the
early sources with which the major points of Richard's life have been gathered. Ottaviano,
Riccardo di S. Vittore, 411-422, 533 also deals with the earliest texts.

[33]John of Toulouse, a seventeenth century prior of the Abbey who collected the
Victorine annals from 1605-1659, is one of the earliest known commentators on Richard's
life. PL 196, prolegomena, ix-xiv. John does not make it clear where Richard's exact origins
lay, but enough is given to affirm what we have here. From his Antiquitates abbatiae S.
Victoris 5.55; (for full bibliographic reference see Cousins, Notion, 4 n.2, 59 n.2. See also,
"Notice sur Richard de Saint-Victor," by Mgr. Hugonin, Ibid., xiii-xxii.

[34]Richard died, leaving "a worthy reputation, from the holiness of his life and the
beauty of his writings" (according to John of Toulouse's rendering of the necrology, see
Cousins, Notion, 63) just after the installation of Guarin, who succeeded the ecclesiastically
deposed Ervisius in 1173. See, Dictionnaire de theologie Catholique, 1936 ed., s.v. "Richard
de Saint-Victor," by E. Levesque. Marvin Colker, "Richard of St. Victor and the
Anonymous of Bridlington," Traditio 18 (1962): 181-227. This hypothesis is found on 196.
Colker has several helpful bibliographies: on the history of the Victorine Abbey, 188 n. 46;
on the life of Richard, 191 n.65; on the history of textual transmission and the Victorine
library, 189 nn.46, 47.

Thagaste, where this new form of monasticism found its origin in the mid-fourth century, and outside the walls of Paris in the mid-twelfth.[35]

An element which is close relation to the personalism discussed in Chap. Four is that of edification, which as Caroline Bynum has elicited is evident in Richard's writings.[36] The thesis here is alluring. Fundamental to it is a shift from the literal interpretation of Augustine's dictum, "Love God, and do as you please." Rather than struggling with the problem inherent in a total devotion to a primary love to God and then forging a niche for love of neighbor, it seems that Richard and others rightly focused on a love for neighbor as an expression, a fulfillment, of a rightly-ordered love for God. Basic to the life of the regular canons was a concern for responsible relational education. Taking the basic Latin meaning of "ex-ducere" to heart, the canons emphasized moral teaching, both verbally, as in preaching, reading and the use of reflective questioning; and demonstrably, by living life with a pattern of godliness, an actual behavior which reflected divine charity.[37] Conduct was seen as more important that speech; the "other" was preeminent in this "imitatio Christi." The communication of virtue had within it a fundamental attitude toward relationships, the love of God made manifest in particular physical acts.[38] Richard was a

---

[35]George Lawless, <u>Augustine of Hippo and his Monastic Rule</u> (Oxford: Clarendon Press, 1987), 56-58, gives a synopsis of the basic tenets of the Augustinian rule. The notion of 'friendship' within the Thagaste experiment may have interesting connections with the Victorine concern for the edification of others we find in Richard's period. For a critical edition of the Victorine Order itself see <u>Liber Ordinis Sancti Victoris Parisiensis</u>, Corpus Christianorum, Vol. 61, ed. Lucas Jocqué and Ludovicus Milis (Brepols, Typographi Brepols Editores Pontificii, 1984). Within the Order, see the pastoral roles of the prior and sub-prior, Ibid., cc.5-8, 25-30. Bonnard, <u>Historie</u>, writes, "Cette vie rythmée était éminemment propre aux fortes études aux forte." 81. Dickinson, <u>Origins</u>, is helpful in distinguishing regular canons and monks and secular clergy. The brothers at St. Victor could claim to be like monks in every respect save ordination, 12. The basic elements of an intimate social group tied together by a rule that was not "a vague authority,"(Ibid., 165) but a guide for the intention behind radical obedience, (Ibid., 175) fed the life and thought of Richard.

[36]<u>Docere Verbo et Exemplo</u> (Missoula, Mont.: Scholars Press, 1979), 55-60.

[37]J. B. Schneyer, Sigeltabellen zu Repertorium der lateinischen Sermones Mittelalters für die Zeit von 1150-1350 in <u>Beiträge zur Geschichte der Philosophie un Theologie des Mittelalters</u>, vol. 43, pt. 5 (München: Aschendorffsche Verlagsbuchhandlung, 1973), 162-170, lists 110 sermons of Richard, most of which were attributed to Hugh until Jean Chatillon's critical work on the <u>Sermones Centum</u> in <u>PL</u> 177: 901-1210 proved that they belonged to Richard.

[38]<u>Docere Verbo et Exemplo</u>, the theme of edification runs throughout, but see esp. Ch. 1, and 77-78, 89, 90-93, for "example" theme as it relates to mutual human love. Bynum explores this form of medieval religion in Ch. 1 of <u>Jesus as Mother</u>, "The Spirituality of Regular Canons in the Twelfth Century," 22-58, esp. 53-58. This was one of the points of contention between the Cistercians and the Victorines. To be "evangelical" was interpreted in two ways. Bernard's followers emphasized acts extrinsic to the Cloister, while the latter saw "intentional" acts of edification mainly within the confines of the

biblical scholar whose emphasis on contemplation drew upon not only the text but also the awareness of mutual and responsibile self-giving.

It may be said that Richard's grammatical analysis, reasoning capabilities and dialectical method were balanced by the existential ballasts of a doctrine of free-will and human relationships. The mutual relationships within the Abbey were objects of sense-data which provided one source for his reflection on divine life. The Rule under which he lived, with its voluntary subordination and mutual encouragement, gave a plethora of ways of visualizing "affectus ordinatus", rightly-ordered love, on a daily basis. By perception, Richard meant the abstracting of sense-data from material objects which are both grounded in and point to things divine.

Undergirding his a priori metaphysics, what some might call a "realist" approach to reality, are his six types of contemplation. None of the symbolism was, for Richard, of any worth if it did not feed the viator in the contemplative life.

-The Victorines and the Via Contemplativa

Synthesizing the Augustinianism of Hugh with the Pseudo-Dionysian tradition, Richard's method of contemplation formed a basis with which nearly every other later medieval mystical work was to interact. It was as a doctor of contemplation that Richard's "ecstatic" methodology is most clearly seen. As the apex of the divine gifts, contemplation was not to be treated lightly. The supreme object of this mystical vision, as found in his Benjamin Minor, Benjamin Major, and De Trinitate is the divine Trinity, and the unity of the Three found there.[39] Speculation precedes contemplation, and that speculation entails an understanding of all of reality which originates within the inner life of the Trinity. It is this principle which elicits Richard's ecstatic mysticism and the theology undergirding it. Following the restoration motif of Hugh, Richard views love as the "all and truth of God," thus "it must be the all and the truth of man," and as such the only means of reforming

---

monastery as fulfillment of that call for the most part. It seemed that those shut off from the world had a heightened sense of moral responsibility and of actual education. Ibid., 56.

[39]The Benjamin Minor is not specifically a treatise on contemplation, but rather a preparatio for it. It is without a doubt, that within the pedagogical framework of the Benjamin Minor the Trinity is the goal of contemplation although Richard does not refer to it as often as in other works, see PL 196:c. 86, 61D]; or, Richard of St. Victor, Selected Writings on Contemplation, trans. Clare Kirchberger (New York: Harper, 1957), 126, where two kinds of contemplation are contrasted. Cf. Benjamin Major, PL:196:Bk. 4, c. 21, 165CD-164A. We must refer to G. Zinn's important addition in the Classics of Western Spirituality series, Richard of St. Victor: The Twelve Patriarchs (Benjamin Minor) The Mystical Ark (Benjamin Major), Book Three of the Trinity, trans. and ed. by Zinn, preface by J. Chatillon (New York: Paulist Press, 1979). His full translation of the Richard's major works on contemplation is a much needed addition to Kirchberger's work, but also, his placing of them alongside Richard's third Book on the Trinity expresses our contention here more than adequately.

the wounded will.[40]

The proper way to know God is by contemplating that Love, that Perfection. Let it be said that this spiritual exercise was not blind affectivity. For Richard, each of the degrees of contemplation demands a corresponding mode by which the different levels of contemplation are reached.[41] Truth, for the canon, was the result of stringently disciplined yet affectively applied meditative contemplation. Against the scholastic tendencies already appearing in his day, the inductive method of apprehending truth was not evident in Richard. It entailed a rigorous "cogitatio" demanding preparation through the purgation of mind and soul. The use of "personification allegory" by both Hugh and Richard served as the points of awareness and purging which a contemplative was to experience in mystical ascent.[42] "Discretio," or the art of self-knowing in comparison to the supreme object of contemplation, was required. This self-knowledge marked by a purity in virtue or heart, is still not adequate for a full knowledge of God. The highest levels of Richard's hierarchical order of objects of contemplation require an "excessus mentis" a union with the divine which transcended reason; a detachment from the sensible alone.[43] Robilliard is convinced that this method is impregnated by Platonic metaphysical structures, especially the doctrine

---

[40]Leclerq, Spirituality of the Middle Ages, 236 check???

[41]Zinn, "Personification Allegory," 203, is a helpful summary of this method according to both Benjamin Minor and Benjamin Major. J. Ebner, Die Erkenntnislehre Richards von St. Viktor, Beiträge Vol.19, pt.4 also deals with these categories, 92-120, esp. 111ff.

[42]Grover Zinn is helpful here in "Personification Allegory and Visions of Light in Richard of St. Victor's Teaching on Contemplation," Univ. of Toronto Quarterly 46:3 (Spring, 1977):190-214. The twelve sons of Jacob correspond to the stages of purifying contemplation. Joseph is the emblem of "discretio" while Benjamin, (following a mistranslation of Ps. 47:28) is the example of ecstatic contemplation. "By Joseph the soul is carefully taught and eventually it is brought to full self-knowledge, just as his half-brother Benjamin is at length brought to the contemplation of God." PL 196: Benjamin Minor, c.71, 51B, Kirchberger, Selected Writings, 109.

[43]Alistair Minnis, "Affection and Imagination in 'The Cloud of Unknowing' and Hilton's 'Scale of Perfection'," Traditio 39 (1983): 323-366, is helpful in accentuating the wholeness of the affectus and the intellectus in Richard's scale of contemplation in contrast to Thomas Gallus and the "Cloud" in a denigration of the sensible, see 328-329, 338-341. Richard maintained a unity between the will and reason in the ascent to "excessus mentis". (Benjamin Major Bk. 5 is central to this point.) With regard to Richard's modes of ascent, Minnis correctly points out, "The human intelligence (intelligentia) increases from the greatness of its dilation so that it is no longer itself - not that it is not intelligence, but that it is no longer human," 329. This is yet another connection to Pseudo-Dionysius and the Greeks in their emphasis on "deification". Though the mystery of union God with perfect souls might be ineffable, the fundamental view of the imago was not a Gnostic one. The senses were created good as well as the intellect and thus while they might be transcended they were never expunged in the theological syntheses of those whose view of sin did not mean the total denial of the good of created beings.

of participation." It is important to note that this method was not a Gnostic denial of matter or reaction to the use of reason. If one contextualizes Richard's major works on contemplation within the framework of the Augustinian Rule, with its emphasis on mutual edification and Augustinian illuminationism, then these steps are far from speculative abstractions. They are primarily pedagogical tools for understanding the "elusive aspects of visionary experience," by natural symbols and mnemonic devices which were to aid the contemplative in interpreting a variety of experiences." To separate Richard's contemplative method from his Trinitarian thought, by saying that the latter is primarily speculative, is to miss the point of his culminative work. Divine love is the source, the means, the object of all contemplation. Thus to ponder that divine essence is not to speculate but to enjoy a communion, however far that may be possible, ineluctably offered by the beckoning presence of the mutual Love which defines that essence.

With this in mind it is also important to see the shift in thinking from the Benjamin Minor and Major to the De Trinitate. The difference mainly lies in Richard's view of reason. The latter work uses a different method in its claim to 'prove' the rationality of the Trinity. In the fifth grade of contemplation, trinitarian unity was perceived as those things that "exceed the mode of human understanding, and yet they are no less fit for reason."[46] It is the sixth level in which the unity of the persons of the Trinity is the object of ultimate contemplation, with evidence of the Victorine approximation of the apophatic tradition, which is both above and contrary to reason: that realm of revelation in which the pondered truth is approaches anti-reason.[47]

Note that when Richard brings these two levels of contemplation together, he at once affirms the tradition of the so-called psychological trinities while laying down reservations about their adequacies. He writes:

> In this rational creature itself, if we pay careful attention, we can find, we believe, some trace of the supreme Trinity. For there is something from the mind itself, namely its wisdom; and there is something there from both the mind and its wisdom, namely their love....
> Surely it ought to be noted that these three things that come together in the

---

"J.-A. Robilliard, "Les six genres de contemplation chez Richard de Saint-Victor et leur origine platonicienne," R.S.P.T. 28 (1939):229-233. His schemata of the objects of contemplation affirms our contention of the centrality which the Trinity plays in Richard's thought. See p. 232. Zinn's article, "Personification Allegory," corresponds with the findings of Robilliard and J. Chatillon in "Les trois modes de la contemplation selon Richard de Saint-Victor," Bulletin de littérature ecclésiastique 41:1 (1940):3-26.

⁴⁵Zinn, "Personification Allegory," 208. See Jean Chatillon's preface to Zinn's Book Three, xv.

⁴⁶PL 196: Benjamin Major, Bk. 4, c. 17, 156BC, Zinn's trans. Richard of St. Victor, 290.

⁴⁷PL196: Benjamin Major, Bk. 4, c. 18, 158A.

consideration of the soul do not make a Trinity of persons; just as those three in God divide into three persons according to a difference of individual properties. See, therefore, that in similitude, the dissimilarity is greater than the similarity to that supreme Trinity.[48]

How is it then that Richard can even disembark on an endeavor like that which he outlines in De Trinitate? This might be answered on different levels but the thrust we are making here is that inherent in, what might be called, Richard's maturing "systematic principle" is the metaphysic of divine love. While it is never fully comprehended, its revelatory nature can be contemplated with reason as a major "handmaiden" in that process.[49] For Richard the more one spent in "speculating" the more intimate the inner reality, and the more likely that the concrete mutuality of divine love was revealed.[50] The plenitude of divine being called the "mens" beyond both the sensate order and itself, to an unsullied union with that which was ever beyond it, yet willing to share the fullness of which it consisted. In this methodology Richard placed himself with the Augustinian and Dionysian traditions of unmediated truth and the accessibility of knowledge of the divine.

There is evidence on some fronts of the Catholic tradition that Richard is gaining new adherents due to his mystical emphases. The marginalization of mysticism must end if the Catholic tradition, or any other for that matter, is to flourish. As von Hügel pointed out, mysticism, institutionalism and intellectualism are all needed for healthy spirituality.

-Richard of St. Victor's Literary Works

All of Richard's texts can be found in Migne, Patrologia Latina volume 196,

---

[48]PL 196: Benjamin Major Bk. 4, c. 20, 162C-D. In c. 19, 169C, Richard makes clear that to speak of different persons is not to speak of different things like Arius had said. Nor had Sabellius's modalism solved the mystery, Ibid. Even though we do not find here the full force of Richard's logic regarding persons there is ample evidence of an underlying dissatisfaction with the prevalent "unity model" which had been accepted for centuries.

[49]Note here that reason is the counterpart of seven other human experiential responses in Benjamin Minor and Major. Phillippe Delhaye, 861-862, states that one of the reasons Richard is not rightly noted for his studious interpretation of the inner psychology of the moral life of the believer was the dominant place of Lombard's Sentences and Thomas' Summa. However, the Council of Trent chose six of the seven, without recognizing their sources which he feels ought to include Richard, in its "Decr. de iustificatione," see c. 6, "Modus preaeparationis," Denzinger, 1526; Neuner, 1930, 522-523. This underscores our contention that much of the thought of Richard was not rejected because of doctrinal flaw but because of the demise of the Victorine school and the overshadowing of more popular works and persons.

[50]See Dorothy Sayers' proper translation of Dante's passage affirming the Florentine's recognition that Richard never claimed to be a contemplative, "In speculation not a man, but more." The Comedy of Dante Alighieri: Cantica 3, Paradise, trans. Dorothy Sayers and Barbara Reynolds (Middlesex: Penguin Books, rep. 1973), 138. She notes on p. 147 D. Butler's helpful distinction between the verifiability of truth latent in contemplation and the pilgrimage toward that truth residing in consideration, which is, I guess, her interpretation of what Dante meant by the use of "considerar".

although many critical texts have appeared due to the manuscript evidence. Generally speaking, it is possible to delineate three periods in the bibliography of Richard: 1) one mainly expository,[51] 2) another more philosophically oriented, and finally, 3) a contemplative period.[52]

1)Prior to 1150 - (Found in PL 196 if not otherwise noted)
 In Expositione Tabernaculi foederis, 211-255
 Explicatio In Cantica Canticorum, 405-524
 Mysticae Adnotationes in Psalmos, 265-402
 In Visionem Ezechielis, 527-600
 In Apocalypsin Joannis, 683-887
 De Emmanuele, 601-666
 Sermones Centum, (PL, 177) 899-1210[53]

2)1150-1160
 De tribus appropriatatis Personis in Trinitate, 992-994
 De Verbo incarnatio, 995-1010
 Liber Exceptionum, PL 175, 177(see Chatillon's ed. for proofs)

3)1162-1173
 De eruditione interioris hominis, 1229-1366
 De statu interioris hominis, 1115-1160
 De gradibus charitatis, 1195-1208
 De quatuor gradibus violentae charitatis, 1207-1224
 Benjamin Minor, 1-64
 Benjamin Major, 63-202
 De exterminatione mali et promotione boni, 1073-1116
 Quomodo Spiritus Sanctus est Amor Patris et Filii, 1011
 De Trinitate, 887-992

---

[51]We give only a representative list here. Ottaviano lists 42 works of different levels in his chronology, Riccardo de S. Vittore, 534. Kirchberger, Selected Writings, admits that the proper ordering of the texts is not yet assured despite the assiduous labor of J. Chatillon (see his Sermons et opuscules inédits, Vol. I, xxxiii-xlv.) and others. She also says of this period that it reveals, "a closer affinity to the general teaching and manner of the period. There is a greater tendency to rely on the moral and ascetical interpretations of the usual authorities," 21.

[52]Apparently Richard wrote up until the final two years of his life. Though it was not his final work, De Trinitate is definitely the culminating masterpiece of this contemplative's endeavors. Dumeige, L'Idée Chretienne de l'Amour, "Chronologie des oeuevres de Richard, sans être absolument indispensable pour l'intelligence de son oeuvre, serait des plus utiles," 168. His abbreviated chronology runs from 168-170. Of special note here is the fact that both De tribus appropriatis personis in Trinitate and Liber de Verbo Incarnato precede De Trinitate. Kirchberger, Selected Writings, says this period is one of "purely dogmatic theology," (23) which turns into a, "consistent concern with purely spiritual questions," 24. We follow Walker's, "Richard of St, Victor: An Early Scottish Theologian?" 39-40. Cf. the delineations of G. Fritz, Dictionnaire de Theologie Catholique, 1936 ed., s.v. "Richard de Saint-Victor," where he follows for the most part Kulesza, La Doctrine mystique de Richard de Saint-Victor; 1) works on the interior life, 2) those which are properly theological, and 3) more or less the exegetical works of Richard.

[53]Javelet classifies these alone as they are marked by the liturgical style of the Abbey at that time, "Sens et Réalité," 2-3.

Bibliography

Collections of Primary Sources

The Ante-Nicene Fathers: Translations of the Writings of the Fathers down to A. D. 325. eds. Alexander Roberts and James Donaldson. 10 vols. Reprint. Grand Rapids: Eerdmans Pub. Co. 1977-1979. Hereafter ANF.

The Fathers of the Church: A New Translation. Various editors. Washington: Catholic University of America Press, Hereafter, FC.

Patrologiae Cursus Completus Series Graeca. ed. J.-P. Migne. 162 vols. Paris: Migne-Garnier, 1857-1912. Hereafter, PG.

Patrologiae Cursus Completus Series Latina. ed. J.-P. Migne. 220 vols. Paris: Migne-Garnier, 1844-1890. Hereafter, PL.

Select Library of Nicene and Post-Nicene Fathers of the Christian Church. ed. Philip Schaff. 14 vols. Reprint. Grand Rapids: Eerdmans, 1978. Hereafter, NPNF.

Select Library of Nicene and Post-Nicene Fathers of the Christian Church. Second Series ed. Philip Schaff. 14 vols. Reprint. Grand Rapids: Eerdmans, 1978. Hereafter, NPNF2.

Primary and Secondary Sources

Abraham, William J. and Steven Holtzer eds. The Rationality of Religious Belief: Essays in Honour of Basil Mitchell. Oxford: Clarendon, 1987.

Actes du premier congrés internationale de philosophie médiévale. Louvain, Brussels, 28 August - 4 September, 1958. L'Homme et son destin d'après les Penseurs du moyen âge. Louvain: Éditions Nauwerlaerts, 1960.

Aghiorgoussis, Maximos. "Applications of the Theme "Eikon Theou" According to Saint Basil the Great." The Greek Orthodox Theological Review 21:3 (1976): 265-288.

_____. "Christian Existentialism of the Greek Fathers: Persons, Essence and Energies in God." The Greek Orthodox Theological Review 22:1 (1978): 15-48.

_____. "Image as "Sign" of God: Knowledge of God Through the Image According to Saint Basil." The Greek Orthodox Theological Review 21:1 (1976): 19-41.

Alfaro, Juan. "Persona y Gracia." Gregorianum 41 (1960): 5-29. trans. "Person and grace." Theology Digest 14:1 (1966): 3-7.

Allchin, A.M. "Trinity and Incarnation in Anglican Theology from the Sixteenth Century Until Today." Sobornost 7:5 (1977): 363-376.

Allport, Gordon Willard. Personality: A Psychological Interpretation. New York: Henry Holt and Co., 1937.

Altaner, B. Patrology. trans. H.C. Graef. 5th ed. Freiburg: Herder-Nelson, 1965.

Altheim, Franz. "Persona." Archiv für Religionswissenschaft 27 (1929): 35-52.

Altizer, Thomas J.J. "Discussion: The Tri-unity of God." Union Seminary Quarterly Review 21:2 (1966): 207-218.

Alverny, M.-Th. de. "Achard de Saint-Victor. De Trinitate-De unitate et pluralitate creaturarum". Recherces de Théologie ancienne et médiévale 21 (1954): 299-306.

American Catholic Philosophical Association. Existential Personalism. vol. 60. ed. Daniel O. Dahlstrom. Washington: American Catholic Philosophical Association, 1986.

_____. The Human Person. vol. 53. ed. George F. McLean. Washington: Catholic Univ. of America Press, 1979.

_____. Thomas and Bonaventure: A Septicentenary Commemoration. vol. 48. ed. George F. McLean. Washington: Catholic Univ. of America Press, 1974.

Anastos, Thomas Leo. "Essence, Energies and Hypostasis: An Epistemological Analysis of the Eastern Orthodox Model of God." Ph.D. dissertation, Yale Univ. 1986.

Anderson, Ray S. On Being Human: Essays in Theological Anthropology. Grand Rapids: Eerdmans Pub. Co., 1982.

Andresen, Carl. "Zur Entstehung und Geschichte des Trinitarischen Person-begriffes." Zeitschrift für die Neutestamentliche Wissenschaft 52 (1961): 1-38.

_____. "The Integration of Platonism into Early Christian Theology." In Studia Patristica 15:1. ed. Elizabeth A. Livingstone, 399-413. Berlin: Akademie-Verlag, 1985.

Ansaldi, Jean. "Approche doxologique de la Trinité de Dieu: dialogue avec J.-L. Marion." Études Theologiques et Religieuses 62 (1987): 81-95.

Anselm of Canterbury. Monologion vol. 1. ed. and trans. Jasper Hopkins and Herbert Richardson. New York: Edwin Mellen Press, 1974.

_____. Trinity, Incarnation, and Redemption. ed. with intro. Jasper Hopkins and Herbert Richardson. New York: Harper and Row, Pub., 1970.

Arendt, Hannah. The Human Condition. Chicago: Univ. of Chicago Press, 1958.

_____. The Life of the Mind: Vol. One/ Thinking, Vol. Two/ Willing. New York: Harcourt Brace and Jovanovich, 1978.

Aristotle. Basic Works of Aristotle. ed. with intro. Richard McKeon. New York: Random House, 1941.

_____. Metaphysica. ed. W. Jaeger. Oxford: Clarendon Press, 1963.

_____. Metaphysics. vol. 3. The Student's Oxford Aristotle. trans. W.D. Ross. New York: Oxford University Press, 1942.

Armstrong, A.H., ed. The Cambridge History of Later Greek and Early Medieval Philosophy. London: Cambridge Univ. Press, 1967.

_____. On the Holy Trinity. NPNF. vol. 3.

_____. De Trinitate. PL. vol. 42.

_____. De Trinitate: Libri XV. ed. W.J. Mountain. Corpus Christianorum, Series Latina, vols. 50, 50A. Turnholt, Belgium: Typographi Brepols Editores Pontificii, 1968.

_____. The Trinity. trans. Stephen McKenna. FC. vol. 45. Washington: Catholic Univ. of America Press, 1963.

Aulén, Gustaf. Christus Victor: An Historical Study of the Three Main Types of the Idea of the Atonement. trans. A. G. Hebert. New York: Macmillan Pub. Co., 1969.

_____. The Faith of the Christian Church. Philadelphia: The Muhlenberg Press, 1948.

Auer, Johann. Person: Ein Schlüssel zum christologische Mysterium. Regensburg: Pustet, 1979.

Ayer, A.J. The Concept of the Person and other Essays. New York: St. Martin's Press Inc., 1963.

Backus, Irena. "Influence of Some Patristic Notions of 'substantia' and 'essentia' on the Trinitarian Theology of Brenz and Bucer (1528)." Theologische Zeitschrift 37:2 (1981): 65-70.

Bailleux, Emile. "La christologie de saint Augustin dans le "De Trinitate"." In Recherches Augustiniennes, vol.7, 219-242. Paris: Études Augustiniennes, 1971.

_____. "Dieu Trinité et son oeuvre." In Recherches Augustiniennes, vol. 7. 185-217. Paris: Études Augustiniennes, 1971.

_____. "Le personalisme de St. Thomas en theologie trinitaire." Revue Thomiste 61 (1961): 25-42, 62 (1962): 27-50, 63 (1963): 165-192.

_____. "Le personalisme trinitaire des pères grecs." Mélanges de Science Religieuse 27 (1970): 3-25.

_____. "La reciprocité dans la Trinité." Revue Thomiste 74 (1974): 357-390.

Baillie, D. M. God was in Christ. New York: Charles Scribner's Sons, 1948.

Baillie, John. The Sense of the Presence of God. New York: Charles Scribner's Sons, 1962.

Balas, David. "Christian Transformation of Greek Philosophy Illustrated by Gregory of Nyssa's Use of the Notion of Participation." In Scholasticism in the Modern World. ed. George McLean, 152-157. Proceedings of the American Catholic Philosophical Association. vol. 40. Washington: American Catholic Philosophical Association, 1966.

_____. "Plenitudo Humanitatis: The Unity of Human Nature in the Theology of Gregory of Nyssa." In Disciplina Nostra: Essays in honor of Robert R. Evans. Patristic Monograph Series, no. 6. ed. Donald F. Winslow, 115-131. Cambridge, Mass.: Philadelphia Patristic Foundation, 1979.

Balthasar, Hans Urs von. "Creation and Trinity." Communio (US) 15 (Fall, 1988): 285-293.

_____. "On the Concept of Person." Communio 13 (1986): 18-27.

_____. Of the Morals of the Catholic Church. NPNF. vol. 4.

_____. On the Holy Trinity. NPNF. vol. 3.

_____. De Trinitate. PL. vol. 42.

_____. De Trinitate: Libri XV. ed. W.J. Mountain. Corpus Christianorum, Series Latina, vols. 50, 50A. Turnholt, Belgium: Typographi Brepols Editores Pontificii, 1968.

_____. The Trinity. trans. Stephen McKenna. FC. vol. 45. Washington: Catholic Univ. of America Press, 1963.

Aulén, Gustaf. Christus Victor: An Historical Study of the Three Main Types of the Idea of the Atonement. trans. A. G. Hebert. New York: Macmillan Pub. Co., 1969.

_____. The Faith of the Christian Church. Philadelphia: The Muhlenberg Press, 1948.

Auer, Johann. Person: Ein Schlüssel zum christologische Mysterium. Regensburg: Pustet, 1979.

Ayer, A.J. The Concept of the Person and other Essays. New York: St. Martin's Press Inc., 1963.

Backus, Irena. "Influence of Some Patristic Notions of 'substantia' and 'essentia' on the Trinitarian Theology of Brenz and Bucer (1528)." Theologische Zeitschrift 37:2 (1981): 65-70.

Bailleux, Emile. "La christologie de saint Augustin dans le "De Trinitate"." In Recherches Augustiniennes, vol.7, 219-242. Paris: Études Augustiniennes, 1971.

_____. "Dieu Trinité et son oeuvre." In Recherches Augustiniennes, vol. 7. 185-217. Paris: Études Augustiniennes, 1971.

_____. "Le personalisme de St. Thomas en theologie trinitaire." Revue Thomiste 61 (1961): 25-42, 62 (1962): 27-50, 63 (1963): 165-192.

_____. "Le personalisme trinitaire des pères grecs." Mélanges de Science Religieuse 27 (1970): 3-25.

_____. "La reciprocité dans la Trinité." Revue Thomiste 74 (1974): 357-390.

Baillie, D. M. God was in Christ. New York: Charles Scribner's Sons, 1948.

Baillie, John. The Sense of the Presence of God. New York: Charles Scribner's Sons, 1962.

Balas, David. "Christian Transformation of Greek Philosophy Illustrated by Gregory of Nyssa's Use of the Notion of Participation." In Scholasticism in the Modern World. ed. George McLean, 152-157. Proceedings of the American Catholic Philosophical Association. vol. 40. Washington: American Catholic Philosophical Association, 1966.

_____. "Plenitudo Humanitatis: The Unity of Human Nature in the Theology of Gregory of Nyssa." In Disciplina Nostra: Essays in honor of Robert R. Evans. Patristic Monograph Series, no. 6. ed. Donald F. Winslow, 115-131. Cambridge, Mass.: Philadelphia Patristic Foundation, 1979.

Balthasar, Hans Urs von. "Creation and Trinity." Communio (US) 15 (Fall, 1988): 285-293.

_____. "On the Concept of Person." Communio 13 (1986): 18-27.

_____. A Theological Anthropology. New York: Sheed and Ward, 1967.

Ban, Joseph D. ed. The Christological Foundation for Contemporary Theological Education. Macon, Ga.: Mercer Univ. Press, 1988.

Banawiratma, Johannes B. Giyana. "Der Heilige Geist in der Theologie von Heribert Mühlen: Versuch einer Darstellung und Würdigung." Ph.D. dissertation, Univ. of Innsbruck, 1980.

Barral, Mary Rose. Merleau-Ponty: The Role of the Body-Subject in Interpersonal Relations. Pittsburgh: Duquesne Univ. Press, 1965.

Barrett, C. K. The Gospel According to St. John. Philadelphia: Westminster Press, 1978.

Barrett, William, Death of the Soul: From Descartes to the Computer. Garden City, New York: Anchor Press/ Doubleday, 1986.

Barth, Karl. Church Dogmatics. eds. Geoffrey W. Bromiley and Thomas F. Torrance. Various trans. 4 vols. Edinburgh: T. & T. Clark, 1936-1969 (1975 edition).

_____. Anselm: Fides Quaerens Intellectum. Pittsburgh Reprint Series. n.p.: Pickwick Press, 1975.

_____. Protestant Theology in the Nineteenth Century: Its Background and History. London: SCM Press Ltd., 1972.

Barth, Timotheus. "Zur Geschicte der Analogie." Franziskanische Studien 37 (1955): 85-97.

Basil of Caesarea, Saint. Letters 1-185. trans. Agnes Clare Way. notes Roy J. Deferrari. FC. vols. 12, 13. Washington: Catholic Univ. of America Press, 1955.

_____. On the Holy Spirit. NPNF2. vol. 8.

Bataillon, L.-J. "Bulletin d'histoire des doctrines médievalés: Le treizième siècle." Revue des Sciences Philosophiques et Théologiques 56 (1972): 265-296, 492-520.

Battenhouse, Roy W. A Companion Guide to the Study of St. Augustine. Reprint. Grand Rapids: Baker Book House, 1955.

Bettenhouse, Henry. ed. Documents of the Christian Church. London: Oxford Univ. Press, 1963.

Bauckham, Richard. " "Only the Suffering God Can Help": Divine Passibility in Modern Theology." Themelios 9:3 (1984): 6-12.

Baum, Gregory. ed. The Future of Belief Debate. New York: Herder and Herder, 1967.

Baur, Jörg. "Die Trinitätslehre als Summe des Evangeliums." Kerygma und Dogma 22 (1976): 122-131.

Bavinck, H. The Doctrine of God. Grand Rapids: Eerdmans, 1951.

Becker, Lawrence C. "Human Being: The Boundaries of the Concept." Philosophy and Public Affairs 4:4 (1975): 334-359.

Bell, David N. "Esse, Vivere, Intelligere: The Noetic Triad and the Image of God." Recherches de Théologie ancienne et médiévale 52 (1985): 6-43.

_____. The Image and the Likeness: The Augustinian Spirituality of William of St. Thierry. Kalamazoo, Michigan: Cistercian Publications, 1984.

_____. "The Tripartite Soul and the Image of God in the Latin Tradition." Recherches de théologié ancienne et mediévale 47 (1980): 16-52.

Bellah, Robert N., Richard Madsen, William H. Sullivan, Ann Swidler, and Steven M. Tipton. Habits of the Heart: Individualism and Commitment in American Life. New York: Harper and Row, Pub., 1985.

Benson, Robert L. and Giles Constable with Carl D. Lanham. Renaissance and Renewal in the Twelfth Century. Cambridge: Harvard Univ. Press, 1982.

Berdyaev, Nicolas. The Destiny of Man. London: Geoffrey Bles, 1948.

_____. Freedom and the Spirit. London: Geoffrey Bles: The Centenary Press, 1935.

_____. Truth and Revelation. trans. R. M. French. London: Geoffrey Bles, 1953.

Berger, Peter. A Rumor of Angels: Modern Society and the Rediscovery of the Individual. Garden City, NY: Doubleday Anchor Books, 1970.

Bergeron, M. "La structure du concept latin de personne." Études d'histoire litteraire et doctrinale du XIIIe siècle. 2 (1932): 121-161.

Bertocci, Peter A. The Person God Is. London: George Allen and Unwin Ltd., 1970.

Bethune-Baker, James Franklin. An Introduction to the Early History of Christian Doctrine to the Time of the Council of Chalcedon. London: Methuen and Co., 1903.

_____. The Meaning of the Homoousios in the Constantinopolitan Creed. In Texts and Studies: Contributions to Biblical and Patristic Literature. vol. 7. ed. J. Armitage Robinson. Cambridge: Cambridge Univ. Press, 1901. Reprint. Nendeln/ Liechenstein: Kraus Reprint Ltd., 1967.

Betz, Otto. Der Paraklet. Leiden: E.J. Brill, 1963.

Bickersteth, Edward Henry. The Trinity: Scripture Testimony to the One Eternal Godhead of the Father, and of the Son, and of the Holy Spirit. Grand Rapids: Kregel Publications, 1976.

Blaise, Albert. ed. Lexicon Latinitatis Medii Aevi. Corpus Christianorum series. Turnholt, Belgium: Typographi Brepols Editores Pontificii, 1975.

Blaser, Klauspeter. "Les Enjeux d'Une Doctrine Trinitaire Sociale." Revue de Théologie et de Philosophie. 113:1 (1981): 155-166.

Bligh, John. "Richard of St. Victor's De Trinitate: Augustinian or Abelardian?" Heythrop Journal 1 (1960): 118-139.

Boethius. The Theological Tractates. trans. H. F. Stewart and E. K. Rand and S.J. Tester. Loeb Classical Library. Reprint. Cambridge, Massachusetts: Harvard Univ. Press, 1978.

_____. PL. vols. 63, 64.

Boigelot, R. "Le mot "personne" dans les écrits trinitaires de saint Augustin." Nouvelle Revue Théologique 57:1 (1930): 5-16.

Bolgar, R.R. The Classical Heritage and its Beneficiaries. Cambridge: Cambridge University Press, 1954.

Bonaventure. Disputed Questions on the Mystery of The Trinity. trans. Zachary Hayes. St. Bonaventure: The Franciscan Institute of St. Bonaventure Univ., 1979.

_____. Itinerarium Mentis in Deum: The Mind's Road to God. trans. George Boas. Indianapolis: Library of Liberal Arts, 1953.

Bongard, Willy. "Zu der philosophisch-theologischen Grundlagen de Personbegriffe." Salzburger Jahrbuch zu Philosophie 23/24 (1978/1979): 167-181.

Bonhoeffer, Dietrich. Christ the Center. trans. John Bowden. New York: Harper and Row, Publishers, 1966.

Bonnard, Fourier. Historie de l'abbaye royale et de l'ordre des chanoines réguliers de Saint-Victor de Paris. 2 vols. Paris: Arthur Savète Editeur, 1904-1907.

Booth E. G. T. "St Augustine's 'de Trinitate' and Aristotelian and neo-Platonist Noetic." In Studia Patristica 16:2. ed. Elizabeth A. Livingstone, 487-490. Berlin: Akademie-Verlag, 1985.

Bossier, F. Images of Man in Ancient and Medieval Thought: Studia Gerardo Verbeke Ab Amicis et Collegis dicata. In Symbolae: facultatis Litterarum et Philosophiae Lovaniensis Series A. vol. 1. Louvain: Louvain Univ. Press, 1976.

Boublík, Vladimír. "Una Mystica Persona." Divinitas 13:3 (1969): 623-653.

Bourassa, Francois. "Personne et conscience en théologie trinitaire. I and II." Gregorianum 55:3 (1974): 471-493, 55:4 (1974): 677-719.

_____. "Théologie trinitaire chez saint Augustin." Gregorianum 58 (1977): 675-725, 59 (1978): 375-412.

Bourke, Vernon. Readings in Ancient Medieval Philosophy. ed. James D. Collins. Westminster, Maryland: Neuma Press, 1960.

Bouyer, Louis. Le Consolateur: Esprit-Saint et la vie de grace. Paris: Les Éditions du Cerf, 1980.

_____. Cosmos: The World and the Glory of God. Petersham, Mass.: St. Bede's Pub., 1988.

_____. Le Père Invisible: Approches du Mystère de la Divinité. Paris: Les Éditions du Cerf, 1976.

Bowman, Robert M., Jr. "Oneness Pentecostalism and the Trinity: A Biblical Critique." Forward (Fall,1985): 23-27.

Braaten, Carl E. and Philip Clayton. eds. The Theology of Wolfhart Pannenberg: Twelve American Critiques with an Autobiographical Essay and Response. Minneapolis:

Augsburg Publishing House, 1988.

Bracken, Joseph A. "The Holy Trinity as a Community of Divine Persons." Heythrop Journal 15:2,3 (1974): 166-182, 257-270.

_____. "Process Philosophy and Trinitarian Theology-I and II." Process Studies 8 (1978): 217-230, 11 (1981): 83-96.

_____. "Subsistent Relation: Mediating Concept for a New Synthesis?" Journal of Religion 64:2 (1984): 188-204.

_____. "The Trinity as Interpersonal Process." Ecumenical Trends 13:7 (July-August 1984): 97-99.

_____. The Triune Symbol: Persons, Process and Community. Lanham: Univ. Press of America, 1985.

_____. What Are They Saying About the Trinity?. New York: Paulist Press, 1979.

Brague, Rémi. "On the Christian Model of Unity: The Trinity." Communio 2 (1983): 149-166.

Braine, David. "Observations on the Trinity: A Response to Professor Lochman." Theology 78:658 (1975): 184-190.

_____. The Reality of Time and the Existence of God: The Project of Proving God's Existence. Oxford: Clarendon Press, 1988.

Braun, René. Deus Christianorum: Recherche sur le vocabulaire doctrinal de Tertullian. Public. de la Fac. des lettres et Sciences Humaines d'Alger. 41. 1962. 2nd ed. Paris: Études Augustiniennes, 1977.

Bray, Gerald. Creeds, Councils and Christ. Downer's Grove: Inter-Varsity Press, 1984.

Breuning, Wilhelm. ed. Trinität: Aktuelle Perspektiven der Theologie. Freiburg: Verlag Herder, 1984.

Bright, Laurence. "St. Thomas on the Trinity: A Study of Philosophical Reasoning in Theology." Dominican Studies 7 (1954): 48-58.

Brightman, Edgar Sheffield. Is God a Person? New York: Association Press, 1932.

_____. Person and Reality: An Introduction to Metaphysics. New York: Ronald Press Co.,1958.

_____. Personalism in Theology: A Symposium in Honor or A. C. Knudson. New York: AMS Press, 1979.

Bromiley, Geoffrey W. Historical Theology: An Introduction. Grand Rapids: Eerdmans Pub. Co., 1978.

Brown C.G. " Objective and Subjective: An Assessment of R.C. Moberly's Atonement and Personality." Scottish Journal of Theology 25:3 (1972): 259-278.

Brown, David. The Divine Trinity. La Salle,Illinois: Open Court Publishing Company, 1985.

_____. "Wittgenstein against the 'Wittgensteinians': A Reply to Kenneth Surin on The Divine Trinity." Modern Theology 2:3 (1986): 257-276.

Brown, Francis, S. R. Driver and Charles A. Briggs. A Hebrew and English Lexicon of the
Old Testament. Reprint. Oxford: Clarendon Press, 1976.

Brown, Peter. Augustine of Hippo. Los Angeles: Univ. of California Press, 1967.

Brueggemann, Walter. Genesis: A Bible Commentary for Teaching and Preaching. Atlanta:
John Knox Press, 1982.

Brühl, Carl Richard. Palatium und Civitas: Studien zur Profantopographie Spätantiker
Civitates vom 3 bis zum 13 Jahrhundert. vol. 1. Cologne: Gallien, 1975.

Brunner, Emil. Dogmatics. trans. Olive Wyon and David Cairns. 3 vols. London:
Lutterworth Press, 1949-62.

_____. Man in Revolt: A Christian Anthropology. Philadelphia: Westminster Press, 1947.

_____. The Mediator. London: Lutterworth Press, 1934.

Buber, Martin. I and Thou. trans. Ronald Gregor Smith. New York: Charles Scribner's Sons,
1958.

Buckley, J.J. "Retrieving Trinitarian Teaching." The Thomist 48 (1984): 274-296.

Bull, George. Defensio Fidei Nicaenae. 2 vols. Oxford: John Henry Parker, 1851-1858.

Burkart, Anna Driver. "The Person in Religion: An Examination of Christianity's
Contribution to the History of Thought." Ph.D. dissertation, Univ. of Pennsylvania,
1930.

Burnaby, John. Amor Dei. London: Hodder & Stoughton, 1960.

_____. The Belief of Christendom: A Commentary on the Nicene Creed. London: SPCK,
1959.

Burns, J. Patout. trans. and ed. Theological Anthropology. Philadelphia: Fortress Press, 1981.

Burrell, David. Aquinas: God and Action. Notre Dame: Univ. of Notre Dame Press, 1979.

Buytaert, E.M. ed. Peter Abelard. Proceedings of the International Conference, Louvain, May
10-12, 1971. In Medievalia Lovaniensia, Series 1, Study 2. The Hague: Louvain
Univ. Press, 1974.

Bynum, Caroline Walker. Docere, Verbo et Exemplo: An Aspect of Twelfth Century
Spirituality. Missoula, Mont.: Scholar's Press, 1979.

_____. Jesus as Mother: Studies in the Spirituality of the High Middle Ages. Berkeley:
Univ. of California Press, 1982.

Cahalan, John C. Causal Realism: An Essay on Philosophical Method and the Foundations
of Knowledge. Sources in Semiotics, vol. 1. Lanham: Univ. Press of America, 1985.

Cahn, Steven M. ed. Philosophy of Religion. New York: Harper and Row, 1970.

Cairns, David S. The Image of God in Man. London: SCM Press, 1953

Calvin, John. Institutes of the Christian Religion. ed. John T. McNeill. trans. Ford Lewis

Battles. The Library of Christian Classics, vols. 20, 21. Philadelphia: Westminster Press, 1960.

Cambridge History of Later Medieval Philosophy: 1100 - 1600. eds. Norman Kretzmann, Anthony Kenny, Jan Pinborg (New York: Cambridge Univ. Press, 1982)

Cambridge Medieval History. various eds. 7 vols. Cambridge: Cambridge Univ. Press, 1911-1936.

Camelot, P. Th. "Le dogme de la Trinité: origine et formation des formules dogmatiques." Lumiére et vie 30 (1956): 9-48.

_____. "La théologie de l'image de Dieu." Revue des Sciences Philosophiques et Théologiques 40:3 (1956): 443-471.

Campbell, C. A. On Selfhood and Godhood. New York: Macmillan Co., 1957.

Cantor, Norman. Medieval History. New York: MacMillan Co.. 1967.

Caputo, John D. "Being and the Mystery of the Person." In The Universe as Journey: Conversations with W. Norris Clarke, S.J. ed. Gerald A. McCool, 93-113. New York: Fordham Univ. Press, 1988.

Carolsfeld, L. Schnorr von, Geschichte der Juristichen Person. vol. 1. Munich: Becci, 1933.

Carlson, Rae. "Where is the Person in Personality Research?" Psychological Bulletin 75:3 (1971): 293-219.

Carrithers, Michael and Steve Collins. eds. The Category of the Person. New York: Cambridge Univ. Press, 1985.

Casey, Robert P. ed. trans. intro. and notes. The "Excerpta ex Theodoto of Clement of Alexandria. In Studies and Documents. eds. Kirsopp Lake and Silva Lake. London: Christophers, 1934.

Casper, B. Das dialogischen Denken: Eine Untersuchung der religionsphilosophichen Bedeutung Franz Rosenzweigs, Ferdinand Ebners und Martin Bubers. Freiburg: Herder, 1967.

Cassiodorus, Expositio Psalmorum I-LXX. In Magni Aurelii Cassiodore Senatoris Opera. Corpus Christianorum Series Latina. Turnholt, Belgium: Typographi Brepols Editores Pontificii, 1968.

Cassirer, Ernst. The Individual and the Cosmos in Renaissance Philosophy. trans. with intro. Mario Domandi. Philadelphia: Univ. of Pennsylvania Press, 1972.

The Catholic Encyclopedia. S.v. "Person," by L.W. Geddes.

Cerfaux, Lucien. Christ in the Theology of St. Paul. trans. Geoffrey Webb and Adrian Walker. New York: Herder and Herder, 1959.

Chadwick, Henry. The Early Church. New York: Penguin Books, 1967.

Charlesworth, James H. ed. and trans. Odes of Solomon: The Syriac Texts. Chico, Ca.: Scholar's Press, 1977.

Chatillon, Jean. Theologie et spiritualité et métaphysiques dans l'oeuvre oratorie d'Achard de Saint-Victor: Études d'histoire doctrinale précédées d'une essai sur la vie et l'oeuvre d'Achard. Études de philosophie médiévale, 58. Paris: Vrin, 1969.

_____. "Les trois modes de la contemplation selon Richard de Saint-Victor." Bulletin de littérature ecclésiastique 41:1 (1940): 3-26.

Chenu, M. D. Nature, Man and Society in the Twelfth Century. Selected, ed. and trans. by Jerome Taylor and Lester K. Little. Midway Reprint, 1968. Chicago: Univ. of Chicago Press, 1983.

_____. La Théologie au douzième siècle. Études de Philosophie Médiévale. vol. 45. Paris: Librarie Philosophique J. Vrin, 1966.

Chestnut, Roberta C. "The Two Prosopa in Nestorius." Journal of Theological Studies n.s. 29 (1978): 392-409.

Chevalier, Irénée. S. Augustin et le pensée grecque: les relations trinitaires. Collectanea Friburgensia Fasciculus 33. n.s. 24. Fribourg en Suisse: Librairie de l'Université, 1940.

Chirico, Pietro F. "The Divine Indwelling and Distinct Relations to the Indwelling Persons in Modern Theological Discussion." Ph.D. dissertation ad lauream, Rome, 1960.

Chisholm, Roderick M. Person and Object: A Metaphysical Study. London: George Allen and Unwin Ltd., 1976.

Christensen, Torben. The Divine Order: A Study in F. D. Maurice's Theology. Leiden: E. J. Brill, 1973.

Church, F. Forrester and Terrence J. Mulry. The Macmillan Book of Earliest Christian Hymns. New York: Macmillan Pub. Co., 1988.

Clark, Mary T. Augustinian Personalism: The Saint Augustine Lecture, 1969. The Saint Augustine Lecture Series. Villanova, Pennsylvania: Villanova Univ. Press, 1970.

_____. "The Human Person and God." The Downside Review 84:274 (1966): 15-30.

_____. "The NeoPlatonism of Marius Victorinus the Christian." In NeoPlatonism and Early Christian Thought: Essays in honor of A.H. Armstrong. eds. H.J. Blumenthal and R.A. Markus, 153-159. London: Variorum Publications Ltd., 1981.

Clark, Stephen B. Man and Woman in Christ: An Examination of the Roles of Men and Women in Light of Scripture and the Social Sciences. Ann Arbor: Servant Books, 1980.

Clayton, Philip. "Being and One Theologian." Thomist 52:4 (Oct.,1988): 645-671

Clines, D. J. A. "The Image of God in Man." Tyndale Bulletin 19 (1968): 53-103.

Cobb, John B. "Reply to Jürgen Moltmann's "The Unity of the Triune God"." St. Vladimir's Theological Quarterly 28:3 (1984): 173-177.

Cochrane, Charles Norris. Christianity and Classical Culture. Reprint. Oxford: Oxford Univ. Press, 1980.

Coffey, David. "The Gift of the Holy Spirit." Irish Theological Quarterly 38:3 (1971): 202-223.

_____. Grace: The Gift of the Holy Spirit. Sydney: Catholic Institute of Sydney, 1979.

_____. "The "Incarnation of the Holy Spirit in Christ"." Theological Studies 45:3 (1984): 466-480.

_____. "The Palamite Doctrine of God: A New Perspective." St. Vladimir's Theological Quarterly 32:4 (1988): 329-358.

_____. "The Proper Mission of the Holy Spirit." Theological Studies 47:2 (1986): 227-250.

Colker, Marvin L. "Richard of St. Victor and the Anonymous of Bridlington." Traditio 18 (1962): 181-227.

Collins, Steven. Selfless Persons: Imagery and Thought in 'Thervada' Buddhism. Cambridge: Cambridge Univ. Press, 1982.

Congar, Yves M. J. I Believe in the Holy Spirit. 3 vols. trans. by David Smith. New York: Seabury Press, 1979-1983.

Connelly, T. Gerard. "Perichoresis and the Faith That Personalizes, according to Jean Mouroux." Ephemerides Theologicae Lovaniensis 62:4 (1986): 356-380.

Congresso Internazionale di studi boeziani. ed. L. Obertello. Pavia 5-8, Oct., 1980. Rome: Editrice Herder, 1981.

Constable, Giles. Religious Life and Thought (11th and 12th centuries). London: Variorum Reprints, 1979.

Cooke, Bernard. Beyond Trinity. The Aquinas Lecture, 1969. Milwaukee: Marquette Univ. Press, 1969.

_____. "The Theology of Person." Spiritual Life 7 (1961): 11-20.

Copleston, F. C. A History of Medieval Philosophy. New York: Harper Torchbooks, Harper and Row Pub., 1974.

Cousins, Ewert H. Bonaventure and the Coincidence of Opposites. Chicago: Franciscan Herald Press, 1978.

_____. "The Coincidence of Opposites in the Christology of Saint Bonaventure." Franciscan Studies Annual 7 (1968): 27-45.

_____. "Fecundity and Trinity: An Appendix to Chapter Three of The Great Chain of Being. In Studies in Medieval Culture 11. eds. J.R. Sommerfeldt and Thomas H. Seiler. Medieval Institute, 103-108. Kalamazoo: Western Michigan Univ., 1977.

_____. "God as Dynamic in Bonaventure and Contemporary Thought." In Proceedings of the American Philosophical Society 48 (1974): 136-148.

_____. "Harmony in Nature and Man." In Person and God. eds. George F. McLean and Hugo Meynell, 227-238. The International Society for Metaphysics vol. 3. Studies in Metaphysics. Lanham: Univ. Press of America, 1988.

_____. "Models and the Future of Theology." Continuum 7:1 (1969): 78-92.

_____. "The Notion of the Person in the 'De Trinitate' of Richard of St. Victor." Ph. D. dissertation, Fordham Univ., 1966.

_____. "The Temporality of God in Process Theology." In Kerygma und Mythos 6:8. Theologische Forschung 59. Hamburg: Herbert Reich, 1976.

_____. "A Theology of Interpersonal Relations." Thought 45 (1970): 56-82.

_____. "The Trinity and World Religions." Journal of Ecumenical Studies 7:3 (1970): 476-498

Couturier, C. "La structure métaphysique de l'homme d'après Saint Augustin." In Augustinus Magister: Congrès International Augustinien 1. 543-550. Paris: Études Augustiniennes, 1954.

Cowburn, John. The Person and Love. New York: Alba House, 1967.

Cramer, Winfrid. Der Geist Gottes und des Menschen in frühsyrischer Theologie. In Münsterische Beiträge zur Theologie, vol. 46. Münster: Aschendorff, 1979.

Crawford, R.G. "Is the Doctrine of the Trinity Scriptural?" Scottish Journal of Theology 20 (1967): 282-294.

Crewdson, Joan O. "Michael Polanyi: A Conservative Revolutionary." Frontier 18:4 (1975/6): 204-207.

Cristiani, Leon. Heresies and Heretics. trans. Roderick Bright. New York: Hawthorn Books Publishers, 1959.

Cross, Nicol. "The Blessed Trinity." Hibbert Journal 55 (1956/57): 233-240.

Crouse, Robert L. "In Multa Defluximus: Confessions X, 29-43 and St. Augustine's Theory of Personality." In NeoPlatonism and Early Christian Thought: Essays in Honor of A.H. Armstrong. eds. H.J. Blumenthal and R.A. Markus, 181-185. London: Variorum Publications Ltd., 1981.

Crouse R. D. "St. Augustine's 'De Trinitate': Philosophical Method." In Studia Patristica 16:2. ed. Elizabeth A. Livingstone, 501-510. Berlin: Akademie-Verlag, 1985.

Cullman, Oscar. Christ and Time. trans. Floyd Filson. Philadelphia: Westminster Press, 1950.

_____. The Christology of the New Testament. rev. ed. and trans. Shirley G. Guthrie and Charles A.M. Hall. Philadelphia: Westminster Press, 1959.

Cunliffe-Jones, H. "Two Questions Concerning the Holy Spirit." Theology 72 (1975): 283-298.

Curran, Rosemary T. "Whitehead's Notion of the Person and the Saving of the Past." Scottish Journal of Theology 36:3 (1983): 363-385.

Curtis, Olin A. The Christian Faith. New York: Eaton and Mains, 1905.

Cuskelly, E.J. "Grace and Person." Australasian Catholic Record 38 (1961): 114-122.

Cyril of Alexandria. Cathechetical Lectures. NPNF2 vol. 7.

Dahlstrom, Daniel O. ed. Existential Personalism. Proceedings of the American Catholic Philosophical Association. vol. 60. Washington: American Catholic Philosophical Association, 1986.

D'Alverny, M.-Th. "Achard de Saint Victor. De Trinitate-De Unitate et pluralitate creaturarum." Récherches de Théologie ancienne et médiévale 21 (1954): 299-306.

Dalmau, José M. "La Analogia en el concepto de persona." Estudios Ecclesiásticos 28 (1954): 195-210.

Danielou, Jean. "La Notion de personne chez les pères grecs." In Problèmes de la Personne. ed. I. Meyerson, 183-191. Paris: Mouton and Co., 1973.

Daniels, Donald E. "The Argument of the De Trinitate and Augustine's Theory of Signs." In Augustine Studies. vol. 8. Villanova: Villanova Univ., 1977.

Davey, J. E. "Lines of approach to a trinitarian ontology." Hibbert Journal 55 (1956/57): 223-232.

Deats, Paul and Carol Robb. The Boston Personalist Tradition. Macon, Ga.: Mercer Univ. Press, 1986.

De Boylesve, Pierre Faucon. Être et Savoir: études du fondement d'intelligibilité dans la pensée médiévale. Paris: Librarie philosophique J. Vrin, 1985.

De Chardin, Pierre Teilhard. The Phenomenon of Man. intro. Sir Julian Huxley. New York: Harper and Row, Pub., 1961.

Dederen, Raoul. "Reflections on the Doctrine of the Trinity." Andrews University Seminary Studies 8 (1970): 1-22.

Degl'Innocente, Humbertus. "De actu essendi substantiali et constitutione personae." In Sapientia Aquinatis: Communicationes IV Congressus Thomistici Internationalis. Rome, 13-17 September, 1955. Rome: Officium Libri Catholici, 1955.

De Halleux, A. "'Hypostase" et 'Personne" dans la formation du dogme trinitaire (ca. 375-381)." Revue d'Histoire Ecclésiastique 29:2 (1984): 313-369.

Delhaye, Philippe. "Les Perspectives Morales de Richard de Saint-Victor." In Mélanges offerts à Rene Crozet. 2 vols. ed. Pierre Gallais and Yves-Jean Rion, 851-862. Poitiers: Société d'études médiévales, 1966.

De Lubac, Henri. Exégèse Medievale: Les quatre sens de l'ecriture. 2 vols. in 4 parts. Paris: Aubier, 1959-1964.

de Margerie, Bertrand. "L'analogie familiale de la Trinite." Science et Esprit 24 (1972): 77-92.

_____. The Christian Trinity in History. Still River, Massachusetts: St. Bede's Pub., 1982.

_____. "Relations humains et relations divines: Reflexions sur la Trinité economique et immanente." Divinitas 18 (1974): 5-39.

_____. "Reflexions sur la Trinite economique et immanente: Relations humaines et relations divines." Esprit et Vie 90:13 (1980): 177-184.

Demers, G.-Ed. "Les divers sens du mot 'ratio' au moyen âge. Autour d'un texte de Maître Ferrier de Catalogne (1275)." In Études d'histoire littéraire et doctrinale du XIIIe siècle. Premiere Serie, I. 105-139. Montreal: Publications de l'Institute des études médiévales, 1932.

Deneffe, August. "Perichoresis, circumincessio, circumisessio: Eine terminologische Unters."

Zeitschrift für katholische Theologie 47 (1923): 497-532.

Denzinger, Henrich and Adolph Schömetzer. Enchiridion Symbolorum: Definitionum et Declarationum de rebus fidei et morum. 33rd ed. Freiburg: Verlag Herder, 1965.

de Régnon, Theodore. Études de théologie positive sur la Sainte Trinité. 4 vols. Paris: Victor Retaux et Fils, 1892.

Descartes, René. Oeuvres de Descartes. vol. 3. Correspondence: Jan 1640-Jan 1643. Paris: Charles Adam and Paul Tannery, 1956.

_____. Philosophical Letters. trans. and ed. Anthony Kenny. Oxford: Clarendon Press, 1970.

Dettloff, Werner. S. Bonaventura: 1274-1974. 4 vols. Rome: Collegio S. Bonaventura Grottaferrata, 1974.

De Vogel, C.J. "The Concept of Personality in Greek and Christian Thought." Studies in Philosophy and the History of Philosophy 2 (1963): 20-60.

Dewart, Joanne M. "The Notion of "Person" Underlying the Christology of Theodore of Mopsuetia." In Studia Patristica 12:1. ed. Elizabeth A. Livingstone, 199-207. Berlin: Akademie-Verlag, 1975.

Dewart, Leslie. The Future of Belief: Theism in a World Come of Age. New York: Herder and Herder, 1966.

De Wulf, Maurice. History of Medieval Philosophy: 2 vols. trans. Ernst C. Messenger. New York: Dover Publications, 1952.

_____. Philosophy and Civilization in the Middle Ages. Princeton: Princeton Univ. Press, 1922.

Dickinson, John Compton. The Origins of the Austin Canons and Their Introduction into England. London: SPCK, 1950.

Dictionary of Christian Ethics. S.v. "Persons and Personality," by G. F. Woods. ed. John MacQuarrie. 1967.

Dictionary of Latin and Greek Terms. ed. Richard A Muller. Grand Rapids: Baker Book House, 1985.

Dictionary of the Middle Ages. S.v. "Richard of St. Victor." ed. Joseph Strayer. New York: Charles Scribner's Sons, 1988.

Dictionary of the Middle Ages. S.v. "Trinitarian Doctrine," by Kenan Osborne. ed. Joseph R. Strayer. vol. 12. New York: Charles Scribner's Sons, 1989.

Dictionary of Moral Theology. S.v. "Person, Human." ed. M. Petro Palazzini. 1962.

Dictionary of Philosophy and Religion: Eastern and Western Thought. S.v. "Person." ed. William Reese. 1980.

Dictionary of Theology. S.v. "Person." ed. Louis Bouyer. trans. Charles Underhill Quinn. New York: Desclee Co., 1965.

Dictionnaire etymologique de la langue grecque: Histoire des Mots. vol.3. S.v. "Personne," by Pierre Chatraine. Paris: Éditions Klincksieck, 1974.

Dictionnaire etymologique de la langue latine: histoire des mots. S.v. "Persona," by A. Ernout and A. Meillet. Paris: Éditions Klincksieck, 1979.

Dictionnaire de Théologie. S.v. "Richard de Saint Victor," by E. Levesque. vol. 13, 1936 edition.

Dictionnaire de Théologie Catholique. S.v. "Hypostase," by A. Michel. vol. 7. col.369-437. Paris: Librairie Letouzey et Ané, 1922.

_____. vol. 15. S.v. "Trinité," by G. Bardy and A. Michel. Paris: Librarie Letouzey et Ané, 1945.

Dietz, Mary G. Between the Human and the Divine: The Political Thought of Simone Weil. Totowa, NJ.: Rowman and Littlefield, 1988.

Dillon, John. The Middle Platonists. Ithaca: Cornell Univ. Press, 1977.

_____. "Origin's Doctrine of the Trinity and Some Later Neo-platonic Theories." In Neo-platonism and Christian Thought. ed. Dominic J. O'Meara, 19-23. Albany: State Univ. of New York Press, 1982.

Dionysius the Areopagite, On the Divine Names and the Mystical Theology. trans. C. E. Rolt. Translations of Christian Literature. Series 1. Greek Texts. New York: Macmillan, 1920.

_____. The Celestial Hierarchies. trans. Editors of the Shrine of Wisdom. Manual 15. London: The Shrine of Wisdom, 1935.

Disandro, C.A. "Historia semántica de 'perikhóresis'." In Studia Patristica 15:1. ed. Elizbeth A. Livingstone, 442-447. Berlin: Akademie-Verlag, 1985.

Dix, Dom Gregory. The Image and the Likeness of God. New York: Morehouse-Gorham Co., 1954.

Dobbin, Edmund J. "Towards a Theology of the Holy Spirit, I." Heythrop Journal 27:1 (1976): 5-19.

Donnelly, Malachi J. "The Supernatural Person." Irish Theological Quarterly 30:4 (1963): 340-347.

Dorenkemper, Mark. The Trinitarian Doctrine and Sources of St. Caesarius of Arles. Fribourg, Switzerland: The University Press, 1953.

Doull, James A. "Augustinian Trinitarianism and Existential Theology." Dionysius. Halifax, N.S.: 3 (Dec., 1979): 111-159.

Dowdall, H.C. "The Word "Person"." The Church Quarterly Review 212 (July,1928): 229-264.

Drobner, Hubertus, R. Person-Exegese und Christologie bei Augustinus: zur herkunft der formal "una persona". Leiden: E.J. Brill, 1986.

Drury, John. "Personal and Impersonal in Theology." Theology (1984): 427-431.

Duclow, Donald F. "Gregory of Nyssa and Nicholas of Cusa: Infinity, Anthropology and the 'Via Negativa'." Downside Review 92:2 (1974): 102-108.

Dumeige, Gervais. Ives Épitre a Séverin sur la charité: Richard de Saint-Victor, Les Quatre degrés de la violente charité. vol. 3. Textes Philosophiques du Moyen Age. Paris: Librarie philosophique J. Vrin, 1955.

_____. Richard de Saint-Victor et l'Idée Chrétienne de l'Amour. Paris: Presses Universitaires de France, 1952.

Dumont, Louis. Essays on Individualism: Modern Ideology in Anthropological Perspective. Chicago: Univ. of Chicago Press, 1986.

Dunne, John. A Search for God in Time and Memory. Notre Dame: Univ. of Notre Dame Press, 1972.

Dunne, Tad. "Trinity and History." Theological Studies 45 (1984): 139-142.

Dunning. H. Ray. Grace, Faith and Holiness: A Wesleyan Systematic Theology. Kansas City: Beacon Hill Press, 1988.

Duns Scotus, Johannes. Opera Omnia ed. Vivès. Paris: 1891-1895.

Dupuy, Bernard. "Trinité et royaume de Dieu: Un nouvel ouvrage de Jürgen Moltmann." Istina 30:1 (1985): 81-89.

Du Roy, Jean-Baptiste. "L'expérience de l'amour et l'intelligence de la foi trinitaire selon Saint Augustin." In Recherches Augustiniennes vol. 2. 415-445. Paris: Études Augustiniennes, 1962.

Du Roy, Olivier. L'Intelligence de la foi en la Trinité selon Saint Augustin. Paris: Études Augustiniennes, 1966.

Durrant, Michael. Theology and Intelligibility. Boston: Routledge and Kegan Paul, 1973.

Dwyer, John C. Son of Man and Son of God: New Language for Faith. New York: Paulist Press, 1983.

Ebner, Joseph. Die Erkenntnislehre Richards von St. Viktor. In Beiträge zur Geschichte du Philosophie des Mittelalters: texte und untersuchungen. vol. 19:4. Münster: Aschendorff, 1917.

Elmore, Floyd. "An Evangelical Analysis of Process Pneumatology." Bibliotheca Sacra 145 no. 577 (Jan-Mar, 1988): 15-29.

Emad, Parvis. "Person, Death and World." In Max Scheler 1874-1928: Centennial Essays. ed. Manfred S. Frings. The Hague: Martinus Nijhof, 1974.

Emilianos, Timiadis. "The Holy Trinity in Human Life." One in Christ 21:1 (1985): 1-18.

Encyclopedia Judaica. S.v. "Man, The Nature of." vol. 11. Encyclopedia Judaica Jerusalem. Macmillan Comp. Jerusalem: Keter Pub. House, 1971.

Ethier, Albert-Marie. Le "De Trinitate" de Richard de Saint-Victor. Paris: Vrin, 1939.

Ettlinger, G. H. "Theos de ouk outos" (Gregory of Nazianzus, "Oratio XXXVII": The Dignity of the Human Person according to the Greek Fathers." In Studia Patristica 16:2. ed. Elizabeth A. Livingstone, 301-304. Berlin: Akademie-Verlag, 1985.

Evans, C. Stephen. Preserving the Person: A Look at the Human Sciences. Grand Rapids: Baker Book House, 1977.

Evans, E. "Tertullian's Theological Terminology." The Church Quarterly Review 139 (Oct-Dec.1944): 56-77.

Evans, G. R. "St. Anselm's Images of the Trinity." Journal of Theological Studies n.s. 27 (1976): 46-57.

Evdokimov, Paul. "Mystère de la Personne Humaine." Contacts 21 (1969): 272-289.

Fairweather, Eugene R. A Scholastic Miscellany: Anselm to Ockham. New York: Macmillan Co., 1970.

Faith and Order Studies: 1964-1967. Reprint from Faith and Order Paper no. 50. New Directions in Faith and Order. Geneva: World Council of Churches, 1968.

Faith and Renewal. Reports and Documents of the Commission on Faith and Order. Stavanger, Norway, 1985. ed. Thomas F. Best. Faith and Order Paper no. 131. Geneva: World Council of Churches, 1986.

Farley, Edward. "God as Dominator and Image-Giver: Divine Sovereignty and the New Anthropology." Journal of Ecumenical Studies 6 (1969): 354-375.

_____. "Toward a Contemporary Theology of Human Being." In Images of Man. ed. J. William Angell and E. Pendleton Banks. n.p.:Mercer Univ. Press, 1984.

Farrell, Walter. A Companion to the Summa. 4 vols. New York: Sheed and Ward, 1945-1947.

Farrer, Austin. Finite and Infinite: A Philosophical Essay New York: Seabury Press, 1979.

_____. "The Prior Actuality of God." In Reflective Faith: Essays in Philosophical Theology. ed Charles C. Conti, 178-191. Grand Rapids: Eerdmans Pub. Co., 1974.

Fatula, Mary Ann. "The Holy Spirit and Human Actualization through Love: The Contribution of Aquinas." Theology Digest 32:3 (Fall,1985): 217-224.

Fay, Thomas. "Imago Dei: Augustine's Metaphysics of Man." Antonianum 49 (1974): 173-197.

Feenstra, Ronald J. and Cornelius Plantinga. eds. Trinity, Incarnation and Atonement: Philosophical and Theological Essays. Notre Dame: Univ. of Notre Dame Press, 1989.

Feiner, Johannes and Magnus Löhrer. eds. Mysterium Salutis vol. 2 of 6 vols. Die Heilsgeschichte vor Christus. Einsiedeln: Benzinger Verlag, 1967.

Ferré, Nels F. S. "Beyond Substance and Process." Theology Today 24:2 (1967): 160-171.

_____. "A Theological Doctrine of Man." Religion in Life 11:4 (1942): 571-583.

Ferruolo, Stephen C. The Origins of the University: The Schools of Paris. Stanford: Stanford Univ. Press, 1985.

Fichtner, Joseph. A Christian Anthropology: Man, The Image of God. New York: Alba House, 1978.

Fiddes, Paul S. The Creative Suffering of God. Oxford: Clarendon Press, 1988.

Finan, Barbara Ann. "The Mission of the Holy Spirit in the Theology of Karl Rahner." Ph.D. dissertation, Marquette Univ., 1986.

Findlay, John N. "The Impersonality of God." In God: The Contemporary Discussion. eds. by Frederick Sontag and M. Darrol Bryant, 181-196. New York: Rose of Sharon Press Inc., 1982.

Fischer, Konrad. De Deo trino et uno. Göttingen: Vandenhoeck and Ruprecht, 1978.

Flew, R. Newton. The Idea of Perfection in Christian Theology: An Historical Study of the Christian Ideal for the Present Life. London: Oxford Univ. Press, 1934.

Ford, David F. "'The Best Apologetics is Good Systematics.' A Proposal About the Place of Narrative in Christian Systematic Theology." Anglican Theological Review 67:3 (1985): 232-259.

Ford, Josephine Massingberd. "The Ray, the Root and the River: A Note on the Jewish Origin of Trinitarian Images." In Studia Patristica 11:2 ed. F.L. Cross, 158-165. Berlin: Akademie-Verlag, 1972.

_____. The Spirit and the Human Person. Dayton, Ohio: Pflaum Press, 1969.

Ford, Lewis. The Lure Of God. Philadelphia: Fortress Press, 1978.

_____. "Process Trinitarianism." Journal of the American Academy of Religion 43 (1975): 199-213.

Ford, Stephen H. "Perichoresis and Interpenetration: Samuel Taylor Coleridge's Trinitarian Conception of Unity." Theology 89:727 (1986): 20-24.

Fortman, Edmund J. The Triune God. Reprint. Grand Rapids: Baker Book House, 1982.

Fourth World Conference on Faith and Order: Montreal 1963. ed. P.C. Rodgers and Lukas Vischer. New York: Association Press, 1964.

Fowler, Dean R. "A Process Theology of Interdependence." Theological Studies 40:1 (1979): 44-58.

Fox, Robert W. "Athanasian Meaning of "Being One Substance with the Father"." Lutheran Quarterly 12:3 (1960): 205-216.

Fraigneau-Julien, B. "Réflexion sur la signification religieuse du mystère de la Sainte Trinité." Nouvelle Revue Theologique 87:7 (1965): 673-687.

Frank, Erich. Philosophical Understanding and Religious Truth. London and New York: Oxford Univ. Press, 1945.

Frank, S. L. Reality and Man: An Essay in the Metaphysics of Human Nature. trans. from the Russian by Natalie Duddington. New York: Taplinger Pub. Co., 1966.

Freeman, Kenneth D. "The Mutuality of Divine Love." Drew Gateway 40:1 (1969): 15-21.

Frend, W. H. C. "The Doctrine of Man in the Early Church: An Historical Approach." The Modern Churchman 45:3 (1955): 216-231.

_____. The Rise of Christianity. Philadelphia: Fortress Press, 1984.

Fuller, Reginald H. "On Demythologizing the Trinity." Anglican Theological Review 43:2 (April,1961): 121-131.

Gaede, S. D. Where Gods May Dwell: Understanding the Human Condition. Grand Rapids: Zondervan Publishing House/ Academie Books, 1985.

Gallagher, Kenneth T. Philosophy of Gabriel Marcel. foreword by Gabriel Marcel. New York: Fordham Univ. Press, 1975.

Galot, Jean. The Person of Christ: Covenant Between God and Man. Chicago: Franciscan Herald Press, 1984.

_____. "Valeur de la notion de personne dans l'expression du mystère du Christ." Gregorianum 55:1 (1974): 69-97.

_____. Who is Christ? Chicago: Franciscan Herald Press, 1981.

Geach, Peter. The Virtues: The Stanton Lectures, 1973-1974. New York: Cambridge Univ. Press, 1977.

Geisler, Norman and Winfried Corduan. Philosophy of Religion. Grand Rapids: Baker Book House, 1988.

Geisser, Hans. "Der Beitrag der Trinitätslehre sur problematik des Redens von Gott." Zeitschrift für Theologie und Kirche 65 (1968): 231-255.

Gelber, Hester Goodenough. "Logic and the Trinity: A Clash of Values in Scholastic Thought, 1300-1335." Ph.D. dissertation, Univ. of Wisconsin-Madison, 1974.

Gelpi, Donald. The Divine Mother: A Trinitarian Theology of the Holy Spirit. Lanham: Univ. Press of America, 1988

Gerlitz, Peter. Ausserchristliche einflüssse auf die Entwicklung des christlichen Trinitätsdogmas. Leiden: E. J. Brill, 1963.

Gersh, Stephen. Middle Platonism and Neoplatonism. In Publications in Medieval Studies. ed. Ralph McInerny. vol.23:1,2. Notre Dame: Univ. of Notre Dame Press, 1986.

_____. "Platonism, Neo-Platonism and Aristotelianism in the Twelfth Century." In Renaissance and Renewal in the Twelfth Century. ed. Robert Benson, et al., 512-534. Cambridge: Harvard Univ. Press, 1982.

Ghellinck, J. de. "L'histoire de 'persona' et d'hypostasis dans un ecrit anonyme porrétain du XIIe siècle." Revue neoscholastique de philosophie. 36 (1934): 111-127.

Giannaras, Christos. "Consequences of an Erroneous Trinitology in the Human World." In Les Études Theologiques de Chambesy. vol. 2, 497-502. La signification et l'actualité du IIe Concile Oecumenique pour le monde Chrètien d'aujourd'hui. Chambesy-Geneve: Editions du Centre Orthodoxe du Patriarcat Oecumenique, 1982.

_____. "The Distinction between Essence and Energies and its Importance for Theology." St. Vladimir's Theological Quarterly 19 (1975): 232-245.

_____. The Freedom of Morality. trans. Elizabeth Briere. Crestwood: St. Vladimir's

Seminary Press, 1984.

_____. Person und Eros: Eine Gegenüberstellung der Ontologie der griechieschen Kirchenväter und der Existenzphilosophie des Westens. Göttingen: Vandenhoeck and Ruprecht, 1982.

Gibbon, Edward. The Decline and Fall of the Roman Empire. 2 vols. In The Great Books. ed. R. M. Hutchins. Chicago: Encyclopaedia Brittanica, 1952.

Gill, Christopher. "Personhood and Personality: The Four-personae Theory in Cicero, de Officiis I." In Oxford Studies in Ancient Philosophy. vol. 6. ed. Julia Annas, 169-199. Oxford: Clarendon Press, 1988.

Gilligan, Carol. A Different Voice: Psychological Theory and Women's Development. Cambridge: Harvard Univ. Press, 1982.

Gilson, Etienne. The Mystical Theology. New York: Sheed and Ward, 1940.

_____. The Spirit of Medieval Philosophy. trans. A. H. C. Downes. New York: Charles Scribner's Sons, 1940.

Gist, Richard. "Soul and the Person in Defining Life." Christian Century 18:32 (Oct. 14,1981): 1022-1024.

Glicksberg, Charles I. The Self in Modern Literature. University Park, Pennsylvania: Pennsylvania State Univ. Press, 1963.

Gonzalez, Olegario. "Sobre las fuentes de Ricardo de San Victor y su influjo en San Buenaventura." La Ciudad de Dios, 176:3-4 (1963): 567-602.

Gonzalez, Severino. La Formula "mia ousia treis hypostaseis" en San Gregorio de Nisa. vol. 21. Series Facultatis theologicae. Sectio B. (n.11). Rome: Typis Pontificiae Universitatis Gregorianae, 1939.

Gorringe, T. J. "'Not Assumed is not Healed': The Homoousion and Liberation Theology." Scottish Journal of Theology 38:4 (1985): 481-490.

Gracia, Jorge J. E. Introduction to the Problem of Individuation in the Early Middle Ages. Washington: Catholic Univ. of America Press, 1984.

Grane, Leif. Peter Abelard. trans. Frederick and Christine Crowley. London: George Allen and Unwin, Ltd., 1970.

Grant, C. David. "Personal and Impersonal Concepts of God: A Tension Within Contemporary Christian Theology." Encounter 49:2 (Spring, 1988): 79-91.

Grant, Robert M. Early Christian Doctrine of God. Charlottesville: Univ. Press of Virginia, 1966.

_____. Gods and the One God. Library of Early Christianity. ed. Wayne A. Meeks. Philadelphia: Westminster Press, 1986.

Gray, Patrick T. R. The Defense of Chalcedon in the East (451-553). Leiden: E. J. Brill, 1979.

_____. "Theodoret on the "One Hypostasis." Studia Patristica 17:3 ed. Elizabeth A. Livingstone. 301-304. Berlin: Akademie-Verlag, 1985.

Gregory of Nazianzus. Orations 1-26. PG. vol. 35.

_____. Orations 27-45. PG. vol. 36.

_____. Funeral Orations. FC. vol. 22.

_____. Repertorium Nazianzenum: Orationes, Textus Graecus. ed. Justin Mossay. In Studien zur Geschichte und Kultur des Altertums, Neue Folge, 2 Reihe: Forschungen zu Gregor von Nazianz, 1. Heft. Paderborn: Schöningh, 1981.

_____. Selected Orations and Letters. NPNF2. vol. 7.

Gregory of Nyssa. The Catechetical Oration of Gregory of Nyssa. ed. James Herbert Strawley. Cambridge Patristic Texts. Cambridge: Cambridge Univ. Press, 1956.

_____. Gregorii Nysseni Opera. ed. Werner Jaeger. Institutum pro Studiis Classicis Harvardianum. 9 vols. Leiden: E. J. Brill, 1958-1972.

_____. Select Writings and Letters. trans., with intro., William Moore and Henry Austin Williams. NPNF. vol. 5.

Grider, Kenneth J. "The Holy Trinity." In Basic Christian Doctrine. ed. Carl F. H. Henry, 35-41. Reprint. Grand Rapids: Baker Book House, 1979.

Griechisches Etymologische Wörterbuch. S.v. "Prosopon," by Hjalmar Frisk. Heidelberg: Carl Winter/ Universitätsverlag, 1970.

Grillmeier, Aloys. Christ in Christian Tradition. trans. John Bowden. 2nd rev. ed. London: Mowbrays, 1975.

Grote, George. Aristotle. 2 vols. London: John Murray, 1872.

Gruenler, Royce Gordon. The Inexhaustible God. Grand Rapids: Baker Book House, 1983.

_____. The Trinity in the Gospel of John: A Thematic Commentary on the Fourth Gospel. Grand Rapids: Baker Book House, 1986.

Guardini, Romano. The World and the Person. trans. Stella Lange. Chicago: Henry Regnery Co., 1965.

Guillet, J. et al. L'Homme Devant Dieu: Mélanges offerts au Père Henri de Lubac. Paris: Aubier, 1963.

Guimet, Fernand. "'Caritas ordinata' et 'Amor Discretus' dans la theologie trinitaire de Richard de Saint-Victor." Revue du Moyen Age latin 4 (1948): 225-236.

_____. "Notes en marge d'un texte de Richard de Saint-Victor." Archives d'Histoire Doctrinale et Littérature vol. 14. 371-394. Paris: Librarie Philosophique J. Vrin, 1943.

Gunten, F. Von. "La notion de personne dans la Trinité d'apres Alexandre de Hales." Divus Thomas 28 (1950): 36-62.

Gunton, Colin E. The Actuality of the Atonement: A Study of Metaphor, Rationality and the Christian Tradition. Grand Rapids: Zondervan, 1991.

_____. "Augustine, The Trinity and the Theological Crisis in the West." Scottish Journal of Theology 43:1 (1990): 33-58.

_____. "Barth, The Trinity and Human Freedom." Theology Today 43:3 (Oct. 1986): 316-330.

_____. Becoming and Being. Oxford: Oxford Univ. Press, 1978.

_____. "Christ the Sacrifice: Aspects of the Language and Imagery of the Bible." In L. D. Hurst and N. T. Wright eds. 228-238. The Glory of Christ in the New Testament: Studies in Christology. Oxford: Clarendon Press, 1987.

_____. Enlightenment and Alienation. Grand Rapids: Eerdmans Pub. Co., 1985.

_____. "Using and Being Used: Scripture and Systematic Theology." Theology Today 47:3 (October, 1990): 248-259.

Gustafson, Scott W. "Gregory of Nyssa's Reformulation of Christian Thought: Some Paradigmatic Implications of his Doctrine of the Divine Infinity." Ph. D. dissertation, Drew University, 1985.

Hadot, P. "L'Image de la Trinité dans l'âme chez Victorinus et chez Saint Augustin." In Studia Patristica 6:4. ed. F.L. Cross, 409-442. Berlin: Akademie-Verlag, 1962.

_____. "De Tertullien à Boèce: le development de la notion de 'personne' dans les controverses theologiques." In Problèmes de la personne. ed. I. Meyerson, 123-134. Paris: Mouton and Co.

Hall, Douglas John. Imaging God: Dominion as Stewardship. Grand Rapids: Eerdmans Pub. Co. and New York: Friendship Press, 1986.

Hamilton, Robert. "Individuation and Co-Inherence: A Manifesto." Theology 89:727 (1986): 15-20.

Hammond, Guy B. "Tillich on the Personal God." Journal of Religion 44 (1964): 289-293.

Hammond, Lewis M. "The Medieval Doctrine of Man." Anglican Theological Review 42:4 (1960): 347-361.

Hankey, W. J. God in Himself: Aquinas' Doctrine of God as Expounded in the Summa Theologiae. New York: Oxford Univ. Press, 1987.

_____. "The Place of the Psychological Image of the Trinity in the Arguments of Augustine's De Trinitate, Anselm's Monologion, and Aquinas' Summa Theologiae." Dionysius 3 (1979): 99-110.

Hanson, Richard P. C. "The Doctrine of the Trinity Achieved in 381." Scottish Journal of Theology 36:1 (1983): 41-57. Found also in Studies in Christian Antiquity, 233-252.

_____. The Search for the Christian Doctrine of God. Edinburgh: T. & T. Clark, 1988.

_____. Studies in Christian Antiquity. Edinburgh: T. & T. Clark, 1985.

_____. "The Transformation of Images in the Trinitarian Theology of the Fourth Century." In Studia Patristica 17:1. ed. Elizabeth A. Livingstone, 97-115. Oxford: Pergamon Press Ltd., 1982. Found also in Studies in Christian Antiquity, 253-278.

Hardy, Daniel and David F. Ford. Praising and Knowing God. Philadelphia: Westminster Press, 1985.

Hardy, Edward. Christology of the Later Fathers. In The Library of Christian Classics. ed. Edward R. Hardy. Philadelphia: Westminster Press, 1954.

Haren, Michael. Medieval Thought: The Western Intellectual Tradition from Antiquity to the Thirteenth Century. New York: St. Martin's Press, 1985.

Häring, N. "A Treatise on the Trinity by Gilbert of Poitiers." Recherches de Theologie Ancienne et Médiévale 29 (1972): 14-50.

Harman, Allan M. "Speech about the Trinity: With Special Reference to Novatian, Hilary and Calvin." Scottish Journal of Theology 26 (1973): 385-400.

Harnack, Adolf. History of Dogma. trans. E.B. Speirs and James Millar. 7 vols. London: Williams and Norgate, 1898.

_____. Outlines of the History of Dogma. trans. Edwin Knox Mitchell. intro. Philip Rieff. Boston: Beacon Press, 1957.

_____. What is Christianity? trans. Thomas Bailey Saunders. intro. Rudolf Bultmann. New York: Harper Torchbooks, 1957.

Haroutounian, Joseph. "Christian Faith and Metaphysics." Journal of Religion 33 (1953): 103-112.

_____. "The Spirit of God and the People of God." Union Seminary Quarterly Review 12:4 (1957): 39-54.

Harré, Rom. Personal Being: A Theory for Individual Psychology. Cambridge: Harvard Univ. Press, 1984.

Hartshorne, Charles and William L. Reese. Philosophers Speak of God. Chicago and London: Univ. of Chicago Press, 1953. Midway Reprint, 1976.

Hasker, William. "Tri-Unity." Journal of Religion (Jan., 1970): 1-32.

Hassel, David J. "Conversion-Theory and Scientia in the "De Trinitate"." In Recherches Augustiniennes vol.2. 383-401. Paris:Études Augustiniennes, 1962.

Hatch, Edwin. The Influence of Greek Ideas on Christianity. New York: Harper Torchbooks, 1957.

Hatch, Edwin and Henry A. Redpath. A Concordance to the Septuagint. Reprint. Grand Rapids: Baker Book House, 1983.

Hauerwas. Stanley. "Happiness, the Life of Virtue and Friendship: Theological Reflections on Aristotelian Themes, 3 Parts." Asbury Theological Journal (Spring, 1990): 5-48

Hawkins, D. J. B. "On Nature and Person in Speculative Theology." The Downside Review 80:258. (1962): 1-11.

Hayen, André. "L'etre de la personne selon B. Jean Duns Scot." Revue philosphes de Louvain 53 (1955): 525-541.

Haymes, B. "The Supernatural is Personal." Baptist Quarterly 26:1 (1975): 2-13.

Hebblethwaite, Brian. "Perichoresis - Reflections on the Doctrine of the Trinity." Theology 80:676 (1977): 255-261.

Hebblethwaite, Brian and Stewart Sutherland. The Philosophical Frontiers of Christian Theology: Essays Presented to D. M. Mackinnon. Cambridge: Cambridge Univ. Press, 1982.

Hegel G. W. F. The Phenomenology of Mind. New York: Harper and Row, Pub., 1967.

Heitmann, Claus and Heribert Mühlen. Erfahrung und Theologie des Heilige Geists. Hamburg: Agentur des Rauhen Hauses, Münich: Verlag-Kösel: 1974.

Hendry, George S. The Holy Spirit in Christian Theology. rev. ed. Philadelphia: Westminster Press, 1965.

Henry, Paul. "The 'Adversus Arium' of Marius Victorinus, the First Systematic Exposition of the Doctrine of the Trinity." Journal of Theological Studies 6:1 n.s.(1950): 42-53.

_____. "Une Comparaison chez Aristote, Alexandre et Plotin." In Les Sources de Plotin. Entretiens. vol. 5. Geneva: Foundation Hardt, 1960.

_____. "On Some Implications of the "Ex Patre Filioque Tanquam Ab Uno Principio"." The Eastern Churches Quarterly 7:supp.2 (1948): 16-31.

_____. Saint Augustine on Personality: The Saint Augustine Lecture, 1959. The Saint Augustine Lecture Series. New York: Macmillan Co., 1960.

Hermann, Ingo. Kyrios und Pneuma: Studie zur Christologie der Paulinischen Hauptbriefe. In Studien zum Alten und Neuen Testament. vol. 2. Münich: Kösel-Verlag, 1961.

Heron, A. I. C. "Who Proceedeth from the Father and the Son: The Problem of the Filioque." Scottish Journal of Theology 24 (1971): 149-166.

Hibbert, Giles. "Mystery and Metaphysics in the Trinitarian Theology of St. Thomas." Irish Theological Quarterly 31 (1964): 187-213.

Hick, John. "Is God Personal?" In God: The Contemporary Discussion eds. Frederick Sontag and M. Darrol Bryant, 169-180. New York: Rose of Sharon Press Inc., 1982.

Hilary of Poitiers. The Trinity. trans. Stephen McKenna. FC. vol. 25. Washington: Catholic Univ. of America Press, 1954.

Hill, Edmund. "Karl Rahner's "Remarks on the Dogmatic Treatise 'De Trinitate' and St. Augustine." In Augustinian Studies 2. 67-80. Villanova: Villanova Univ. Press, 1971.

_____. The Mystery of the Trinity. London: Geoffrey Chapman, 1985.

_____. "Our Knowledge of the Trinity." Scottish Journal of Theology 27 (1974): 1-11.

Hill, William J. "Does the World Make a Difference to God?" The Thomist 38 (1974): 146-164.

_____. Knowing the Unknown God. New York: Philosophical Library, 1971.

_____. The Three-Personed God: The Trinity as a Mystery of Salvation. Washington: Catholic Univ. of America Press, 1982.

Hirzel, Rudolf. Die Person: Begriff und Name derselben im Altertum. Reprint. New York: Arno Press, 1976.

Hoban, James Henry. The Thomistic Concept of Person and Some of its Social Implications. In The Catholic University of America Philosophical Studies, vol. 43. Washington: Catholic Univ. Press, 1939.

Hodgson, Leonard. The Doctrine of the Trinity. New York: Charles Scribners Sons, 1944.

_____. "The Metaphysics of Nestorius." Journal of Theological Studies 19:1 (1918): 46-55.

Hofmann, Peter. "Analogie und Person: zur Trinitätspekulation Richards von St. Victor." Theologie und Philosophie 59 (1984): 191-234.

Hofmeier, Johann. Die Trinitätslehre des Hugo von St. Viktor. In Munchener Theologische Studien Pt. 2 Systematische Abteilung. vol. 25. Münich: Max Hueber Verlag, 1963.

Holmes, Arthur F. Contours of a World View. Grand Rapids: Eerdmans Pub. Co., 1983.

L'Homme et son destin d'après les penseurs du moyen âge: Actes du premier congrès internationale de philosophie Médiévale. Louvain-Brussels 28 August - 4 September, 1958. Louvain/Paris: Éditions Nauwelaerts, 1960

Horst, Friedrich. "Face to Face: The Biblical Doctrine of the Image of God." trans. John Bright. Interpretation 4:3 (1950): 259-270.

Houlden, J.L. "The Doctrine of the Trinity and the Person of Christ." The Church Quarterly Review 169 (1968): 4-18.

Houston, J. "On Being Human." Scottish Journal of Theology. 38:4 (1985): 471-479.

Houston Declaration, December 14-15, 1987.

Howe, Leroy. "Ontology, Belief and the Doctrine of the Trinity." Sophia (Melbourne) 20 (1981): 5-16.

Hufnagel, Alfons. "Die Wesensbestimmung der Person bei Alexander von Hales." Freiburger Zeitschrift für Philosophie und Theologie 4 (1957): 148-174.

Hugh of Saint Victor. PL. vols. 175, 176, 177.

_____. The Didascalion of Hugh of St. Victor: A Medieval Guide to the Arts. ed. and trans. Jerome Taylor. New York: Columbia Univ. Press, 1961.

_____. On The Sacraments of the Christian Faith. English Version by Roy J. Deferrari. Cambridge, Massachusetts: Mediaeval Academy of America, 1951.

The Human Agent. Royal Institute of Philosophy Lectures. vol. 1. 1966-1967. New York: St. Martin's Press, 1968.

Hume, David. An Inquiry Concerning Human Understanding. ed. Charles W. Hendel. New York: Liberal Arts Press, Inc., 1955.

Hummel, Horace D. "The Image of God." Concordia Journal 10:2 (1984): 83-93.

Hussey, Edmund M. "The Persons - Energy Structure in the Theology of St. Gregory Palamas." St. Vladimir's Theological Quarterly 18:1 (1974): 22-43.

Interpreter's Dictionary of the Bible. "Man, The Nature of." vol. 3. Abingdon: Nashville,

1962.

Jacobs, Alan Darwin. "Hilary of Poitier and the Homoousians: A Study of the Eastern Roots of his Ecumenical Trinitarianism." Ph. D. dissertation, Emory Univ., 1968.

Jaeger, Werner. Gregor von Nyssas Lehre vom Heiligen Geist. Leiden: E.J. Brill, 1966.

Jansen, Francois. "Le concept de 'personne' chez les latins entre 1150 et 1250." Nouvelle Revue Théologique, Tournai: Louvain 61 (1934): 389-395.

Jaspers, Karl. Plato and Augustine. New York: Harcourt, Brace and World Inc., 1957.

Javelet, Robert. "Psychologie des auteurs spirituels du deuxieme siècle." Revue des Sciences Religieuses 33:1,2,3 (1959): 18-64, 97-164, 209-268.

_____. "La réintroduction de la liberté dans les notions d'image." In Der Begriffe der Repraesentatio im mittelalter. ed. A Zimmerman, 1-34. Miscellanea Medievalia vol. 8. New York: Walter de Gruyter, 1971.

_____. "Sens et realité ultime selon Richard de Saint-Victor." Ultimate Reality 6:3 (1983): 221-243.

Jennings, Theodore W. Jr. Beyond Theism: A Grammar of God-Language. New York/Oxford: Oxford Univ. Press, 1985.

Jenson, Robert W. "Creation as a Triune Act." Word and World 2:1 (1982): 34-42.

_____. "Three Identities of One Action." Scottish Journal of Theology 28 (1975): 1-15.

_____. The Triune Identity. Philadelphia: Fortress Press, 1982.

Jerphagon, Lucien. "L'Histoire de la notion de Personne dans l'oeuvre de Maurice Nédoncelle." Revue de Théologie et de Philosophie 110 (1978): 99-109.

Jocque, Lucas and Ludovicus Milis, eds. Liber Ordinis Sancti Victoris Parisiensis. Corpus Christianorum. Continuatio Mediaevalis 61. Turnholt: Typographi Brepols Editores Pontificii, 1985.

John of Damascus. Exposition of the Orthodox Faith. NPNF2 vol. 9, Reprint. 1976.

_____. Writings. Trans. Frederich H. Chase. FC vol. 37, 1958.

Johnson, A. R. The One and the Many in the Israelite Conception of God. 2nd ed. Cardiff: Univ. of Wales Press, 1961.

Johnston, George. The Spirit-Paraclete in the Gospel of John. Cambridge: Cambridge Univ. Press, 1970.

Jones, O. R. The Concept of Holiness. London: George Allen and Unwin Ltd., 1961.

Jüngel, Eberhard. The Doctrine of the Trinity. Grand Rapids: Eerdmans Pub. Co., 1976.

_____. God's Being is in Becoming. trans. Horton Harris. Edinburgh: Scottish Academic Press, 1976.

_____. Gott als Geheimnis der Welt: Zur Begründung der Theologie des Gekreuzigten im Streit zwischen Theismus und Atheismus. Tübingen: J. C. B. Mohr, 1977.

_____. God As the Mystery of the World: On the Foundation of the Theology of the Crucified One in the Dispute between Theism and Atheism. Grand Rapids: Eerdmans Pub. Co., 1983.

_____. "The Relationship Between 'Economic' and 'Immanent' Trinity." Theology Digest 24 (Summer, 1976): 179-184.

Justin Martyr. Dialogue with Trypho. ANF vol. 1.

Kaiser, Christopher B. "Christology and Complementarity." Religious Studies 12 (1976): 37-48.

_____. "The Development of Johannine Motifs in Hilary's Doctrine of the Trinity." Scottish Journal of Theology 29:3 (June 1976): 237-247.

_____. "The Discernment of Trinity." Scottish Journal of Theology 28:5 (Oct. 1975): 449-460.

_____. The Doctrine of God. Westchester, Illinois: Crossway Books, 1982.

_____. "The Ontological Trinity in the Context of Historical Religions." Scottish Journal of Theology 29 (1976): 301-310.

Kant, Immanuel. Religion Within the Limits of Reason Alone. trans. with intro. and notes by T. M. Greene and H. H. Hudson. New York: Harper and Row, 1960.

Kantzer, K. and S. Gundry. Perspective in Evangelical Theology. Grand Rapids: Baker Book House, 1977.

Kaser, M. Roman Private Law. trans. Rolf Dannenberg. I, 271. London: Butterworths, 1968.

Kasper, Walter. The God of Jesus Christ. trans. Matthew J. O'Connell. New York: Crossroads Pub. Co., 1986.

Kaufman, Gordon D. Systematic Theology. New York: Scribners, 1968.

Kaufmann, Yehezkel. The Religion of Israel. New York: Schocken Books, 1972.

Keane, Kevin. "Ordo Bonitates: The Summa Fratris Alexandre and Lovejoy's Dilemma." In Jacob's Ladder and the Tree of Life: Concepts of Hierarchy and the Great Chain of Being. eds. Marion Leathers Kuntz and Paul Grimley Kuntz, 55-71. New York: Peter Lang, 1986.

Kee, Alistair. The Roots of Christian Freedom: The Theology of J.A.T. Robinson. London: SPCK, 1988.

Kee, Alistair and Eugene T. Long, eds. "Being and Truth: Essays in honor of John Macquarrie." London: SCM Press Ltd., 1986.

Kegley, Charles W. and Robert W. Bretall. eds. The Theology of Paul Tillich. New York: Macmillan Co., 1961.

Kehoe, Kimball. The Theology of God Sources. New York: Bruce Publishing Co., 1971.

Kelly, Anthony J. "God: How Near a Relation?" The Thomist 34:2 (1970): 191-229.

_____. "Trinity and Process: Relevance of the Basic Christian Confession of God." Theological Studies 31:3 (1970): 393-414.

_____. The Trinity of Love: A Theology of the Christian God. Wilmington: Michael Glazier, 1989.

Kelly, John Norman Davidson. The Athanasian Creed: The Paddock Lectures for 1962-3. London: Adam & Charles Black, 1964.

_____. Early Christian Doctrines. rev. ed. San Francisco: Harper & Row, Publishers, 1978.

Kerr, Fergus. Theology After Wittgenstein. New York: Basil Blackwell, 1986.

Kilcourse, George. "Interpersonal Love and Created Sanctifying Grace." Thought 48:189 (Summer, 1973): 240-255.

Kilian, Sabbas J. "The Holy Spirit in Christ and in Christians." American Benedictine Review 20 (1969): 99-121.

Kilmartin, Edward. Christian Liturgy, vol. 1 Systematic Theology of Liturgy. Kansas City: Sheed & Ward, 1988.

King-Farlow, John. "Is the Concept of the Trinity Obviously Absurd?" Sophia (Melbourne) 22 (1983): 37-42.

Kirkpatrick, Frank G. Community: A Trinity of Models. Wahington D.C.: Georgetown Univ. Press, 1986.

_____. "Toward a Metaphysic of Community." Scottish Journal of Theology 38:4 (1985): 565-581.

Kittel, Gerhard and Gerhard Friedrich, eds. Theological Dictionary of the New Testament. trans. and ed. Geoffrey W. Bromiley. 9 vols. Grand Rapids: Eerdmans, 1964-1974.

Kitwood, T.M. What is Human? Downers Grove, Illinois: Inter-Varsity Press, 1970.

Klappert, Bertold. "Tendenzen der Gotteslehre in der Gegenwart." Evangelische Theologie 35:3 (1975): 189-208.

Klibansky, Raymond. The Continuity of the Platonic Tradition during the Middle Ages, vol. 1. London: Warburg Institute, 1950.

Kline, Meredith. Images of the Spirit. Grand Rapids: Baker Book House, 1980.

Klinger, Elmar and Klaus Wittstadt, eds. Glaube im Prozess: Christsein nach dem II. Vatikanum: Für Karl Rahner. Freiburg: Herder Verlag, 1984.

Knight, G. A. F. A Biblical Approach to the Doctrine of the Trinity. Scottish Journal of Theology Occasional Papers, no. 1. Edinburgh: Oliver & Boyd, 1953.

Knowles, David. The Evolution of Medieval Thought. Baltimore: Helicon Press, 1962.

_____. The Historian and Character. Cambridge: Cambridge Univ. Press, 1963.

König, Adrio. Here Am I. London: Marshall, Morgan and Scott/ Grand Rapids: Eerdmans, 1982.

Koernke, Theresa F. "The Pneumatological Dimension of the Eucharist: The Contribution of Modern Catholicism on the Relationship Between Office, Eucharist, and Holy Spirit." Ph.D. dissertation, Univ. of Notre Dame, 1983.

Kolp, A. L. "Partakers of the Divine Nature." In Studia Patristica 17:3. ed. Elizabeth A. Livingstone, 1018-1023. Oxford: Pergamon Press Ltd., 1982.

Konidaris, G. "The Inner Continuity and Coherence of Trinitarian and Christological Dogma in the Seven Ecumenical Councils." The Greek Orthodox Theological Review 13:2 (1968): 263-277.

Kosman, L. A. "Substance, Being, and Energies." In Oxford Studies in Ancient Philosophy. vol. 2. ed. Julia Annas. Oxford: Clarendon Press, 1984: 121-149.

Kothgasser, Alois M. "Aktuelle Perspektiven der Trinitätslehre: Ein Tagungsbericht." Salesianum 45 (1983): 359-363

Kretschmar, George. "Le développment de la doctrine du Saint-Esprit du Nouveau Testament à Nicée." Verbum Caro 22 (1968): 5-55.

Kretzmann, Norman. "Goodness, Knowledge and Indeterminacy in the Philosophy of Thomas Aquinas." Journal of Philosophy 80 (1983): 631-649

Kreyche, Gerald F. "Culture," The Humanities and Personhood 18 (1983): 158-171.

Krivocheine, B. "Simplicité de la nature divine et les distinctions en Dieu selon S. Grégoire de Nysse." In Studia Patristica 16:2. ed. Elizabeth A. Livingstone, 389-399. Berlin: Akademie-Verlag, 1985.

Kroger, Athanasius. Mensch und Person: Moderne Personbegriffe in der katholischen Theologie. Recklinghausen: Paulus Verlag, 1967.

Kühneweg, Uwe. "Trinitätsaufweis Richards von St. Victor." Theologie und Philosophie 62 (1987): 401-422.

Kuntz, Marion Leathers and Paul Grimley Kuntz. Jacob's Ladder and the Tree of Life: Concepts of Hierarchy and the Great Chain of Being. Bern and New York: Peter Lang, 1986.

Kuykendall, George. "Thomas' Proofs as 'Fides Quaerens Intellectum'": Towards a Trinitarian 'Analogia'". Scottish Journal of Theology. 31:2 (1978): 113-131.

Lacey, T. A. Nature, Miracle and Sin. London: Longman's, Green & Co., 1916.

Lacordaire, Henri-Dominique. O.F.P. Jesus Christ, God, God and Man. Manchester: James Robinson, 1907.

LaCugna, Catherine Mowry. "Baptists, Feminists and Trinitarian Theology." Ecumenical Trends 17:5 (May 1988): 65-68.

_____. "Current Trends in Trinitarian Theology." Religious Studies Review 13:2 (April 1987): 141-147.

_____. "Philosophers and Theologians on the Trinity." Modern Theology 2:3 (1986): 169-181.

_____. "Placing Some Trinitarian Locutions." Irish Theological Quarterly 51:1 (1985): 17-37.

_____. "Problem of a Trinitarian Reformulation." Louvain Studies 10:4 (Fall 1985): 324-340.

_____. "Re-Conceiving the Trinity as the Mystery of Salvation." Scottish Journal of Theology 38:1 (1985): 1-23.

_____. "The Relational God: Aquinas and Beyond." Theological Studies 46 (1985): 647-663.

LaCugna, C. M. and Kilian McDonnell. "Returning from the Far Country: Theses for a Contemporary Trinitarian Theology." Scottish Journal of Theology 41 (1988): 197-215.

Ladner, Gerhart B. "Homo Viator: Medieval Ideas on Alienation and Order." Speculum 40:2 (April 1967): 233-259.

_____. The Idea of Reform. Cambridge, Massachusetts: Harvard Univ. Press, 1959.

_____. "Philosophical Anthropology of St. Gregory of Nyssa" In Dunbarton Oaks Papers: Washington 12 (1958): 59-94.

_____. "St. Augustine's Conception of the Reformation of Man to the Image of God." In Augustinus Magister: Congrès International Augustinien 2. 867-878. Paris: Études Augustiniennes, 1954.

Lampe, G. W. H. God as Spirit: The Bampton Lectures, 1976. Oxford: Clarendon Press, 1977.

Lapierre, M. J. "'The Divine Trinity": A Critique." Science Et Esprit 36 (1984): 125-130.

Lash, Nicholas. "Considering the Trinity." Modern Theology 2:3 (1986): 183-196.

Lateinisches Etymologisches Wörterbuch. S.v. "Persona." ed. A. Walde und J. B. Hofmann, vol. 2. Heidelberg: C. Winter/Universitasverlag, 1972.

Lauer, Eugene and Joel Mlecko. eds. A Christian Understanding of the Human Person. New York: Paulist Press, 1982.

Lauer, Quentin. Hegel's Concept of God. Albany: State Univ. of New York Press, 1982.

Layman, Steven. "An Ontology for Trinitarian Theories." Los Angeles (1978). (Mimeographed)

_____. "Tritheism and the Trinity." Faith and Philosophy. 5:3 (July 1988): 291-299.

Lawless, George. Augustine of Hippo and his Monastic Raule. Oxford: Clarendon Press, 1987.

Leclerc, Ivor. "God and the Issue of Being." Religious Studies 20:1 (1978): 63-78.

Leclerq, Jean. Love, Learning and the Desire for God. Reprint. New York: Fordham Univ. Press, 1985.

_____. Monks and Love in Twelfth-Century France. New York: Oxford Univ. Press, 1979.

_____. Francois Vandebroucke and Louis Bouyer. The Spirituality of the Middle Ages. New York: Desclée Co.: 1968.

Leech, Kenneth. The Social God. London: Sheldon Press, 1981.

Lefèvre, Charles. "La personne comme être en relation chez Platon et Aristote." Mélanges de Science Religieuse 30 (1973): 161-183.

_____. "La relation personelle chez saint Thomas D'Aquin." Mélanges de Science Religieuse. 31 (1974): 121-144.

Leff, Gordon. The Dissolution of the Medieval Outlook. New York: Harper & Row, 1976.

Le Guillou, M.J. "Réflections sur la théologie trinitaire: à propos de quelques livres anciens et récents." Istina 17 (1972): 457-464.

Lehmann, Paul. "The Tri-unity of God." Union Seminary Quarterly Review 20:1 (1965): 35-49.

Levinas, Emmanuel. Otherwise Than Being or Beyond Essence. trans. Alphonso Lingis. The Hague: Martinus Nijhoff Publishers, 1981.

Lewis, C. S. The Allegory of Love. New York: Oxford Univ. Press, 1958.

_____. The Discarded Image. Cambridge: Cambridge Univ. Press, 1964.

_____. Mere Christianity. New York: Macmillan Pub. Co., 1943.

Lexikon für Theologie und Kirche vol.8. S.v. "Person," by A. Halder, A. Grillmeier and H. Erharter.

Liddell, Henry George and Robert Scott. A Greek-English Lexicon. New York: Harper and Bros., 1878.

Lightfoot, J. B. The Apostolic Fathers. London: MacMillan and Co., 1907.

Lindbeck, George. The Nature of Doctrine: Religion and Theory in a Post-Liberal Age. Philadelphia: Westminster Press, 1984.

Lochman, Jan Milic. "Zum praktischen lebenszug der Trinitätslehre." Evangelische Theologie 35:3 (1975): 237-248.

_____. "The Trinity and Human Life." Theology 78:658 (1975): 173-183.

Lock, Charles. "Review of John Zizioulas' Being as Communion." St. Vladimir's Theological Quarterly 30:1 (1986): 91-94.

Locke, John. "An Essay Concerning Human Understanding." ed. with intro. Peter Nidditch. Oxford: Clarendon Press, 1975.

Löffler, Paul. "Die Trinitätslehre des Bischofs Hilarius von Poitiers zwischen Ost und West." Zeitschrift für Kirchengeschicte 71 (1960): 26-36.

Lohse, Eduard. "Prosopon." TDNT. vol. 6. Grand Rapids: Eerdmans, 1968: 768-780.

Lonergan, Bernard J. F. "Dehellenization of Dogma." Theological Studies 28 (1967): 336-351.

_____. De Deo Trino. Rome: Gregorianae, 1964.

_____. Divinarum Personarum Conceptionem Analogicam. Rome: Gregorian Univ., 1957.

_____. The Way to Nicea. trans. by Conn O'Donovan. Philadelphia: Westminster Press, 1976.

Lopez, Robert. The Birth of Europe. New York: M. Evans & Co., 1966.

Lossky, Vladimir. In the Image and Likeness of God. Crestwood, New York: St. Vladimir's Seminary Press, 1985.

_____. "The Procession of the Holy Spirit in the Orthodox Triadology." The Eastern Churches Quarterly 7:suppl.2 (1948): 31-53.

_____. The Vision of God. trans. Asheleigh Moorhouse. London: The Faith Press, 1963.

Lotz, Johannes Baptist. "Person und Verkündigung." In Wahrheit und Verkündigung: Michael Schmaus zum 70 Geburstag. ed. Leo Scheffczyk, et. al., 1241-57. Munich, Paderborn, Vienna: SchÖningh, 1967.

Louth, Andrew. Denys the Areopagite. Wilton, CT.: Morehouse-Barlow, 1989.

_____. Discerning the Mystery: An Essay on the Nature of Theology. Oxford: Clarendon Press, 1983.

_____. The Origins of the Christian Mystical Tradition. Oxford: Clarendon Press, 1981.

Lovejoy, Arthur. The Great Chain of Being: A Study of the History of an Idea. Cambridge: Harvard Univ. Press, 1936.

Lowry, Charles W. "Origen as Trinitarian." Journal of Theological Studies. (1936): 225-240.

_____. The Trinity and Christian Devotion. New York: Harper and Row, 1946.

Lull, Timothy F. "The Trinity in Recent Theological Literature." Word and World 2:1 (1982): 61-68.

Luscombe, D.E. The School of Peter Abelard. Cambridge: Cambridge Univ. Press, 1969.

Luther, A. R. Persons in Love: A Study of Max Scheler's "Wesen und Formen der Sympathie." The Hague: Martinus Nijhoff, 1972.

Lynch, John. J. "Prosopon and the Dogma of the Trinity: A study of the background of the conciliar use of the word in the writings of Cyril of Alexandria and Leontius of Byzantium." Ph. D. dissertation, Fordham Univ., 1974.

_____. "'Prosopon' in Gregory of Nyssa: A Theological Word in Transition." Theological Studies 40:4 (1979): 728-738.

McBrien, Richard P. Catholicism. 2 vols. Minneapolis: Winston Press Inc., 1966.

McCallum, J. Ramsay. Abelard's Christian Theology. Oxford: Basil Blackwell, 1948.

McClendon, James W. "Some Reflections on the Future of Trinitarianism." Review and Expositor 63:2 (1966): 149-156.

McCool, Gerald A. "The Ambrosian Origin of St. Augustine's Theology of the Imagae of God in Man." Theological Studies 20:1 (March, 1959): 62-81.

McCulloch, Joseph. "Persons in Relation." The Modern Churchman n.s. 12:1 (1968): 32-41.

McDonnell, Kilian. pref. and intro. Open the Windows: The Popes and the Charismatic Renewal. South Bend: Greenlawn Press, 1989.

_____. "A Trinitarian Theology of the Holy Spirit." Theological Studies 46 (1985): 191-227.

MacDonald, H. D. The Christian View of Man. Westchester, Ill.: Crossway Books, 1981.

McFadyen, Alistair, I. The Call to Personhood. Oxford: Oxford Univ. Press, 1991.

McFague, Sallie. Metaphorical Theology: Models of God in Religious Language. Philadelphia: Fortress Press, 1982.

McGinn, Bernard and John Meyendorff, eds. Christian Spirituality: Origins to Twelfth Century. New York: Crossroad, 1985.

McGrath, Alister. Understanding the Trinity. Grand Rapids: Zondervan Academie, 1988.

McInerny, Ralph M. "Metaphor and Analogy." In Inquiries into Medieval Philosphy: A Collection in Honor of Francis P. Clarke. ed. James F. Ross, 75-96. Westport, Conn.: Greenwood Publishing Co., 1971.

Mackay, Donald G. M. "The Relation of God and Man in the Writings of Nicolas Berdyaev." Scottish Journal of Theology 3 (1950): 380-396.

McKelway, Alexander J. "Perichoretic Possibilities in Barth's Doctrine of Male and Female." "Princeton Seminary Bulletin" 7:3 n.s. (1986): 231-243.

McKenzie, J. L. Dictionary of the Bible. Milwaukee: Bruce Pub. Co., 1965.

McKeon, Richard. Selections from Medieval Philosophers. 2 vols. ed. and trans. with intro, notes and glossary by McKeon. New York: Charles Scribner's Sons, 1930.

Mackey, James P. The Christian Experience of God as Trinity. London: SCM Press Ltd., 1983.

_____. "The Holy Spirit: Relativizing the Divergent Approaches of East and West." Irish Theological Quarterly 48:3/4 (1981): 256-267.

MacKinnon, Donald M. "Aristotle's Concept of Substance." In New Essays on Plato and Aristotle. ed. Bambrough Renford. London: Routledge and Kegin Paul, (1965) 1967: 97-119.

_____. Borderlands of Theology and other Essays. Philadelphia: J. B. Lippincott Company, 1968.

_____. "The Relation of the Doctrines of the Incarnation of the Trinity." In Creation, Christ and Culture: Studies in Honour of T. F. Torrance. ed. Richard W. A. McKinney. Edinburgh: T & T Clark Ltd, 1976.

_____. "Substance in Christology—A Cross-bench View." In Christ, Faith and History:

Cambridge Studies in Christology. eds. S. W. Sykes and J. P. Clayton, 279-300. Cambridge: Cambridge Univ. Press, 1972.

Mackrell, G. F. "The Trinity and Human Love." New Blackfriars 53 no. 625 (1962): 270-75.

McLean, George F., ed. The Human Person: Proceedings of the American Catholic Philosophical Association vol. 53. Washington D.C.: Catholic Univ. of America, 1979.

McLean, George F. and Hugo Meynell. "Person and God." In The International Society for Metaphysics: Studies in Metaphysics 3. Lanham: Univ. Press of America, 1988.

McLean, Stuart D. "The Humanity of Man in Karl Barth's Thought." Scottish Journal of Theology 28:2 (1975): 127-147.

McMullin, Ernan., ed. The Concept of Matter in Greek and Medieval Philosophy. Notre Dame: Univ. of Notre Dame Press, 1963.

MacMurray, John. The Form of the Personal: Gifford Lectures, 2 vols. 1953-54, 1961. Reprint. Atlantic Highlands, NJ: Humanities Press, 1979.

_____. Persons in Relation. Atlantic Highlands, N.J.: Humanities Press, 1979.

McMurrin, Sterling M. "Is God a Person?" in Great Issues Concerning Theism. ed. Charles H. Monson, Jr. Salt Lake City: Univ. of Utah Press, 1965.

Macquarrie, John. God-Talk: An Examination of the Language and Logic of Theology. London: SCM Press Ltd., 1967.

_____. In Search of Humanity: A Theological and Philosophical Approach. New York: Crossroad Pub. Co., 1983.

_____. Principles of Christian Theology. New York: Charles Scribner's Sons, 1966.

Malet, A. Personne et amour dans la theologie de Saint Thomas d'Aquin. Paris: Vrin, 1956.

Malet, Albert. La synthèse de la personne et de la nature dans la theologie trinitaire de Saint Thomas. Revue thomiste 54 (1954): 483-522, 55 (1955): 43-84.

Maloney, George. "Ecumenical Implications for the Doctrine of the Trinity." Ecumenical Trends (July-August, 1983).

_____. Man, the Divine Icon: The Patristic Doctrine of Man Made According to the Image of God. Pecos, New Mexico: Dove Publications,1973.

Mantzarides, G.I. "The Ethical Significance of the Trinitarian Dogma." Sobornost n.s. 5:10 (1970): 720-729.

Marcel, Gabriel Being and Having. Westminster [London]: Dacre Press, 1949.

_____. The Mystery of Being. vol. 1. Reflection and Mystery. Gifford Lectures 1949-50. London: Harwill Press Ltd., 1950.

Marenbon, J. "Making Sense of the "De Trinitate": Boethius and Some of his Medieval Interpreters." In Studia Patristica 17.1. ed. Elizabeth A. Livingstone, 446-452. Oxford: Pergamon Press Ltd., 1982.

Marías, Julian. A Biography of Philosophy. trans. Harold C. Raley. Univ. of Alabama: University of Alabama Press, 1984.

Markus, R. A., ed. Augustine: A Collection of Critical Essays. Garden City, New York: Anchor Books, 1972.

_____. "Trinitarian Theology and the Economy." Journal of Theological Studies n.s. 9:1 (April, 1958): 89-102.

Marsella, Anthony, George DeVos, Francis I. K. Hsu. Culture and Self: Asian and Western Perspectives. New York: Tavistuck Pub., 1985.

Marshall, Mary Hatch. "Boethius' Definition of "Persona" and Medieval Understanding of the Roman Theater." Speculum 25:3 (1950): 471-482.

Masiello, Ralph J. "Reason and Faith in Richard of St. Victor." New Scholasticism 48 (1974): 233-242.

Martin, Ralph. comp. Spirit and the Church. New York: Paulist Press, 1976.

Martin, Vincent. "Reciprocal Relationships in Trinitarian Theology." Monastic Studies 17 (Christmas, 1986): 7-29.

Martinich, A. P. "Identity and Trinity." Journal of Religion 58 (April, 1978): 169-181.

Martland, T. R. "A Study of Cappadocian and Augustinian Trinitarian Methodology." Anglican Theological Review 47 (1965): 252-263.

Mascall, E. L. Existence and Analogy. New York: Longmans, Green & Co., 1949.

_____. He Who Is: A Study in Traditional Theism. London: Darton, Longman, & Todd, 1962.

_____. The Openness of Being. Philadelphia: Westminster Press, 1971.

_____. The Triune God: An Ecumenical Study. Allison Park, PA: Pickwick Pub., 1986.

Mastermann, Margaret. "Theism as a Scientific Hypothesis, I, Theoria to Theory 1:1 (Oct. 1966): 76-87; II, 1:2 (Jan. 1967): 165-186; III, Icons: The Nature of Scientific Revelation." 1:3 (1967): 232-250; IV, 1:4 (July, 1967): 338-353.

Maximus the Confessor, Quaestiones ad Thalassium, Corpus Christianorum, Greek Series 7-8 Turnholt: Typographi Brepols Editores Pontificii, 1980.

Mayr, Franz K. "Die Einseitigkeit der traditionellen Gotteslehre: zum Verhältnis von Anthropologie und Pneumatologie" In Erfahrung und Theologie des Heiligen Geistes. Hamburg: Agentur des Rauhen Hauses, Munich: Kösel Verlag, 1974.

_____. "Trinitätstheologie und Theologische Anthropologie." Zeitschrift für Theologie und Kirche 68 (1971): 427-477.

_____. "Trinität und Familie in De Trin. XII." Revue des études Augustinniennes 18 (1972): 51-86.

Meijering, E. P. "The Doctrine of the Will and of the Trinity in the Orations of Gregory of Nazianzus." Nederlands Theologische Tijdschrift 27 (1973): 224-234.

_____. Hilary of Poitiers on the Trinity. Leiden: E. J. Brill, 1982.

Meredith, Anthony. "The Pneumatology of the Cappadocian Fathers and the Creed of Constantinople." Irish Theological Quarterly 48:3 & 4. n.s. 1981: 196-211.

Meslin, M. "L'autonomie de l'homme dans la pensée pelagienne." In Problèmes de la Personne. ed. I. Meyerson, 135-165. Paris: Mouton & Co., 1973.

Metz, J. B. and E. Schillebeeckx. eds. God as Father? Concilium 143:3 (1981).

Meyendorff, John. Byzantine Theology: Historical Trends and Doctrinal Themes. New York: Fordham Univ. Press, 1974.

_____. "Reply to Jürgen Moltmann's "The Unity of the Triune God"." St. Vladimir's Theological Quarterly 28:3 (1984): 183-187.

Meyerson, I. ed. Problèmes de la Personne. In Congrès et Colloques XIII, Colloque du centre de récherches de psychologie comparative. Paris: Mouton & Co., 1973.

Meynell, Hugo. "The Holy Trinity and the Corrupted Conciousness." Theology 79:669 (1976): 143-151.

Migliore, Daniel L. Called to Freedom: Liberation Theology and the Future of Christian Doctrine. Philadelphia: Westminster Press, 1980.

_____. "The Trinity and Human Liberty." Theology Today 36:4 (1980): 488-497.

Milano, Andrea. Persona In Teologia: Alle Origini del Significato di Persona nel Cristianesimo Antico. Universita Degli Studi Della Basilicata-Potenza. Saggi e Recherche. vol. 1. Naples: Edizone Dehoniane, 1984.

Milbank, John. "The Second Difference: For a Trinitarianism Without Reserve." Modern Theology 2:3 (1986): 213-234.

Miles, Margaret. "Vision: The Eye of the Body and the Eye of the Mind in Saint Augustine's De trinitate and Confessions." Journal of Religion 63 (April, 1983): 125-142.

Milis, Ludo. "The Regular Canons and Some Socio-Religious Aspects About the Year 1100." In Étude de Civilisation Médiévale (Ninth-Twelfth centuries): Mélanges offerts à Edmond-René Labande. B. Jeanneau, et al., 553-561. Poitiers: C. E. S. C. M., 1975.

Miller, David L. Three Faces of God: Traces of the Trinity in Literature and Life. Philadelphia: Fortress Press, 1986.

Min, Anselm K. "The Trinity and the Incarnation: Hegel and Classical Approaches." The Journal of Religion 66:2 (1986): 173-193.

Minkus, Peter. Philosophy of the Person. Oxford: Basil Blackwell, 1960.

Minnis, Alastair. "Affection and Imagination in 'The Cloud of Unknowing' and Hilton's Scale of Perfection." Traditio 39 (1983): 323-366.

Miregeler, Albert. Mutations of Western Christianity. trans. Edward Quinn. Montreal: Palm Publishers, 1964.

Misch, G. A History of Autobiography in Antiquity. 2 vols. trans. E. W. Dickes. London:

Routledge & Kegan Paul, 1950.

Mischel, T. ed. Understanding Other Persons. Totowa, New Jersey: Rowmen and Littlefield, 1974.

Mitchell, Richard. The Gift of Fire. New York: Simon & Schuster, 1987.

Moberly, R. C. Atonement and Personality. New York: Longmans, Green and Co., 1901.

Modras, Ronald. "The Thomistic Personalism of Pope John Paul II." Modern Schoolman 59 (1982): 117-127.

Moingt, Joseph. "Théologie Trinitaire de Tertullien." Recherches de Science Religieuse 54 (1966): 337-369.

Moltmann, Jürgen. The Crucified God: The Cross of Christ as the Foundation and Criticism of Christian Theology. trans. R. A. Wilson and John Bowden. New York: Harper & Row, Pub., 1974.

_____. "The Fellowship of the Holy Spirit - Trinitarian Pneumatology." Scottish Journal of Theology 37:3 (1984): 287-300.

_____. "Gedanken zur "trinitarischen Geschicte Gottes"." Evangelische Theologie 35:3 (1975): 208-223.

_____. Gott in der Schöpfung. Münich: Chr. Kaiser Verlag, 1985. English trans. God in Creation: An Ecological Doctrine of Creation. London: SCM Press, 1985.

_____. Man: Christian Anthropology in the Conflicts of the Present. trans. John Sturdy. London: S.P.C.K., 1974.

_____. "The Trinitarian History of God." Theology 78 (1975): 632-646.

_____. The Trinity and the Kingdom. trans. Margaret Köhl. San Francisco: Harper & Row, Pub., 1981.

_____. "The Unity of the Triune God." St. Vladimir's Theological Quarterly 28:3 (1984): 157-171.

Moltmann- Wendel, Elisabeth and Jürgen Moltmann. Humanity in God. New York: Pilgrim Press, 1983.

Montagu, Ashley. On Being Human. New York: Hawthorn Books, 1966.

Morreal, John S. Analogy and Talking About God: A Critique of the Thomistic Approach. Washington: Univ. Press of America, 1979.

Morris, Colin. Discovery of the Individual: 1050-1200. New York: Harper & Row, 1972.

_____. "Individualism in Twelfth-Century Religion: Some Further Reflections." Journal of Ecclesiastical History 31 (1980): 195-206.

Morris, Thomas. "Incarnational Anthropology." Theology 87:719 (1984): 344-350.

_____. "Philosophers and Theologians at Odds." Asbury Theological Journal 44:2 (1989): 31-41.

Moule, C. F. D. "The New Testament and the Doctrine of the Trinity: A Short Report on an Old Theme." Expository Times 88 (1976-77): 16-20.

Mühlen, Heribert. A Charismatic Theology: Initiation in the Spirit. London: Burns and Oates, 1978.

_____. "El concepto de Dios." Estudio Trinitarios 6 (1972): 535-59.

_____. L'Esprit dans L'Église. trans. A. Liefooghe, M. Massart and R. Virrion. 2 vols. Paris: Les Éditions du Cerf, 1969.

_____. "Der gegenwärtige Aufbruch der Geisteserfahrung und die Unterscheidung der Geisten." In Gegenwart der Geistes: Aspekte der Pneumatologie. ed. Walter Kasper, 24-53. In Quaestones Disputate vol. 85. eds. K. Rahner und Heinrich Schlier. Freiburg: Herder, 1979.

_____. "'Gottesbeweis' heute: Überlegungen zu einem personologischen Aufweis der Existenz Gottes." In Martyria, Leiturgia, Diakonia: Feschrift für Hërmann Volk. ed. Otto Semmelroth, 40-58. Mainz: Matthias-Grünewald Verlag, 1968.

_____. Der heilige Geist als Person: Beitrag zur Frage nach der dem heiligen Geiste eigentümlichen Funktion in der Trinität, bei der Inkarnation und im Gnadenbund. Münsterische Beiträge zur Theologie, vol. 26. Münster: Aschendorff, 1963.

_____. "Der Heilige Geist und Maria." Catholica (Münster) 29 1975: 145-163.

_____. "Modelle Der Einigung: Auf dem Weg zu einem universalen Konzil aller Christen." Catholica 27:2 (1973): 111-134.

_____. "Das Mögliche Zentrum der Amtsfrage: Überlegungen zu vier ökumenischen Dokumenten." Catholica 27:3 & 4 (1973): 329-358.

_____. "Die 'Okumenishen Skizzen' Lukas Vischers." Catholica 28:1 (1974): 78-84.

_____. "Person und Appropriation - Zum Verständnis des Axioms: In Deo omnia sunt unum, ubi non obviat relationis oppositio." Münchener Theologische Zeitschrift 16 (1965): 37-57.

_____. "Das Pneuma Jesus und die Zeit: zur theologie des Amtes." Catholica (Munster) 17 (1963): 249-276.

_____. Sein und Person nach Johannes Duns Scotus: Beitrage zur Grundlegung einer Metephysik der Person. Franziskan Forschungen Vol. 47. Werl: Dietrich - Coelde - Verlag, 1954.

_____. "Soziale Geisterfahrung als Antwort auf eine einseitige Gotteslehre." In Erfahrung und Theologie des Heiligen Geistes. 253-272. Munich: Kosel Verlag, 1974.

_____. Una Mystica Persona: Eine Person in vielen Personen. Munich: Verlag Ferdinand Schöningh, 1968.

_____. "Das unbegrenzte Du: Auf dem Wege zu einer Personology." In Wahrheit und Verkundigung: Michael Schmaus zum 70 Geburstag. ed. Leo Scheffczyk, et. al., 1259-1285. Munchen, Paderborn, Wien: Schoningh, 1967.

_____. Die Veränderlichkeit Gottes als Horizont einer zukunftigen Christologie: Auf dem Wege zu einer Kreuzestheologie in Auseinandersetzung mit der altkirchlichen

Christologie. Münster: Aschendorff, 1969. Found also in "Christologie in Horizont der Traditionelle Seinsfrage?" In Catholica 23 (1969): 205-279.

_____. "Das Vorverständis von Person und die Evangelisch-Katholische Differenz." Catholica 18 (1964): 108-142.

Mühlen, Heribert and A. Bittlinger. Einubung in Die Christliche Grunderfahrung. 2 vols. 40 & 49 in Topos-Taschenbucher Series. Mainz: Matthias-Grünewald-Verlag. 1976.

Müller, Max. Biographies of Words and the Home of the Aryans. London: Longmans, Green & Co., 1888.

Murdoch, Iris. The Sovereignty of the Good. 1970. London: Ark Paperbacks, (1985).

_____. The Sovereignty of the Good Over Other Concepts. The Leslie Stephens Lectures, 1967. Cambridge: Cambridge Univ. Press, 1967.

Murray, John Courtney. The Problem of God: Yesterday and Today. New Haven: Yale Univ. Press, 1964.

Nabe, Clyde. Mystery and Religion: Newman's Epistemology of Religion. Lanham: Univ. Press of America, 1988.

Narum, William H.K. "The Trinity, The Gospel and Human Experience." Word and World 2:1 (1982): 43-52.

Nédoncelle, Maurice. Explorations Personalistes. In Philosophie de l'esprit. Paris: Aubier Editions Montaigne, 1970.

_____. Intersubjectivité et Ontologie: Le Defi Personnaliste. Louvain/Paris: Nauwelaerts, 1974.

_____. "L'intersubjectivité humaine est-elle pour saint Augustin une image de la Trinité?" In Augustinus Magister: Congrès International Augustinien 2. 595-602. Paris: Études Augustiniennes, 1954.

_____. Love and the Person. trans. by Sr. Ruth Adelaide. New York: Sheed & Ward, 1966.

_____. The Personalist Challenge: Intersubjectivity and Ontology. trans. François C. Gérard and Francis F. Burch. Allison Park, Pennsylvania: Pickwick Publications, 1984.

_____. Prosopon et persona dans l'antiquité classique: essai de bilan Linguistique." Revue des Sciences Religieuses (Strasburg) 22 (1948): 277-299.

_____. "Les variations de Boèce sur la personne." Revue des Sciences Religieuses. 29 (1955): 201-38.

Neidhardt, W. Jim. "The Creative Dialogue Between Human Intelligibility and Reality - Relational Aspects of Natural Science and Theology." Asbury Theological Journal 41:2 (Fall, 1986): 59-83.

Neuner, J. and J. Dupuis, eds. The Christian Faith in the Doctrinal Documents of the Catholic Church. Westminster, MD: Christian Classics, 1975.

Neville, R. C. "Creation and the Trinity." Theological Studies 30 (March, 1969): 3-26

New Catholic Encyclopedia vol.11. S.v. "Person (in Philosophy)," by L. W. Geddes and W. A. Wallace. Washington: Catholic Univ. of America, 1967:

New Catholic Encyclopedia vol.11. S.v. "Person (in Theology)," by M. J. Doremkemper, and "Person, Divine," by A. M. Bermejo.

New Dictionary of Christian Theology. eds. Alan Richardson and John Bowden. London: SCM Press, 1983. S.v. "Trinity" by J.P. Mackay.

New Dictionary of Christian Theology. S.v. "Person." eds. Alan Richardson and John Bowden. London: SCM Press (1983): 442-443.

New Encyclopedia Britannia: Macropaedia vol. 1. S.v. "Anthropology," and "Anthropology, Philosophical."

Newlands, George. Theology of the Love of God. London: Collins, 1980.

Newman, Paul W. "Humanity with Spirit." Scottish Journal of Theology 34:5 (1981): 415-426.

Newman, Robert C. "Perspectives on the Image of God in Man from Biblical Theology." Evangelical Journal 2:2 (1984): 66-76.

Newton, John Thomas. "The Importance of Augustine's Use of the Neoplatonic Doctrine of the Hypostatic Union for the Development of Christology." Augustinian Studies 2 (1971): 1-15.

Niebuhr, H. Richard. "The Doctrine of the Trinity and the Unity of the Church." Theology Today 3:3 (Oct. 1946): 371-384.

Niebuhr, Reinhold. The Nature and Destiny of Man: A Christian Interpretation. New York: Charles Scribner's Sons, 1951.

Nielsen, Lauge Olaf. Theology and Philosophy in the Twelfth Century: A Study of Gilbert of Porreta's Thinking and the Theological Expositions of the Doctrine of the Incarnation during the Period 1130-1180. In Acta Theologica Danica vol. 15. Leiden: E. J. Brill, 1982.

Noble, T. A. "Gregory Nazianzen's Use of Scripture in Defense of the Deity of the Spirit." Tyndale Bulletin 39 (1988): 101-123.

Noll, Mark A. and David F. Wells, eds. Christian Faith and Practice in the Modern World: Theology from an Evangelical Point of View. Grand Rapids: Eerdman Pub. Co., 1988.

Norris, R. A. "The Problem of Human Identity in Patristic Christological Speculation." In Studia Patristica 17:1. ed. Elizabeth A. Livingstone, 147-159. Oxford: Pergamon Press Ltd., 1982.

Novak, Michael. Belief and Unbelief. New York: The Macmillan Co., 1965.

Niceta of Remesiana. Writings. FC. vol. 7.

Nygren, Anders. Agape and Eros. trans. Philip S. Watson. Philadelphia: The Westminster Press, 1953.

Oakley, Francis. The Medieval Experience. New York: Chas. Scribner's and Sons, 1974.

Oberman, Heiko Augustinus. The Harvest of Medieval Theology. Durham, North Carolina: The Labyrinth Press, 1983.

O'Carroll, Michael. Trinitas: A Theological Encyclopedia of the Holy Trinity. Wilmington, Delaware: Michael Glazier, Inc., 1987.

O'Collins, Gerald. What are they Saying About Jesus? New York: Paulist Press, 1983.

O'Connell, Robert J. St. Augustine's Early Theory of Man, A.D. 286-391. Cambridge: Belknap Press, Harvard University, 1968.

O'Connor, Terrence R. '"Homoousios" and "Filioque": An Ecumenical Analogy." The Downside Review 83:270 (1965): 1-19.

O'Daly, Gerard J.P. Plotinus' Philosophy of the Self. Shannon, Ireland: Irish Univ. Press, 1973.

Odeberg, Hugo. The Fourth Gospel. Amsterdam: B. R. Grüner, 1968.

Oden, Thomas C. Agenda for Theology: After Modernity... What? Grand Rapids: Zondervan, 1990.

_____. Systematic Theology, vol. 1-3. The Living God. vol. 1. The Word of Life. vol 2. Life in the Spirit. vol. 3. (forthcoming) San Francisco: Harper & Row Publishers, 1987 and 1989.

O'Donnell, John J. "The Doctrine of the Trinity in Recent German Theology." Heythrop Journal 23 (1982): 153-167.

_____. "In Him and Over Him: The Holy Spirit in the Life of Jesus." Gregorianum 70:1 (1989): 25-45.

_____. The Mystery of the Triune God. New York: Paulist Press, 1989.

_____. The Trinity as Divine Community. Gregorianum 69:1 (1988): 5-34.

_____. Trinity and Temporality. Oxford: Oxford Univ. Press, 1983.

O'Donovan, Leo J. ed. Word and Mystery. New York: Newman Press, 1968.

O'Donovan, Oliver. The Problem of Self-Love in St. Augustine. New Haven: Yale Univ. Press, 1980.

Oeing-Hanhoff, Ludger. "Trinitarische Ontologie und Metaphysik der Person" in Quaestiones Disputatae series. eds. K. Rahner and H. Schleer, 73-182. Trinitat: Aktuelle Perspektiven der Theologie. ed. Wilhelm Browning. Freeburg: Herder, 1984.

Offermanns, Helga. Der christologische und trinitarische Personbegriffe der frühen Kirche. Bern/Frankfurt: Herbert Lang/Peter Lang, 1976.

Ogden, Schubert. "On the Trinity". Theology 83:691 (1980): 97-102.

Olson, Roger. "Trinity and Eschatology: The Historical Being of God in Jürgen Moltmann and Wolfhart Pannenberg." Scottish Journal of Theology 36:2 (1983): 213-227.

_____. "Wolfhart Pannenberg's Doctrine of the Trinity." Scottish Journal of Theology 43:2 (1990): 175-206.

O'Malley, John B. "The Fellowship of Being: An Essay on the Concept of Person in the Philosophy of Gabriel Marcel. The Hague: Martinus Nijhoff, 1966.

Oman, John. Grace and Personality. New York: The Macmillan Co., 1925.

One Lord, One Baptism: World Council of Churches Commission in Faith and Order. preface by Keith Bridston. Minneapolis: Augsburg Publishing House, 1961.

Osthathios, Geervarghese Mar. Theology of a Classless Society. Guildford and London: Lutterworth Press, 1979.

Ott, Heinrich. God. Edinburgh: St. Andrew Press, 1971.

Ottaviano, Carmelo. Riccardo di S. Vittore, la vita, le opere, il pensiero. Classe di scienze morali, storiche e filologiche, Serie VI, vol 4. Fascicolo V. Rome: Dott, Giovanni Bardi, 1933.

Otto, Stephan. Die Funktion des Bildbegriffs in der Theologie des 12 Jahrhunderts. Beitrage zur. Geschichte der Philosophie und Theologie des Mittelalters, vol. 40:1. Munster/Westfalen: Aschendorffsche Verlagsbuchhandlung, 1963.

Ouspensky, Leonide. Theology of the Icon. Crestwood, New Jersey: St. Vladimir's Seminary Press, 1978.

Outka, Gene. Agape: An Ethical Analysis. Yale Publications in Religion 17. New Haven and London: Yale Univ. Press, 1972.

Outler, Albert. "The Beginnings of Personhood: Theological Consider- ations." Perkins Journal 27:1 (1973): 28-34.

Oxford-Carpenter, Rebecca. "Gender and the Trinity." Theology Today 41:1 (Apr.1984-Jan. 1985): 7-25.

Pailin, David A. "The Humanity of the Theologian and the Personal Nature of God." Religious Studies 12: 141-158.

Pannenberg, Wolfhart. Anthropology in Theological Perspective. trans. Matthew J. O'Connell. Philadelphia: Westminster Press, 1985.

_____. "Atom, Duration, Form: Difficulties with Process Philosophy." Process Studies 14:1 (Spring, 1984): 21-30.

_____. "The God of History." trans. M.B. Jackson. Cumberland Seminarian 19:2,3 (1981): 28-41.

_____. Jesus - God and Man. trans. Lewis L. Wilkins and Duane A. Priebe. Philadelphia: Westminster Press, 1968.

_____. "Person and Subjekt: Zur Überwindung des Subjektivismus im Menschenbild und im Gottesverständnis." Neue Zeitschrift für Systematische Theologie und Religionsphilosophie 18 (1976): 133-148.

_____. "The Question of God." Interpretation 21:3 (1967): 289-314.

_____. "Die Subjektivität Gottes und die Trinitatslehre." Kerygma und Dogma 23 (1977): 25-40.

Pannikar, Raymond. The Trinity and World Religions: Icon- Person- Mystery. Madras, India: The Christian Literature Society, 1970.

Pape, Roy W. "The Origins of Trinitarian Doctrine." Theology. 78 (1975): 429-430.

Parent, J. M. "La Notion de Dogme au XIII siecle." In Etudes D'Histoire Litteraire et Doctrinale du XIII sciècle. vol. 1. Publications de L'Institut D'Etudes Médiévales D'Ottawa. Ottawa: Inst. D'Études Médiévales, 1932.

Parker, Thomas D. "The Political Meaning of the Doctrine of the Trinity: Some Theses." Journal of Religion 60:2 (1980): 165-184.

Pastrana, Gabriel. "Personhood and the Beginning of Human Life." The Thomist 41:2 (1977): 247-294.

Patfoort, Albert. "La 'fonction personnelle' du Saint-Esprit." Angelicum 45 (1968): 316-327.

_____. "Un projet de "traité moderne" de la Trinité: Vers une réevaluation de la "notien" de personne? Angelicum 48 (1971): 93-118.

Paulys Real-Encyclopädie der Classichen Altertumswissenschaft. S.v. "Persona," by Rudolph Düll. ed. Wilhelm Kroll. Stuttgart: J. B. Metzler Jerlagbuchandlung (1937): 1036-1042.

Pederson, Johannes. Israel: It's Life and Culture I-II (of 4 vols.). London: Oxford Univ. Press, 1964.

Pelikan, Jaroslav. The Christian Tradition: A History of the Development of Doctrine. 5 vols. Chicago and London: The Univ. of Chicago Press, 1971-1989.

_____. "The Doctrine of the Image of God." In The Common Christian Roots of the European Nations vol. 1. 53-62. Florence: Le Monnier, 1982.

_____. "Imago Dei: An Explanation of Summa Theologiae Part 1, Question 93." In Calgary Aquinas Studies. ed. Anthony Parel. Toronto: Pontifical Institute of Medieval Studies, 1978.

Penido, M. T. L. "Prélude que à la thèorie 'psychologique' de la Trinité." Revue Thomiste 45 (1939): 665-74.

_____. "La valeur de 'La theorie 'psychologique' de la Trinite.'" Ephemerides Theologicae Lovanienses 8 (1931): 5-16.

Peter, Carl J. "A Shift to the Human Subject in Roman Catholic Theology." Communio (US) 6 (1979): 56-72.

Peters, Albrecht. "Die Trintätslehre in der reformatischen Christenheit." Theologische Literaturzeitung 94:8 (1969): 562-570.

Petry, Ray C., ed. Late Medieval Mysticism. Philadelphia: The Westminster Press, 1957.

Phillips, D. Z. Faith after Foundationalism. New York: Routledge, 1988.

Piault, Bernard. What is the Trinity? New York: Hawthorn Books, 1959.

Pietri, Ch. "Personne, analogie de l'âme humaine et théologie de l'esprit. Brèves remarques sur Augustin, Mühlen, et Rahner." Les quatres fleuves 9 (1979): 111-124.

Pikaza, Javier. "Notas sobre la Trinidad en Ricardo de San Victor." Estudios Trintiarios 6:1 (1972): 63-101.

Pinnock, Clark. Tracking the Maze. San Francisco: Harper and Row, 1990.

Pittenger, Norman. The Divine Triunity. Philadelphia: United Church Press, 1977.

_____. "Trinity and Process: Some Comments in Reply." Theology Digest 32 (1971): 290-296.

Plantinga, Alvin. Does God Have a Nature? The Aquinas Lectures, 1980. Milwaukee: Marquette University Press, 1980

Plantinga, Cornelius Jr. "Gregory of Nyssa and the Social Analogy of the Trinity." Thomist 50:3 (July, 1986): 325-352.

_____. The Hodgson-Welsh Debate and the Social Analogy of the Trinity. Ph.D. dissertation, Princeton Theological Seminary, 1982.

_____. "The Perfect Family." Christianity Today (March 4, 1988): 24-27.

_____. "The Threeness/Oneness Problem of the Trinity." Calvin Theological Journal 23:1 (April, 1988): 37-53.

Plato. The Works of Plato. Bohn's Classical Library. 6 vols. London: G. Bell and Sons, 1880-85.

Polanyi, Michael. Personal Knowledge: Toward a Post-Critical Philosophy. Chicago: Univ. of Chicago Press, 1958.

_____. The Study of Man. Chicago: Univ. of Chicago Press, 1958.

Pollard, T. E. "Logos and Son in Origin, Arius and Athanasius." In Studia Patristica Vol 2. eds. Kurt Aland and F. L. Cross, 282-287. Akademie-Verlag: Berlin, 1957.

Pollard, William G. "Rumors of Transcendence in Physics." American Journal of Physics 52:10 (October, 1984): 877-881.

Portalie, Eugene. A Guide to the Thought of Saint Augustine. Chicago: Henry Regnery Co., 1960.

Porter, Lawrence B. "On Keeping 'Persons' in the Trinity: A Linguistic Approach to Trinitarian Thought." Theological Studies 41:3 (1980): 530-48.

Pourrat, Pierre. Christian Spirituality in the Middle Ages. Westminster: The Newman Press, 1953.

Powell, Samuel. "The Doctrine of the Trinity in Nineteenth Century American Wesleyanism." Wesleyan Theological Journal. 18:2 (1983): 33-46.

Power, William L. "The Doctrine of the Trinity and Whitehead's Metaphysics." Encounter 45:4 (1984): 287-302.

Prestige, George Leonard. "Clement of Alexandria, Stromata 2. 18, and the Meaning of 'Hypostasis'." Journal of Theological Studies 30 (1929): 270-72.

Prestige, G. L. Fathers and Heretics. London: SPCK, 1940.

_____. God in Patristic Thought. London: S.P.C.K., 1959.

_____. "'Perichoreo" and "Perichoresis" in the Fathers." Journal of Theological Studies 29 (1928): 242-252.

Principe, Walter H. "The Dynamism of Augustine's Terms for Describing the Highest Trinitarian Image in the Human Person." In Studia Patristica 17:3. ed. Elizabeth A. Livingstone, 1291-1299. Oxford: Pergamon Press Ltd., 1982.

_____. "Odo Rigaldus, A Precursor of St. Bonaventure on the Holy Spirit as "effectus formalis" in the Mutual Love of the Father and the Son." Medieval Studies 39 (1977): 498-505.

_____. "The Theology of the Hypostatic Union in the Early 13th Century." Alexander of Hales' Theology of the Hypostatic Union. Vol 2 (of 4). Toronto: Pontifical Institute of Medieval Studies, 1967.

Przywara, Erich. Schriften. vol. 3. Einseideln: Johannes-Verlag, 1962

Quasten, Johannes. Patrology. 4 vols. Reprint. Westminster, Maryland: Christian Classics, 1986.

Rahner, Karl. Foundations of Christian Faith: An Introduction to the Idea of Christianity. trans. William V. Dych. New York: Seabury Press, 1978.

_____. "Remarks on the Dogmatic Treatise 'De Trinitate'." Theological Investigations. vol. 4. trans. Kevin Smyth. 77-102. Baltimore: Helicon Press, 1966.

_____. "Theology and Anthropology." In The Word in History. ed. T.P. Burke, 1-23. New York: Sheed and Ward, 1966.

_____. The Trinity. Trans. Joseph Donceel. New York: Herder & Herder, 1970; Reprint. New York: Seabury Press, 1974.

Ramm, Bernard L. An Evangelical Christology: Ecumenic and Historic. Nashville: Thomas Nelson Publishers, 1985.

Ranson, Guy H. "F. D. Maurice on the Social Nature of Man." Canadian Journal of Theology 11 (1965): 265-276.

Rashdall, Hastings. The Universities of Europe in the Middle Ages. eds. F. M. Powicke and A. B. Emden, vols. 1-3. London: Oxford University Press, 1936 (1895).

Ratzinger, Joseph. Introduction to Christianity. trans. J. R. Foster. New York: Herder and Herder, 1969.

Rawlinson, A. E. J., ed. Essays on the Trinity and the Incarnation. New York: Longmans, Green & Co., 1933.

Reardon, Bernard M. C. "A Comment." Theology 72 (1975): 298-301.

Reeves, Marjorie. "The Originality and Influence of Joachim of Fiore." Traditio 36 (1980):

269-319.

Die Religion Geschicte und Gegenwart, S.v. "Person," by W. Pannenberg. ed. Kurt Galling, 1969.

Relton, H.M. Studies in Christian Doctrine. London: MacMillan, 1960.

Renehan, Robert. "The Greek Anthropocentric View of Man." Harvard Studies in Classical Philology 85 (1981): 239-259.

Rey, B. "Trinité." Revue de sciences philosophique et theologique 49 (1965): 527-533.

Rheinfelder, Han. Das Wort "Persona". In Beihefte zur Zeitschrift für Romanische Philologie. vol. 77. Halle: H. Niemeyer, 1928.

Rhodes, J. Stephen. "Christ and the Spirit: "filioque" reconsidered." Biblical Theology Bulletin 18 (July, 1988): 91-95.

Richard of St. Victor. Liber Exceptionum, texte critique avec introduction, notes et tables. ed. Jean Chatillon. Paris: Vrin, 1958.

_____. De Tribus appropriatis personis in Trinitate. PL 196.

_____. De Trinitate, texte critique avec introduction, notes et tables. ed. Jean Ribaillier. Paris: Vrin, 1958.

_____. Richard de Saint-Victor, la Trinité, texte latin, introduction, traduction et notes. vol. 63. Sources Chrétiennes. ed. and trans. Gaston Salet, S.J. Paris: Editions du Cerf, 1959.

_____. Opuscules Theologiques: Texte critique avec introduction, notes et tables par I. Ribaillier. vol. 15. Textes philosophiques du Moyen Age. Paris: J. Vrin, 1967.

_____. Selected Writings on Contemplation. trans. Clare Kirchberger. New York: Harper, 1957.

_____. The Twelve Patriarchs, The Mystical Ark, Book Three of the Trinity. trans. with intro. Grover A. Zinn. Preface by Jean Châtillon. In The Classics of Western Spirituality. New York: Paulist Press, 1979.

_____ and Brother Yves. Les Quatres degres de la violent charite. Paris: J. Vrin, 1955.

Richard, Robert. L. The Problem of an Apologetical Perspective in the Trinitarian Theology of St. Thomas Aquinas. vol. 131. Series Facultatis Theologicae: sectio B. n.43. Rome: Gregorian University Press, 1963.

Richards, M. L, Sr. trans. A Christian Anthropology by Joseph Goetz, et al. St. Meinrad, IN: Abbey Press, 1974.

Richardson, Alan. Creeds in the Making. Philadelphia: Fortress Press, 1981.

Richardson, Cyril C. The Doctrine of the Trinity. New York: Abingdon Press, 1958.

_____. "The Trinity and the Enhypotasia." Canadian Journal of Theology 5:2 (April, 1959): 73-78.

Richardson, R.D. "The Doctrine of the Trinity: Its Development, Difficulties, and Value."

Harvard Theological Review 36 (1943): 109-134.

Ridderbos, Hermann. Paul: An Outline of His Theology. trans. John Richard De Witt. Grand Rapids: Eerdmans, 1975.

Rist, John M. Platonism and its Christian Heritage. London: Variorium Reprints, 1985.

_____. "Theos and the One in some texts of Plotinus." Medieval Studies 24 (1962): 169-180.

Robb, J. Wesley. "That Haunting Problem of the Self." Religion in Life 42:2 (1973): 212-223.

Roberts, Robert. "Kierkegaard on Becoming an 'Individual'". Scottish Journal of Theology 31:2 (1978): 133-152.

Robilliard, J. A. "Les six genres de contemplation chez Richard de Saint-Victor et leur origine platonicienne." Revue des sciences philosophiques et theologiques 28 (1939): 229-233.

Robinson, H. Wheeler. The Christian Experience of the Holy Spirit. London: Nisbet and Co., 1930.

_____. The Corporate Personality in Ancient Israel. Philadelphia: Fortress Press, 1964.

Robinson, John A. T. The Priority of John. ed. J. F. Coakley. Oak Park, Il: Meyer-Stone Books, 1987.

_____. "Thou Who Art." Ph. D. dissertation, Cambridge Univ., 1946.

Robinson, N. H. G. "Trinitarianism and Post-Barthian Theology." Journal of Theological Studies 20 (1969): 186-201.

Rodd, Cyril S. ed. Foundations Documents of the Faith. Edinburgh: T. & T. Clark, 1987.

Rohls, Jan "Die Persönlichkeit Gottes und die Trinitätslehre." Evangelisch Theologie 45:2 (1985): 124-139.

Rorty, A. O. ed. The Identities of Persons. Berkeley: Univ. of California Press, 1976.

Rosenthal, Klaus. "Bermerkungen zur gegenwärtigen Behandlung der Trinitätslehre." Kerygma und Dogma 22 (1976): 132-148.

Roth, Robert J. ed. Person and Community: A Philosophical Exploration. New York: Fordham Univ. Press, 1975.

Rouët, M. J. de Journel. Enchiridion patristicum. Barcinone-Frieburgi: Br.-Romae-Neo-Eboraci, 1969.

Rougier, Louis. "Le sens des termes "Ousia", "Hypostasis" et "Prosopon" dans les controverses trinitaires Post-Nicéenes." Revue de l'Histoire des Religions 73 (1916): 133-189.

Ruether, Rosemary Radford. Gregory of Nazianzus; Rhetor and Philosopher. Oxford: Clarendon Press, 1969.

Rusch, William G., trans. and ed. The Trinitarian Controversy. Philadelphia: Fortress Press, 1980.

Rust, Eric C. "The Holy Spirit, Nature, and Man." Review and Expositor 63:2 (1966): 157-176.

Rydstrom-Poulsen, Age. "Kaerlighad og Treenighed: Et hovedtema i Richard af St. Victor's "De Trinitate"." Dansk Theologisk Tidsskrift 47 (1984): 265-281.

_____. "Tro, Fornuft og erfaring: Richard af St. Victor's Teologiske Metode." Dansk Theologisk Tidsskrift 47:2 (1984): 109-130.

Sacramentum Mundi. S.v. "Person." ed. Karl Rahner. 4 vols. New York: Herder and Herder, 1968-70.

Sacramentum Verbi. S.v. "Man," by Robert Koch. ed. Johannes B. Bauer. New York: Herder & Herder, 1970.

Salmann, Elmar. "Trinität und Kirche." Catholica 38 (1984): 352-374.

_____. "Wer is Gott? zur Frage nach dem Verhaltnis von Person und Natur in der Trinitätslehre." Münchener Theologische Zeitschrift 35 (1984): 245-261.

Sanday, W. Christology and Personality. Oxford: Clarendon Press, 1911.

Sartorius, Ernest. The Doctrine of Divine Love. trans. Sophia Taylor. In Clark's Foreign Theological Library, Edinburgh: T. & T. Clark, 1984.

Saward, John. "Towards an Apophatic Anthropology." Irish Theological Quarterly 46:3 (1974): 222-234.

Sawyer, John. "The Meaning of "Beselem Ha'Elohim" ('in the image of God') in Gen. I-XI." Journal of Theological Studies. n.s. 25 (1974): 418-426.

Sayers, Dorothy. Further Papers on Dante. Reprint. Westport, Conn.: Greenwood Press, 1979.

_____. The Mind of the Maker. New York: Harcourt, Brace and Co., 1941.

Schaberg, Jane. The Father, the Son and the Holy Spirit: The Triadic Phrase in Mt. 28:19b. Chico, Calif.: Scholar's Press, 1982.

Schacten, W. "Das Verhaltnis von "immanenter und ökonmischer" Trinität in der neueren Theologie." Franziskanische Studien 61 (1979): 8-27.

Schadel, Erwin. Bibliotheca Trinitariorum. International Bibliography of Trinitarian Literature. 2 vols. New York: K. G. Saur, 1984-1988.

Scharlemann, Robert P. "Hegel and Theology Today." Dialog 24:4 (1984): 257-262.

Scheler, Max. Formalism in Ethics and Non-Formal Ethics of Value. trans. Manfred S. Frings and Roger L. Funk. Evanston: Northwestern Univ. Press, 1973.

Schierse, Franz Josef. "Die neutestamentliche Trinitätsoffenbarung." In Mysterium Salutis. vol 2. ed. Johannes Feiner, 85-131. Einseideln: Benzinger Verlag, 1967.

Schillebeeckx, Edward and Bas van Iersel, ed. A Personal God? New York: The Seabury Press, 1977.

Schilling, S. Paul. Contemporary Continental Theologians. Nashville: Abingdon Press, 1966.

Schiltz, Eugene. "La notion de personne d'après Saint Thomas." Ephemerides theologicae lovanienses. 10 (1933): 409-26.

Schinzer, Reinhard. "Objektification der Existenz: Versuch über die Trinitarischen Personen bei Heinrich von Gent." Neue Zeitschrift für Systematische Theologie und Religionsphilosophie 18:2 (1976): 225-245.

Schleiermacher, Friedrich. The Christian Faith. eds. H. R. Mackintosh and J. S. Stewart. New York: Harper & Row, Pub., 1963.

Schlette, Heinz Robert. "Das unterschiedliche Personverständnis im theologischen Denken Hugos und Richards von St. Viktor." In Mitteilungen des Grabmann-Institute der University München. vol. 3. 55-72. Munich: Max Hueber Verlag, 1959.

Schlossmann, Siegmund. Persona und 'Prosopon': im Recht und im christlichen Dogma. Darmstadt: Wissenschaftliche Buchgesellschaft, 1968.

Schmaus, Michael. Die Denkform Augustins in Heft 6 seinem Werk De Trinitate. Munich: Verlag der Bayerischen Akademie der Wissenschaft, 1962.

_____. Dogma Vol. 3: God and His Christ. New York: Sheed and Ward, 1971.

_____. Die psychologische Trinitätslehre des heiligen Augustinus. Münster: Aschendorffsche Verlagsbuchhandlung, 1967.

Schmaus, Michael and Max Seckler eds. Begegnung: Beitrage zu einer Hermeneutik des theologischen Gesprächs. Graz, Austria: Verlag Styria, 1972.

Schmidt, Erik. "Hegel und die kirchliche Trinitätslehre." Neue Zeitschrift für Systematische Theologie und Religionsphilosophie 24 (1982): 241-260.

Schmidt, Martin Anton. "Zur Trinitätslehre der Früscholastik." Theologische Zeitschrift 40:2 (1984): 181-192.

_____. "Verstehen de Unbegreiflichen in den beiden ersten Büchern "De Trinitate" des Richard von Saint-Victor." In Abendlandische Mystik im Mittelalter. Symposium Kloster Engelbery, 1984. ed. Kurt Ruh Germanishe Symposien, Berichts-Bonde. vol. 7. Stuttgart: J. B. Metzler, 1986.

Schneyer, Johannes Baptist. "Sigeltabellen zu Repertorium der lateinischen Sermones des Mittelalters für die Zeit von 1150-1350." In Beitrage zur Geschichte der Philosophie und Theologie des Mittelalters. vol. 43, pt. 5. Munich: Aschendorff, 1974.

Schoedel, William R. and Robert L. Wilken. Early Christian Literature and the Classical Intellectual Tradition: In Honorem Robert M. Grant. Paris: Editions Beauchesne, 1979.

Schoonenberg, P. J. A. M. "Process or History in God?" Theology Digest 23 (1975): 38-44.

_____. "Zur Trinitätslehre Karl Rahners." In Glaube in Prozess. eds. Klinger and Wittstadt, Freiburg: Herder Verlag, 1984.

_____. "Trinity - The Consummated Covenant: Theses on the Doctrine of the Trinitarian God." Studies in Religion 5 (1975-76): 111-116.

Schütz, Christian. Einführung in die Pneumatologie. Darmstadt: Wissenschaftliche Buchgesellschaft, 1985.

Schütz, Christian and Rupert Sarach. "Der Mensch als Person." In Mysterium Salutis. vol 2. ed. Johannes Feiner, 637-655. Einseideln: Benzinger Verlag, 1967.

Schwarz, Balduin V. ed. The Human Person and the World of Values. New York: Fordham Univ. Press, 1960.

Sciacca, M. F. "Trinité et unité de l'esprit." In Augustinus Magister: Congrès International Augustinien vol. 1. 521-533. Paris: Études Augustiniennes, 1954.

Scott, David A. "The Trinity and Ethics: The Thought of Helmut Thielicke." Lutheran Quarterly 29:1 (1977): 3-12.

Scuiry, Daniel E. "The Anthropology of St. Gregory of Nyssa." Diakonia 18:1 (1983): 31-42.

Sears, Robert T. "Spirit: Divine and Human. The Theology of the Holy Spirit of Heribert Mühlen and its Relevance for Evaluating the Data of Psychotherapy." Ph. D. dissertation, Fordham Univ., 1974.

_____. "Trinitarian Love as Ground of the Church." Theological Studies 37 (1976): 652-679.

Seeberg, Reinhold. Text-Book of the History of Doctrines. 2 vols. trans. Charles E. Hay. Grand Rapids: Baker Book House, 1977.

Segundo, Juan Luis. Our Idea of God. A Theology for Artisans of a New Humanity, vol. 4. Maryknoll, New York: Orbis Books, 1974.

Sengler, D. "Die ontologische und ökonomische Trinität und die Natur in Gott." Theologie Studien und Kritiken 35 (1862): 791-800.

Serralda, Vincent. La Philosophie de la Personne chez Alcuin. Paris: Nouvelles Éditions Latines, 1978.

Shafer, Ingrid. ed. The Incarnate Imagination: Essays in Theology, The Arts and Social Sciences in Honor of Andrew Greeley. A Festschrift. Bowling Green, Ohio: Bowling Green State Univ. Press, 1988.

Shahan, Robert W. and Frances J. Kovach. eds. Bonaventure and Aquinas: Enduring Philosophers. Norman, OK.: Univ. of Oklahoma Press, 1976.

Sherrard, Philip. Latin East and Greek West: A Study in Christian Tradition. London: Oxford Univ. Press, 1959.

Shideler, Mary McDermott. The Theology of Romantic Love. Grand Rapids: Eerdmans, 1962.

Shoemaker, Sydney. Self-Knowledge and Self-Identity. Ithaca, New York: Cornell Univ. Press, 1963.

Shoemaker, Sydney and Richard Swinburne. Personal Identity. Oxford: Basil Blackwell, 1984.

Shutte, Augustine. "Indwelling, Intersubjectivity and God." Scottish Journal of Theology 32:2 (1979): 201-216.

_____. "A Philosophy of the Human Person for Contemporary Theology." Journal of

Theology for Southern Africa 41 (Dec.1983): 70-77.

_____. "What Makes Us Persons." _Modern Theology._ 1:1 (1984): 67-79.

Sider, Robert. "Approaches to Tertullian: A Study of Recent Scholarship." _The Second Century_ 2:4 (1982): 252-253.

Siebel, Wigand. _Der Heilige Geist als Relation: Eine Soziale Trinitätslehre._ Münster: Aschendorff, 1986.

Simonis, Walter. _Trinität und Vernunft: Untersuchungen zur Möglichkeit einer rationalen Trinitätslehre bei Anselm, Abaelard, den Viktorinen, A. Günther und J. Frohschammer._ In _Franfurter Theologische Studien._ vol. 12. Frankfurt am Main: Verlag Josef Knecht, 1972.

Skutsch, F. "Persona." _Archiv für Lateinische Lexicographie_ 15 (1908): 145-146.

Slesinski, Robert. _Pavel Florensky: A Metaphysics of Love._ Crestwood, New York: St. Vladimir's Seminary Press, 1984.

Slusser, Michael. "The Exegetical Roots of Trinitarian Theology." _Theological Studies_ 49 (1988): 461-476.

Smail, Thomas A. _The Forgotten Father._ Grand Rapids: Eerdmans Pub. Co., 1980

Smalley, Beryl. _The Study of the Bible in the Middle Ages._ New York: Philosophical Library, 1952.

Smalley, Stephen S. _John: Evangelist and Interpreter._ Nashville: Thomas Nelson Pub., 1984.

Sommerfeldt, John R. _Studies in Medieval Culture_ 8 & 9. Medieval Institute, Western Michigan Univ. (Conf. on Medieval Studies, 8th, 1973, 9th, 1976), 1976.

Snook, Lee E. "A Primer on the Trinity: Keeping Our Theology Christian." _Word and World_ 2:1 (1982): 5-16.

Snowden, James H. _The Personality of God._ New York: Macmillan Co., 1920.

Southern, R. W. _Western Society and the Church in the Middle Ages._ Grand Rapids: Eerdmans Pub. Co., 1970.

Spicer, Malcolm. "The Trinity: A Psychological God." _Studies in Religion_ 5:2 (1975/6): 117-133.

Spicq, C. _Equisse d'une histoire de l'exégèse latine au Moyen Age._ Paris: Vrin, 1944.

Splett, Jörg. "Uber die Einheit von Nächsten und Gottesliebe laienhaft (Idiota de unitate.)" In _Wagnis Theologie: Erfahrung mit der Theologie Karl Rahners._ ed. Herbert Vorgrimler. Freiburg: Herder, 1979.

_____. _Die Trintätslehre G. W. F. Hegels._ In _Symposion: Philosophische Schriftenreihe._ vol. 20. Munich: Verlag Kari Alber, 1965.

Squire, A. K. "Personal Integration in the Latter Books of Augustine's 'De Trinitate'." In _Studia Patristica_ 16:2. ed. Elizabeth A. Livingstone, 565-569. Berlin: Akademie-Verlag, 1985.

Stead, Christopher. "The Concept of Divine Substance." Vigiliae Christianae 29 (1975): 1-14.

_____. Divine Substance. Oxford: Clarendon Press, 1977.

_____. "The Origins of the Doctrine of the Trinity." Theology 77 (1974): 508-17, 582-588.

_____. "The Significance of the "Homoousios"." In Studia Patristica 3:1. ed. F. L. Cross, 397-412. Berlin: Akademie-Verlag, 1961.

_____. Substance and Illusion in the Christian Fathers. London: Variorum Reprints, 1985.

Stephens, Bruce M. "The Doctrine of the Trinity from Jonathan Edwards to Horace Bushnell: A Study in the Eternal Sonship of Christ." Ph.D dissertation, Princeton Theological Seminary, 1976.

_____. God's Last Metaphor: The Doctrine of the Trinity in New England Theology. Chico: Scholars Press, 1981.

Stephenson, A. A. "S. Cyril of Jerusalem's Trinitarian Theology." In Studia Patristica 11:2. ed. F. L. Cross, 234-241. Berlin: Akademie-Verlag, 1972.

Stock, Brian. "Hugh of St. Victor, Bernard Silvester and M.S. Trinity College, Cambridge, 0.7.7." Medieval Studies 34 (1972): 152-173.

Stocks, J.L. "Plato and the Tripartite Soul." Mind n.s. 24 (1915): 207-21.

Stohr, A. "Die Hauptrichtungen der Spekulativen Trinitätslehre in der Theologie der 13. Jahrhunderts." Theologische Quartalschrift 106: 1-2 (1925): 113-135.

Sträter, Carl. "Le point de départ du traité thomiste de la Trinité." Sciences Ecclésiastiques 14 (1962): 71-87.

Strawson, P.F. Individuals: An Essay in Descriptive Metaphysics. London: Metheun and Co. Ltd., 1964.

Streetman, Robert F. "Friedrich Schleiemacher's Doctrine of the Trinity and its Significance for Today." Ph. D. dissertation, Drew University, 1975.

_____. "Some Questions Schleiermacher Might Ask About Karl Barth's Trinitarian Criticisms." In Barth and Schleiermacher: Beyond the Impasse? ed. James O. Duke and Robert F. Streetman. Philadelphia: Fortress Press, 1988.

Studer, Basil. "Der Person-Begriff in der frühen Kirchenamtlichen Trinitätslehre." Theologie und Philosophie 57 (1982): 161-177.

Suchocki, Marjorie Hewitt. God, Christ, Church: A Practical Guide to Process Theology. New York: Crossroad, 1988.

_____. "The Unmale God: Reconsidering the Trinity." Quarterly Review. 3:1 (Spring, 1983): 34-49.

Sullivan, John Edward. The Image of God: The Doctrine of St. Augustine and its Influence. Dubuque, Iowa: Priory Press, 1963.

Surin, Kenneth. "The Trinity and Philosophical Reflection: A Study of David Brown's The Divine Trinity." Modern Theology 2:3 (April, 1986): 235-256.

Swete, H.B. The Holy Spirit in the Ancient Church. London: Macmillan, 1912.

Swinburne, Richard. "Could there be more than One God?" Faith and Philosophy 5:3 (July, 1988): 225-241.

Szemerényi, O. "The Origins of Roman Drama and Greek Tragedy." Hermes 103 (1975): 300-332.

Tavard, George H. The Vision of the Trinity. Washington: Univ. Press of America, 1981.

_____. A Way of Love. Maryknoll: Orbis, 1977.

Taylor, Mark Lloyd. God is Love: A Study in the Theology of Karl Rahner. American Academy of Religion Academy Series. ed. Carl A. Raschke. no. 50. Atlanta: Scholars Press, 1986.

Teichman, Jenny. "The Definition of Person." Philosophy 60 (1985): 175-185.

Teresa of Avila, St. The Complete Works of St. Teresa of Avila. trans. and ed. E. Allison Peers. 3 vols. New York: Sheed and Ward, 1944.

Tertullian. Adversus Praxean. PL. 2.

_____. Tertullian's Treatise Against Praxeas. ed. with an intro., trans., and comm. Ernest Evans. London: S. P. C. K., 1948.

TeSelle, Eugene. Augustine·the Theologian. New York: Herder & Herder, 1970.

Thatcher, Adrian. "The Personal God and a God Who is a Person." Religious Studies 21:1 (1985): 61-73.

Theological Dictionary. S.v. "Person," K. Rahner and H. Vorgrimler. ed. Cornelius Ernst, O.P. trans. Richard Strachan. New York: Herder and Herder, 1965.

Theological Dictionary. S.v. "Trinity." ed. Cornelius Ernst, O.P., trans. Richard Strachan. New York: Herder and Herder, 1965.

Theological Dictionary of the New Testament. S. v. "Prosopon," Eduard Lohse. ed. Gerhard Frederick. trans and ed. Geoffrey w. Bromiley, vol. 6. 768-780. Grand Rapids: Eerdmans Publishing Company, 1968.

Thielicke, Helmut. The Evangelical Faith. 3 vols. trans. and ed. Geoffrey W. Bromiley. Grand Rapids: Eerdmans Pub. Co., 1977.

Thiemann, Ronald F. Revelation and Theology: The Gospel of Narrated Promise. Notre Dame: University of Notre Dame Press, 1985.

Thistlethwaite, Susan Brooks. "Comments on Jürgen Moltmann's "The Unity of the Triune God"." St. Vladimir's Theological Quarterly 28:3 (1984): 179-182.

Thomas Aquinas, Saint. Basic Writings of Saint Thomas Aquinas. ed. and annotated, with intro. by Anton C. Pegis. 2 vols. New York: Random House, 1945.

_____. Summa Contra Gentiles. Book One: God. trans. with intro. by Anton C. Pegis. Notre Dame: Univ. of Notre Dame Press, 1975.

_____. The "Summa Theologica" of St. Thomas Aquinas. trans. The Fathers of the English Dominican Province. Part I, QQ. 37-49. London: Burns, Oates and Washbourne,

1921.

_____. Summa Theologiae. Blackfriars edition. Vol. 6. The Trinity. trans. and intro. Ceslaus Velecky. Vol. 7. 1a 33-43: Father, Son and Holy Ghost. trans and intro T. C. O'Brien. New York: McGraw Hill Book Co., 1965.

_____. The Trinity and the Unicity of the Intellect. trans. Sister Rose Emmanuella Brennan. London: B. Herder Book Co., 1946.

Thompson, John. "The Holy Spirit and the Trinity in Ecumenical Perspective." Irish Theological Quarterly 47:4 (1980): 272-285

Thompson, William M. The Jesus Debate: A Survey and Synthesis. Mahwah, NJ.: Paulist Press, 1985.

Thornton, L. S. The Incarnate Lord. London: Longmans, 1928.

Thurmer, J.A. "The Analogy of the Trinity." Scottish Journal of Theology 34:6 (1981): 509-515.

_____. Detection of the Trinity. Exeter: Paternoster Press, 1984.

_____. "Letter to the Editor" Theology 72 (1975): 426-427.

Tillich, Paul. History of Christian Thought. New York: Simon and Schuster, 1967.

_____. Systematic Theology. 3 vols. Chicago: Univ. of Chicago Press, 1951-63.

Tixeront, J. A Handbook of Patrology. trans. S. A. Raemers. St. Louis and London: B. Herder Book Co., 1947.

Toon, Peter and James D. Spiceland, eds. One God in Trinity. Westchester, Illinois: Cornerstone Books, 1980.

Torrance, Thomas F. Christian Theology and Scientific Culture. New York: Oxford Univ. Press, 1981.

_____. "The Goodness and Dignity of Man in the Christian Tradition." Modern Theology 4:4 (July, 1988): 309-322.

_____. The Mediation of Christ. Grand Rapids: Eerdmans Pub. Co., 1983.

_____. Reality and Evangelical Theology. Philadelphia: Westminster Press, 1982.

_____. Reality and Scientific Theology. Edinburgh: Scottish Academic Press, 1985.

_____. "Theological Realism." In The Philosophical Frontiers of Christian Theology: Essays presented to D.M. Mackinnon. eds. Brian Hebbelthwaite and Stewart Sutherland, 169-190. Cambridge: Cambridge Univ. Press, 1982.

_____. Theological Science. London: Oxford Univ. Press, 1969.

_____. Theology in Reconciliation: Essays towards Evangelical and Catholic Unity in East and West. Grand Rapids: Eerdmans, 1976.

_____. Theology in Reconstruction. Reprint. Grand Rapids: Eerdmans Pub. Co., 1975.

_____. "Toward an Ecumenical Consensus on the Trinity." Theologische Zeitschrift 31 (1975): 337-350.

Torrance, Thomas F. ed. Theological Dialogue Between Orthodox and Reformed Churches. Edinburgh: Scottish Academic Press, 1985.

Tournier, Paul. The Meaning of Persons. trans. Edwin Hudson. Guildford and London: Billing and Sons Limited, 1957.

Tracy, David. The Analogical Imagination. New York: Crossroad, 1981.

_____.Blessed Rage for Order: The New Pluralism in Theology. New York: Seabury Press, 1975.

Tracy, Thomas. God, Action, Embodiment. Grand Rapids: Paternoster/ Eerdmans, 1984.

Trapè, A. "I termini "natura" e "persona" nella teologia trinitaria di S. Agostino." Augustinianum 13 (1973): 577-587.

Trendelburg, Adolf. "A Contribution to the History of the Word Person." Monist 20 (1910): 336-363.

Trethowan, Illtyd. "In Defence of Traditional Trinitarianism." Monastic Studies 17 (Christmas, 1986): 143-154.

Trierer Thelogische Studien. Petrus Abaelardus. vol. 38. ed. Rudolf Thomas. Trier: Paulinus-Verlag, 1980.

Trinkaus, Charles. In Our Image and Likeness. 2 vols. Chicago: The Univ. of Chicago Press, 1970.

Tritik, Zdenek. "Der Personbegriff im dogmatischen Denken Karl Barths: eine kritische Untersuchung." Neue Zeitschrift für Systematische Theologie und Religionsphilosophie 5 (1963): 263-295.

Turner, J. E. Personality and Reality. New York: Macmillan Co., 1926.

Tweedale, Martin M. Abailard on Universals. New York and Oxford: North-Holland Publishing Co., 1976.

Ugolnik, Anthony. The Illuminating Icon. Grand Rapids: Eerdmans, 1989.

Ullmann, S. "Le vocabulaire, moule et norme de la pensée." In Problèmes de la Personne. ed. I. Meyerson, 251-269. Paris: Mouton and Co., 1973.

Uppsala Report, 1968. ed. Norman Goodall. Geneva: W.C.C., 1968.

Vanderwelde, George. "The Grammar of Grace: Karl Rahner as a Watershed in Contemporary Theology." Theological Studies 49 (1988): 445-459.

Van Inwagen, Peter. "And Yet They are Not Three Gods but One God." In Philosophy and the Christian Faith. ed. Thomas V. Morris. University of Notre Dame Studies in the Philosophy of Religion: 5. Notre Dame: Univ. of Notre Dame Press, 1988.

Van Leeuwen, Mary Stewart. The Person in Psychology: A Contemporary Christian Appraisal. Grand Rapids: Eerdmans Pub Co., 1985.

Van Straaten, Zak. ed. Philosophical Subjects: Essays presented to P. F. Strawson. Oxford: Clarendon Press, 1980.

Verkhovsky, Serge S. "Procession of the Holy Spirit According to Orthodox Doctrine of the Trinity." St. Vladimir's Seminary Quarterly 2:1 (1953): 12-26.

Victorinus, Marius. Theological Tractates on the Trinity. In FC. vol. 69. trans. Mary T. Clark.

Vignaux, Paul. Philosophy in the Middle Ages. trans. E. C. Hall. New York: Meridian Books, 1959.

Vincent of Lerins. Commonitories. FC. vol. 7. trans. Rudolph E. Morris.

Vischer. Lukas. Spirit of God, Spirit of Christ: Ecumenical Reflections on the "Filioque" Controversy. Faith and Order Paper No. 103. London: SPCK/ Geneva: W.C.C., 1981.

Vitz, Paul. "A Covenant Theory of Personality: A Theoretical Introduction." In The Christian Vision: Man in Society. ed. Lynne Morris, 79-99. Hillsdale: Hillsdale College Press, 1984.

Vitz, Paul C. Psychology As Religion. Grand Rapids: Eerdmans Pub. Co., 1977.

Wainwright, Arthur W. The Trinity in the New Testament. London: S.P.C.K., 1962.

Wainwright, Geoffrey. Doxology. New York: Oxford Univ. Press, 1980.

Wainwright, G. "From Pluralism towards Catholicity? The United Methodist Church after the General Conference of 1988." Asbury Theological Journal 44:1 (Spring, 1989): 17-27.

Walgrave, Jan. Unfolding Revelation: The Nature of Doctrinal Development. Philadelphia: Westminster Press, 1972.

Walgrave, John H. Person and Society: A Christian View. Pittsburgh: Duquesne Univ. Press, 1965.

Walker, Williston. A History of the Christian Church. New York: Charles Scribner's Sons, 1930.

Ward, Keith. "Recent Thinking on Christian Beliefs II.The Concept of God." The Expository Times 88 (Oct.1976-Sept.1977): 68-71.

_____. The Concept of God. New York: St. Martin's Press, 1974.

Ware, Kallistos. "Image and Likeness." Parabola 10:1 (1985): 62-71.

_____. The Orthodox Way. Crestwood, New York: St. Vladimir's Seminary Press, 1980.

Warfield, B. B. "The Biblical Doctrine of the Trinity." In Biblical and Theological Studies. ed. Samuel G. Craig, 22-59. Philadelphia: Presbyterian and Reformed Pub. Co., 1952.

Warnach, Viktor. Agape: Die Liebe als Grunmotiv der neutestamentlichen Theologie. Düsseldorf: Patmos-Verlag, 1951.

Wassmer, Thomas A. "Platonic Thought in Christian Revelation as seen in the Trinitarian

Theology of Augustine." American Ecclesiastical Review 139 (1958): 291-298. Identical article found as "The Trinitarian Theology of Augustine and His Debt to Plotinus." Scottish Journal of Theology 13 (1961): 248-255.

Watson, Gerard. "The Theology of Plato and Aristotle." The Irish Theological Quarterly 37:1 (1970): 56-64.

Watts, Fraser and Mark Williams. The Psychology of Religious Knowing. New York: Cambridge Univ. Press, 1988.

Webb, Clement C. J. Divine Personality and Human Life. New York: Macmillan Co., 1920

_____. God and Personality. New York: Macmillan Co., 1918.

_____. Problems in the Relations of God and Man. Reprint. London: Nisbet and Co. Ltd., 1924.

Webster, J. B. Eberhard Jüngel: An Introduction to His Theology. Cambridge: Cambridge Univ. Press, 1986.

Webster, John. "The Identity of the Holy Spirit: A Problem in Trinitarian Theology." Themelios 9:1 (1983): 4-7.

Weinandy, Thomas G. Does God Change?. Still River, Massachusetts: St. Bede's Publications, 1985.

Weingart, Richard E. The Logic of Divine Love. Oxford: The Clarendon Press, 1970.

Welch, Claude. ed. and trans. God and Incarnation in Mid-Nineteenth Century German Theology. New York: Oxford Univ. Press, 1965.

_____. "The Holy Spirit and the Trinity." Theology Today 8:1 (April 1951-January 1952): 29-40.

_____. In This Name: The Doctrine of the Trinity in Contemporary Theology. New York: Charles Scribner's Sons, 1952.

_____. Protestant Thought in the Nineteenth Century: Vol. I. 1799-1870. New Haven and London: Yale Univ. Press, 1972.

Wendebourg, Dorothea. "From the Cappadocian Fathers to Gregory Palamas: The Defeat of Trinitarian Theology." In Studia Patristica 17:1. ed. Elizabeth A. Livingstone, 194-198. Oxford: Pergamon Press Ltd., 1982.

West, Delno and Sandra Zimdars-Swartz. Joachim of Fiore: A Study in Spiritual Perception and History. Bloomington: Indiana Univ. Press, 1983.

Westminster Dictionary of Christian Theology. S.v. "Person," by R.A. Norris. eds. A. Richardson and John Bowden. Philadelphia: Westminster Press, 1983.

_____. S.v. "Trinity, Doctrine of the." by J.P. Mackay.

Wetter, Friedrich. "Amor mutuus und amor reflexus: Uberlegungen zum Hervorgang des Heiligen Geistes." In Wahrheit und Verkundigung: Michael Schmaus zum 70 Geburstag. ed. Leo Scheffczyk, et al., 707-731. Munich: Schöningh, 1967.

_____. Die Trinitätslehre des Johannes Duns Scotus. In Beitrage zur Geschichte der

Philosophie und Theologie des Mittelalters. vol. 41. pt. 5.Münster: Ascendorffsche Verlagsbuchhandlung, 1967.

Whitehead, Alfred North. Process and Reality. New York: The Free Press, 1957.

Whitlock, Glenn. "The Structure of Personality in Hebrew Psychology." Interpretation 14 (1960): 3-13.

Widmer, Gabriel. "L'essence trinitaire et l'histoire trinitaire de Dieu." Revue d'Histoire et de Philosophie Religieuses 56 (1976): 495-508.

Wiles, Maurice F. "Psychological Analogies of the Fathers." In Studia Patristica vol. 11. ed. F. L. Cross, 264-267. Berlin: Akademie Verlag, 1972.

_____. The Remaking of Christian Doctrine. London: SCM Press, 1974.

_____. "Some Reflections on the Origins of the Doctrine of the Trinity." Journal of Theological Studies n.s. 8 (April, 1957): 92-106.

Wiles, Maurice and Mark Santer. Documents in Early Christian Thought. Cambridge: Cambridge Univ. Press, 1975.

Wilhelmsen, Frederick D. "Modern Man's Myth of Self Identity." Modern Age 24 (Winter 1980): 39-46.

Wilken, Robert L. "The Resurrection of Jesus and the Doctrine of the Trinity." Word and World 2:1 (Winter 1982): 17-28.

Williams, Arthur H. "The Trinity and Time." Scottish Journal of Theology. 39:1 (1986): 65-81.

Williams, Charles. The Descent of the Dove. London: Faber and Faber, Ltd., 1950.

_____. The Forgiveness of Sins. Grand Rapids: Eerdmans Pub. Co., 1984.

_____. He Came Down From Heaven. Grand Rapids: Eerdmans Pub. Co., 1984.

Williams, Paul L. The Abelardian Perspective: A Moral View of Christ's Work. Ph.D. dissertation, Drew Univ., 1976.

Williams, Rowan. "Trinity and Revelation." Modern Theology 2:3 (1986): 197-212.

Willis, W. Waite. Theism, Atheism and the Doctrine of the Trinity: The Trinitarian Theologies of Karl Barth and Jürgen Moltmann in Response to Protest Atheism. Atlanta: Scholars Press, 1987.

Wilson, R. Mcl. "The Early History of the Exegesis of Gen. 1:26." In Studia Patristica. vol. 2. eds. Kurt Aland and F. L. Cross, 420-437. Berlin: Akademie Verlag, 1957.

Wingren, Gustaf. "Fragen um das Personsein Gottes." Theologische Literaturzeitung 101:10 (1976): 721-728.

Wipfler, Heinz. Grundfragen der Trinitätsspekulation: Analogiefrage in der Trinitätstheologie. Regensburg: Verlag Habbel, 1977.

_____. Die Trinitätsspekulation des Petrus von Poitiers und Die Trinitätsspekulation des Richard von St. Viktor: Eine Vergleich. In Beiträge zur Geschichte der Philosophie und Theologie des Mittelalters. vol. 41. pt. 1. Munich: Aschendorffsche Verlagsbuchhandlung, 1965.

Wippel, John F. and Allan B. Wolter. Medieval Philosophy: From Augustine to Nicholas of Cusa. New York: Free Press, 1969.

Wölfel, Eberhard. Seinsstruktur und Trinitätsproblem. Beiträge zur Geschichte der Philosophie und Theologie des Mittelalters. vol. 40. pt. 5. Munich: Aschendorffsche Verlagsbuchhandlung, 1965.

Wolf, Herbert C. "An Introduction to the Idea of God as Person." Journal of Bible and Religion 32:1 (1964): 26-33.

Wolfson, Harry Austryn. The Philosophy of the Church Fathers. vol. 1: Faith, Trinity, Incarnation. Cambridge, Massachusetts: Harvard Univ. Press, 1956.

Wolter, Allan. Life in God's Love. Chicago: Franciscan Herald Press, 1958.

Wong, Joseph H.P. "Karl Rahner's Christology of Symbol and Three Models of Christology." Heythrop Journal 17:1 (1986): 1-25.

Wood, Laurence W. "The Panentheism of Charles Hartshorne: A Critique." The Asburian Seminarian 37:2 (1982): 20-46.

_____. Pentecostal Grace. Wilmore, Ky.: Francis Asbury Press, 1980.

Wood, Nathan R. The Secret of the Universe: God, Man and Matter. Grand Rapids: Eerdmans Pub. Co., 1955.

Woodhouse, H.F. "The Limits of Pluralism." Scottish Journal of Theology 34:1 (1981): 1-15.

Wright, George Ernest. The God Who Acts. London: SCM Press, 1952.

Yamamura, Kei. "The Development of the Doctrine of the Holy Spirit in Patristic Philosophy: St. Basil and St. Gregory of Nyssa." St. Vladimir's Theological Quarterly 18:1 (1974): 3-21.

Note: For Yannaras, Christos see Giannaras

Young, Frances M. From Nicaea to Chalcedon: A Guide to the Literature and its Background. Philadelphia: Fortress Press, 1983.

Zagzebski, L. "Christian Monotheism." Faith and Philosophy 6:1 (January, 1989): 3-18.

Zimany, Roland. "Human Love and the Trinity: Jüngel's Perception." Dialog 21:3 (1982): 220-223.

Zinn, Grover. "Book and Word: The Victorine Background of Bonaventure's Use of Symbols." In Sanctus Bonaventura: 1274-1974. vol. 2. ed. Anton C. Pegis, 143-169. Rome: Collegio S. Bonaventura Grottaferrata.

_____. "Personification Allegory and Visions of Light in Richard of St. Victor's Teaching on Contemplation." University of Toronto Quarterly. 46:3 (Spring: 1977): 190-214.

Zizioulas, John D. Being as Communion: Studies in Personhood and the Church. Crestwood, New York: St. Vladimir's Seminary Press, 1985.